W9-BQU-933

Special Edition
Using
AutoCAD
2000

Ron House

Paul W. Richardson

John Brooks

Dylan Vance

que ®

A Division of Macmillan USA
201 W. 103rd Street
Indianapolis, Indiana 46290

Contents at a Glance

Associate Publisher
Greg Wiegand

Acquisitions Editor
Todd Green

Development Editor
Jeff Durham

Managing Editor
Thomas F. Hayes

Project Editor
Nancy E. Sixsmith

Copy Editors
Kate Givens
Krista Hansing

Indexers
Larry Sweazy
Tim Tate

Proofreaders
Maribeth Echard
Harvey Stanbrough

Technical Editor
Art Liddle

Team Coordinator
Julie Otto

Book Designer
Louisa Klucznik
Ruth Lewis

Cover Designer
Dan Armstrong
Ruth Lewis

CONTENTS

ABOUT THE AUTHORS

Ron House has more than 12 years of working experience with AutoCAD including help-desk support, training, application development, and consulting. He has presented hundreds of AutoCAD seminars to audiences on varying disciplines, including the initial rollouts of Release 13 and 14 in the Kansas City area. As an Autodesk Certified Instructor, Ron has taught AutoCAD to students throughout the United States and from Russia and Mexico. He has been a beta tester of AutoCAD since Release 12 and has recently beta-tested Autodesk's Actrix Technical and Volo View software; he is currently testing the Mapguide 5.0 software product.

Ron has also served as adjunct professor at Johnson County Community College in Overland Park, Kansas, where he has taught all levels of AutoCAD, 3D, customizing, AutoLISP, and engineering classes. Ron is currently the GIS\CAD Supervisor in the Real Estate Technology Group at Sprint, and he is considered the resident expert on AutoCAD and the Autodesk Mapguide products. Ron holds a B.S. in Architectural Engineering from Kansas State University in Manhattan, Kansas.

Paul W. Richardson has 18 years of experience in the CAD industry. During the past 12 years, he has specialized in AutoCAD programming (AutoLISP and VBA), creating productivity tools and CAD Standards automation applications. Recent projects include San Francisco Basemap (GIS) Project and CADD Standards Development project. He is the co-author of the *AutoCAD 13 Instant Reference* and *Mastering AutoCAD LT* and has contributed to *Mastering AutoCAD 14* and an online version of the classic *ABC's of AutoLISP*.

John Brooks is a product designer who hails from London, England, and now resides permanently in the United States. John has worked in the electronics industry for almost 30 years—designing products for the consumer, computer, and communications industries. He has used many different manufacturing techniques such as molding, casting, and sheet metal. His experience has been gained working as a Consultant Designer on three continents (Europe, North America, and Asia). Part of John's work has involved evaluating CAD and 3D CAD systems and advising companies on how 3D technology will improve their productivity and which system is best suited for their needs.

John now lives close to Kansas City—in Smithville, Missouri—where he runs his own consultancy business called Designs Midwest Inc. He is also the Director of Engineering for a large multinational telecommunications company based in Kansas City.

Dylan Vance has worked in the computer industry for the last eight years in such areas as technical support, quality assurance, and product design. He is the author of *Inside Autodesk World* and the forthcoming *Inside AutoCAD Map*. Dylan currently works for Autodesk in the GIS Solutions Division.

DEDICATION

From Ron:

To my wife and sons, with love.

ACKNOWLEDGMENTS

From Ron:

I would like to thank a number of individuals for assisting me in creating *Special Edition Using AutoCAD 2000*. I truly am grateful for their support and hard work on this project.

Many thanks go to everyone at Macmillan Computer Publishing—I could not have chosen a better team to work with on a project of this size. I would especially like to thank Todd Green, acquisitions editor, and Jeff Durham, development editor, for keeping me focused and on track during the creation of this book. Thanks also to Art Liddle, Paul Richardson, Dylan Vance, and John Brooks for going over the book with a fine-tooth comb as technical editors.

Special thanks also to contributing authors Paul Richardson and his talented wife, Christine Meredith, at Technical Publications in Portland, for pitching in and helping out when I needed it the most. I am indebted to both of them for their efforts.

I truly could not have finished the book without those who contributed to the book. Thanks go to Autodesk employees Clay Freeman for his insight on the book and on Architectural Desktop; to Dylan Vance, for the wonderful job he did on the plotting chapter; to John Brooks, who put forth his best effort on the Mechanical Desktop and Visualization chapters; and to Paul Richardson, who did an incredible job throughout the entire book. I wish to also thank Cynde Hargrave of Autodesk for her efforts in getting the software together for the companion CD.

I would also like to thank those who were instrumental in giving me support from the onset of this project. Many thanks go to Brian Gill and Jeff Leinbach for believing in me, as well as to the many individuals at Sprint—especially Brian Jordan, Pam Hatcher, Bob Phillips, and Paul Savastano—for their ongoing support and advice.

A heartfelt thanks to my family for their encouragement. Finally, and most importantly, I thank my loving wife, Rose, and my two incredible sons, Aaron and Alex, for supporting me throughout the fulfillment of a dream come true.

From Dylan:

Thanks to Shawn Kirkpatrick (www.shawnk.com) for the use of his architectural drawings.

TELL US WHAT YOU THINK!

As the reader of this book, *you* are our most important critic and commentator. We value your opinion and want to know what we're doing right, what we could do better, what areas you'd like to see us publish in, and any other words of wisdom you're willing to pass our way.

As an Associate Publisher for Que, I welcome your comments. You can fax, email, or write me directly to let me know what you did or didn't like about this book—as well as what we can do to make our books stronger.

Please note that I cannot help you with technical problems related to the topic of this book, and that due to the high volume of mail I receive, I might not be able to reply to every message.

When you write, please be sure to include this book's title and author as well as your name and phone or fax number. I will carefully review your comments and share them with the author and editors who worked on the book.

Fax: 317-581-4666

Email: office_que@mcp.com

Mail: Greg Wiegand, Associate Publisher
            Que
            Macmillan USA
            201 West 103rd Street
            Indianapolis, IN 46290 USA

INTRODUCTION

In this introduction

WHO CAN USE THIS BOOK

Special Edition: Using AutoCAD 2000 is designed specifically for two types of users. First, this book is for those users who are looking to learn AutoCAD the right way the first time, efficiently and effectively. This book covers each command in detail, using examples that assist the user to jump-start the AutoCAD learning process, gaining valuable knowledge quickly to become productive in a short time frame. And it is also for those who have used AutoCAD in the past who now want to enhance their skills and get up to speed on the new features of AutoCAD 2000. Each feature is discussed with expert advice, giving those users the "inside track" on how to use the new commands with ease.

Other users will find *Special Edition: Using AutoCAD 2000* is a great reference book they can refer to when needed for specific AutoCAD functions, features, or settings. And there are those who want to try out the software and aren't quite sure whether they want to make the investment. This book provides them with an evaluation copy of AutoCAD 2000 included on the companion CD, allowing them to "test drive" the software while providing expert advice about how to get started.

HOW THIS BOOK IS ORGANIZED

Special Edition: Using AutoCAD 2000 is geared to assist you in mastering the numerous features of AutoCAD, describing in detail how each command works using real-world examples. Each chapter is embellished with tips and tricks from AutoCAD experts, taking you beyond just learning how operate the command. As you advance through the chapters, you will become more productive and efficient, and learn techniques that allow you to work smarter and faster. To assist you in becoming a master of AutoCAD, this book is presented in six parts, each dealing with a specific feature set of AutoCAD 2000.

PART I: GETTING STARTED

Part I gets you started by covering the interface and the various tools you will use to become proficient using AutoCAD 2000. You will get well-acquainted with the drawing setup commands and learn how to use layers and linetypes expertly within your drawings. Learn how to open drawings and other files within AutoCAD 2000, whether they are on your local disk or on the Internet.

PART II: OBJECT CONSTRUCTION

This section covers the object construction commands in detail with real-world examples, with specific applications showing you how to get the most out of each operation. Learn how to create and edit complex object types, with tips on when best to use these objects regardless of what you are drawing.

PART III: EDITING YOUR DRAWING

This section illustrates each command in full, with tips and notes to increase your productivity. Use the advanced techniques in these chapters to learn how to quickly manipulate the drawing objects professionally.

PART IV: AUTOCAD MECHANICS

This part discusses the mechanics of AutoCAD 2000 in full detail. The viewing, hatching, dimensioning, and inquiry commands are illustrated step by step, showing you how to become more productive and efficient with each chapter. The sections on creating and editing blocks and external reference files show you how to take full advantage of these features. Chapter 19, "Internet Publishing," then shows you how to interact and work with colleagues using the Internet. Working with Autodesk's new Volo View Explorer software, you can take your native AutoCAD drawing files and safely and securely collaborate with others working on your project.

PART V: BECOMING A MASTER OF AUTOCAD

Learn how to master AutoCAD with these advanced chapters on customizing and programming with Visual LISP and Visual Basic for Applications. Then, discover how to link your drawings to external databases and how to leverage the full potential of AutoCAD 2000.

PART VI: BEYOND AUTOCAD

This part gives you a glimpse beyond using AutoCAD 2000 with previews of working with Autodesk's Architectural Desktop and Mechanical Desktop software products. Each chapter is written by experts in the fields of architectural and mechanical design, giving you a top-notch understanding of what these applications can do for you.

PART VII: APPENDIXES

There are three appendixes in *Special Edition Using AutoCAD 2000:*

- Appendix A, "Taking Advantage of AutoCAD's Keyboard Shortcuts," is a quick reference for the default shortcuts available in AutoCAD 2000.

- Appendix B, "AutoCAD Environment Options," explains the parameters and setting variables that affect the workings of AutoCAD. Use this appendix as a quick reference to find exactly what you are looking for.

- Appendix C, "AutoCAD Migration Assistance," contains information on each of the tools used to migrate your drawings to AutoCAD 2000.

CONVENTIONS USED IN THIS BOOK

This book contains various conventions that point out specific features:

Note	Notes contain information or alternative techniques for performing tasks that we feel will enhance your use and/or understanding of the current topic.

Tip #1001 from *Ron House*	Tips point out a shortcut or another way to access a feature or an AutoCAD secret.

→ Cross-references refer you to other chapters in this book that contain additional information about the topic or feature.

Caution	Cautions alert you to times when extra consideration needs to be given to an action or operation. Reader, beware!

The style conventions used throughout this book exist to help you to learn many of the AutoCAD shortcuts. The following rules have been maintained as part of this effort:

- Commands that are typed at the keyboard are in boldface: type **Stretch**.
- Menu hotkeys appear underlined: <u>M</u>odify pulldown.
- Command-line prompts are displayed in a different font: `Select objects`.

As each command is discussed, I have also indicated the different ways to activate that command, either by pull-down menu, toolbar, shortcut menu, or via the command line.

Although the main focus on using AutoCAD 2000 is through the heads-up display features, which minimize the use of the keyboard, I have still included the keyboard shortcuts for two reasons. First, this was done to accommodate those users of previous versions of AutoCAD, who are familiar with activating commands and options by using keyboard shortcuts. I suspect that many users who have used AutoCAD in the past will continue to use this feature while learning that there are other means to access a command or option.

Second, I have included them to familiarize new readers with the options they have available to them. My intent was to present the information to users so they could decide which mode of operation works best for them, which may include a combination of command-activation techniques.

The many options to activate a command and the ability to customize the interface to your liking are among the best features of AutoCAD. Use these features to your advantage and you will find you can quickly increase your productivity—whether you have used previous versions of AutoCAD or if you are using AutoCAD for the first time.

GETTING STARTED

CHAPTER 1

WORKING WITH THE INTERFACE

In this chapter

THE AUTOCAD 2000 INTERFACE

Although AutoCAD Release 14 was the first release to ship as a Windows only software product, only now has AutoCAD been capable of taking full advantage of what that environment has to offer. With a complete Windows interface, labeled as a "Heads-Up Design" environment, the AutoCAD 2000 interface has a totally efficient feel and look to it. Much emphasis has been given to enabling the user to access all the commands from the screen, similar to the way any of the Microsoft Office software products work. This permits the user to concentrate on the drawing, thus minimizing keyboard dependence.

AutoCAD initially adopted the Microsoft Windows interface sometime after AutoCAD Release 12 was introduced to the market. At that time, the program was offered as an option with what was then considered the standard Microsoft DOS (MS-DOS) operating system. Many of the commands were available only by typing them from the keyboard. Since accepting the Windows interface standards, however, each new release of the software has been getting closer to total compliance with those standards. With AutoCAD 2000, the transition to Windows is now complete.

With any software product, the key to mastering the software lies in taking the time to become familiar with the interface. Knowing where to choose the commands—and knowing how to use them efficiently—enables you to master the software. But to truly understand the software, you must look beyond the interface. Mastering the software begins when you start to comprehend what happens behind the scenes when you press a button, access a menu, or type a command.

To accomplish this, you first need to be an expert working with the various AutoCAD interfaces discussed in this chapter. To get you started, let's examine the different ways to access the various commands. You can access commands in four ways using specific interfaces: toolbars, pull-down menus, the keyboard, and the Screen Menu.

TOOLBARS

Toolbars are small pallets that contain a series of icons representing various commands. Twenty-four toolbars are available, and each contains specific groups of commands, such as drawing, editing, inquiry, and so on. By default, four toolbars open automatically when you open a drawing file. These are known as the Standard, Object Properties, Draw, and Modify toolbars. The Standard toolbar is shown in Figure 1.1.

As with any Windows-based software, it is not very practical to have all the toolbars open at once. To avoid cluttering the screen with toolbars, you will want to open and close them as needed. You can open toolbars in one of three ways, the quickest of which is by right-clicking an open toolbar (see Figure 1.2).

This gives you the complete list of toolbars; those that are already open show a check mark next to their name. To open another toolbar, simply select its name from the list.

Figure 1.1
The AutoCAD Standard toolbar is similar to what you would find in any Windows application.

Figure 1.2
Right-clicking a toolbar brings up this list of all toolbars, making it easy to select which toolbar to open.

Tip 1 from
Ron House

When you end a drawing session, AutoCAD remembers which toolbars you had opened. When you launch AutoCAD again, it opens those same toolbars, allowing you to start right where you left off.

Tip 2 from
Ron House

To avoid docking a toolbar into the Drawing Editor frame, you can hold down the Ctrl key while dragging the toolbar. This allows the toolbar to overlap the frame rather than becoming part of it. To undock the toolbar, select a part of its frame and move the toolbar towards the center of the screen. When the toolbar is released, it reverts back to floating mode.

You also can access toolbars from the View pull-down menu; simply choose Toolbars and select the checkbox for the desired toolbar from the Toolbar dialog box (see Figure 1.3).

You may also type **TOOLBAR** at the command prompt to access that dialog box. The Toolbar dialog box contains two check boxes that control the size of the toolbar icons (if you find them hard to read in their default size) and the display of ToolTips.

Two extremely useful features of the toolbars are ToolTips and flyouts. As you examine the Standard toolbar, notice that each button has a ToolTip, a small box that appears as the mouse cursor passes over the button. This ToolTip indicates the command associated with that button. Considering there are hundreds of buttons, this assists you in learning which command is activated when the button is picked.

Figure 1.3
The Toolbars dialog box gives you control over the size of icons and the display of ToolTips.

Flyouts are buttons that represent multiple options for a particular command. Notice that the Standard toolbar contains five buttons with small black triangles located in their lower-right corner.

Figure 1.4
Flyouts options are available from the Standard toolbar.

This designates that these buttons are flyouts. When a flyout button is continually depressed, the option buttons for those commands appear. All the command options are available from one button location, making it quick and easy to access them.

PULL-DOWN MENUS

Across the top of the Drawing Editor are a series of menus called pull-down menus. Similar to the toolbars, each pull-down menu represents a specific group of AutoCAD commands. From these you can select the majority of commands, something that is not available with the toolbars.

Helpstrings are also available for the pull-down menus as you move your cursor over the options listed within a menu. The pull-down menus also support cascading menus and the use of ellipsis buttons to indicate which menu options will open dialog boxes, (displayed in Figure 1.5).

Tip 3 from
Ron House

To close a pull-down menu you accidentally selected, either select another menu or press the Esc key. You may need to press Esc several times to exit a cascading menu.

Figure 1.5
Cascading pull-down menus display additional commands or options available.

USING THE COMMAND LINE

As commands are activated during a drawing session, the command line displays the prompts for user input (see Figure 1.6). As new commands are accessed, the previous commands and prompts scroll up, creating a command history of the drawing.

The command line (or command prompt, as it has been referred to in the past) is a carry-over from earlier versions of AutoCAD—the primary way to activate commands in previous releases of the software was to actually type in the desired command using the command prompt. AutoCAD is somewhat unique in relation to other Windows software products because it still has a command line. This is necessary to respond to certain prompts for many of the commands.

AutoCAD utilizes the effectiveness of the command line and has built in some pretty unique features. Let's discuss these features and explore how you can use them to become more efficient.

ARE YOU PROMPTING ME?

Every time a command is activated, the command line updates to show the prompt for that command. The command prompt either asks you for a value or a specific action, or displays the options for that command, as shown in Figure 1.6.

The options available are contained within straight brackets; default options are shown in angled brackets. These can be quickly activated by typing the capitalized letter or the whole word of that option. For example, let's examine the command prompt for the Text command:

```
Command: text
Current text style:  "Standard"
Text height:  0.2000
Specify start point of text or [Justify/Style]:
Specify height <0.2000>:
```

Figure 1.6
The command line leads you through the various command prompts.

To access the Style option, you would type **S** at the command line and press the Enter key. To accept the default height in the last line of the example, you would need only to press the Enter key. In both cases, the command line would then prompt you to complete the next step. Various options are available, depending on the command you chose. Many of these options are accessible only through the command line, and many are available on the right-click shortcut menus, which are discussed later in this chapter.

Tip 4 from
Ron House

Remember to always look at the command line when you are working on a drawing. This is where the program communicates with you by prompting you for information. Each command that is activated uses the command line to prompt you for further action. If at any time you are not certain about what the next step is, refer to the prompt displayed in the command line.

To view the other command-line options, right-click in the Command Line window (see Figure 1.7).

Figure 1.7
A convenient option from the shortcut menu enables you to repeat a command; just right-click and choose the command from the pop-up menu.

RECENT COMMANDS

The command line gives you quick access to a list of recent commands. To repeat a command, right-click in the Command Line, select the Recent Commands option, and choose the command from the list.

COPY

This option enables you to copy selected text from the command line to other applications via the Windows clipboard.

PASTE TO CMDLINE

You can paste text from the previous commands and values you've typed back to the command line. This is especially handy when you need to enter incorrectly typed coordinates. Just select the part of the text that is correct, the copy and paste it back at the command prompt. Then continue to type the rest of the coordinate and press Enter to accept.

PASTE

Similar to Paste to CmdLine, this option pastes text from an external application, such as the Windows Clipboard, to the command line.

COMMAND-LINE EDITING

Standard Windows editing methods, such as insert, overwrite, and backspace, can be used in the command line to correct typing errors. This saves a considerable amount of time when typing commands and values.

COMMAND-LINE RECALL

You can repeat previous command-line entities by using the up and down arrow keys, much like the DOSKEY function available in DOS. This function keeps in memory a list of recently accessed commands, and the arrow keys can be used to scroll through the commands previously entered. Pressing the Enter key simply activates the command again.

COPY HISTORY

This option copies all the text currently in the text screen to the Clipboard, or the history of the command line. This can also be done by typing the command **Copyhist**. This is convenient when you want to track all commands activated during a drawing. This might be done to view the number of mistakes a user made while working on a drawing to determine whether training is needed for that individual or to view how another user completed a particular task.

OPTIONS

Options, the last selection from the shortcut menu, activates a dialog box that provides quick access to the program settings.

KEYBOARD SHORTCUTS

One of the quickest ways to activate a command via the command line is through the use of a keyboard shortcut. A keyboard shortcut is an abbreviation of a command, where the command has been shortened to make typing the command quicker. Table 1.1 shows the shortcuts available in AutoCAD. Keying in the shortcut and pressing the Enter key activates the associated command.

→ You can learn how to customize this list and add your own keyboard shortcuts in Chapter 20, "Customizing Made Easy."

TEXT SCREEN

The text screen is a larger version of the command line, from which you can view the entire command history of the drawing session. You can toggle between the text screen and the command line by pressing the F2 function key (see Figure 1.8).

Figure 1.8
The options available from the command line are also available at the text screen.

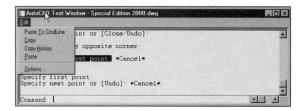

Because the text screen and the command line are one and the same, you also can type in commands from the text screen.

Both the command line and the text screen have scrollbars for scrolling through the command history. In addition, the Page Up and Page Down keys can be used to page through the contents when these windows are active.

Tip 5 from
Ron House

You cannot close the Command Line window, although you can minimize it to show just one line of text.

Now let's look at the rest of the AutoCAD interface, starting with the Screen Menu.

THE SCREEN MENU

An optional menu is not initially displayed when a drawing is opened, but commands also can be selected from here. This menu is called the Screen Menu. To display the Screen Menu, right-click in the command line and select the Options menu item. This opens the Options dialog box, in which you should choose the Display tab. Click the check box to Display Screen Menu. The Screen Menu will then appear on the right side of the Drawing Editor after you select the Apply button(see Figure 1. 9).

THE STATUS BAR

The status bar contains a series of tiles, or toggle buttons, and can be used to toggle various drawing functions off and on. Located at the bottom of the Drawing Editor, the status bar is easily accessible while you are working on a drawing (see Figure 1.10).

Clicking on the tiles activates a specific function; each of these features are covered in the Chapter 2, "Drawing Setup." The status bar also has an X, Y, and Z coordinate readout to indicate cursor location in relation to the overall drawing.

Figure 1.9
The Screen Menu can be turned on to provide another way to access commands.

Figure 1.10
To turn on a function from the status bar, click on the appropriate tile.

| SNAP | GRID | ORTHO | POLAR | OSNAP | OTRACK | LWT | MODEL |

ICON MENUS

Icon menus display a graphical representation of the result of activating a command or option. A good example of this is the Hatch Pattern palette (see Figure 1.11).

Figure 1.11
The Hatch Pattern palette is an example of an icon menu in which the options are shown graphically.

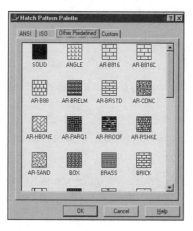

Each icon on the palette resembles a hatch pattern, which displays a preview of the pattern before it is applied to the drawing. Using an icon menu enables you to make a quick decision based on graphical commands or options.

MODEL AND LAYOUT TABS

Layouts give you the ability to arrange how the model will look on a virtual sheet of paper. The Model and Layout tabs toggle between the Model and Layout design areas. You can use these tabs to set up and create the layouts; simply right-click on a tab to access the menu shown in Figure 1.12.

Figure 1.12
Right-clicking on a tab brings up the Layout menu and allows you to edit the layout tab properties.

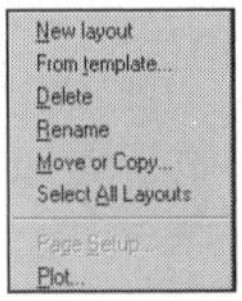

UCS ICON

When a drawing is loaded, an icon appears in the lower-left corner (see Figure 1.13).

Figure 1.13
The User Coordinate System (UCS icon) indicates the current orientation of the x- and y-axes for the drawing.

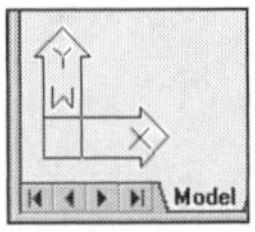

This is the User Coordinate System, or UCS, icon. This icon indicates the x- and y-axes direction for the drawing. You can toggle off the UCS icon by selecting the View pull-down menu, choosing the Display option, choosing the UCS icon, and the clicking On. This removes the check mark next to the On option on the menu and turns off the display of the UCS icon.

→ See "Defining the User Coordinate System," p. 691, to learn more about defining your own UCS.

RIGHT-CLICK OR CONTEXT MENUS

The right-click shortcut, context menus, or can be used to access many of the options available for the current command or drawing (see Figure 1.14).

Context menus save considerable time by giving you quick access to the options, eliminating the need for keyboard entry. Five types of shortcut menus are available depending on when and where you right-click:

- Command-mode—The menu shown in Figure 1.15 appears while you are working with a command.

- Edit-mode—This menu appears when objects are selected but no command is applied (see Figure 1.16).

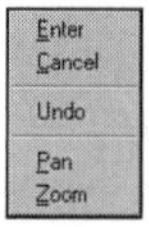

Figure 1.14
The right-click short-cut menu displays the options available for quick access to the Polyline command.

Figure 1.15
The right-click shortcut menu displays the options available during the Zoom command.

Figure 1.16
The edit-mode right-click menu is accessed when objects have been selected but no command is activated.

- Default-mode—The default mode menu appears when you right-click in the drawing area when no objects are selected and you have no command applied (see Figure 1.17).

Figure 1.17
The default-mode menu shows the basic right-click menu options; notice that the specific-object editing options are not available.

- Dialog-mode—This menu appears when you right-click inside a dialog box (see Figure 1.18).
- Other menus—These menus are available from the command line by right-clicking (see Figure 1.19).

Figure 1.18
Right-clicking inside a Select File dialog box gives you the dialog-mode menu, which enables you to modify how the files are displayed.

Figure 1.19
An example of another right-click menu available from the command line, which gives you access to specific options for that interface.

Now that we've examined the various menu types, let's look at the different facets of opening a drawing.

THE VARIOUS WAYS TO OPEN A DRAWING

There are multiple ways to open or import a drawing into AutoCAD 2000, depending on what format the file is in and where the file is located. Most familiar is the process of opening an existing drawing by selecting the Open icon from the Standard toolbar. (The Standard toolbar is similar to what you see in other Windows products, so you should be familiar with many of the buttons.)

This opens the Select File dialog box, illustrated in Figure 1.20, which has some unique features that assist you in finding the right file. One of these features is the drawing previewer, which allows you to preview a drawing files by selecting it from the list, shown in Figure 1.20.

Figure 1.20
The Select File dialog box with the drawing previewer makes it easy to locate the file you are looking for.

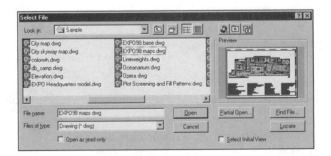

Tip 13 from	The drawing previewer, first introduced in Release 13, provides a quicker and more efficient way for users to locate drawing files. Unfortunately, this tool works only on those drawing files that have been saved in a Release 13 or higher format.
Ron House	

Similar to other Windows applications, you can also modify how the file properties are viewed within the dialog box. Right-clicking the mouse button while the cursor is located inside the Select File dialog box brings up a shortcut menu, which enables you to create new subdirectories and to view the file listing, as well as the entire folder, in various ways. Selecting on a specific file or folder and right-clicking gives you even more standard Windows options to choose from.

To open additional filetypes other than drawing files with AutoCAD 2000, use the Files of Type: selection list. This enables you to view both DXF and Template files within the Select File dialog box. DXF files are the Drawing Exchange Format for transferring files from one design software to another. Template files are drawing files with a .DWT extension used to "quick start" the creation of new drawing files.

Note	See Chapter 2, "Drawing Setup," for more information on Template files. DXF files are covered in more detail later in this chapter in "Options for Converting a Drawing File to DXF Format."

Both of these filetypes can be viewed within the Select File dialog box by selecting the desired type from the Files of type: select list. Now that it is becoming more common and even standard within many firms, the next section discusses how to access drawing files from the Internet or from a company's internal Intranet.

ACCESSING DRAWINGS FROM THE INTERNET

The Select File dialog box for the Open command also recognizes Uniform Resource Locators (URLs), which enables you to open drawing files via the Internet (see Figure 1.21).

Figure 1.21
AutoCAD 2000's
Internet buttons available from the Select File dialog box give quick access to Internet and intranet Web sites.

The URL is the address where the files are located on the Internet, similar to a path on your local drive. You can access these files by typing in the complete address in the File name edit box, or by browsing the Web for the file you want. The following example illustrates the process of opening a file from the Internet.

EXAMPLE: ACCESSING A FILE VIA A URL

1. Click the Open command from the Standard toolbar, or type Open at the Command Line.

2. There are two ways to access a drawing from the Internet. The most efficient way is when you know the name of the drawing file you want. Then you can type the complete address of the file in the File name: edit box. For example, type in the following URL to open the sample file from Autodesk's website:

   `http://www.autodesk.com/exercise/expo98e.dwg`

3. The other way is to browse the Internet till you find the desired file. When the Select File dialog box opens, select the Launch Browser button. This will open the Browse the Web - Open dialog box (See Figure 1.22. Depending on the default URL set within the Options dialog box, this internal browser will go to that site. Else, you can type in another URL to browse to in the Look in: edit box.

Tip 7 from
Ron House

You can set the default URL to point to when using the Launch Browser button on the Standard toolbar. See Appendix B, "AutoCAD Environment Options," for additional information on using this feature.

Figure 1.22
Using the Browse the Web - Open dialog box to browse for drawing files located on the World Wide Web.

Tip 8 from
Ron House

AutoCAD assumes you are already connected and have access to the World Wide Web when you try to access a drawing file from the Internet. If not, you will need to connect prior to selecting the Launch Browser button. Check with your system administrator or the Windows documentation for information.

When you find the files you need, you can easily add the visited site names to your browser favorites list by selecting the Add to Favorites button.

→ For more information on accessing drawing files via the Internet, check out Chapter 19, "Internet Publishing."

SEARCHING FOR SPECIFIC FILES

When you are not careful, there are those occasions when files get misplaced or unfortunately, just downright lost. To accommodate for this, the Select File dialog also has a Find File... button. This opens a dialog box with two tab options: *Browse* and *Search*. The *Browse* option allows you to easily preview an entire directory of drawing files (see Figure 1.23).

Figure 1.23
Browsing an entire drawing directory using the Find File option within the Select File dialog box.

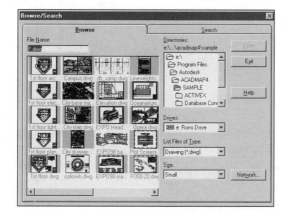

You will also find the Size and Network options handy for locating files. The Size option changes the size of the drawing preview in the directory list. Selecting the size from the pull-down list makes it easier to view those complex drawings when the files shown are hard to distinguish from one another. The Network option is great for looking across the network for files that are not located on your computer. When you are trying to locate a specific file, you'll find the Search option indispensable.

The Search option searches for a specific drawing file based on the filename or the date and/or time the file was created (see Figure 1.24). Files can also be located by local drive or network drives, or by specifying a directory path.

Once you've located the file you want, click the Open button or select Exit to close the Browse/Select dialog box.

ADDITIONAL WAYS TO FIND A FILE

You can also search for a specific file that you believe to be located in a directory listed in the Support file path. This is done using the Locate button, found in the Select File dialog box. To find a file using the Locate button, type in a known drawing name and then click Locate. The support file path will be searched to locate the file. If the system locates the file, the directory in which the file was located is displayed. If the file is not found, an alert box appears, indicating the directories searched to locate the missing file.

Figure 1.24
You can search for a drawing file by a specific creation date or by using wildcards in the Search tab in the Browse/Search dialog box.

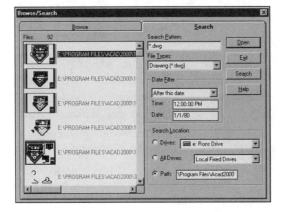

MORE OPEN FILE OPTIONS

In addition to the Locate button, two check boxes also are located at the bottom of the Select File dialog box. The Open as read-only check box permits files to be opened only in read-only mode. When this option is checked, drawing files can be viewed, but not modified. This is typically used when someone needs to view your drawing files, but you do not want that person to accidentally modify them.

Tip 9 from
Ron House

The Open as read only option is also handy when you want to open a file, modify it, and save it under a different name. This gives you an added sense of comfort knowing you won't unintentionally modify and overwrite your original file.

The other check box, Select Initial View, enables you to open a drawing file with a predefined view. Drawing files can be saved with views, which are snapshots of specific areas of the drawing with a certain magnification. Selecting this option shows you the list of pre-defined views read from the drawing (See Figure 1.25).

Picking a view from the list opens the drawing to that view. You might want to use this option when you are working on a very complex drawing and want to go back to the same spot you previously were working when you opened the file. Use the Select Initial View to open the drawing and return to that same work area.

MULTIPLE DESIGN ENVIRONMENT

A Multiple Design Environment allows multiple files to be opened in individual windows during a single session, which has been the Windows standard for some time. Finally, with AutoCAD 2000, you can now open and edit more than one drawing file. The ability to edit or view multiple files has its advantages, many of which are listed below.

Figure 1.25
The Select Initial View option makes it convenient to return to an area designated by a view upon opening the drawing.

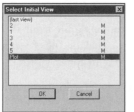

Caution

Although you may find that opening and working between multiple drawings can increase productivity, having too many windows open at one time can be counterproductive. Use good judgement when using this feature.

You can open multiple drawings from the file list in the Select File dialog by using the Shift or Control keys.

Figure 1.26
The AutoCAD Multiple Design Environment enables you to open several drawings at one time.

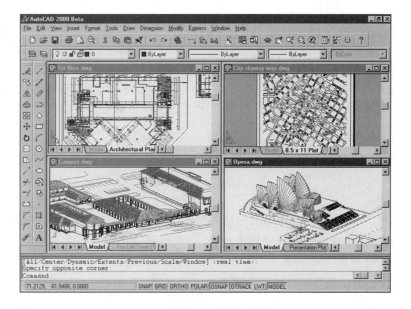

By taking advantage of this capability of opening several files at once, we can use the features listed below to increase functionality between drawings:

- Drag-and-drop from Windows Explorer
- Concurrent command execution
- Cut, copy, and paste

Each of these features is discussed in the following sections.

OPENING A FILE USING DRAG-AND-DROP

You can move or copy objects by dragging and dropping a file from Windows Explorer into a drawing. To move or copy an object, simply right-click on the object and drag it into the drawing. When you "drop" the object, a shortcut menu appears with these options:

- Insert Here—The object can be inserted into the drawing as an AutoCAD block.

- Open—The drawing file can be opened in the current window.

- Create Xref—The file can be externally referenced to the drawing in the current window.

- Create Hyperlink Here—The object can be defined as a hyperlink in the drawing into which it is inserted.

- Cancel—Cancel the current operation.

As you can see, these options are useful defining exactly what you want to do with the drawing file. Other advantages of using AutoCAD Multiple Design Environment are discussed in the following sections.

CONCURRENT COMMAND EXECUTION

Concurrent Command Execution enables you to switch between drawings without canceling a command. This means you can start a command in one drawing, move to another and start a different command, and return to the first drawing and finish the initial command. This greatly increases productivity when you are working with multiple drawings.

CUT, COPY, AND PASTE

You also can transfer objects between drawings using the cut, copy, and paste functions. Right-clicking on a file during the drag-and-drop operation opens a shortcut menu containing these options:

- Copy Here—This feature copies the file into the drawing at the user-defined location.

- Paste as Block—This inserts the file into the drawing as a block at a user-defined insertion point. Using this option, entire drawings could be pieced together by dragging and dropping other drawings as blocks into the receiving drawing.

Note
A block can be defined as a group of objects that can be reused in the same drawing as well as in multiple drawings. In Chapter 16, "Creating and Using Blocks," you can learn more about blocks and their specific uses.

- Paste to Orig Coords—This feature pastes the object into the recipient drawing at the original coordinates at which the object was located in the host drawing. This makes it convenient because you do not need to know the original coordinates of the object, yet you can position it in the same location in the receiving drawing.

- Cancel—Cancels the cut, copy, or paste operation.

Again, using the shortcut menu broadens the number of options available to you when using these functions. There are times, though, when you just want to open a portion of a file, especially when you know exactly what you want to access within a drawing file. For these times you'll want to use the Partial Load command covered in the next section.

PARTIAL OPEN AND LOAD

When working with large drawing files, sometimes it is advantageous to partially open a file rather than open it entirely. This both conserves computer resources and enhances productivity, allowing you to pick and choose objects you want loaded into your current drawing.

From the Select File dialog box, the Partial Open button, which is new with AutoCAD 2000, offers access to a drawing's layers and views before the drawing is opened. From here, you can choose what portion of the file you want to open, either from the Saved view or from the Layer list. Placing a check mark in the box next to the layer name toggles layer geometry to be loaded after a View has been selected (see Figure 1.27).

Tip 10 from	The Partial Open and Load feature only works with drawings that have been either created in or opened and saved as an AutoCAD 2000 file. This is not possible with older drawings you might try to partially open.
Ron House	

Figure 1.27
With the Partial Open command, you can choose what specific part of the drawing file to open.

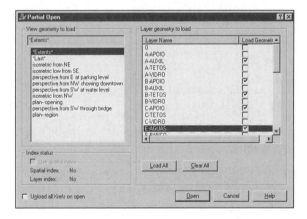

After a file is opened, the Partial Load command can also be used to load additional parts of the file. You can even specify a specific area to be searched for geometry by selecting the Pick an Area button shown in Figure 1.28.

You will find many advantages to loading only the portion of the file that you want, especially when you are working with large files that take time to load and maneuver within.

Once a file is loaded into AutoCAD, look at different ways to save a drawing file in another format

Figure 1.28
You can choose geometry from a specific area of a drawing using the Pick an Area button from the Partial Load dialog box.

SAVING A DRAWING IN ANOTHER FORMAT

Once a drawing file has been loaded and after it has been modified, you can change the name of the file using the SaveAs command. This command not only enables us to save a drawing file with a new name, but it can also save a drawing ino other formats, as shown in Figure 1.29.

Figure 1.29
You can save an AutoCAD 2000 drawing in one of the many DWG or DXF formats available.

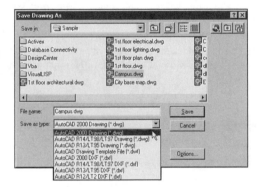

These formats include earlier versions of AutoCAD (Releases 13 and 14) drawing files, the Drawing Exchange Format (DXF) files, and Templates files, which are discussed in detail in Chapter 2, "Drawing Setup."

There are occasions where you may need to save your drawing files into another format. This might occur when you are working with a client or consultant who needs to export your AutoCAD drawing file into a format that can be read by other design software packages. If you have the need to save a drawing in one of these formats, you should specify the parameters of the chosen format. By default, AutoCAD is set to save drawings in AutoCAD 2000 format. You can change the output format by clicking the Options... button in the Save Drawing As dialog box (see Figure 1.30).

There are two tabs available, each dealing with specific parameters for the DWG or DXF formats.

Figure 1.30
Parameters for the DWG and DXF file formats can be set when you select the Options... button from the Save Drawing As dialog box.

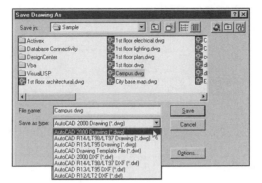

PART I

THE DWG FILE OPTIONS WITH THE SAVEAS COMMAND

These options are available when saving a drawing file:

- Save proxy images of custom obje—When saving a file to Release 13 or older formats, you need to determine how "custom" will be saved with the drawing file.

- Custom objects are files imported into AutoCAD, such as an Excel spreadsheet or an image file. Older versions of AutoCAD did not have the capability of referencing these filetypes like you can now with AutoCAD 2000. Therefore, you must decide how these custom objects will appear when these drawings are opened in an earlier version of the software. Depending on the value set in the Proxygraphics setting variable, AutoCAD determines how these objects will be saved in the drawing file. A value of 0 creates a bounding box that is displayed in the file, and a value of 1 creates an image of the custom object.

- Index type—*Indexes* can be used to help speed up the process of loading a drawing file during demand loading.

→ Demand loading is used in reference to External Reference Files. Please see Chapter 17, "External Reference Files and Importing Images," for detailed information.

This option determines whether a *spatial* or *layer* index will be saved with the file. The descriptions below will help define the differences between the two types of index files. There are four index types available:

- None—No index is created for the file.

- Layer—Only On and Thawed layers are loaded when this option is set.

- Spatial—Only the portion of the drawing within the clipped boundary is loaded.

- Layer & Spatial—A combination of the two indexes. This specifies that only those layers that are On and Thawed within a clipped boundary of the drawing are displayed.

- Save All Drawings As—This sets the default file format all drawings will be saved to. This can save you a considerable amount of time if you are required to save the majority of your drawings in a format other than AutoCAD 2000 drawing format. The available formats are listed in Table 1.1:

TABLE 1.1   THE DEFAULT FILE FORMATS AVAILABLE WITH THE SAVEAS COMMAND

File Format	Extension
AutoCAD 2000 Drawing	(*.dwg)
AutoCAD R14/LT98/LT 97 Drawing	(*.dwg)
AutoCAD R13/LT 95 Drawing	(*.dwg)
AutoCAD Drawing Template File	(*.dwt)
AutoCAD 2000 DXF	(*.dxf)
AutoCAD R14/LT98/LT 97 DXF	(*.dxf)
AutoCAD R13/LT 95 DXF	(*.dxf)
AutoCAD R12/LT2 DXF	(*.dxf)

There are also specific options available when saving a file to the DXF format, which are discussed in the next section.

OPTIONS FOR CONVERTING A DRAWING FILE TO DXF FORMAT

DXF, the Drawing Exchange Format, was designed specifically for exporting drawing files for use into other CAD packages. The DXF process converts the drawing file into text-based files that contain information, such as included objects, layer structure, and specifics about the drawing file, so it may be imported.

Note

The DXF file format was developed by Autodesk to create a standard file format that could be read and utilized by other design software companies to import AutoCAD drawings. Using the DXF file, developers could determine how to convert the AutoCAD object types into similar entities within their own software and vice-versa. This means that if a similar object type does not exist in the importing software, portions or all of the object could be lost. Extreme care should be taken when importing and exporting drawing files so that important information within the drawing is not lost during the conversion process.

Here are the DXF options available:

- Format—Two different types of DXF files can be created; ASCII and Binary. ASCII DXF files are text-based files and can be opened and edited using a text editor. Binary DXF files, on the other hand, contain the same information but are compressed and can be opened within AutoCAD more quickly. The purpose of the file will depend on the format to be used.

- Selected Objects—Certain objects within the file can be saved in this format rather than the entire drawing.

- Save Thumbnail Preview Image—With AutoCAD 2000, DXF files can now be saved with a preview image when this option is selected. This will make them viewable from within the Select File - Open dialog box.

- Decimal Places Of Accuracy—Determines the precision required for the file. This typically depends on the application for which the DXF file is intended. The higher the precision, the larger the DXF file.

These options allow you to conveniently set the parameters of how you want a DWG or DXF file to be saved and enable you to adjust these value depending on the application.

SUMMARY

With all of the different menu options available, it can take some time to get comfortable working with the AutoCAD interface. Once you know how to access the commands you need, you will become more and more proficient, and will have taken the first step toward mastering AutoCAD 2000.

In the next chapter, you'll explore the various settings and options available to set up a drawing, and how to become more efficient in creating and setting up projects.

DRAWING SETUP

In this chapter

USING TEMPLATES

There are numerous settings that can be set within a drawing. This chapter introduces you to these settings and the numerous facets of setting up a drawing, building templates, and to the basic drawing objects and viewing commands. First, let's discuss creating templates and the potential time savings they can save you when creating project drawings.

Files that contain preset drawing settings are called *templates*. Essentially, templates are base drawing files with a .DWT extension. Templates can contain settings, such as units, size of drawing, pre-defined layers, text and dimension styles, default angle direction, and more. They can also contain drawing objects, such as titleblocks and base drawing information. Using a template to create a new drawing can save a considerable amount of time, speed up production time, and allow consistency throughout your project drawings.

When a new drawing is created, information contained in the template is transferred to the new drawing, which takes on the template drawing settings. This proves extremely handy when you are creating multiple new drawing files that share the same drawing format. Using a template keeps you from having to set up a new drawing each time.

Let's examine the process of creating a new drawing using a template by clicking on the New button from the Standard toolbar (see Figure 2.1).

Figure 2.1
Access the New button from the Standard toolbar.

Select the Use a Template button from the Create New Drawing dialog box (see Figure 2.2).

Figure 2.2
You can use a template to quickly create a new drawing file using the New command.

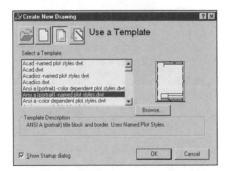

This enables you to view a list of pre-defined templates that ship with AutoCAD 2000. A template previewer and description box make it easy to locate the right template for the job. You can also click the Browse button to use templates created for similiar projects or templates located in a directory other than the one specified by the default location.

Tip 11 from
Ron House

When you select the Use a Template button, AutoCAD displays all templates located in the path set by the Drawing Template File Location. To set this path, right-click in the command line and select <u>O</u>ptions from the shortcut menu. Once the options dialog box opens, click on the Files tab and then double-click on the folder labeled Drawing Template File Location. Double-click again on the current template path, which opens a Browse for Folder dialog box, enabling you to search for the directory you want to set as the default template directory. After you've selected the path you want, click on the OK button on all dialog boxes to exit.

Project-specific templates can also be defined by creating your own templates. This process is described in the next section.

CREATING YOUR OWN TEMPLATE

One of the easiest ways to create a template is to modify a drawing from a similar project. This drawing should have similiar if not the same settings you want in your new project. These settings might include units, drawing limits, or drawing objects you want to include on all the drawings in a project. For example, say you are designing a multistory building. The building is 10 stories tall, and the exterior walls and location of other components, such as elevator shafts and stairwells, do not change from one floor to the next. Your template could also include these building components, so whenever this template is used to create a new drawing for the project, the integral building objects would already be in the drawing, enabling you to quickly focus on the items that do change on each floor.

Tip 12 from
Ron House

In Chapter 17, "External Reference Files and Importing Images," you'll learn about external reference files and how these enable you to reference other drawing files within a template or drawing. The advantage to doing this is that changes can be made to the original file and saved independently of the files that reference it. These changes could then be dynamically updated throughout all of your project drawings, insuring drawing consistency and considerable time savings. This is definitely a chapter worth reading when setting up your project.

Before creating your own template, you must first understand the numerous settings that can be set and how they can be used within a drawing. To help illustrate this, let's look at the Advanced Setup Wizard, also available from the Create New Drawing dialog box and covered in the next section.

USING A WIZARD TO CREATE A NEW DRAWING

Next to using a template, using the Setup Wizard is the best way to set up a drawing. You can use two wizard types: Advanced or Quick, both available from the Create New Drawing dialog box (see Figure 2.3).

The Quick Setup Wizard enables you to set the units and drawing area for your drawing, relying on the default setting in the Acad.dwt file. The Advanced Setup Wizard is more specific by giving you options to modify the angle, angle measure, and angle direction in addition to the units and drawing area. Both are based on the template ACAD.DWT, which is the default 9×12-inch template with no titleblock.

Figure 2.3
The Advanced Setup Wizard creates a drawing by prompting you for values to specific drawing settings.

Follow these steps to create a new drawing using the Advanced Setup Wizard:

EXAMPLE: WALKING THROUGH THE ADVANCED SETUP WIZARD

1. Create a new drawing by clicking on the New button from the Standard toolbar. Select the Use a Wizard button from the Create New Drawing dialog box.

2. Click the Advanced Setup wizard option from the Select a Wizard list; then click the OK button.

3. Choose a unit format for the drawing. Five unit formats, or units of measurement, are available for a drawing: Decimal, Engineering, Architectural, Fractional, and Scientific. A preview of each of the formats is shown to the right of the list as they are selected (see Figure 2.4).

Figure 2.4
You can choose between five different units formats using the Advanced Setup wizard.

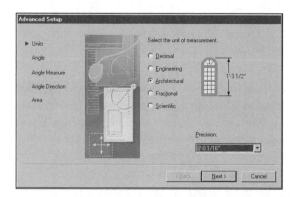

4. Once a unit format is selected, you'll also need to set the unit precision. The unit precision is defined as the smallest increment you will be working with in your drawing.

5. Then select an angle format and the angle precision. Just as with the drawing unit formats, there are also five types of angle measurement: Decimal Degrees, Degrees/Minutes/Seconds, Grads, Radians, and Surveyors Units. You also can set angle precision, which determines the smallest angle increment you wish to work with.

6. Set the angle measurement. The drawing angle measurement is the starting direction from which all angles are measured. For example, architectural drawings are set to use due East as the starting direction, whereas civil drawings typically use due North as the starting point for angle measurement.

7. Determine an angle direction. The default direction is counterclockwise, which is also referred to as the positive angle direction for all angles in the drawing.

8. Define the boundary of the drawing by providing the length and width of the paper. The last dialog box within the Advanced Setup wizard prompts you to enter the length and width of the drawing area using full-scale units. In other words, you will need to chose a drawing area large enough for your drawing to accommodate whatever you want to draw.

After you become familiar with creating new drawings, you may wish to turn off the Startup dialog box. You can do this by selecting the Show Startup dialog check box in the lower-left corner of the Startup dialog box.

Tip 13 from *Ron House*	After turning off the Startup dialog box, the next time you try to create a new file, you will be prompted at the command line to type the name of the prototype you want to use. If you wish to use the standard Windows File dialog box to select the template, type a tilde (~) at the Enter template file name or [. (for none)] prompt. You can also type a period and press Enter at the prompt if you do not wish to use a template.
	To turn on the Startup dialog box again, go to the Tools pull-down menu and select Options. This opens the Options dialog box. Click the System tab, and then click the Show Startup dialog check box in the General Options frame. First click the Apply button, and then click OK button to close the Options dialog box.

The Advanced Setup wizard is great when you first start using AutoCAD, but eventually you will want to modify some, if not all, of the settings automatically created for you to match your own project standards. To better understand what is actually happening when the wizard is activated, let's walk through the setup process step by step.

WALKING THROUGH THE DRAWING SETUP PROCESS

Now that we know how to use the Setup Wizard, let's examine what occurred in the background as we ran through the steps. Using the Advanced Setup option as an example, we'll examine the commands that were used to define the drawing, starting with the Units command.

THE UNITS COMMAND

The Units command is used to set the drawing and angle units, angle mode, angular direction, and precision. The first four steps of the Setup Wizard deal mainly with this command. To access this command independently of the Wizard, go to the Format pull-down menu and select the Units menu option. Figure 2.5 shows the Drawing Units dialog box.

Figure 2.5
The Units command sets the drawing and angle units, angle mode, angular direction, and precision.

Through pull-down menus, you can set the modes of the units length and angle. Notice that the dialog box displays sample output so you can see how the units will be formatted. Choose the Direction button to bring up the Direction Control dialog box shown in Figure 2.6.

Figure 2.6
Use the Direction Control dialog box to set a default or a custom base angle.

Once the Units have been set, you can determine the working area for the drawing with the Limits command.

THE LIMITS COMMAND

The limits define a drawing's outer boundary, or the working space of the file. The working space of the file is also considered to be the extent of the drawing. By default, limits are set to 9×12 inches in landscape mode. For each drawing, depending on the working area size desired, the limits will need to be adjusted. From the Format pull-down menu, select Drawing Limits. The following prompts for the limits command are displayed at the command line:

```
Command: limits
Reset Model space limits:
Specify lower left corner or [ON/OFF] <0'-0",0'-0">:
Specify upper right corner <1'-0",0'-9">: 144',96'
```

PART

I

CH

2

Tip 14 from
Ron House

To set the limits using the desired unit type, you must first use the Units command. If the units for an architectural drawing are set to Decimal format, you will not be able to key in an architectural value—AutoCAD will give you an "Invalid 2D Point" error. You must first set the units to Architectural format to key in architectural values.

This is why the Setup Wizard prompts you for the drawing area in full-scale units. The best philosophy to consider in dealing with AutoCAD drawings and scale is that drawings are always drawn at full scale. This philosophy works great when using the Setup Wizard, yet you must consider other factors when a scale is determined. Let's now review those factors.

When using the Setup Wizard, you are never prompted for the scale of the drawing. You are however, prompted for the overall drawing area. The Advanced Setup wizard assumes that you want to draw at a 1:1 scale, and no options are given to define the scale. Of course, the scale of the drawing will affect a number of settings, and scale is definitely a factor when plotting. What you are setting with the Setup Wizard is the overall area of the drawing, which is completely different from the plot scale. Although these values are distinct, they are definitely related. Plot scale is actually a combination of paper size and the desired scale for the drawing.

To determine any drawing scale, first determine the orientation of your drawing in relation to the sheet of paper you want to plot to.

Next, compare the largest overall dimension of what you want to draw with the longest side dimension of your paper. Be certain to allow extra room for the titleblock, dimensions, and notes, as well as spacing around the entire drawing.

Use Table 2.1 to determine the plot sheet size based on paper size and scale factor. The selected scale should allow the largest overall dimension, plus whatever extra room is needed to fit within the length of the paper.

TABLE 2.1 LIMIT SETTINGS BASED ON STANDARD SHEET SIZES

Architectural Scales

	"A"	"B"	"C"	"D"	"E"
Dwg. Scale	**8.5"x11"**	**11"x17"**	**17"x22"**	**34"x22"**	**34"x44"**
1/32"=1'-0"	272',352'	352',544'	544',704'	704',1088'	1088',1408'
1/16"=1'-0"	136',176'	176',272'	272',352'	352',544'	544',704'
1/8"=1'-0"	68',88'	88',136'	136',176'	176',272'	272',352'
1/4"=1'-0"	34',44'	44',68'	68',88'	88',136'	136',176'
1/2"=1'-0"	17',22'	22',34'	34',44'	44',68'	68',88'
1'=1'-0"	8.5',11'	11',17'	17',22'	22',34'	34',44'

Decimal Scales

Dwg. Scale	**8.5"x11"**	**11"x17"**	**17"x22"**	**22"x34"**	**34"x44"**
.125=1	68,88	88,136	136,176	176,272	272,352
.25=1	34,44	44,68	68,88	88,136	136,176
.5=1	17,22	22,34	34,44	44,68	68,88
1=1	8.5,11	11,17	17,22	22,34	34,44
2=1	17,22	22,34	4,44	44,68	68,88

Use the information in Table 2.1 to quickly determine the plot scale for a drawing. Let's look at how each of the scales in the table were calculated. To make this easy, we'll use the following example:

Say that we want to create a floor plan of a house in which the overall dimensions are to be 80×125 feet. We also want to plot the drawing onto a standard architectural "D" size, or a 22×32-inch sheet of paper. A scale must be determined so that we can fit our drawing onto this size sheet of paper with the 125-foot length along the x-axis and the 80-foot width along the y-axis. Therefore, the 125-foot side will be placed along the 34-inch side of our paper. The scale we need will have to be small enough to fit the 125-foot length of the house within 34 inches.

Let's start with an architectural scale of ¼ inch = 1 foot–0 inches. Using this scale means that every ¼ inch on our paper would equal 1 foot. Because there are four ¼-inch segments to every inch, and because our paper length is 34 inches, multiply 34×4 to determine the maximum length. Based on this calculation, we can fit a house with a maximum length that is 136 feet long onto our paper. Allowing a little more room for annotating the drawing, this scale should work well. Before we decide to use this scale, though, we must also check to see if it will work with the width of the house. Taking our scale of ¼ inch = 1 foot–0 inches and applying it to 22 inches gives us a plotted scale of 88 feet, which again falls well within our desired size.

The plotted scale of this drawing is ¼ inch = 1 foot–0 inches. Now that we know this, we can apply it to other settings. Some of the settings that would need to be modified are Text Height, Linetype Scale, and Plot Scale, just to name a few. I'll save the discussion of those for their respective chapters.

Note

To learn more about these settings and how each of these is affected by drawing scale, see Chapter 3, "Working with Layers and Linetypes," for information on linetype scale; see Chapter 12, "Annotating the Drawing," for determining text height; and see Chapter 18, "Plotting and Layouts," for details on plot scale.

PART

I

CH

2

Now that you've covered how to set up the drawing limits, let's discuss the drafting settings, which affect the drawing and editing commands, in the next section.

DRAFTING SETTINGS

The Drafting Settings dialog box contains a series of commands designed to assist you while drawing in AutoCAD. To access these settings, click on the Tools pull-down menu and select Drafting settings, or type **Dsettings** at the command line. You may also right-click on the Snap or Grid tile located on the status bar and choose Settings from the shortcut menu. Each of these actions open the Drafting Settings dialog box. As shown in Figure 2.7, three separate tabbed dialog boxes make up this dialog box:

The drafting settings are grouped into three categories:

- Snap and Grid
- Polar Tracking
- Object Snap

Figure 2.7
The various options that affect how objects are drawn and edited are available through the Drafting Settings dialog box.

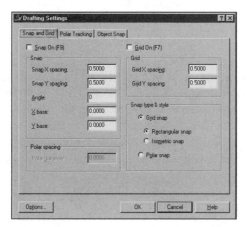

The next sections discuss these tabs and their features in greater detail.

SNAP AND GRID

The Snap feature sets the increment at which the crosshairs will move across the screen. Typically the increment is set to either the smallest denominator you want in the drawing or the desired accuracy. Notice that after this value is set, the crosshairs will not go to any location in the drawing smaller than that value when the Snap is turned on. Essentially, you have told AutoCAD that there is no need to go any smaller than that increment.

The following sections cover the specific Snap settings.

SNAP SPACING

The X and Y values can differ, but if the X value is set and you press the Enter or Tab keys, the Y value will be set equal to the X value. If the Y value needs to be different, you must set the Y value independently.

SNAP ANGLE

The snap angle is the angle by which the snap, grid, and crosshairs will be rotated in the drawing. This enables you to work at this angle with the axis rotated at this angle.

X AND Y BASE

These set the origin for the snap angle. They do not change the origin of the drawing; they just set the base for the snap to be rotated at, such as a specific point on an object in a drawing.

GRID X AND Y SPACING

This feature places a grid in the drawing at the spacing desired. The grid is a series of dots in the background of the drawing. The grid dots can be used for alignment and spacing, yet they cannot be plotted. You can toggle the grid on and off by double-clicking the Grid tile on the status bar. The X and Y values can differ, but the default is that the Y value is set equal to the X value. Similar to the Snap spacing values, the Y value should be set first if it must be different than the X value.

Tip 15 from
Ron House

These commands can be accessed at one time and transparently with dialog boxes. *Transparently* means that the values for these commands can be modified without having to cancel the current command to access the dialog box.

ORTHO

Three other drawing settings should also be discussed. The first of these is the Ortho setting. Although it is not available from this dialog box, it can be quickly accessed from the drawing editor. This feature can be a very important and extremely handy tool to use while drawing.

You can toggle the Ortho setting on or off easily by either clicking the Ortho tile in the status bar or by pressing the F8 function key. When this setting enabled, only straight horizontal or vertical lines can be drawn. This also affects the way an object can be dragged or rubberbanded in the drawing, such as with the editing commands.

OBJECT SNAPS

Object snaps enable you to snap to specific features on an object, such as an endpoint, the midpoint, or the center of a circle. Two types of object snap modes exist: running and single action.

A running object snap is a constant mode in which specified object snaps are applied to every action, whether it be creating a line or moving an object.

Single action object snaps are object snaps applied for a single particular action, which override any running object snaps you may have set. You can select these features from the Object Snap toolbar, or by right-clicking while holding the Shift key during a command to access the Object Snap menu, shown in Figure 2.8.

Figure 2.8
Right-clicking while holding the Shift key during a command brings up the Object Snap shortcut menu.

Tip 16 from
Ron House

The Drafting Settings dialog box can be quickly opened to the Object Snap tab by typing **OS** and pressing Enter at the command line.

You can also open the Object Snap toolbar from the list of available toolbars by right-clicking on any toolbar.

Figure 2.9
The Object Snaps toolbar makes it convenient to snap to objects as you are drawing.

The following is a list of all object snaps, either available from the Object Snap toolbar or shortcut menu:

- Temporary track point—Serves as a temporary base point or reference point from which you can define a specific distance.

- From—Enables you to specify a base point and a direction from that point in which to place a starting, from, or center point for the current operation.

- Point Filters—Enables you to specify a base point and a direction from that point. These are only available from the shortcut menu.

- Endpoint—Snaps to the nearest endpoint of the selected line.

- Midpoint—Locates the midpoint of the selected line.

- Intersection—Snaps to the existing intersection of two or more elements.

- Apparent Intersection—Enables you to find the apparent intersection in space of two entities when the intersection is not visually apparent.

- Extension—Finds and snaps to the extension of a line or arc.

- Center—Snaps to the center point of the selected circle. The circumference of the circle must be selected for this object snap to work.

- Quadrant—Snaps to the nearest quadrant (defined as 0°, 90°, 180°, or 270°) on the selected circle.

- Tangent—Enables you to place a line tangent to the selected circle.

- Perpendicular—Allows the current line, polyline, or similar item to snap perpendicular to the selected element.

- Parallel—Snaps to parallel lines while using the Line command. Activate the Line command; at the From point prompt, select this object snap. Then pass over the line you want to be parallel with until the parallel line symbol appears. As you move away from that line, you will see a dashed line that indicates the parallel line path. Move the cursor along that path to define the length of the new parallel line.

- Insert—Snaps to the insertion point of the selected block or text.

- Node—Enables you to find the insertion point of a point node.

- Nearest—Snaps to the nearest object, which overrides the Ortho drawing aid.

- None—Overrides the current object snap, and is used when no object snap is desired.

- Osnap Settings—Activates the Object Snap settings in the Drafting Settings dialog box.

In addition to the object snaps, the Autotrack feature assists you in drawing objects in relation to other objects in the drawing, based on the object snaps that are set.

AUTOTRACK

Autotracking enables you to draw with precision by aligning the crosshairs with alignment paths. These alignment paths make it easy to align particular points on the screen with other elements in the drawing (see Figure 2.10).

Figure 2.10
Alignment paths, indicated by the dashed lines, make drawing easy when aligning the crosshairs with a path defined by an object in the drawing.

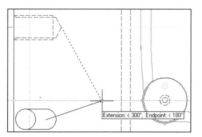

Alignment paths occur whenever the crosshairs come near a path defined by an element or an object snap point (refer to the "Object Snap Tracking Settings" section later in this chapter). Alignment paths appear whenever the path comes within a distance defined by the Aperture size, or the object snap target box that is located at the center of the crosshairs. This is set from the Options dialog box under the Drawings Tab (see Figure 2.11).

Figure 2.11
Alignment paths are visible when a path defined by an element falls within a distance defined by the Aperture Size setting, which can be set in the Options dialog box by selecting the Drafting tab.

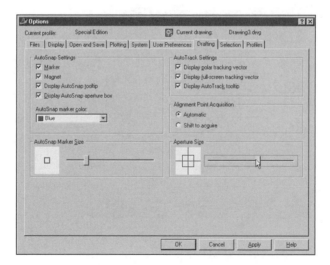

To access the Options dialog box, right-click on the Otrack or Osnap tiles from the status bar, choose Settings from the pop-up menu, and then select the Option button.

POLAR TRACKING

Polar tracking is a feature very similar to the Ortho setting, yet it is available at any angular value. The Ortho feature allows you to draw only at right angles, and polar tracking enables you to predefine other angle settings to assist you by aligning a point at any angle (see Figure 2.12).

Figure 2.12
Polar tracking alignment paths enable you to align with other objects in the drawing at specific angles.

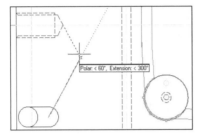

You can set this option by clicking the Polar tile in the status bar or by pressing the F10 function key. A number of available options determine how this feature will act.

Use the Polar function when you are working with quadrant angles of 0°, 90°, 180°, and 270°. Use Polar tracking when you want to align with a specific angle other than those at the quadrants, such as 33° or 45°. Figure 2.13 shows the polar tracking functions accessed from the Drafting Setting dialog box.

Figure 2.13
The polar tracking functions are available though the Drafting Settings dialog box.

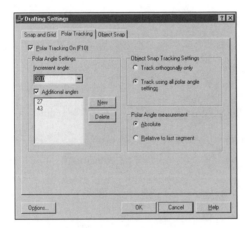

These functions are split into three groups:

- Polar Angle Settings
- Object Snap Tracking Settings
- Polar Angle measurement

The following sections illustrate these groups in more detail.

POLAR ANGLE SETTINGS

The polar angle settings set the angles for what are called alignment paths. With these alignment paths, you can lock onto a specific angle, making it easy to place a point along this path. You can select increment angles from the common angles list, or you can add new angles to the Additional angles list.

Tip 17 from *Ron House*	AutoCAD allows only 10 additional angles to be set in the Additional angles list. When you exceed this limit, AutoCAD prompts you to delete an angle from the list.

OBJECT SNAP TRACKING SETTINGS

Object snap tracking settings provide alignment paths based on the current Object Snap setting. Two options are available: Track orthogonally only, or Track using all polar angle settings.

When Tracking orthogonally only is enabled, object snap alignment paths appear only when a horizontal or vertical path is found in relation to the location of the cursor and other object features.

The Track using all polar angle settings option finds alignment paths based on any angle, in addition to horizontal and vertical relationships between entities.

POLAR ANGLE MEASUREMENT

This option determines how polar tracking angles are measured, and two different types of measurement are involved. These types are listed as absolute and relative measurements, and they are defined as follows:

- Absolute—Polar tracking angles are based on the x- and y-axes of the current User Coordinate System.
- Relative to last segment—The x- and y-axes of the line formed by the last two object points are used to determine the polar angle measurement. For example, if you use the endpoint or the midpoint of a line to start a new line segment, the angle is based on the x- and y-axes of that existing line.

Now that you've been introduced to many of the drafting settings set within the Setup Wizard, let's create an architectural template for an 8-1/2 × 11 sheet of paper using some of the settings.

EXAMPLE: CREATING AN ARCHITECTURAL TEMPLATE

1. Start AutoCAD and create a new drawing by clicking <u>N</u>ew from the <u>F</u>ile pull-down menu. From the Create New Drawing dialog box, select the Start from Scratch button.

2. Select the English (feet and inches) option and then click the OK button. This will create a blank drawing with units of feet and inches.

3. From the Format pull-down menu, choose Units, which opens the Drawing Units dialog box. In the Length section, set the Type: to Architectural, then click the OK button.

4. Next, select Drawing Limits from the Format pull-down menu. Accept the default lower left corner coordinate of 0,0 by pressing Enter. Then type **88',68'** at the Specify upper right corner prompt and press Enter.

5. Right-click on the Snap tile from the status bar and choose Settings from the shortcut menu.

6. From the Snap and Grid tab in the Drafting Settings dialog box, click the Snap On (F9) and Grid On (F7) options.

7. Set the Snap X spacing and Snap Y spacing to 1 inch, and then the Grid X Spacing and Grid Y spacing to 12 inches.

Tip 18 from *Ron House*	After entering the X spacing for either or both the Snap and Grid settings, by default the Y value will automatically match that value if you press the Tab key.

8. Click the OK button to close the Drawing Settings dialog box.

Tip 19 from *Ron House*	After setting the Snap values, it's a good idea to zoom the extents of the drawing. Because the current zoom magnification is saved with the drawing, this will set up your drawing to be viewed at its extents the next time it is opened.

9. Choose View, then Zoom, and then Extents from the pull-down menus.

10. Select Save As from the File pull-down menu. In the Save As dialog box, choose AutoCAD Drawing Template File from the Save as type drop-down list. Store the file in the default Template subdirectory.

11. Enter a name of Arch-A-8 and press Enter. This will save the settings and the name of the template based on the unit type of the file, size, and scale factor.

Now that you've defined your own template, you will create a new drawing using this template to create the outline of an architectural building in the next section. But before creating the outline, let's first examine the various ways to place a line in a drawing.

WORKING WITH THE LINE COMMAND

One of the most basic of all AutoCAD commands is the Line command. This command can be used for a number of different functions wherever you might want a line drawn between two user-defined points. After that, more points can be specified to create a series of continuous lines connected by their endpoints.

The Line command can be accessed by selecting the Line button from the Draw toolbar.

Figure 2.14
The Line command can be accessed from the Draw toolbar.

Tip 20 from	For quick access to the Line command, type **L** at the command line and press the
Ron House	Enter key.

The options available with the Line command are listed here:

- Specify first point—Designates the starting point of the line segment.
- Specify next point, or [Undo]—Designates the endpoint of the line segment, which is also the starting point of the next line segment.
- Undo—Undoes the last line segments and enables you to redesignate the end of the line. This is activated when you type a **U** at the command line and press Enter. It is important that you are still in the Line command. If you choose the Undo option after you exit the Line command, you will undo the last command.
- Close—Closes the current group of lines, drawing a line from the end of the last segment to the beginning of the first line drawn. This option is available only after two or more segments have been drawn. Choose this option from the Screen menu (if available), or type it in at the command prompt.

Other options available from the shortcut menu (available by right-clicking during the command) are listed here:

- Enter—Ends the Line command.
- Cancel—Cancels the current Line segment and exits the Line command.

Tip 21 from	To repeat the last command applied in AutoCAD, right-click and select the Repeat
Ron House	Command option.

Tip 22 from	To continue a line segment after exiting the Line command, right-click to access the short-
Ron House	cut menu and select the Repeat Line command. Right-click again to start the next line from the end of the last line drawn.

Placing Lines by Coordinates

You can use three different types of coordinates systems while placing lines:

- Absolute   This is typically used to place a starting point; it uses the origin, or the lower-left corner of the drawing, as its reference point. It has the format of "x coordinate, y coordinate." This coordinate is always used in reference to the origin of the drawing to locate a specific point.

- Relative   This references the last point picked on the screen and is indicated by an "at" symbol (@). The total distances, or displacements, along the x-axis and the y-axis are used in this format. It has the format of "@distance along the x-axis, distance along the x-axis." If you know the distance along the x axis and the y axis, this type of coordinate is the one to use.

Tip 23 from *Ron House*	If there is no displacement along an axis, this should be indicated with a zero. As an example, say that you wanted to draw a line straight to the right. You would key in at the **@3,0** prompt. This would draw a line 3 units horizontally along the x-axis.

- Polar   This format is used when you know the true distance and angle from the last point. It has the format of "@distance<angle." The number preceding the symbol is an angle in degrees, so only the numerical value of the angle needs to be typed.

Which format you use depends on what you know about the displacement. Another method to indicate the position of a line is the direct distance input feature. This enables you to indicate the distance and angle of the new line segment by using the crosshairs and providing the distance of the line.

Direct Distance Input

Direct Distance Input now gives AutoCAD users a much needed and quicker way to input distances. You can enter distances and obtain the angle desired from the location of the crosshairs from the last point chosen on the screen.

For example, when using this with the Line command at the Specify first point prompt, you only need to locate the crosshairs in the direction the line is to be placed and then type in the distance desired. When you press the Enter key, the line is drawn at that distance and angle. This input function works well when the Ortho drawing aid is activated. Use polar tracking when you are using this feature when drawing elements at an angle that is not located at the quadrants.

Tip 24 from
Ron House

You should be careful having any object snaps set in running mode when using the direct distance input feature. Since you are using the location of the crosshairs to locate the line segments, you can unsuspectingly snap to an object. Rather than the line being drawn in the direction you want, it will go in the direction of the object snap. You may want to turn off all object snaps while using direct distance input.

To do this, right-click on the Osnap tile from the status bar and select settings from the menu. Click the Clear All button from the Object Snap tab in the Drafting Settings dialog box, then click the OK button.

This feature works well when working only with straight lines, such as drawing the outline of a building or mechanical part. To illustrate this, let's use direct distance input in addition to the other coordinate placement formats to create the outline for a building in the following example.

EXAMPLE: USING DIRECT DISTANCE INPUT WITH THE LINE COMMAND

1. Let's use the architectural template created earlier in this chapter to create a new drawing. From the Standard toolbar, select the New button. Click on the Use a Template button, and select the Arch_A_8.dwt template.

2. When you are done with this example, you should have a drawing that looks similar to the one shown in Figure 2.15.

Figure 2.15
The outline of a house created using the Line command, direct distance input, and the line coordinate placement formats.

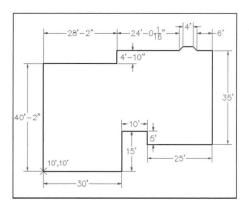

3. Once the drawing has opened, select the Line button from the Draw Toolbar. At the following prompt, supply a relative coordinate of **10',10'** and press Enter to start the line:

```
Specify first point: 10',10' <Enter>
```

4. Drag the crosshairs to the right. Note that the line is rubberbanded from the first point. Toggle the Ortho mode on by pressing the F8 key or by clicking the Ortho tile on the status bar.

5. At the To point prompt, type **30'** and press Enter.

   `To point: 30' <Enter>`

Tip 25 from
Ron House

It is important that you remember to type the foot symbol at the end of each distance. If you do not, AutoCAD will assume you meant inches and will draw your line accordingly. If this happens, don't worry because the Line command contains the Undo option. Just type a **U** at the To point prompt to undo the last line segment, press Enter, and then type the correct distance and continue.

---

6. A line is drawn 30' feet to the right. Drag the crosshairs straight up.

7. Type **15'** and press Enter after positioning the crosshairs.

   `To point: 15' <Enter>`

8. A line is drawn 15' units to top of the page. Drag the crosshairs to the right and then type **10'** at the command line and press Enter:

   `To point: 10' <Enter>`

9. A line is drawn 10' units to the left. Now let's try some of the other coordinate placement formats.

10. From the last point, you'll want to indicate the endpoint of the new line segment to be 5 feet in the negative Y direction, with no displacement in along the X axis. This is indicated by typing **@0,-5'**.

    `To point: @0,-5' <Enter>`

11. Next type **@25',0** and press Enter to draw a line horizontally to the right 25 feet.

12. Now type **@35',0** to draw the right hand side of the house.

    `To point: @35',0 <Enter>`

13. Type **@6'<180** to the draw a line over to the right-hand side of the bay window.

    `To point: @6'<180 <Enter>`

14. To create a bay window on the rear of the house, let's switch to using polar coordinates. The window is 6 feet from the right back corner of the house. Using Figure 2.16 as a reference, start by typing **@2'<135**.

    `To point: @2'<135 <Enter>`

15. Enter **@4'<180** to create the large window section of the bay, then type **@2'<225** for the opposite side.

    `To point: @4'<180 <Enter>`
    `To point: @2'<225 <Enter>`

16. To complete the rear of the house, you'll need to type in a coordinate that includes a fraction. The next line segment is 24'-1/16" long. For this, type **@24'1/16**. No inches symbol is needed; it is assumed that the fraction is in inches.

Figure 2.16
The dimensions of the bay windows created in this example using the Line command and the line polar coordinate format.

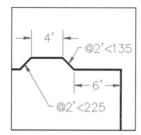

PART

1

CH

2

Tip 26 from
Ron House

When using feet, inches, and fractional inches all in the same coordinate for an architectural drawing, you would separate the inches and the fraction with a hyphen. For example, say the distance is 24'3-1/16 inches, you would type **24'3-1/16**. Remember to type the foot symbol or the length of your line will be incorrect.

17. The next segment is 4'10" long straight down, so type **@0,-4'10** and press Enter. Type **@28'2<180** for the next segment.

18. To complete the outline, you can now type **C** to close the line segment.

       To point: **C <Enter>**

At times it is convenient, and many times necessary, to magnify the drawing when working on detailed areas, such as the bay window you created on the house outline in the last example. The Real time Zoom and Pan commands give you this ability without the need to cancel the current command. This functionality is discussed in the next section.

NAVIGATING THE DRAWING

To magnify a portion of a drawing, you can use the real-time Zoom and Pan commands. They are called *real time* because of their capability to work either within the current command or transparently. Let's look at how these viewing commands are used while working in conjunction with the various drawing and editing commands.

THE DYNAMIC VIEWING COMMANDS

The dynamic or real-time viewing commands can be accessed by right-clicking and selecting either the Zoom or Pan options from the shortcut menu, shown in Figure 2.17.

Selecting these options does not interrupt the immediate command, so you can modify the present view magnification or position as often as needed. This is convenient if you are working on a small detail and need to zoom out to view the entire drawing without canceling the current command.

After selecting the viewing option, you will immediately see the cursor change to a small magnifying glass with a plus and a minus sign, shown in Figure 2.18.

Figure 2.17
You can easily access the Dynamic Pan and Zoom options from the Standard toolbar while operating the current command.

Figure 2.18
The cursor changes during the Real-time Zoom command to indicate cursor direction to increase or decrease view magnification.

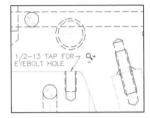

The Dynamic Zoom function has two modes, depending on which way you move the mouse while holding down the left mouse button:

- Zoom Out—When you drag the mouse toward the bottom of the screen, the view magnification decreases.

- Zoom In—When you drag the mouse toward the top of the screen, the view magnification increases.

As an example, if you constantly hold down the left mouse button and move the cursor toward the top of the screen, you increase the magnification scale factor. Alternately, if you move the cursor toward the bottom of the screen, the scale factor decreases and the drawing appears smaller on the screen.

When you are in Realtime mode, the command prompt displays the following:

```
>>Press ESC or ENTER to exit, or right-click to display shortcut menu.
```

If you right-click, the menu shown in Figure 2.19 appears.

Figure 2.19
The Display shortcut menu is available by right-clicking during the Real time commands.

PANNING THE DRAWING

From this menu, you can also select the Real time Pan command, or you can select the Pan Realtime button from the Standard toolbar (see Figure 2.20).

Figure 2.20
Choose the Pan Realtime button from the Standard toolbar.

If you just want to shift the drawing but you do not want to change the current view scale factor, you will need to use the Real time Pan command. The Real time Pan option shifts the current drawing view without changing the view magnification. Using this function changes the cursor to a small hand icon. Holding down the left mouse button when you move the mouse in any direction, the drawing view shifts in that direction.

Both of these functions are available through the right-click menus for the Drawing and Editing commands. This gives the user quick and easy access to the Real time Pan and Zoom commands when viewing the drawing, without interrupting the command process.

Note

See Chapter 11, "Viewing the Drawing," for in-depth information on the additional viewing commands.

SUMMARY

There are numerous drafting settings that can be set within a drawing. Using templates, you can eliminate much of the time needed to create a new drawing. Once the drawing is set up, you can save time using the various line coordinate input formats and object snaps to quickly lay out a drawing. You were also introduced to the Real time Zoom and Pan functions to view the drawing from different magnification factors while drawing. In the next chapter, you'll learn about creating layers and loading linetypes for a drawing to complete the drawing setup.

WORKING WITH LAYERS AND LINETYPES

In this chapter

LAYERS

Now that you've gotten familiar with the interface, learned how to create new drawings, how to open existing ones, and how to set up a drawing, let's look at some of the more specific AutoCAD features that have an overall effect on multiple objects, starting first with layers.

Imagine a stack of thin glass sheets that could individually be drawn on. Each sheet, or layer, would be the same size so that the sides could easily be aligned with each other. When you looked straight down through the stack of glass layers, you would be able to see everything that was drawn on each layer. This concept can be used to define drawing layers, in which you can control both the visibility of the layers and the linetype and color of the objects on each of the layers. This is achieved through the use of the Layer Properties Manager dialog box, which is opened via the Layers button on the Object Properties toolbar (see Figure 3.1).

Figure 3.1
Accessing the Layer Properties Manager via the Layers button on the Object Properties toolbar.

LAYER PROPERTIES MANAGER

The Layer Properties Manager dialog box lists all the layers contained in the current drawing. From here you can toggle the display of layers and also modify their properties. As we work our way through all the options available in the Layer Control Manager dialog box, let's first examine the New, Delete, Current, and Hide\Show details buttons in the upper-right corner of the dialog box.

NEW

To create a new layer, click the New button, which adds a new layer with the default name of Layer1. If you want to duplicate an existing set of layer properties and apply them to a new layer, highlight the layer from the list and click the New button. A new layer with duplicate properties is added to the list. If a layer exists with the same name, AutoCAD numbers them in consecutive order by adding the next-higher number to the end of the layer name, as shown in Figure 3.2.

Layers in AutoCAD follow the standard Windows naming conventions. When a name is given to a layer that exceeds the layer name column width, the name is abbreviated. The abbreviation shows the beginning and the end of the layer name, separated by an ellipsis. The layer name is displayed in a ToolTip when the cursor passes over the abbreviation.

Figure 3.2
Creating a new layer,
in addition to managing all properties of
the drawing layers, is
easy using the Layer
Properties Manager.

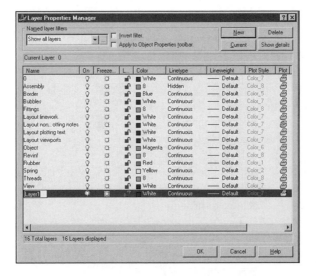

Tip 27 from
Ron House

More than one new layer can be added to the list by keying in a comma after the new
layer name.

After you name the layer, you can modify its properties. The properties shown are the properties for the entire layer, so every object residing on the layer will have these characteristics
by default. The next option deals with setting a layer to be the current layer.

CURRENT

The Current property sets the highlighted layer to be the current layer or the layer new
objects are placed on. This also lists that layer as current above the list of layers.

DELETE

When you select a layer from the list, you can delete the highlighted layer name if it meets
certain criteria. The criteria for deleting a layer are listed here:

- The layer cannot be current.
- No objects can exist on the layer.
- The layer cannot be named 0 or Defpoint.
- The layer also cannot belong to an externally referenced file.

→ See Chapter 17, "External Reference Files and Importing Images," for more information on external reference files.

The last option available is Hide\Show details.

Hide/Show Details

By selecting the Show details button, you can open the Details dialog box within the Layer Properties Manager, as Figure 3.3 illustrates.

Figure 3.3
The Details dialog box provides easy access to the layer properties.

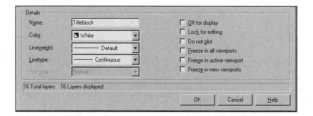

> **Note**
>
> Note that now the Show button changes to say Hide details. Clicking the Hide details button closes the Details dialog box.

The Details dialog box contains the various properties of each layer. These are described in the next section.

LAYER PROPERTY TYPES

Opening the details section of the Layer Manager dialog box gives you access to the individual layer property types. Each layer has five properties and six display states that can be set, which define the color, linetype, lineweight, or visibility of the layer. The individual properties are set by pull-down lists that contain the possible layer values or check boxes that set a current state. These layer properties are as follows:

- Name
- Color
- Lineweight
- Linetype
- Plot style

The layer display states include the following:

- Off for display
- Lock for editing
- Do not plot
- Freeze in all viewports

- Freeze in active viewport
- Freeze in new viewports

Each property is discussed in further detail in the following sections. The layer display states will be discussed in detail in "Layer Display States" later in this chapter.

NAME

The name of the layer is displayed here unless the name of the layer is 0 or Defpoints or unless the layer is part of an external reference file. Layers can be renamed through this edit box by selecting the layer from the list, highlighting the old layer name, and typing in the new name. When you exit the dialog box or highlight another layer, the modified layer name is updated.

When you create multiple new layers and after you key in the layer name, type a comma to add a new layer to the list. This is convenient because you need to provide only the names of the layers separated by a comma to quickly create new layers.

PART

I

CH

3

COLOR

The color assigned to the layer can be selected from here. The default color for a new layer is white. You can choose a different color from a list of colors; alternatively, you can select the Other option to bring up a color palette that contains a broader choice of colors to pick from.

LINEWEIGHT

Lineweight can best be described as the thickness or width of an object. The thickness of an object determines how the object is displayed on the screen, as well as how it will be plotted. Selecting a varying thickness from the list defines the default thickness for all objects on the layer. Lineweights can be used to specify an area or significant part, or just to outline the part you want to bring attention to—for example, referencing a detail on a plan with a thick dashed line surrounding the area of concern.

Linetype requires more explanation than the previous layer properties did. Therefore, before moving on to discuss the next layer property, plot styles, let's take some time to discuss working with linetypes.

LINETYPES

The *linetype* can be defined as the physical description of the object and typically is used to represent how an object is displayed in a drawing. Examples of a linetype are dashed, hidden, and continuous; numerous linetypes can be assigned in AutoCAD beyond what is listed here. Linetypes are typically used to indicate what is occurring within the drawing, such as hidden lines to represent a hole not visible from the side the part is viewed from, or a centerline to indicate the alignment of a series of holes.

The next section discusses the process of loading a linetype so it can be easily accessed within a drawing.

LOADING LINETYPES

Before assigning a linetype to a layer, you must load the linetype definition. The standard linetype file is located the ACAD.lin file. Note that linetype files have an .LIN extension. These files define the characteristics of the linetype definitions. To load a linetype file, select the Other option from the Linetype pull-down menu in the Object Properties dialog box (see Figure 3.4).

Figure 3.4
Accessing the Linetype Manager by selecting Other from the list of available linetypes.

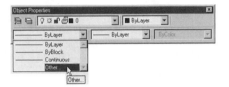

This opens the Linetype Manager, displayed in Figure 3.5.

Figure 3.5
The linetypes that are loaded are shown in the Linetype Manager dialog box.

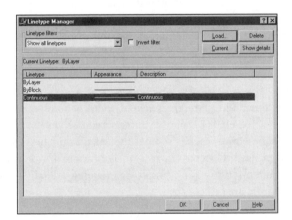

Click the Load button to bring up the Load or Reload Linetypes dialog box, shown in Figure 3.6.

From here you can select which linetypes from the default ACAD.LIN file you want to have available in the current drawing. Select the linetypes using the Shift or Ctrl keys, and then click the OK button. The selected layers will then appear in the Linetype Manager dialog box. You can load a different linetype file from here by clicking the File button and selecting a new linetype file from the Select Linetype File dialog box.

Figure 3.6
Clicking the Load button allows you to load a new linetype from the Load or Reload Linetypes dialog box.

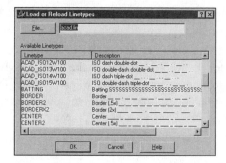

Tip 28 from
Ron House

Linetypes can easily be loaded in a project template drawing and saved with the drawing. This makes the linetypes available in any drawing that uses this template. This is one of the advantages of using template drawings; the linetypes do not need to be loaded at the onset of creating a new drawing.

→ You can learn more about using templates in Chapter 2, "Drawing Setup," in the section "Creating And Using Templates."

If you select the Hide/Show Details button from the Linetype Manager, you gain access to the properties of the individual linetypes. These properties are available via the Details section in the Linetype Manager dialog box (see Figure 3.7):

Figure 3.7
Selecting the Show details button from the Linetype Manager dialog box displays the specific properties of a linetype available in the drawing.

- Global scale factor
- Current object scale
- Use paper space units for scaling

The details of each of these properties are discussed in the following paragraphs.

GLOBAL SCALE FACTOR

This is the linetype scale factor for the whole drawing, or the Ltscale variable. This setting enables you to set a scale factor to increase or decrease the spacing of all linetypes throughout the drawing. Because the Ltscale factor directly affects the way a linetype is displayed, use this option to adjust the display of all linetypes in the drawing.

CURRENT OBJECT SCALE

Current Object Scale is the individual linetype scale factor, which can be applied to individual objects as needed. This is a factor of the Global Scale Factor, so objects that have this value set will change as the Ltscale variable is changed.

USE PAPER SPACE UNITS FOR SCALING

This setting uses the viewport scale factor to determine the size of the linetype, which affects how the linetype is displayed.

→ For more information on working in paper space, see Chapter 18, "Plotting and Layouts," in the section called "Model Space and Paper Space."

Now let's return back to our list of layer properties with the next section on plot styles.

PLOT STYLES

Plot styles classify the plotted characteristics of objects that determine how they will appear on the plotted sheet. Through the Layer Properties Manager, you can assign plot styles to individual layers.

→ You can find more information on Plot styles in Chapter 18, "Plotting and Layouts."

Next, you'll learn about the layer display states available in the drawing.

LAYER DISPLAY STATES

The *layer display states* for a layer define the visibility and selectability of objects on each layer. These states can easily be changed, or toggled, to the opposite effect to display or select objects from the drawing. The different states available are discussed in the next section, "Changing Layer Display States."

APPLYING SPECIFIC DISPLAY STATES

The specific layer display states are available from the Show details option within the Layer Properties Manager dialog box. These enable you to apply certain display states to layers during these situations:

- Off for display—When this check box is selected, the objects on this layer will not be displayed.

- Lock for editing—Lock for Editing defines a layer as noneditable, which essentially makes the layer read-only; it can be displayed but not modified.

- Do not plot—Layers can also be marked to not plot using this check box. This can be used to not plot non-essential layers, such as a personal notes layer you may use to contain notes about the drawing but that you do not want plotted.

- Freeze in all viewports—This option turns off the visibility of the layer, making the items on this layer nonselectable, enabling you to quickly apply this to all viewports you have in the drawing.

→ Look in the section labeled "Viewports" in Chapter 11, "Viewing the Drawing" for details on working with viewports in the drawing.

The next two options pertain only to those drawings that have paperspace viewports created.

→ For more information on working with paperspace viewports, see the section called "Model Space and Paper Space" in Chapter 18, "Plotting and Layouts."

- Freeze in active viewport—This option turns off the selected layer visibility in only the active viewport.

- Freeze in new viewports—This option turns off the visibility of the highlighted layer in every new viewport created in the layout.

CHANGING LAYER DISPLAY PROPERTIES

Three sets of layer display properties can be modified:

- On/Off
- Thaw/Freeze
- Lock/Unlock

These properties can be toggled to various states when the symbol for that state is selected in the Layer Properties Manager dialog box or the layer pop-up list, as shown in Figure 3.8.

Figure 3.8
Setting layer display properties using the layer pop-up list makes modifying a layer display property easy.

Note

You can select multiple layers and apply display properties to the selected group by using the Shift and Ctrl keys when picking layers from the Layer Properties Manager dialog box. This make it convenient to apply a certain color or linetype to multiple layers at one time.

Let's discuss the effects of each of the display properties in detail.

ON/OFF

This option turns the visibility of the selected layer off, and items on the layer cannot be selected. When the layer state is toggled back on, only the items on this layer are regenerated. This property is represented by a lighted light bulb when on, and an unlighted light bulb when off.

Caution

The All selection set mode can select objects on a layer that has been turned off. Take care when you have layers in this state and you are using this selection set mode. Objects that exist on this layer can accidentally be erased, and you may not realize it until the layer is turned back on. See Chapter 10, "Selecting Objects," for more detail.

THAW/FREEZE

Like the Off state, when a layer is frozen, objects on that layer cannot be viewed or selected. The difference exists when the layer is thawed: The entire drawing will regenerate, not just the items on the layer. This property is represented by a sun when thawed and a snowflake when frozen.

Caution

Take care with frozen layers when using the All selection set mode. For example, if you move all items on a thawed layer, consider the alignment with those objects on a frozen layer since the frozen objects will not be selected and moved and the situation may be difficult to correct.

UNLOCK/LOCK

When a layer is locked, the objects on that layer cannot be selected even though they are visible on the screen. Object snaps can still be applied to objects on a locked layer.

Now that you know more about the layer display states and how they can be used in the drawing, let's look at some specific settings in which the layer display states can be applied.

NAMED LAYER FILTERS

This feature allows you to determine which layers will be displayed in the list by filtering the layers that are in the drawing by a specific property. Clicking the ellipsis button from the Named layer filters box (see Figure 3.9) opens the Named layer filters dialog box.

From the Named layer filters dialog box, shown in Figure 3.10, filter criteria can be chosen based on layer property or state.

With the Named layer filters dialog box, you can set which layers are displayed in the Layer Properties Manager based on property setting or state.

Figure 3.9
You can apply filters from the Named layer filters box on the Layer Properties Manager to control the display of layers.

From the Named Layer Filters dialog box, shown in Figure 3.10, filter criteria can be chosen based on layer property or state.

Figure 3.10
With the Named Layer Filters dialogue box, you can set which layers are displayed in the Layer Properties Manager based on property setting or state.

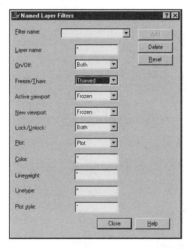

When applied, this displays only those layers affected. This dialog box enables you to set only specific layer criteria, so filter criteria must be saved to a file and recalled in the Layer Properties Manager dialog box.

To apply filter criteria to the list of layers, select the filter criteria name from the Named layer filters pull-down menu. You'll notice three default choices available to you, in addition to the named filters you have created:

- Show all layers—No filter is applied, and all layers in the drawing (including external reference file layers) are visible.

- Show all used layers—This shows only those layers that are being used in the drawing. In other words, only those layers that have objects on them will be shown in the list.

- Show all Xref dependant layers—This lists only those layers that are part of an external reference file. See Chapter 17, "External Reference Files and Importing Images," for more information.

Looking at the rest of the Named Layer Filters box, you'll see two other options that control how the Named layer filters affect the layer listing shown in the Layer Properties Manager.

- Invert filter—This option gives you the inverse, or opposite, of the current filter criteria. For example, if the filter criteria were set to show only those layers that were frozen, inversing the filter would then show you only the layers that are thawed.

- Apply to object properties toolbar—This option applies the layers matching the filter criteria to the Object properties toolbar. Only those layers that have not been filtered out will appear when you access the toolbar.

Using the options available in the Layer Properties Manager enables you to modify the properties of the layers. Now let's look at modifying the properties of individual objects in the drawing.

THE PROPERTIES WINDOW

The Object Properties dialog box, or the Properties window, is a dialog box designed to easily modify the properties of objects. With this dialog box, you can modify objects by object type on a per-object basis.

This is accomplished in two ways: by overall drawing or by selectioning objects from the drawing.

MODIFYING THE PROPERTIES OF THE OVERALL DRAWING

The Properties command is activated by selecting the Tools pull-down menu, Properties option, which opens the Properties dialog box, as shown in Figure 3.11.

Figure 3.11
The Properties dialog box accesses the general properties of the drawing when a selection set is not found.

These drawing properties can be modified:

- General—Deals with overall properties of the drawing file, such as color, layer, linetype, and lineweight.

- Plot style—Modifies the properties of the plot style and plot table. See Chapter 18, "Plotting and Layouts," for more information on plot styles.

- View—Lists the properties of the current view—such as location, height, and width—and enables you to modify these properties.

- Misc—Deals mainly with the User Coordinate System (UCS) settings. Properties such as UCS Icon visibility (UCS per Viewport) are available here.

In addition to these options for modifying the drawing as a whole, you can also modify the properties of objects selected from the drawing.

MODIFYING OBJECT PROPERTIES BY SELECTION SET

When you have created a selection set, which is a group of objects you've selected from the drawing to be modified, you can access the Properties dialog box by right-clicking and choosing Properties from the shortcut menu. If the Properties dialog box is already opened, it automatically updates to show the properties of the object selected during the creation of the selection set.

Note that you can access the sets of objects from the pull-down menu; these sets have been grouped by object type with the number of objects in that group, shown in Figure 3.12.

PART

I

CH

3

Figure 3.12
You can easily modify the properties of a selection set via the Object Properties dialog box.

The properties that can be modified depend on the objects selected. All characteristics of the objects can be edited from here. To modify the properties of a specific selection set of objects or to quickly select objects from the drawing, you can filter the drawing using the Quick Select command covered in the next section.

QUICK SELECT

To select a particular group of objects from the drawing, type Qselect at the command line to open the Quick Select dialog box. The Quick Select dialog box enables you to filter a group of objects based on property settings from the current selection set or the entire drawing, see Figure 3.13.

Figure 3.13
The Quick Select dialog box is used to filter objects based on property settings.

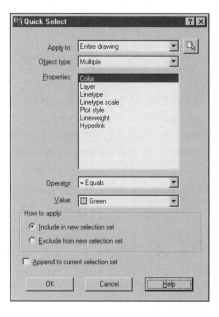

The objects filtered can then be added or removed from a new selection set. This gives you a simple and fast method of selecting objects from the drawing file via their object type or property.

→ To learn about additional ways to select objects from a drawing, advance to Chapter 10, "Selecting Objects," for more information.

SUMMARY

Using layers efficiently enables you to expand the functionality of a drawing. You can, if desired, maintain all the information about a project contained within a single drawing. By toggling the visibility of layers off and on, you can change the drawing to display the information you want to convey. For example, all of the discipline drawings for a single building floor, such as architectural, structural, electrical, and so on, can easily be managed in this way. Using this in combination with linetypes allows specific information in the drawing to be highlighted. And, by modifying properties of certain objects, either on layers or individually, gives you complete control of how the drawing can be displayed.

OBJECT CONSTRUCTION

CHAPTER 4

THE BASIC DRAWING OBJECTS

In this chapter

WORKING WITH CONSTRUCTION LINES

On some occasions, construction lines are needed to visually demonstrate relationships within the drawing. Although the Object Tracking feature works similarly to having a temporary construction line, you may need an actual drawing object when setting up a drawing to represent an association between two or more drawing elements (for example, laying out the top, front, and side views of a mechanical drawing). AutoCAD has two line elements, Xlines and rays, specifically for this purpose.

XLINES

Xlines, or construction lines, enable you to create horizontal, vertical, or diagonal lines that run in both directions from a midpoint to infinity. Although they run beyond the boundary of your defined working space, Xlines are not taken into consideration when viewing the extents of your drawing. Xlines can be extremely handy when used in a drawing, either by offsetting a specific distance from an element or when bisecting angles. Figure 4.1 illustrates the use of Xlines in a three view instrumental drawing.

Figure 4.1
Xlines, shown here with a dashed line-type and light color, were used in this drawing to quickly lay out the front, top, and side views of this mechanical block.

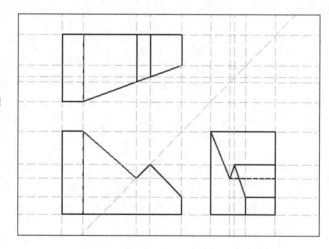

The Xline command can be selected from the Draw toolbar, chosen from the Draw pull-down menu, or activated by typing XL and pressing Enter at the command line.

Selecting the Construction Line button gives you the default Xline prompt (see Figure 4.2):

```
Specify a point or [Hor/Ver/Ang/Bisect/Offset]:
Specify through point:
```

With the default options you can pick two points, one that locates the Xline midpoint and another that specifies the angle the construction line will go through. Picking more points at the Specify through point prompt draws another construction line that passes through the same midpoint of the first Xline. You can access the other Xline placement options through the right-click shortcut menu, shown in Figure 4.3.

Figure 4.2
Access the Construction Line button from the toolbar.

Figure 4.3
The Xline command options are also available through the right-click menu.

This right-click shortcut menu makes it easy to quickly choose any of the following Xline options:

- Hor—Draws a horizontal construction line after a point is picked to define the location the Xline will pass through. This enables you to quickly layout the horizontal elements of your drawing.
- Ver—Inserts a vertical construction line wherever a location point is picked.
- Ang—Allows you to type in the angle of the construction line, or is defined when you pick a point. This option is great for creating auxiliary views.
- Bisect—Creates a construction line that bisects an angle after the angle vertex, angle start point, and angle endpoint are selected.
- Offset—After an offset distance is specified, the construction line or other line to be offset is selected and the side it is to be offset is picked.

Two options enable you to place Xlines by bisecting an angle or by offsetting the Xline from another object. These two options are discussed in further detail in the next two sections.

BISECTING AN ANGLE

Let's follow through the steps it takes to completely bisect an angle with an Xline. After the command is invoked, right-click to access the shortcut menu and then select Bisect.

EXAMPLE: BISECTING AN ANGLE

1. At the prompt Specify the angle vertex point, select the intersection of the two elements using an Intersection object snap, if an intersection exists, or select a chosen vertex point that the Xline will pass through.

2. Pick a point on one leg of the angle when prompted to Specify the angle start point, and then drag the bisector into place.

3. Next, specify the angle endpoint and select the other angle leg. As you move the cursor to pick the angle endpoint, the angle bisector is placed in position. Now the Xline can be used as the bisector and can be edited as needed.

This option allows you to easily arrange construction lines at a angle in relation to other object lines or Xlines. The other Xline option, Offset, is great way to "rough in" a drawing or to set up vertical, horizontal, or angular relationships between elements, using an existing object in the drawing to offset from.

Let's now examine the process of offsetting an Xline.

OFFSETTING AN XLINE

In this example, you offset an Xline.

EXAMPLE: OFFSETTING AN XLINE

1. Pick the Xline (Construction Line) icon from the Draw toolbar to call up the command; then right-click and click the Offset option.

2. Type in the offset distance and the following prompt:

   `Specify the offset distance or [Through] <1.0000>:`

   The Through option enables you to pick two points that represent the offset distance.

3. Pick the linear object that you want to offset from, which can be either a line or an Xline.

4. Pick a point onscreen that represents the side you wish to offset to at the Specify the side to offset prompt.

5. Right-click and select Enter to exit the command, or press Enter.

In addition to using Xlines to layout a drawing, you can also place rays when only half a construction line is needed.

RAYS

Rays are similar to Xlines, except that rays begin at a point you specify and extend in one direction to infinity. Essentially, rays can be considered one-half of an Xline.

> **Note**
> When a construction line (Xline) is broken in two using an editing command, such as Break or Trim, the two segments are converted into rays. When a ray is broken, the segment closest to the start point is converted into a line; the remainder is still a ray segment.

The Ray command must be keyed in at the command prompt or chosen from the Draw pull-down menu; no button is available for it on the Draw toolbar.

Figure 4.4
To activate the Ray command, choose Ray from the Draw pull-down menu.

The following prompt lines describe the actions taken during the Ray command:

```
Command: RAY
Specify start point:
Specify through point:
```

As indicated by the prompts, you first select a start point for the ray, and then select another point as you drag the ray into position. The second point specifies the rotation angle for the ray. The command will repeat, prompting you to select another throughpoint for the next ray. A good example of using rays to create a mounting base is shown in Figure 4.5.

Figure 4.5
Multiple rays emanate from a single point, which is ideal when using construction lines to create circular, symmetric parts.

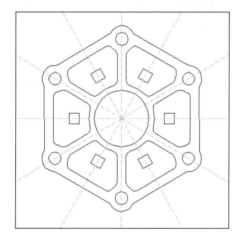

The next ray will be drawn from the same start point of the last until you right-click or press Enter, which terminates the command.

Tip 29 from
Ron House

If you use Xlines and rays as construction lines in a drawing, consider placing them onto a separate, locked layer. This enables you to draw and edit your object lines on a different layer, keeping them separate from the construction lines, and allows the layer with the construction lines to be turned off when not needed.

Now that you have learned how to use the Xline and Ray commands as construction lines for a drawing, let's look at the basic drawing commands.

THE BASIC DRAWING COMMANDS

We've already covered the Line command in the Chapter 2, "Drawing Setup," so now it's on to circles and arcs. Both of these elements have various options that enable you to create the circle or arc you desire. You can create these objects by either dragging or rubberbanding the object into shape, or by providing a specific coordinate to define points along their boundaries. Let's look at each of these commands in detail.

THE CIRCLE COMMAND

The Circle command is accessed from the Draw toolbar or pull-down menu, or by simply typing **C** and pressing Enter at the command line.

Figure 4.6
Access the Circle command from the Draw toolbar.

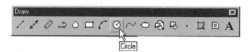

The Circle command places a circle by radius or diameter, or based on specified points you have chosen to define the circle. You can choose from various options, mainly depending on how you wish to draw the circle.

After providing a center point for the circle, you can specify the size of a circle by its radius or by its diameter through the right-click menu shown in Figure 4.7.

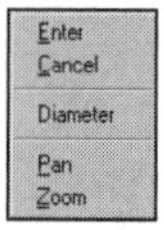

Figure 4.7
With the right-click Circle shortcut menu, you can specify a diameter value to create a circle.

You can type in a value or the circle can be dragged, or "rubberbanded," to its desired size. This process is called rubberbanding because you can actually see the shape of the circle change, similar to stretching a rubberband.

Note

The default value will appear as the size of the last circle placed in the drawing. To place another circle of the same size, all you need to do is select Enter from the right-click menu to accept the default value.

After initiating the command and selecting a center point, the options discussed in the next sections are also available by activating the right-click menu, shown in Figure 4.8:

Figure 4.8
The options available with the Circle command are readily accessible with the right-click menu.

Note

Figure 4.8 illustrates the capability to quickly access additional options via the right-click shortcut menu. This functionality is part of the "heads-up display" feature in AutoCAD, allowing you to focus more on your design and not on the keyboard.

ADDITIONAL OPTIONS AVAILABLE WITH THE CIRCLE COMMAND

Three options are available with the Circle command:

- 3P—Three points determine the boundary of the circle, or its circumference. After placing the first and second points, the circle can be dragged to its desired size.

- 2P—Creates a circle from two supplied points that define its circumference. A relative or polar coordinate can be used to interpret the second point on the diameter.

- Tangent, Tangent, Radius—The circle is created by selecting two tangent objects that define the size of the circle.

Let's examine the last option in more detail in the next section.

CREATING A TANGENT, TANGENT, RADIUS CIRCLE

The Tangent, Tangent, Radius circle command provides a convenient way to place a circle tangent to two other objects. This option is great for determining a turn radius when designing parking lots and to check to see whether there is enough room for a wheelchair in restrooms (see Figure 4.9).

Figure 4.9
An example of the Tangent Tangent Radius option used to create a circle to represent the turning radius of a wheelchair.

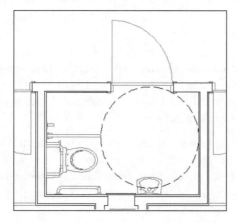

PART
II

CH
4

Creating this type of circle is easy if you follow these steps:

EXAMPLE: CREATING A CIRCLE

1. When the Circle command is invoked, select the Ttr (tan tan radius) option from the right-click menu.

2. Pick a relative point on the first tangent object at the Specify point on object for first tangent of circle prompt.

Tip 30 from
Ron House

When selecting the tangent points on an object using the Tangent Tangent Radius option, you do not need to use object snaps. AutoCAD determines the exact location on the object where the circle will be tangent when the circle is drawn.

---

3. Select the second tangent reference object.

4. Type in the desired radius at the Specify radius of circle prompt.

5. You also can pick two points on the screen to represent the distance. The circle is drawn based on the parameters you've provided.

Tip 31 from
Ron House

If it is not possible to draw this circle, AutoCAD will simply state at the command line that this circle does not exist. Check your circle radius to determine a probable cause, keeping in mind the units set for the drawing. If you have the units for the drawing set to feet and you key in a value in inches, this could keep the circle from being drawn. This is common when working on drawings where you want to switch between unit types, such as a site plan. The units might be engineering feet when working on the site, yet switched to architectural inches when placing the floorplan into the site. Reference the Units command, discussed in Chapter 2, "Drawing Setup."

Arcs can be placed in the drawing when just a portion of a circle will do, and you have eleven distinct ways to create them. Arc options are discussed in the next section.

CREATING ARCS

Arcs are one of the more flexible AutoCAD commands because there are so many options available to create them, each depending on the specific purpose for that arc. To begin, you can access the Arc command from the Draw toolbar (see Figure 4.10) or pull-down menu, or type **C** and press Enter at the command line.

The ARC command places an arc in the drawing where you provide the details about the arc, such as the start, center, or endpoints and the angle, radius, direction, or length of chord. The options you choose depend on the information you know about the arc to be drawn. As you are prompted to further define the arc, certain characteristics such as those listed previously can be used to specify how the arc will look.

Figure 4.10
Access the Arc command from the Draw toolbar.

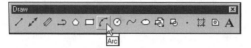

Let's start by examining the default Arc option, which enables you to draw a three-point arc, the easiest type of arc to create. Then we'll look at the remaining Arc options.

The three-point arc is defined by picking three points along the path of the arc. The arc is drawn by picking the first (start), second (arc circumference midpoint), and third (endpoint) points of the arc at the corresponding prompts.

```
Specify start point of arc or [CEnter]:
Specify second point of arc or [CEnter/ENd]:
Specify end point of arc:
```

Note that other options were available as we were creating the three-point arc. These other options allow you to create other types of arcs when the information known about the arc isn't as straightforward as that of the three-point arc. All these options are available through the right-click menu, and the menus change depending on which option we choose. Let's run through some examples of creating an arc with these options.

CREATING ARCS VIA A KNOWN CENTER POINT AND ANGLE

Another way to create an arc is by its center point. Start by selecting the Arc button from the Draw toolbar; then select the Center option from the right-click menu shown in Figure 4.11 and follow these steps:

Figure 4.11
Once the Arc command is invoked, the right-click shortcut menu is a quick way to access additional arc options or display commands.

EXAMPLE: CREATING AN ARC VIA A KNOWN CENTER POINT AND ANGLE

1. Pick a point in the drawing or type the absolute coordinate to specify the center point of the arc.

2. Provide the starting point for the arc. This can be done by typing in an absolute, relative, or polar coordinate, or by picking a point.

3. Specify the endpoint of the arc, then

4. Access the right-click menu and choose the Angle option, as shown in Figure 4.12.

PART
II

CH

4

Figure 4.12
This right-click menu changes depending on which arc option was selected before-hand; in this example the Angle and Chord Length options are now available.

5. Drag the arc to its desired size, or key in the included angle.

CREATING ARCS VIA A KNOWN CENTER POINT AND CHORD LENGTH

Follow steps 1–3 in the previous example to draw an arc by providing the chord length. This time, however, instead of selecting Angle from the right-click menu, let's pick the chord Length option.

EXAMPLE: CREATING AN ARC VIA A KNOWN CENTER POINT AND CHORD LENGTH

1. Right-click and select the chord Length option at the following prompt:
   ```
   Specify the endpoint of the arc or [Angle/chord Length]:
   ```

2. Key in the desired chord length, and then press Enter to place the arc. The chord length can be used to create a major or minor arc based on a positive or negative chord length. This is shown in Figure 4.13.

Figure 4.13
Two arcs created with the same starting point but with positive and negative chord lengths of the same value.

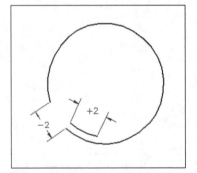

If the chord length is positive, the minor arc is drawn counterclockwise by defining the distance from the start point to the end point. If the chord length is negative, the major arc is drawn counterclockwise but measured in a clockwise direction.

CREATING ARCS VIA A KNOWN CENTER POINT AND ANGLE

Another alternative is to create an arc by its center point. Select the command from the Draw toolbar; then select the Center option from the right-click menu and follow these steps:

EXAMPLE: CREATING ARCS VIA A KNOWN CENTER POINT AND ANGLE

1. Start by selecting a center point for the arc.

2. Then pick where you want the arc to start.

3. Right-click and select Angle from the list.

4. Specify the included angle by keying it in or by dragging to the angle desired.

Tip 32 from
Ron House

You can simplify the process of making arcs if you turn on polar tracking by double-clicking the Polar tile in the status bar. You also can set the polar angle by right-clicking on this same tile and selecting Settings from the list. This opens the Drafting Settings dialog box to the Polar Tracking tab. Here you can adjust the polar settings as needed. Typing OS at the command line and pressing Enter also opens the Drafting Settings dialog box, yet you will need to click on the Polar Tracking tab.

Note

Arcs are drawn in a counterclockwise direction from the starting point. Therefore, the order in which you pick points plays a part in how the arc is drawn. Pay close attention when creating arcs to avoid unexpected results.

DRAWING ARCS WITH A KNOWN STARTING POINT, ENDPOINT AND EITHER ANGLE, DIRECTION, OR RADIUS

The last arc example we'll walk through is one in which you know the start and endpoints of the arc, and one of three other available parameters. These parameters are listed here:

- Angle—Indicates the included angle of the arc. Whether this value is positive or negative determines how the arc is drawn. A positive included angle draws the arc from the start point counterclockwise. A negative included angle draws the arc in a clockwise direction. This is illustrated in Figure 4.14.

Figure 4.14
The direction an arc is drawn depends on whether a positive and negative value is given for the included angle using the Start, End, and Angle Arc options.

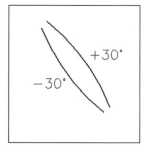

- Direction—Draws the arc tangent to the starting direction you specify.

- Radius—Draws a major or minor arc in a clockwise direction from the start point. To create a major arc, or the largest arc drawn between the start and endpoints, provide a negative radius. A positive value for the radius produces a minor arc, or the smallest arc drawn between the points (see Figure 4.15).

Figure 4.15
The major (negative radius) and minor (positive radius) arcs created with an Start, End, Radius Arc.

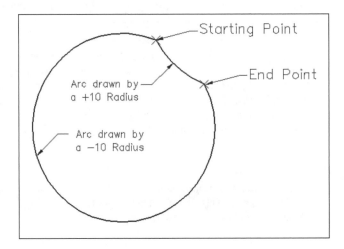

As you can see, you can use a number of different ways to create an arc. The best way to determine how you will draw the arc depends on what you know about it. The old saying rings true in creating arcs: "Practice makes perfect!" It may take a while before you develop a process to create arcs efficiently, or to determine which arc to use. Don't hesitate to experiment with all the arc options; it is time well spent and can only lead to increased productivity in the long run.

SUMMARY

The commands in this chapter represent the object types you can use to layout and create a basic drawing. Many of these commands are used to build the base objects of the drawing, which are then elaborated on using the addition drawing objects. The next three chapters discuss these additional drawing object types, increasing in degree of complexity and purpose. In Chapter 5, "More Drawing Objects," you'll expand your knowledge of the different drawing objects available as we continue the Object Construction section of this book.

CHAPTER **5**

MORE DRAWING OBJECTS

In this chapter

DRAWING OBJECTS

Each of the drawing types in this chapter has some very specific uses and are typically considered the basic drawing objects. However, some of these objects can be created using equations, such as with complex ellipses. This allows you to draw a full range of objects based on your needs, as you will find in this chapter.

BUILDING MULTISIDED POLYGONS

Polygons are multisided objects in which each side is of equal length. The lines that make up the side of the polygon are grouped to form a single object, and the number of sides for a polygon can vary from 3 to a maximum of 1,024. Objects such as square rivet holes, revision triangles, or simple bolt heads are easily created with this command. To activate the Polygon command, choose the Polygon button from the Draw toolbar or select it from the Draw pull-down menu.

Figure 5.1

Access the Polygon
button from the Draw
pull-down menu.

Tip 33 from
Ron House

You can also start this command by typing **POL** at the command line.

After keying in the number of sides for the polygon, the various options available are as follows:

- Specify center of polygon or [Edge]—A polygon can be created either by specifying its center or an edge by defining its start point and endpoints.

- Enter an option [Inscribed in circle/Circumscribed about circle]—This option determines whether the polygon will be drawn inscribed or will be circumscribed about a circle radius:

    - Inscribed—Inscribed means that the corners, or vertices, of the polygon will be placed on the circumference of the circle radius.

    - Circumscribed—This option locates the midpoint between the edges of the polygon touching on the circle radius.

Examples of inscribed and circumscribed polygons are shown in Figure 5.2.

- Specify first endpoint of edge/Specify second endpoint of edge—When the edge option is chosen, you can specify the beginning point and endpoint of the edge.

Figure 5.2
This figure illustrates the differences between an inscribed and circumscribed polygon.

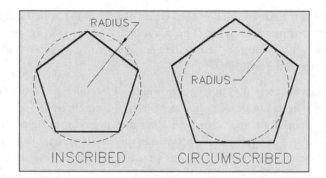

Tip 34 from
Ron House

The direction of the edge determines the orientation of the polygon. The length runs in the positive X direction, and the edge is the bottom edge of the polygon. If the direction or length is negative, the edge drawn forms the top edge of the polygon.

To illustrate how easy it is to use the Polygon command, let's look at the next example—creating a bolt head.

EXAMPLE: DEFINING A BOLT HEAD WITH THE POLYGON COMMAND

1. Start AutoCAD and open the drawing ch5_01.dwg from the accompanying CD. Start the Polygon command by selecting it either from the Draw toolbar or from the Draw pull-down menu.

2. In this example, let's simply create a six-sided bolt in Plan view to complete the framing detail and to emphasize the process of creating a circumscribed polygon. At the Enter Number of Sides prompt, type **5** and press Enter:

```
POLYGON Enter number of sides <4>: 5 <ENTER>
```

Tip 35 from
Ron House

To set the default number of sides for a Polygon, use the Polysides system variables. Just type **Polysides** at the command line, enter the value, and press Enter.

3. Say the center of the bolt is given, so we should use the default, or center option:

```
Specify center of polygon or [Edge]: 52'7,66'5-5/8<ENTER>
```

4. Because the size of the bolt head is determined by the distance across the flats, or from center of edge to center of edge, use the Circumscribed ellipse option to draw the bolt. Right-click to access the shortcut menu and select Circumscribed:

```
Enter an option [Inscribed in circle/Circumscribed about circle] <C>: C <ENTER>
```

5. Key in the **.75** radius that will be used to define the bolt head:

```
Specify radius of circle: .75 <ENTER>
```

Following this process, you can easily create a 3/4-inch radius bolt head.

PART
II

CH
5

One way to check the size of the bolt is to create a circle of the same radius you specified for the bolt using the same center point. The circle should touch only the center of the circumscribed polygon edges. Using the same circle on an inscribed polygon, the circle would touch each corner of the polygon.

Polygons are actually created as polylines in which all the sides are formed to make a single object. Polyline objects can be described as a series of continuous line segments and are discussed in more detail in the next chapter. Rather than polygons being composed of separate lines, they are created as a polyline, which makes this object type more efficient, taking up less physical drawing space than if polygons were multiple individual line segments.

→ If you want to work on the individual lines of the polygon, you must first "explode" the object with the Explode command. You'll learn more about working with polylines and the Explode command in Chapter 6, "Complex Drawing Objects."

Polygons are extremely flexible objects that can be used to create numerous items within a drawing—essentially any object that has even sides. Experiment with the Polygon command to determine just how you might apply this type of object throughout all of your drawings.

Another versatile yet complex object that has a number of applications is the ellipse, which is covered in the next section.

CREATING WHOLE AND PARTIAL ELLIPSES

Ellipses are complex elements that can be created in one of two ways: either as a whole ellipse or as a segment of an ellipse, an elliptical arc. Let's look at the ellipse options available. Select the Ellipse button from the Draw toolbar, shown in Figure 5.3, to get the following prompt:

Figure 5.3
Access the Ellipse button from the Draw toolbar.

```
Command: _ellipse
Specify axis endpoint of ellipse or [Arc/Center]:
```

At this point, you are ready to define what type of ellipse you want to draw. Using the default option, ellipses can be defined by the endpoints that determine the boundaries of the ellipse's major and minor axis.

You can also right-click to access the other ellipse options from the shortcut menu:

- Arc—This option creates an elliptical arc, which is defined by the angle of the first axis used to create the ellipse.
- Center—The center of the ellipse can be specified using this option.

The next example walks you through creating an ellipse by two endpoints, which define its axis.

EXAMPLE: CREATING AN ELLIPSE BY AXIS ENDPOINTS

1. Create a new drawing and start the Ellipse command by selecting the Ellipse button or by choosing the command from the Draw pull-down menu.

2. At the prompt, pick or key in the first axis point:

   `Specify axis endpoint of ellipse or [Arc/Center]:` **3,2 <ENTER>**

3. Now, enter the opposite endpoint of the axis:

   `Specify other endpoint of axis:` **1,4 <ENTER>**

4. After the first axis has been created, define the other axis from the center of the first:

   `Specify distance to other axis or [Rotation]:` **5,2 <ENTER>**

   The ellipse created in this example should look like the one in Figure 5.4.

Figure 5.4
This figure displays an example of an ellipse created by axis end-points showing the major and minor axes.

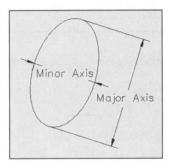

Now, let's follow through the next example to create an ellipse by defining a center point.

EXAMPLE: CREATING AN ELLIPSE USING THE CENTER OPTION

1. Using the same drawing you created for the last example, select the Ellipse button on the Draw toolbar.

2. At the Specify Axis Endpoint of Ellipse or [Arc/Center] prompt, right-click and select the Center option.

3. Enter the center point for the ellipse or pick a point:

   `Specify center of ellipse:` **7,3 <ENTER>**

4. Enter the endpoint of either the major or minor axis from the center:

   `Specify endpoint of axis:` **@2<45 <ENTER>**

5. Now that the first axis has been defined, you'll need to create the other axis to complete the process:

   `Specify distance to other axis or [Rotation]:` **8.5,3 <ENTER>**

The other available option, the Rotation option, enables you to specify the rotation around the major axis of the ellipse based on a ratio between the major and minor axes. A value of 0 or a low ratio leads to a more circular ellipse object, and a high ratio tends to flatten the ellipse, with a maximum possible value of 89.4. Figure 5.5 illustrates the difference between a high- and low-ratio ellipse.

Figure 5.5
The two ellipses shown in this figure were created with a high rotation value of 80.0 (the thinner ellipse) and a low ratio value of 0 (the outside circular ellipse).

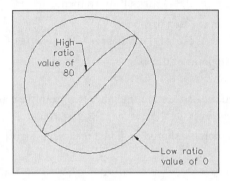

Another option of the Ellipse command is the capability to create partial or elliptical arcs, discussed in the next section.

DRAWING ELLIPTICAL ARCS

You can draw a specific portion of an ellipse using the Arc option of the Ellipse command. The following example illustrates how:

EXAMPLE: CREATING AN ELLIPTICAL ARC

1. Still using the drawing from the last example, type **EL** at the command line and press Enter. At the prompt, right-click and select the Arc option.

2. Type in the first axis endpoint:
   `Specify axis endpoint of elliptical arc or [Center]:` **3,1 <ENTER>**

3. Define the opposite axis endpoint:
   `Specify other endpoint of axis:` **3,2 <ENTER>**

4. Use the Rotation option to create the ellipse by right-clicking and selecting Rotation from the menu:
   `Specify distance to other axis or [Rotation]:` **r**

5. For this example, use a low ratio value of 30:
   `Specify rotation around major axis:` **30 <ENTER>**

6. The start angle is measured from 0°:
   `Specify start angle or [Parameter]:` **45 <ENTER>**

7. Finally, you'll need to specify the end angle, which is also measured from 0°:
   `Specify end angle or [Parameter/Included angle]:` **270 <ENTER>**

The values of the last two steps either can be keyed in or can be picked off the screen. Notice when you get to this point in the command that there are two additional options when you specify the rotation around the major axis: Parameter and Included Angle.

Using the Parameter option, the start angle of the elliptical arc is determined using this vector equation:

```
p(u) = c + a* cos(u) + b* sin(u)
```

Here, c is the center of the arc, a represents the limits of the major axis, and b represents the limits of the minor axis. Values are given to the variables, and an angle is calculated via this equation (see Figure 5.6).

Figure 5.6
The parameters of the equation are used to determine the start point and endpoint of an elliptical arc.

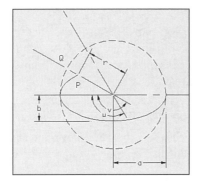

When in this mode, the following prompt is given:

```
Specify start parameter or [Angle]:
```

PART

II

CH

5

At this point you are expected to key in a value, specify a point, or provide the length of the major axis (or a), which is then plugged into the equation.

At this point you can toggle between Parameter mode and Angle mode. The mode you are in determines how AutoCAD calculates the start angle for the elliptical arc. The Parameter mode uses the vector equation listed previously to determine the angle; the Angle mode uses the angle you provide. Both option modes are available via a right-click menu for the start and end angle of the arc. The prompt for the Angle mode is this:

```
Specify end angle or [Parameter]:
```

Here you are expected to key in a value, specify a point, or provide the value for p.

Using the Included Angle, you define the angle relative to the start angle rather than 0°.

As you can see, a number of options are available depending on the type of ellipse you want to draw. Another use of the Ellipse command is in drawing circles used in isometric drawings, which are actually ellipses placed in the Isometric drawing mode, shown in Figure 5.7.

Figure 5.7
Ellipses can be used to give the illusion of holes in isometric drawings.

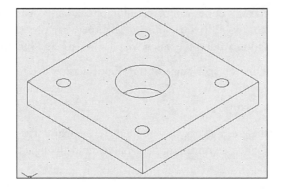

To create these circles, you must first place AutoCAD into an isometric mode. When AutoCAD is set in this mode, the crosshairs, snap, and grid align with the isometric axes of 30°, 90°, and 150°. In the next example, you'll learn how to quickly setup an isometric drawing and how to create isometric circles.

EXAMPLE: PLACING THE DRAWING IN ISOMETRIC MODE

1. From within the current drawing, click the Tools pull-down menu, and select the Drafting Settings option. This opens the Drafting Settings dialog box, where you can set up the isometric settings.

2. On the Snap and Grid tab, toggle the Isometric Snap from the Snap Type and Style box to ON. Notice that when this is done, the Snap X and Grid Spacing edit boxes are set to a value of 0.8660. This locks the crosshairs at an angle of 30° from the horizon. It might also be a good idea to turn on the grid so you can see how it is affected.

3. You may toggle between the different isoplanes, or isometric planes, such as top, left, and right by pressing Ctrl+E. These settings enable you to draw in that plane, which defines the axis and angle where your objects are placed.

Tip 36 from
Ron House

You may toggle between the different isometric planes by also activating the Isoplane command transparently. Just type a single quote before the command to temporarily suspend your current command and set the plane you want to work in. The following prompt will be displayed in the command line:

```
Current isoplane: Left
>>Enter isometric plane setting [Left/Top/Right] <Top>:
```

Note that the two greater-than symbols at the beginning of the prompt indicate that the command is being run transparently.

Now that you've set up an isometric drawing, let's walk through the process of creating an isometric circle.

EXAMPLE: CREATING AN ISOMETRIC CIRCLE

1. Open drawing ch5_02.dwg, which you copied from the accompanying CD. You will need to place a 0.5-diameter isometric circle at the center of the part. First, follow the steps listed previously to set up the drawing in isometric mode, with the left isoplane current. Type **EL** at the command line. This gives the following prompt:

   ```
   Specify axis endpoint of ellipse or [Arc/Center/Isocircle]:
   ```

> **Note**
>
> The Isocircle option of the Ellipse command is not available from the Draw pull-down menu. You must first set the drawing in Isometric mode and then access the Ellipse command from either the Draw pull-down menu or the command line. Only then will the Isocircle option be available.

2. Right-click to select the Isocircle option.

3. Locate the isocircle at the point 3.5, 1.45:

   ```
   Specify center of isocircle: 3.5,1.45 <ENTER>
   ```

4. Type in a radius of **0.5** for the isocircle at the Specify radius of isocircle or [Diameter] prompt, and press Enter:

   ```
   Specify radius of isocircle or [Diameter]: .5 <ENTER>
   ```

> **Tip 37 from**
> *Ron House*
>
> You may toggle between the different isoplanes by holding down the Ctrl button and pressing the E key repeatedly while being prompted to specify the radius or diameter of the isocircle.

5. Create a smaller ellipse on the right face of the part by using CRTL+E to toggle to the Right isoplane, then place an isocircle at 4.67,1.6 with a radius of 0.125.

6. Complete the part by placing the next isocircle under the last at 4.67,1.0 with a radius of 0.125.

Your part should look similar to the one in Figure 5.8.

Figure 5.8
An ellipse can be placed into an isometric drawing to create the illusion of a hole.

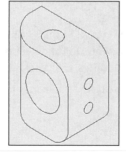

Tip 38 from
Ron House

Using polar tracking while in Isometric mode makes it easier to work in the different iso-planes. Right-click the POLAR tile from the status bar, and select the Settings option from the menu to configure the angle to be used while in this mode. In the case of isometric drawings, you would want to set the increment angle to 30° and select the Track Using All Polar Angle Settings check box.

This option simplifies the process of creating isometric circles when the radius or diameter is known, which normally would be difficult in an Isometric setting.

The next section discusses two additional drawing objects and explains how setting variables affect the creation of and display of drawing objects.

Using Setting Variables to Define the Size and Shape of Drawing Objects

The next two objects, donuts and points, are very basic elements that can be mastered shortly after you create them. In the context of this book, these objects are used to show how setting variables can modify the display of certain drawing objects, which is illustrated in the next section.

Donuts and the Fillmode Setting

Donuts can be used to create a filled circle in a drawing, and is typically used when you want a hole to be represented as such. Instances of when you might use this command are when drawing rivet holes or conduit coming up through a wall. Creating a donut is as easy as specifying the inner and outside diameter and then defining where you want the center of the donut to be located. The value for the inside diameter of the donut is saved in the variable DONUTID and the outside diameter in the system variable DONUTOD.

Tip 39 from
Ron House

Unlike the other drawing commands, the Donut command is not available from the Draw toolbar, although it can be accessed from the Draw menu or by typing **DO** at the command line.

The value determining whether the donut is filled is saved in the variable called Fillmode, which controls how polylines are displayed. Because the Donut object is actually a polyline, the value of this variable affects the display of both donuts and polylines in a drawing.

→ See "Creating Polylines," in Chapter 6, "Complex Drawing Objects," for more information on the Polyline object.

Example: Creating a Donut and Using the System Variables to Control Its Display

1. Using the current drawing, select the Donut command from the Draw pull-down menu. Following the prompts listed here, set the desired inner and outer diameters of the donut and place at least two donuts into the drawing:

```
Specify inside diameter of donut <0.5000>:
Specify outside diameter of donut <1.0000>:
Specify center of donut or <exit>:
```

2. Now use the DONUTID and DONUTOD system variables to change the current inner and outer diameter settings for any newly created donuts. Type in each system variable in the command line and set the inner diameter to now be 0 and the outer diameter to be 1.0:

```
Command: donutid
Enter new value for DONUTID <0.5000>: 0 <ENTER>
Command: donutod
Enter new value for DONUTID <0.0000>: 1 <ENTER>
```

3. Placing new donuts into the drawing will demonstrate that the new values for the system variables have been modified. Now, let's place a few donuts in the drawing accepting the defaults for the donut inner and outer diameter that you set in the last step:

```
Command: donut<ENTER>
Specify inside diameter of donut <0.5000>:<ENTER>
Specify outside diameter of donut <1.0000>:<ENTER>
Specify center of donut or <exit>:
```

Place a few random donuts into the drawing. Notice that currently they are filled. Now modify the system variable Fillmode by activating it transparently from within the Donut command. Remember to type a single quote (') before the command to activate it transparently:

```
Command: 'fillmode
Enter new value for FILLMODE <1>: 0 <ENTER>
```

Place a few more donuts to see the effect of the Fillmode variable on the Donut objects. You will notice that as you place new donuts into the drawing, they will have no fill applied to them (see Figure 5.9). The donuts previously placed will remain the same until the drawing is regenerated. This variable is different from the DONUTID and DONUTOD variable because it affects all donuts as well as all polylines in the drawing.

4. Type the **Regen** command at the command line and press Enter. As the drawing is regenerated, notice that all the donuts and polylines currently display no fill. Regenerating the drawing after setting the FILLMODE variable back to 1 displays the objects with a fill.

Figure 5.9
This figure displays the difference between donuts created before and after setting the Fillmode variable to 1.

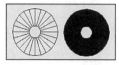

Similar to donuts, points can also be affected by the value of settings. As you'll see in the next section, a setting variable also determines the shape and size used to represent points placed into the drawing.

MARKING THE DRAWING WITH POINTS

Points are symbols that are typically used as construction markers in a drawing. If you wish to mark a location that you can reference later, use the Point command to place a point into the drawing. These points are also referred to as nodes, and they can be "snapped" to using the object snaps in both two- and three-dimensional drawings.

The display of points is controlled by two setting variables, PDMODE and PDSIZE. These two variables make up the overall point style for the drawing. Both of the point setting variables can be accessed through the Point Style dialog box or can be typed individually at the command line. Choose Format, Point Style to open the Point Style dialog box shown in Figure 5.10.

To place a point into the drawing, you can type **PO** at the command line, or select the button from the Draw toolbar, as shown in Figure 5.11.

Four different point nodes are available and are displayed in the top row of icons shown in the Point Style dialog box. Starting from the left and moving to the right, these are numbered 0, 2, 3, and 4; a value of 1 displays nothing. The remaining three rows represent the other three types of point types that define what the point node will be contained within. Each row has an equivalent PDMODE numeric value, which, when added to the point node value, determines the composite point symbol to be used for all points in the drawing.

Figure 5.10
Both the PDMODE and PDSIZE system variables can be set from the Point Style dialog box.

Figure 5.11

The Point Style dialog box button resides on the Draw toolbar.

Each row is numbered in groups of 32, so the second row has a value of 32, the third row has a value of 64, and the last row has a value of 96.

For example, to place a point displayed as a circle with an X defining the center of the node, you would add the value for the X node type, which is 3, to the value of 32 for the circle point group, resulting in a total value of 35. You would type this at the prompt for the PDMODE setting variable:

```
Enter new value for PDMODE <0>: 35
```

Handily, the Point Style dialog box enables you to choose from the list of point icons to determine this value. You can also set the PDSIZE variable from here in one of two ways. By selecting the Set Size Relative to Screen button, the size is determined as a percentage of the current view scale. Because the view scale changes constantly throughout a drawing's life cycle, this means the size of the points placed in the drawing are dynamic. They will change in size when the view magnification scale is modified, such as with the Zoom command. Activating the Regen command will also update the point to its modified scale.

→ See Chapter 11, "Viewing the Drawing," for more on the Zoom and Regen commands.

This constant changing of point size can also be achieved by typing in a negative value for the PDSIZE setting variable at the command line.

The Set Size in Absolute Units option sets an absolute size for the point. This is true except when the value is set to 0, which creates a point that is 5% of the current view scale.

Summary

This chapter covers some very unique object types. Polygons can be used in variety of ways to create objects that have equal-length sides. Ellipses can be used to create various shapes and can be combined into irregular arcs that can be defined by mathematical equations. Donuts and points can be utilized to assist in marking the drawing when other the use of other objects types would be excessive. This chapter concludes the basic drawing types, and in the next chapter you'll learn about the more complex object types in AutoCAD.

PART

II

CH

5

6

COMPLEX DRAWING OBJECTS

In this chapter

DRAWING OBJECTS

Although most AutoCAD drawings consist of elementary object types such as those discussed in previous chapters, objects that provide the capability to draw complex shapes also are needed—especially when you need to draw smooth, asymmetrical curves beyond what can be achieved with the basic and elliptical arc commands.

Actually, two distinct types of curves can be produced in AutoCAD, each with different commands. The first type of curve can be created with the Polyline command. Polylines are a step above the primary commands because they offer a greater degree of flexibility and can be made up of continuous segments. Polylines, by default, are linear objects that can be converted to represent a curve. They are typically used where multiple lines or arc segments would be tedious to edit as compared to editing a single polyline object. An example of when a polyline might be used to portray a curve would be contour lines on a topographical map.

Splines, the second type of curve, are continuous, irregularly shaped curves that offer a greater amount of adaptability depending on project needs. One example of a spline would be the profile of a plastic container where a smooth, adaptable object type is needed to define the part. You'll find both object types discussed in this chapter.

DRAWING POLYLINES

Polylines consist of continuous line and arc segments that can have either common or varying widths. These give you the ability to combine multiple line and arc segments into one, which means the segments can then be edited as a whole, taking you beyond what can be achieved with the individual line and arc commands. Use polylines when you want to combine lines and arcs as one or when you wish to work with one element rather than multiple, separate objects.

A single polyline object can replace multiple arc segments, which can save considerable editing time when working with complex objects. Another advantage of using polylines is that they can form a continuous, closed boundary, which might be used to define a functional space on an architectural drawing or a profile of a mechanical part.

You can access this command by selecting the Polyline button from the Draw toolbar, shown in Figure 6.1.

After specifying a start point, the current width is displayed. A right-click opens a shortcut menu (see Figure 6.2) with the following options that are used to create polylines:

- Arc—Toggles to the PolyArc mode, where arcs with the characteristics of polylines can be created. These objects actually have a separate set of options, which will be discussed later in this chapter. Use polyarcs when you want to curve or bend a polyline object.

- Close—Joins, or draws a segment between the first and last segments of the polyline when one does not exist. This will create a single, continuous, closed boundary free of any gaps or overlaps, making your polyline objects clear and concise.

- Halfwidth—Defines the width of the polyline from its centerline to one of its edges, quickly enabling you to define the width from a polyline's center.

- Length—Draws a polyline segment at the same angle as the previous segment and at a specified length, which can be used easily to extend an existing polyline segment.

- Undo—Undoes the last segment, allowing it to be redefined.

- Width—Specifies the edge-to-edge width of the polyline segment. Tapered widths can be set by providing a different starting width than ending width. This value can also be set with the Plinewid system variable.

Figure 6.1
Polylines, accessed from the Draw toolbar, consist of multiple line or arc segments that can be edited as a whole object.

Figure 6.2
Six options are available to aid in the creation of polylines and polyarcs.

> **Note**
>
> If a specific or varying width is set for the polyline, the ending width of the last segment is continued through to the next segment.

When placing polylines in a drawing, you can toggle back and forth between the polyline and polyarc options, depending on which object type you wish for that segment. Polyarcs are used when you want to combine the features of polylines with arcs (see Figure 6.3).

For example, you might use a polyline to represent a conduit in a drawing when you want to show the bends in the conduit. Typically, you'll find that them useful in those instances when you want to curve a polyline. Because this is not possible, insert polyarcs wherever needed to give the appearance of a curve, or when you need to draw an arc with varying beginning and ending widths. The direction arrows marking a parking lot are an example of polyarcs (see Figure 6.4).

Figure 6.3
An example of combining polylines with polyarcs to create circuit paths on a circuit board.

Figure 6.4
Polyarcs can be created with varying starting and ending widths, used to represent parking lot direction arrows in this figure.

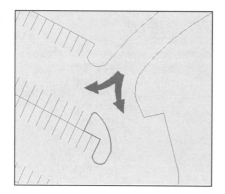

You'll find that polyarcs have characteristics similar to standard arcs in that they are typically placed with a center point and a radius, although more options are available. Here are the options for polyarcs, which are accessed by choosing the Arc option after selecting a starting point for the Polyline command:

- Endpoint of Arc—Defines the endpoint of the arc segment tangent to the last polyline segment, enabling you to define exactly where you want the polyarc to end.

- Angle—Prompts you to specify the included angle of the arc drawn in a clockwise direction. A negative value draws in a counterclockwise direction. Options to define the center or the radius of the arc to the endpoint of the arc are available in addition with this selection.

- Center—Enables you to locate the center of the arc and can be instrumental when the endpoint of the arc is not known. Other options within this selection allow you to enter the included angle or length of chord.

- Close—Closes the polyline with an arc segment and ends the command, forming a closed boundary made up of polyarcs.

- Direction—Prompts for the starting direction of the polyarc tangent to the last segment, which determines the curve of the arc.

- Halfwidth—Similar to the option of same name for the Line mode, defines the width of the polyarc from the centerline to the edge of the arc. This provides a quick way to transition between two polyarcs, using the starting and ending halfwidths. This can be used to represent a transition between two pieces of ductwork, for example.

- Line—Toggles you conveniently back to the Line mode for drawing straight polyline segments.

- Radius—This option prompts you for the radius of the next polyarc, which uses the endpoint of the last polyarc as its starting point.

- Second Pt.—Enables you to define the shape of the arc by specifying the second point of the arc and then the endpoint. This is one of the more straightforward options, allowing you to pick the second point and endpoint the polyarc passes through rather than defining it by specific radius and centerpoint.

- Undo—This undoes the last polyarc segment, which enables you to place the segment again.

- Width—Prompts you for the continuous width of the polyarc—at this point the starting width becomes the ending width. This width value remains in effect for all new polyarcs until changed to a different value.

This example walks you through creating a clip using a combination of polylines and polyarcs using many of these options.

EXAMPLE: DRAWING POLYLINES AND POLYARCS AS ONE

1. Open the drawing ch6_01.dwg that you copied from the accompanying CD.

2. Start the Polyline command by choosing the Polyline button from the Draw toolbar.

3. Snap to the endpoint of the existing polyline indicated by a mark at point A. At the Specify next point prompt, type **A** and press Enter to draw a polyarc:

   `Specify next point or [Arc/Close/Halfwidth/Length/Undo/Width]:` **A <Enter>**

4. Right-click and choose Center from the shortcut menu at the Options prompt to place the arc by using a center point.

5. Place the center point 1.25 inches at 270° from the existing polyline endpoint:

   `Specify center point of arc:` **@1.25<270 <Enter>**

6. Right-click and select Angle to specify the angle of the arc.

7. Type **180** at the prompt to Specify included angle:

   `Specify included angle:` **180<Enter>**

8. Select Line from the shortcut menu to toggle back to the Polyline options. Create a polyline segment of 7.5 at an angle of 0°:

   `Specify next point or [Arc/Close/Halfwidth/Length/Undo/Width]:` **@7.5<0 <Enter>**

9. Create another polyarc by accessing Arc from the shortcut menu. This time you will create the arc by dragging the rubber band straight down (toggle the Ortho mode on if

PART

II

CH

6

needed) from the last point and typing the direct distance value of **1.0** at the Specify next point prompt:

```
Specify endpoint of arc or [Angle/CEnter/CLose/Direction/Halfwidth/Line/
Radius/Second pt/Undo/Width]: 1.0 <Enter>
```

10. Toggle back to the polyline options again and create a segment that is seven inches long at 180° by typing **@7<180**.

```
Specify next point or [Arc/Close/Halfwidth/Length/Undo/Width]: @7<180 <Enter>
```

11. Create one more polyarc by right-clicking and selecting Arc from the shortcut menu.

12. Select Radius from the shortcut menu to place a polyarc of .89 units.

13. Next, type in the coordinates of the endpoint of the arc: **@5.4,2.4**.

14. Press Enter to end the polyline command. You should have something that looks similar to Figure 6.5.

Figure 6.5
The outline of a clip created using a combination of polylines and polyarcs with the Polyline command.

Next you will use this example to demonstrate editing polylines using the many features of the Pedit command.

MODIFYING POLYLINES WITH PEDIT

After you have placed a polyline in a drawing, you can edit it with the Pedit command. Because the polyline is a complex object, the Pedit command is an extensive tool with numerous options. This command can be used to edit two- and three-dimensional polylines as well as 3D meshes, which are covered in "Using Polylines in Three-Dimensional Space" later in this chapter. It can also be used to convert lines and arcs into polylines. Let's begin by accessing the Pedit option from the Modify pull-down menu or the Pedit button from the Modify toolbar (see Figure 6.6).

Tip 40 from
Ron House

Use the Pedit command shortcut by typing **PE** at the command line. Shortcuts are useful when a toolbar is currently not open in the drawing, and this is sometimes easier to do than selecting the command from the pull-down menus.

Figure 6.6
The Pedit command can be accessed from the Modify II toolbar.

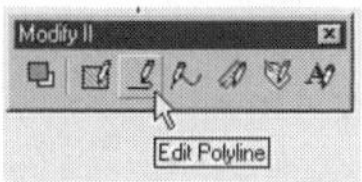

Tip 41 from
Ron House

Another way to quickly edit a polyline or spline is to select the object; then right-click and choose Polyline or Spline Edit, respectively, from the menu.

→ Refer to Chapter 1, section "Accessing Commands Using Toolbars," for a refresher on how to open toolbars currently not displayed if needed.

Many of the Pedit options deal with the polyline as a whole, but some deal with the individual segments of the polyline and the vertices of those segments. This section first covers the options pertaining to the overall polyline. The options dealing with the polyline at a sublevel will be discussed in detail in "Editing the Vertices of the Polyline" later in this chapter.

During the process of editing a polyline, if an object other than a polyline is selected, such as an arc or line, you will be prompted to convert the object into a polyline. After doing so, or if you have selected a polyline, the following editing prompt appears:

```
Enter an option [Close/Join/Width/Edit vertex/Fit/Spline/Decurve/Ltype gen/Undo]:
```

These options are displayed from left to right:

- Close—Closes an open-ended polyline, creating a polyline segment that extends from the beginning of the polyline to its end. Closing the polyline changes the option to Open so you can reopen the polyline within this command session.

- Join—Joins lines, arcs, or other polylines to a polyline. Again, if a line or arc is selected, AutoCAD will prompt you to specify whether you want to covert it to a polyline. It is important to remember that objects can be joined to the existing polyline only if the endpoints match up exactly. This option is for 2D polylines only.

- Width—Changes the width for all segments of the selected polyline. This option is for 2D polylines only.

- Edit vertex—Deals with the individual vertices of the polyline, which can be modified in various ways. Because there are numerous options for the editing of specific segments of the polyline, these will be discussed later in this chapter.

- Fit—Creates a continuous curve made up of a series of arcs that connect at each vertex point. Any curve fitting done with the Tangent option is applied to the arcs passing through the vertex (see Figure 6.7). This option is for 2D polylines only.

- Spline—Converts the polyline into an approximated B-spline curve. Figure 6.8 shows an example of a polyline converted to a spline curve. See "Creating Splines from a Polyline" later in this chapter, for more details.

PART
II

CH
6

Figure 6.7
A polyline, illustrated here with the heavier line, and its associated fit curve. Note that the fit curve passes through the vertices points on the polyline.

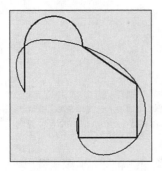

Figure 6.8
A spline-curve polyline, shown here as a heavier line, and its associated polyline.

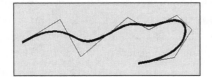

- Decurve—Reverts a polyline converted into a fit or spline curve back into its original polyline-based shape.

- Ltype gen—Allows a uniform linetype pattern to be applied to the polyline. By default, this option is turned off, which applies the linetype to each individual segment rather than to the polyline as a whole. Figure 6.9 illustrates the difference between the settings for this option.

The top polyline illustrates linetype generation turned off, whereas the bottom polyline has the linetype generation turned on. Note that the dashes passing through the vertices on the top polyline are longer and inconsistent with the other dashes in the polyline. The dashes on the bottom polyline are consistent throughout.

Figure 6.9
These polylines represent the difference between linetype generation settings.

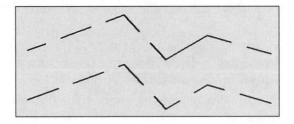

- Undo—Undoes the previous operation.

Let's now look at an example that illustrates how to combine multiple polyline segments.

EXAMPLE: JOINING OTHER OBJECTS TO A POLYLINE

1. Use the drawing you created from the previous example. In this example, you will join the two polyline segments, make an offset copy of the new combined polyline, and connect all the polyline segments to form one polyline object. After the segments are joined, you can set an overall width for the polyline.

2. Start the Pedit command by selecting it from the Modify pull-down menu. At the Select Polyline prompt, pick one of the polyline segments. This displays the following prompt:

   ```
   Enter an option [Close/Join/Width/Edit vertex/Fit/Spline/Decurve/Ltype
   gen/Undo]: J <ENTER>
   ```

3. Right-click and select Join to join this polyline with the other. Then, when you are prompted to select objects, select the other polyline and press Enter again. To indicate the successful joining of the two polylines, the command line will display a prompt like this:

   ```
   5 segments added to polyline.
   ```

4. Press Enter once more to end the Pedit command. Next you will use a command called Offset to make a copy of the combined polyline and offset it a specific distance. Type **Offset** at the command line and press Enter. You will be prompted to specify the offset distance, at which you will reply a distance of **.25**.

   ```
   Specify offset distance or [Through] <Through>: .25 <ENTER>
   ```

5. At the following prompt, select the polyline:

   ```
   Select object to offset or <exit>:
   ```

6. After the polyline is selected, you will be prompted to pick a point on the side you want the polyline to be offset. At the next prompt, pick a point below the polyline:

   ```
   Specify point on side to offset:
   ```

   Your drawing should now look like Figure 6.10.

Figure 6.10
Offsetting the polyline segment to form the opposite edge of the clip cuts in half the amount of time needed to draw the part.

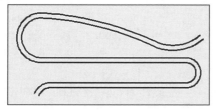

7. Now draw two lines that cap the ends of the two polyline segments. Use the Line command to draw the two lines, one on each end of the polylines.

Tip 42 from
Ron House

> Make certain to use the Endpoint object snap to align the endpoints of the lines with the polylines. At the Specify First Point prompt, hold down the Shift key and right-click, which opens the Object Snap toolbar. Select the Endpoint object snap, and then pick the endpoint of one of the polyline segments.

8. Repeat this to snap to the corresponding end of the opposite polyline. Press Enter to end the Line command, and repeat the entire process to cap the other polyline end of the clip.

Tip 43 from
Ron House

> If the endpoints of the line and polyline segments do line up exactly, you will not be able to join the all segments as a whole.

9. After the lines are in place, convert one of the lines to a polyline using the Pedit command. From the Modify pull-down menu, select Polyline, which also launches the Pedit command. Select one of the line segments you just drew at the Select Objects prompt.

10. To convert the line to a polyline, answer Yes to the following prompt:

   `Object selected is not a polyline. Do you want to turn it into one? <Y>`

11. When the selected line is converted, select Join from the shortcut menu to join all the segments. Selecting all the line and polyline segments during this process converts the remaining line segment automatically into a polyline and joins all the segments into one.

Tip 44 from
Ron House

> When selecting polylines that have a width, you will find it easier to select the polyline by clicking its outline rather than clicking between the sides of the polyline.

12. AutoCAD then displays how many segments were added to the polyline:

   `15 segments added to polyline`

13. After the objects have been selected, press Enter to end the Select Objects part of the command. AutoCAD then displays the polyline options again. From the shortcut menu, select Width to use the width option to change the width of the overall polyline.

14. Type **.125** to set the width:

   `Specify new width for all segments: .125 <ENTER>`

15. Press Enter to end the Pedit command. The finished clip is shown in Figure 6.11.

Figure 6.11
The finished clip from the previous example created with the Polyline, Offset, Line, and Pedit commands.

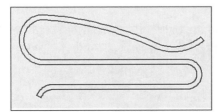

EDITING THE VERTICES OF THE POLYLINE

One of the advantages of using the Polyline command instead of the Line command is that you have the ability to modify the polyline as a whole object. The Pedit command was created to edit the many features of a polyline, including the location of the polyline vertices. The Edit Vertex option of the Pedit command has a number of tools designed specifically to edit vertices of individual polyline segments.

After entering the Edit Vertex option, a small X marks the vertex closest to the beginning of the polyline within the current view.

Note
If the entire polyline segment is not visible in the Drawing Editor, only the vertices that are shown are editable, starting with the vertex closest to the beginning of the polyline.

The X marker indicates vertex, which can be edited with one of the following options:

- Next—Moves the X indicator to the next vertex on the selected polyline, allowing you to select the vertex you wish to modify.
- Previous—Returns you to the previous vertex.
- Break—Cuts the selected polyline between the two vertex points specified. The Next and Previous options let you choose the beginning and ending vertices, and the Go option breaks the polyline at these points.
- Insert—Permits you to insert a new vertex after the highlighted vertex into the polyline.
- Move—Relocates the selected vertex to the new location.
- Regen—Regenerates the polyline segment. This is useful when multiple changes have been made to the polyline and you wish to update the polyline if the changes are not visually apparent.
- Straighten—Removes any vertices between the selected beginning and ending vertices, straightening the polyline segment.
- Tangent—Enables you to assign a tangent direction to the vertex you are editing. The tangent direction is used to control curve fitting. You will be prompted to specify the direction of the vertex tangent, which can be set either by dragging or by typing an angle at the command line. An arrow that represents the angle will appear at the vertex.
- Width—Enables you to set the starting and ending width of the individual polyline segment.
- eXit—Ends the Edit Vertex menu and returns you to the main PEDIT menu.

This next example demonstrates editing a polyline vertex.

PART

II

CH

6

EXAMPLE: ADDING TO AND EDITING VERTICES OF EXISTING POLYLINES

1. Return to the clip drawing you created from the two proceeding examples. To complete this example drawing, you will modify the top end of the clip by moving and adding vertices to the polyline.

2. Use the Zoom Window command to magnify the portion of the polyline you will be editing. Using the pull-down menus, select View, Zoom, and then Window. At the Specify first corner prompt, type **15,6** and press Enter:

   `Specify first corner: `**`15,6 <Enter>`**

3. Then specify the opposite corner to be **14,5**:

   `Specify opposite corner: `**`14,5 <Enter>`**

4. The polyline end that will be modified is magnified on the screen. Use the Pedit command again to edit the vertices. Start the command by typing **PE** at the command line, press Enter, and select the polyline at the Select polyline prompt.

5. The Pedit command options appear. Right-click and select Edit Vertex. You will see an X or vertex marker appear on the vertex closest to the beginning of the polyline, indicating the vertex you want to edit.

6. Right-click again and select Move:

7. You will be prompted to specify the new location for the vertex. Type **@.625<38** and press Enter:

   `Specify new location for marked vertex: `**`@.625<38 <ENTER>`**

8. The polyline vertex will update to show the new location. Now insert a new vertex into the polyline by accessing the shortcut menu and choosing Insert at the Options prompt:

9. Type **@.15<180** for the location of the new vertex:

   `Specify location for new vertex: `**`@.15<180 <ENTER>`**

10. After inserting the new vertex, right-click and select Next to move to the next existing vertex.

11. Right-click and choose Move from the menu. Move the existing vertex to a new location by typing **@.4<38**:

    `Specify new location for marked vertex: `**`@.4<38 <ENTER>`**

12. Right-click and select Exit to exit the Edit Vertex options, and then press Enter to end the Pedit command. The modified polyline end should look like the one shown in Figure 6.12.

TURNING OFF THE FILL FOR POLYLINES

When a width is given to a polyline, you have the option of seeing polylines with a solid fill between their edges. The Fill command controls how polylines will be displayed. If the Fill command is turned off or set to 0, only the edges of the polyline are displayed (see Figure 6.13).

Figure 6.12
This is the end of the clip that was modified using the Edit Vertex option of the Pedit command in the last example.

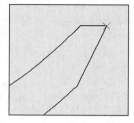

Figure 6.13
The top clip has Fill turned on; the bottom clip has it turned off.

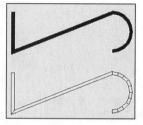

Tip 45 from
Ron House

When the Fill command is set to a value of 1, only those polylines drawn afterward will have a solid fill applied. When the drawing is regenerated, as with a Zoom operation, all polylines in the drawing will be converted to the current Fill setting.

If a polyline is exploded, it is converted into lines and all width data is lost. After exploding a polyline, you will see the following prompt:

```
Exploding this polyline has lost width information.

The UNDO command will restore it.
```

The Undo command returns the polyline back to its original state. Sometimes it is necessary to explode a polyline when the advantages of having it are no longer needed and when line objects will suffice for the intended purpose.

The rectangle is actually a polyline used to create objects with four linear sides. Although a rectangle is a polyline, it has its own options used to define the rectangular shape, which are discussed in the next section.

WORKING WITH RECTANGLES

Rectangles are also created with the Polyline command. The Rectangle command was designed to speed the creation of four-sided objects rather than having to draw each side of the rectangle with the Line or Polyline command.

To start the Rectangle command, select the Rectangle button from the Draw toolbar. You can also select it from the Draw pull-down menu.

PART

II

CH

6

Tip 46 from
Ron House

You can key in **Rectang** at the command line to activate the Rectangle command.

You will see the following prompts:

```
Command: rectang
Current rectangle modes:  Elevation=2.0000  Fillet=0.5000  Width=0.2500
Specify first corner point or [Chamfer/Elevation/Fillet/Thickness/Width]:
```

The prompt displays the current rectangle mode values, and these options are available:

- Specify first corner point—Locates the first corner of the rectangle based on the current rectangle settings. When the first corner is specified, you will be prompted for the opposite corner.

- Chamfer—Creates chamfers at each corner of the rectangle, which prompts for the chamfer distances to be applied:
  ```
  Specify first chamfer distance for rectangles <0.5000>:
  Specify second chamfer distance for rectangles <0.5000>:
  ```

Note

The default chamfer option is to create a chamfer with equal distances, although you can set different distances by typing in a value for the second chamfer distance. These chamfer values are applied to all the rectangle corners.

- Elevation—Sets the z-axis height level above the current drawing plane for the rectangle to be drawn. See Chapter 23, "Visualization," for more information on this setting.

- Fillet—Prompts for the radius of the fillet to be applied to all corners of the rectangle.

- Thickness—Prompts for the z-axis height of the rectangle. This represents the extrusion of the rectangle above the current drawing plane. See Chapter 23 for more information on this setting.

- Width—Sets the width for the polyline. This is the equivalent of using the PLINEWID command to set the width prior to creating a polyline.

The next example uses many of the options mentioned above to create a rectangle.

EXAMPLE: CREATING A RECTANGLE WITH FILLETED EDGES

1. Pick the Rectangle button from the Draw toolbar.

2. Right-click and select the Fillet option from the shortcut menu.

3. Key in a value of **0.25** for the fillet radius and press Enter.

4. Set the rectangle width by right-clicking and choosing the Width option. Type in a value of **0.125** and press Enter.

5. To place the rectangle, type in a value of **3,2** for the first corner point:
   ```
   Specify first corner point or [Chamfer/Elevation/Fillet/Thickness/Width]: 3,2
   <Enter>
   ```

6. At the Specify other corner point prompt, type the relative coordinate **@6,3**:

```
Specify other corner point: @6,3 <Enter>
```

You should end up with a rectangle with rounded edges with a 1/8-inch thickness. Use this command to quickly create four-sided objects, which will save you considerable time over conventional methods.

One other polyline object type needs to be discussed before moving on: the three-dimensional polyline. The vertices points of 3D polylines contain a Z-axis component, unlike their 2D counterparts, enabling them to create three dimensional objects.

USING POLYLINES IN THREE-DIMENSIONAL SPACE

Polylines can be created in three dimensions with the 3dpoly command, which cannot be done with the standard polyline command. The vertices of these polylines can have different x, y, and z coordinates, although they cannot have a width or thickness assigned to them as can two-dimensional polylines.

Using the Pedit command on three-dimensional polylines gives you a different set of options to work with than if you had selected a two-dimensional polyline. Options available for editing a three-dimensional polyline are Close, Edit Vertex, Spline Curve, Decurve, and Undo. These options are similar to the options given for a two-dimensional polyline, except that you are dealing with an object in three dimensions rather than two.

Now that you have worked with the different options used to create and edit polylines, let's look at how to manage older-style polylines from earlier versions of AutoCAD.

CONVERTING OLDER AUTOCAD DRAWING FILES CONTAINING POLYLINES

A new type of polyline, called a *lightweight polyline*, was introduced with Release 14. These new polyline objects replace the older polyline elements found in drawing files prior to Release 14. Because of the way the vertex information was stored, the older polylines added considerably to the overall file size. These polylines have been reworked to create the newer type of polyline, which act just like the older polylines but take up less space—thus the term *lightweight* polyline.

By default, when an older drawing file is opened in AutoCAD 2000, the older polylines are automatically converted to the newer type of polylines.

PART

II

CH

6

Tip 47 from *Ron House*	You can use the system variable Plinetype to define when older polylines are converted from the older type of polylines to the newer, optimized, lightweight polylines when a Release 13 or later drawing is opened. This system variable will convert all polylines at once.

The Convert command was created to change associative hatching and polylines into light-weight polylines. Hatching is a group of polylines bound together to form a fill pattern for a specific user-defined boundary. These objects are not converted when using the Plinetype system variable.

→ See Chapter 13, "Hatching," for more specifics on placing hatch patterns into a drawing.

This command also gives you the option of selecting which polylines or hatched areas will be converted.

Tip 48 from	In some instances you might not want to convert polylines to the new optimized version. The most common reason is when a third-party application was used to create the drawing you are opening. Converting the polyline might cause the loss of data associated with the polyline when it was created. Check with your third-party application vendor when converting older version drawings to the newer format in AutoCAD 2000.
Ron House	

Typing **Convert** at the command line yields the following prompt:

```
Enter type of objects to convert [Hatch/Polyline/All] <All>:
```

Right-click and select Polyline, and then determine whether to select all or specific individual polylines in the drawing at the Select/All prompt. This converts all polylines except those that are fit or spline curves and those that contain extended entity data. The command will then tell you how many polylines were converted.

Next you'll examine how to create advanced shapes with smooth curves using the Spline command.

SPLINES

Splines are smooth curves that pass through a series of points and are typically used to create irregularly shaped curves. Although you can convert a polyline into a spline-fit polyline, which you will see later in this book, this is done by approximation, and the result does not give you what is defined as a true spline. The Spline command generates true splines, or nonuniform rational b-splines (NURBS). These spline elements are more accurate mathematically, and they also help create smaller drawing files than spline-fit polylines.

Tip 49 from	One of the best reasons to use splines over fit or spline-curve polylines is that splines maintain their true shape after editing. Using editing commands such as Trim or Break, which are discussed in Chapter 9, "Not All Objects Can Be Edited This Way," remove the spline definition of fit or spline-curve polylines. Splines, on the other hand, retain their shape.
Ron House	

A spline is placed by placing a minimum of three vertices, or fit points, through which the spline passes. These fit points also define the location of the spline's control points, which determine the curvature of the spline at that location.

To create a spline, choose the Spline button from the Draw toolbar, shown in Figure 6.14.

Figure 6.14
Splines are activated by using the Spline button from the Draw toolbar.

The Spline command offers the following prompt:

```
Specify first point or [Object]:
```

The default option is to place a point that defines the starting location of the spline. After providing the starting point, you will be prompted for the second point of the spline. Then you are prompted to place additional fit points or you can choose from two more options that are available:

- Close—This option closes the spline, in which the start and end of the spline are coincident and tangent. You will be prompted for tangent information that defines both the start point and endpoint.

- Fit tolerance—This determines how close the spline fits in relation to the fit points you have located. With a tolerance of 0, the spline passes through the fit points. The higher the tolerance, the more flexibility the spline has around its fit points.

When you have finished providing a fit point for the spline, AutoCAD prompts for the tangent information for the start point and endpoint, which determine the shape of the spline.

Yet another option is available when you first activate the command. The Object option prompts you to select a spline-fit polyline, which is converted into a true spline.

Look at the following example to see how to create a spline.

EXAMPLE: PLACING A SPLINE INTO THE DRAWING

1. Create a new drawing and choose the Spline button from the Draw pull-down menu.

2. Specify the start point of the spline:
   ```
   Specify first point or [Object]: 3,2
   ```

3. Then specify the second fit point of the spline (2):
   ```
   Specify next point: 4,5
   ```

4. Now specify the third point (3):
   ```
   Specify next point or [Close/Fit tolerance] <start tangent>: 6,3
   ```

5. Also specify the fourth point (4):
   ```
   Specify next point or [Close/Fit tolerance] <start tangent>: 9,4
   ```

6. Finally, specify the last fit point (5):
   ```
   Specify next point or [Close/Fit tolerance] <start tangent>: 13,2
   ```

PART

II

CH

6

7. Now tell AutoCAD that point 5 was the last fit point for the spline by pressing Enter.
   ```
   Specify next point or [Close/Fit tolerance] <start tangent>: <ENTER>
   ```

8. Now you will need to define the tangency of the start point:
   ```
   Specify start tangent: 2.5,1.5
   ```

9. Also specify the tangency of the endpoint:
   ```
   Specify end tangent: 10,2.5
   ```

   You should have a spline that looks similar to the one in Figure 6.15.

Figure 6.15
This figure displays a spline created with a fit tolerance of 0.

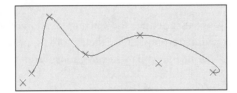

The last example creates the spline by placing points in the drawing. Now let's create a more detailed spline object by modifying the Fit tolerance.

EXAMPLE: CREATING A SPLINE WITH A FIT TOLERANCE

1. In this example, apply a fit tolerance of 1 to a spline of the same dimensions. Create another new drawing and select the Spline button from the Draw toolbar.

2. Use the same fit points as in the last example (1):
   ```
   Specify first point or [Object]: 3,2
   ```

3. Point 2 will be located at **4,5**:
   ```
   Specify next point: 4,5
   ```

4. Now apply the fit tolerance. Right-click and select Fit tolerance from the shortcut menu:
   ```
   Specify fit tolerance <0.0000>: 1
   ```

5. Then continue with the fit points (3):
   ```
   Specify next point or [Close/Fit tolerance] <start tangent>: 6,3
   ```

6. Now specify the fourth point (4):
   ```
   Specify next point or [Close/Fit tolerance] <start tangent>: 9,4
   ```

7. Finally, specify the last fit point (5):
   ```
   Specify next point or [Close/Fit tolerance] <start tangent>: 13,2
   ```

8. Right-click and select Enter to indicate that you are done supplying fit points:
   ```
   Specify next point or [Close/Fit tolerance] <start tangent>: <ENTER>
   ```

9. Now define the tangency of the start point (6):

   `Specify start tangent:` **2.5,1.5**

10. Also specify the tangency of the endpoint:

    `Specify end tangent:` **10,2.5**

    Notice the difference between the spline shown in Figure 6.15 and the one in Figure 6.16.

Figure 6.16
This spline was created using the same fit points as in the previous example with a fit tolerance of 1.0.

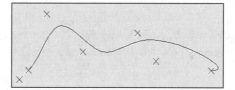

As you can see, splines are extremely flexible objects that can be used for a number of applications. Disciplines that require the use of irregularly shaped curves, such as mechanical and civil engineering, typically use splines for a wide variety of applications, such as plastic-injected molding and contours.

CREATING SPLINES FROM A POLYLINE

Polyline objects can be interpolated into splines or B-splines. This is done using the Pedit Spline option, which is similar to the Fit option, yet the curves of the polyline do not pass through the vertices. With B-splines, the curve is pulled near the vertices. The vertices of the polyline make up a frame for the spline-fit curve. The more control points on the frame, the more definition the curve has. The frame for the curve is initially not displayed, yet it can be viewed using the SPLFRAME variable. When this variable is set to 1 and after the drawing is regenerated, the frame can be seen with the spline-fit curve (see Figure 6.17).

Tip 50 from
Ron House

You can force a regeneration of the drawing to update certain settings, such as Splframe, by typing **Regen** at the command line, which may not display the after making the changes to this setting.

Note

Width information assigned to individual polyline segments is disregarded when the polyline is converted to a spline or fit curve.

Figure 6.17
This figure illustrates a polyline converted to a spline curve with its associated frame made visible using the Splframe system variable.

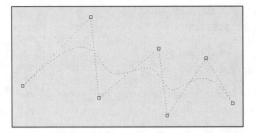

AutoCAD can generate two types of B-splines: quadratic and cubic. The type of B-spline that is generated is controlled by the Splinetype system variable. Setting the Splinetype variable to a value of 5 creates an estimated quadric B-spline, and a value of 6 gives an estimated cubic B-spline.

> **Note**
>
> AutoCAD can only approximate true quadric and cubic B-splines by using this conversion. Using the Spline command to create nonuniform rational B-splines—NURBS, for short—will give you a more accurate representation of curved boundaries than will spline-fit polylines. In addition, splines take up much less disk space than polylines, making the overall drawing size smaller.

EDITING SPLINES WITH THE SPLINEDIT COMMAND

As you have seen so far, the advantage of working with splines is that they are flexible and can be modified easily. The Splinedit command is used to change the shape, edit vertices, and add new vertices to a spline object.

Similarly to how you could change a polyline with the Pedit command, you can specifically edit splines with the Splinedit command.

> **Note**
>
> If you select a spline-curve polyline after activating the Splinedit command, the polyline will automatically be converted into a spline.

These options are available from the shortcut menu after selecting a spline. Note that as soon as a Spline is selected, the control points for the object appear:

- Fit data—This option enables you to edit the fit data for the spline, which has a separate menu. These options are discussed later in this chapter.
- Close—If the Spline is open, this closes the spline, joining the beginning and ending control vertices. When the Close option is selected, this option is replaced with the Open option to reopen the spline. This function is similar to the option with the same name that is available with the Polyline and Line commands.
- Move vertex—This option enables you to select a point and move it to a new location. Similar to the Pedit and Edit Vertex options, these options will be discussed in the next example.

- Refine—Finer adjustments to the spline can be made with this option, allowing you to add control points or adjust the weight of control points. The higher the number of the weight, the closer the spline comes to the control point.

- Reverse—This option reverses the direction for the spline and is used by some third-party applications.

- Undo—This option undoes the last editing operation.

In this example, you'll use a spline to represent a contour line on a site plan.

EXAMPLE: CREATING A SPLINE WITH A FIT TOLERANCE

1. Open the drawing ch6_02.dwg that you copied from the companion CD. The north-ernmost contour shown in the drawing needs to be modified. Start by selecting the Edit Spline button from the Modify II toolbar.

2. Select the spline at point A (shown in Figure 6.18) at the Select spline prompt:

   ```
   Select spline: (Select Point A)
   ```

Figure 6.18
Control points are shown on a selected spline, which makes it easy to adjust the display of the contour.

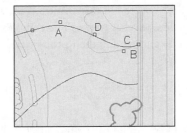

3. Right-click and select the Move Vertex option from the menu:

4. Note that the control point at point B is highlighted, indicating it is to be moved. At the prompt, type in the coordinates **591',1174'** and press Enter:

   ```
   Specify new location or [Next/Previous/Select point/eXit] <N>: 591',1174'
   <ENTER>
   ```

5. Change to the next control point located at point C, and type the coordinate value **575',1158'**. Then press Enter:

   ```
   Specify new location or [Next/Previous/Select point/eXit] <N>: n <ENTER>
   Specify new location or [Next/Previous/Select point/eXit] <N>: 575',1158'
   <ENTER>
   ```

6. Right-click and select Next to move to the next control point, and supply the next coordinate value **559',1149'**, and press Enter after typing the value:

   ```
   Specify new location or [Next/Previous/Select point/eXit] <N>: 559',1149'
   <ENTER>
   ```

PART

II

CH

6

7. Right-click and choose eXit to exit the Move Vertex option, and press Enter again to exit the Splinedit command. The relocation of the contour is now complete and should look similar to Figure 6.19.

Figure 6.19
This figure represents what your drawing should look like after modifying the spline contour.

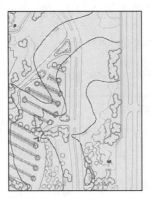

One other complex object type that will be covered in this chapter is the multiline object. Multilines are similar to polylines and splines in that they can be complex in nature and they require special editing tools to specify and modify their properties. The next section discusses multilines in detail.

MULTILINES

Multilines are multiple parallel lines that can vary in centerline offset, color, and linetype. These lines are combined to act as a single object, similar to polyline segments, and are also chosen from the Draw toolbar, shown in Figure 6.20.

Figure 6.20
The Multiline command is easily accessed using the Draw toolbar.

Up to 16 elements can be used to define a multiline, which then becomes a single object (see Figure 6.21).

Multilines are unique in that they have certain characteristics that set them apart from other AutoCAD objects. Multilines are different because they are made up of multiple parallel line segments that act as one. To accommodate for this, the Mledit command specifies the properties of the individual line segments, or elements, that make up the multiline. In addition, the Mledit command was created to specifically edit multilines, which is covered in "Multiline Editing" later in this chapter.

Figure 6.21
Up to 16 elements of the multiline can be assigned different properties.

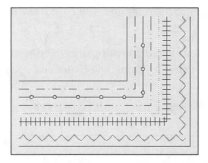

Figure 6.22
An example of a multiline used to represent a wall section.

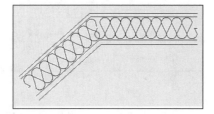

PLACING MULTILINES IN THE DRAWING

First let's examine how to create a multiline. From the Draw toolbar, select the Multiline button.

```
Command: MLINE
Current settings: Justification = Top, Scale = 1.00, Style = STANDARD
Specify start point or [Justification/Scale/STyle]:
```

With the default options, you can define the justification, the scale factor, the multiline style, or the start point of the multiline. Let's look at these options:

- Specify start point/next point—This option defines the path or location of the vertices for the Multiline.
- Justification—Sets top, zero, or bottom justification to place the multiline, as shown in Figure 6.23. Top or bottom justification depends on what direction the multiline is placed. Zero justification places the multiline centered on the line initially representing the multiline.
- Scale—Sets the scale for the multiline, depending on how it was defined in the current Multiline Style box. This enables you to define a multiline that can be used on any scale drawing.
- Style—Allows the current multiline style to be changed to another existing style.

PART
II

CH

6

After you place the first two segments of the multiline, you have these options available through the right-click menu:

- Close—This option closes the multiline segment by drawing a segment from the endpoint of the multiline back to the starting point, and closes any open-ended joints in the process.

- Undo—Undoes the last multiline segment so it can be redrawn.

Figure 6.23
The three possible justification types of a multiline that also define how the multiline will be drawn depending on the justification chosen.

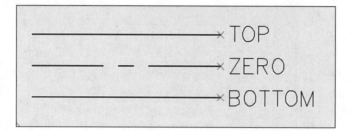

Using these options allows you to place multilines just as you would a line or polyline into drawings at any scale. Now let's look at the main feature of multilines, which is the capability to create a style that defines the overall look of a multiline.

MULTILINE STYLES

You can create the characteristics of individual multiline elements using the Multiline Style, or Mlstyle, command. This command enables you to set the element properties, such as number of lines, color, and linetype of each line to be set (see Figure 6.24). You also can set the characteristics of the overall multiline, such as the fill and capping properties. The capping properties come in handy when using multilines to represent walls in plan view in an architectural floorplan. This option allows multiline walls to be capped as the multiline preview is available so you can view the multiline before placing it into the drawing.

Tip 51 from
Ron House

After modifying the current properties of the multiline, you must type a new name in the Name Edit box and then select the Add button. This adds the new multiline to the Current drop-down list. The Save button will add a multiline to the multiline definition file .mln file *only* if the changes have been added first. Just selecting the Save button will not save the current changes unless a name for the changes has been provided.

Caution

An existing Multiline Style option cannot be redefined if a multiline with that style exists in the current drawing file. All multilines in the drawing representing that style must either be erased or exploded before the style can be updated. If you attempt to modify an existing multiline style, the multiline and element properties for that style are disabled and not editable.

The following options are available from the Multiline Styles dialog box shown in Figure 6.24:

Figure 6.24
You can set the element and multiline properties in the Multiline Style dialog box.

- Current—This lists the current Multiline Style and allows a different style to be selected from the list if available.

- Name—Allows the changes made to the current Multiline Style to be saved under a different style name.

- Description—Enables you to give a description to the multiline to define the multiline's intended purpose.

- Load—Loads an existing multiline from the chosen .mln file. Multilines style can be saved to an external file with a .mln extension, which by default is the acad.mln file. This enables you to utilize multiline styles in more than one project by loading the multilines saved in a .mln file into other AutoCAD drawings.

- Save—Saves the changes to the Multiline Style and adds it to the current .mln file. This will open the Save Mulitline Style dialog box, enabling you to save the multiline to a .mln file.

- Add—Adds the new Multiline Style to the Current drop-down list making it the current multiline style.

- Rename—Renames the current Multiline Style option to a new user-defined name. This name must be unique or "Invalid Style" will appear in the lower-left corner of the dialog box.

Now that we know the various style functions, let's look at the different multiline element properties.

MULTILINE ELEMENT PROPERTIES

Selecting the Multiline Element button opens the Multiline Element Properties dialog box, which enables you to determine how the multiline will be displayed in the drawing (see Figure 6.25).

Figure 6.25
You can set color, line-types, and the multi-line element offsets with the Element Properties dialog box.

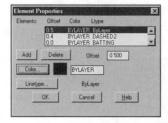

Element offsets, color, and linetype properties are available as follows:

- Add—Adds a new element to the multiline. By default, the new element is placed at the center (offset equals 0.0) of the multiline with bylayer color and linetype properties. Bylayer indicates the current properties are set by the layer the objects reside on.

- Delete—Deletes the highlighted element from the multiline.

- Offset—Enables you to modify the offset or the spacing between the highlighted element and the other elements in the multiline. You can set the new offset value in the Offset Edit box. A positive or negative value designates the location of the element in relation to the centerline, depending on how the multiline is drawn.

- Color—Changes the color of the highlighted element in the multiline. When you click this button, you can select the color you want from the color palette.

- Linetype—Allows you to select the linetype for the highlighted element from the Select Linetype dialog box. This is based on the loaded linetypes available in the current drawing.

In addition to the element properties, there are also Multiline Properties, which define how the multiline is placed into the drawing and the multiline will have a fill applied to it, similar to the fill available with polylines. Multiline Properties are discussed in the next section.

MULTILINE PROPERTIES

Multiline Properties define how the multiline will be created and displayed in the drawing. Selecting the Multiline Properties button opens the dialog box, shown in Figure 6.26.

Figure 6.26
You can set multiline properties, such as Fill and Display Joints, within the Multiline Properties dialog box.

These options are available as multiline properties:

- Display joints—Displays the joints of the multiline, similar to what you would see at the corners of a picture frame or window trim. This is also a good option to enable when using multilines to define a roof line in a landscaping plan.

- Line—Places a line cap at the start or end of the multiline at the angle specified. This option can automatically "cap" the multilines at each end at a specified angle. This angle can be from 10 to 70°.

The next two options enable you to use multilines to represent oval or circular objects with concentric arcs, such as a swimming pool or a running track. The advantage to this is that you can create a multiline style to place the entire object with one multiline. This can save you a considerable amount of time with some advance thought on how to use the multiline object to your advantage.

- Outer arc—Places an arc joining the two outermost lines of the multiline. This can be placed at the start or the end of the multiline at the angle specified. You can utilize this option when using multilines to create slots in a part.

- Inner arcs—Places an arc joining the two innermost lines of the multiline. This can be placed at the start or end of the multiline at the angle specified. This is a convenient option when using multilines to create curbs and islands in a road design.

- Angle—Allows the angle to be set for the specified cap at the start or end of the multi-line.

- Fill—Sets the fill color for the multiline, which can save you from hatching the multiline shape after placing it into the drawing if desired. After a color is chosen from the color palette, the fill floods the inside boundary of the multiline.

To provide more detail on the multiline properties, let's discuss each option before you continue. The first option listed at the top of the dialog box is the Display joints option. When you select this check box, the joints of the multiline are displayed (see Figure 6.27).

Figure 6.27
The multiline on the left has the Display joints option toggled off; the one on the right has that feature toggled on.

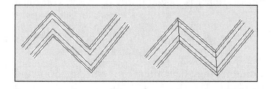

The Caps section of the dialog box defines how the multiline ends are to be capped, whether by a line or by an arc. Multiline caps are user-specified via the Start and End check boxes. The Line option places a line at either end of the multiline, and a different angle can be set for each multiline cap using the Angle edit boxes. Two arc options are available, depending on how the multiline was created. Outer arc draws an arc between the two outside lines of the multiline. Inner arcs creates an arc using two inside lines if they exist in the multiline definition (see Figure 6.28).

Figure 6.28
Examples of the Line, Outside arc, and Inner arcs options of a multiline and how they affect the display of a multiline.

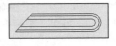

The Fill option also can be set to fill in the multiline with a color. Selecting the Color button brings up a color palette from which you can choose a color. The pool in Figure 6.29 was created using two multilines, one to create the water in the pool and the other to create the sidewalk around the pool.

Figure 6.29
A multiline shown with the Fill option enabled and Inner and Outer arc options turned on.

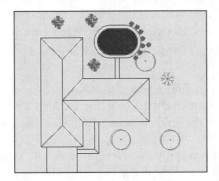

If you wish to edit a multiline after it is placed into a drawing, you must use the Mledit command to modify a multiline.

MULTILINE EDITING

Because multilines are so unique, they have their own editing command. The Mledit command deals only with multilines in which 12 editing functions are available (see Figure 6.30). These functions are typically used to edit how one multiline intersects with another, or to add, delete, or insert vertices of the multiline. A good example of this is using multilines to represent walls in plan view, and how the wall intersections are treated in reference to the other multiline walls. To edit a multiline, choose the Multilines option from the Modify pull-down menu. Reference Table 6.1 for descriptions of all of the Mledit editing functions.

Figure 6.30
There are 12 different multiline editing options available using the MLEDIT command.

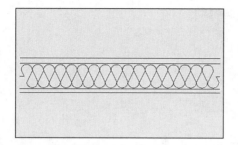

TABLE 6.1   THE MULTILINE EDITING FUNCTIONS

Figure	Description
	Closed Cross—Creates a closed-cross intersection between two multilines. The first multiline selected is the primary, or overlapping, multiline.
	Open Cross—Creates an open-cross intersection between two multilines.
	Closed Tee—Creates a closed-tee intersection between two multilines. The first multiline selected is the primary, or capping, multiline.
	Merged Cross—Creates a merged-cross intersection between two multilines.
	Open Tee—Creates an open-tee intersection between two multilines.
	Merged Tee—Creates a merged-tee intersection between two multilines.
	Corner Joint—Creates a corner joint intersection combining two multilines.
	Add Vertex—Adds a new vertex to an existing multiline.
	Delete Vertex—Deletes a vertex from an existing multiline.
	Cut Single—Cuts the selected element of the multiline.
	Cut All—Cuts all the elements of a multiline.
	Weld All—Welds all the elements of a cut multiline.

These editing functions enable you to edit multilines depending on the operation desired. One of the most unique features of multiline editing is that the multiline object has the ability to combine element linetypes and colors in one object when two multilines are edited.

Create the multiline shown in Figure 6.31.

Figure 6.31
An example of a multi-line used to represent a wall section with 4″ batting and 1/2″ wall board on each side.

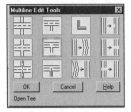

This is a typical wall section, made up of a 2-by-4-inch wood stud, with ¾-inch interior gypsum wall board and ½-inch exterior wood sheathing. You will also place three inches of batt insulation into the wall cavity (see Figure 6.32).

Figure 6.32

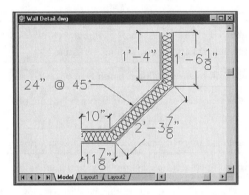

The Multiline Style 2-by-4 wall insulation is used in the next example.

EXAMPLE: CREATING A MULTILINE

1. Open the Multiline Style dialog box to create the multiline style for this drawing. The default multiline style Standard is shown; you will modify this style and save your changes as **2x4 Wall Section with Insulation**.

2. Replace the name in the Name Edit box with **2x4_Wall_Insulation.**

   It is best to use the name of the multiline to represent its function. AutoCAD only allows 31 characters per multiline; however, you can use the Description field to elaborate on the function.

3. In the Description field, type **2x4 Wall Section, 3/4″ Gypsum Board, 3-1/2″ Wall Cavity with Insulation, and 1/2″ Sheathing.**

4. Next, select the Add button. This should add the name of your multiline to the Current Name pop-up list and should set it as the current multiline.

5. Click the Element Properties button. First you will define the top line as the ¾-inch gypsum wall, or the innermost part of the wall. Change the 0.5 offset line from the Standard multiline definition to 2.5. This modifies the first element of the multiline to be 2.5 inches above the centerline of the wall.

6. The next line will be the opposite side of the gypsum board, or the start of the wall cavity. Select the –0.5 element definition. This adds the 2.5 offset element to the list and readies the –0.5 element to be modified. Type **1.75** for this line.

7. The next element defines the insulation, which will use no offset. Click the Add button, which adds a new element to the list with 0.00 offset. You will use the Batting linetype for this element, but first you must check whether the Batting linetype is loaded for this drawing. Select the Linetype button to open the Select Linetype dialog box. If the Batting linetype is listed, select it from the list and click the OK button. Proceed to step 9.

8. If the linetype is not loaded, click the Load button and select the Batting linetype from the list of available linetypes in the Load or Reload Linetypes dialog box. Click the OK button to load the linetype. Now that you have loaded the linetype you need, select it from the list (make certain it is selected) and press the OK button.

9. Finish the wall segment by adding the remaining two lines to the opposite side of the wall. Click the Add button, and change the offset to –1.75.

10. Again select the Add button, and modify the offset for the last element to –2.25. Press the Tab key to update the element list, and use the scrollbar to view the changes you have made. Click the OK button to close the Element Properties dialog box.

11. At this point, select the Save button to save these multiline properties to an external file for use in other drawing files if you desire. Also, you will not need to set any of the Multiline Properties for this example, so click the OK button to save the changes. Now you can use the MLINE command to try out your multiline.

Note

When you preview a multiline in the Multiline Styles dialog box, you may not be able to see the linetype applied to the elements. The best way to check is to actually draw a segment of the multiline. Also remember that the LTSCALE and CELTSCALE setting variables that control overall and individual object linetype scale, respectively, play a large part in how the multiline will look. You may need to experiment to get the desired look for your multiline based on the current drawing scale.

PART

II

CH

6

SUMMARY

Whether you choose polylines or splines to represent a curve on the drawing, you'll find these elements are easier to manage than standard lines and arcs. When you have the process down for creating and editing polylines and splines, you'll find that you will use them to define more complex shapes.

Use multilines to define a single object that contains multiple linetype definitions, such as a road or the plan view of a wall. You'll be surprised by the uses you find for these object types when you learn how to master them.

EDITING YOUR DRAWING

Editing Commands

In this chapter

ERASING OBJECTS

One of the most used commands, regardless of your experience level, is the Erase command. This command is used to remove objects from the drawing—and if you accidentally remove an object you didn't want to, you can use the Oops or Undo command to restore it. Let's first look at these commands and then continue on to learn about two other basic editing commands, Move and Copy.

REMOVING OBJECTS FROM THE DRAWING

You can use the Erase command to remove a single object or multiple objects from the drawing by selecting the Erase button from the Modify toolbar or from the Modify pull-down menu (see Figure 7.1).

Figure 7.1
To remove unwanted objects from the drawing, use the Erase command available from the Modify toolbar.

Tip 52 from
Ron House

To expedite launching the Erase command, try using its command alias. Type **E** at the command line and press Enter.

When the specific objects you want to erase have been selected, pressing the Enter key erases them. This process is fairly straightforward, although selecting exactly what you want to modify can become more involved.

→ Use the advanced object-selection methods discussed in Chapter 10, "Selecting Objects," to learn how to select any object you want from a drawing.

Caution

Objects can also be erased by first selecting what you want to erase and then choosing the Erase command. You must be careful when erasing objects in this fashion because no warning will be given when the objects are erased. You can learn more about this method of editing objects in the "Grips: Another Way of Editing" later in this chapter.

At times, you may accidentally erase some of your work. Fortunately, you have two commands available to retrieve what was lost. The Undo and Oops commands, covered in the next two sections, will assist you in these situations.

UNDOING WHAT WAS DONE

The Undo command undoes an action or a group of actions. This is extremely useful when you are uncertain of changes you make to a drawing and want to revert back to a specific point in the current drawing session. The Undo command is also listed on the shortcut menu of many commands—such as Line, Polyline, and Multilines—allowing you to reverse the effects of that particular command. This use of the Undo command will be covered as part of the individual commands as they are discussed in this book. This chapter focuses on the use of the command and it options. To start, type **Undo** at the command line.

You'll see the following options at the command line:

```
Enter the number of operations to undo or [Auto/Control/BEgin/End/Mark/Back] <1>:
```

- Number of operations to undo—The default option prompts you to enter how many operations you wish to undo. This will be referred to in this text as the Undo Multiple Operation option.

Tip 53 from *Ron House*	You can select the Undo button from the Standard toolbar, shown in Figure 7.2, to back up one operation at a time if you don't know exactly how many operations you want to undo. You may also type **U** and press Enter to achieve the same functionality at the command line.

Figure 7.2
Click the Undo command button on the Standard toolbar.

- Auto—The Auto option enables you to set the Auto mode on or off. When Auto mode is on, which is the default, it groups the operations activated by a menu pick, and Undo then undoes these operations as a whole as if they were a single command.

- Control—This option enables you to define the operation of the Undo command. To help explain each option listed, they are described here:

  - All—The All option allows the full operation of the Undo command.

  - None—This setting turns off the Auto, Begin, and Mark options of the Undo command. In addition, this option disables use of typing U to activate the Undo command from the command line. The Control prompt appears only if the None option is set when the Undo command is run, allowing you to change the current setting:

    ```
    Enter an UNDO control option [All/None/One] <All>:
    ```

- One—This limits the Undo command to single operations, of which only the Control and default Undo Multiple Operation options are available.

  `Control/<1>:`

  If the control option is accessed from here, you will be returned to the prompt shown in the None option.

- Begin\End—You can set begin and end marks for the Undo command by using these options. All the commands between a begin and end mark are subsequently treated as a single operation by the Undo or U commands.

Tip 54 from
Ron House

If you activate an Undo Multiple Operation before placing an Undo End, you can only back up to where the Undo Begin has been placed. To undo beyond that, you must place an Undo End to finish the group, although there may not be any operations to be undone within the current group.

- Mark—You can place a mark in the drawing indicating where the Undo command, when activated as a multiple undo, cannot go beyond. The Undo command will end upon reaching a mark. To remove the mark, run the Undo command again.

- Back—This option undoes all operations back to the most recent Undo mark.

Tip 55 from
Ron House

It is good practice to set an Undo mark before doing an operation or group of operations that you are unsure of. If the result of a group of operations was not what you wanted, you can easily restore the drawing back to the way it was by issuing an Undo Back. Doing so will unavoidably regenerate the drawing once, yet this process is less time-consuming than activating a number of single Undo commands, which would regenerate the drawing each time. You may create as many Undo marks as you would like as you work.

Tip 56 from
Ron House

It may appear that typing **U** and pressing Enter three individual times is the same as typing **Undo 3** at the command line. Actually, there is a big difference and a distinct time savings to be gained by typing the command using the Number of undo operations format. Because this option does not involve three separate regenerations as the first operation does, you can save a considerable amount of time avoiding the regenerations altogether.

There are certain commands that are not affected by the use of the Undo command, which are listed in Table 7.1.

TABLE 7.1 COMMANDS UNAFFECTED BY THE UNDO COMMAND

ABOUT	GRAPHSCR	PSOUT	REINIT
AREA	HELP	QSAVE	RESUME
ATTEXT	HIDE	QUIT	SAVE

COMPILE	ID	RECOVER	SAVEAS
CVPORT	LIST	REDRAW	SHELL
DBLIST	NEW	REDRAWALL	STATUS
DELAY	OPEN	REGEN	TEXTSCR
DIST	PLOT	REGENALL	

To reverse the operation that was previously undone, use the Redo command. This command can be activated only immediately after the Undo command, and exists to provide you with a way to restore the drawing back to its original condition before the use of the Undo command. The Redo command can be accessed from the Standard toolbar, shown in Figure 7.3, or from the Edit pull-down menu. You can also press the keyboard shortcut Ctrl+Y or simply type **R** and press Enter at the command line to undo the effects of the Undo command.

Figure 7.3
The Redo command, available from the Standard toolbar, is used to restore the drawing after the use of the Undo command.

The next command, called Oops, is similar to the Undo command, yet it restores only the last-removed objects from the drawing.

THE APPROPRIATELY NAMED OOPS COMMAND

The Oops command unerases or restores the last object or objects erased from the drawing. This is important to remember because this command is different than the Undo command, which remembers what operations have occurred in the drawing and allows you to undo those operations. The Oops command restores only what was just erased from the drawing. This provides a simpler and faster way of restoring the object, but only if it occurs immediately after using the Erase command.

Note   You can activate the Oops command only from the command line. It is not available from the Modify pull-down or toolbar menus.

For example, say that you accidentally erased a group of objects from a drawing. You do not realize this immediately, and you continue to modify and add to the drawing without erasing anything else. When you do become aware of what you have done, you have already spent a considerable amount of time working on the drawing. You could use the Undo

PART

III

CH

7

command, yet that would force you to undo everything you just worked on to get back to the point before you erased the objects. Using the Oops command restores what had been erased, allowing you to bring those objects back into the drawing without having to undo back to that point. This will save you a considerable amount of time and rework of the drawing.

Tip 57 from
Ron House

Use the Oops command rather than the Undo command when restoring accidentally erased objects from the drawing. This enables you to restore objects to the drawing without having to undo work done following the accidental erase.

Now that you know how to erase and restore objects to the drawing, next you'll learn how to move objects around in the drawing.

MOVING OBJECTS AROUND IN THE DRAWING

The Move command displaces objects from one area of the drawing to another. This can be done either by graphically selecting where you want the objects to be moved onscreen or by entering a specific displacement. Let's examine moving objects by entering a specific displacement.

Start the Move command by selecting the Move button from the Modify toolbar.

Figure 7.4
As you might expect, the Move command is available from the toolbar.

After selecting the objects you want to move, you have two options available:

- Specify second point of displacement—With this option, AutoCAD prompts you for the final destination of the object in relation to the base point selected. An absolute, relative, or polar coordinate can be supplied to indicate the second point of displacement. Also, the use of Direct Distance Input can prove invaluable when quickly moving an object, especially when used in conjunction with polar tracking.

- Use first point as displacement—This option enables you to use the coordinate of the base point as a relative displacement point. When a base point is picked, the x, y, and z coordinate values of that point are used as relative coordinates to move the selection set from the initial base point.

The following example shows you how to move a group of objects by using the group's base point to define its displacement.

EXAMPLE: MOVING A GROUP USING THE BASE POINT AS A DISPLACEMENT

1. In this example, you create a reference line that you will use to indicate where the destination point will be located if you use the base point as a displacement. Open the drawing ch07_01.dwg that was copied from the companion CD. Use the ID command to learn the coordinate point of the base point, which is found at location A in the drawing. Use your object snaps to get an exact point. The command line will display the x, y, and z values, which should read

   ```
   X = 3.0     Y = 4.0     Z = 0.0000.
   ```

2. Access the Line command from the Draw pull-down menu, and start the line at the base point of the group using an absolute coordinate:

   ```
   Specify first point: 3.0,4.0<ENTER>
   ```

3. Define the endpoint of the line using these same values in a relative coordinate:

   ```
   Specify next point or [Undo]: @3.0,4.0 <ENTER>
   ```

4. Right-click to end the Line command by selecting the Enter option.

5. This creates a reference line that defines how far the group will be moved using the base point as a displacement option. Next, select the Move command from the Modify pull-down menu.

6. At the Select Objects prompt, type G at the command line and press Enter. You are prompted to type the group name you wish to select, which is a group that has been created for you in this drawing named SEUACAD2000.

   ```
   Enter group name: SEUACAD2000 <ENTER>
   ```

7. Next, specify the base point:

   ```
   Specify base point or displacement: 3.0,4.0<ENTER>
   ```

8. At the following prompt, press Enter to use the base point as the displacement:

   ```
   Specify second point of displacement or
   <use first point as displacement>: <ENTER>
   ```

9. Note that the group of objects was moved to the endpoint of the line, which represented the displacement by using the base point to provide the distance in along the x- and y-axes. Your drawing should look like Figure 7.5.

This can save you considerable time when you know that the base point of the group or selection set also represents the amount of displacement.

Tip 58 from
Ron House

The value of the base point may not always be apparent when using this option. Therefore, if you suspect that you might want to use the base point as the displacement and you have already started your command, use the ID command transparently by typing a hyphen (') before the command. AutoCAD will display the base point coordinates, allowing you to make a determination without needing to exit the command.

Figure 7.5
You can move objects using the base point of the object to define the displacement.

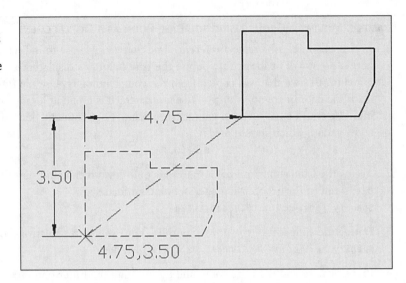

In addition to using the steps shown in the last example to edit an object, where the command is activated first and then the objects are selected, there is an alternative editing process you may find easier and quicker to use. This involves a feature called Grips (discussed in the next section).

GRIPS: ANOTHER WAY OF EDITING

Before you go on to more of the editing commands, let's look at a faster way to edit drawing objects. The process for using the Move command discussed previously was that the command was chosen first and then the objects to be modified were selected. This process is called verb/noun selection, where the command is selected before the objects. You can also reverse this process and work in a noun/verb mode, where the objects are selected first and then the command is chosen. This functionality is actually controlled by a system variable called Pickfirst. When this variable is on, or set to 1, objects can be selected before choosing a command. Turning this variable off reverts AutoCAD back to verb/noun selection mode. Table 7.2 displays a list of commands that can be used with noun/verb selection:

TABLE 7.2 NOUN/VERB-ENABLED COMMANDS		
ALIGN	DVIEW	PROPERTIES
ARRAY	ERASE	ROTATE
BLOCK	EXPLODE	SCALE
CHANGE	LIST	STRETCH
CHPROP	MIRROR	WBLOCK
COPY	MOVE	

Toggling the selection mode to noun/verb also introduces you to grips. When the Pickfirst variable is set to 1, grips are activated on the selected drawing objects and appear as small squares located at specific points on the individual objects.

Tip 59 from	Multiple objects can be added or removed from the selection set created using Grips by
Ron House	pressing the Shift key while selecting the objects.

Picking a grip on a selected object, which becomes the base grip, enables you to choose from five editing commands. These commands are listed here with their prompts:

```
** STRETCH **
Specify stretch point or [Base point/Copy/Undo/eXit]:

** MOVE **
Specify move point or [Base point/Copy/Undo/eXit]:

** ROTATE **
Specify rotation angle or [Base point/Copy/Undo/Reference/eXit]:

** SCALE **
Specify scale factor or [Base point/Copy/Undo/Reference/eXit]:

** MIRROR **
Specify second point or [Base point/Copy/Undo/eXit]:
```

These commands, in addition to the Copy command discussed in the section "Copying Objects Within the Drawing" later in this chapter, can be toggled through by pressing the Enter key or the spacebar. They are also available from the right-click shortcut menu, shown in Figure 7.6.

Figure 7.6
The commands and options available using grips via the shortcut menu.

Note	The Rotate, Scale, and Mirror commands are discussed in further detail in Chapter 8,
	"More Editing Commands," and the Stretch command is discussed in Chapter 9, "Not All
	Objects Can Be Edited This Way."

These commands can be used multiple times during one editing session in any order using grips, a significant advantage over the verb/noun selection mode.

TYPES OF GRIPS

As items are selected and grips appear on those items, you can define how the grips function during the editing process. Clicking a grip defines that grip as the base grip, or the hot grip. This is similar to the base point used in conjunction with the Move command discussed earlier in this chapter, and becomes the origin or anchor point for that object or objects. When a grip becomes the base grip, its color changes to indicate that this is the hot grip. The hot grip is one of three types of grips shown in Figure 7.7.

Figure 7.7
This figure illustrates the differences between the hot, cold, and warm grips.

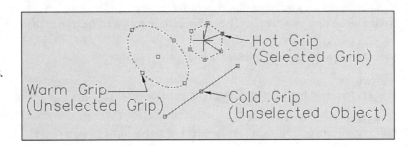

- Hot—This is the base grip, or the grip that has been selected as the base point for the editing commands.
- Warm—This grip on a highlighted object has not been selected as the base grip.
- Cold—These are defined as grips on an object that has not been highlighted. These grips are typically used as object snap points on objects that are not part of the selection set.

Cold grips can be created by holding down the Shift key while selecting anywhere on the highlighted object except on a grip box. These are typically objects that were initially selected as part of the selection set and removed, although the grips are kept so they can be used as points to snap to on those objects, similar to object snaps.

Use of grips can definitely decrease production time, especially when needing to apply numerous editing commands to one selection set. The next example shows you how to use grips to move an object in the drawing.

EXAMPLE: MOVING A DRAWING OBJECT USING GRIPS

1. Using the drawing used in the previous example, click an object or select multiple objects with the mouse to create a window or crossing selection window. The selection set will be highlighted, and grips will appear at specific points on the objects.
2. Select a base or hot grip of your choice.
3. Right-click to select the primary command desired. When that command is activated, right-click again and select the Copy option. As an example, the prompt for the Move command would change to read as follows:

```
** MOVE (multiple) **
```

This indicates that you can now create multiple copies of the object while working with this Grip command. In this case, multiple copies of the selection set can be made (see Figure 7.8).

Figure 7.8
Grips can be used to place multiple copies of any object using the Move and Copy commands.

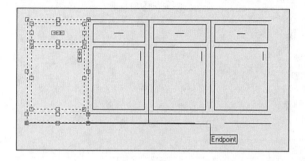

Tip 60 from
Ron House

Grips can be canceled by pressing the Esc (Cancel) button twice or by activating any drawing command.

In addition, the base point can be respecified as many times as desired, as the following example illustrates.

EXAMPLE: CHOOSING A DIFFERENT BASE POINT FOR AN EDITING COMMAND USING GRIPS

1. Create a new drawing and draw some objects of your choice.
2. Select one of the objects to edit, and then pick an initial hot grip.
3. Right-click and select the Move command. The selection set can be moved using the initial base point. Right-click again and select Base Point; then pick another base point to move about.
4. The selection set now moves using the new base point. This can be done for any of the commands using grips, as many times as desired.

This enables you to modify the base point, depending on the command chosen while grips are applied to the selected objects. Because you can activate multiple commands with grips, the base point you used with the Move command may not be the base point you want to use for the Stretch command. This option gives you the flexibility to adjust the base point as needed. Now let's look at some of the options available when using grips.

MODIFYING THE GRIP OPTIONS VIA THE PREFERENCES DIALOG BOX

Right-click in the command line and chose the Options command. Select the Selection tab from the Option dialog box, shown in Figure 7.9.

Figure 7.9
The settings available for the grip can be set in the Options dialog box.

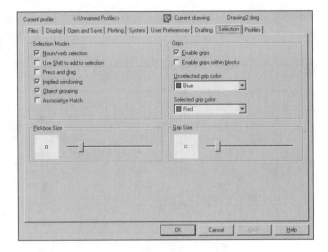

This section contains many of the options that affect how grips function. Although some deal with how objects are selected, other options control the display of the grips. Starting with the selection modes, this list discusses each mode in detail.

- Noun/verb selection—As discussed earlier in this chapter, this mode defines how objects can be selected, either before or after selecting a command. A check mark next to this option is the same as setting the Pickfirst variable to 1.

- Use Shift to add to selection—This option utilizes the Shift key to add or subtract objects from a selection set. If this option is left unchecked, attempting to add more items to the selection set will deselect the initial objects. With this option checked, more objects can be added by holding down the Shift key while selecting objects. If an object is already selected, it will remain highlighted when selected in conjunction with a new object added to the selection set. The equivalent system variable for this command is Pickadd.

- Press and drag—This allows a selection window to be created by picking a point and dragging from that point around the objects you wish to select. If this option is not selected, the selection window is defined by picking two points that define its boundary, with no dragging required. This option can also be set by using the Pickadd system variable.

- Implied windowing—This determines whether a selection window will be drawn if no object is selected. Dragging to the right selects all objects completely inside the window. Dragging to the left simulates a crossing box, where objects crossed by the boundaries of the box and those completely inside the box are selected.

The following options available in the Grips section under the Selection tab control the display of grips:

- Enable grips—This controls whether grips are displayed on a selected object. This can also be set by the use of the GRIPS system variable.

- Enable grips within blocks—This setting enables grips on every object within the block. If the option is not enabled, a grip is displayed only at the insertion point of the block.

- Unselected grip color—This sets the color for unselected grips, either cold or warm grips, depending on whether they exist on an object that is highlighted.

- Selected grip color—This determines the color for selected grips, or hot grips.

- Grip Size—This slider bar enables you to set the size of the grip.

Editing objects using grips provides definite advantages over using the standard noun/verb editing command process, such as activating multiple editing commands within one function and the ability to reassign the base point of the selected objects. Although you will find grips useful, working with them takes practice to determine exactly how they can be utilized in your day-to-day practices. After you learn them, you'll find that grips are an invaluable tool in making your editing processes more efficient. In Chapters 8 and 9, you'll learn how to work with the other editing commands available using grips. First, however, let's look at the Copy command in more detail.

COPYING OBJECTS WITHIN THE DRAWING

The Copy command duplicates an object or objects previously existing in the drawing. This command can be used to create a single copy or multiple copies of the objects selected. Let's examine using these options while dealing with complex selection sets.

Start the Copy command by selecting the Copy button from the Modify toolbar (see Figure 7.10), by choosing the Copy option from the Modify pull-down menu, or by simply typing **CP** at the command line and pressing Enter.

Figure 7.10
The Copy command is available on the Modify toolbar.

When the objects you want to copy have been selected, you have two options:

- Specify base point or displacement—With this option, you can either provide a base point or define a displacement for the copied objects. To specify a base point, pick a base point on or near the selection set that will act as the handle by which these objects will be displaced. To define a displacement, pick two points in the drawing that represent where you want the copied objects to be located.

■ Multiple—This option enables you to make multiple copies of the selected items. You may continue to make as many copies as you want until you press the Enter key, or right-click and choose Enter.

You can use object snap tracking with the editing commands to assist in the placement of objects. The next example walks you through working with the Copy command using object tracking to make and position a copy of a tap screw.

EXAMPLE: COPYING OBJECTS USING OBJECT SNAP TRACKING

1. Open the drawing ch7_02.dwg that you copied from the companion CD. You will make a copy of the tap screw point A and locate the copy by aligning it with point B using object snap tracking. First, select the Copy command from the Modify pull-down menu.

2. Select the tap screw A and specify the base point to be at bottom midpoint of the screw, indicated by point A.

3. When you are prompted to specify the second point of displacement, turn on object snap tracking by clicking the OTRACK tile on the status bar. Move the cursor to the bottom midpoint indicated by the X at point B that will be used to locate the tap screw. Do not click at this point—you'll just need to pause briefly to toggle the alignment path on. As you move off center and straight down, notice that the path appears. Move down, making sure the alignment path is still showing, until you are perpendicular with the horizontal direction of the tap screw.

4. When the alignment paths meet, this is the location for the second point of displacement. Click to locate the screw and to end the command.

Object tracking works well when you have objects in the drawing that you can align with. Typically, though, objects are placed in relation to other objects using specific distances. Follow through the next example to learn how to copy objects using direct distance input and the polar snap feature.

EXAMPLE: COPYING MULTIPLE OBJECTS AT AN ANGLE USING DIRECT DISTANCE INPUT

1. Open drawing ch7_03.dwg from the CD. In this example, you will make multiple copies of the door spaced at 5 feet along the wall.

2. Use the polar snap to assist in laying out the windows. You will need to set the polar snap equal to the angle of the wall, which is 30°. Right-click the Polar tile on the status bar, and choose Settings from the shortcut menu that appears. This opens the Drafting Settings dialog to the Polar Tracking tab. Set the increment angle to 30.0, and make certain the Polar Tracking On check box has been selected. Then click the OK button.

3. Start the Copy command by selecting the Copy option from the Modify pull-down menu. Select the first door at point A, and press Enter.

4. Next, you want to make multiple copies of this window, so type **M** at the Specify Base Point or Displacement or [Multiple] prompt. and press Enter.

5. Pick the base point to be the center of the fixture. As you start to move the crosshairs in a direction parallel to the wall, notice that the alignment path is displayed.

6. At the Specify Second Point of Displacement prompt, type **5'** and press Enter. With this, the first copy of window is placed. As long as the alignment path is pointing in the direction you wish to place the window, you will need to provide only the absolute spacing from the base point for each window.

7. Next type **10'**, and press Enter. This will place the windows in their desired locations. To end the command, press Enter. Your drawing should look similar to Figure 7.11.

Figure 7.11
Placing windows at an angle is easy using the Copy command with the direct distance input and polar snap functions.

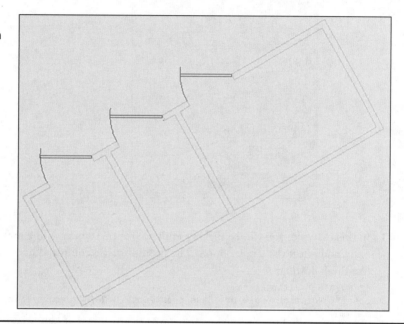

The Using grips with the copy command allows the added benefit of redefining the base point for the copied objects, as the next example demonstrates.

EXAMPLE: ACTIVATING THE COPY COMMAND WITH GRIPS VIA THE MOVE COMMAND

1. To perform a standard Copy function, let's begin by first opening drawing ch7_04.dwg from the CD. Select the object shown in Figure 7.12 by selecting on the arm, which has been grouped together as one object.

2. Grips should appear on the arm. Select the grip shown at point A, making it the Hot grip. Right-click and select the Rotate command from the menu.

Figure 7.12
This example demonstrates how to make multiple copies of this arm while rotating the arm at different angles using point A as the base point.

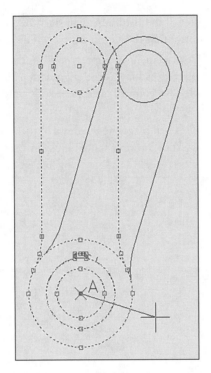

3. In this example, you will be making multiple rotated copies of the arm, so right-click again and select the Copy option. The prompt at the command line should now look like the following:

```
** ROTATE (multiple) **
Specify rotation angle or [Base point/Copy/Undo/Reference/eXit]:
```

4. When prompted for a rotation angle, key in **–30**, **–60**, and **–90**, respectively. Then press Enter.

Tip 61 from
Ron House

Step 5 in this example assumes you have your drawing units configured so that the counter-clockwise direction is the positive direction for angles. To check this, select Units from the Format pull-down menu. After the Unit dialog box opens, make certain the Clockwise button is not checked. This is the default mode, yet this needs to be mentioned to avoid any confusion.

5. The finished drawing should look like Figure 7.13.

Figure 7.13
This figure illustrates another advantage of using grips by combining the Rotate and Copy commands.

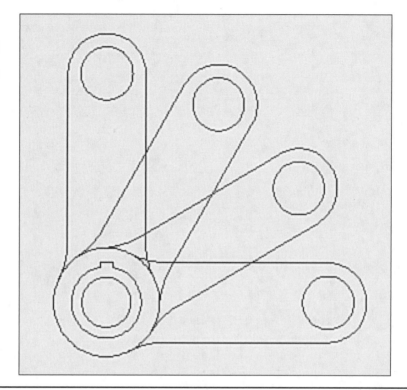

The examples in this chapter only begin to give you an idea of what can be accomplished using grips. Consider using grips for any editing function to increase your productivity and especially when you want to combine multiple commands in one operation.

SUMMARY

The Erase, Move, Undo, Oops, and Copy commands form the core editing commands. With these commands, you can complete the bulk of editing operations within AutoCAD 2000. Combined with the use of grips, you have a powerful way to quickly edit objects within the drawing. Now let's take what you've learned with this chapter and expand your knowledge of the Rotate command and other editing commands in the next chapter.

PART

III

CH

7

MORE EDITING COMMANDS

In this chapter

ADVANCED EDITING COMMANDS

There are two distinct groups of commands used to edit objects in AutoCAD: basic and advanced. The basic editing commands can be used to edit the majority of AutoCAD drawing objects. This chapter deals with the remainder of the basic editing features, beyond the elementary Erase, Move, and Copy commands. The advanced commands deal only with specific objects, and these are covered in the next chapter.

ROTATING OBJECTS

Anytime you want to rotate an object or a group of objects within a drawing, you will want to use the Rotate command. This is typically used when an object is placed in the drawing and then needs to be rotated into a different position or angle, such as the rotation of a new building on a site plan or furniture on a furniture plan. One of the more common ways to access the command is to select the Rotate button from the Modify toolbar, shown in Figure 8.1. You are prompted to select the object or objects you want to rotate, as well as to select a base point from which the objects are rotated about. You then supply the angle you want the items to be rotated either by typing the value or by dragging the crosshairs to the desired angle.

Figure 8.1
Choose the Rotate button from the Modify toolbar.

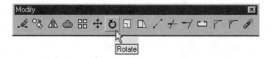

Tip 62 from
Ron House

You can also access the Rotate command by selecting it from the Modify pull-down menu or by typing **RO** at the command line.

MODIFYING THE ROTATE COMMAND WITH SETTING VARIABLES

When the command is accessed, you will see the following prompts:

```
Current positive angle in UCS:  ANGDIR=counterclockwise  ANGBASE=0
Select objects:
```

The Rotate command displays the current settings that affect how objects will be rotated in the present User Coordinate System (UCS).

→ The UCS defines the direction of the x and y axis, which gives you a base coordinate system to work with. It is called the User Coordinate System because the user can define multiple coordinate systems within a drawing. Refer to Chapter 23, "Visualization," for a brief overview on this feature.

These settings are listed here:

- ANGDIR—This system variable sets the direction all angles are rotated.
- ANGBASE—ANGBASE defines the angle from which all angles are measured.

Tip 63 from *Ron House*	Both of these variables, ANGDIR and ANGBASE, can also be set from the Drawing Units dialog box, accessed from the Format pull-down menu, Units… option.

Note	When using the Rotate command with grips, the current settings for these setting variables are not displayed. These are shown when you enter the command at the command line or when you choose from the Modify toolbar or pull-down menu.

Knowing the current settings for these variables will assist you in determining how the items you select will be rotated.

ROTATING WITH GRIPS

When the Rotate command is used with grips, the functionality of the command is greatly enhanced. The capability to change the base point as often as desired, and the fact that you can create multiple copies of the objects being rotated help to illustrate this point. The following example demonstrates this:

EXAMPLE: ROTATING AND COPYING WITH THE ROTATE COMMAND

1. In this example, open the drawing ch08_01.dwg. Currently there are two chairs, represented by a block called CHAIRS, located at the head of the table. Suppose you want to copy and rotate a pair of the chairs to each of the table's other three sides.

2. Use the Rotate command to not only rotate each pair of chairs, but also to copy them around the dining table. First, select the chairs so the grip handles appear. Only one grip handle should appear, and that is at the insertion point of the block.

Tip 64 from *Ron House*	Although this is not necessary for this example, if you want to see all the grips available on this block, right-click within the command line and select the Options command from the menu. This opens the Options dialog box; from here you will need to select the Selection tab. Then you can select the option Enable Grips Within Blocks check box and toggle this option on (see Figure 8.2). This allows all of the objects within the block to display their grip handles, making them selectable. Click the OK button to apply this to the drawing.

Figure 8.2
You can toggle on the display of grips within blocks through the Options dialog box.

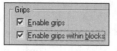

3. Select the grip on the chairs and right-click to open the shortcut menu. Select the Rotate command option. You should see this prompt displayed:

   `Specify rotation angle or [Base point/Copy/Undo/Reference/eXit]:`

4. Type **C** for the Copy option. This allows you to make multiple copies of the rotated objects.

5. You will want to select a base point that will enable you to place all the chairs at once. A base point selected at the middle of the table would allow this, so type **B** to relocate the current base point. At the Specify Base Point prompt, you should make certain your Object Snap settings are set to Midpoint only. To check this, right-click the OSNAP tile located in the status bar. This opens the Drafting Settings dialog box, with the Object Snap tab selected.

6. Click the Clear All button, and then click the Midpoint check box and select the OK button. Check to also make sure the OSNAP and OTRACK tiles are depressed, turning both these options on. You will want to quickly find the center point of the table to use as the base point.

7. Drag your cursor over one edge of the table until a triangular object snap marker appears along with a tracking vector. Pause briefly to make the tracking vector appear. Now, without selecting anything, drag the cursor to the adjacent edge 90° from the first and locate the object snap marker on this edge as well. Move the cursor to the approximate intersection of these two vectors until the tracking vectors line up. Click at this point, selecting the center of the table as the base point. This is shown in Figure 8.3.

Figure 8.3
Using Object Tracking and Object Snaps to locate the center of the table while rotating with grips.

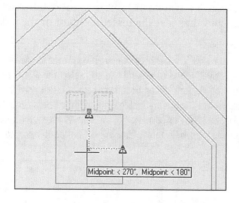

8. You will notice the chairs now rotate about the center of the table, not about the insertion point of the block as before. Turn on your Ortho setting by clicking the Ortho tile from the status bar if it's not already activated. Now you can drag the chairs into position or type in the corresponding angles of 90, 180, and 270, to place a pair of chairs at each end of the table.

Tip 65 from
Ron House

You can also hold down the Shift key to evenly space objects after the first object has been rotated, similar to a polar array. This can save you time, rotating objects at an equal spacing, such as bolt holes on a flywheel or rivet holes on a structural framing member.

In the previous example, you had a good indication where the chairs were going to be placed, so it was easy to establish what the rotation angle should be. The next section covers the Reference Angle option of the Rotate command, which references the rotation angle of another object in the drawing to determine the amount of rotation.

ROTATION VIA A REFERENCE ANGLE

Another feature, the Reference Angle option, is very useful in aligning objects to a specific angle, especially when you might not know what angle the objects are currently rotated at. The Reference option enables you to rotate an object to a precise angle after you furnish the angle to which the object is currently rotated. If you do not know that angle, you can select two points that the angle will be derived from, as the following example shows:

Tip 66 from
Ron House

The order in which you select the two points that determine the angle makes a difference in the way the angle will be calculated. A general rule of thumb is that the first point picked is the angle base point; the second point defines the direction the angle is given as well as the value of the angle. The same holds true for the use of the Dist command to determine angles. Use this rule to ensure that you will get the desired results every time.

EXAMPLE: ROTATING OBJECTS USING A REFERENCE ANGLE

1. Open the drawing ch08_01.dwg, if it's not already open. The table in the conference room needs to be rotated so the bottom edge of the table is parallel with the angled wall. Start by selecting the Rotate command from the Modify pull-down menu.

2. Select the table and chairs, and find the center of the table the same way you did in the previous example; use that as the base point (refer to Figure 8.3).

3. The wall you want to align the table with should be rotated at 30°. If it's not, the Dist command can be used to determine the angle of the wall. Access the Reference option by typing **R** and pressing Enter.

Tip 67 from

Ron House

You can use the Dist command to find the angle between two points in addition to the distance. When you select two points that define a distance, the distance along that line, the distance in the X, Y, and Z axis are given, and the angle between the two points selected. Remember, this command can be run transparently by typing a single quote before the command, such as 'Dist.

4. Assume you do not know the current angle of the table, so you will select two points that will provide AutoCAD with the current angle of the table. At the following prompt, select the table at point A. When you are prompted for the second point, click near point B.

```
Specify the reference angle <0>:
```

5. Type **135** for the angle of the wall at the prompt to specify the new angle. The table should rotate to the new angle and should look like the table in Figure 8.4.

Figure 08.4
Rotating a table to match the reference angle of an existing wall is an easy task using the Rotate command.

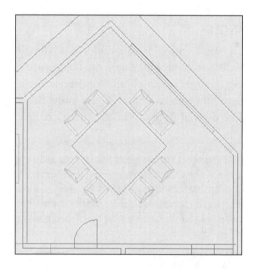

Note

Three-dimensional objects can be rotated in along a specific axis or two points defining an axis of rotation using the Rotate3D command. This command is accessed from the Modify pull-down menu, 3D Operation, Rotate 3D.

Use this option at times when you know the angle by which you want to rotate, yet you do not know the amount of rotation needed.

CHANGING THE SIZE OF OBJECTS WITH THE SCALE COMMAND

The Scale command increases or decreases the size of an object or a selection set of objects (see Figure 8.5). The objects are always scaled proportionately in the X, Y, and Z directions.

PART
III

CH

8

Figure 8.5
The Scale command increases or decreases the size of an object or a selection set of objects.

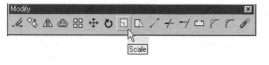

By default, you are prompted for the object or objects to scale. Then, by clicking a base point to scale from, you can key in or drag to define the scale factor. A scale factor larger than 1 increases, and a factor less than 1 decreases the scale of the objects, which is illustrated in Figure 8.6.

Figure 8.6
Distance from the origin point to the selected objects must be taken into consideration when increasing or decreasing the scale.

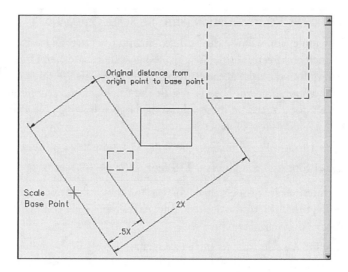

Note

It is important to remember that if a base point is placed away from the objects you are scaling, the distance from the base point to the objects will be scaled by the same scale factor (see Figure 8.6). If this is not taken into consideration, not only will the objects be scaled, but they will relocate from their original position as well.

Tip 68 from
Ron House

When accessing this command using grips, you can invoke the Copy option while scaling your objects, allowing you to make copies of the selection set as they are scaled. For example, suppose you've drawn a tree on a site plan, and now you want to use this to place multiple trees, changing the scale of the tree with each copy. Using grips to access both the Scale and Copy commands can save a considerable amount time, enabling you to apply two operations on a selection set at one time.

Using this option is great if you know the scale factor, yet what do you do if you do not know what scale factor to use? The next section shows you how to use the Scale command to determine the desired scale factor in relation to other objects in the drawing.

USING A REFERENCE LENGTH TO SCALE AN OBJECT

The Reference Length option scales objects based on a user-provided reference length and a new length. The reference length refers to the current size of a reference object, and the new size is the size you want the object to be. AutoCAD compares the two values and computes the scale factor for you. The following example illustrates using the Relative option:

EXAMPLE: USING THE RELATIVE OPTION WITH THE SCALE COMMAND

1. In this example, you will use the Scale command to convert a landscape-oriented 11 × 17-inch architectural titleblock from one scale to another. Open the drawing ch08_2.dwg found on the accompanying CD. Currently, the titleblock is at a scale of 1/4 inch = 1 foot. You will need to rescale the titleblock to accommodate a drawing at 1/8 inch = 1 foot. Based on these values, the largest drawing area available at both scales on a 11 × 17-inch sheet of paper is

   1/4 inch = 1 foot = 17 × 4 inches = **68 feet,** 11 × 4 inches = **44 feet**

   1/8 inch =1 foot = 17 × 8 inches = **136 feet,** 11 × 8 = **88 feet**

2. Because the sizes are proportional, you can use the Scale Relative option to easily convert the titleblock to the desired scale. Access the Scale command by selecting it from the Modify pull-down menu.

3. Then use the All selection set filter to select all objects in the drawing, in this case all objects that make up the titleblock. At the Select Objects prompt, type **ALL** and press Enter.

   `Select objects: ALL <ENTER>`

   Press Enter once more to end the selection process.

4. Type **0,0** at the Specify Base Point prompt and press Enter.

5. At the Specify Scale Factor or [Reference] prompt, right-click and select Reference from the shortcut menu.

6. Enter the current reference length, which is 68 feet, at the Specify Reference Length prompt and press Enter.

7. Then specify the new length:

   `Specify new length: 136' <ENTER>`

   The drawing area and titleblock are now adjusted for use with a / inch = 1 foot drawing, as shown in Figure 8.7.

Figure 8.7
Modifying the existing scale of a titleblock using the Scale Relative option to a new scale factor.

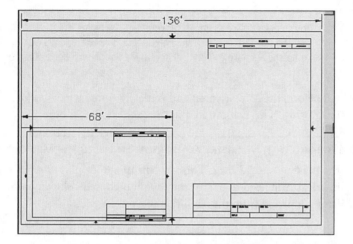

Use the Dist command transparently by typing **'DIST** at the Specify New Length prompt to determine the value for an unknown reference length.

This option also comes in pretty handy when scaling an entire drawing from one format to another. For example, if you want to convert a drawing from metric to imperial format, you would specify a reference length of 25.4 and a new length of 1.

MIRRORING OBJECTS IN THE DRAWING

The Mirror command is used to create a mirror image of selected objects. An example of when you could use this command is to mirror one side of a completed duplex floor plan to create the entire unit when the duplicated side is symmetrical of the other. This command is found on the Modify toolbar and pull-down menu (see Figure 8.8). After selecting the objects you want to mirror, you are prompted to define a mirror line. This mirror line represents the axis about which the objects will be mirrored or "flipped." This does not need to be an existing line, and it is created by the user selecting two points on the screen.

Figure 8.8
The Mirror command is used to create a mirror image of selected objects.

Tip 69 from
Ron House

You can quickly access the Mirror command by typing **MI** at the command line or (taking this one step further) select the objects first, type **MI**, and press Enter. This will activate the command and take you immediately to the Specify first point of mirror line: prompt.

As mentioned before, the Mirror command is ideally suited when working with symmetrical areas of your drawing. This is illustrated in the exercise shown here:

EXAMPLE: WORKING WITH SYMMETRICAL AREAS WHEN USING THE MIRROR COMMAND

1. Open the drawing ch08-3.dwg. This is a part of a floor plan where the restroom layout is symmetrical. You need to mirror the highlighted items shown in Figure 8.9. Launch the Mirror command from the Modify pull-down menu.

Figure 8.9
The Mirror command is ideal for symmetrical rooms where the objects can be mirrored about a common centerline.

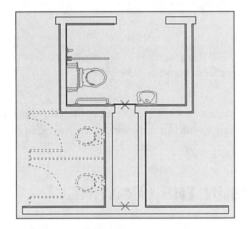

2. The highlighted items in Figure 8.9 have already been saved as a group in this drawing called RESTROOM. All of these objects have been saved together as one object, making them easier to select. You will use this group to easily select what you want to mirror. At the Select Objects prompt, type **G** and press Enter. Then, at the Enter Group Name prompt, type **RESTROOM**, as shown here:

```
Select objects: G <ENTER>
Enter group name: RESTROOM <ENTER>
```

→ You'll find more information on the Group command in Chapter 10, "Selecting Objects." This function can be used to group objects together as one, which is similar to using the Group command in PowerPoint or Word Draw.

3. Press Enter again to move to the definition of the mirror line. Start the mirror line at point A, and then turn on your Ortho to draw a straight line 90° from point A to point B.

4. When you are prompted to specify the second point of the mirror line, click point B.

5. AutoCAD asks whether you wish to delete the source objects.

```
Delete source objects? [Yes/No] <N>:
```

Answer No to retain the original objects.

Tip 70 from
Ron House

Just as with the Rotate and Scale commands discussed earlier in this chapter, when using the Mirror command with grips you can activate the Copy option to make a copy of the mirrored objects. This is similar to using the Mirror command from the command line and declining the option to delete source objects.

MIRROR TEXT OR MIRRTEXT

The Mirrtext option is available with the Mirror command. When text is selected for use with the Mirror command, it is reversed or turned upside down along with the other objects selected. The Mirrtext option allows the text to be mirrored, yet you can control the correct orientation of the text by setting the Mirrtext command to 1, as illustrated in Figure 8.10.

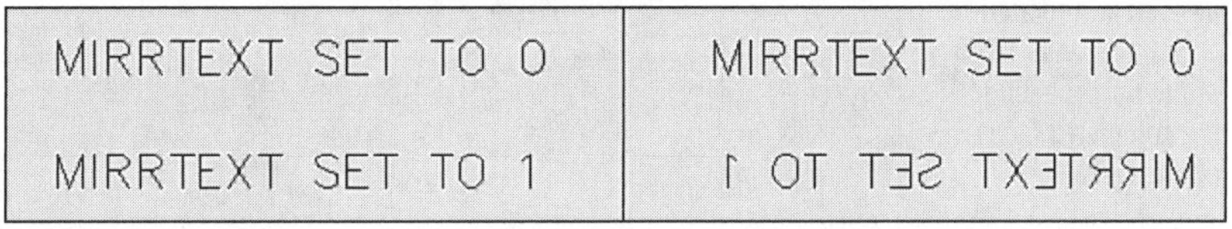

Figure 8.10
Setting Mirrtext to 1 forces the text to be oriented correctly when it is mirrored.

Note

Objects can also be mirrored in three dimensions by using the Mirror 3D command. Options for mirroring objects along the Z axis, three points, or a specified combination of two axes (such as XY, YZ, or XZ) are available. This command is accessed from the Modify pull-down menu, 3D Operation, Mirror 3D.

The next two commands discussed in this chapter can be used to duplicate an existing object multiple times, based on a user-defined spacing.

CREATING ARRAYS

The Array command creates multiple copies of an object at a defined spacing. This comes in handy when you wish to copy a number of objects and you notice that the spacing between your objects is uniform. In defining the spacing, two formats are available: polar and rectangular.

To view the prompts for these two options, select the Array button from the Modify toolbar, or choose the Array command from the Modify pull-down menu (see Figure 8.11).

Figure 8.11
The Array command creates multiple copies of an object at a defined spacing.

Tip 71 from
Ron House

Type **AR** at the command line for quick access to the Array command.

After you have selected some objects to array, the following spacing options are displayed:

- Polar—The Polar format enables you to array in a circular pattern about a center point. You are prompted for the center point of the array, the number of objects to be arrayed, and the angle in degrees that the array will pass through. The last prompt asks if you want the objects rotated as they are arrayed. Answering Yes to this option rotates the objects about the center point as they are being arrayed, as shown in Figure 8.12.

Figure 8.12
The objects in the figure on the left are arrayed and rotated about the center point of the part, creating the completed figure on the right.

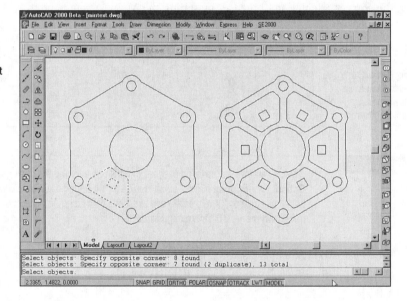

- Rectangular—This option arrays the objects in a series of rows and columns. You are prompted to give the number of columns and rows, as well as the spacing between them, which can also be defined as the *unit cell*. The user is prompted to select two points that create a rectangular-shaped *unit*. The width of the unit cell outlines the distance between columns, and the height is the distance between rows.

> **Note**
>
> The column spacing includes the height of the object (and respectively, the row spacing includes the width of the object) you array, as well as the spacing between objects. Make certain you take this into consideration when determining these distances, as illustrated in Figure 8.13.

Figure 8.13
The spacing between columns and rows should include the width of the object in addition to the spacing to the same location on the adjoining object in the next row or column, illustrated by this unit cell.

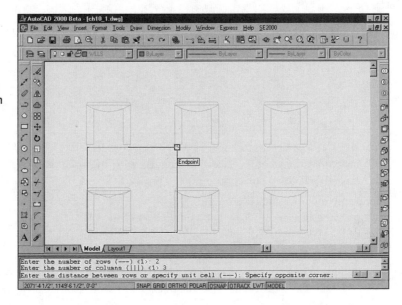

CREATING AN ARRAY AT A ROTATED ANGLE

At times, you may need to place an array that is rotated at a certain angle, such as when you are placing a ceiling grid in rooms rotated at different angles in a building. This can be accomplished by being a little creative with the Snap command options, as the following example illustrates:

EXAMPLE: ROTATING A RECTANGULAR ARRAY

1. This example details how to create a rotated rectangular array. For this example, say you want to place two rows of fluorescent lights in a conference room that is rotated at an angle of 135°. Open the drawing ch08_01.dwg used earlier in this chapter and restore the Conference View.

2. Turn on both the Lighting and Notes layers. Begin by setting the snap angle to match that of the conference room. From the Tools pull-down menu, select the Drafting Settings... option. On the Snap and Grid tab, key in a value of **135** in the Angle: edit box, and then click the OK button. Notice that the crosshairs are now rotated to that angle.

3. Start the Array command by choosing it from the Modify pull-down menu. At the Select Objects prompt, select the light fixture indicated at point A, shown in Figure 8.14, and press Enter.

Figure 8.14
Use a rotated rectangular array to evenly space hallway light fixtures by changing your snap angle to equal the rotation angle of the room.

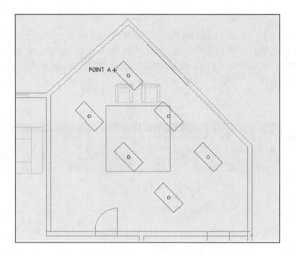

4. Specify that you want to place a rectangular array by typing **R** at the Enter the Type of Array [Rectangular/Polar] prompt, and press Enter.

5. Specify the rows and columns:

```
Enter the number of rows (—·) <1>: 2 <ENTER>
Enter the number of columns (¦¦¦) <1> 3 <ENTER>
```

6. Next, you will want to define a unit cell to represent the spacing between rows and columns. When you are prompted to specify a unit cell, snap to the corner intersection of the light fixture at point A. At the Specify Opposite Corner prompt, type **@-8',8'** and press Enter.

7. Return the snap rotation back to its original settings by entering an angle value of 0 from the Drafting Setting dialog box.

The spacing provided will evenly lay out the light fixtures to cover the conference room.

Note
You can also array objects in three dimensions by using the 3D Array command. In addition to what you provide for the two-dimensional Array command, you also need to provide the number of levels along the Z axis and spacing between levels. This command is accessed from the Modify pull-down menu, 3D Operation, 3D Array.

When you want to copy an object at a specific spacing in one direction, use the Offset command, which is discussed in the next section.

OFFSETTING OBJECTS AT A SPECIFIED DISTANCE

The Offset command places a copy of the selected object parallel to itself at a user-defined distance. This command easily creates concentric circles and parallel lines and curves, and cannot be used on three-dimensional faces or objects.

This command is available from the Modify toolbar or pull-down menu (see Figure 8.15).

Figure 8.15
The Offset command places a copy of the selected object parallel to itself at a user-defined distance.

The two options for defining the offset distance are listed here:

- Specify Offset Distance—After you type in the desired offset distance, AutoCAD prompts you to select the object to be offset and to click the side of the object you want to offset. You can also pick two points to define the offset distance, or click one point and type in a relative distance.

- Through—With this option, you define the offset distance by clicking a point you want the offset object to pass through.

In both instances, the respective prompts for the options are repeated so you can select a new object to be offset and set a new offset distance.

Note Because the Offset command cannot be used on three-dimensional objects, use the 3D Array command to offset objects along a specific axis.

OFFSETTING VARIABLES

Two setting variables affect the operation of the Offset command. First, the Offsetdist variable controls the offset distance. When you set a distance during the Offset command, this is the system variable that contains that distance. Second, the variable called Offsetgaptype deals with polylines and how polylines are affected by the Offset command. When a polyline is offset, gaps are created in a polyline at its vertices. To remedy this, the Offsetgaptype variable was created to specify how these gaps would be treated. Not only does this fix the gaps, but it also provides a quick way to apply a fillet or chamfer to a polyline while offsetting. The following values can be set for the Offsetgaptype variable:

- 0—AutoCAD extends the individual polyline segments to fill the gaps.
- 1—A radius equal to the offset distance is used to fill the gap.
- 2—The polyline is chamfered to fill the gap.

Suppose you have drawn a polyline that represents the boundary of a parking lot, and you want to offset this polyline to depict the curb surrounding the parking lot. Using a value of 1 for the Offsetgaptype variable would allow you to create the curb without the need to modify the offset polyline and round its vertices points. The following example illustrates the different types of offset polylines that can be created using the Offsetgaptype variable:

EXAMPLE: OFFSETTING A POLYLINE

1. Open the drawing ch08_4.dwg from the companion CD. This is a part that has a polyline edge that will be offset with each of the different Offsetgaptype settings.

2. Type **Offsetgaptype** at the command line, and set the value to 1.

3. Use the Offset command to offset the outside edge of the part 0.5 inch to the outside. You should now have something that looks similar to Figure 8.16.

Figure 8.16
An offset polyline with the results of the various Offsetgaptype values can be used to modify the display of the offset polyline.

4. Next, set the Offsetgaptype value to 2. Offset the original part edge a distance of 1 inch to the outside. Notice that the now polyline has chamfered edges instead of filleted edges as before.

5. Finally, set the Offsetgaptype variable to 1 and offset the original part edge a distance of 1.5 inches to the outside. Your final part should look like the one shown in Figure 8.17.

Figure 8.17
The finished part, created by varying the value of the Offsetgaptype variable and using the Offset command.

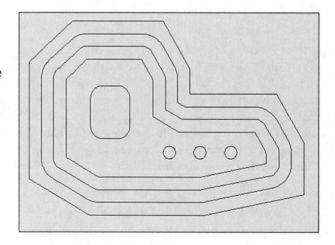

The next command can align objects in relation to each other. This command is invaluable when the specific distances to move, scale, and rotate are unknown.

ALIGN: MOVE AND ROTATE IN ONE COMMAND

The Align command is one of the more dynamic editing commands at your disposal. Because this command can move, rotate, and scale in one operation, you can do some very creative editing and save some time as well. Before using this command, you should apply some thought as to how the selected objects will be aligned. When you start to use the Align command regularly, you'll naturally start to look for ways to apply it. The Align command is also one of those commands that can act on three-dimensional features as well as two-dimensional objects.

This command is available from either the Modify pull-down menu under 3D Operation, or by typing **AL** at the command line. While using this command, you will be prompted for three types of points: source, destination, and alignment. Source points are points on the object you want to align, destination points are points on the object you want to align to, and alignment points are points that define how the objects will be scaled.

WORKING WITH SOURCE AND DESTINATION POINTS

Now that you know what these points do, the Align command can be applied in two different ways:

■ **Defining the first and second source and destination points**—This allows the objects to be moved, rotated, and scaled. The first set of source and destination points defines how the objects will be moved and also determines the base point for the rotation. The second set of points establishes how the objects will be rotated. If you answer No to the Scale Objects Based on Alignment Points? [Yes/No] prompt, the objects are moved and rotated. If you answer Yes to this prompt, the distance between the first and the second source points is used as the reference length. AutoCAD then uses the distance between the first point and destination points as the new length to calculate the scale factor. Use this feature to combine the Move, Rotate, and Scale commands into one to save time, whether you are working in two or three dimensions.

Tip 72 from
Ron House

If you define the first source and destination point, and then press Enter at the Specify second source point prompt, the command acts like the Move command. The source point will be moved to match up with its corresponding destination point. Any Rotate or Scale operations are not allowed by defining only one set of points.

■ **Defining three sets of points**—This procedure allows the alignment of objects in three-dimensional space, although this can also be done with only two sets of points. The first set of source and destination points outlines how the objects will be moved. The second set of points defines how the source object will be rotated in relation to the destination object. The last set of source and destination points determines how the object will be rotated again, typically along a third axis. This option is very useful when working in three dimensions when you want to rotate along two axes. This enables you to take advantage of one command to complete multiple operations, increasing your productivity.

You can see how this command can be very flexible and, if not well thought out, can provide some undesirable results, especially in dealing with objects in three dimensions. If you select the incorrect source and destination points, the object may be rotated at the incorrect angle. Use the Undo command to return the objects back to their original position and repeat the command again. The example that follows illustrates using the Align command to manipulate an object along the X, Y, and Z axes.

EXAMPLE: ALIGNING AND SCALING A TWO-DIMENSIONAL OBJECT

1. Open ch08_4.dwg, supplied with the companion CD. This drawing contains two parts, a wood base and metal sleeve, that will be attached together by screws. Use the Align command to move, rotate, and scale the oversized wood screw to fit into the drilled hole.

2. Start by launching the Align command by typing **AL** at the command line. Select the screw at the Select Objects prompt and press Enter.

   Be certain to turn on your Node Object Snap and snap to the node at point A. This will allow you to snap to the point node at point A. Snap to the node at point B for the destination point (see Figure 8.18).

4. For the second source point, snap to the node at point C, and then select the node at point D for the destination point (see Figure 8.18).

Figure 8.18
The use of object snaps is essential when aligning objects with the Align command, especially when working in three dimensions.

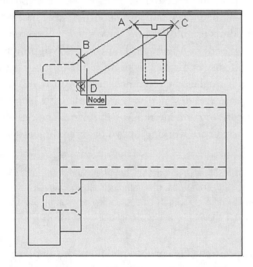

5. Press the Enter key to continue when prompted to specify third source point.

6. Answer Yes and press Enter when the following prompt is displayed:

```
Scale objects based on alignment points? [Yes/No] <N>: y
```

Although it is easier to visualize working in the XY plane, with practice you can also master using the Align command in three dimensions. Try your hand at using the Align command manipulating objects in three-dimensional space with the next example.

EXAMPLE: ALIGNING AN OBJECT IN THREE-DIMENSIONAL SPACE

1. Open the drawing ch08_05.dwg that you copied from the companion CD. In this example, you will move and rotate the column so it is aligned with the center of the top face of the cube. You will use object snaps and object tracking to assist in locating the column onto the cube.

2. First, launch the Align command, either by selecting it from the Modify pull-down list, or by typing **AL** at the command line.

3. At the Select Objects prompt, select the column and press the Enter key.

4. Now you will need to define the source and destination points. When you are prompted for the first source point, select the center of the base of the column at point A (see Figure 8.19).

Note

Make sure the Center and Midpoint object snaps are active during this step. Right-click the OSNAP tile in the status bar to confirm this.

5. To define the destination point, use object tracing to locate the center of the top face of the cube.

This can be accomplished by moving the cursor near the midpoint on one of the edges of the cube and pausing briefly. You will see the midpoint icon appear, along with a tracking vector, as you drag the cursor away from the midpoint. Move your cursor toward the edge adjacent or 90° from the last edge until the midpoint icon appears on this edge. Now, move away from the edge until you reach the estimated center of the cube the tracking vectors intersect. Select this point to define the center of the top face of the cube. This will define the first source and destination points (see Figure 08.19).

Figure 8.19
Locating the center of the base using object tracking provides a quick and easy way to furnish the source and destination points during the Align command.

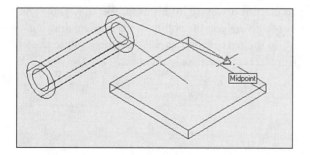

6. In determining the second set of points, select a Quadrant point on the base of the column (Shift + right-click to access the Object Snap pull-down menu, and choose QUAD to temporarily select the quadrant object snap) shown at point C (see Figure 8.19).

7. Align this point with a midpoint on one of the top edges of the cube, shown in Figure 8.20. This tells AutoCAD you want the quadrant point on the column to be at the same level as the midpoint of the edge on the cube, which defines the rotation angle.

8. Press Enter to continue at the Specify Third Source Point or <continue> prompt.

9. Type **N** at the following prompt to decline scaling the object:

   `Scale objects based on alignment points? [Yes/No] <N>:`

   You should have something that looks like the object in Figure 8.20.

Figure 8.20
Rotating a column to align with another object in three-dimensional space is easy with the Align command.

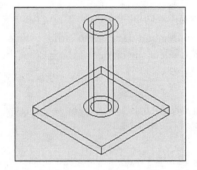

The Align command can be extremely useful while working with objects in two and three dimensions. More importantly, it allows you to combine multiple commands into one, enabling you to increase your productivity. Although there are benefits to be gained from using this command, it may take you some time before you master its use. But the time saved can pay off in the long run, once you learn to recognize when to use the command.

SUMMARY

The basic editing commands discussed in this chapter enable you to modify objects in the drawing in several ways, giving you the ability to manipulate drawing objects to fully represent your ideas. In the next chapter, you'll learn how to use the advanced editing commands and what objects you can apply them to.

CHAPTER 9

NOT ALL OBJECTS CAN BE EDITED THIS WAY

In this chapter

More Editing Commands

This chapter deals with commands that work on a specific group of objects. Unlike the editing commands discussed in Chapter 7, "Editing Commands," these commands work only with specific objects. These commands are covered in detail in this chapter: Stretch, Lengthen, Trim, Extend, Break, Fillet, and Chamfer.

The Stretch Command

The Stretch command elongates or stretches objects that fall within a selection window or polygon. The Stretch command is activated by selecting the Stretch button from the Modify toolbar shown in Figure 9.1. This displays the following prompt at the command line:

```
Select objects to stretch by crossing-window or crossing-polygon...
```

The object must have a point, side, or edge completely within a selection window to be stretched. A selection window is created by clicking a blank area in the drawing and dragging to the left a dashed box, or window, around what you want to edit. When you click the opposite corner of the window, it selects what is inside. When selecting an object to be stretched, you cannot select the object just by clicking it; what you want to edit must be completely inside a selection window.

To further illustrate this, let's examine two examples. If the vertex of an object such as a line or polyline is included inside the selection window, only that vertex will be moved and the other segments that are attached to it will be stretched. The same goes for a polyline or line segment completely contained within the selection window. It will be moved while the other segments it is joined to are stretched.

The following objects can be stretched:

- Lines
- Polylines
- Arcs
- Rays
- Splines
- Elliptical arcs
- Dimensions

Figure 9.1
Access the Stretch command from the Modify toolbar.

On very detailed drawings, you might find it hard to use a selection window to select what you want to stretch. Therefore, rather than selecting objects you want to stretch by dragging a selection window around them, you can also select objects by using an editing tool called *grips*.

STRETCHING WITH GRIPS

Certain objects can also be stretched using grips, depending on the type of object. When using grips with the Stretch command, some objects are moved rather than stretched, based on the grip location for that object. The following list defines these objects:

- Midpoints of lines
- Centers of circles
- Centers of ellipses
- Text objects
- Blocks
- Point objects

PART III

CH 9

To stretch with grips, click on an object while no command is active. Grips, or small editing boxes, will appear on the object. Select a grip on the portion of the object you wish to stretch. Selecting that grip makes that handle active, from which you can access the shortcut menu and the Stretch command. After clicking the new location of where you want the grip to be placed, the selected object or portion of the object is stretched. This enables you to quickly stretch an object, such as a polyline vertex or a quadrant point on a circle, that affects the size or location of the object.

STRETCHING MORE THAN ONE GRIP

Stretching using grips is a quick way to edit an object, although typically you will find that multiple grip handles must be selected to stretch the entire object. A good example is a case where you might want to stretch a wall to a desired length. Say that if the wall were made up of two separate lines, both line endpoints or vertices would need to be selected in order for both sides of the wall to be stretched in unison. This can easily be done by selecting the grips as you hold down the Shift button, as shown in Figure 9.2.

Figure 9.2
Multiple highlighted grips are selected and used to stretch both sides of a wall.

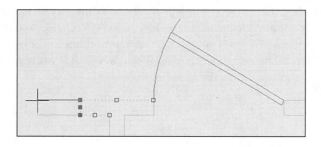

After the grips have been selected, release the Shift key and pick the one grip you want to use as the base grip. As you drag the base grip, the other highlighted grips follow in unison until the second displacement point is picked.

EXAMPLE: USING MULTIPLE GRIPS TO STRETCH A GROUP OF OBJECTS

1. Open drawing ch09_01.dwg that you copied from the accompanying CD.

Figure 09.3
This is an example of using multiple grips in combination with the Stretch command to stretch the top of the retaining wall.

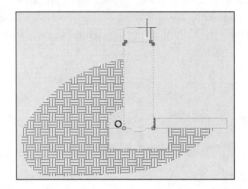

2. In this instance, you want to extend the retaining wall up by 12 inches. Start the Stretch command by choosing it from the Modify pull-down menu. Use a crossing or polygon selection window to place grips on the top portion of the retaining wall. Four grips should be highlighted.

3. While holding down the Shift key, select the four grips that will be used to stretch the object

4. Release the Shift key and pick one of the grips.

5. Key in a second point of displacement of **@12<90** and press Enter. This stretches only the top portion of the retaining wall, leaving the remainder of the wall in its original position.

STRETCHING WITH THE MOVE COMMAND

Objects can also be moved using the Stretch command. If objects are completely inside the selection set window, those objects will be moved during the Stretch operation, as shown in Figure 9.4. Using the Stretch command to move objects in relation to other objects near or in the selection set can save you a considerable amount of time as compared to using just the Move command. The next example helps illustrate why it is easier to move objects using the Stretch command than the Move command.

Figure 9.4
Objects are moved during the Stretch operation.

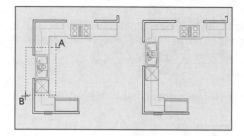

EXAMPLE: USING STRETCH TO MOVE A GROUP OF OBJECTS

1. Open drawing ch09_02.dwg after it has been copied from the companion CD.

2. Say for this example that you want to shift the placement of the sink and the dishwasher to the right by two feet. Start the Stretch command and place a crossing window around these objects from point A to B. Then press Enter using Figure 9.4 as a reference.

3. Select a point anywhere near the sink for a base point.

4. Key in a second point of displacement of **@2'<90**. This moves only the sink from its original position.

If you had moved the sink and dishwasher instead of stretching, you would now need to clean up the wall and counter to accommodate this move. This is not necessary if you use the Stretch command to move objects, saving you editing time.

STRETCHING DIMENSIONS

Dimensions can also be modified using the Stretch command. This is typically done when the size of an object has changed and the associated dimension needs to be updated, or if the placement of the dimension needs to be modified. You can use the Stretch command to lengthen or shorten the dimension, to reposition the location of the dimension line in relation to the object, or to change the default location of the dimension text. Even the length of extension lines can be modified using the Stretch command with grips.

Making these changes can easily be done by using grips or by including either of the extension lines of the dimension inside the Stretch selection window. As you stretch objects in the drawing, consider selecting the associated dimension with the object. An *associated dimension* is a dimension that updates its text value when modified. If the dimensions were placed as associative dimensions, the value of the dimension will automatically update as the dimension (and object) are stretched.

Tip 73 from
Ron House

To make the dimensions associative, the dimension variable DIMASO must be turned on before the dimension is placed into the drawing. See Chapter 14, "Dimensioning," for more information on associative dimensions.

The process of stretching a dimension is illustrated in Figure 09.5.

Figure 9.5
Modifying dimensions by using the Stretch command provides a quick way to adjust dimensions already placed in the drawing.

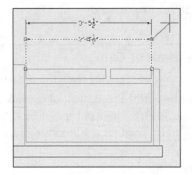

In the same category of the Stretch command is the Lengthen command. This command also enables you to stretch a line, but only along its current direction, with a variety of options that define the new length of the line. These options are discussed in detail next.

THE LENGTHEN COMMAND

The Lengthen command is designed to alter the length and the included angle of the following objects:

- Arcs
- Elliptical arcs
- Open lines
- Open polylines
- Open splines

You can increase or decrease the length or angle of the selected object by selecting the command from the Modify toolbar or pull-down menu.

Figure 9.6
Access the Lengthen command from the toolbar.

Tip 74 from	You can also quickly access the Lengthen command by typing **LEN** at the command line.
Ron House	

When the command is activated, several options are available from the shortcut menu. Using these options, you can adjust the length of an existing line based on its original length. The option used depends on the information you have that dictates the length of the object; for example, do you know the actual change in length, or percentage change in length? The option you use is going to depend on the situation.

- Select object—This prompts you to select the object you wish to edit. After you select the object, its current length is displayed. If an arc is selected, the arc length and the included angle are displayed.

By default, the following options all assume that the arc length will be modified when an arc is selected. Only the Delta and Total options have Angle suboptions that deal with the included angle.

- Delta—This option enables you to change the length of an object or arc length by a specific amount. This is used when you want to change the length of the object by a known distance.

- Percent—You can change the selected object by providing the percent increase or decrease with this option, which is based on the current length or arc length. This enables you to change the object by a percentage, given that the original length is 1.

- Total—This option defines the total length or arc length of the selected object. This enables you to change the object by knowing the total length desired.

- Dynamic—You can graphically increase or decrease the object length or included angle by *rubberbanding* the object with the cursor. Rubberbanding is the term used to describe how the object can actually be dynamically dragged with the cursor, enabling you to see the change in length. This is used when you do not know the length and want to be able to view it dynamically onscreen.

Tip 75 from	Polylines and polyarcs cannot be lengthened using the Dynamic option.
Ron House	

- Angle—This suboption is available only through the Delta and Total options. The angle value you enter alters the included angle of the selected arc. As you might guess, a negative value decreases the included angle, and a positive value increases the included angle.

When the values for these options have been set, the prompts will repeat until you press the Enter key. The following example depicts the use of the Lengthen command to modify a part that has an arc length constraint, as shown in Figure 9.7.

Figure 9.7
The arc that makes up the top portion of this key can be extended to an exact length to fit design criteria using the Lengthen command.

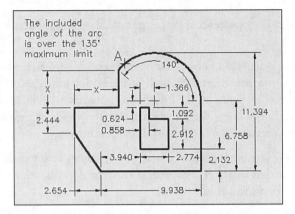

EXAMPLE: USING THE LENGTHEN COMMAND

1. Open drawing ch09_03.dwg that you copied from the companion CD. In this drawing, a redesign has been issued for this part. Based on design constraints, the arc on the top part of this key is limited to a maximum included angle of 135°. You need to modify the part to accommodate this change.

2. Start the Lengthen command by typing **LEN** at the command line.

3. Select the arc to determine its original included angle. The current angle is displayed as follows:

```
Select an object or [DElta/Percent/Total/DYnamic]:
Current length: 11.3315, included angle: 140
```

4. Right-click and select the Total option from the shortcut menu. Right-click again and select Angle to change the included angle of the arc. Because the maximum angle length cannot exceed 135°, enter a value of 135 at the Specify Total Angle prompt:

```
Select an object or [DElta/Percent/Total/DYnamic]: t <ENTER>
Specify total length or [Angle] <1.0000)>: a <ENTER>
Specify total angle <50>: 135 <ENTER>
```

5. You will now want to select the arc endpoint you want to adjust. Select the arc near point A.

6. This modifies the arc to the exact angle required. Use additional editing commands to change the unconstrained lines, dimensioned with an "X", to match the updated arc endpoint.

You will find that the Lengthen command typically comes in handy when modifying existing objects in the drawing, when a specific length is desired. You can use the next two commands to extend or trim drawing objects to another object when the actual length of the object does not need to be specified.

The Trim command, instead of lengthening an object, trims objects to other selected objects used to define a "cutting edge."

THE TRIM COMMAND

The Trim command enables you to cut an object exactly at an edge identified by one or more additional objects. This is very useful when dealing with overlapping lines. Only the following objects can be cut using the Trim command:

- Arcs
- Circles
- Elliptical arcs
- Floating viewports
- Lines
- Polylines (3D and open 2D)
- Rays
- Splines
- Regions
- Text

The command can be launched by selecting the Trim option from the Modify pull-down menu or by picking the Trim button from the Modify toolbar, shown in Figure 9.8.

Figure 9.8
You can quickly access the Trim command via the Modify toolbar.

There are numerous options available after you define a cutting edge:

- Select object to trim—This is the default option, allowing you to select the objects to be trimmed.

- Project—This option defines what AutoCAD projects the cutting edge onto when trimming objects. There are three different ways to define the projection; None, UCS, and View:

  - None—No projection is defined; objects must physically intersect the cutting edge.

  - UCS—This projects onto the current UCS to determine whether any objects intersect the cutting edge.

  - View—This option projects onto the current view to determine whether the cutting edge intersects any objects.

- Edge—The option set establishes whether a cutting edge is implied or actual. There are two options for defining the cutting edge; Extend or No Extend:

  - Extend—Extends the cutting edge along its current direction to intersect the nearest object.

  - No Extend—Stipulates that the cutting edge must intersect another object.

- Undo—Undoes the last operation completed by the Trim command and returns you to the Select object to trim prompt.

Now let's examine how some of these options can be utilized.

TRIMMING TO IMPLIED INTERSECTIONS

You can define the cutting edge by selecting an object, by choosing multiple edges, by letting AutoCAD calculate the closest object to be used as the cutting edge, or by trimming to the implied intersection. To trim by an implied intersection, press the Enter key at the Select cutting edges prompt. When you select an object, AutoCAD assumes the closest edge found is the cutting edge.

EXAMPLE: TRIMMING WITH IMPLIED INTERSECTIONS

1. Open the file ch09_04.dwg copied from the companion CD. This example wills use the Trim command to clean up a ceiling grid that overlaps the walls of a conference room, shown in Figure 9.9.

Figure 9.9
Use the Trim command to clean up the overlapping lines, such as these lines that define a ceiling grid that extends beyond a wall.

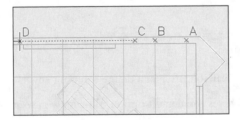

2. Start the command by selecting the Trim option from the Modify pull-down menu.

3. This example skips the first part of this command and lets AutoCAD find the nearest object to use as the cutting edge. This is done as you select the objects you want trimmed. This specific use of the Trim command saves considerable time because it saves you from having to select multiple cutting edges. At the Select cutting edges prompt, press the Enter key.

4. When AutoCAD prompts you to select an object to trim, pick the desired objects. Select point A and B. AutoCAD immediately determines the intersection or intersections and trims the object you selected to that point. After you select an object, it returns you to the Select object to trim prompt.

5. You can also use the Fence selection filter to select multiple objects to trim at one time. At the Select objects to trim prompt, type F to activate the Fence mode. Pick point C, and then drag the fence line and pick point D. Press the Enter key after you select point D. The selected objects are trimmed back to the nearest intersection.

The result is shown in Figure 9.10.

Figure 9.10
The conference room wall shows the corrected ceiling grid, a result of using the Trim command.

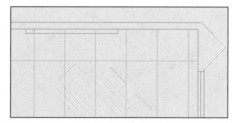

The opposite of Trim is the Extend command, which extends objects to a defined edge. This command is covered in detail in the next section.

EXTENDING OBJECTS TO A BOUNDARY

Similar to the Trim command is the Extend command, yet this command extends objects to a selected boundary edge. This feature enables you to extend an object exactly to an edge identified by one or more objects. Using the scenario in the previous section as a example, you could use the Extend command to project ceiling grid lines to an edge. This comes in very handy also when you are extending lines to a boundary on the other edge of the drawing. The command is accessed by selecting the Extend option from the Modify pull-down menu or by picking the Extend button from the Modify toolbar, shown in Figure 9.11.

Figure 9.11
You can select the Extend button from the Modify toolbar to access the Extend command.

The following list contains objects that can be extended:

- Arcs
- Elliptical arcs
- Lines
- Polylines (3D and open 2D)
- Rays

Similar to the Trim command, three options are available after you define a boundary edge:

- Select boundary edges—As the default option, this enables you to select one or multiple boundary edges using the selection set filters. The list that follows defines all the objects that can be used as a boundary edge:
  - Arcs
  - Circles
  - Ellipses
  - Floating viewports
  - Lines
  - Polylines (2D and 3D)
  - Rays
  - Regions
  - Splines
  - Text
  - Xlines

The following options are available for the Extend command:

- Project—This option defines the projection of the boundary edge, in which there are three options:
  - None—With this option, no projection is defined, so objects must physically intersect the boundary edge.
  - UCS—This option uses the User Coordinate System, which could be defined as the current drawing plane bounded by the X and Y axis, to determine how the selected objects will be extended. In this case, objects are extended to an edge in the current UCS rather than a boundary edge defined by an object.
  - View—Like the UCS option, this option projects onto the current view to determine how the selected objects will be extended.
- Edge—This option has two settings that establish whether a boundary edge is implied or actual. There are two options to define the edge:
  - Extend—The boundary edge is extended along its current direction to form an implied edge that the selected object will extend to.
  - No Extend—When this option is set, the selected object must intersect the actual boundary edge.
- Undo—This undoes the last operation completed by the Extend command and returns you to the Select boundary edges prompt.

The next section describes a process that expedites the use of the Extend command by using AutoCAD to determine the closest edge to extend to rather than choosing a boundary edge.

EXTENDING TO IMPLIED INTERSECTIONS

In addition to defining the boundary edge by selecting a single or multiple objects, AutoCAD can also calculate the closest object found along the path of the selected object to be used as the boundary edge. To extend to this implied intersection, press the Enter key at the Select Boundary Edges prompt. Then, when selecting objects to extend, AutoCAD will follow the path of that object until an intersection point is found and will extend the object to that point.

PART

III

CH

9

EXAMPLE: EXTENDING TO IMPLIED INTERSECTIONS

1. Open the drawing ch09_05.dwg from the companion CD. Use the Extend command to complete the part, shown in Figure 9.12.

Figure 9.12
Using the Extend command to quickly update this drawing by extending the hidden lines that indicate grooves on the underside of this part.

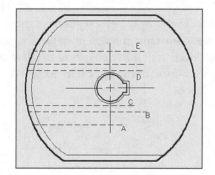

2. Start the command by selecting the Extend option from the Modify pull-down menu.

3. At the Select boundary edges prompt, press the Enter key to let AutoCAD determine the nearest object to use as the boundary edge. As you select objects to extend, AutoCAD will determine the closest object and will extend the object to the intersection of the two objects. Click the objects at points A, B, and C to extend the hidden lines to the edge of the part.

4. You can also use the Fence selection filter to select multiple objects to extend at one time. Type **F** at the First fence prompt and drag a Fence line over the objects between the objects at points D and E. Pressing Enter extends the lines to the outside edge of the object. The completed part is shown in Figure 9.13.

The next command break objects at selected points to provide a way of placing a gap in a boundary.

Figure 9.13
The finished part drawing after using the Extend command to extend the lines to an implied edge.

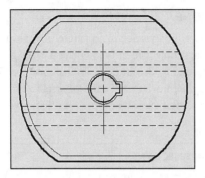

THE BREAK COMMAND

The Break command breaks an object in two or erases a segment of the selected object. This command can be used to create an opening in a wall or to place a gap in an object where that is not determined by the location of other objects in the drawing like with the Trim or Extend commands. Using the button from the Modify toolbar shown in Figure 9.14, you can break the following objects:

- Lines
- Circles
- Arcs
- Ellipses
- Elliptical arcs
- Polylines
- Rays
- Splines
- Xlines

Figure 9.14
Access the Break command from the toolbar.

Tip 76 from
Ron House

Type **BR** at the command line to quickly start the Break command.

Two modes exist in which to break an object. The default mode prompts you to select the object you wish to break and uses that selection point as the first break point. Then you are prompted to select the second break point on the object:

```
Specify second break point or [First point]:
```

You can override this and specify the first break point again by right-clicking and choosing First point from the shortcut menu. The First point option is the second mode, where you can define both the first and second points of the break.

When selecting an object to break, how you select the object determines which mode and which associated prompt you will be given at the command line. If the object is selected using the pick box, AutoCAD assumes the selected point is also the first break point. On the other hand, if you select the object with a selection window by typing W and Enter at the Select object prompt, AutoCAD then prompts you to define the first break point.

→ In addition to Window, you'll find all of the Selection set filters discussed fully in Chapter 10, "Selecting Objects," by referring to "Selection Set Filters," p. 196.

Tip 77 from *Ron House*	If the second break point is picked beyond the object to be broken, AutoCAD selects the nearest point on that object and uses this as the second break point. This is more efficient when you want to remove one end of an object, and it is quicker to pick a point beyond the object than to specify a specific point.

Tip 78 from *Ron House*	To break an object without erasing a portion of the object, use the same point for the first and second points. This is done using an at symbol (@) at the prompt for the second break point.

BREAKING A PORTION OF A CIRCLE OR AN ARC

When removing a section of a circle or an arc, how the points are selected determines which part of the object is removed. The key rule to remember is to pick the second break point in a counterclockwise direction from the first. A good rule of thumb to follow is counterclockwise to remove, clockwise to keep. To elaborate on this, the portion of the circle or arc between the points you choose in a counterclockwise direction will be removed. That portion between the points selected in a clockwise direction will remain. Use this rule of thumb to quickly determine the order in which you should pick break points when breaking a circle or arc.

To illustrate this, Figure 9.15 shows two ellipses, both the same size and shape. The portion that is removed is represented by the dashed lines. If you wish to break the first ellipse so that the top part of the ellipse remains, you must first select the break point at point A and then at point B. If this order is reversed, the bottom portion of the ellipse remains and the top part is removed, as illustrated in the second ellipse.

The next example walks you through an exercise dealing with the Break command.

PART
III
CH
9

Figure 9.15
Reversing the order of break points changes what section of the arc is removed.

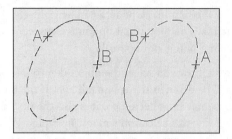

EXAMPLE: REMOVING A SECTION OF A LINE WITH THE BREAK COMMAND

1. Open drawing ch09_06.dwg that you copied from the companion CD. In this example, the ductwork passes over the light fixture in the ceiling plenum. You will need to indicate this on the drawing by applying a hidden linetype to some of the lines. The lines of the light fixture will need to be broken, so the linetype can be applied to only that part of the fixture that is covered by the HVAC duct. These break points are indicated by points A, B, C, and D, shown in Figure 9.16.

Figure 9.16
Use the Break command to break the lines of the light fixture shown under the ductwork.

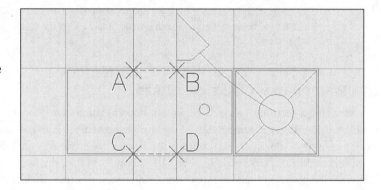

2. Start the Break command and select a point between the letters A and B on the light fixture.

3. Right-click and select First point from the shortcut menu. Use the node object snap to snap to the node at point A by pressing the Shift key while right-clicking. Choose Node from the object snap menu, then pick the node.

4. At the Specify second break point prompt, type an at symbol (@) and press Enter. This instructs AutoCAD to use the previous point selected as the second break point. Using this process, you can separate this portion of the line so its linetype can be changed to hidden.

5. Repeat steps 3 and 4 for the remaining three break points, B, C, and D, activating the Break command each time and selecting the line the point lies on.

6. After these line segments have been broken out, select both of the lines and use the Linetype drop down list to change their linetype property to Hidden. This time, select point B and then point A using your intersection object snap to remove the right portion of the circle. Your part should look similar to the bottom figure in Figure 9.17.

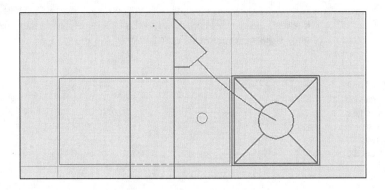

Figure 9.17
This detail is now complete after the lines have been broken and the correct linetype is applied.

Continuing with the editing commands, the Fillet command, which enables you to round the edges of objects, is covered in the next section.

SMOOTHING AND ROUNDING CORNERS

The Fillet command places an arc of a user-specified radius at the intersection of two selected objects, with the option of trimming those objects to the fillet endpoints. You can also use the Fillet command to quickly generate a slot from two parallel lines, which you will do later in one of the examples in this chapter.

The command can be activated by selecting the Fillet button from the Modify toolbar (see Figure 9.18) or by choosing the Fillet command from the Modify pull-down menu.

Figure 9.18
Access the Fillet command from the toolbar.

The following is a list of objects that can be filleted:

- Arcs
- Circles
- Elliptical arcs
- Lines
- Polylines

- Rays
- Splines
- Xlines

Tip 79 from
Ron House

When specifically working with polylines, you cannot fillet two separate polylines together. However, you can fillet polyline segments of the same polyline if they are separated by a single segment, as shown in Figure 9.19.

Figure 9.19
The Fillet command can be used to fillet two polyline segments separated by one segment of the same polyline.

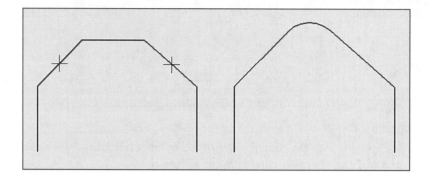

Four main options are available with the Fillet command:

- Select first object—This prompt enables you to pick the first of two objects needed to create a 2D fillet or a 3D edge to fillet. After selecting the first object, AutoCAD then prompts you for the second object when working with a two-dimensional object. In dealing with a three-dimensional solid, multiple edges can be selected individually after entering the desired fillet radius. This provides you with three options:
  - Select an edge—This option enables you to select individual edges of the 3D object until you press Enter.
  - Chain—This option, available only when a solid model is selected, lets you select tangential edges related to the initial selected edge, allowing you to define the path of the fillet along multiple edges. This assists AutoCAD in determining how the fillet will interact with chained fillets.
  - Radius—This option defines the radius of the fillet.
- Polyline—This option tells AutoCAD it is working with a polyline and that the fillet radius should be applied to all polyline vertices.
- Radius—This sets the value of the fillet radius for all fillets created afterward.
- Trim—The value of this setting determines whether the selected objects will be trimmed to the fillet endpoints.
  - Trim—This trims the selected objects to match the endpoints of the fillet.

- No Trim—No trimming occurs, and the selected objects are left as is. Selected lines are also not modified to match the fillet endpoints.

Figure 9.20 illustrates the differences in setting the trim values.

Figure 9.20
The result of using the Trim/No Trim options (respectively) of the Fillet command on two intersecting lines.

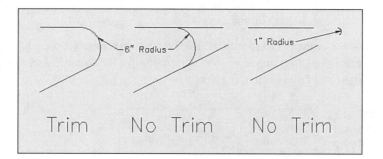

Note

The properties of a newly created fillet—such as layer, linetype, color, and lineweight—depend on the properties of the lines selected to create the fillet. For example, when a fillet is generated, that fillet is placed on the same layer as the selected lines if they exist on the same layer. If they do not, the fillet is placed on the current layer.

FILLETING TWO PARALLEL LINES TO CREATE A SLOT

When you apply the Fillet command to two parallel lines, AutoCAD determines the radius of an arc and places the arc to match the nearest endpoints of the two lines to make a slot. Rounded edges for two parallel lines and slots can be quickly and easily created this way, such as a pad on a casting with a milled slot (see Figure 9.21).

Figure 9.21
The Fillet command can be used to quickly create a slot from two parallel lines.

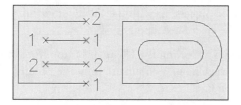

Tip 80 from
Ron House

It is important to make certain that the lines you select to create the slot are parallel. If the lines are almost parallel, AutoCAD will place the fillet at the point where the two lines intersect, which typically is not going to be within your drawing limits.

USING THE FILLET COMMAND TO ROUND 3D EDGES

You can also apply fillets to mechanical and architectural solid models to round corners or edges. When the edge of a solid model is selected, the following prompts are displayed:

```
Enter fillet radius <0.2500>:

Select an edge or [Chain/Radius]:
```

You first are prompted to specify the fillet radius, then to select the edges to fillet. Remember, the Chain option enables you to group a number of edges to be filleted at one time. Figure 9.22 shows an example of this.

Figure 9.22
The Chain option was used to round the top edge of this drill base with the Fillet command.

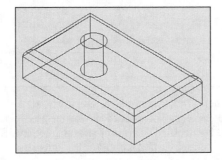

Similar to the Fillet command is the Chamfer command. You will find the options pretty much the same, yet the result is a beveled edge rather than a rounded one. The next section discusses the options for the Chamfer command in detail.

CHAMFERING EDGES

As mentioned earlier, the Chamfer command places a beveled edge at the intersection, implied or actual, of two selected objects. As with the Fillet command, you have the option of trimming those objects to the chamfer endpoints.

The command can be activated by selecting the Chamfer button from the Modify toolbar (see Figure 9.23), by choosing the Chamfer command from the Modify pull-down menu, or by typing **CHA** at the command line.

Figure 9.23
Access the Chamfer command from the toolbar.

The following is a list of objects that can be chamfered:

- Lines
- Polylines

- Rays
- Xlines

> **Tip 81 from**
> *Ron House*
>
> Similar to the Fillet command, you cannot chamfer two separate polylines together since they are separate objects with different properties, although you can chamfer polyline segments of the same polyline if they are separated by a single segment.

When you start the Chamfer command, these options are displayed at the command line:

```
Select first line or [Polyline/Distance/Angle/Trim/Method]:
```

- Select first line—Click the first of two lines, either 2D or 3D, to make the chamfer. After you select the first line, AutoCAD prompts you for the second line.
- Polyline—This option applies the chamfer to all polyline vertices. See the example on chamfering polylines later in this chapter.

> **Note**
>
> When you chamfer lines that make up a hatch boundary, the hatch association is lost. This is not true if a polyline is used for the hatch boundary because it can be chamfered and will cause the associated hatch to update.

- Distance—This option prompts you to set the value of the chamfer distances. The default values are set for a chamfered angle of 45°, as shown in the following prompts:
```
Specify first chamfer distance <0.5000>:
Specify second chamfer distance <0.5000>:
```

- Angle—With this option, you can specify the chamfer by a chamfer length and angle rather than two chamfer distances. These prompts are displayed when this option is chosen:
```
Specify chamfer length on the first line <1.0000>:
Specify chamfer angle from the first line <0>:
```

- Trim—The value of this setting determines whether the selected objects will be trimmed to the chamfer endpoints. Figure 9.24 shows an example of both.
  - Trim—The selected objects are trimmed to match the endpoints of the chamfer.
  - No Trim—The selected lines are not modified to match the chamfer endpoints.

Figure 9.24
This figure displays the result of using the Trim/No Trim options (respectively) of the Chamfer command on two intersecting lines.

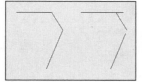

■ Method—This defines the trim method for the chamfer, which determines whether distances or an angle will be used to create the chamfer. This prompt sets the desired option:

```
Enter trim method [Distance/Angle] <Angle>:
```

Note

A chamfer is placed on the same layer as the lines selected to create the chamfer, if they exist on the same layer. If they do not, the chamfer is placed on the current layer. This also applies to other properties, such as linetype, color, and lineweight.

APPLYING A CHAMFER TO ALL VERTICES OF A POLYLINE

When you apply the Chamfer command to a polyline using the Polyline option, AutoCAD creates a chamfer at all the vertices of the polyline, if possible (see Figure 9.25). AutoCAD then displays the total number of vertices that were chamfered and those that were not.

Figure 9.25
You can chamfer all the vertices of a polyline at once with the Chamfer command's Polyline option.

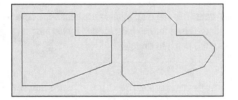

Similar to the Fillet command, you can also chamfer three-dimensional solid objects or parts. The next section describes how.

CHAMFERING SOLID MODELS

The Chamfer command can also be used to bevel edges of three-dimensional solid models, like a 3D retaining wall or a mechanical part. These are the prompts you will see when a solid model is selected during the Select First Line prompt:

```
Base surface selection...
Enter surface selection option [Next/OK (current)] <OK>:
```

AutoCAD highlights a surface adjacent to the edge you selected. Accept this surface as the one you wish to chamfer, or right-click and select Next from the shortcut menu to highlight the next face. Repeat this until the desired surface is highlighted, and then press Enter to accept. Then you will need to set the chamfer distances:

```
Specify base surface chamfer distance <1.0000>:
```

```
Specify other surface chamfer distance <1.0000>:
```

After the distances have been set, select the edges to be chamfered. The Loop option automatically finds all edges associated with the selected surface, making it easy to chamfer an entire face.

```
Select an edge or [Loop]: l

Select an edge loop or [Edge]:
```

Selecting an edge highlights the entire surface associated with it. Press Enter to accept, and the edges will be chamfered, similar to the model shown in Figure 9.26.

Figure 9.26
This figure illustrates the use of the Loop option with the Chamfer command to chamfer the top edge of the part.

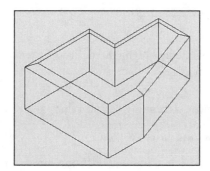

EXAMPLE: APPLYING A CHAMFER TO AN EDGE LOOP

1. Open the drawing ch09_07.dwg located in the directory where you copied the drawing files from the companion CD.

2. You will chamfer some of the edges on the solid model of this guide, with the end result being a better defined model. Start the Chamfer command and select the top edge indicated at point A.

3. You will see the following prompt displayed:

```
(TRIM mode) Current chamfer Dist1 = 0.5000, Dist2 = 0.5000
Select first line or [Polyline/Distance/Angle/Trim/Method]:
```

4. AutoCAD highlights the edges it believes you want chamfered. Right-click and select Next to toggle to the next set of surface edges until the desired surface is highlighted, shown in Figure 9.27, as the prompt indicates:

```
Base surface selection...
Enter surface selection option [Next/OK (current)] <OK>: N
```

Figure 9.27
The Chamfer command allows you to toggle to the face you want to chamfer on three-dimensional objects.

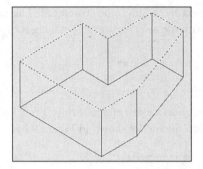

5. You should now see the top surface edges highlighted. Press Enter or right-click and select Enter to accept the current edges.

   ```
   Enter surface selection option [Next/OK (current)] <OK>:
   ```

6. Next, define the chamfer distances. Accept the default values:

   ```
   Specify base surface chamfer distance <0.5000>:
   Specify other surface chamfer distance <0.5000>:
   ```

7. Right-click and select Loop at the Select an Edge or [Loop] prompt to indicate that you want to create a chamfered edge loop:

   ```
   Select an edge or [Loop]: L
   ```

8. Click again a point located at point A. The top surface edge is highlighted again. Press Enter to accept, and the chamfer is applied to the edge.

9. Repeat the same set of steps to place a chamfer at the base of the cylinder. When finished, your part should look like Figure 9.28.

Figure 9.28
The finished guide after chamfering the top and bottom edges using the Loop option of the Chamfer command.

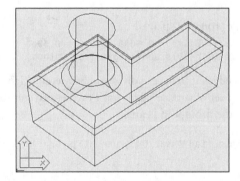

As you can see with the last example, the Chamfer command can quickly apply a beveled edge to transition from one three-dimensional face to another, enabling you to create complex solid models in addition to chamfering between two-dimensional linear objects.

SUMMARY

The commands in this chapter are unique in that they only work with specific objects, yet they enable you to further define how these objects can be applied in your drawings, such as with the Chamfer and Fillet commands. The next chapter, "Selecting Objects," discusses how to filter the drawing based on individual object types or properties to create distinct selection sets for editing.

CHAPTER 10

SELECTING OBJECTS

In this chapter

SELECTION SET FILTERS

Selection sets, which are defined as drawing objects chosen to be edited, can be created by clicking a single object or a group of objects. Likewise, selection sets can also be created by filtering the drawing based on a particular object property, such as its color or linetype. This chapter discusses in detail the different ways to create selection sets and how to save them so they can be applied to multiple drawings. Let's start with looking at the different types of selection filters.

Two of the filters listed here, Window and Crossing, are essentially the default filters—both are automatically available at any Select objects prompt. To create a selection set using either of these filters, first pick a starting corner for the selection window; then you can easily decide which filter you want, depending on which way you drag the cursor. If you drag the cursor to the right, the Window selection set filter is activated. When the cursor is dragged to the left, the Crossing filter can be used to select objects. If you want to use a more specific type of filter, access the remaining filters by typing question mark (**?**) at a Select objects prompt.

```
Window/Last/Crossing/BOX/ALL/Fence/WPolygon/
CPolygon/Group/Add/Remove/Multiple/
Previous/Undo/AUto/Single
```

The following are detailed descriptions of the filters available from the command line:

- Window—Creates a selection window that selects everything completely encompassed inside the window.
- Last—Selects the last object created. This provides a quick way of selecting and editing the last object placed into the drawing.
- Crossing—Similar to the Window option, except this selection window selects every object it crosses over, in addition to everything inside the window. This is a quick way to select a group of objects located in the same area.
- Box—Combines the Window and Crossing filters, depending on which direction the box corner points are defined. Specifying the corner points from left to right creates a Window selection box, and from right to left defines a Crossing box.
- All—Selects all objects within the current drawing, including those on layers that have been turned off. Use this option to quickly select all drawing objects to edit.
- Fence—Selects all objects the Fence line crosses. This option is typically used to select those objects you cannot select with the Window and Crossing filters.

The next two options are great for selecting objects randomly spaced throughout the drawing with a polygon of any shape:

- WPolygon—Selects all objects completely within the polygon.
- CPolygon—Selects all objects within and crossing the polygon.
- Group—Specifies a specific group created with the Group command.

Note

All of the filters discussed here, except Group, create temporary selection sets. This means that once a new selection set has been created, it overwrites the last selection set. Groups are essentially permanent selection sets that can be recalled and used when needed. These are covered in "Creating Groups" later in this chapter.

- Add—Enables you to add objects to the current selection set. If you are in the Remove selection mode, selecting this filter toggles you back to this default mode. This selection set filter, combined with the Remove option discussed next, enables you to toggle between adding and removing objects from the set until finished.

- Remove—Toggles the selection mode to remove selected objects. After selecting this filter, you can use any of the other selection set filters to select the objects you wish to remove. While in the Remove mode, any filter chosen will remove objects until the mode is toggled back to Add.

- Multiple—Selects objects without the initial highlight, speeding up the process of selecting objects. When you're finished selecting the desired objects and you press Enter, the objects are highlighted. Use this filter when adding or removing large numbers of objects to or from the selection set.

- Previous—Re-selects the previous selection set created. This option is convenient when you need to apply another command to the previous objects selected in the drawing.

- Undo—Undoes the last selected objects in order until there are no more objects in the selection set—good for backing up through the selection and removing an unintended object.

- Auto—Is the default mode. If a point is selected with either the Selection tool or the Select Objects pickbox, the small box that appears when selecting objects, and nothing is found at that point, the Box selection filter is activated.

- Single—Selects a single object rather than prompting for multiple objects.

These filters give you great flexibility in selecting specifically what you want to select. Creating a selection set using the Multiple selection set filter, which provides a quick way to select objects from a large, complex drawing, is examined in the next example.

PART
III

CH
10

EXAMPLE: SELECTING OBJECTS WITH THE MULTIPLE SELECTION SET FILTER

1. Open the 1st floor.dwg file in the ACAD2000 Sample directory.

2. Start the Move command. At the Select objects prompt, type **M** (the shortcut key for Multiple) and press Enter.

3. Start picking objects from the drawing, selecting at least three objects. Note that as you select the objects, they are not highlighted after they are selected.

4. Press Enter. You'll notice the selected objects are now highlighted.

Note

Prior to ACAD2000, there was no selection set filter similar to Multiple. This could cause a delay when you selected a large number of objects, forcing you to wait until every object was highlighted. A solution to this problem was to turn off the highlighting by setting the value for the Highlight variable to 0 and then creating your selection set, remembering to toggle the highlight mode back to on when you were done. The Multiple command is a welcome feature in AutoCAD because it saves a number of steps and a lot of time when creating large selection sets.

5. Press Esc to cancel the Move command.

Make the Multiple option your primary selection set filter when selecting large groups of objects. This will save you a considerable amount of time, making you more productive when editing huge selection sets.

On the opposite side of the spectrum, let's examine how to select a specific object when it is overlapped by another by using object cycling.

OBJECT CYCLING

Another feature that is invaluable when you are trying to select an object from a group of overlapping objects is called object cycling. Using the Object Cycle feature can assist you in selecting exactly what you want when the desired object is obstructed by another object. Clicking two or more overlying objects while pressing the Ctrl key highlights the first object. Picking another point anywhere on the screen highlights the next object found at that selection point. This process continues until you press the Enter key, which selects the highlighted object.

This feature is great when selecting one object at a time, yet searching the entire drawing, you can use the Quick Select command to find specifically what you're looking for. This enables you to filter the drawing and select a particular object type, based on a property or feature like color or linetype. The next section discusses the Quick Select command in detail.

CREATING QUICK SELECTION SETS

A quick way to create a selection set is to use the Quick Select, or Qselect command. With this command, you can set criteria drawing objects must meet to be added to the selection set. Right-click in the drawing editor to access the Qselect command from the shortcut menu, shown in Figure 10.1.

Figure 10.2 shows the Quick Select dialog box, in which there are five sets of filtering criteria that determine what you want to select.

Figure 10.1
Right-click in the drawing editor to access the Quick Select command from the menu.

Figure 10.2
The Quick Select filter criteria in the Quick Select dialog box enables you to define exactly what you are looking for in the drawing.

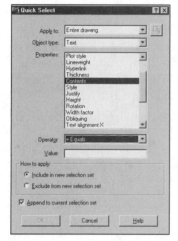

These criteria are described in detail here:

- Apply to—Select what you want to apply the filter to. You can apply the filter to the entire drawing or to the current selection. The default option is Current selection, unless this does not exist, in which case the Entire drawing option is the default. You can create a current selection by selecting the Select Objects button, which clears the Quick Select dialog box and enables you to select objects from the drawing.

- Object type—Lists the available object types that have been selected. If no objects are selected, all object types in the current drawing are listed. If there is a current selection, only the objects in the selection are listed. The Multiple option defines that the filter be applied across multiple object types. This is also the default option.

- Properties—Determines the object property for the selected object(s) available for filtering. The property selected sets the values available for the next two options: Operator and Value.

- Operator—Enables you to set a range for the filter. Depending on the selected object property, these options are possible:
  - Equals—When this object property option is set, the chosen property must equal the value for any objects to be added to the selection set.
  - Not equal to—Selects everything except the objects whose property type matches the Value.
  - Greater than—Selects those objects whose property is greater than the selected value, such as an object's lineweight greater than 0.125.
  - Less than—Selects objects where the property is less than the chosen value. For example, you might set the Less Than operator to select all arcs in a drawing whose radius is less than .25 units.
  - Wildcard match—Available only if text is set for the object type and if Contents is set for the property. Searches the drawing and selects text objects that match the wildcard criteria. (See " Using Wildcard Characters to Search Specific Text Strings in a Drawing" later in this chapter.)
- Value—Sets the value for the filter. You can select from a list of values if you know the values for the selected property.

Other options define how the filter will be applied to the drawing only if you are creating a new selection set:

- Include in new selection set—Those objects that match the filter criteria will be added to the new selection set.
- Exclude from new selection set—The new selection set includes every object that does not match the filter criteria.

The last option available on this dialog box, Append to current selection set, defines whether the filtered objects replace the current selection set or are appended to it. If the option is selected, the only Apply to option is Entire drawing.

The following example helps illustrate the use of the Quick Select command.

EXAMPLE: SELECTING FILTERED OBJECTS FROM A DRAWING

1. Open the City base map drawing from the Sample subdirectory from the ACAD2000 directory. You will use the Qselect command to create a selection set of all the polylines in the drawing on the Freeways layer.
2. Right-click and select the Quick Select option from the menu.
3. From the Quick Select dialog box, set the Apply to option to Entire drawing.
4. Select Polyline from the Object type list.
5. Choose Layer from the Properties list.
6. Set the Operator to =Equals.
7. Pick Freeways from the Value list.

8. In the How to apply section of the Quick Select dialog box, click the Include in new selection set radio button (see Figure 10.3).

Figure 10.3
You can determine whether the selected objects will be appended to or made into a new selection set.

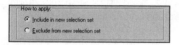

9. Press the OK button to start the filtering process. The command line should display this:

   `367 item(s) selected.`

10. At the completion of this command, grips are applied to the filtered objects ready to be edited.

Note
When changing the properties of multiple objects, reference "Modifying Object Properties" discussed later in this chapter to modify the group as a whole.

Follow through the next example to learn how to filter from a selected set of objects.

EXAMPLE: CREATING A NEW SELECTION SET BY FILTERING THE CURRENT SELECTION

1. Now, open the ch10_01.dwg that you copied from the companion CD. In this example, you'll use the Quick Select command to select all polylines that have an area of greater than 10,000 square inches, and then hatch the selection set. A group of cubicles have polylines encompassing their perimeter, defining the rentable space on this floor.

2. Right-click in the drawing editor and select Quick Select from the shortcut menu.

3. In this example, you define a current selection rather than filter the entire drawing as in the last example. Make certain the Append to current selection set check box is not selected, and then click the Select objects button.

4. Approximately define an area starting in the upper-left corner of the office space to the center of the building, and then press Enter.

5. The Apply to option should be set to Current selection. If not, select that option from the list.

6. Select Polyline from the Object type selection list.

7. From the Properties list, select Area.

8. Set the Operator to > Greater than.

9. You will want to locate those polylines areas that are greater than 10,000 square inches. Supply the number of square inches a cubicle occupies by entering **10,000**.

Note

Although this example can be modified for a number of different uses to indicate total area spaces or parts, when working with architectural drawings you must convert the standard area reference of square feet into square inches. Mechanical drawings are already set up to use decimal units, so no conversion is needed.

10. Click the Include in new selection set check box, and then click the OK button.

11. After AutoCAD has selected those polylines with an area greater than 10,000 square inches, start the Bhatch command by choosing Hatch from the Draw pull-down menu.

12. Click the Select objects button, and then type **P** for Previous at the Select objects prompt. Press Enter.

13. After defining your desired hatch properties, such as Pattern, Angle, and Scale, click the OK button to see the hatch applied to the selected polylines.

→ See "Defining the Hatch Pattern Style," p. 277 in Chapter 13, "Hatching."

Note

Because of the scale of this drawing, you'll want to use a hatch scale of 120 or greater so the hatch will be the correct size. A value of 120 is correct for the hatch pattern scale factor shown in Figure 10.4.

The polylines boundaries hatched should be similar to Figure 10.4.

Figure 10.4
The Quick Select feature was used to select and hatch cubicles whose areas exceeded a specific size.

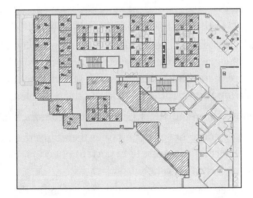

USING WILDCARD CHARACTERS TO SEARCH SPECIFIC TEXT STRINGS IN A DRAWING

In this next example, you'll really put the Quick Select command to work. Say that for a presentation you want to change the color of all text that matches the wildcard criteria "*AV" to a different color to indicate the avenues shown on the City base map drawing. Refer to Table 10.1 when using wildcard characters to search for specific character matches in text:

TABLE 10.1   WILDCARD CHARACTERS

Character	Definition
*	Finds any character string
?	Finds a specific single character or replaces a character in the string
#	Finds a numeric digit
@	Finds an alphabetic character
.	Finds any nonalphanumeric character
~	Finds anything except the pattern following the tilde
[ ]	Finds anything found within brackets
[-]	Finds a range of characters separated by the hyphen within brackets
[~]	Finds anything except the pattern following the tilde within brackets
'	Finds exactly what is shown after the quote

EXAMPLE: USING THE *WILDCARD MATCH FILTER CRITERIA TO SELECT TEXT

1. Open the City base map sample drawing again, or switch to it using the Windows pull-down menu and select it from the list of opened drawings.

2. Right-click in the drawing and choose Quick Select from the menu.

3. Set the Apply to filter criteria to Entire drawing.

4. Select Text from the Object type list.

5. From the Properties list, click Contents.

6. Set the Operator filter to *Wildcard match.

7. Enter the wildcard criteria *AV*.

   The second asterisk is needed to select the text after the letters AV for those North and South avenues that have a direction indicator, such as N for north, appended to the end of their name. If this were left off, AutoCAD would select only the East-West avenues.

8. Click Include in new selection set button.

9. Click the OK button. Text objects with AV in their name are selected.

10. Right-click in the drawing and select Properties from the shortcut menu.

11. The Object drop-down list should read Text(25), indicating that 25 text objects have been selected. Click in the box to the right of the Color box and select Blue from the Color drop-down menu (see Figure 10.5).

12. The text objects with AV in their name should turn blue. Close the Properties window.

Figure 10.5
The Properties command can be used to easily modify the properties of objects selected with the Qselect.

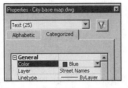

You can now see how powerful the Quick Select command can be, enabling you to quickly search through entire drawings and select specific objects based on unique property values.

For more advanced filter criteria options, or for combining multiple filter criteria, check out the Object Selection Filter command in the next section.

OBJECT SELECTION FILTER

The Object Selection Filter (or Filter command, as it is referred to), enables you to filter for specific object types by combining multiple filter criteria sets. For example, you can use the Filter command to select all the lines in a drawing that are dashed and all the circles of a certain radius and of a specific color. Whereas the Qselect command could select one type of object based on its properties, the Filter command uses Boolean operators such as *And*, *Or*, and *Not* to chain together different property criteria, going beyond the basic functionality of the Quick Select command.

This command can be run either independently from the command line or transparently while using the Erase command. To activate the filter transparently at the Select objects prompt, type **'Filter**. The single quote is required to activate the command transparently. This opens the Object Selection Filters dialog box, shown in Figure 10.6.

Figure 10.6
The Object Selection Filters dialog box assists in the selection of specific drawing objects based on element properties.

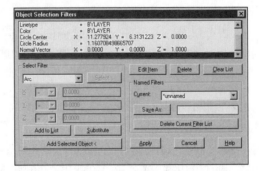

This dialog box enables you to define a filter that will create a selection set of those objects matching the filter criteria. The Select Filter pull-down list contains every object type that is possible within an AutoCAD drawing. As the object type is selected from the list, you will then need to click the Add to List button to start the filter definition list. Next, you will choose attributes or parameters of the object selected to further define what you want to find.

When the filter is complete, click the Apply button to select all or a portion of the drawing to apply the filter to. The next example illustrates the use of this command.

EXAMPLE: CREATING A SIMPLE FILTER QUERY

1. Open drawing ch10_2.dwg that was copied from the accompanying CD. Say for example you have a drawing that includes circles with a radius greater than 20 inches that exist on a layer called Preliminary. These circles were used for some preliminary design work and now need to be erased from the drawing. Unfortunately, other preliminary linework overlaps these circles, making them harder to erase from the drawing. You'll need to create and apply a filter to select these circles so they can be easily erased from the drawing.

2. Type **Filter** at the command line. From the Select Filter pull-down list, choose the Circle object type, and then click the Add to List button. You will see the filter criteria Object = Circle added to the filter list.

3. Next, select the Layer object type from the pull-down list. You need to be able to define which layer you want to search—in this example, it is the Preliminary layer. Click the Select button to the right of the pull-down list. A dialog box appears that contains all the layers that exist in the drawing. Select Preliminary from the list and click the OK button. This lists the layer name as the x coordinate value to define that this is the layer you want to search for the circles. Then, click the Add to List button.

4. Now, define the circle radius. Select Circle Radius from the Select Filter pull-down menu and type in the value of **20** in the x coordinate edit box. Make certain the x relationship indicator reads greater-than or equal-to (>=), and click the Add to List button. Your Filter dialog box should look similar to the one in Figure 10.7.

Part

III

Ch

10

Figure 10.7
The Object Selection Filters dialog box shows the filter query to select all circles with a radius of 20 inches or greater on the layer Preliminary.

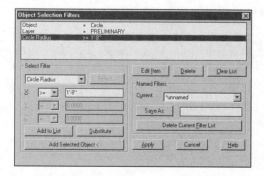

5. Before you apply this filter query to the drawing, save the query so you can apply this to multiple drawings. Type **Overlapping Circles** in the Save As edit box. You are

allowed a total of 18 characters to name your filter. Then click the Save As button, which adds your filter query to the list of available named filters in the default file filter.nfl. Using this external file, you can transfer filter queries between drawings.

6. Click the Apply button to apply the filter to your drawing. You can use any of the selection set filters to define what part of the drawing you want to apply the filter to. In this example, you use the All selection set filter to search the entire drawing for these overlapping circles. Type **All** at the Select objects prompt and press Enter. AutoCAD responds by prompting the total number of objects that were selected and the number of objects that matched your filter criteria. Press Enter again to exit the filtered selection.

7. At this point, you have selected the objects with grips that can now be edited with any editing command. Right-click and choose Erase from the shortcut menu to erase the selected circles.

8. Use the Undo command to restore the drawing back to its original state for the next example.

Note

See "Undoing What Was Done" in Chapter 7, "Editing Commands," for more information on the use of the Undo command.

Now, let's take this process one step farther by making the selection query more complex.

MORE ADVANCED FILTER QUERIES

You can expand the filter queries you apply to the drawing by utilizing the grouping operators AND, OR, XOR, and NOT in your filter. This enables you to combine multiple filters and expand the capability of the filter. Continuing with the previous example, let's take a look at what would happen if you wanted to select all the circles on the Preliminary layer except those that have a radius of 20.

Tip 82 from
Ron House

Use the Substitute button to modify the filter list by replacing an existing filter criteria with new criteria you want to add to the list.

You would need to apply the NOT grouping operator to create this selection set. You would start by applying the **BEGIN NOT grouping operator to the list, then add the filter properties you want to apply, and then end the list with the **END NOT operator. This will select all circles except those that have a radius of 20 inches.

Tip 83 from
Ron House

You can nest the AND and OR grouping operators within each other to further narrow your filter criteria.

EXAMPLE: CREATING AN ADVANCED FILTER

1. In this example, you select all the circles on the Preliminary layer except those that have a radius of 20. Run the command transparently inside the Erase command by starting the Erase command: Type **E** at the command line and press Enter.

2. Next, type **'Filter** at the Select objects prompt. (Remember that to run the command transparently, you will need to type the single quote before the command.)

3. To create your filter, select the Circle object type from the Select Filter object type list. Object = Circle is added to your list. You want to tell the filter to not select those circles with a radius of 6.75, so enclose this inside a set of NOT grouping operators. Create the following filter list:

```
Object = Circle
**BEGIN NOT
Circle Radius = 20
**END NOT
**BEGIN AND
Layer = Preliminary
**END AND
```

4. The filter you have created will select all circles on the Preliminary layer except those that have a radius of 20. Apply this to the drawing by selecting the Apply button and then typing **All** at the Select objects prompt; then press Enter. AutoCAD responds by telling you how many objects where selected and how many were filtered out.

5. To erase those objects selected, press Enter twice to erase the circles and to end the command.

Using the Filter command, either transparently or individually, is a quick way for you to filter through entire drawings for a specific object or group of objects to modify. When you master creating filter lists, you may find it hard to do without this command when editing large and complex drawing files.

APPLYING MULTIPLE EDITS TO OBJECTS WITH GRIPS

One extremely quick way to apply multiple edits to objects in a drawing is to use grips. First, place grips on the objects you want to edit, and then right-click. Then select the editing command you want from the list. You can use the Filter command to first select the objects and then right-click to access the shortcut menu and edit the objects. To edit the same group of objects, use the Previous selection set filter to reselect the objects.

Note

Prior to the Filter and Quick Select commands, the Select command allowed you to create a selection set outside the editing commands. You can still type **Select** at the command line and select the objects you want in the selection set. When you press Enter, the objects are saved into a selection set that can be accessed using the Previous selection filter. You'll find that the Filter and Quick Select commands give you increased functionality and greater flexibility selecting specific objects than the standard selection set filters using the Select command.

PART

III

CH

10

Although the Filter and Quick Select commands enable you to create a temporary selection set, at times you will need to create a more permanent type of selection set that you can access more than once. The Group command enables you to save selection sets and use them when needed.

CREATING GROUPS

Grouping several objects within AutoCAD can be done on a temporary basis using the Group command. This command enables you to select any AutoCAD object and group it with one or more objects. Any object of a group can be part of multiple groups. For example, suppose you are trying to determine the location of a series of light fixtures within a room. By grouping the fixtures together, you can easily move them as a whole to decide where they will be located.

Typing **Group** at the command line launches the command and brings up the Object Grouping dialog box, shown in Figure 10.8.

Figure 10.8
The Object Grouping dialog box creates groups of multiple objects within a drawing.

The options available through the Object Grouping dialog box are described in detail here:

- Group Identification—All groups can be denoted by a name and a description. When you enter this information, the group is created after you select the New button. You then can query an object to determine what group it belongs to by using the Find Name< button. Also, you can highlight the entire group the object belongs to by using the Highlight< button.

- Create Group—Groups can be created in two different ways: named or unnamed, and selectable or unselectable.

- Unnamed groups are designated *anonymous*, or *An*, where n indicates the number of groups currently defined. This number increases with each new group. Clicking the Include Unnamed check box adds the unnamed groups to the list of available groups.

- Selectable groups are those in which, if one item of the group is selected, the entire group is also selected if they are not on a locked layer.

→ See "Layer Display Properties" in Chapter 3, "Working with Layers and Linetypes," to find out more information about editing objects on locked layers.

- Unselectable groups—Unselectable groups are groups in which, if one item of the group is selected, just that item is selected and the other members of the group are unaffected.

- Change Group—After a group has been created, it can be modified using the options in the Change Group box.

- Remove—This removes an object or objects from the already defined group.

- Add—This adds an object or objects from the already defined group.

  - Rename—This enables you to rename the selected group from the list.

  - Re-Order—This reorders the number assigned to the objects in a group. This number is assigned when the objects are selected and added to the group.

  - Description—This enables you to modify the description for the selected group.

  - Explode—This deletes the group from the list of available groups in the current drawing. This just deletes the group definition; it does not delete the objects in that group.

  - Selectable—This changes the selectability of the selected group.

PART

III

CH

10

EXAMPLE: CREATING A SELECTABLE GROUP

1. Open a drawing with a number of objects. Once open, type **Group** at the command line.

2. The Object Grouping dialog box appears. Type the name **GROUP1** and add an optional description for the new group you will create. You cannot duplicate a group name listed in the Group Name list box.

3. Make certain the Selectable button is checked, and click the New button. Select objects A, B, and C, and press Enter. These items have now become part of group GROUP1, and the Object Group dialog box reappears.

4. Name the next group **GROUP2**. Note that if you select the Unnamed check box, you cannot edit the Group Name box because AutoCAD will assign a name for the group. For this example, you want your groups to be named. Therefore, unclick the Unnamed check box.

5. Click the New button and select objects A, D, and E.

6. Both groups should be listed in the list of group names, and both should have YES in the Selectable column.

7. You can click the Find Name< button and select an object to determine which group or groups it is part of (see Figure 10.9).

8. Selecting the Highlight< button enables you to select a group from a list and highlight every object in that group. A group must first be selected in order to make the Highlight< button active.

Figure 10.9
The Group Member List dialog box displays the group or groups an object is a member of.

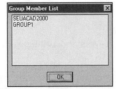

To select a group at the Select objects prompt for the editing commands, type **G** at the command line and press Enter. This gives the following prompt:

`Enter group name:`

You can enter a specific group name or an asterisk (*) if all groups are to be selected. If an individual object from a group is to be selected without selecting the entire group, you can toggle off Groups by entering Ctrl+A. After the object has been selected, you can use Ctrl+A again to turn Groups back on. This turns off only the grouping feature and does not affect the groups themselves. This is a dynamic toggle and can be used while in any command to control the selection of objects within groups.

Note

Use extreme care when editing a drawing with groups. Selecting one item in the group selects the other members of the group. You may find it wise to toggle Groups off using Ctrl+A to avoid selecting any objects that are part of a group if you are not familiar with the groups in a drawing.

The last section examines how to modify the properties of a single object or multiple objects using the Properties command.

MODIFYING OBJECT PROPERTIES

When you need to quickly modify the properties of an object, use this new AutoCAD Properties feature. In previous releases of AutoCAD, you either were limited or had to use multiple commands to change specific object properties. In AutoCAD 2000, you can select a single object and modify all the properties of that object, or you can select multiple objects to modify the common properties of those objects.

The fastest way to access the properties of an object or objects is to use the Properties command in conjunction with grips. Place a grip on a single object, right-click, and select Properties from the menu (see Figure 10.10).

The Properties window appears, listing all the properties of the an object you select (see Figure 10.11).

If multiple objects are selected, use the Object selection list at the top of the Window to choose the object properties you want to modify. The Quick Select button also enables you to define the selection set of objects you want to change. Two tabs, Alphabetic and Categorized, alter the display of the property types within the window, depending on your preference.

Figure 10.10
Access the properties of an object by using the shortcut menu after selecting an object with grips.

Figure 10.11
The Properties window gives you quick access to an object's properties.

Use this feature to quickly modify the properties of objects within the drawing. When combined with the Quick Select command, this enables you to easily edit anything placed in a drawing.

SUMMARY

Use the selection set filters to temporarily select objects to edit. Bind objects together using the Group command, giving you the power of complex grouping but the flexibility of still being able to select individual objects from the group. Now that you've covered the basic editing commands and the various ways to select objects in the drawing, let's move on to more editing commands.

AutoCAD Mechanics

CHAPTER 11

VIEWING THE DRAWING

In this chapter

VIEWING DRAWINGS

One of the most flexible features of AutoCAD is its capability to display a drawing at different magnification scale factors using multiple commands. This chapter deals with those commands, whether you want to magnify the drawing up close for more detail or to view the entire drawing, ranging from the simple to the more complex viewing commands. The workhorse of these commands is the Zoom command, which is discussed in the next section.

THE ZOOM COMMANDS

Regardless of scale, you can view the drawing at whatever level of detail you want. There are many viewing options to choose from, giving you the opportunity to decide which is the best. Chapter 1, "Working with the Interface," introduced you to the Realtime Zoom and Pan commands. These commands are pretty much the mainstay as far as quickly manipulating the magnification of the drawing. Yet a number of options are available with the Zoom command that give you more specific ways to change how you can view a drawing. These can be selected from a flyout on the Standard toolbar, shown in Figure 11.1.

Figure 11.1
The Zoom flyout contains many of the Zoom commands.

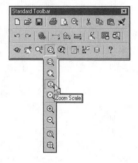

All these commands can be activated transparently or while working simultaneously with another command.

Tip 84 from
Ron House

Of all the commands in AutoCAD, Zoom is one of the easiest to access because you can do so in a multitude of ways.

You may find it more productive to access the Zoom command options from an undocked or floating Zoom toolbar, especially when you are working on the entire drawing rather than just a small portion. When in this mode, the toolbar can be located where it is easiest to access, allowing you to quickly manipulate the portion of the drawing you are working in. Zoom can be accessed in this way by choosing View, Toolbars, and then selecting Zoom from the list of available toolbars.

You also can activate the Zoom options via the shortcut menu and the command line. Right-clicking in the drawing editor while no objects are selected, and choosing Zoom from the shortcut menu gives you access to all the options listed in this section.

Or if you are comfortable typing commands from the keyboard, you can type **z** and press Enter. This lists the Zoom options at the command line, giving you easy access by typing the capital letter for the option you want.

Note

Appendix A, "Taking Advantage of AutoCAD's Keyboard Shortcuts" lists all the standard keyboard shortcuts you can use in AutoCAD. Use this as a reference for these commands. If you are interested in creating your own shortcuts, see Chapter 20, "Customizing Made Easy," to learn how.

The Zoom command options available from the shortcut menu are these:

- Zoom Realtime—This is the default Zoom command, allowing you to rapidly change the magnification of the drawing by dragging the cursor in one direction or another. When this command is activated, the cursor changes to a magnifying glass with a plus and minus sign (see Figure 11.2).

Figure 11.2
When using Realtime Pan and Zoom, the cursor changes to a magnifying glass—and the plus and minus signs indicate the direction in which you need to move the cursor to change the magnification factor.

Notice the location of these signs, which refers to the direction in which you need to move the cursor to either increase (plus sign) or decrease (minus sign) the magnification. When you've achieved the desired scale factor, you can cancel the command by right-clicking and selecting Exit from the menu, or by just pressing the Esc key. Note that when you access the shortcut menu, you can activate some of the other Zoom options, all of which are discussed here. Use this command to quickly magnify an area of interest in the drawing.

Note

The Realtime feature combines the functionality of both the Pan and the Zoom commands. Although these can be accessed separately from the Standard toolbar, you can easily toggle back and forth between commands using the right-click shortcut menu. Either of these Realtime features can be easily activated during a command or transparently, enabling

continues

continued

you to dynamically zoom and pan around in the drawing without canceling the current command.

This transparent function allows the realtime commands to be used anytime you need to zoom or pan. You'll find more information about the Realtime Pan option in the next section, "Panning Around in the Drawing."

Tip 85 from
Ron House

AutoCAD 2000 takes advantage of the functionality of Microsoft IntelliMouse or compatible pointing devices. These devices contain a scrolling wheel, which enables you to change the magnification scale factor during the Realtime Zoom and Pan commands.

Tip 86 from
Ron House

You can control the display of raster images during the use of the Realtime Pan and Zoom commands with the system variable Rtdisplay. If this variable is set to 0, the raster image is displayed normally during the use of these commands. If the value is set to 1, only an outline of the raster image is shown. Depending on the number of raster images used in the drawing, you may want to consider using this function to speed up the amount of time it takes to pan and zoom the drawing.

- Zoom Window—This enables you to specify the view magnification by dragging a window around what you want to want magnify. When the command is activated, you are prompted to pick one corner of the Zoom window and then the opposite corner. A box appears on the screen as you drag the window, representing the area to be magnified, allowing you specify the view area of the drawing. Whereas the realtime pan and zoom allows you to first zoom to an area of the drawing and then pan to what you want to view, the zoom window option "zooms" you right to where you want to go in the drawing.

- Zoom Dynamic—Zoom Dynamic modifies the current zoom magnification by showing you the current magnification window in relation to the extents of the drawing. By default, you are placed into View Panning mode. A dashed blue rectangle indicates the extents, and a dashed green rectangle defines the current magnification window. A black rectangle with an X located at its center, called the panning view box, represents the current Zoom window magnification. This box can be repositioned onscreen to define the location and scale factor you wish to view in the drawing (see Figure 11.3). Use this zoom option to magnify a general area of the drawing that you want to work in.

This gives you the ability to reapply the present magnification factor to other areas of the drawing. If you wish to change the magnification factor, click the screen and you'll notice that the panning view box can be resized by moving the cursor. An arrow appears on the right side of the box, defining the zoom scale factor.

Notice that the sides of the box stay at a relative scale in relation to the size of the box. Clicking onscreen again locks the size of the box into the new size or magnification scale, in which it can then be relocated. Press the Enter key while in View Panning mode to change the drawing to the updated magnification scale factor. The advantage of this option is that it shows you the current magnification factor in relation to the overall drawing and enables you to change the zoom scale relative to this.

Figure 11.3
The Zoom indicators used during View Panning mode with the Zoom Dynamic command; the blue rectangle displays the extents of the drawing, and the green rectangle displays the current magnification view.

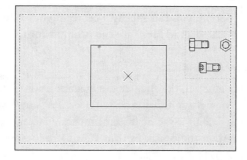

- Zoom Scale—The Zoom Scale option prompts you to manually supply the zoom scale factor. After you give the scale factor, the zoom factor is applied to the view using the center of the view as a basepoint. Selecting the Zoom Scale button gives the following prompt:

```
Enter a scale factor (nX or nXP):
```

The zoom scale factor changes the current view based on a value relative to the scale factor of the drawing limits. In other words, the drawing zoom scale changes from what it was to a zoom scale factor multiplied by the given value. For example, if a value of 2 is given, the zoom scale is doubled relative to the zoom scale viewing the drawing limits, shown in Figure 11.4.

Figure 11.4
This illustrates how the current view appears before (left) and after (right) applying a value of 2x using the Zoom Scale command.

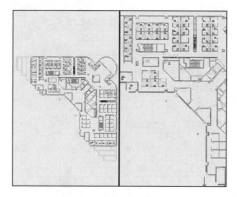

Adding an x after the scale factor modifies the zoom scale factor relative to the current view scale factor, instead of the drawing limits. Thus, if a value of 2x is given, the current view scale factor is increased by 2. On the other hand, a value of .5x would reduce the current zoom scale by one-half, decreasing the magnification. This is the more typical use of the command because it is easier to relate to the current view rather than the drawing limits' view. Use this option when you know exactly how much you want to zoom in or out relative to the current view.

- Zoom Center—With this option, you can specify a center point for the drawing view along with a magnification scale factor. Here are the prompts for this command:

```
Specify center point:
Enter magnification or height <4.5000>:
```

The larger the value that is entered, the smaller the magnification factor. The smaller the value, the larger is the view magnification scale factor. Pressing Enter at the magnification prompt accepts the default value or the current scale factor. This option is used when you know where you want the center of your view to be located and what the magnification scale factor is to be from that point.

The next two options are available only from the Zoom toolbar and provide a quick way to double the magnification factor or decrease it by half:

- Zoom In—This increases the magnification scale factor by 2, which increases the current scale factor of the view.

- Zoom Out—This decreases the magnification scale factor by half, decreasing the scale factor of the current view.

- Zoom All—This changes the current drawing view to include all elements in the drawing. This option displays either the drawing limits or the extents, whichever is the greater of the two. Although this command can be run transparently, doing so forces a regeneration of the drawing. Use this option when you want to view the entire drawing.

- Zoom Extents—This zooms to the extents of the drawing, which is the total physical space of any drawing elements within the drawing; any empty space beyond a drawing element is ignored. This option is used when you want to view all of the objects you have in a drawing—not necessarily the drawing extents.

Zoom Window and Extents can be accessed from within the Realtime Zoom and Pan commands using the Zoom shortcut menu shown in Figure 11.5.

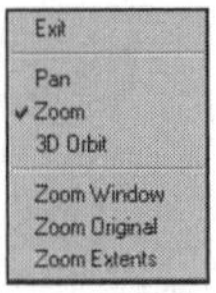

Figure 11.5
The Zoom Original option, available from the shortcut menu, restores the original zoom scale factor to the drawing view.

The next example illustrates the use of the Zoom Dynamic command:

EXAMPLE: CHANGING THE ZOOM SCALE FACTOR OF THE DRAWING BY USING THE ZOOM DYNAMIC COMMAND

1. Open a drawing file of your choice from the ACAD2000 Sample directory. Then select the Zoom Dynamic button from the Zoom toolbar.

2. Immediately, you will be placed in View Panning mode. A blue rectangle is shown to represent the extents of the drawing; a green rectangle displays the current zoom scale factor.

3. To change the current View location without changing the zoom scale factor, use the mouse to relocate the panning view box to the desired location and press Enter.

4. To change the current zoom scale factor, click on the screen, which enables you to resize the panning view box. Use the mouse to resize the box, and then click again to set the scale factor, which is relative to the size of the box.

5. Move the box to the desired view location and then press Enter to apply the new scale factor and location to the current drawing view.

Next, you'll examine the Pan command, which is used typically with the Zoom command to adjust the location of the current view.

PANNING AROUND IN THE DRAWING

The compliment of the Zoom command is the Pan command. After you've defined the magnification scale factor you want with the Zoom options, you can use the Pan command to adjust your view by shifting the focus point of your drawing. This is done by "pulling" the drawing in the direction you want, which is better described by using the Pan commands listed here as reference. Select the Pan button from the Standard toolbar, shown in Figure 11.6.

Figure 11.6
Select the Pan button from the Standard toolbar.

- Pan Realtime—This is the other dynamic mode when using the Realtime Zoom command. When the Realtime Pan command is selected from the Standard toolbar, the cursor changes to a small hand, which enables you to "pull" the drawing view in the direction you want. To pan the view, hold the left mouse button as you move the mouse in the desired direction. When you release the button, the panning stops. The right-click shortcut menu can be used to toggle between the two realtime modes.

n Pan—The same functionality is achieved activating the command from the command line by typing **Pan**, or **P** using the keyboard shortcut. When the Pan command is accessed this way, the following prompt is displayed at the command line:

```
Press ESC or ENTER to exit, or right-click to display shortcut menu.
```

Tip 87 from
Ron House

Both the Zoom and the Pan commands can be run from the command line without canceling the command you are working with. Typing a single quote before the command, such as '**Zoom** or '**Pan**, enables you to manipulate the drawing view while remaining in the current command. Activating a command in this way is called *transparently activating* a command. Not all commands can be accessed like this, but Zoom, Pan, and many of the system variables discussed at the end of each chapter are transparent commands.

You'll typically use the Zoom and Pan commands to accomplish the majority of your navigation needs. On occasions, however—especially when working with large, complex drawings—it is advantageous to see where your current view is in relation to the entire drawing. For example, this command is convenient when you are routing conduit or piping in a building, and you need to see not only where you are currently working, but also where to you are in regard to the overall building. For these times, you will want to use the Aerial View command, which is discussed in the next section.

AERIAL VIEWER

The Aerial Viewer gives the user an easy-to-use separate interface for viewing a drawing, showing the location of the current view in relation to the drawing extents. The Aerial View window is a convenient function to have on large drawings with extraordinary amounts of detail. Not only can this floating window be run transparently, but it also allows you to view the entire drawing to determine the next view location. The Aerial View is similar in functionality to the Zoom Dynamic command in that the drawing extents can be viewed while determining zoom magnification.

To activate the Aerial View command, choose the Aerial View option from the View pull-down menu. This brings up the Aerial View Window shown in Figure 11.7.

Three viewing options are available from either the View pull-down menu or the Aerial View toolbar:

■ Zoom In—Magnifies the zoom scale factor of the drawing in the Aerial View by a factor of 2, doubling the magnification.

■ Zoom Out—Decreases the zoom scale factor of the drawing in the Aerial View by a factor of 2, decreasing the magnification by half.

■ Global—Displays the extents of the drawing in the Aerial View.

Figure 11.7
The Aerial View window enables you to view the extents of the drawing in relation to the current drawing magnification.

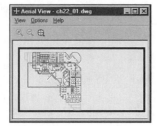

Each of these options centers the view about the location of the panning view box. This appears as a solid gray box in the Aerial View window. The panning view box is similar in functionality to the one used in the Zoom Dynamic command. The initial click in the window enables you to relocate the panning view box. Clicking again in the window enables you to resize the panning view window, changing the view scale factor. Pressing the Enter key or right-clicking during these two modes changes the view location and magnification of the drawing.

When initially opening the Aerial View window, right-clicking inside the window not only gives you the three options listed, but it also gives three additional options via a shortcut menu, shown in Figure 11.8.

Figure 11.8
Both the display and the dynamic updating options are available from the right-click shortcut menu in the Aerial View window.

These options deal with the automatic updating of the viewport display to match the current view and dynamic updating of the drawing. They are as follows:

- Auto Viewport—Automatically updates the drawing view to match the Aerial View. When this option is toggled off, the drawing view is not updated.

- Dynamic Update—Updates the Aerial View window while the drawing is edited. When toggled off, an update is not performed until the focus is returned to the Aerial View window.

- Realtime Zoom—Dynamically updates the drawing view as you modify the location and size of the panning view box or magnification scale of the current view window.

Using the Aerial View command is useful when you want to see the current view in relation to the overall drawing, such as in pipe or conduit routing, and when you want to transparently change the zoom scale factor in a separate window, dynamically updating the drawing view.

When working with a drawing, it is convenient to be able to save a particular view location and magnification in a drawing, allowing you to quickly return to that section of the drawing. The next section discusses the View command, which offers this functionality.

VIEWS

Views give you a way to save a previously defined zoom location and magnification. This is useful when you want to return to a location in the drawing and you want to have the same zoom scale factor when viewing that area. To access the View dialog box, choose the Named Views tab from the View pull-down menu, shown in Figure 11.9.

Figure 11.9
The View dialog box give you access to the previously defined views in the drawing.

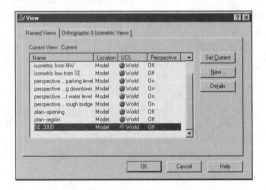

Tip 88 from
Ron House

This command can also be accessed by typing **v** at the command line.

The View dialog box contains two tabbed sections: one for user-defined Named Views and another for Orthographic and Isometric Views. Selecting the tab enables you to view the views listed in each section. The view lists also contain information on the location (Model space or Layout) of the view, the name of the User Coordinate System (UCS) saved with the view and tells whether the views are three-dimensional perspective views or whether they have been clipped.

→ Refer to Chapter 18, "Plotting and Layouts," for detailed information on using layouts. Chapter 23, "Visualization," covers the use of the User Coordinate System. Use these chapters for references when using View in relation to plotting or viewing three-dimensional drawings.

To set a current view, select a view from the list, click the Set Current button, and select the OK button to apply that view to the drawing screen.

To create a new view, follow these steps:

EXAMPLE: CREATING AND SETTING VIEWS IN THE DRAWING

1. Open a drawing of your choice from the ACAD2000 Sample directory; then open the View dialog box by selecting the Named Views option from the View pull-down menu.

2. Click the Named Views tab.

3. Select the New button, which opens the New View dialog box (see Figure 11.10).

Figure 11.10
From the New View dialog box, you can create a view based either on the current display or on a defined window.

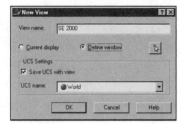

4. Type in a name for the view in the View name edit box.

5. Select the Current display or Defined window option. If you want to specify a defined window, the Define New Window button temporarily dismisses the dialog box so you can drag a window box around the elements in the view.

6. You can also save a specific UCS with the new view by selecting the Save UCS with view button. The desired UCS can then be selected from the list of defined UCSs in the drawing. See Chapter 23, "Visualization," for detailed use of the UCS command.

7. Clicking the OK button adds the new view to the named view list.

8. Select the view from the list and then click the Details button to open the View Details dialog box, which gives you specific details about the view in relation to a selected UCS that can be chosen from the Relative to list. This dialog box is shown in Figure 11.11.

Figure 11.11
The View Details dialog box gives you specific information about the selected view relative to an UCS.

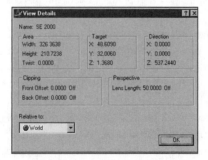

Tip 89 from
Ron House

When a view is saved with a drawing, you can check the option to Select Initial View on the Select File dialog box when that drawing file is reopened using the Open command. This opens the drawing with the Select Initial View dialog box, shown in Figure 11.12. From here you can select which view to open the drawing with.

Figure 11.12
The Select Initial View dialog box gives you the choice of opening a drawing to a particular view.

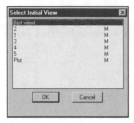

➔ Chapter 1, "Working with the Interface," discusses the Select Initial View option with the Open command. Refer to this chapter if needed for details on the use of this option.

The Orthographic and Isometric Views tab displays the list of predefined views that are available with any drawing relative to a chosen UCS. The Restore Orthographic UCS with View toggle restores a saved UCS with the view when an orthographic view is made current. These types of views are essential when emphasizing the specifics of a drawing, such as a single part or assembly of parts or the overall piping in a building.

Another way to effectively use views is to split the viewing area into multiple screens called *viewports*, in which multiple views can be displayed. This is discussed in the next section.

VIEWPORTS

Viewports enable you to divide the viewing area into multiple screens, in which each screen can display the current view or be assigned a saved view. This makes it possible for you to interact with the whole drawing rather than one specific portion.

➔ Two different types of viewports are available within AutoCAD: tiled and floating. This chapter deals specifically with tiled viewports. Chapter 18, "Plotting and Layouts," discusses floating viewports and the advantages of using these with layouts combined with plotting. Check out this chapter to determine when to use this type of viewport.

At this point, you may question when and why you would need to use a feature like this. The reasons are more obvious than you might think. When a new drawing is created, you are actually viewing the drawing through a single viewport. As your drawing starts to get more detailed, you might want to split the drawing into multiple viewports to examine how other parts of the drawing relate to the current viewport. You only need to select in a viewport to make it active, allowing you to work on that portion of the drawing without changing the current view magnification or location. As you draw in the current viewport, changes to the drawing are automatically displayed in the other viewports.

One good example of this is when you need to draw a line starting at one side of the drawing and ending on the other side. You can create two viewports, one showing a close-up of where the line starts and the other showing the area of the drawing where the line ends. This would enable you to draw the line without the need to zoom in and out; you would simply start the line in one viewport, then click in the opposite viewport to provide the endpoint of the line.

If you start a command in one viewport and want to finish it in another viewport, just select the desired viewport to make it active and finish the command. This allows you to jump to another section of the drawing rather than having to adjust the magnification of the view. This also saves you considerable time, regardless of the drawing size.

This section looks at how to set up the viewports for a drawing and also examines the different ways to utilize the command.

APPLYING VIEWPORTS TO A DRAWING

To view the different viewport configurations, select the Viewports button, shown in Figure 11.13, from the Standard toolbar, or type **VPORTS** at the command line and press Enter.

Figure 11.13

The Viewports dialog box opens, displaying the default New Viewports tab. This tab displays the list of standard viewports and the configuration of the current drawing screen (see Figure 11.14).

Figure 11.14
The Viewports dialog box enables you to define a viewport configuration for the drawing.

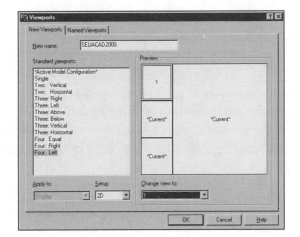

Selecting a viewport from the Standard viewports list changes the Preview window to that configuration, which displays the possible arrangement of the viewports in the drawing. Four options apply to the viewports:

- Apply to—This option enables you to define where the selected viewport configuration will be applied, to the current display or a specific viewport.

- Setup—Clicking the Setup selection list enables you to toggle between a 2D and 3D setup, depending on the viewport configuration you choose. When you select a configuration, notice that each viewport is set with the default current viewport. If the 3D option is selected from the Setup list, the viewports toggle to a 3D-related view, such as Top, Front, and Isometric views, automatically setting the standard views you might want for this type of drawing.

The Setup option highlights the advantage of using viewports when working with three-dimensional drawings. This option enables you to view the drawing from multiple views, allowing you to work between the viewports, depending on which view gives the best viewing angle. Figure 11.15 helps illustrate working with multiple viewports on a three-dimensional drawing.

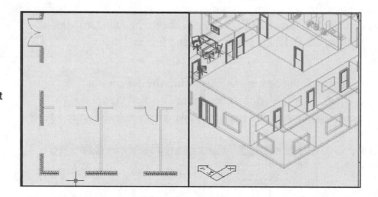

Figure 11.15
Working with viewports on a three-dimensional drawing gives you the advantage of viewing the drawing from different angles.

- Change view to—If you have saved views in the drawing, a specific view can be assigned to a viewport. Select a viewport by clicking inside the viewport boundary, and then select the Saved View from the Change view to list. That view will be applied to the viewport, enabling you to set up your viewports before applying them to the drawing.

Tip 90 from
Ron House

The Ctrl+R keys enable you to set which viewport is active. Each time you consecutively press these keys, you transfer the active mode to the next viewport.

- New name—When you've defined how to set up the drawing viewports, you can give your new configuration a name. Not only does this allow you to easily remember a configuration by name, but you also can assign multiple viewport configurations for a drawing. You can create multiple viewport configurations for specific operations and easily toggle between them using this command.

After you have created and named multiple viewport configurations in the drawing, use the Named Viewports tab to toggle which configuration you want active. This tab contains a list of configurations and a Preview window. As you select the from the Named Viewports list, the Preview window displays the layout of the viewport configuration. The following example lists the steps to create and set a viewport configuration.

EXAMPLE: CREATING AND SETTING A VIEWPORT CONFIGURATION

1. Open the drawing Ch11_01.dwg you copied from the companion CD. Select the Model Layout tab at the bottom of the drawing editor.

2. Click the Display Viewport Dialog button from the Standard toolbar. Enter a name for the Viewport called **Southwest Entrance**.

3. Select the "Three: Left viewport" configuration for the list of Standard viewports.

4. Make certain the Apply to option is set to Display and that the Setup list is set to 2D.

5. In the Preview window, click inside the large left viewport. Choose Camera01 from the Change to View selection list.

6. Click the upper-right viewport and assign it the view Model.

7. Then set the view "Plan" to the lower-right viewport.

8. Clicking the OK button then updates the drawing using this viewport configuration with each of the views within their respective viewports.

9. If you change to a different viewport configuration and you want to return the drawing to the Southwest Entrance configuration, reopen the Viewports dialog box. Click the Named Viewports tab, select this configuration from the list, and then click the OK button.

10. Your drawing should look like the one in Figure 11.16.

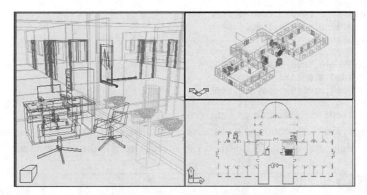

Figure 11.16
By using the Viewports command, you can easily divide the screen to display multiple views.

If you have given a configuration the wrong name or if you find you no longer need a viewport configuration, continue to the next section to accomplish either of these functions.

DELETING AND RENAMING VIEWPORT CONFIGURATIONS

A viewport configuration, or layout of the views within the viewports, can be deleted or renamed from the Named Viewports tab. Just select the configuration from the list and then right-click and select the Delete or Rename option from the menu. If you select the Rename option, you can edit the name of the configuration within the Viewports dialog box.

CHECKING A VIEWPORT CONFIGURATION

To apply the selected viewport configuration to the drawing, click the OK button. The drawing will update to match those settings.

You can check the settings for each viewport configuration by typing **–Vports** at the command line. This lists the viewport options at the command line. Placing a hyphen (–) at the beginning of this command forces the command to be run from the command line rather than through a displayed dialog box. Typing a question mark (?) at the Enter an option prompt displays information about each configuration, such as name and viewport location. This is displayed on the text screen:

```
Enter an option [Save/Restore/Delete/Join/SIngle/?/2/3/4] <3>: ? <ENTER>
Enter name(s) of viewport configuration(s) to list <*>:<ENTER>
Current configuration:
id# 3
   corners: 0.5000,0.0000 1.0000,0.5000
id# 2
   corners: 0.5000,0.5000 1.0000,1.0000
id# 4
   corners: 0.0000,0.5000 0.5000,1.0000
id# 5
   corners: 0.0000,0.0000 0.5000,0.5000
Configuration "VP 3":
    0.5000,0.5000 1.0000,1.0000
    0.5000,0.0000 1.0000,0.5000
    0.0000,0.0000 0.5000,1.0000
Configuration "VP 4":
    0.5000,0.5000 1.0000,1.0000
    0.0000,0.5000 0.5000,1.0000
    0.0000,0.0000 0.5000,0.5000
    0.5000,0.0000 1.0000,0.5000
```

The current configuration and any saved configurations are listed, indicating number and relative viewport location. The location coordinates are displayed as the lower-left and upper-right corner points, based on the coordinates for the entire screen.

Note

The location format for the viewports—which sets 0,0 as the coordinate for the lower-left corner, and 1,1 as the coordinate for the upper-right corner—makes it easier to relate to the location of each viewport within the configuration.

Accessing the list of viewport configurations using this method enables you to filter out all the configurations except those desired using wildcard characters. You could easily type *VP at the Enter name(s) of viewport configuration(s) to list prompt to get a listing of those viewport configurations that start with VP. Of course, this all depends on how you name your viewport configurations. It's a good idea to think about the naming convention of your viewports so that the name gives you an indication of what the configuration displays.

When you've finished editing the drawing with a viewport configuration, you may find you no longer need a viewport, or maybe you created one too many. Rather than deleting the viewport, you can join the unwanted viewport with another. The options that were available by accessing the viewport command from the command line—such as Restore, Delete, and Join—are covered in the next section.

JOINING VIEWPORTS TO FORM ONE

One other viewport option that needs to be discussed is the Join option. This feature enables you to combine two viewports to form a single viewport. The following steps walk you through the process of joining two viewports to form a single viewport.

JOINING TWO VIEWPORTS TO FORM ONE VIEWPORT

1. From within a drawing with two or more viewports, select <u>V</u>iew, <u>V</u>iewports, <u>J</u>oin.

2. You can click inside a viewport boundary to define it as the dominant viewport, which can be defined as the parent viewport that will be merged with the child viewport.
   ```
   Select dominant viewport <current viewport>:
   ```

3. After selecting the dominant viewport, you are prompted for the viewport to join.
   ```
   Select viewport to join:
   ```

4. The drawing then updates to combine the two viewports.

Whichever view was the dominant viewport fills the area of the combined viewports. Rather than joining all the viewports until you return to one, the process described in the next section covers when you want to remove all other viewports from the screen.

RESTORING THE SCREEN TO A SINGLE VIEWPORT

If you find it easier to work with a single viewport, you can revert the drawing screen back into a single viewport by using the 1 Viewport or Single Viewport option. Select <u>V</u>iew, <u>V</u>iewports, and then <u>1</u> Viewport. All other viewports except the current viewport are removed.

Four commands assist you in viewport maintenance: Redraw, Regen, RedrawAll, and RegenAll. Each is discussed in the following section.

REFRESHING THE VIEWPORTS

Whether you are dealing with a single viewport or multiple viewports, at times stray pixels remain onscreen. This typically occurs if you have moved a large number of objects and you can see remaining pixels from where the objects were moved. Or you may have erased a number of items from the drawing and it appears that the Erase command did not get everything. Use the Redraw command to clean up these pixels, giving you a clear view of your drawing. In the case of multiple viewports, if you want to refresh all the viewports at once rather than separately, use the RedrawAll command. This refreshes the display in the current viewport.

REGENERATING THE VIEW

At times, the view needs to be regenerated so AutoCAD can recalculate the location of all objects in the drawing. Unfortunately, this is a necessary process for AutoCAD. You have already seen this occur although you may not have realized it. Changing a viewport configuration regenerates a drawing, or this also may occur when you toggle to thaw a layer that was previously frozen. You can also force this to happen when needed, and doing so helps AutoCAD speed up the process of selecting large sets of objects in the drawing.

REGEN AND REGENALL

Similar to the Redraw and RedrawAll commands, you also have Regen and RegenAll. Use Regen when you wish to regenerate a single viewport, and use RegenAll when you want to regenerate all your viewports. Because these commands enable you to force a regeneration of the drawing, you should limit your use of this command, especially when working with large drawings. Each time this command is activated, no other command can be run until it is finished, thus reducing your productivity. However, you can tell AutoCAD to notify you when a regeneration needs to occur. The RegenAuto command enables you to temporarily postpone the regenerations until a convenient time. This command has two options: ON and OFF. When RegenAuto is turned on, AutoCAD automatically regenerates the drawing when needed. When this option is toggled off, AutoCAD informs you that a regeneration is needed by displaying the following prompt:

```
About to regen--proceed?
```

If you answer no to the prompt, AutoCAD cancels the current command that would have forced a regeneration. This gives you the option of using another command, such as using Zoom Dynamic or trying to run the command transparently to avoid the regeneration.

SUMMARY

Use these commands to navigate a drawing with ease. Taking the time to learn the different Zoom commands will save you time and effort, allowing you to focus exactly what you want to see in the drawing. Creating views can save a considerable amount of time, and using viewports can extend your productivity, regardless of whether the drawing is small or large. Although the commands discussed in this chapter deal mainly with objects in two-dimensional space, there are additional ways to manipulate a drawing view when working with three-dimensional drawings. If you are working with these types of drawings, turn to Chapter 23, "Visualization," for details on using these commands.

CHAPTER 12

ANNOTATING THE DRAWING

In this chapter

ANNOTATING DRAWINGS

No AutoCAD 2000 drawing can successfully communicate without some form of annotation. Maps, mechanical drawings, buildings, title blocks, details, and even blocks and symbols all require some kind of key, legend, labeling, or definition to assist the user in understanding and interpreting the lines and shapes on the page. AutoCAD 2000 provides a variety of options for creating, positioning, formatting, and editing text in drawings. Underlying all these options, only two basic methods exist for adding annotation: Text may be added to a drawing as either as a *single-line* text object or as extended paragraphs of *multiline* text.

This chapter provides a hands-on comparison of each of these kinds of text objects. You will learn how to draw and edit both lines and paragraphs of text, and when it is best to use single-line or multiline text. This chapter also reviews two different ways to create text styles, and the pros and cons of each approach. Finally, you will learn how to reuse text styles in new drawings and how to share text styles with other users.

ADDING LINE TEXT

Line text is preferred for short, simple text elements in a drawing, such as labels or single-line entries. In this section, you will start by adding line text to a drawing; you will then review all the different properties of text that you can manipulate, such as style, position, height, and rotation angle. You will also practice moving and changing text, and modifying the properties of existing line text.

The Line Text command can be started from the Draw menu or from the command line. If you don't already have AutoCAD 2000 running, start it now. Locate the file CH12EX01. DWG on the CD that accompanies this book, and copy it to a practice folder on your hard drive. In the following exercise, you will use this sample drawing to practice adding line text.

Note

Users who are familiar with the Text and Dtext commands in previous versions of AutoCAD should note that the AutoCAD 2000 Text command now performs the same way as Dtext: you may add consecutive lines of text with the simple Text command. Dtext is still available on the command line but is largely redundant.

1. Select File, Open, and then browse to your practice folder and open CH12EX01. DWG. This drawing is a simple technical illustration that requires some labels.

   Step through the practice example. You will have a chance to review each of the prompts in more detail after you have completed this exercise.

2. Select <u>D</u>raw, Te<u>x</u>t, <u>S</u>ingle Line Text, or type **text** at the command line and press Enter. The following prompt appears:

```
Current text style:  "Romans"  Text height:  0.0900
Specify start point of text or [Justify/Style]:
```

3. Using your mouse, select a point in the drawing area to enter the caption **FIGURE 1**, as shown in Figure 12.1. (You may also enter the start point coordinates at the command line: **1.8,0.025**) The next prompt appears:

```
Specify height <0.0900>:
```

4. Press Enter to accept the default text height of 0.09. The next prompt appears:

```
Specify rotation angle of text <0>:
```

5. Press Enter to accept the default rotation angle of 0°. You are finally prompted to start entering text:

```
Enter text:
```

6. Type **FIGURE 1** and press Enter. When you are prompted a second time to enter text, press the Enter key again to end the Text command.

Figure 12.1
Use the Text command to add a line of text to an AutoCAD 2000 drawing.

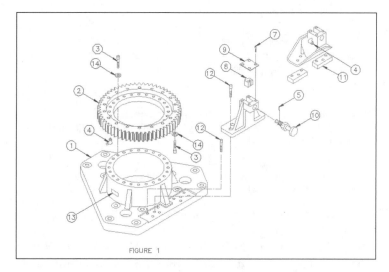

When you use the Text command, whatever you type will be entered as a single line of text until you press the Enter key. If you make a mistake as you type, use the Backspace key to back up and remove the error, and then type in the correction. In the previous short exercise, you accepted all the text defaults as defined in the text style. Now take a look at where and how these defaults are stored.

TEXT STYLE

All AutoCAD 2000 text has a style associated with it; this style is a predefined group of settings that controls the font, size, and alignment of the text. If you do not have any particular text preferences of your own, you may continue to use the default AutoCAD 2000 "STANDARD" style, varying only the height of text to distinguish headings or detail and section callouts. Alternatively, CAD users may prefer to use different text *styles* for varying text items (headings, notes, or callouts, for example) to improve the readability and overall appearance of their drawings.

When you start the Line Text command, it instantly informs you of your current settings for text style and text height. In the practice drawing, they are as follows:

```
Current text style:  "Romans"  Text height:  0.0900
Specify start point of text or [Justify/Style]:
```

Before you start entering any text, you have the option of choosing another style, by typing **s** at the command line. If you type **s** and press Enter, AutoCAD 2000 will prompt you to enter a style name. At this point, you should enter the name of a pre-existing style—and one that is available in the current drawing. To see which type styles are available in the current drawing, follow these steps:

1. Type **?** and press Enter.

2. Then type ***** and press Enter again. Details of the text styles are displayed in the AutoCAD Text window.

```
Text styles:

Style name: "Romans"     Font files: romans.shx
  Height: 0.0000  Width factor: 1.0000  Obliquing angle: 0
  Generation: Normal

Style name: "STANDARD"    Font files: txt
  Height: 0.0000  Width factor: 1.0000  Obliquing angle: 0
  Generation: Normal
```

3. Press Esc to terminate the command when you have reviewed the list.

Just two styles are listed in the current drawing: STANDARD and Romans. The only difference between these styles is the font file used. Both use standard AutoCAD fonts.

- The STANDARD style is the default text style supplied in the AutoCAD 2000 template drawings. It uses the plainest font available—the TXT font—which is a widely used although not particularly attractive font.

- Romans is a style created for use in this drawing. It uses the AutoCAD Romans font, a more readable typeface.

There is no advantage to changing the text style at this point because Romans is well suited to this drawing. You will learn how to develop your own text styles later in this chapter in "Creating Text Styles."

JUSTIFICATION AND ALIGNMENT

At the same command line prompt, you may also choose a different text alignment.

```
Specify start point of text or [Justify/Style]:
```

If you simply press Enter at this point, AutoCAD 2000 will use the default insertion point for text, as shown in Figure 12.2.

Figure 12.2
By default, text is positioned left-aligned, with the text baseline at the selected start point.

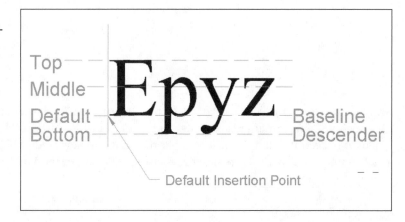

To review all of the alignment options type **j** [Justify] and press Enter. A string of options is displayed:

```
Enter an option [Align/Fit/Center/Middle/Right/TL/TC/TR/ML/MC/MR/BL/BC/BR]:
```

Skip over the Align and Fit options for now; these are reviewed in the next section of this chapter. The remaining Justify options are depicted graphically in Figure 12.3. The X-mark adjacent to each option indicates the insertion point as selected by your mouse-click.

- The Center and Right options (shown on the top line of Figure 12.3) operate in a similar way as the default text justification. The baseline of the text is aligned with the insertion point, and the text is centered on or right-aligned with the selected point. (While you are entering the text, it looks as if it is left-aligned, but when you hit the final Enter key, the text string jumps into the correct position.)

- The Middle option positions text slightly differently from the Center option; text is centered vertically as well as horizontally with the start point. This option is useful for centering text within a symbol—such as a grid bubble—or in a table cell.

- The TL/TC/TR/ML/MC/MR/BL/BC/BR options provide a 3×3 matrix of justification choices as shown in Figure 12.3. These options enable you to position the top, middle, and bottom of the text at a selected point. Notice that *bottom* means the bottom of the descenders (y, p, and so on), not the text baseline.

Figure 12.3
In addition to the default text position, you have 12 alternate justification options.

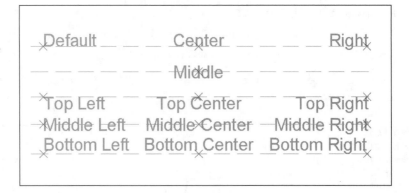

You may observe that Middle and Middle Center appear to be essentially the same option. However, one important difference exists: All the TL/TC/TR/ML/MC/MR/BL/BC/BR options are effective with horizontal text, but the results are less predictable with nonhorizontal annotation. If you have vertical or otherwise rotated text, the Middle option should be used to center the text.

ALIGN AND FIT OPTIONS

The Align and Fit options both enable you to make text fit into a specified length. You may use these options to squeeze a single line of text into a limited area or create the effect of justified text (text that fills from the left to the right margin in a column of text). Whereas a word processing program would manipulate the space between words and letters to accomplish these ends, AutoCAD changes the overall size of the text to make it fit—the Align option calculates what *height* of text will give the best fit, and the Fit option calculates what *width* of text will give the best fit.

- The Align option shrinks or expands the overall height of the text to make it fit between specified points in the line. When you choose this option, AutoCAD 2000 prompts you to pick two endpoints for the line of text. You are not prompted for a text height because AutoCAD 2000 calculates the text height that is required to fill the space. Figure 12.4 shows in a somewhat exaggerated fashion how the Align option works. Typically, you will use this option to make minor adjustments in text size to make it fit or match.

- The Fit option works in a similar fashion, but it keeps the text height constant (at the currently specified height) and manipulates the width of the text. Figure 12.4 shows how the Fit option manipulates text width.

These options will make more sense to you if you try out a quick example. You can complete the following exercise in the practice drawing CH12EX01.DWG. You don't need to keep the results of this practice, so erase it at the end of the exercise.

Figure 12.4
The Align option varies the height of text, and the Fit option varies the width of text to fill a given space.

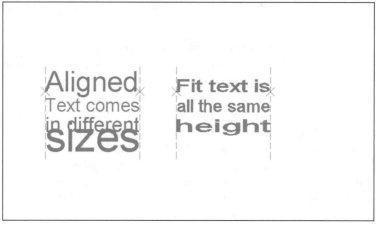

EXAMPLE: USING ALIGN AND FIT OPTIONS

1. Type **text**, type **j**, and press Enter. Then, type **a** and press Enter. You will be prompted for two points:

   ```
   Specify first endpoint of text baseline:
   Specify second endpoint of text baseline:
   ```

2. Pick two points fairly close together on the drawing editor. (You may also type in the coordinates, such as **5.0,2.0** and **7.0,2.0**.)

3. Type the following statement: **The quick brown fox jumps over the lazy dog.** Then press Enter twice.

   As you complete the command, the text will shrink in size to fit into the length defined.

4. Repeat the previous three steps, but this time type **f** instead of **a** in step 1. Start the text directly below the aligned text, and specify the same start point and endpoint in the X-axis. (For example, you might use **5.0, 1.0** and **7.0,1.0** as the start point and endpoint.)

Actually, using these command options will give you a better sense of the different effects of Fit and Align, instead of just reading about them. You will be better able to decide which option to use when you need to fit text into a fixed space.

Note

If you know which justification or alignment option you intend to use, you do not need to type **j** before selecting an option. You need to type **j** only if you wish to review the options; otherwise, simply type the required option code (**tc**, **r**, or **a**, for example) directly at the first prompt.

CALCULATING THE APPROPRIATE TEXT HEIGHT

Determining the appropriate height for text is one of the more challenging aspects of annotation. Before you start adding text to a drawing, there is nearly always some setup to do. If

PART
IV
CH
12

you are working with a scaled drawing, you will need to calculate the size of your text so it plots at the correct size.

There are no hard-and-fast rules about the height of plotted text. Different work groups establish their preferred text sizes, and the process of standardizing text heights within a company or government body is often a lengthy one. Text heights usually are defined in 1/32-, 1/16-, or 1/8-inch increments, and typical heights range from as small as 3/32 inch to as much as 1/4 inch. A lot of factors determine the final choice of text height, which usually involves a compromise between achieving maximum readability and fitting all of the required text in the available space. A further consideration in determining text height is that the same drawings are often plotted at different scales, which means that the same AutoCAD 2000 text will print at different sizes. So, although the final choice of text height may be a little smaller than optimal for one scale and a little bigger than optimal for another, it can be made to work for both situations.

After you have selected the desired height for plotted text, you have to determine how to accomplish it in AutoCAD 2000. Calculating text height for a particular drawing scale is not as simple as you might expect. If you want to have 1/8-inch-height text in your plotted drawing, you cannot simply select 1/8 inch, or even 0.125. You must compensate for the scale adjustment that happens when a drawing is plotted. Most geometry is drawn full size in model space; then a floating viewport is used in a layout to shrink the drawing so it fits on the selected paper size.

→ For more information on plotting, see Chapter 18, "Plotting and Layouts," starting on page **481**.

What you need to know is the scale factor used in the viewport; then multiply your text size by the *inverse* of that scale factor. For example, if your drawing scale is 1:20, your model space geometry will be reduced by 1/20 to fit your paper size. Your text will need to be drawn 20 times larger for it to plot at the correct height. If you convert these numbers to decimals, the math is not too hard. You can use the command line to do the math for you. Type the following line at the command prompt to divide 1.0 by 8.0 to get the decimal equivalent of 1/8 inch:

```
Command: (/ 1.0 8.0)
0.125
```

Obviously, you can also use a calculator to get the decimal equivalents of fractions. Choose the method you find most convenient. Now multiply the result by 20 to get your text height for model space:

```
Command: (* 20.0 0.125)
```

(Or 20×0.125 on your calculator.) The answer is 2.5. If you have a 1:50 scale drawing, you can multiply 0.125 by 50 to get the text height for 1/8 inch. When you see the pattern, it's fairly easy to make up a table of values for your commonly used scales and text heights. If you have a spreadsheet on your computer, you can have it do the calculations for you as well. The following tables (grouped as Table 12.1) provide examples for three typical scales.

The first example can be used also as a standard decimal scale—1:10 is the same as 1 foot = 10 inches, and so on. In each of the tables, the values for text height are expressed in AutoCAD units.

TABLE 12.1 TEXT HEIGHT FOR VARIOUS DRAWING SCALES

Engineering Scales with Model Space Units as Feet

Scale	3/32-inch Text	1/8-inch Text	3/16-inch Text	1/4-inch Text
1 foot = 10 feet	0.9375	1.25	1.875	2.5
1 foot = 20 feet	1.875	2.5	3.75	5
1 foot = 30 feet	2.8125	3.75	5.625	7.5
1 foot = 40 feet	3.75	5	7.5	10
1 foot = 50 feet	4.6875	6.25	9.375	12.5
1 foot = 100 feet	9.375	12.5	18.75	25
1 foot = 200 feet	18.75	25	37.5	50

Engineering Scales with Model Space Units as Inches

Scale	3/32-inch Text	1/8-inch Text	3/16-inch Text	1/4-inch Text
1 inch = 10 feet	11.25	15	22.5	30
1 inch = 20 feet	22.5	30	45	60
1 inch = 30 feet	33.75	45	67.5	90
1 inch = 40 feet	45	60	90	120
1 inch = 50 feet	56.25	75	112.5	150
1 inch = 100 feet	112.5	150	225	25
1 inch = 200 feet	225	300	450	600

Architectural Scales with Model Space Units as Inches

Scale	3/32-inch Text	1/8-inch Text	3/16-inch Text	1/4-inch Text
1/32 inch = 1 foot	36	48	72	96
1/16 inch = 1 foot	18	24	36	48
1/8 inch = 1 foot	9	12	18	24
3/16 inch = 1 foot	6	8	12	16
1/4 inch = 1 foot	4.5	6	9	12
3/8 inch = 1 foot	3	4	6	8
1/2 inch = 1 foot	2.25	3	4.5	6

continues

TABLE 12.1   CONTINUED

Scale	3/32-inch Text	1/8-inch Text	3/16-inch Text	1/4-inch Text
5/8 inch = 1 foot	1.8	2.4	3.6	4.8
3/4 inch = 1 foot	1.5	2	3	4
1 inch = 1 foot	1.125	1.5	2.25	3
1.5 inches = 1 foot	0.75	1	1.5	2
3 inches = 1 foot	0.375	0.5	0.75	1
6 inches = 1 foot	0.1875	0.25	0.375	0.5
12 inches = 1 foot	0.09375	0.125	0.1875	0.25

Calculating text height can be a dizzying experience. The best approach is to develop a table for the sizes most commonly used in your discipline. Develop standards for text height for typical drawings, and make your own table of standard values that work.

With the exception of special headings, most text in a given drawing will be the same size. When you set the text height at the Specify Height prompt, it will remain as your default. After you have set it, you can simply press Enter when the prompt appears to keep using the default value. When you want to use a different height, type in a new value, which will then become the new default.

Note If you are experimenting with the Text command in one of your own pre-existing drawings, you may find you sometimes do not get a prompt for text height. The reason for this is discussed later in this chapter, in "Creating Text Styles."

ROTATING TEXT

You may also rotate line text to any angle. Before you enter the actual text, AutoCAD 2000 issues a final prompt:

```
Specify rotation angle of text <0>:
```

Three choices are available at this prompt:

- Press Enter to accept the default rotation angle (shown in <> brackets).
- Type a number to position the text anywhere between 0° and 360°. You may even enter a negative value, and AutoCAD will calculate the required position. Some standard choices are shown in Figure 12.5.
- Use the cursor to specify the required rotation by clicking on the screen.

Any text rotation you choose will become the default until you select another value when this prompt appears.

A very useful application for rotated text is in aligning street names within or along street boundaries. The AutoCAD 2000 sample drawing \ACAD 2000\SAMPLE\City skyway map.DWG shows a wide variety of text orientations (see Figure 12.6). To align text with a given street, drag your mouse along the middle of the street at the Specify Rotation prompt. (It is a good idea also to set the justify option to Middle.)

Figure 12.5
Text may be rotated to any angle, from 0° to 360°.

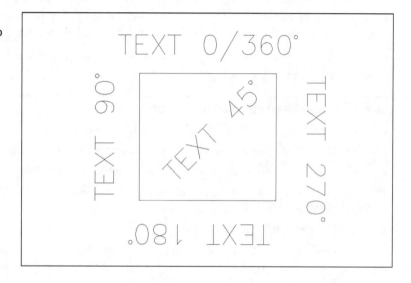

Figure 12.6
Use the text rotation option to line up text objects with other drawing objects.

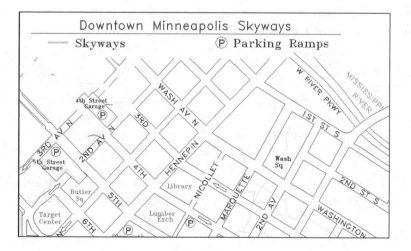

ADDING MULTIPLE LINE TEXT OBJECTS

Line text is most appropriately used to enter short, simple pieces of text. As you will be aware—from the repeated Enter Text prompt—the Text command enables you to add more than one line of text at a time. In fact, you can add as many lines of text as you wish. This is not to suggest that this command is the desired way to enter extended passages of text—the multiline text command is designed for that. However, there are a number of situations where line text is the most efficient way to add several lines of text. You often have to make short, last-minute additions and revisions to a drawing, and it is faster to use the Text command than to start the multiline text command and editor. When you are adding a series of one- or two-line labels to a drawing (a common occurrence in CAD), using the Text command is the most effective approach, as demonstrated in the exercise that follows.

In this exercise, don't exit the command until you have completed all the steps. Follow the positioning of the text shown in Figure 12.7:

EXAMPLE: ADDING MULTIPLE LINE TEXT OBJECTS

1. If it is not already open, open the CH12EX01.DWG once more.

2. Select Draw, Text, Single Line Text, or type **text** at the command line and press Enter.

3. Click in the space between callout 5 and callout 11 to position your text.

4. Press Enter twice to accept the default height of 0.09 and rotation of 0°, and then type **BRAKE WELDMENT** and press Enter.

5. Type **W/ SPACERS** and press Enter.

   The second line of text appears underneath your first line. This is an automatic feature of single-line text; text objects are spaced at 1 2/3 the height of the text. (In decimal terms, this would be 1.6666 recurring.)

6. Move your cursor to the area below callouts 5 and 10, and click to start a new line of text. Then type **BRAKE CASTING** and press Enter.

7. Move your cursor once again to a position under callout 13 and type **SERIAL NUMBER**. Then press Enter twice to exit the command.

The previous practice example gives you a sense of how you could annotate an entire drawing with a single instance of the Text command (presuming all the text was the same style, height, and rotation). After you have started the Text command, you can keep moving around the drawing and adding different pieces of text without having to restart the command. Line text provides a speedy and flexible way to add a lot of text elements in one pass. When you complete the Text command, each line of text is a separate text object. This feature is an asset because you may wish to edit individual labels separately.

FORMATTING LINE TEXT

Line text is formatted as a single unit, using the text style and the command-line options that you have just reviewed. Style determines, in particular, the text font; Justify controls the position of the text; and the height and rotation values can be manipulated as you enter each piece of text.

All these formats apply to all the text entered at one time. You can also apply a limited range of formats to portions of line text as you enter it by using special formatting codes, prefixed by %%. The format codes are shown in Table 12.2; these codes toggle the text effect on and off. If you do not toggle the effect off, it will automatically turn off at the end of the line.

Figure 12.7
You can add multiple text objects with a single Text command.

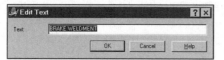

In the same way, you can insert some standard symbols (see Table 12.2) into your text. The degree symbol shown in Figure 12.5 was created using the %%d code.

TABLE 12.2   SPECIAL LINE TEXT CODES

Formatting Codes

Code	Produces	Description
%%utext%%u	text	Toggles underline on/off
%%otext%%o	text	Toggles overscore on/off
%%u%%otext%%u%%o	text	Toggles underline and overscore combined

Symbol Codes

Code	Produces	Description
%%d	o	Adds degree symbol
%%c	Ø	Adds diameter symbol
%%p	±	Adds plus/minus symbol
%%%	%	Adds a single percent sign
%%nnn		Adds ASCII character *nnn*

PART

IV

CH

12

EDITING LINE TEXT

Although adding line text to a drawing is a somewhat laborious process, line text can be changed using a few efficient commands: The grip editing commands, Ddedit, and the new AutoCAD 2000 Properties command are particularly useful. Take a look at each of these in turn.

MOVING LINE TEXT

You may reposition text the same way you reposition any other AutoCAD 2000 object—using the grip editing commands. Just select the text object, highlight the grips, and move the text to a new position.

1. Open CH12EXO1.DWG again, and click FIGURE 1 to show its grip point. Click a second time to turn the grip red. The following prompt appears:

   ```
   ** STRETCH **
   Specify stretch point or [Base point/Copy/Undo/eXit]:
   ```

2. Move your cursor down about 0.5 units (the distance is tracked in the status line). The text follows the cursor; when you click, FIGURE 1 repositions to that point.

3. Press the Esc key twice to exit Grip mode.

Tip 91 from
Paul Richardson

If the cursor keeps snapping back to the original position, you probably have the Object Snap option on, with a snap setting that is interfering with your new positioning. You can turn off object snaps in mid-command by simply clicking the OSNAP button on the AutoCAD 2000 status bar or by pressing the F3 key. Likewise, if your cursor will move only horizontally or vertically, you probably have Ortho mode on; you can turn this off by clicking the ORTHO button on the status bar or by pressing the F8 key while still in Grips mode.

CHANGING LINE TEXT

If you wish to edit the actual text in a single-line object, the easiest way is to click it to highlight the text, and then right-click and select Text Edit on the shortcut menu. Try changing the text in a few labels:

EXAMPLE: CHANGING LINE TEXT

1. Click the BRAKE WELDMENT label, and then right-click to open the shortcut menu.

2. Click Text Edit on the shortcut menu. This opens the Edit Text dialog box (see Figure 12.8).

   You have actually started the Ddedit command. You could type Ddedit at the command prompt and then pick a line-text object and end up in the same place.

3. Backspace over MENT and type **ING** in its place; then press OK. You are still in the Edit Text command.

4. Without exiting the Edit Text command, click on the W/ SPACERS label and change it to **WITH SPACERS**; press OK.

5. Without exiting the Edit Text command, change FIGURE 1 TO **FIGURE A**, and change SERIAL NUMBER to **SERIAL NUMBERS**; press OK.

6. When you have changed all the required text, press the Enter key to exit the Edit Text command.

Using the Edit Text command, you may quite efficiently edit all single-line text in a drawing at one pass.

Figure 12.8
Use the Edit Text command (Ddedit) to change the text in one or more text objects.

CHANGING OTHER TEXT PROPERTIES

AutoCAD 2000 introduces the Properties command (a huge improvement over the Properties button of AutoCAD 14), which enables you to review and edit any of the properties of any selected objects—including text objects.

The "properties" of an object store information about the current appearance or behavior of the object—the current *settings* for the object. In the case of a text object, the properties include all of the formatting options you reviewed in the earlier part of this chapter: style, justification, height, rotation, width, obliquing, and so on. They also include standard AutoCAD 2000 characteristics: color, layer, linetype, and lineweight—and also the X, Y, and Z coordinates of the text insertion point. Even the actual text itself, the words and characters, are stored in the "Content" property.

You can view all of the properties of any selected object via the Properties window, as shown in Figure 12.9. In the following exercise, you will use the Properties command to edit the properties of a piece of text in the drawing:

EXAMPLE: CHANGING OTHER TEXT PROPERTIES

1. Press the Esc key twice to make sure no other objects are selected, and then click again on the label SERIAL NUMBERS. Then, right-click to open the shortcut menu for this object.

2. This time, click the Properties option at the bottom of the shortcut menu. This pops up the Properties window for the text object you selected (see Figure 12.9). If necessary, drag the Properties window so it does not obscure the text you are editing.

   This window displays everything you want to know about the text object, including style, height, rotation, and justification. By clicking any of these items, you may select or enter a different value. You may change the text back to SERIAL NUMBER, or change the style to STANDARD (the only other style in this drawing) if you choose.

3. Click the Justify property, currently set at Left.

4. Click the arrow to drop down a list of the justification options. This contains the same information as the command-line list you saw earlier in the chapter—but it is much easier to follow.

PART

IV

CH

12

Figure 12.9
The AutoCAD 2000 Properties command enables you to view and update all the properties of a selected text object.

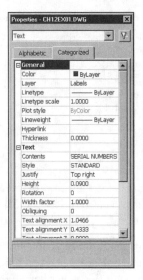

5. Try clicking different justification options. As you click Center or Top Right, for example, the selected text moves instantly. If you don't like the position selected, you may immediately try another one.

6. When you have positioned the text satisfactorily, close the window and press the Esc key twice to de-select this text.

7. Click the FIGURE A label, and open the Properties window again. This time you will change the height of the label.

8. Click Height and change the height value to 0.25. This changes onscreen immediately. Close the Properties window and press Esc twice to deselect this text.

Note

You can also open the Properties window without selecting a specific object. The Properties command may be started by typing **Properties** at the command prompt, by pressing Ctrl+1, or by clicking the Properties button on the Standard toolbar—the button with a hand pointing at the letter A. This approach initially opens a list of the properties of the drawing. When you select a specific text object, the Properties window generates the relevant properties for that object. You may keep the Properties window open while you work in AutoCAD 2000. It will continuously update the Properties information, depending upon which objects are selected.

CHANGING MULTIPLE TEXT OBJECTS

So far, you have made changes to only one object at a time. It is possible to change the style, the height, or any common property of multiple text objects at one pass. The common properties of text objects are all the properties shown in the Properties window when text is selected. (Most of the properties shared by text objects are displayed in Figure 12.9.) If you select a text object and a line object, a smaller set of common properties will be shown, typically only the properties classified as "General" in Figure 12.9.

In this exercise, you will change the Obliquing property (currently set at 0) of all the text in CH12EX01.DWG at once, as shown in Figure 12.10:

EXAMPLE: CHANGING MULTIPLE TEXT OBJECTS

1. Select all the (5) text objects, right-click to open the shortcut menu, and then select the Properties option. When the Properties window opens, you will notice that some fields are blank—Contents, for example. Fields for which the selected text objects have different values are left blank.

2. Click the Obliquing property (which enables you to set the slant of the text) and change the value to **15**. All the text slopes to the right. Your drawing should now look like Figure 12.10.

Caution

If you are practicing with a different drawing, make sure all the text you select is single-line text, or else the Properties window will not display the Obliquing property because it is not a common property shared with multiline text.

3. Close the Properties window and click Esc twice to deselect the text.

Figure 12.10
All the text is slanted at one time using the Properties command.

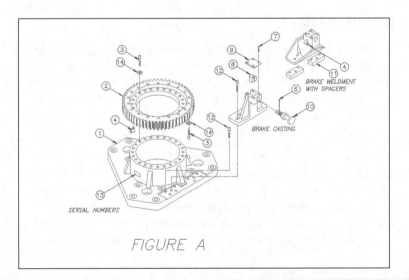

Note

> When you select more than one text object, only the properties that are identical in all objects are displayed in the Properties window; properties that are different for each object are left blank. For example, when you select more than one text object, the "Contents" field will always be blank because the actual words are different in each object; the Geometry fields (X, Y, and Z coordinates) will also be blank. If the text objects are on different layers, the Layer field will be blank, and so on. Even when a field is blank, you may still enter a new value, and it will be applied to all of the selected text objects. For example, if the different text objects are on different layers, you may change them all onto a single layer.

As you can see, it is relatively easy to make global changes to text elements in a drawing. If you have many text objects to change (not just five), you will probably want to use the Quick Select option. This enables you to quickly set up a selection set of objects. To access Quick Select, choose Tools, Quick Select, or type **qselect** at the command prompt. (You may also click the filter funnel icon in the Properties window to open the Quick Select dialog box.) Use the Quick Select dialog box to identify and select the set of text objects that you wish to change. Then proceed with the Properties command. You will work further with the Quick Select command later in this chapter.

You have spent a considerable amount of time reviewing the features and options of single-line text. However, many of these same properties and some of the procedures apply also to multiline text. It is now time to look at multiline text and the ways in which the Mtext command both differs from and complements the Line Text command.

MULTILINE TEXT

It is clear from the previous exercises that each line created using the Text command is a separate object. There is nothing to stop you from adding a series of line objects to create paragraphs of text. Problems arise, however, if lengthy sections of line text are edited; this can require reconstruction of many of the lines. If the text height in a drawing is changed, each individual object may have to be repositioned. Multiline text offers a better solution for entering extended passages of text.

Multiline text— or Mtext—was introduced as a new object in AutoCAD Release 13. Unlike line text, multiline text can store many lines of text as a *single object*. Detailed drawing labels, or Notes that accompany a drawing, frequently run to many lines of text, and Mtext provides a flexible and easy-to-use interface for entering blocks of text. It enables users to edit paragraph text more easily, and Mtext has more extensive formatting options than line text, although both types of text object share many of the same properties.

ADDING MULTILINE TEXT

Like line text, multiline text can be accessed via the Draw menu (Draw, Text, Multiline Text) or the command line. In addition, multiline text is available on the Draw toolbar (see Figure 12.11).

Figure 12.11
Multiline text can be started from the Draw toolbar.

You will use another example file from the CD that accompanies this book to explore multiline text. If you have not already done so, you should copy CH12EX02.DWG onto your hard drive in a practice folder:

EXAMPLE: ADDING MULTILINE TEXT

1. Start AutoCAD 2000 and open CH12EX02.DWG. This is a more complicated mechanical drawing with more extensive labeling than the previous drawing. A label at the center top of the diagram is missing. You will add this text.

2. Click the Multiline Text button on the Draw toolbar, or type **mtext** at the command line. The following prompt appears:

```
Current text style:  "STANDARD"  Text height:  0.1000
Specify first corner:
```

The Specify First Corner prompts you to enter the first corner—the top left margin—of the Mtext window.

Figure 12.12
Before adding multiline text, you position a window in the drawing to define the start point and width of the Mtext.

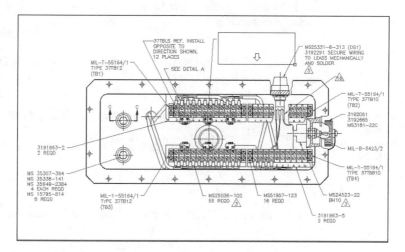

3. Look at Figure 12.12. It shows an outline box in the space where you will be adding the Mtext. Pick a *first* point corresponding to the top left corner of the box. You will be prompted:

```
Specify opposite corner or [Height/Justify/Line spacing/Rotation/Style/Width]:
```

This prompt enables you to change some text settings at the command line before you enter the second corner of the Mtext window. You are offered the same command-line

PART

IV

CH

12

options as in line text—plus some extras: Line Spacing and Width. Type **j** and press Enter to review the Justification options, although you will not actually change any settings at this point.

```
Enter justification [TL/TC/TR/ML/MC/MR/BL/BC/BR] <TL>:
```

As noted in step 2, top left is the default insertion point for multiline text. (You may remember that the line text default is left baseline, as shown in Figure 12.2.)

4. For now, press Enter to accept the default. (You can comfortably ignore these options because they are all available in the Mtext Editor in a much more flexible format.) Pick a *second* point that corresponds to the bottom right corner of the box in Figure 12.12.

The second corner essentially defines your right margin. The depth of the window you create is unimportant because there is no restriction on how many lines of multiline text you can enter. Observe the window created onscreen; this defines your top, left, and right margins.

Note

As you define the Mtext window in the AutoCAD 2000 drawing editor, a hollow arrow appears temporarily in the window. This arrow shows the direction in which the multiline text will flow. If you use the default insertion point for multiline text (top left) the arrow points *downward*. If you choose a *bottom* insertion point (BL/BC/BR), the arrow points *upward*. If you choose a *middle* justification, two arrows display, pointing out from the center of the box to indicate that the text will flow from the center to the top and bottom edges of the window.

As you complete your Mtext window definition, the Multiline Text Editor opens for you to start entering text (see Figure 12.13).

Figure 12.13
The Multiline Text Editor enables you to enter and format paragraphs of text.

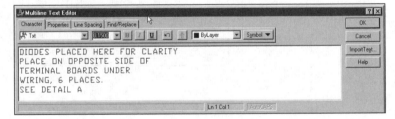

5. Type in the following piece of text, observing the line breaks as shown. You will usually type in Mtext as a continuous string and allow the text editor to use word wrap to make the appropriate breaks. In this example, follow the breaks indicated to fit the text into the space shown.

DIODES PLACED HERE FOR CLARITY
PLACE ON OPPOSITE SIDE OF
TERMINAL BOARDS UNDER
WIRING, 6 PLACES.
SEE DETAIL A

Take a quick look at the Mtext Editor. It provides a standard Windows-type interface with the usual buttons and drop-down list boxes. You can use the standard Windows editing Ctrl-key commands in the Mtext Editor. Additionally, you may convert selected text to upper- or lowercase using the Ctrl and Shift keys.

Ctrl+A	Selects all the text in the eEditor
Ctrl+B	Toggles bold on/off for selected text
Ctrl+C	Copies selected text to the Windows Clipboard
Ctrl+I	Toggles italic on/off for selected text
Ctrl+U	Toggles underline on/off for selected text
Ctrl+V	Pastes contents of Clipboard to selected point
Ctrl+X	Cuts selected text to the Windows Clipboard
Ctrl+Shift+L	Converts selected text to lowercase
Ctrl+Shift+U	Converts selected text to uppercase

You will have a chance to experiment with the Mtext Editor later in this chapter.

6. Click OK to exit the editor and position the paragraph text in the drawing.

ADJUSTING THE MTEXT WINDOW

If you copied exactly the window size shown in Figure 12.12, your text will break awkwardly. This is easily remedied:

EXAMPLE: ADJUSTING THE MTEXT WINDOW

1. Select the new Mtext object so its grips are showing.

2. Click the top-right grip point to activate it.

3. When the grip point turns red and the grip editing commands appear on the command line, stretch the top-right grip until it is over the 25 of MS25331 in the adjacent text label. The text will now position appropriately.

4. Press the Esc key twice to deselect the Mtext object.

PART

IV

CH

12

USING AN EXTERNAL EDITOR FOR MULTILINE TEXT

If you find you don't like the Multiline Text Editor, you can tell AutoCAD to use your preferred editor for multiline text, such as Windows Notepad or Edit.COM. There is little to be gained from choosing a powerful word processor, such as MS Word, as your editor because the formatting codes are not automatically compatible with AutoCAD 2000.

EXAMPLE: USING AN EXTERNAL EDITOR FOR MULTILINE TEXT

1. Select Tools, Options, or type **options** at the command prompt.

2. Select the Files tab, and expand Text Editor, Dictionary, and Font File Names.

3. Click Text Editor Application.

4. Browse to the location of your preferred editor's .EXE file and select it.

Next time you start the Mtext command, your own editor will appear. If you choose to use a third-party editor, use the control codes shown in Table 12.3 to preformat your text to be sure your formats translate into something AutoCAD 2000 understands.

TABLE 12.3 CONTROL CODES FOR EXTERNAL EDITORS

Code	Function
\O	Begin overline
\o	End overline
\L	Begin underline
\l	End underline
\~	Nonbreaking space
\\	Backslash
\{	Open brace
\}	Close brace
\C###	Change to color ###
\Ffontname	Change font to specified fontname
\Hheight	Change text height
\H##x	Change text height by scale factor ##
\S	Stack the following text surrounding the \, #, or ^ symbol
\Tvalue	Adjust kerning, from 0.75 to 4 times
\Qangle	Change oblique angle
\Wvalue	Change width
\A#	Alignment value: (0 = bottom, 1 = center, 2 = top)
\P	End paragraph

To maintain consistency, always use the same editor you used to create the text when you make any changes. If you decide to switch back to the regular Mtext Editor, start the Options command again, click the Remove button to remove the third-party editor, and then type **Internal** as the value for Text Editor application.

FORMATTING AND EDITING MULTILINE TEXT

You may apply formatting to text as you enter it or go back into the Mtext Editor at any time to re-format your text. Typically, you will format the text as you enter it, according to your usual standards. If the text needs to be changed or resized to fit, you can start the Mtext Editor at any time to make the changes.

Tip 92 from *Paul Richardson*	An even easier way to open the Mtext Editor is to simply select the Mtext object and then right-click. When the shortcut menu drops down, select Mtext Edit. The Multiline Text Editor opens.

EXAMPLE: FORMATTING AND EDITING MULTILINE TEXT

1. To open the Mtext Editor, choose Modify, Text, or type **ddedit** at the command prompt and press Enter. You will be prompted:

```
Command: _ddedit
Select an annotation object or [Undo]:
```

2. Select any piece of text in CH12EX02.DWG to experiment with. When you have selected a block of Mtext, the Multiline Text Editor opens and displays that piece of text.

3. Make any desired changes to the text or the formatting and then press OK to return to the drawing editor.

The Ddedit command keeps prompting you to select more text objects; this enables you to edit different pieces of multiline text one after another without having to restart the command. Check out each of the formatting options described here on any (or all) of the text blocks in this drawing. Remember that you can always use the Undo button in the Mtext Editor—or the one on the Standard toolbar—to return any Mtext object to its original settings.

The text-formatting commands are grouped onto four tabs. Let's take a look at each tab in turn.

CHARACTER TAB

Click the Character tab to bring it to the front if it is not already displayed. The Character tab is shown in Figure 12.13. The text you selected is displayed with the default text style (TXT font, height 0.1, and so on). You can override these defaults using the options on this tab.

FONTS   Click the font list box at the left of the Character tab; you will see a list of all the fonts available. This includes standard AutoCAD fonts and Microsoft TrueType fonts, which are used increasingly in AutoCAD drawings. The TrueType fonts are marked with a TT symbol, and the AutoCAD-compiled shape fonts have the drawing dividers symbol. Select all the text (Ctrl+A) or highlight just a part of the text, and then select a new font. You can change the font in a paragraph as often as you like. The text window will immediately display the result. (Remember, you can use the Undo key to reverse the preceding font change.)

TEXT HEIGHT   Next to the font list box is the font height edit box. This field contains the default height for the displayed text. As with text fonts, you can select a portion of text and override the height property with a new height value. Select a word in your text window and then enter a value of 0.05 in the font height list box. Press the Tab or Enter key to display the result. (Undo will undo the preceding text height change.)

If you change a whole block of text, you will observe that the line spacing adjusts proportionately so the text is not too close together or too far apart.

BOLD, ITALIC, AND UNDERLINE   To the right of the height list box are the Bold, Italic, and Underline buttons. These are active only if the current font (or the font of the currently selected text) allows those options. Generally, many of the TrueType fonts allow these options because the font families include a bold, italic, and bold italic version. If an option is not available, AutoCAD 2000 will gray out the button so it can't be selected.

STACKED FRACTIONS   Beyond the Mtext Undo button is a grayed-out button with a fraction on it. You have to add a fraction to activate this button:

EXAMPLE: USING STACKED FRACTIONS

1. In the Mtext Editor, type **2/3** and press the Spacebar. (If the fraction is part of a block of text, always leave a space between the fraction and any preceding numbers so the Mtext Editor knows which part is the fraction.)

   The first time you enter a fraction in the Mtext Editor, AutoCAD 2000 will ask for your preferences for handling stacked fractions.

2. When the AutoStack Properties dialog box appears (see Figure 12.14), check Enable AutoStacking, check Remove leading blank, and click Convert it to a diagonal fraction. Click OK when you are done.

Figure 12.14
The AutoStack Properties dialog box enables you to select your preferred fraction format.

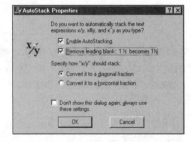

Enabling AutoStacking means the text editor will automatically adjust any numbers separated by ^, /, or # symbols into stacked fractions. Try a few more fractions; notice that the AutoStack Properties dialog box pops up each time. This will get tedious, so when you have seen enough, check Don't show this dialog again, and you won't see it again.

The Stack/Unstack button on the toolbar will remain grayed out until you highlight either a stacked fraction or a string of text formatted as a fraction. You can then toggle the fraction as stacked or unstacked. If a string of numerals with a / in it is formatted as a fraction in error, select the text and right-click to open the shortcut menu. Then click Unstack. In the process, the Mtext Editor usually converts the / to a # sign, and you must change it back manually.

If you wish to disable stacking on a more permanent basis (and you have turned off the AutoStack Properties dialog box), you will have to go via the Stack Properties interface. Highlight a stacked fraction, right-click your mouse, and then choose Properties from the shortcut menu. This opens the Stack Properties dialog box (see Figure 12.15). From there you can open the AutoStack dialog box, via the AutoStack button, and disable stacking.

Figure 12.15
The Stack Properties dialog box enables you to modify fraction style as you work.

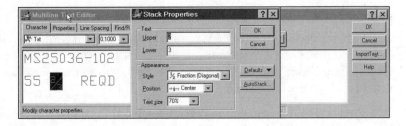

The Stack properties dialog box also enables you to change the fraction settings for the selected fraction. Notice that you can edit the text and fine-tune the style, change the position of the fraction relative to its parent text line, and also vary its size (the default is 70%) relative to the base text. You can save these settings as defaults if you wish.

TEXT COLOR   The Text Color list box enables you to set a color for new text or change the color of selected text. These settings override the default AutoCAD settings for the current text object. You can select as many text strings as you like in a single text object, and specify a different color for each.

SYMBOL   The Symbol button enables you to select and insert symbols that are outside the basic text alphabet. The first three items on the Symbols menu are the traditional AutoCAD symbols:

%%d	Degree symbol	100°
%%p	Plus/minus symbol	±
%%c	Diameter symbol	Ø

The Other option on the Symbols button gives you access to the Windows Character Map (see Figure 12.16). When you click the Other option, the Windows Character Map interface appears. First, use the Select button to select any character(s) you want to insert into the Mtext. Then click the Copy button. This copies the selected character(s) to the

Windows Clipboard. You may now close the Character Map window. Back in the Mtext Editor, place your cursor at the desired insertion point and press Ctrl+V. This copies the contents of the Clipboard into your block of text.

Figure 12.16
You can insert symbol characters into Mtext using the Windows Character Map.

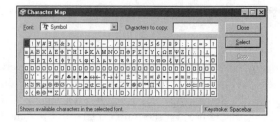

PROPERTIES TAB

Select a new piece of text to edit and open the Mtext Editor again. Now, click the Properties tab to bring it to the front of the editor (see Figure 12.17). The Properties tab gives you some more formatting options, but these apply to the *overall* block of text rather than to the individual characters.

TEXT STYLE The first item on the Properties tab is the text Style list box. This list box shows the default AutoCAD style (STANDARD) and enables you to select from all the currently defined text styles in the drawing. You will review the processes involved in developing a text style in the "Creating Text Styles" section later in this chapter.

Figure 12.17
The Properties tab enables you to change the overall characteristics of multiline text.

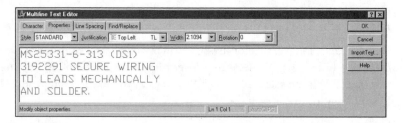

JUSTIFICATION You reviewed briefly the text justification options as you started the first Mtext exercise. Now, click to open the Justify list box and review the nine options. Mtext can be aligned at the left, center, or right of the window; additionally, the text can be top-, bottom-, or middle-aligned relative to the insertion point of the Mtext object.

It should be clear that it is much easier to select or change the text justification in this tab than at the command line. Just click the arrow at the right of the Justification option and select the type of justification you require. The text will reposition in the Mtext Editor to give you a preview of how it will look.

Caution

> If you are aligning multiple-line text with single-line text, you may run into some problems aligning horizontally. This situation can occur when you update an older drawing in which the text was all entered as line text. Particularly if the text is in columnar or tabular format, it is important to align the text baselines. The default vertical position for single-line text relative to the insertion point of the text object is along the *baseline*. This is true for left-, center-, and right-aligned text objects. The closest justification option that multiline text uses is *Bottom*, which aligns the text at the bottom of the lowest part (the descender) of the text object.

WIDTH   The Width option enables you to change the width of the text window you initially specified. The value shown in the width field is the window size corresponding to the points selected onscreen. You can make this wider or narrower as you choose. The drop-down list box contains all the recently selected width values. When you change the width value, the text block in the editor is repositioned to reflect this new value.

At the bottom of the drop-down list is the No Wrap selection. If you choose this option, the Mtext window has no width, and all the text will be entered as a single line unless you add hard returns in the text.

ROTATION   The Rotation option in Mtext is identical to the Rotation option for line text. The drop-down list box, provided in the Properties tab, contains all the values from 0° to 360° in 15-degree increments. You may also enter any other (positive or negative) value of your choice. The Mtext Editor cannot provide a preview of text rotation. You will have to return to the drawing editor to view your new setting.

LINE SPACING TAB

When you practiced adding line text in the early exercises of this chapter there was no variable to control line spacing. This is because line text is automatically spaced at 1 2/3 times the height of the text. With line text, the user has no control over line spacing. Also, when you change the height of the line text, the original spacing remains the same; it does not adjust proportionately as it does with multiline text. The Mtext Line Spacing tab offers you a set of choices for line spacing that are comparable to any other Windows text editors:

- At Least—This is the default option. This option adjusts the space between the lines based upon the height (in units) of the largest character in the line. This can lead to variations in the line spacing in a given set of text.

- Exactly—If you want to control the line spacing for the whole Mtext object, you should select this option. As long as all the text in a drawing is approximately the same height, you can match the line spacing for all text objects.

- Single (1x, and so on)—The default setting is single-space or 1 2/3 times the text height (baseline to baseline). You may change the specification by picking from the preset choices (1.5x and 2x) or enter a value of your choice.

PART

IV

CH

12

It is also possible to enter a fixed value (in units) of 1 or 3, which will not vary even when text height changes.

FIND/REPLACE TAB

This final tab in the Mtext Editor enables you to perform a quick find-and-replace operation on the text that is currently in the Editor.

Click the Find/Replace tab to bring it to the front. The example shown in Figure 12.18 shows a find-and-replace operation involving 3 and Z. You may vary this according to the text that you are editing. Enter the appropriate text for the find and/or replace you want to perform. To find text, click the binoculars icon; the cursor jumps to the first instance. To replace text, click the **A-B** icon on the right of the text input field. Keep pressing the Replace button until all the 3s have been changed.

Figure 12.18
The Find/Replace tab enables you to search for and modify text in individual Mtext objects.

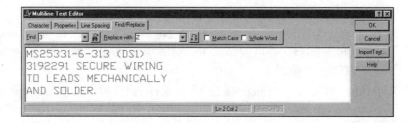

You may narrow your search by being specific about only locating whole words or matching the case of text.

At times you may need to find and replace text throughout the drawing, and it would be rather tedious to have to call up each object in the Mtext Editor and perform this process item by item. Fortunately, AutoCAD 2000 has some other ways of making global changes in a drawing.

CHANGING MTEXT GLOBALLY

Although many changes you make to multiline text apply to only one object, from time to time a term used throughout a drawing will be changed (or misspelled), or the text height throughout the whole drawing needs to be changed. Fortunately, there are ways to accomplish these tasks without unnecessary repetitions of the Mtext command.

FINDING AND REPLACING TEXT

A comprehensive find-and-replace option is available on the Edit menu. This version searches multiple text objects or the entire drawing for specific text strings:

EXAMPLE: FINDING AND REPLACING TEXT

1. With CH12EX02.DWG open in AutoCAD 2000, select <u>E</u>dit, <u>F</u>ind to open the Find and Replace dialog box (see Figure 12.19).

Figure 12.19
The Find and Replace dialog box enables you to search for and modify text in multiple Mtext objects at one time.

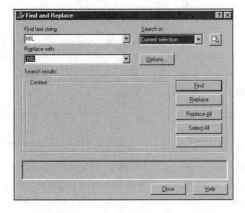

You may select the text you wish to search before opening this dialog box, or else use the Select Objects button to pop out into the drawing editor at any point and select specific objects. If you do not select any objects, AutoCAD 2000 will search all the text in the drawing.

2. Click the Options button and review the different types of objects that will be included. The find and replace may be applied to any of the following:

   - All regular annotation objects, both line text and multiline text
   - Block attribute text
   - Dimension text
   - Hyperlinks and hyperlink descriptions

3. Click to turn off all these text categories except Text (Mtext, Dtext, Text); click to turn on Match Case and then press OK.

4. In the <u>F</u>ind text String field, type **MIL**.

5. In the <u>R</u>eplace With field, type: **NIL**.

6. If you are fairly confident that this selection will not accidentally change text you did not intend to change, click the Replace <u>A</u>ll button.

   Otherwise, use the <u>F</u>ind and the <u>R</u>eplace buttons to step through all the text items in turn. Each item is displayed in the Context field. You can decide whether to replace that item or find the next item.

PART

IV

CH

12

Because the text objects used here are very short, the entire item is displayed in the Context field. In longer text passages, AutoCAD 2000 displays as much text as will fit in the context window to assist you in deciding whether to change a given item of text. To see this in action, you will need to import a longer text file into this drawing.

IMPORTING TEXT The Multiline Text Editor has an option that enables you to import external text files (up to 16K in size) into an AutoCAD 2000 drawing. The imported text becomes an Mtext object, which you may modify in the editor. This means you can save and reuse standard text files in different drawings. Often, many of the drawings in a project will share a standard set of notes, or a legend. Rather than re-creating this file over and over, you may import the same text file into each drawing:

EXAMPLE: IMPORTING TEXT

1. Pan over to the right side of the drawing editor in CH12EX02.DWG.

2. Choose <u>D</u>raw, <u>T</u>ext, <u>M</u>ultiline Text, and pick two points to position the top left and right margins of the Mtext, as shown in Figure 12.20. (You do not need to be too precise because you can adjust the width of the Mtext window in the Properties tab of the Mtext Editor.)

3. When the Multiline Text Editor opens, click the Import Text button, and browse to the \ACAD 2000 \EXPRESS folder.

4. Select the text file AUGI.TXT and press Open. The text file appears in the Mtext Editor.

5. Click the Properties tab and adjust the Width setting to **4.0000**, and then press OK to exit the Mtext Editor.

6. Save CH12EX02.DWG with this imported Mtext object. You will need it for the practice exercises that follow.

Figure 12.20
The Multiline Text Editor enables you to import .TXT or .RTF files from external sources.

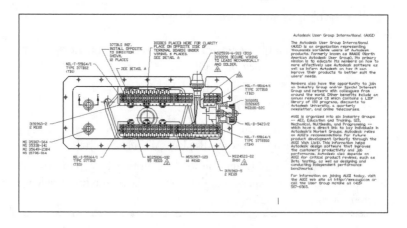

Tip 93 from
Paul Richardson

> If you want the imported text to be converted to uppercase, toggle the AutoCAPS button (at the bottom of the Mtext Editor) to On. This option applies to all text that you add in the Mtext Editor, as well as to imported text files. If you leave this option set to On, it will turn on the Caps Lock function on your keyboard every time you open the Mtext Editor.

Now, try a find-and-replace on this piece of text:

1. Highlight the imported text file (see Figure 12.20), and then choose Edit, Find. (All the options you previously set remain as defaults.)

2. In the Find Text String field, type **Autodesk**.

3. In the Replace With field, type **AutoCAD**.

4. Press Find to locate the first instance of the search text. The Context window fills with text. Press Replace to move on to the next instance and its context.

You may continue through each instance (11 of them) or press Replace All to speed up the process.

EDITING MULTIPLE TEXT OBJECTS

You practiced using the Properties command to change multiple-line text objects earlier in this chapter. You can use the same command to perform multiple Mtext edits at one time. To preselect the text objects in CH12EX02.DWG, you will want to use the AutoCAD 2000's new Quick Select method to create a selection set:

EXAMPLE: EDITING MULTIPLE TEXT OBJECTS

1. Select Tools, Quick Select, or type **qselect** at the command prompt. The Quick Select dialog box opens (see Figure 12.21).

2. Click the Object type arrow to open the list box and select Mtext. At this point, you may narrow your search to Mtext on a specific layer, or color or any of the items listed in the Properties list box. None of these properties is critical in the current selection set.

3. Press OK to return to the drawing editor. All the Mtext is highlighted.

   You may now use the Properties command to modify any common features of these selected Mtext objects.

4. Right-click to open the shortcut menu and then select the Properties option. The Properties window opens and displays all the properties shared by these objects, as shown in Figure 12.22.

5. Click the Style property and select the BOLD style. All the text in the drawing will change immediately to this style.

6. Click the Height property and change the value to **.11**.

7. Close the Properties window and click Esc twice to deselect the Mtext.

Figure 12.22

The AutoCAD 2000 Properties command enables you to view and update the properties of multiple Mtext objects.

The exercise you have just completed demonstrates an elementary example of the combined use of the Quick Select and Properties commands. This methodology provides a very powerful tool for text selection and modification.

USING THE AUTOCAD 2000 SPELLING CHECKER

Because you have an extended block of text in your drawing (CH12EX02.DWG), now is a good time to review AutoCAD 2000's spelling checker.

1. Select the imported Mtext object (AUGI.TXT).

2. Choose Tools, Spelling, or type **spell** at the command prompt. The Check Spelling dialog box opens.

   This spelling checker operates like any standard Windows-type spelling checker. It identifies any words that do not occur in its dictionary, offers alternatives, and allows you to ignore or change the flagged items.

3. Run the spell check on the imported text file. Most of the items flagged are CAD industry-related acronyms, and you should either ignore them or add these items to a custom dictionary.

CUSTOM DICTIONARIES

The spelling checker also enables you to add new words to a custom dictionary. For this option to be functional, a Custom Dictionary must be specified in addition to the Main Dictionary. The Main Dictionary governs the overall language (American English/English English/French) that is checked, and you may not add words to this dictionary; the Custom Dictionary contains all the additional terminology you wish to include as valid. AutoCAD

2000 includes a default custom dictionary SAMPLE.CUS to start you off. It contains a basic set of AutoCAD-related terminology, such as AutoLISP, AutoSketch, and so on.

- If you want to create or use your own custom dictionary, choose Change Dictionaries, Custom Dictionary. Then either type in a dictionary name (with a .CUS extension), or use the Browse button to locate a previously saved dictionary.

- You may edit the Custom Dictionary using the Add and Delete buttons in the Change Dictionaries dialog box.

You have now mastered the fundamentals of adding, formatting, and editing single-line text and multiline text. In the process, you have also experimented with almost all the elements that make up a text style, such as font, height, and rotation. It's time to learn how to put these elements together and to create a text style from scratch.

CREATING TEXT STYLES

Throughout this chapter, you have encountered many references to text style: the ways in which style defines the appearance of text, and the ways in which the default settings may be modified. A text style stores settings for font, text height, and other special effects, such as backward text. Every text object you create is based on a text style, whichever one is current when the text object is created. This section reviews all of the elements and issues pertaining to text styles, with particular attention on the selection of fonts and whether it is best to create many fixed-height styles versus a single flexible height style for each font. After these issues have been considered in some depth, you may try your hand at creating a text style or two and then look at the options available for transporting text styles between different drawings and different users.

AutoCAD Standard Fonts and TrueType Fonts

The most fundamental aspect of a text style is the font (or typeface) that it uses. Two basic types of fonts are supplied with AutoCAD 2000: standard AutoCAD fonts and TrueType fonts.

- Standard fonts—Some examples of the standard AutoCAD fonts are shown in Figure 12.23. Check the User's Guide in the AutoCAD Help system for more information about these standard fonts. In addition to the fonts shown, the standard library of AutoCAD fonts contains several symbol fonts for mapping, meteorology, music, and math. Each font resides in a separate compiled shape file with the name *font*.SHX.

- TrueType fonts—A set of about one hundred TrueType fonts is supplied with AutoCAD 2000; forty of these can be reviewed in a drawing file Truetype.DWG in the \ACAD 2000\SAMPLE folder. The TrueType fonts supplied include: Swiss (an Arial-like font), Dutch (a Times New Roman look-alike), Monospace, Bank Gothic, Commercial Script, and Universal Math Pi.

Figure 12.23
AutoCAD 2000 help provides a list and examples of the standard fonts that are supplied with AutoCAD.

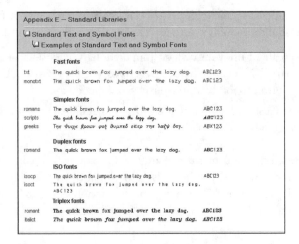

From your experiments with the Mtext Editor, you will be aware that a much more extensive range of TrueType fonts is available to the AutoCAD 2000 user. You have access to the full range of Windows fonts and may select from more than 200 different TrueType fonts.

SOME FONT CONSIDERATIONS

Before creating a text style, you should consider the fonts you typically use in your drawings. Select a few fonts that you will use consistently; this will give a professional look to your drawings. Don't use multiple fonts just because you can. Also consider plotting time when you are selecting fonts.

- Romans is probably the most widely used font for architectural and engineering drawing. You can use this for all your model space work, notes, labels, dimension text, and so on.

- Some users prefer to use a font that simulates a hand-drawn look, such as the TrueType Stylus or Country BluePrint fonts. These fonts add a little style to a drawing but can be more difficult to read.

- If you still use a pen plotter, you would be well advised to stay with standard AutoCAD fonts. TrueType fonts look good but can take many more strokes of the pen to plot.

TITLE BLOCK FONTS

Most companies like to have one or two good-looking fonts for the Title Block. Common choices are Times New Roman (or Dutch) for a font with serifs, and Arial (or Swiss), for a cleaner, sans serif font.

Creating text to match a company logo can be very time consuming. Often the fonts don't quite match or the logo is made up of partial letters. The Express tools provide a program for exploding text, txtexp. This program converts text to a polyline outline, which can then be edited with all the usual AutoCAD commands. When you have the desired outline you can use the Solid Fill hatch pattern to fill in the shapes.

→ For more information on this and other text-related Express tools, see the "The Express Text Menu" section in Chapter 15, "Making Drawing Easier," on page **383**.

TABLE TEXT

If you are creating text that is in a tabular form, you should use a monospaced font, in which the space for each character is the same. This makes all the text and numbers line up vertically. In this situation, you could use either the standard AutoCAD font Monotxt, or the TrueType font Monospace.

SPECIFYING TEXT HEIGHT

After font, text height is the next most significant setting to determine in a text style. There are two distinct schools of thought on how this is best handled:

- Fixed-height text style—This approach prefers to define a new text style with a fixed height for each size of text in a drawing. This approach names each style according to its function. For example, a different style could be created for dimension text, for Labels, one for notes, all with fixed heights. If you are doing a lot of drawings with the same text requirements, this makes some sense. This method can be used to enforce standards for text usage.

- Flexible-height text style—This approach prefers to define a single text style with a text height of 0. It is called a flexible-height text style, and it enables you to define one style for each font used in a drawing (rather than each type of text). For example, the Romans style you used in CH12EX01.DWG is a zero-height style, which uses the ROMANS.SHX font file.

Note

> The Line Text command (Text) and multiline text command (Mtext) respond to fixed-height and zero-height text styles differently. The Line Text command prompts the user for text height *only* if the style is set to 0 height; with a fixed-height style, there is no option to change the height. Multiline text is always flexible and allows you to change text height whichever way the style is defined.

PART

IV

CH

12

If you choose to create fixed height text styles, this is akin to the way styles are used in a word processing program, in which you might create a style for headings, a style for notes, a style for general text, and so on. This process is easy to understand intuitively.

The concept of flexible-height (or zero-height) styles is less easy to grasp. It is as if you created a single style in your word processor for Times New Roman, and then changed the height on-the-fly each time you needed a different size. Nonetheless, after you get used to the idea, this approach works well in a CAD environment. There are some definite advantages to creating zero-height styles:

- A flexible-height text style can be used to create text of any height. Therefore, only one text style is needed per font used in a drawing. This stops the proliferation of differently named text styles in a CAD drawing. Naming the text style to the same name as the font allows users to instantly see what they are getting when selecting a text style.

- Another key reason for using flexible-height styles is for dimension text. With a flexible-height style, the text height of dimension text can be automatically adjusted using the DIMSCALE variable.

CREATING A NEW TEXT STYLE

When you create a new style, it is always based on an existing style. All new AutoCAD 2000 drawings contain a copy of the AutoCAD Standard text style, which uses the TXT font. Start a new drawing and take a look at this style.

EXAMPLE: CREATING A NEW TEXT STYLE

1. Choose File, New, and select the ACAD.DWT template to base the new drawing on.

2. Save the new drawing as **Text Styles.DWG** in your practice folder.

3. Choose Format, Text Style, or type **style** at the command prompt. The Text Style dialog box is displayed, as shown in Figure 12.24.

Figure 12.24
The Text Style dialog box displays the settings of the current text style.

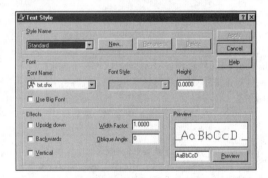

The following attributes of the Standard text style are displayed:

- Style Name—This field allows a style name up to 255 characters.

- Font Name—This list box enables you to select from all the AutoCAD Standard fonts (.SHX files) and the Windows TrueType fonts (prefixed by the TT icon). When you select a font name, the Preview window (at bottom right) immediately displays the font for your review.

- Font Style—This field is an extension of the previous one. For TrueType fonts, you may specify further whether the regular, italic, or bold (as available) is to be used.

- Use Big Font—This check box is accessible only when you are using an .SHX font file; it is not relevant for TrueType fonts. Big Font is a special shape-definition file that is required to create non-ASCII characters, such as Asian text characters.

- Height—AutoCAD 2000's Standard text style is a zero-height style. For a fixed-height style, a character height value is entered here.

- Upside down/Backwards/Vertical—Using these three options, you can develop a text style for use in varied orientations.

- Width Factor—This value applies to the actual character width (expansion or compression). This is a different application from the Mtext width setting, which controls the width of the paragraph of text.

- Oblique Angle—This option enables you to preset the slant of the characters in a text style.

Notice that there is no setting for text justification. The justification defaults of line text and multiline text are AutoCAD 2000 defaults and are not specified in the text style.

CREATING A FLEXIBLE-HEIGHT STYLE

The most versatile multipurpose text style is a flexible-height style. For this approach to work best, you should create a single style for each font you use and give each style the same name as the font. If you create a flexible (zero-height) style for each font you want to use in a drawing, you can use the same style(s) over and over again for any height of text the drawing requires. To start your own library of text styles, create a style for the Romans font.

Caution

You might be tempted to just change the font of the Standard style, but this can get you into trouble later. If you copy geometry from one drawing to another and you have text styles of the same name using different fonts, text objects will use the definition in the current drawing.

PART

IV

CH

12

EXAMPLE: CREATING A FLEXIBLE-HEIGHT STYLE

1. In the Text Style dialog box, click the New button to define a new style name, and type **Romans** in the New Text Style edit box. Then press OK.

2. Click the down arrow on the Font Name list box to scroll down the list box, or type **R** to jump to font names beginning with R, and then select Romans.shx.

3. Skip the Height field. The default value for height is 0.0000; you should leave it at that.

4. In the Effects section, change the Width Factor to **0.8**. This slightly narrows the text characters. (Romans is a font that actually looks better given a width factor. Most TrueType fonts do not improve with width applied.) Leave the other effects as defaults.

5. Press the Apply button now to create your new text style.

6. Press Close to complete the command.

Romans is now the current text style. Any new text you create in this drawing will use the Romans font. Repeat this process for each font you wish to use in the current drawing. Use a new style for each font, and name the style with the same name as the font.

CREATING FIXED-HEIGHT STYLES

Fixed-height styles are created in essentially the same way—but the height is specified using the Height setting, which was described in the previous section. With fixed-height styles, you may also use the font's name in the style name and then add the height value to the name. For example, Romans with 1/8-inch height could be named ROMANS 1_8 or ROMANS ONE-EIGHTH INCH. Note that you may use spaces in style names of AutoCAD 2000, but you may not use slash or inch characters. Naming your text styles in this fashion makes them more multipurpose and ensures that you and others know which style to use.

RENAMING AND DELETING TEXT STYLES   Typically, because of the pressures of production deadlines—to make text fit and to match other users' text on-the-fly—users add and borrow text styles in a rather haphazard fashion. Hopefully you have been inspired to clean up at least the text style naming conventions that you use. You may wish to rename some styles and remove others from your collection. This can be accomplished easily using the Rename and Delete buttons in the Text Style dialog box. When a text style is renamed, the style property of all the text objects in the drawing is changed at the same time.

Note   It is not possible to rename the Standard AutoCAD text style–the Rename button grays out when the Standard style is selected. Additionally, a text style cannot be deleted as long as there are still text objects in the drawing that reference the style; the Delete button is grayed out until all such objects are deleted.

SHARING TEXT STYLES

Text styles are stored in the drawing where they were created. You may be wondering if you have to go through this same text style setup process for each new drawing. Fortunately, there are a couple of ways to avoid this repetition:

- You can create an AutoCAD 2000 template drawing (.DWT) containing all your standard styles. You could save the current practice drawing as a template drawing (File, Save As, and then click the *.DWT option). Then use the template as a basis for all new drawings

- The AutoCAD 2000 Design Center provides another option. You can drag a text style from any drawing to your current drawing. A convenient way to set up your CAD standards is to store your text styles in a clearly named drawing. Store them in a specified folder, on the server if appropriate.

SHARING TEXT STYLES VIA TEMPLATE DRAWING FILES

Template drawings provide an easy method for reusing text styles. A template drawing can store anything a drawing can; it is just used by AutoCAD in a different way. Templates are used as a starting point for a new drawing. AutoCAD has a Template folder with template drawing files designed to conform to various standards. (You probably see these in the Startup dialog box every time you open AutoCAD.)

You can open a template just like a regular drawing file. Often, there is not a lot to actually see in a template because they typically contain nongraphical objects, such as text styles and dimension styles. Choose File, Open, and select Drawing Template file (*.DWT). Browse to the \ACAD 2000\TEMPLATE folder and pick (for example) ACAD.DWT to open. Then save it as TEXT STYLES.DWT.

You can now create as many text styles as you wish in this template. When you have defined your template drawing and saved it to the defined folder for templates, it will appear in the Startup dialog box in the Template folder (see Figure 12.25).

Figure 12.25
A template drawing can be used to start each new drawing you create.

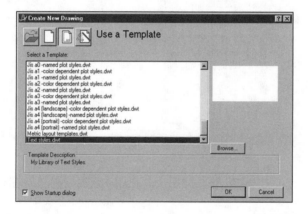

PART
IV
CH
12

Note

If you wish to set up your own folder for templates, you can do so with the Options command. Right-click anywhere and select Options from the menu, or just type **options**. Select the File tab. Scroll down to Drawing Template File Location. You can specify only one folder, so if you want to create your own location, you will lose the path to the default folder, which contains all the template drawings supplied with AutoCAD 2000.

USING THE DESIGN CENTER TO SHARE TEXT STYLES

To get you started, AutoCAD 2000 includes a drawing called TrueType.DWG in the \SAMPLE folder. It contains text styles for all the standard TrueType fonts supplied with AutoCAD 2000. You can copy this nongraphical "content" from one drawing to another:

EXAMPLE: SHARING TEXT STYLES

1. Click the AutoCAD DesignCenter button on the Standard toolbar, or select Tools, AutoCAD DesignCenter from the menus. (You can also type **Ctrl+2** to start the DesignCenter.)

2. Click the Load button on the DesignCenter toolbar. Browse to the \ACAD 2000\SAMPLE folder.

3. Select the TrueType drawing and click Open, or simply double-click the TrueType drawing. In the right window of the DesignCenter, a list of the objects that you copy from a drawing is displayed (see Figure 12.26).

4. Double-click the Text Styles folder. It displays a library of the TrueType text styles.

Figure 12.26
AutoCAD 2000 DesignCenter makes it easy to transfer text styles between drawings.

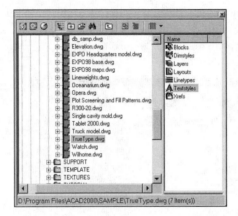

5. Select any fonts in the Text Styles list; drag them to the open drawing area and release them there.

    If you have been following through with this chapter, you probably have a template file open in the drawing editor. You may copy content from drawing files in the DesignCenter into both templates and regular drawing files.

6. Move back into the regular drawing area and open the Text Style dialog box. All the styles that you dragged from the DesignCenter are now included in the Style Name list box.

As you review the text styles you have imported, you should notice a couple of features:

■ Each text style for each of the TrueType fonts is named by its font name: Swiss Light, Monospace Bold, and so on.

■ The text height for all these styles is set to 0, giving you flexible-height text styles.

Here you have a ready-made library of text styles to build from. The drawing itself has a sample of each font, and you may want to print this on your own printer and take a look at it.

When you have developed a library file for DesignCenter or have your Text Styles organized into template drawing files, you won't have to create any more text styles—simply use them.

SUMMARY

AutoCAD 2000 supplies a range of options for adding and modifying annotation in a drawing. This chapter covered the steps involved in adding single lines of text, and also how to add longer blocks of text by efficiently using the Mtext Editor. The chapter reviews everything you need to know about formatting text: how to choose the correct text height, how to position and orient text, how to create the text styles that will work for you, and how to share these styles with other users.

CHAPTER 13

HATCHING

In this chapter

THE HATCH COMMAND

Hatching enables the user to bring a higher level of visual interest to a drawing by embellishing a defined boundary with a pattern. This allows the user to focus on an area of interest, to indicate the use of a particular material, or to differentiate between multiple boundaries formed in the drawing. In earlier versions of AutoCAD, hatching was more of an art than a science, and it was typical that the novice user obtained unexpected results when using this command. Within the last few releases of AutoCAD, the process of hatching a drawing has improved considerably. This chapter describes in detail how to achieve the expected results every time.

Hatching is commonly used to place a repetitive pattern within a defined area, adding graphic detail to the drawing. For example, suppose you are working on a part that is composed of various materials and you want to illustrate graphically where those materials are used in the drawing. The easiest way to do this is with the boundary hatch command, or Bhatch.

You can activate the Bhatch command by selecting Hatch from the Draw toolbar (see Figure 13.1). This opens the Boundary Hatch dialog box, shown in Figure 13.2.

Figure 13.1
You can easily access the Boundary Hatch dialog box for the Bhatch command from the Draw toolbar.

Figure 13.2
All options for defining hatch style and boundary mode are available from the Boundary Hatch dialog box.

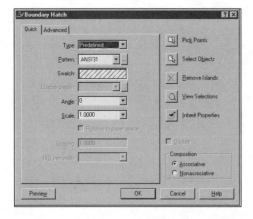

This dialog box contains numerous options that enable you to control how a hatch is created and how the hatch will look. These options are discussed in the next sections.

DEFINING THE HATCH PATTERN STYLE

By selecting the Quick tab, you can set the hatch pattern, scale, and angle. Combined, these establish how the hatch pattern will look in your drawing.

These are the options available under the Quick tab:

- Type—This defines whether the pattern chosen will be a predefined pattern, which is the one supplied with AutoCAD, or a user-defined or custom hatch pattern. Both user-defined and custom hatch patterns will be discussed later in this chapter.

→ You may want to reference "Creating Your Own Hatch Patterns" later in this chapter to learn more about build-your-own hatch patterns.

- Pattern—This option enables you to select which predefined pattern will be applied to the hatch boundary. The pattern can be selected either by name from the pop-up list or by graphically selecting a pattern by choosing the Pattern ellipses button. This opens the Hatch Pattern Palette, from which you can choose the desired pattern. Four different types of patterns are available:

  - ANSI—The patterns shown in Figue 13.3 represent a repetitive set of symbols or lines that make up a generic hatch pattern that is commonly used to represent a building material such as steel, copper, and aluminum. These typically should be scaled in relation to the plot scale.

Figure 13.3
The ANSI hatch patterns are typically used to represent a generic building material.

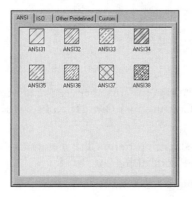

  - ISO—The ISO, or Metric, patterns are specifically designed for use on metric drawings. These patterns are based on millimeters as the drawing units (see Figure 13.4). Because of this, the ISO pen width can be set when these patterns are used. The ISO Pen Width setting sets the scale equal to that of the chosen pen width, which is ideal when working with metric drawings due to the large-scale factors used.

  - Other Predefined—Many of these patterns represent architectural building materials and are defined by a 1 to 1 scale factor. For example, the hatch pattern AR-B88 at a scale of 1 creates a pattern of blocks that are 8 inches wide by 8 inches long (see Figure 13.5). .

PART

IV

CH

13

Figure 13.4
The ISO hatch patterns are used when working with a metric drawing or other drawing with large scale factors.

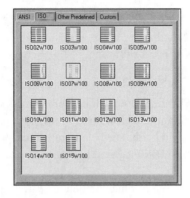

Figure 13.5
Other predefined hatch patterns can designate a specific building material type in look and size.

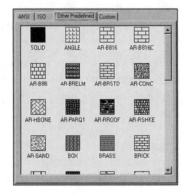

- Custom—After you create custom patterns, they are stored here. These pattern types will be discussed in "Creating Your Own Hatch Patterns" later in this chapter.

- Swatch—This displays the selected hatch pattern. Click the swatch to view the patterns available from the Hatch Pattern Palette dialog box.

- Custom pattern—This enables you to select the custom pattern. This option is available only when Custom is selected from the Type pull-down menu.

- Angle—This defines the angle at which the hatch pattern will be placed into the drawing.

- Scale—This sets the scale of the hatch pattern based on the current scale of the drawing.

- Relative to Paper Space—This determines whether the scale of the pattern is relative to the paper space viewport scale. When this option is off, the scale is defined by the current drawing scale. This option is available only when creating a hatch in a layout view. (See Chapter 14, "Dimensioning," for more information on layouts.)

LOOKING AT THE ADVANCED HATCH OPTIONS

Choosing the Advanced tab gives options to define how AutoCAD will hatch the selected boundary and how you want to retain the boundary used to determine the hatch. Essentially, there are three different ways to define a hatch boundary. You can select the boundary itself (if the boundary is a polyline or a region), have AutoCAD determine the boundary for you, or select points to make up a boundary called the direct hatch option.

USING THE DIRECT HATCH OPTION

Use the direct hatch option to specifically place a hatch pattern into an area where the first two options will not work. These instances might occur when the hatch boundary is not closed or when the objects you want to use to define the boundary do not form a closed boundary.

Here are the steps used to place a hatch pattern using the direct hatch option by selecting points in the drawing:

EXAMPLE: USING THE DIRECT HATCH OPTION

1. Start the Hatch command by typing the command at the command line, which displays the following prompt:

   ```
   Enter a pattern name or [?/Solid/User defined] <ANSI31>:
   ```

Tip 94 from
Ron House

A list of hatch patterns can be viewed by typing a question mark (**?**) at this prompt and pressing Enter. (See Table 13.1 for a complete list of hatch pattern names and descriptions.)

A solid fill can be applied to the hatch boundary in place of a pattern by typing **S** at the prompt.

2. Type the name of the pattern you want to use and press Enter.
3. Specify the hatch scale and angle by using <u>S</u>cale and Angle at the corresponding prompts.
4. At the following prompt, press Enter to activate the direct hatch option:

   ```
   Select objects to define hatch boundary or <direct hatch>,
   Select objects: <Enter>
   ```

5. The direct hatch option enables you to create a polyline that defines the hatch boundary. First, AutoCAD will prompt you to retain the polyline boundary:

   ```
   Retain polyline boundary? [Yes/No] <N>:
   ```

6. Answer the prompt to view the direct hatch polyline options:

   ```
   Specify next point or [Arc/Close/Length/Undo]:
   ```

PART

IV

CH

13

> **Note**
>
> The direct hatch polyline options are the same as those used to place a polyline into the drawing. See Chapter 6, "Complex Drawing Objects," for details on how to place a polyline in a drawing. Be certain to use the Close polyline option to ensure that the boundary is closed.

7. Choose an option or pick points in the drawing to determine the extent of the hatch boundary.

   After closing the polyline boundary with the Close option, AutoCAD will prompt you to place another boundary or to apply the hatch.

Table 13.1 lists the available hatch pattern names and descriptions that can be used with the direct hatch option.

TABLE 13.1   HATCH PATTERN NAMES AND DESCRIPTIONS

Name	Description
SOLID	Solid fill
ANGLE	Angle steel
ANSI31	ANSI Iron, Brick, Stone masonry
ANSI32	ANSI Steel
ANSI33	ANSI Bronze, Brass, Copper
ANSI34	ANSI Plastic, Rubber
ANSI35	ANSI Fire brick, Refractory material
ANSI36	ANSI Marble, Slate, Glass
ANSI37	ANSI Lead, Zinc, Magnesium, Sound/Heat/Elec Insulation
ANSI38	ANSI Aluminum
AR-B816	8x16 Block elevation stretcher bond
AR-B816C	8x16 Block elevation stretcher bond with mortar joints
AR-B88	8x8 Block elevation stretcher bond
AR-BRELM	Standard brick elevation english bond with mortar joints
AR-BRSTD	Standard brick elevation stretcher bond
AR-CONC	Random dot and stone pattern
AR-HBONE	Standard brick herringbone pattern @ 45°
AR-PARQ1	2x12 Parquet flooring: pattern of 12×12
AR-RROOF	Roof shingle texture
AR-RSHKE	Roof wood shake texture

Name	Description
AR-SAND	Random dot pattern
BOX	Box steel
BRASS	Brass material
BRICK	Brick or masonry-type surface
BRSTONE	Brick and stone
CLAY	Clay material
CORK	Cork material
CROSS	A series of crosses
DASH	Dashed lines
DOLMIT	Geological rock layering
DOTS	A series of dots
EARTH	Earth or ground (subterranean)
ESCHER	Escher pattern
FLEX	Flexible material
GRASS	Grass area
GRATE	Grated area
HEX	Hexagons
HONEY	Honeycomb pattern
HOUND	Houndstooth check
INSUL	Insulation material
ACAD_ISO02W100	dashed line
ACAD_ISO03W100	dashed space line
ACAD_ISO04W100	long dashed dotted line
ACAD_ISO05W100	long dashed double dotted line
ACAD_ISO06W100	long dashed triplicate dotted line
ACAD_ISO07W100	dotted line
ACAD_ISO08W100	long dashed short dashed line
ACAD_ISO09W100	long dashed double-short-dashed line
ACAD_ISO10W100	dashed dotted line
ACAD_ISO11W100	double-dashed dotted line
ACAD_ISO12W100	dashed double-dotted line

continues

TABLE 13.1   CONTINUED

Name	Description
ACAD_ISO13W100	double-dashed double-dotted line
ACAD_ISO14W100	dashed triplicate-dotted line
ACAD_ISO15W100	double-dashed triplicate-dotted line
LINE	Parallel horizontal lines
MUDST	Mud and sand
NET	Horizontal / vertical grid
NET3	Network pattern 0-60-120
PLAST	Plastic material
PLASTI	Plastic material
SACNCR	Concrete
SQUARE	Small aligned squares
STARS	Star of David
STEEL	Steel material
SWAMP	Swampy area
TRANS	Heat transfer material
TRIANG	Equilateral triangles
ZIGZAG	Staircase effect

Tip 95 from
Ron House

If you select the objects that make up a hatch boundary and the objects overlap, you might `end up with some unexpected results. In other words, the pattern may not completely fill the selected boundary or the pattern may not be complete. It is typically best if the end-points of the objects match exactly to form the boundary. Try defining the same boundary with the direct hatch method for better results.

If you choose to have AutoCAD create the boundary (which may find be the quickest method), the options on the Advanced tab define how that boundary is calculated. Before learning about these options, take a look at the alternatives you have to place the hatch into the drawing. These methods and options are available on the right side of the Boundary Hatch dialog box under the Advanced tab:

■ Pick Points—This determines the hatching boundary from the existing objects within a closed area. How this boundary is determined depends on the settings based on the Island Detection mode, which is set from the Advanced Options tab, discussed later in this chapter.

- Select Objects—This selects the objects used to define the hatch boundary. If text is selected during this mode, the hatch is placed around the text so the text is visible.

Tip 96 from *Ron House*	Hatching does not pass through text, attributes, solids, or shapes when selected by the Select Objects hatching mode.

Figure 13.6 helps illustrate the Select Objects feature when hatching around text. The objects on the left have been hatched using the Pick Point option, which did not detect the text object within the rectangle. Using the Select Object option, you can select the text with the other objects. Therefore, AutoCAD avoids placing the pattern on top of its boundary, shown on the right.

Figure 13.6
Text placed within a hatch boundary will be avoided if selected during the Bhatch Select Objects mode.

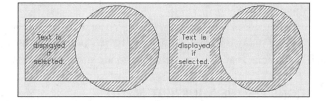

- Remove Islands—Islands are boundaries found inside the outermost boundary, and you can define whether they will be hatched. After a hatch boundary has been initially defined to contain islands, this option allows you to remove any or all of the islands from the selection.

- View Selections—You can view the selection made with this option. The selections are highlighted, making it easy to view the overall selection group.

- Inherit Properties—This option enables you to inherit the properties from an existing hatch after selecting the hatch pattern.

- Double—The Double option is available only when the Type is set to User Defined from the Quick tab. This creates a crosshatch, placing lines perpendicular to the original hatch lines.

- Composition—This defines the hatch boundary characteristics, either Associative or Nonassociative.

Here are the definitions of the two Composition options:

- Associative—This type of hatch updates to match the new boundary area when the hatch boundary is modified.

- Nonassociative—This hatch type is static and will not update. It remains in its initial position regardless of changes made to the hatch boundary.

The following steps are used to create a user-defined cross-hatched area:

PART

IV

CH

13

EXAMPLE: CREATING A USER-DEFINED CROSS-HATCHED AREA

1. Type **Bhatch** at the command line or choose the bHatch button from the Draw toolbar.

2. Set the type of hatch pattern to User Defined from the Type pull-down menu.

3. Note that the Double option is now available. Toggle this option on by selecting the Double checkbox.

4. Set the desired angle and spacing and then click on the Associative composition option radio button.

5. Use any of the hatch-placement options to define the boundary for this hatch. Press Enter to return to the Boundary Hatch dialog box. Use the Preview option to view the hatch pattern before it is applied to the drawing.

6. Once you are satisfied with the appearance of the hatch, choose the OK button to apply the hatch to the drawing.

The process of choosing many of these options can be streamlined by using the Bhatch shortcut menu. The options available from this menu are discussed in the next section.

SETTING HATCH OPTIONS VIA THE SHORTCUT MENU

The Bhatch shortcut menu can be accessed by right-clicking while using any of the Pick Points, Select Objects, and Remove Island boundary placement options from the dialog box (see Figure 13.7). This makes it easy to toggle between the Pick Internal Point and Select Objects boundary selection options when defining multiple hatch boundaries.

Figure 13.7
From the Pick Points shortcut menu, you can undo the last or all point selections, change the selection method and the island detection style, or preview the hatch.

- Enter—Selecting this option returns you to the Boundary Hatch dialog box.

- Undo Last Select/Pick—This undoes the last selection or pick, enabling you to remove the last selection but not the entire selection.

- Clear All—This clears the entire selection and enables you to start anew.

- Pick Internal Point—This default option enables you to return to picking an internal point.

- Select Objects—This toggles the selection mode from Pick Point to Select Objects mode.

- Normal, Outer, and Ignore Island Detection—These modes determine how islands are detected, thus defining how the area will be hatched. Having these modes available on the shortcut menu enables you to quickly toggle among the various modes. These options are covered in more detail later in this chapter.

- Preview—This enables you to preview the hatch based on the definition of the boundary area up to this point.

DEFINING THE ISLAND DETECTION STYLE

From the Advanced tab, you can define the way islands are defined within the selected boundary (see Figure 13.8). Here are the options available:

Figure 13.8
The Advanced tab on the Boundary Hatch dialog box contains options that define how objects within boundaries, called islands, are hatched, as well as how AutoCAD detects them.

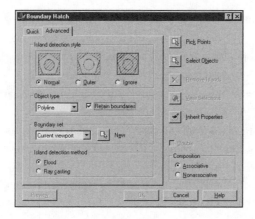

- Island Detection Style—This determines how the area will be hatched. Three styles are available:
  - Normal—This style hatches every other area or boundary.
  - Outer—Only the outermost boundary is hatched.
  - Ignore—Everything inside the outermost boundary is hatched.

These options are used to modify the placement of a hatch boundary, depending on the area the hatch is applied to. For example, suppose you are trying to hatch a part section that has a recessed area with holes. The island detection modes could quickly be set by using the shortcut menu to define how the area will be hatched. The next example illustrates the differences between these island detection styles:

EXAMPLE: DEFINING THE APPEARANCE OF A HATCH USING ISLAND DETECTION STYLES

1. Create a new drawing using the acad.dwt template.

2. Draw a rectangle that contains a number of circles. Enclose this rectangle within another larger rectangle, as shown in Figure 13.9.

PART

IV

CH

13

Figure 13.9
This figure shows the different island detection styles available with the Bhatch command.

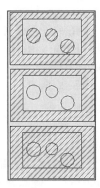

3. Activate the Bhatch command and use the default options for type, pattern, angle, and scale.

4. Click on the Advanced tab to view the Island detection style options, for which the default option is Normal.

5. Choose the Select Objects boundary placement option and window around both the rectangle and circles.

6. Right-click and select Preview from the shortcut menu. Your drawing should look like the top figure shown in Figure 13.9, in which every other boundary is hatched.

7. Right-click again, select the Outer island detection style from the Advanced tab, and select the Preview button. This time, the hatch should change to look like the middle hatched boundary shown in Figure 13.9.

8. Finally, right-click and select the Ignore Island Detection option and then select the Preview button. The hatch boundary should have changed and should look similar to the bottom boundary shown in Figure 13.9.

The last island-detection mode simply ignores any islands or boundaries detected within the outer boundary, giving you more control over the way a hatch is placed in the drawing.

Tip 97 from
Ron House

Hatching concave curves using either the Outer or the Ignore hatching styles can typically give inconsistent results.

In addition to the island-detection options, these boundary options are available under the Advanced tab from the Boundary Hatch dialog box:

■ Object Type/Retain Boundaries—When the Retain Boundaries button is selected, the boundary used to define the area that is hatched can be converted into either a polyline or a region. You can select which boundary you prefer from the Object Type pull-down menu, which is available only when you select the Retain Boundaries button.

- Boundary Set—This option defines what AutoCAD will use to determine the hatch boundary. When the Pick Points mode is used to define the boundary, AutoCAD analyzes everything in the current viewport. This means you can disregard certain items from consideration in the creation of the hatch boundary without having to remove those items. This option has no effect if you choose the Select Objects mode to create the hatching boundary. There are three separate ways to define what is used to determine the boundary:

  - Current Viewport—AutoCAD uses everything in the current viewport to define the boundary. This is the default option.

  - New—This enables you to pick which objects you want to use to determine the boundary. When you have selected the objects, use the Pick Points option to define the hatching boundary. AutoCAD ignores all objects other than those selected to establish the boundary.

  - Existing Set—The existing set of objects is used to determine the boundary. This is available only after you have used the New option to select the objects defining the boundary. The existing set is used until you select the New option to create a new set of objects to define the boundary, which then replaces the previous set.

Tip 98 from	Only the items selected in the boundary set are considered to create a boundary when
Ron House	using the Pick Points boundary creation mode.

SETTING THE ISLAND DETECTION METHOD

The last set of options available under the Advanced tab are those that define how the islands are determined in the hatch boundary:

These two options are used in determining islands:

- Flood—This option allows the islands found to be considered as boundary objects.

- Ray Casting—This determines the boundary by "casting" a line from the point you pick until an object is found, and then outlines the boundary in a counter-clockwise direction. The direction the ray is initially cast can be set by running the –Bhatch command from the command line.

PART

IV

CH

13

Tip 99 from	Setting the ray casting direction is not available from the Bhatch dialog box. Remember that
Ron House	island detection is turned off during ray casting.

The following are the prompts you'll see when directing the direction of the ray accessed from the Advanced options:

```
Command: -bhatch

Current hatch pattern:  ANSI31

Specify internal point or [Properties/Select/Remove islands/Advanced]: A

Enter an option [Boundary set/Retain boundary/Island
detection/Style/Associativity]:I

Do you want island detection? [Yes/No] <Y>: N

Enter type of ray casting [Nearest/+X/-X/+Y/-Y/Angle] <Nearest>:
```

The Nearest option finds the nearest object from the point that was picked. These options—+X, –X, +Y, and –Y—define the ray direction along the x and y axes. The last option, Angle, allows the ray to be cast at a specific angle.

As with all object types in AutoCAD, if it can be drawn, then it can be edited. This holds true for hatching, which the next section discusses in detail.

EDITING A HATCH PATTERN

To edit an existing hatch pattern placed in a drawing, use the Hatchedit command. To edit a hatch using this command, select the Modify pull-down menu and click the Hatch option.

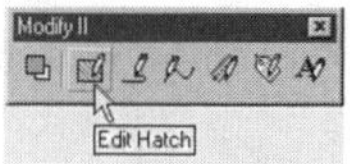

Figure 13.10
You can also access the HatchEdit command from the Modify II toolbar.

Tip 100 from
Ron House

You may find it quicker to access this command using Grips. Apply Grips the hatch pattern you wish to edit, then right-click and select <u>H</u>atch Edit… from the menu.

Using this command you will be prompted to select an existing hatch object from the drawing. A dialog box similar to the one used to place the hatch appears, with some of the options grayed out (shown in Figure 13.11).

From here you can change the type, pattern, angle, scale, and composition of the hatch object. After you have made the modifications inside the dialog box, select the OK button to update the hatch object. Selecting the Advanced tab enables you to modify the island detection style of the hatch.

Figure 13.11
You can quickly edit existing hatch objects with the Hatch Edit dialog box.

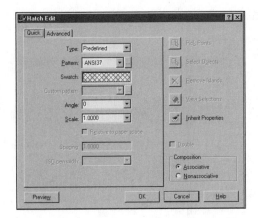

Tip 101 from

Ron House

Hatch objects can also be redefined using the Ddmodify command. After selecting the hatch object, the Hatch Edit dialog box appears to modify.

Another quick way to edit a hatch pattern is to use the Properties window. This window give you access to all the Hatch properties, making it easy to edit an existing hatch pattern. The following example walks you through the steps using this feature to edit the pattern:

EXAMPLE: USING THE PROPERTIES WINDOW TO EDIT A HATCH PATTERN

1. Open the drawing ch13_01.dwg that you copied from the companion CD.

2. Magnify the front entrance area of the house. Select the honeycomb brick hatch pattern shown in Figure 13.12.

Figure 13.12
This honeycomb hatch pattern resembling brick inset pavers can easily be changed to a herring bone pattern using the Hatch Edit command.

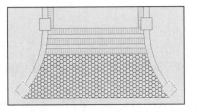

PART

IV

CH

13

3. Right-click and choose Properties from the shortcut menu. From the Properties window, you can modify numerous properties of the hatch (see Figure 13.13).

4. To modify the pattern, click the pattern name, and then click the ellipses button that appears.

5. The Hatch Pattern Palette appears from which you can select another pattern. Select the AR-HBONE pattern and click the OK button.

Figure 13.13
An existing hatch can easily be modified using the Properties window.

6. Using the Properties window, change the scale for the pattern to a value of 1.0. The hatch pattern will automatically update.

7. The type of hatch pattern can also be modified from the Properties window. Click the type and then click the ellipsis button, which opens the Hatch Pattern Type dialog box (see Figure 13.14).

Figure 13.14
The hatch pattern type can also be modified by selecting Type from the Properties window.

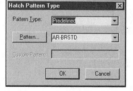

8. You can change the hatch type to Predefined, User-defined, or Custom.

9. After you have completed making your changes to the hatch pattern, close the Properties window and press the Esc key twice to clear the grips.

You can also use the Properties window to edit the properties of any object, not just hatch patterns.

Now that you know how to redefine a hatch pattern, continue on to the next section to learn how to edit existing hatch boundaries.

EDITING HATCH BOUNDARIES

As the drawing is updated throughout the design cycle, you may need to modify existing hatch boundaries. By placing grips on a hatch boundary and using the Stretch command to modify the boundary, AutoCAD automatically revises the hatch associated with the boundary, as shown in Figure 13.15.

Figure 13.15
When modifying an associative hatch boundary, the hatch dynamically updates to fill the stretched hatch boundary.

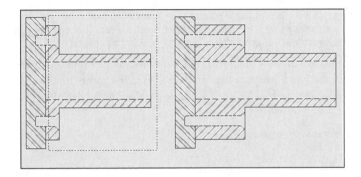

Tip 102 from
Ron House

If the Retain Boundaries option was off when the hatch was created, objects that were used to create the boundary can be modified and cause the associate hatch to update as long as no holes are created in the boundary. If the Retain Boundaries option was on, only the polyline created with the hatch can be modified.

The more you work with AutoCAD, the greater the odds that you will need to work with older drawings. AutoCAD 14 introduced a new polyline and hatch object type, one that was optimized and has some significant improvements over the old polyline and hatch patterns. The following section discusses how to convert the older objects into the new format.

USING THE CONVERT COMMAND TO OPTIMIZE YOUR DRAWING

With the release of AutoCAD 14, both hatch and polyline objects were updated to an enhanced format, reducing the amount of memory and disk space required for a drawing. If you are working with a drawing created before Release 14, you may wish to use the Convert command to update the drawing's hatch and polyline objects, reducing the size of the drawing. You can access this command by typing **CONVERT** at the command line.

→ Refer to the section "Converting Older AutoCAD Drawing Files Containing Polylines" in Chapter 6, "Complex Drawing Objects," for more information and an example of how to use the Convert command.

Now that you have worked with the Bhatch command and its options, the next section investigates what it takes to create your own hatch patterns.

CREATING YOUR OWN HATCH PATTERNS

It can be a rather elaborate process to create your own hatch patterns, adding to the 67 hatch patterns provided in AutoCAD. Sometimes, however, a predefined pattern in

AutoCAD just won't do. Maybe you want to use a pattern that better illustrates a specific material or new technique used on the project, and you are willing to invest the time and effort to create your own hatch pattern. So let's spend some time and look at this process.

→ If you find you want a different hatch pattern than AutoCAD provides but you don't necessarily want to create your own hatch pattern, try using the Super Hatch Express Tool described in the "Using the Super Hatch Command to Create Hatch Patterns" section later in this chapter.

Hatch patterns are defined in an external file called ACAD.PAT. This file contains the definitions of all the hatch patterns used in AutoCAD. To modify this file, you will need to open it with a text editor, such as Windows Notepad. Here is the definition for the CROSS hatch pattern:

```
*CROSS, A series of crosses
0, 0,0, .25,.25, .125,-.375
90, .0625,-.0625, .25,.25, .125,-.375
```

You can see that three sentences of text make up the hatch pattern, and each line depicts what is called a *line family*. Each line family in a pattern definition can contain up to 80 characters, and blank lines are ignored within the pattern definition. The first line family defines the name and description of the pattern, and the next two line families represent an actual line in the pattern. The first line family describes the horizontal portion of the pattern, and the second defines the vertical portion.

Each line family consists of four numbers or coordinates, each separated by a space. The first coordinate value, 0.25, defines the angle of the first line in the hatch pattern. The next coordinate defines the origin of the first line family, which is used to reference other line families that make up the entire pattern. The following set of coordinates represents the spacing of the line family. The first coordinate value, or delta-x, defines the spacing in the direction of the hatch. Delta-y, or the second value in this coordinate, indicates the perpendicular spacing, or create spacing between the line families of this hatch pattern.

The last value denotes the actual line that draws the hatch pattern. The positive value represents the length of the line, and a negative value indicates the spacing between the line segments drawn. Note that both of these line families repeat the spacing and line values after specifying their angle and origin, which is illustrated in Figure 13.16.

Figure 13.16
This figure illustrates the spacing indicated by the hatch pattern definition.

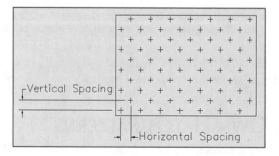

Tip 103 from
Ron House

> You can also document your hatch patterns by entering descriptive text after typing a semi-colon. AutoCAD ignores any text to the right of a semicolon in a line family.

The Express Tools, which enhance a multitude of functions in AutoCAD 2000, also contain a tool called Super Hatch. This Express Tool simplifies the process of creating a hatch pattern, discussed in the next section.

USING THE SUPER HATCH COMMAND TO CREATE HATCH PATTERNS

Included with the bonus routines shipped with AutoCAD 2000 is a command called Super Hatch. This command makes the process of creating custom hatch patterns simpler by using images, blocks, wblocks, externally referenced files, or an object called a wipeout as the hatch pattern. It also makes the process of creating a new hatch pattern simpler by using objects in the drawing or actual raster images to create the hatch. This allows you to avoid typing alphanumeric code to define the appearance of a hatch pattern. The hatch pattern can be defined graphically, which is much easier to do and better-looking if you have an image that resembles the pattern you want to use.

Tip 104 from
Ron House

> A wipeout is a polygon with a white, solid fill that can be used to hide or "wipe out" other objects in the drawing so they do not display.
>
> See "Express Tools" in Chapter 15, "Making Drawing Easier," for more information on the wipeout tool.

This tool can be launched by selecting the Super Hatch command from the Bonus toolbar or by choosing the Super Hatch option from the Express pull-down menu (see Figure 13.17).

Figure 13.17
You can choose the Super Hatch Option from the Express pull-down menu.

PART
IV
CH
13

Let's use the Super Hatch command to create a hatch pattern using an image in the next example.

EXAMPLE: CREATING A HATCH PATTERN USING AN IMAGE

1. Using the ch13_01.dwg from the previous example, create a marble hatch pattern using the grybrick.tga raster image.

2. Select the Super Hatch command from the Express pull-down menu, Draw sub-menu, or choose it from the Express Standard toolbar. Figure 13.18 shows the interface for the Super Hatch command.

Figure 13.18
The Super Hatch dialog box, which enables you to use objects from the drawing or pre-defined images to quickly create hatch patterns.

3. In the Select Image File dialog box, click the Image button and select the image grybrick.tga, found in the Program Files\ACAD2000\Textures subdirectory (see Figure 13.19).

Figure 13.19
The Super Hatch command can use any image from multiple formats to define a hatch pattern.

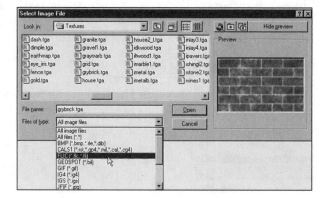

4. Click OK to accept the image, which opens the Image dialog box. You can set the image insertion point, scale, and rotation angle from here, or you can specify these values onscreen (see Figure 13.20).

5. Set the image insertion point to:
```
X = 100 feet 0 inches
Y = 18 feet 6 7/8 inches
Z = 0
```

6. Set the scale for the image to 30° and rotation angle for the image to 0° and click the OK button.

Figure 13.20
You can set the insertion point, scale, and rotation angle of the image for the hatch pattern using the Super Hatch command.

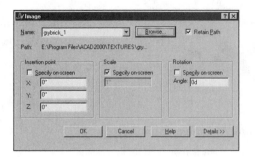

7. You will be prompted to accept the position of the image:

   `Is the placement of this IMAGE acceptable? [Yes/No] <Yes>:`

   If you reply No to the prompt, AutoCAD will repeat steps 2 through 4 to allow you to re-enter the correct values.

8. If you answer Yes to the prompt, AutoCAD prompts you to pick a point inside the area that you want to hatch to define the hatch boundary. Select a point near the center of the entryway, shown in Figure 13.21.

Figure 13.21
This figure illustrates the process of picking a point within a group of objects used to define the hatch boundary for the image.

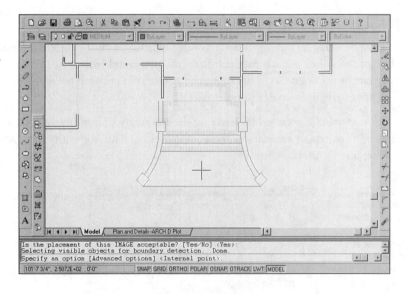

PART

IV

CH

13

9. Press Enter to accept the proposed hatch boundary. You should see something similar to what is shown in Figure 13.22.

Figure 13.22
Using an image to hatch the entry way for a house by using the Super Hatch command Express Tool.

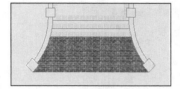

After placing the hatch, AutoCAD displays this prompt:

`Use TFRAMES to toggle object frames on and off.`

When an image is used instead of a hatch pattern to create a hatch, Tframes are used to represent the extents of each image used in the hatch. If you would prefer that the Tframes not show on the drawing, use the Tframes command to toggle off the display of the image frames.

Another object uses the ray casting method mentioned earlier in this chapter to determine a boundary. Although no hatch pattern is placed within this boundary, it has a number of uses when dealing with abstract shapes enclosed within a boundary. The following section discusses the use of these object types.

USING POLYLINES TO CREATE BOUNDARIES

The ray-casting technique to determine a boundary is also used by the Boundary command. Rather than place a hatch pattern within the newfound boundary, this command creates a polyline at the boundary. This command is useful in creating polylines that are formed by the boundary made up of multiple objects.

This command is accessed by selecting the Boundary option from the Draw pull-down menu, or by typing **Boundary** at the command line. This opens the Boundary Creation dialog box shown in Figure 13.23.

Figure 13.23
You can use the options available within the Boundary Creation dialog box to place a polyline or region where a boundary is found.

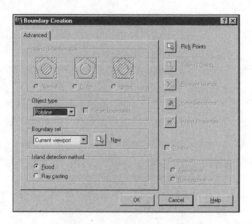

Many of the options available here are similar to those supplied with the Bhatch command. One specific difference is the object types that can be created from this command. There are two options: Polylines and Regions.

→ Regions are composite objects formed as a single object, which can be created by performing various Boolean functions to create the final shape. These object types are covered in Chapter 23, "Visualization."

The Boundary command can be used to define a boundary to which you do not want a hatch pattern applied, but that you do want the ray-casting feature to create for you.

SUMMARY

Although many options are available while hatching, you can greatly enhance the look of your drawings with minimal practice. Take care not to overload your drawings with excessive hatch patterns, which can detract from your drawings main emphasis. Use the Boundary command to create a polyline boundary formed by numerous objects.

The next chapter discusses creating dimensions and all aspects of dimensioning the drawing.

CHAPTER 14

DIMENSIONING

In this chapter

DIMENSIONING BASICS

In the dim and distant days of early AutoCAD, dimensioning was one of the most troublesome aspects of the application. There was a host of cryptic dimension variables to memorize, tricky calculations, constant switching of settings, and arcane command-line functions. Most users never managed to master more than a few of the variables involved, if at all. Since AutoCAD R11—which introduced the concept of dimension styles—the handling of dimensioning has improved with each subsequent release, culminating in the AutoCAD 2000 Dimension Style Manager. With this new interface, and with the excellent addition of the Quick Dimension command, dimensioning has become an almost enjoyable experience.

Note

> Although the old-style dimension mode (DIM mode) is still available in AutoCAD 2000, it is now regarded as obsolete and is not covered in this chapter. If you need more information on DIM mode, look under "DIM and DIM1" in the AutoCAD 2000 online help.

You will learn about dimension styles in considerable detail later in the chapter. Before you start to create dimension styles, you should gain a better understanding of the types of dimensions you will be working with. First, let's open a drawing and try out some of the basic dimensioning commands. For this practice, you should open the first example file (CH14EX01.DWG) from the CD that accompanies this book. Use this simple mechanical drawing to step through the basic dimensioning commands on the Dimension toolbar and menu. As you work through the exercises in this chapter, the example drawing may become a little cluttered. You may use the Undo or Erase commands to remove your practice dimensions as you go, or simply exit AutoCAD 2000 (at convenient points) without saving the changes. This will give you a fresh copy of the example drawing for each practice.

EXAMPLE: OPENING A DRAWING AND USING BASIC DIMENSIONING COMMANDS

1. Start AutoCAD 2000 and open CH14EX01.DWG, which you will find on the CD that comes with this book.

   The line work and labels in this drawing are in the layers LINE and TEXT. You will notice that the current layer is an empty layer called DIMS. Use this layer to add your dimensions. The dimensions will be displayed in red, making them easier to distinguish. (In general, it is good practice to add any form of annotation on a different layer from the line work. That way, you have more flexibility in what you display onscreen at any time: if you want to display only the line work without the additional distractions of text or dimensions, the option is available.

2. To open the Dimension toolbar, select View, Toolbars and then click the check box beside Dimension in the Toolbars list box.

   Alternatively, you may right-click any toolbar in AutoCAD 2000. When the drop-down menu of toolbars appears, click Dimension. The Dimension toolbar is displayed in the drawing (see Figure 14.1).

Figure 14.1

The AutoCAD 2000 Dimension toolbar provides access to all the dimensioning commands.

3. Move your mouse slowly across the buttons on the Dimension toolbar, but don't click yet. A ToolTip appears as you hover over each button, telling you the function of each button.

4. On the AutoCAD 2000 menu, click Dimension to drop down the dimensioning menu (see Figure 14.2). This menu contains the same dimensioning commands as the toolbar shown in Figure 14.1.

You may use either of these interface methods to select the dimensioning commands in the practices that follow.

Figure 14.2

The AutoCAD 2000 pull-down Dimension menu provides access to the same commands as the Dimension toolbar.

Although the original command-line dimensioning has essentially been superseded by the graphical user interfaces (menus and toolbars), there is still a command-line equivalent for all dimensioning commands. In fact, whenever you click a button on a toolbar or an option on a menu, the command is activated at the command line, and you are prompted step by step at the command line. For example if you click the first button on the Dimension toolbar (Linear Dimension), _dimlinear appears at the Command prompt. You probably do not want to type in the lengthy commands, but it is useful to know the actual commands if you plan to customize AutoCAD 2000 by programming your own commands and macros.

PART

IV

CH

14

Note

Knowing the actual dimensioning commands is of particular value to users who want to develop programs and menus within the AutoCAD 2000 environment to meet their unique production requirements. The command-line versions are used to automate commands in menus, toolbars, and AutoLISP macros (see Chapter 21, "A Primer for AutoLISP and VBA," page **589**). For example, to create a macro to obtain a linear dimension by typing **DL**, you would add the following line to an AutoLISP file:

```
(defun c:DL()(command "_dimlinear"))
```

LINEAR DIMENSION

The first button on the Dimension toolbar activates the most frequently used command: the Linear Dimension command (_dimlinear). Although there are a number of different kinds of dimensions, users often need to measure the distance between two points on a line. This command measures and annotates a specified length, either horizontally or vertically. When you start this command, you may either specify two points or select an object to dimension.

EXAMPLE: USING THE LINEAR DIMENSION COMMAND

1. Click the Linear Dimension button, or select Dimension, Linear if you prefer to use the menu.

   The command prompt should show the following lines:

   ```
   Command: _dimlinear
   Specify first extension line origin or <select object>:
   ```

   The Linear Dimension command offers a choice that may not be clear at first: You may either pick a couple of points in the drawing to define your dimension object, or you can press the Enter key and select an AutoCAD object. In this exercise, you will choose the second option <select object>.

2. Press the Enter key. At the select object prompt, pick the line between point A and point B in the lower-left section of the drawing.

Note

When you choose the <select object> option on the Linear Dimension command, the object you select must be a line (including polylines), an arc, or a circle. With lines and polylines that have more than one segment, the linear command will dimension only the selected segment; if you select a circle, this command will dimension the diameter. If you select an object the linear command cannot dimension, it will display the message Object selected is not a line, arc or circle, and will prompt you to select again.

3. The dimension lines and text appear—moving around as you drag your cursor—and you are offered the following options:

   ```
   Specify dimension line location or
   [Mtext/Text/Angle/ Horizontal/Vertical/Rotated]:
   ```

   Ignore these options for now, while you complete the basic command.

4. Drag the mouse to the left of line AB. The image of the dimension will follow your cursor until you click a point to fix it.

5. Click the mouse to position the dimension.

You may position this dimension either to the right or to the left of the object you are dimensioning. In this case, to the left is more appropriate. The result is shown in Figure 14.3 at the left side of the drawing. The dimension object you have created is composed of four lines and a text string: The lines with the arrow tips are the actual *dimension lines*; the lines that extend from the ends of the object you selected are called the *extension lines*.

TEXT AND POSITION OPTIONS

Now take a look at the options available for editing and positioning the dimension text and lines. You may select one or more of these options before you finally place the dimension. For now, simply review these options. You may experiment with them later.

- M—This option opens the Multiline Text Editor and enables you to add text before or after the dimension text—in this case, <1.1955>. For example, you might want to annotate **Height =** before the dimension value <>. The angle brackets represent the calculated measurement. If you delete the <> brackets, the dimension measurement will not be displayed. As the name of this option suggests, you may enter more than one line of text to your dimension by pressing Enter at the end of each line. Press OK to exit the Multiline Text Editor and save your edits.

- T—This option provides the command-line equivalent of the Multiline option but is not quite so flexible. You may enter only a single line of text, and you must remember to type in the angled brackets <> if you want to include the measured dimension as part of your text. Press Enter when you have completed your text edit. The new text will be displayed.

- A—This option enables you to rotate the dimension text. Type **a**, and then enter the text rotation angle. In the current example (see Figure 14.3), the default text position is perpendicular to the dimension line; if you want to rotate the text to run parallel to the measured object, you would enter **90** (for 90°) at this prompt and press Enter.

- H and V—These options enable you to specify a horizontal or vertical dimension. A horizontal dimension measures between two points on the x-axis, and a vertical dimension measures the distance between two points on the y-axis. Typically, AutoCAD 2000 will decide automatically whether a vertical or a horizontal dimension is to be calculated, based upon the relative position of the two points selected. For example, if one point is higher on the y-axis than the other, a vertical dimension is calculated. But you may use the H and V options to override the default choice.

  As you will see in the next exercise, you can also determine whether a horizontal or a vertical dimension is calculated by dragging your mouse in one direction or another.

- R—This option enables you to rotate the entire dimension to a specified orientation. Type **r**, and then enter the dimension rotation angle. You may use this option to align

PART

IV

CH

14

the dimension better with the selected object or to display the dimension better in the drawing.

If you want to experiment with these options, you may do so at this time. Repeat the Linear Dimension command and try out the different options. Use the Undo or Erase command to remove any dimensions you do not want to keep.

DRAWING A VERTICAL DIMENSION

In the first exercise, you selected an object and dimensioned it. In the next exercise, you will pick specific points to create a vertical dimension. (A *vertical dimension* measures between two points on the y-axis.) The sample drawing is already set up with all object snaps (osnaps) on so you can easily pick points and align them accurately with the drawing geometry.

Tip 105 from
Paul Richardson

You can toggle the object snaps on and off using the OSNAP button on the Status bar or via the F3 function key. For the current exercises, it is helpful to have the osnaps on to assist you in precisely locating specific endpoints, midpoints, and intersections. If you want to check the osnap settings, right-click the OSNAP button, and then select Settings from the shortcut menu.

EXAMPLE: DRAWING A VERTICAL DIMENSION

1. Press Enter, which repeats the previous (_dimlinear) command, or click the Linear Dimension button again.
2. This time, click point A on the right side of the drawing. (With the osnaps on, it is easy to locate the point.)
3. Move the mouse until point B is highlighted, and select it.
4. Drag the dimension line sideways so it is away from the line AB, and click once.

The result is shown in Figure 14.3 at the right side of the drawing. The dimension should be identical to the first exercise you completed because these right and left portions of the drawing are mirror images of each other.

DRAWING A HORIZONTAL DIMENSION

Now you should create some horizontal dimensions in the same way. A *horizontal dimension* measures between two points on the x-axis. See also horizontal linear dimensions>. This time, select points or objects in a horizontal plane on the screen, and drag the dimension baseline up or down from the object being dimensioned. You may want to erase the dimensions you have just created to prevent the drawing from becoming too cluttered.

Figure 14.3
Vertical linear dimensions can be created by selecting an object or by picking points.

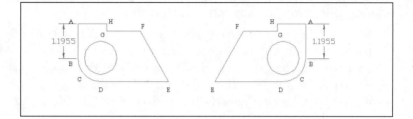

EXAMPLE: DRAWING A HORIZONTAL DIMENSION

1. Start the Linear Dimension command, press Enter, and then select the horizontal line between A and H on the left part of the diagram.
2. Drag the dimension baseline upward, and position it as shown in Figure 14.4.
3. Repeat the process, this time selecting the actual points H and A in the right segment of the drawing.

   Again, your results should be identical.
4. Now, repeat step 3, this time selecting the points F and H.

   To avoid conflict with the H-to-A dimension, you could position this dimension below the objects selected. However, it works more neatly to pull this dimension above the H-to-A dimension line. Notice that the dimensions share an extension line at point A (see Figure 14.4).

Figure 14.4
You can create horizontal dimensions by dragging the dimension up or down from the selected object.

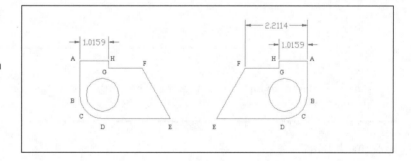

DIMENSIONING ARCS AND ANGLED LINES

In the preceding exercises, the lines selected were all parallel to the x- or y-axis, so there was only one choice: either vertical or horizontal. When the object is angled, the Linear Dimension command can be used to generate either vertical or horizontal dimensions.

PART
IV
CH
14

EXAMPLE: DIMENSIONING ARCS AND ANGLED LINES

1. Start the Linear Dimension command, press Enter, and then select the angled line FE (on the left section of the diagram). Before you click to establish the position of the dimension line, drag the dimension below FE. The dimension displays as a horizontal dimension. Now move your mouse to the right of the angled line (FE). The dimension displays a vertical dimension (1.7500, as shown in Figure 14.5). Click to complete the command.

2. Repeat step 2, this time selecting the EF angled line on the right section of the drawing. Drag the dimension down to display the horizontal dimension. The result (1.0104) is displayed in Figure 14.5.

   When you create a linear dimension from an arc, the result is identical whether you dimension it horizontally or vertically.

3. Press Enter to repeat the Linear Dimension command, and this time select the arc BCD. Pull the dimension to the left side of the arc. This gives the vertical dimension (0.8045).

4. Repeat step three, selecting arc DCB to generate a horizontal dimension this time (also 0.8045). The results are displayed in Figure 14.5.

Figure 14.5
You can also use the Linear Dimension command to create dimension angled lines and arcs.

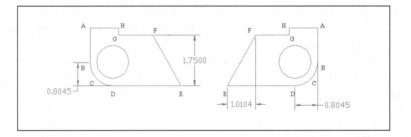

That's all there is to linear dimensioning. The actual process involves only two or three clicks of the mouse.

DISPLAY OPTIONS

Before you move on to the next dimension command, take a look at the ways the dimensions are displayed (refer to Figures 14.3 through 14.5). For these exercises, you have been using the AutoCAD 2000 default dimension settings, stored in the default dimension style Standard. The dimension style determines elements such as text size, arrow size, and start and finish points for the extension lines, alignment of dimension text, and many other variables. After you have practiced using the different dimensioning commands, you will learn how to modify these features and develop your own dimension style.

→ Techniques for creating and overriding dimension styles settings are described later in this chapter. See "Creating a New Dimension Style," page **315**, later in this chapter.

Other aspects, such as the position of the dimension line and extension lines, are constrained by the size and position of the object you are dimensioning. Typically in vertical dimensions (refer to Figure 14.3), the dimension text and lines are placed *within* the extension lines. If they do not fit (as in the horizontal dimensions in Figure 14.4), the dimension lines will automatically be positioned *outside* the extension lines. You will see later that the user may specify preferences about what should be positioned inside or outside the extension lines, but ultimately the reality of the drawing will determine some of the choices AutoCAD 2000 will make. Notice that in dimensioning the arcs (BCD and DCB), AutoCAD 2000 determined that the best fit could be obtained by positioning the text *outside* the dimension lines and the dimension lines *inside* the extension lines.

ALIGNED DIMENSION

The second button on the Dimension toolbar starts the Aligned Dimension command (dimaligned), which works much the same way as the Linear Dimension command. If you use the Aligned Dimension on vertical or horizontal objects (for example, lines AB or AH in the previous examples), you will get a result identical to the Linear Dimension command. When you use this command on angled lines or arcs, the results are different. The Aligned Dimension draws the dimension parallel to the line (or object) that is being dimensioned. The steps used to create an Aligned Dimension are identical to those you use to create a linear dimension, but the result is different.

EXAMPLE: CREATING AN ALIGNED DIMENSION

1. Erase the dimension lines you have drawn on the left side of the sample drawing. You may leave the linear dimensions on the right side for comparison.

2. Click the Aligned Dimension button on the Dimension toolbar, or select Dimension, Aligned if you prefer to use the menu. The command prompt should show the following lines:

```
Command: _dimaligned
Specify first extension line origin or <select object>:
```

3. Press Enter and select the angled line FE.

4. Again, you will be offered some options prior to finally placing the dimension. In the Aligned Dimension, you may edit and position the text using the Mtext/Text/Angle options reviewed earlier.

5. Drag the dimension line outward from the angled line FE, and click to position the dimension. (You may not drag an aligned dimension from side to side or rotate it. The orientation of an aligned dimension is fixed by the orientation of the dimensioned object.)

You can see that Aligned Dimension has given you the actual measurement of the line FE, not just the vertical or horizontal distance between points E and F (see Figure 14.6). This is why this kind of dimension is also called the "true length" dimension. Repeat steps 2 through 5 to add an aligned dimension to arc BCD.

PART

IV

CH

14

Figure 14.6
The Aligned Dimension (or "true length" dimension) command can be used to dimension angled lines and arcs.

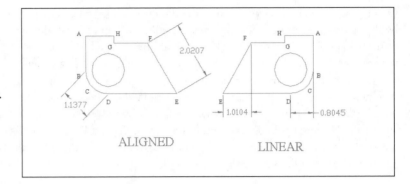

ALIGNED   LINEAR

ORDINATE DIMENSION

The third button on the dimension toolbar actives the Ordinate Dimension command (dimordinate). The Linear and Aligned commands are used to dimension lines, arcs and circles. The Ordinate Dimension command is applied to points; it measures from a common origin (or datum) to any selected point and labels the point's exact X or Y coordinate (or ordinate). The *X-datum* ordinate measures the distance of the point from the datum along the x-axis; The *Y-datum* ordinate measures the distance of the point from the datum along the x-axis.

DISPLAYING X OR Y COORDINATES OF ANY POINT

Each time you activate the Ordinate Dimension command, you must choose to display either the x or the y coordinate of your point because, although this command generates both coordinates, it displays only one at a time on the screen. Before you start the Ordinate Dimensioning command, make the following preparations, so the following exercise will work seamlessly.

EXAMPLE: DISPLAYING X OR Y COORDINATES OF ANY POINT

1. Clean up the sample drawing by undoing or erasing your previous dimensions.
2. Zoom out to view the entire example drawing. The drawing contains four components, not just the two segments you have been working with. (The full drawing is shown in Figure 14.7).
3. Check that Ortho is on for the first practice exercise. Check also that the object snaps are on, to make sure you are selecting the endpoints and center points you require. The Ordinate Dimension command will give you the dimension of any location on the screen. Without the snaps on, you can easily miss a specific point.

Tip 106 from
Paul Richardson

You can toggle Ortho mode on or off using the ORTHO button on the status bar, or via the F8 function key. When Ortho mode is *on,* it constrains your cursor to be either vertical or horizontal in relation to the last point selected, and it gives you straight leader lines. When

Ortho is *off,* your leader lines can jog and zigzag about. If you have a lot of ordinate dimensions crowded close together, you may want to set the Ortho mode to off so your leaders can offset to accommodate the dimension text.

4. Click the Ordinate Dimension button, or select Dime*n*sion, *O*rdinate from the menu. The command prompt should show the following lines:

```
Command: _dimordinate
Specify feature location:
```

5. Pick the center of the circle in the bottom left portion of the drawing. Again, you are prompted at the command line to select from a number of options. Ignore these for now. They are used only if you want to override the command defaults.

6. Drag the dimension image to the left, and click to complete the command. The ordinate dimension consists of a straight leader line with the Y-datum displayed as text. (The Y-datum is the distance from the origin to the selected point, along the y-axis. When you drag the ordinate dimension to the left or right, it displays the Y-datum (1.9103).

7. Repeat steps 4 to 6 and derive the y coordinates for points A and D in the same segment of the drawing. (The results (3.1093 and 1.1093) are shown in the bottom left diagram in Figure 14.7.)

8. Repeat the Ordinate Dimension command for the center of the circle, but this time drag the dimension image *above* the point; the X-datum for the center point is displayed. When you drag the ordinate dimension up or down, it displays the X-datum. You can repeat this process for other points (H, F, and E). These results are also displayed in the bottom left diagram in Figure 14.7.

Figure 14.7
The Ordinate Dimension command enables you to identify the x and y coordinates of selected points.

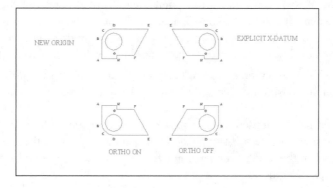

Take a quick look at what happens if Ortho is off.

9. Toggle off Ortho mode via the ORTHO button on the status bar or via the F8 key.

10. Position some ordinate dimensions on the bottom right segment of the drawing.

PART

IV

CH

14

You will notice that the leader line jogs around as you drag the mouse about, offering a much wider range of positions. This can be useful if you have a lot of dimensions and need to juggle for space. Some typical results are shown in the bottom right diagram of Figure 14.7.

COMMAND-LINE OPTIONS

So far, you have been generating ordinate dimensions without accessing any of the command-line options. In the next exercise you will experiment with the X and Y command-line options. The Ordinate Dimension command—like the Linear and Aligned Dimension commands—uses default settings unless you instruct it otherwise. The command-line options allow you to override the defaults if your dimensioning requires this. After you select a point, the following message always appears at the command prompt:

```
Specify leader endpoint or [Xdatum/Ydatum/Mtext/Text/Angle]:
```

You are already familiar with the Mtext, Text, and Angle options, which were reviewed in detail in the Linear Dimension command.

- M—This option opens the Multiline Text Editor and enables you to add text before or after the dimension text.
- T—This option provides a command-line equivalent of the Multiline option.
- A—This option enables you to rotate the dimension text to a specified angle.

The X- and Y-datum options are specific to ordinate dimensioning. They force or make explicit the chosen x or y value, regardless of the cursor movement or final positioning of the dimension.

- X—The X-datum option enables you to force an ordinate dimension to use the horizontal (or x-axis) measurement to a point when it would otherwise choose a vertical measurement. If you want to position an x ordinate to the left or right (rather than above or below) the selected point, type **x** and press Enter. Wherever you position the mouse (up or down, left or right), the x coordinate will be displayed.
- Y—The Y-datum option gives you the opposite of the X-datum option: If you select **y,** wherever you position the cursor, it will force a vertical measurement (y-axis).

You can experiment with these options in the top-right segment of the practice drawing. The example shown in the top-right diagram in Figure 14.7 forces the X value to be displayed even when the leader is dragged horizontally. Some text was added using the Mtext option to emphasize this point.

MOVING THE ORIGIN

In the previous practices, you have been measuring the distance of points from a somewhat arbitrary drawing origin. In practice, you may want to calculate distances between components of a mechanical part or from the outside wall of a building to various interior locations. You can accomplish this by moving the UCS of your drawing to the origin point, or datum, of your choice.

In this final exercise with the Ordinate Dimension command, you will move the origin to the corner A in the top left segment of the example drawing.

EXAMPLE: MOVING THE ORIGIN TO THE CORNER A

1. Select Tools, Move UCS. You will be prompted with this:

   ```
   Specify new origin point or [Zdepth] <0,0,0>:
   ```

2. Type **int** to select the Intersection object snap.

3. Pick the lower-left corner of the drawing part (point A). This moves the UCS origin to this point.

   If your UCS icon is turned on, it will immediately jump to this spot. You may want to turn off the UCS icon for now, to relieve the crowding in this part of the drawing (Type **ucsicon** and press Enter. Then type **off** and press Enter.) If your UCS icon is currently off, you can test whether you have successfully moved the origin with the next steps.

4. Type **id** at the Command prompt, and press Enter.

5. Then pick the corner of at A. It should read as follows:

   ```
   Command: id
   Specify point:  X = 0'-0"     Y = 0'-0"     Z = 0'-0"
   ```

Alternatively, you could generate the x and y coordinates of this point using the Ordinate Dimension command. When you have proved to your satisfaction that the origin has been moved, you should try dimensioning some new points from this new datum point. Your results should correspond to the top-left quadrant of the practice drawing, as shown in Figure 14.7.

OTHER DIMENSION COMMANDS

The remaining basic dimensioning commands are self-explanatory and can be mastered fairly quickly. They deal with nonlinear objects: circles, arcs, and angles. These commands are grouped together on the Dimension toolbar (see Figure 14.8) and on the Dimension menu: Radius Dimension, Diameter Dimension, and Angular Dimension. Frequently, in construction details or mechanical drawing, you are required to provide the diameter of a pipe or an anchor bolt, or the radius of a curb; in the CADD/CAM environment precise angular information is needed for the machining of parts. The non-linear dimensioning commands are used here.

You should clean up the sample drawing or load a fresh copy of CH14EX01.DWG before practicing these commands. Zoom back to the bottom half of the drawing because there are only a few options to test.

PART

IV

CH

14

Figure 14.8

These three buttons on the Dimension toolbar (Radius, Diameter, and Angular Dimension) serve very specific purposes.

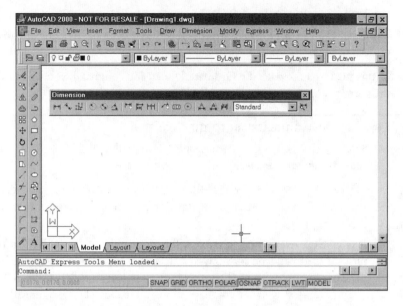

RADIUS DIMENSION

The Radius Dimension command (dimradius) dimensions a radius on an arc or circle object. It does not attempt to dimension complex curves such as splines or ellipses. The command requires two points: The first identifies the arc or circle, and the second determines the position of the dimension line and text. The appearance of the text depends on how you drag your final point, inside or outside the arc or circle.

EXAMPLE: CREATING A RADIUS DIMENSION

1. Click the Radius Dimension button on the Dimension toolbar, or select Dimension, Radius on the menu.

2. At the Select Arc or Circle prompt, click the arc BCD.

3. Again, you are prompted to make adjustments to the text and text angle. You do not need to make changes here unless you want to modify the typical default text or text position.

4. Click to the left of the arc to position the Radius Dimension.

5. Repeat these steps, this time selecting the small circle above the arc. Position its radius dimension below the circle.

Check your results in the lower-left corner of Figure 14.9. Notice that the Radius Dimension command adds a center mark when it dimensions the circle radius, and it automatically adds the radius notation (R) ahead of the text.

Figure 14.9
Non-orthogonal objects such as circles and arcs are dimensioned using the Radius, Diameter and Angular Dimension commands.

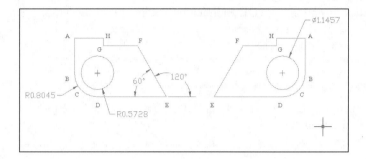

DIAMETER DIMENSION

The Diameter Dimension command (dimdiameter) is very similar in use to the Radius Dimension. Its parameters and mode of operation are identical. However, because this command measures the *diameter* of an object, it can be used to dimension circles only, and not arcs.

EXAMPLE: CREATING A DIAMETER DIMENSION

1. Click the Diameter Dimension button on the Dimension toolbar, or select Dimension, Diameter on the menu.
2. Click the circle on the right of the drawing, and create a Diameter Dimension this time.

Again, the Diameter Dimension command adds a center mark. This time, the diameter notation precedes the text—a circle with a diagonal line through it (see the diagram on the right of Figure 14.9).

Note Farther along the toolbar, you will notice another button with a circle icon and a ToolTip that says Center Mark. This button does not calculate any dimension values; it simply positions a center mark—either a small cross or longer lines, depending on the default setting.

ANGULAR DIMENSION

The Angular Dimension command (dimangular) calculates the angle between any two non-parallel lines. You may use existing geometry in the form of circles, arcs, and lines to get three or four points to define the two lines.

EXAMPLE: CREATING AN ANGULAR DIMENSION

1. Click the Angular Dimension button on the Dimension toolbar, or select Dimension, Angular on the menu.

2. Click first on the line DE and then on the line FE in the left diagram. You should see the following prompts as you select your two lines:

```
Command: _dimangular
Select arc, circle, line, or <specify vertex>:
Select second line:
Specify dimension arc line location or [Mtext/Text/Angle]:
```

You are already familiar with the Mtext, Text, and Angle options, so you do not need to practice them here.

3. Position your cursor sufficiently far from the vertex that the dimension text and arrows can fit within the angle, then click to complete the command. The angular dimension should read 60° as shown in the center of Figure 14.9.

4. Repeat these three steps, this time measuring the angle between the line FE and the horizontal. Your result should show 120°, as shown in Figure 14.9.

The Angular Dimension command is quite diverse. The command prompt asks for circle, line, or arc objects, but in fact it will work with a number of other objects. Here are a few more applications for Angular Dimensions. You may test these if you want.

■ The Angular Dimension command works with polyline and multiline objects. If these complex objects have more than one vertex, the command will create the angular dimension between the segments selected. (Create a couple polylines with multiple segments, and draw some angular dimensions between them to check this out.)

■ You can even define angular dimensions between two closed polygons.

■ In fact, you don't need any objects at all to create an Angular Dimension. After you have activated this command, you may press Enter (to utilize the <specify vertex> option), and then simply pick any points in the drawing area. The command will calculate and display the angle specified.

On the other hand, the Angular Dimension command will reject some AutoCAD 2000 objects—splines and ellipses, for example. A solid object has flat sides, so you might expect this to work, but it doesn't. In this situation, you can use the <specify vertex> option to simply select points for the command.

You are now familiar with each of the basic dimensioning commands. All the dimensioning work you have completed so far has been accomplished using the default dimension settings stored in the AutoCAD 2000 default dimension style, named Standard. On the Dimension Toolbar is a list box (new for AutoCAD 2000). Click the down arrow at the side of the list box, and you will find that Standard is the only dimension style available in this drawing. It's time to take a look at developing a style or two of your own before you progress to the more complex dimensioning commands.

DIMENSIONING WITH STYLE

Since AutoCAD Release 12, the Dimension Style command (dimstyle) and the Dimension Style dialog box have been available to users. However, the earlier versions of this command and interface were limited in versatility and were somewhat confusing in terminology. With each subsequent release of AutoCAD, the features available and the functionality of the dialog box have consistently improved. Click the Dimension Style button—at the far right on the Dimension toolbar—to take a quick look at the new Dimension Style Manager.

The AutoCAD 2000 Dimension Style Manager (shown in Figure 14.10) provides a user interface that is easy to comprehend and to use. Dimension settings are organized into groups of intuitively similar settings via a tabbed interface. Additionally, the Dimension Style Manager provides realistic and immediate visual feedback on any features selected so you can make valid decisions without exiting back and forth into AutoCAD. For your first new dimension style, you will make a few modifications to the existing Standard style and save these changes as My Standard.

CREATING A NEW DIMENSION STYLE

You should keep your most recent practice exercise open while you are creating your new style so you will be able to apply the new style to this drawing.

EXAMPLE: CREATING A NEW DIMENSION STYLE

 1. Click the Dimension Style button on the Dimension toolbar, or select Dimension, Style on the menu. (You may also type **dimstyle** at the command prompt.)

2. When the Dimension Style Manager appears (see Figure 14.10), click the New button.

Figure 14.10
The Dimension Style Manager enables you to create new styles and modify existing styles.

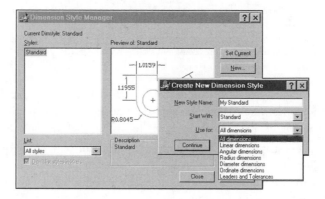

3. Click the Use for list box. You may optionally create a style that applies to specified dimensions only, such as Radius Dimensions. For now, you will create a style for all dimensions.

4. In the New Style Name box, type **My Standard** and then press Continue.

PART

IV

CH

14

You have now created a new style that is identical to the existing AutoCAD 2000 Standard style. You may have observed that the sample drawing in the Dimension Style Manager bears a remarkable resemblance to your practice exercise. It is not actually your drawing that is visible there. The practice drawing was based on this model drawing.

The Dimension Style Manager opens a new dialog box containing six tabbed sections. You will be using four of these tabs in defining your new style: Lines and Arrows; Text; Fit; and Primary Units.

LINES AND ARROWS

If the Lines and Arrows tab is not topmost, click the tab to bring it forward. This tab contains all of the settings that control the appearance of dimension lines and arrows: color and lineweight; how dimension and/or extension lines are displayed; and style and size of arrowheads. You should experiment with each of the dimension variables shown on the tab. The original settings are shown in Figure 14.11, if you need to return to these.

Figure 14.11
This Dimension Style Manager tab shows all the aspects of dimension lines and arrows that can be modified.

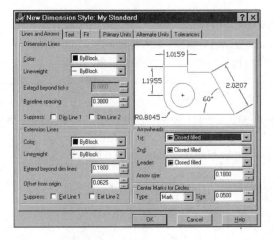

- Color/Lineweight—See what happens when you change the color of dimension lines or the extension lines. The change is reflected immediately in the graphic. Try the same with the lineweights. Return these settings to Byblock before you exit this tab.

- Suppress Lines—Experiment with suppressing either or both of the dimension and extension lines. (Turn them back on again before exiting this tab.) You can vary the offset and length of the dimension lines. Reset the defaults before you exit the Lines and Arrows tab, unless you prefer your own settings.

- Center Mark—You may remember a passing reference to the Center Mark command in the "Radius Dimension" and "Diameter Dimension" sections. The setting for the Center Mark can be specified in this dialog box (bottom right corner). Try clicking the list box and selecting Lines in place of Mark. Much longer centerlines appear in addition to the small cross in the center. Change back to Mark, and experiment with changing the size of the Center Mark. Choose a lower value of 0.5.

- Arrowheads—Now try some different arrow styles. Change the 1st arrowhead from Closed filled to Closed blank. Notice that the 2nd arrowhead setting also changes. (You may select a different arrowhead for the first and second arrows, but this is seldom done.)

- Arrow size—The size of the arrowheads is on the large side for the current drawing. Change the setting from 0.1800 to 0.1250 (or 1/8th).

Press OK to accept the new arrow style and size, plus any other style changes you want to implement.

DEFINING A CUSTOM ARROWHEAD   AutoCAD 2000 offers a wide range of arrow styles to choose from. The choice of arrowhead style is often simply a matter of personal or work-group preference, but there are some discipline- and task-specific styles. For example, architectural drawings typically will use the "tick" arrowhead and the circular "origin indicator" is frequently used in ordinate dimensioning.

If none of these works for you, you have the option to import a User Arrow. Scroll right to the very bottom of the arrowhead list box to locate this option. The User Arrow option dates back to when there were relatively few arrow choices available. AutoCAD 2000 provides such a wide range of arrowhead styles that the User Arrow is almost redundant now. However, you still have the option of designing your own special arrowhead symbol to meet very specific design requirements. The arrowhead shown in Figure 14.12 has curved lines— a feature that is not available in the standard choices.

If you do make your own arrowhead block, you should follow these principles:

- Draw your arrow in a box one AutoCAD unit square.

- Draw the arrow in layer zero and color Byblock so the arrow can inherit color from its insertion layer or from its user-assigned block color.

- Use the Block command to create the new block: Click the Select Objects button, and select the parts of your block. Click the Pick Point button to define the insertion point of your arrow and select the end of the point, which should be facing right (see Figure 12).

In the Lines and Arrows dialog tab, select the User Arrow option and load the new arrow definition. Remember that this user-defined arrowhead will be available only in drawings into which you have inserted the arrow block.

Caution

Using a custom arrowhead can create problems if you are working on a project with other companies or users. It is usually a better idea to use standard AutoCAD arrowheads and avoid any compatibility problems. A possible solution is to save the arrowhead block to a template drawing and distribute the template as a standard to other users.

Figure 14.12
Use the User Arrow option to create your own arrow block for use in a dimension style.

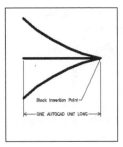

When you press OK to exit the Lines and Arrows tab, AutoCAD 2000 returns you to the opening screen of the Dimension Style Manager. In the Description field, you will see a record of all the changes you have made to the AutoCAD 2000's Standard dimension style. Now let's make some changes on the other tabs, starting with the text settings.

TEXT

This time, select the Modify button; when the Modify Dimension Styles dialog box opens, click the Text tab to bring it to the front. This tab contains all of the settings that control the appearance (color, height, and so on), the placement (vertical, horizontal and offset), and the alignment of dimension text. You should experiment with each of the dimension variables shown on the tab. Figure 14.13 shows the existing default settings for dimension text, if you need to return to these.

Figure 14.13
The Text tab in the Dimension Style Manager shows all the aspects of dimension text that can be modified.

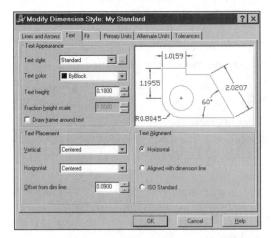

- Text style—Click the Text Style list box. Only two text styles are loaded in this drawing: the AutoCAD 2000 Standard text style and the Labels style, created for the point labels. Continue with the Standard text style, which is more typical for dimensioning.

- Color—You may experiment with text color, bearing in mind that you will lose some flexibility if you choose a fixed color rather than allowing color to be controlled.

■ Text height—The text height in the AutoCAD 2000 Standard style is a little too large for this drawing. Change text height to **0.125** for My Standard dimension style.

Experiment with the other text variables: text frame, text placement, and text alignment. Different disciplines have different preferences for these text standards. You do not need to change these for the present exercises unless your personal preferences dictate doing so.

At this point, you may click OK and return to the first screen before continuing. Or you may carry on with defining your style by moving directly to the next tab.

FIT

Click the Fit tab to bring this part of the dialog box to the front. The Fit tab enables the user to specify alternate preferences as to the placement of dimension text, arrows, dimension lines, and leader lines. The preferences specified on the Fit tab come into play only when AutoCAD 2000 cannot fit text and lines in their usual default positions. Often, when you dimension a small object or a number of adjacent objects—and particularly if the dimension displays a high level of precision—AutoCAD 2000 cannot squeeze the text and arrows inside the extension lines and has to place them somewhere else. Figure 14.14 shows the range of alternate options available via this tab.

Figure 14.14
The Fit tab contains a series of radio buttons with which the user may specify preferences concerning dimension placement.

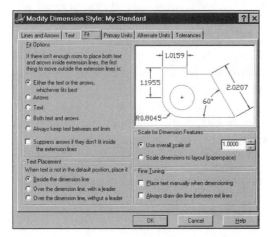

You can experiment with the radio buttons on the left panel of this tab and observe the changes that occur in the sample graphic. You will not always see the graphic change because these Fit preferences are used only when AutoCAD cannot implement the typical default because of space considerations. Most of the preferences stated here represent a want list rather than an implementation directive. AutoCAD 2000 will do its best to implement your preferences, but will not always succeed.

If you want to retain more direct control of dimensioning, you should consider the following options in the Fine Tuning panel:

PART

IV

CH

14

- Place Text Manually When Dimensioning—If you check this box, AutoCAD 2000 will ignore any other horizontal text settings and allow you to place text wherever you click the cursor.

- Always Draw Dim Line Between Ext Lines—This option always places the dimensions lines between the selected points, even when the arrowheads don't fit and are positioned outside.

The topic that follows is an important one. However, it does not have an effect on the practice drawing you are working on at this time because this drawing has no scale. If you want, you can skip over this section for now and proceed to the Primary Units section so you can complete your new dimension style. You should return to read this section when you have finished.

SETTING OVERALL DIMENSION SCALE

Applying dimensions in AutoCAD 2000 is a relatively straightforward operation. You pick the kind of dimension you want from the Dimension toolbar, and then you click one or two points and press Enter. The hard part is specifying the dimension settings so the components of a dimension object (arrows, text, and so on) are scaled correctly so they plot out at the size you want.

A common approach is just to start dimensioning and then to adjust whatever looks obviously wrong onscreen, eventually getting a dimension that looks about right. The problem here is that what looks OK on screen may look very different when plotted. Onscreen, you cannot objectively determine what is the correct text size for output because the zoom factor controls the size of the text you are viewing. Unfortunately, the onscreen magnification has no relationship to the plotting magnification. Also, this approach tends to produce inconsistencies in dimensions within a drawing and between one drawing and another because users may well be using a different zoom factor at different times. To achieve consistent and predictable results, you cannot simply eyeball a dimension on screen—you must do the calculations.

Professional-looking drawings should have all the dimension objects plot with the same size text and arrowheads and all other gaps, spaces, and line lengths should be consistent. This is where the Overall Dimension Scale Factor comes into play.

Hidden away on the bottom right side of the Fit tab is a very important dimension variable: Dimscale, or Overall Dimension Scale. This variable sets the scale factor for all dimension style settings that specify size, distance, or spacing, including text and arrowhead size.

In the practice dimension style exercise, you specified the text (0.125) and arrowhead size (0.125), which corresponds to the size you wanted it to plot (1/8 inch). It is a little confusing to figure out where this scale factor fits into the picture. Two aspects are at work here:

- The individual values you set for text and arrow size should correspond to the size you want them to plot out. Remember to set them to the size you want to see on output (not onscreen).

- The overall dimension scale is used to compensate for layout scaling. When you specify an overall scale value, the scale changes the size of the dimension geometry relative to the drawing. AutoCAD 2000 multiplies the text height, arrowhead size, offsets, and gaps by the overall scale value.

The practice drawing you have been working with (CH14EX01.DWG) is a nonscaled drawing, and the default dimension scale of 1 is appropriate here. There is no need to get into viewports and viewport magnification and adjusting the dimension scaling for this drawing. The text and arrow sizes are correctly set at the size you want them to plot out: 0.125 or 1/8 inch.

In real life, dimension scaling is rarely as uncomplicated as that. To understand how dimension objects should be scaled, you must first understand how an AutoCAD 2000 drawing uses scale, as well as how AutoCAD units affect scale. Although dimension scale is independent of drawing scale, it is derived in the same way and should be identical to drawing scale.

CALCULATING A SCALE FACTOR   Drawing scale (and also dimension scale) covers the relationship between real-size objects, the AutoCAD model, and the plotted drawing size. In AutoCAD terms, the model is represented in model space and the plotted drawing is represented in a layout. AutoCAD drawings are generally drawn full-size in model space and are then reduced for plotting using a Layout Viewport. If you want a 1:10 plot of a model space drawing, the viewport magnification (XP) is the inverse of the plot scale—that is, 1/10 or 0.1.

In addition to taking into account the viewport magnification, there are two further issues that can complicate your calculations: converting feet to inches and converting fractional measurements to decimal measurements.

- Inches versus feet—Calculating the scale factor gets more complicated if your units in model space are different from your plotting units. Inches are the most common units used for plotting, whereas feet are often the units used in engineering drawings. If the AutoCAD units are inches, the scale factor is increased by a factor of 12 compared to a comparable drawing that uses feet as units. Take a look at the top two sections of Table 14.1 for a comparison.

- Decimal versus fractions—Architectural scales involve even more calculation. Typical plot scales are in fractional units (1/4 inch or 1/8 inch). You need to derive a decimal magnification from a fractional scale. For example, a plot scale of 1/8 inch = 1 foot requires you to calculate the number of 1/8-inch lengths in 1 foot ($8 \times 12 = 96$).

Obviously, this is an unwieldy process to go through every time you start a new drawing or create a new dimension style. Ideally, you should develop a chart (comparable to the charts in Table 14.1) that contains the significant numbers you need to make things work for any scale you might need for your discipline. The tables that follow give the appropriate dimension scale for each viewport magnification. They also supply the sample scaled text height to use in each case. By a process of extrapolation, you can calculate any other values you might require when you are creating a dimension style.

PART

IV

CH

14

TABLE 14.1   CALCULATING DIMENSION SCALE VALUES FOR DIFFERENT APPLICATIONS

Engineering Scales: 1 AutoCAD unit = 1 foot

	Dimension Scale	Viewport Scale	1/8-inch Text	1/4-inch Text
10 scale	10	1/10	1.25	2.5
20 scale	20	1/20	2.5	5
30 scale	30	1/30	3.75	7.5
40 scale	40	1/40	5	10
50 scale	50	1/50	6.25	12.5
100 scale	100	1/100	12.5	25
200 scale	200	1/200	25	50

Engineering Scales: 1 AutoCAD unit = 1 inch

	Dimension Scale	Viewport Scale	1/8-inch Text	1/4-inch Text
10 scale	120	1/120	16	30
20 scale	240	1/240	30	60
30 scale	360	1/360	45	90
40 scale	480	1/480	60	120
50 scale	600	1/600	75	160
100 scale	1200	1/1200	160	25
200 scale	2400	1/2400	300	600

Architectural Scales

	Dimension Scale	Viewport Scale	1/8-inch Text	1/4-inch Text
1/32 inch =1 foot	384	1/384	48	96
1/16 inch = 1 foot	192	1/192	24	48
1/8 inch = 1 foot	96	1/96	12	24
3/16 inch =1 foot	64	1/64	8	16
1/4 inch =1 foot	48	1/48	6	12
3/8 inch = 1 foot	32	1/32	4	8
1/2 inch = 1 foot	24	1/24	3	6
5/8 inch =1 foot	19.2	1/19.2	2.4	4.8
3/4 inch = 1 foot	16	1/16	2	4

Architectural Scales

	Dimension Scale	Viewport Scale	1/8-inch Text	1/4-inch Text
1 inch =1 foot	12	1/12	1.5	3
1.5 inches = 1 foot	8	1/8	1	2
3 inches = 1 foot	4	1/4	0.5	1
6 inches = 1 foot	2	1/2	0.25	0.5

When you have a viewport scale, you also have the number for your dimension scale. When the viewport scales a drawing, your model space dimension objects will be shrunk by the same amount. If your drawing scale is 1/8 inch = 1 foot, your viewport scale will be 1/96. If you have specified 1/8-inch text for your dimension object, with the default scale of 1.0, your plotted text and arrows will be reduced to an infinitesimal size. If the dimension scale is set to 96, this increases the size of the arrows and text to compensate for the viewport scaling.

Note

The underlying assumption here is that you will be plotting from paper space (or layout) via a viewport because this is rapidly becoming the norm for plotting. If you are plotting directly from model space, the same principles apply. Determine the scale at which you need to plot, and then set your dimension scale to compensate by the same amount. In the discussion and tables in this section, you should substitute Plot Scale for Viewport Magnification.

→ For further information on plotting, see Chapter 18, "Plotting and Layouts."

SCALING FOR DIFFERENT PAPER SPACE LAYOUTS In the Scale for Dimension Features panel, you may have noticed another option: Scale Dimensions to Layout (Paper Space). At this point, you may be asking yourself if this option would perform the scaling task for you—without all the previous calculations.

The answer is a qualified "yes." In fact, you must establish a basic dimension scale value in your dimension style before you can use this option. The option then allows you to update the dimension scaling automatically for different plotting scenarios. You can use this option as a quick fix in the following scenarios:

- You may receive a set of drawings from another user and want to plot them at a scale that is different from the original setup.
- Although your standard scale for an architectural drawing is 1/8 inch = 1 foot, you may want to temporarily enlarge and plot selected areas of the drawing at 1/4 inch = 1 foot.

Essentially, you first calculate the appropriate dimension scale value for typical output at, say, 100 scale. If you then want to plot the drawing—or part of it—at 40 scale, you can instruct AutoCAD 2000 to adjust the dimensions by activating the Scale Dimensions to Layout button. The procedure is as follows. First, establish your basic dimension style and overall scaling.

PART

IV

CH

14

EXAMPLE: ESTABLISHING THE DIMENSION STYLE AND SCALING

1. In the Dimension Style Manager, select <u>N</u>ew or <u>M</u>odify, depending upon whether you are starting a new style or modifying an existing style.

2. Select the Fit tab, and enter an appropriate value for the Overall <u>S</u>cale. (This is calculated using your typical plotting scale/viewport magnification, as discussed in the preceding section.)

3. Check that you have specified your text and arrow size to reflect the desired output (that is, plotted) size.

4. Save the dimension style.

5. Add any required dimensions to your drawing. (Existing dimensions in the drawing will be updated with the scale value unless you have created an entirely new dimension style.)

So far, the procedure follows the standard procedure for creating or modifying a dimension style. You could go ahead and plot your drawing at the typical scale, and the dimensions would be appropriately scaled.

When you want to plot the drawing—or part of it—at a different scale, complete the following steps.

EXAMPLE: PLOTTING THE DRAWING AT A DIFFERENT SCALE

1. Click a layout tab and then double-click in the viewport to re-enter model space.

2. Set the new plotting scale using the Viewports toolbar, and establish the desired view for plotting.

Tip 107 from
Paul Richardson

An important point to note is that changing the dimension scaling in this way will work only if the text style used for the dimension text is a flexible-height–not a fixed-height–text style. Text styles should be created with a height of zero to ensure that they are flexible in situations such as this. (The default AutoCAD 2000 Standard text style is a zero-height style, unless a user changes it.) If you are using a text style of your own creation for dimension text and it is a fixed-height style, the size of the dimension text will *not* change when you activate the Scale Dimensions to Layout option.

3. Now, click the Dimension Styles button on the toolbar to open the Dimension Style Manager, click <u>M</u>odify, and select the Fit tab.

4. Select Scale Dimension to Layout (Paper Space) in the Scale panel.

5. Press OK to close the Dimension Style Manager.

6. Click the <u>U</u>pdate button on the Dimension toolbar, or select Update on the menu. (The Dimension Update command is reviewed in the "Updating Dimensions" section in this chapter.)

7. Select the dimensions in your current view that need to change—you can type **all** or use a crossing window—and press Enter.

AutoCAD 2000 will now apply a scale factor to the dimensions based on the current paper space viewport scaling.

Caution

When you use the Scale Dimensions to Layout (Paper Space) option in the Dimension Style Manager, it applies a scale factor derived from the current paper space viewport. If you change the scale in the viewport, AutoCAD 2000 will not automatically update the scale factor. You need to click the Update button on the Dimension toolbar and select all of the dimensions each time you change the scale in the viewport.

Additionally, this option will only partially scale leader objects; it will scale the arrowhead, but not the text part of the leader object. You should adjust the leader text via the Properties command, for example.

Before you go back to regular model space, remember to turn off the Scale Dimensions to Layout option. Open the Fit tab again (step 3 in the procedure). Type in the original Overall Dimension scale, and click the radio button. If you don't reset this option, the regular dimensioning in model space will malfunction.

This may seem like a lot of work, but the first five steps are part of creating the basic dimension style for general-purpose use. Steps 3 to 7 are the ones that enable you reset your dimension style for a new plot scenario. Even given all the caveats noted here, this workaround enables you to quickly adapt your underlying dimension scale to different plotting options—without going through the calculations each time. It can also be useful when you receive drawings from other sources and you don't know how they have scaled the viewport(s).

When you use the Dimension to Layout (Paper Space) option, all your dimensioning activities still occur in model space: The dimensions are added in model space and are manipulated via a model space viewport. You are not adding or changing the dimensions in paper space. Dimensioning in paper space per se involves a different set of processes—and is not without its own pitfalls. This topic is covered later in the chapter. (See "Adding a Dimension in Paper Space," on page **355**.) To add dimensions successfully in paper space, you need to know how to modify the linear dimension scale. The linear dimension scale variable (Dimlfac) is on the next tab of the Dimension Style Manager, the Primary Units tab. It is time now to review this group of dimension variables.

This has been a lengthy detour into dimension scaling. As noted before, you do not have to make any complex adjustments to the dimension scaling in the practice drawing (CH14EXO1.DWG) because this drawing has no scale. You may now proceed to the Primary Units tab to complete your new dimension style.

PART

IV

CH

14

PRIMARY UNITS

Click the Primary Units tab in the Modify Dimension Style dialog box to bring it to the front. The variables on this tab enable you to specify the style of linear and angular dimension units, the level of precision required, plus other custom features. Again, you should check through the range of options offered. The default settings are shown in Figure 14.15, if you need to return to these.

Figure 14.15
The Primary Units Tab allows the user to select the style of annotation to be used for dimensioning.

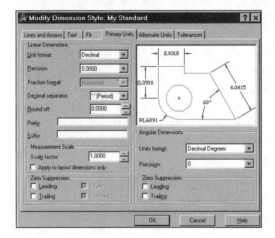

- Unit format—The most significant decision on this tab is which type of unit format is appropriate for your dimension style. The format used in the current dimension style is Decimal, with four decimal places displayed. You may retain this format or change it to another format, such as Engineering—or, to Fractional, if your real-life drawings typically use this dimension format: Engineering and architectural dimensions are displayed in feet and inches; fractional dimensions convert the decimal data to sixteenths or thirty-seconds, or to whichever level of precision you select. (Precision is selected in the next list box.)

Note

The Units setting is not automatically transferred from AutoCAD 2000 into your dimension style, and vice versa. Even if you have already selected architectural or engineering units for your drawing, you will have to select them again in the Dimension Style Manager.

- Precision—This option enables you to select from up to nine levels of precision. The values offered in this list box change, depending on the unit format you have selected. Select a level of accuracy appropriate for your discipline and/or type of drawing. For example, if you choose Engineering format, you should change the number of decimals displayed to 0'0.00".

- Fraction Format—If you choose Fractional or Architectural format, take a look at the different ways fractions may be displayed: Horizontal, Vertical, or Not stacked.

- Prefix/Suffix—These options allow you to include repetitive text (such as mm.) or symbols (such as a degree symbol) that you want to append to your dimensions.

- Measurement Scale—This setting enables you to manipulate *linear* dimension measurements by the specified scale factor. If you enter **5** here, all the linear dimensions in your drawing (including the radii, but not the angular dimension) will increase by a factor of 5. (You will see this reflected immediately in the sample graphic.) Possible applications for this are explored in the "Overriding Dimension Styles" section on page **336**, later in this chapter.

- Apply to Layout Dimensions Only—If you check this item, the scale factor will not be applied to your dimensions in model space. (Notice that the sample graphic does not change when this box is checked.) The scale value is applied only to dimensions created in paper space (layout). You will have a chance to practice dimensioning in paper space in the "Adding a Dimension in Paper Space" section on page **355**, later in this chapter.

- Angular Units Format/Precision—This option enables you to express angular dimensions as decimal degrees; degrees/minutes/seconds; grads; or radians. Change the format to degrees/minutes/seconds with a high number of decimal places.

- Zero Suppression—This option enables you to suppress leading and trailing zeros for linear and angular dimensions.

When you are satisfied with the appearance and format of your dimension style, click the OK button at the bottom of the tabs and return to the opening dialog box of the Dimension Style Manager. You can now compare your new dimension style with the Standard style you started with.

EXAMPLE: COMPARING THE NEW STYLE WITH THE STANDARD STYLE

1. Click the Compare button on the left side of the Dimension Style Manager. The Compare Dimension Styles dialog box opens (see Figure 14.16).

2. From the list boxes, select the two styles you want to compare. AutoCAD 2000 immediately provides a detailed list of the differences (including the names of the dimension system variables that control and store the changes). If you click the Copy icon on this screen, it will copy the results to the Windows Clipboard for pasting into other Windows applications.

Figure 14.16
The Compare Dimension Styles dialog box gives a variable-by-variable comparison of two dimension styles.

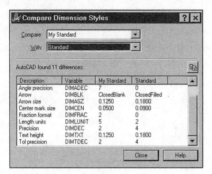

3. Click the Close button to return to the Dimension Style Manager.

4. Select the Set Current button to make your new style the current dimension style.

5. Press the Close button to return to your practice drawing in AutoCAD 2000.

UPDATING DIMENSIONS

When you return to the drawing editor, the first thing that is obvious is that nothing has changed. Your new dimension style's name is displayed in the list box on the Dimension toolbar, showing it is the current style, but the existing dimensions are still in the AutoCAD 2000 Standard style. All AutoCAD dimension styles and text styles are effective only from the time they are created and set current. You can test this by adding a couple new dimensions to the drawing.

If you want to convert your existing dimensions to the new style, use the Dimension Update command located to the left of the list box on the Dimension toolbar.

EXAMPLE: UPDATING DIMENSIONS

1. Click the Dimension Update button on the Dimension toolbar, or select Dimension, Update from the menu. The following prompt appears:
```
[Save/Restore/STatus/Variables/Apply/?] <Restore>: _apply
Select objects:
```

2. Type **all** and press Enter, or use a crossing window to select all the dimension objects.

3. When all the dimensions have been highlighted, press Enter again to terminate the command.

The dimensions are re-drawn using the new dimension style variables. If you have missed any dimensions, repeat the command by pressing the toolbar button or using the menu again. If you try to repeat the Update command by simply pressing Enter, you will need to respond to the command-line prompt and select the Apply option before proceeding.

Note

> The Dimension Update command activates the command-line version of the Dimstyle command, (–dimstyle, or minus dimstyle). Dimension Update starts the command and also selects the Apply option so you have to respond only to the Select Objects prompt (see step 1 in the previous list). If you press Enter to repeat the command, AutoCAD 2000 repeats the –dimstyle command, but then *you* must select the Apply option before selecting any objects.

DIMENSION STYLE FAMILIES

In the Dimension Style Manager, you can create dimension style families as well as individual styles. When you have created a *parent* style, you can develop variations upon the style for different types of dimension. If you want to use a different text height or arrow style for your radius dimensions, there is no need to create a whole new style: You can make a new radial *child* style. AutoCAD 2000 allows up to six different types of child styles for each parent style:

- Linear
- Angular
- Radius
- Diameter
- Ordinate
- Leader and tolerance

Each child style is stored as a subset of the parent style, so they are all active when the parent dimension style is set to current. If the parent dimension style is called My Standard, then each child dimension style will have a name starting with My Standard: (stylename).

Note

> For the user, AutoCAD 2000 displays the child style names as, for example, My Standard: Radial and My Standard: Ordinate. For programming purposes, AutoCAD refers internally to the child styles via a numerical suffix: My Standard$n, where n is a number that refers to the *type* of child dimension involved. A radial child style is $4, an ordinate child style is $6, and so on. This way AutoCAD 2000 can track which styles belong in the same family. If you are developing programs or macros that involve parent and child styles, you can check the internal style name by using the List command.

Follow these steps to add a child style to your new dimension style:

EXAMPLE: ADDING A CHILD STYLE TO THE DIMENSION STYLE

1. Open the Dimension Style Manager with your new dimension style (My Standard) as the current style.

2. Click the <u>N</u>ew button. When the Create New Dimension Style dialog box opens, select Radius Dimensions from the <u>U</u>se for list box. My Standard: Radial appears in the New Style Name text box (see Figure 14.17).

Figure 14.17
In the Create New Dimension Style dialog box, you can select a subgroup of dimensions and create a variation of the parent dimension style.

3. Press the Continue button and make any desired changes for radial dimensions. For example, on the Lines and Arrows tab, change the type of arrowhead to None for radial dimensions. You will see this change in the sample graphic.

   You will observe as you click from tab to tab that only the relevant variables for radial dimensions are highlighted; all other input boxes and buttons are grayed out. Only the radius portion is displayed in the sample graphic.

4. Click OK to return to the opening page of the Dimension Style Manager. The parent-child relationship is shown in the list of available styles, and the changes you have made are shown in the Description panel.

5. Click close to return to the AutoCAD 2000 drawing editor.

The new style is automatically updated to the existing radius dimensions. Although you have created a new child style, AutoCAD 2000 regards this as a modification because it is dependent upon an existing parent. Hence, you do not need to update your existing dimensions.

DELETING AND RENAMING DIMENSION STYLES

By now you have probably created a number of dimension styles and children of dimension styles that you no longer want to keep in your drawing. If you decide you want to delete or rename a dimension style, it is not immediately obvious how to do so.

EXAMPLE: DELETING AND RENAMING DIMENSION STYLES

1. Click the Dimension Style button or select Dimension, Style from the menu. All the dimension styles in the drawing are displayed in the <u>S</u>tyles list box.

2. Highlight the style you want to delete or rename, and then right-click to open the shortcut menu for that style.

3. When the shortcut menu appears, click Rename and overtype the existing name with a new name, or click Delete to remove the dimension style.

Take care: If you rename a dimension style that is a member of a family, it will no longer have an association with the parent. Once renamed, it will become an independent dimension style, and the parent group will lose its specific subset of dimension controls.

IMPORTING AND EXPORTING DIMENSION STYLES

It seems that quite a bit of work is involved in creating a dimension style, especially if you are creating a family of styles. Unfortunately, any dimension styles you create are associated with the particular drawing in which you create them, but fortunately, there are three different ways you can transport them from drawing to drawing.

- Templates—You may save dimension styles—and any other standards you require—in a template drawing. Each time you start a new drawing, you may load the template and thereby load the dimension style into your new drawing. You will review this process in the next section in this chapter.

- DesignCenter—You can drag and drop dimension styles—and other design elements such as layers and linetypes—from drawing to drawing via the AutoCAD 2000 DesignCenter. This process is reviewed in the section "Transferring Dimension Styles via the DesignCenter," on page 333 later in this chapter.

- Express Tools—Two programs in the AutoCAD 2000 Express tools are specifically for exporting and importing dimension styles. These programs are described in the section "Importing and Exporting via the Express Tools" on page 334 later in this chapter.

SAVING DIMENSION STYLES IN A TEMPLATE

It is a good practice to save any drawing standards and styles you have developed in a template (.DWT) file for future use. Try this with the styles you created in CH14EX01.DWG. Before you save the template, you should erase the line work and dimensions from the drawing.

EXAMPLE: SAVING DIMENSION STYLES IN A TEMPLATE

1. Select File, Save As, and select AutoCAD Drawing Template file in the Type list box.

   When you select the .DWT option, AutoCAD 2000 opens the \TEMPLATE directory.

2. Enter a name for your template in the File Name list box.

   You may simply copy the drawing filename, but it makes more sense to give it a name that will describe its purpose. This drawing might be called **Standard No Scale**, another might be **Mechanical 1** or **City Library Project**, and so on.

3. When prompted, enter a description of the main features of this style—for example, **Engineering Units; eighth-inch text and arrows**, and so on. This description will help you identify the template you require in future. Then press OK to save the template.

When you want to start a new drawing with your saved dimension style(s), open the Template drawing as described in the following steps.

EXAMPLE: STARTING A NEW DRAWING WITH THE SAVED DIMENSION STYLES

1. Click the New Document icon, or select File, New, and then page down through the templates displayed in the Create a New Drawing dialog box (see Figure 14.18). (If the templates are not automatically displayed, click the Use a Template icon.)

2. Select the template drawing (.DWT) you saved, and click OK. (In Figure 14.18, the template drawing is shown as CH14EX01.DWT.)

   AutoCAD 2000 opens an empty drawing that contains all the style elements you saved in the template.

3. Save the new drawing under an appropriate new name.

Figure 14.18
You may load the dimension styles you want into a new drawing via a stored template drawing.

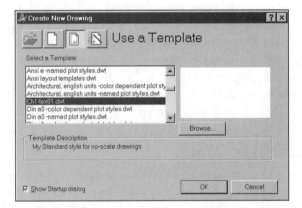

Note

You may be wondering why it is necessary to create a template in order to transfer a "style" from one drawing to another. This is because within the AutoCAD 2000 environment, a style has no independent existence outside of a drawing. A template drawing provides a vehicle that can contain styles and other kinds of drawing content you want to reuse in different drawings.

A template (or drawing prototype) can contain a library of dimension styles, text styles, linetypes, symbols, and so on. Rather than starting a new drawing from scratch, you can open a template drawing and start with all the styles in place. Just remember to save the template under a regular drawing name (.DWG) before you start to add any objects.

TRANSFERRING DIMENSION STYLES VIA THE DESIGNCENTER

Using a template is very effective when you are starting a new drawing. But what about importing a dimension style you have created or received into an existing drawing? The AutoCAD 2000 DesignCenter facilitates reusing and sharing drawing content, such as blocks, layers, and styles. With the DesignCenter, you can locate any drawing, inspect its content, and then drag and drop any design elements you choose from the source drawing into another drawing.

Take a look at how simple it is to move your new dimension style from one drawing to another:

EXAMPLE: MOVING THE NEW DIMENSION STYLE

1. First, open a drawing that does not contain the dimension style My Standard.

2. Select Tools, AutoCAD DesignCenter, or press Ctrl+2 to open the DesignCenter.

   The first time AutoCAD DesignCenter opens, it is docked at the left side of the drawing area. You should undock it by double-clicking the title bar and then dragging the DesignCenter interface away from the docking region. When you drop the title bar, it will become a floating window that you can resize, enlarge, and generally move around on the screen. (You may re-dock the DesignCenter when you are through by double-clicking the title bar again.)

   The left panel of the DesignCenter displays all of the graphical objects stored on your computer system, such as drawings, bitmaps, and GIF files. It is organized in a tree-type hierarchy like the Windows Explorer. (If Tree view is turned off on your system, click the Tree View toggle button at the top left of the panel.)

3. Browse through the folders displayed in the DeisgnCenter to locate the CH14EX01.DWG file, which contains the dimension style(s) you want.

4. Click the drawing name.

   Yet another level in the hierarchy opens up; the DesignCenter displays a set of folders within the AutoCAD 2000 drawing that contain the drawing content.

5. Click the Dimstyles folder.

   All the dimension styles in this drawing are displayed in the adjacent window. This is shown in Figure 14.19.

6. Select My Standard and drag it from the DesignCenter onto the destination drawing, which is currently open in AutoCAD 2000.

After you have dragged all the styles you require into your open drawing, you may re-dock or close the DesignCenter. When you check your drawing, you will see that My Standard has been imported: Click the arrow on the style list box on the Dimension toolbar to verify which dimension styles are loaded in your drawing.

The DesignCenter is a very versatile tool. If you are working in a networked environment, you can set up standard dimension styles for company-wide use and distribute them from

PART

IV

CH

14

the office file server via the DesignCenter. You can even use the DesignCenter across your company intranet or the Internet to access drawing content from FTP or Web sites.

Figure 14.19
The AutoCAD 2000 DesignCenter enables you to drag dimension styles from one drawing to another.

IMPORTING AND EXPORTING VIA THE EXPRESS TOOLS

AutoCAD 2000 comes with a set of productivity programs and utilities called Express Tools. If you have not installed these yet, you should consider doing so now—you will see a menu item Express on the AutoCAD 2000 menu if the tools are loaded. The Express Tools contain a number of dimensioning utilities, including a program to export a dimension style and one to import a dimension style.

→ For more information on installing and using the Express Tools, see Chapter 15, "Making Drawing Easier," p. 357.

To export dimension style(s), follow these steps:

EXAMPLE: EXPORTING DIMENSION STYLES

1. Select Express, Dimension, Dimstyle Export.

   The Dimension Style Export dialog box is displayed.

2. This utility creates a default .DIM file (with the same name as the drawing) that contains all the styles in the drawing. You may optionally choose to do the following:

   - Rename the .DIM file to a more meaningful filename.
   - Export the .DIM file to another folder. By default, the .DIM file will be saved in the same folder as the drawing.
   - Save full Text Style information with the .DIM file.

3. Click OK to export the style(s) and then exit your source drawing.

To import dimension style(s) into another drawing, follow these steps:

EXAMPLE: IMPORTING DIMENSION STYLES INTO ANOTHER DRAWING

1. Open another drawing and select Express, Dimension, Dimstyle Import.

   The Dimension Style Import dialog box is displayed.

2. Browse to the folder where you saved the .DIM file, and select it.

   You may choose to overwrite any existing dimension styles.

This utility works effectively, but with some limitations. As you will no doubt discover, this utility truncates style names with spaces in them—for example, My Standard becomes My—and is probably best used to import/export single dimension styles rather than more complex parent-child-style families. By now, you are thoroughly familiar with all aspects of creating dimension styles and reusing them in different drawings. Take a look now at some situations in which you will need to create modifications to styles you have created.

MAKING CHANGES IN DIMENSION STYLES

In an ideal world, you will create a dimension style (or dimension family) for every standard type of drawing that you produce. However, the real world occasionally comes up with non-standard situations in which it doesn't make sense to create a new dimension style just for one drawing or a part of a drawing.

For these situations, AutoCAD 2000 has some other options: You may either modify the existing dimension style for that drawing only, or use the dimension override option to change a few dimensions within the drawing. In the next two sections, you will take a look at some common scenarios where you will need to vary your underlying dimension styles to meet short-term needs.

MODIFYING A STYLE

If you need to change some aspect of the dimension style in an existing drawing, it is not necessary to create a new style and then go through the Dimension Update process.

For example, for a specific presentation, you may need to include metric as well as imperial (feet and inches) dimensions on your drawing. This option is available on the Alternate Units tab of the Dimension Style Manager, but it is not a part of your standard dimension style.

You can simply make a modification to the current style via the Dimension Style Manager. When you exit from the Dimension Style Manager, the changes are automatically put into effect in your drawing. There is no need to use the update procedure.

From this point forward, any dimensions you add will display the new dimension settings. You have made a permanent change to the style for this drawing—unless you reverse the modification, in which case all dimensions will revert to the original settings.

PART

IV

CH

14

If you want to experiment with this process, open your practice drawing again and start the Dimension Style Manager. Choose Modify, click the Alternate Units tab, and check the Display Alternate Units check box. The two sets of units will be displayed in your drawing for each *linear* dimension you add, as shown in Figure 14.20.

If you need to make a temporary change specific to only a subset of dimensions in the drawing, do not modify your dimension style; instead use the Dimension Override command.

OVERRIDING DIMENSION STYLES

Sometimes when you are dimensioning, you need to make a temporary change to some aspect of a dimension style: For example, if you want to highlight a set of critical dimensions in a drawing, you could change the color or the lineweight so they plot more heavily. Or you might need to increase or decrease the text size to make it easier to read or to make dimensions fit in a particular part of a drawing.

In any of these situations, you will need to create a temporary variation on the default style. This is accomplished by using a dimension override, which involves a three-step process:

EXAMPLE: OVERRIDING DIMENSION STYLES

1. First, set the override. Start the Dimension Style Manager, click the Override button and make any changes in the style tabs you require, and then press OK. (The Dimension Style Manager shows the <style overrides> you have made.) Click Close to return to your drawing.

2. Then, you add (or update) the subset of nonstandard dimensions. Any *new* dimensions added will be based on the override settings. To update *existing* dimensions, click on the update button on the Dimension toolbar and then select the dimensions to change.

3. Finally, you clear the override and carry on with normal dimensioning. Open the Dimension Style Manager again. In the Styles list box, highlight <Style Overrides> and then delete it.

WORKING WITH MULTIPLE SCALES

A particularly useful application of the Dimension Override command is when different parts of your drawing are drawn at different scales. This very common situation can cause inaccuracies in dimension measurements if not handled correctly. A typical instance of this is when you have a building plan, elevations, and construction details all on the same sheet. Each of these items is drawn to a different scale and yet all of the dimensions should be the same size on the plotted output. In the next example, you will enlarge a part of the sample drawing, note how this affects the dimensioning, and learn how to compensate for the scaling differences. (This problem arises in scaled drawings typically, but you can use this nonscaled drawing to demonstrate the principles.)

EXAMPLE: WORKING WITH MULTIPLE SCALES

1. Open CH14EX01.DWG, and add a linear dimension to the segment AH on the lower-left section of the drawing for comparison purposes.

2. Type **scale** and then select the bottom-right section using a crossing window. Specify a Scale Factor of **1.5**.

   The line work and the text both enlarge 160%—you may have to move this part of the drawing over a bit. Use the Property Painter (paintbrush icon on the Standard toolbar) to match the text size to the rest of the drawing. (Select the Property Painter, select a piece of the original text, and then click each piece of enlarged text in turn to reduce their size.)

3. Add a linear dimension to segment HA.

   Because AutoCAD does not realize that this drawing part is 1.5 scale, it measures the dimension at 1.52 feet instead of the true 1.02 feet (see Figure 14.20). To compensate, you will set an override (multiplier) in the linear scale factor.

Figure 14.20
When different parts of a drawing are scaled differently, the dimension calculations will be inaccurate if the appropriate adjustments are not made.

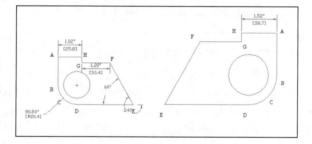

4. Open the Dimension Style Manager and click the Override button.

5. Open the Primary Units tab and adjust the Scale factor in the Measurement Scale panel to **0.6666** (or 1/1.5).

   Because the drawing part is 1.5 scale, you must multiply *down* the linear scale measurement.

   This variable controls only the linear scale, not the overall dimension scale. The appearance of the dimension will stay the same and only the calculation will change.

6. Click OK to return to the opening dialog box, where you will see that the style override is noted and described in the <u>S</u>tyle and <u>D</u>escription boxes.

7. Press Close to return to the AutoCAD 2000 drawing editor, click the Dimension Update button, and select the dimension HA.

   The measurement will now read accurately at 1.02.

PART

IV

CH

14

When you have completed dimensioning the nonstandard drawing section, open the Dimension Style Manager and delete the override: Select the <style overrides> in the Styles list box. Then right-click to open the shortcut menu and select Delete. Your dimension style now reverts to normal. If you have another drawing part at a different scale, repeat this procedure for the new scale.

SETTING AN OVERRIDE AT THE COMMAND LINE   The preceding process is a fairly lengthy series of steps to go through just to change one dimension—four steps to set the override and another couple to remove it. Before the advent of the Dimension Style Manager, users performed this task at the command prompt using the Dimoverride command, which was actually faster than navigating through pages of dialog boxes. However, it required some understanding of the underlying dimension variables. If your work involves a lot of temporary adjustments to dimension styles, you may find it worthwhile to learn more about the dimension system variables so you can use this command-line alternative, which requires only two keyboard entries.

EXAMPLE: SETTING AN OVERRIDE AT THE COMMAND LINE

1. Type **dimoverride**, or select Dimension, Override on the menu.

   You are prompted with this line:

   ```
   Enter dimension variable name to override or [Clear overrides]:
   ```

   The dimension variable that controls linear scale is Dimlfac.

2. Enter **dimlfac** and then a new value of **.6666,** and you are in business.

3. When you have completed dimensioning the nonstandard drawing part, repeat these steps to revert to the original linear scale setting of 1.0.

If you have only one dimension variable to override, it's even faster to simply type **dimlfac** at the command prompt and enter a new value. When you are finished, remember to type **dimlfac** again and reset the value.

Tip 108 from
Paul Richardson

When you receive a drawing from another source and cannot figure out what is going on with the dimensions, the answer may lie in the overrides. Use the List command on any problem dimensions, and it will show the overrides that are in place. A listing of your practice dimension shows the following:

```
default text
dimension style: "My Standard"
dimension style overrides:
  DIMLFAC     0.6666
```

If you want to be able to use the command line Dimoverride option, you will need at least a rudimentary understanding of dimension system variables—or the knowledge of where to find the necessary information when you need it. Throughout this chapter, in all of the exercises you have completed to date, you have been working with dimension variables without actually knowing it. As you created dimension styles, modified specific elements of styles, and scaled your dimensions, you were setting and manipulating the underlying system variables. To learn more about the specific functions performed by dimension variables, you should read the following section.

DIMENSION SYSTEM VARIABLES

Using and understanding the dimension system variables is entirely optional nowadays, because AutoCAD 2000 enables you to dimension quite successfully without using any dimension variables. If you plan to do any programming in the AutoCAD 2000 environment that involves dimensioning, you need to understand dimension variables because you will have to read and write to them directly without the assistance of the user interface. Otherwise, you may prefer to skim through this section and proceed to the following section.

The Dimension Style Manager is essentially a front end for dealing with dimension system variables. The Command Reference in AutoCAD 2000 help provides a useful graphic that depicts the relationship between dimension system variables and the Dimension Style Manager. Open the AutoCAD 2000 help and select Command Reference in the Contents tab. Then, open the Dimension Style Quick Reference. All the components of the dialog box are labeled with the corresponding dimension variable. Figure 14.21 shows the first page of this reference. You should check through all the pages to get a better grasp of the functions of dimension system variables. For more detailed information about the actual values, refer to Table 14.2.

Figure 14.21
The AutoCAD 2000 online help provides a useful cross-reference between the Dimension Style Manager and the system variables.

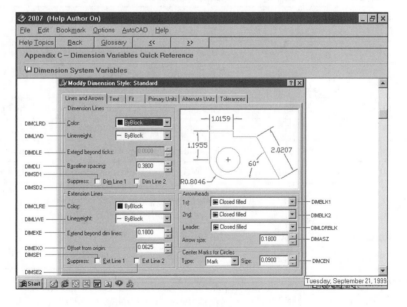

Users may manipulate these variables directly by typing the name of the variable at the command prompt and entering a value. This achieves the same result as clicking the

Override button in the Dimension Style Manager. If you do change a dimension variable setting in this way, the new setting becomes an override to the current dimension style. For example, if you change the Overall Dimension Scale, or DIMSCALE setting, to 48, any new dimensions created will have a dimension scale of 48. An override is not saved as a part of the dimension style, but it remains in effect as if it were until you turn it off.

Using dimension system variables does require that you become familiar with the name and function of each variable. The following table groups the variables by function to make it easier to browse for the appropriate settings. This is not intended as an exhaustive explanation of dimension variables, but rather as a guide to help you find the variables you need.

TABLE 14.2   DIMENSION VARIABLES

General

Variable	Values	Description
DIMSCALE	1.0000	Specifies the scale multiplier for arrows, text, spacing, and so on. Zero enables automatic scale from paper space viewport.
DIMSHO	ON	Displays the changing value of a dimension while re-sizing.
DIMSTYLE	Standard	Gives the name of the current dimension style.
DIMASO	ON	Creates dimensions as a single associated object.

Dimension and Extension Lines

Variable	Value	Description
DIMDLE	0.0000	The overlap distance of the baseline beyond the extension lines when ticks are used.
DIMDLI	0.3800	Offset spacing for baseline dimensioning.
DIMEXE	0.1800	The distance beyond the baseline for extension lines when diagonal ticks are used.
DIMEXO	0.0625	The gap between the extension lines and the dimension point.
DIMSE1	OFF	ON value suppresses the display of the first extension line.
DIMSE2	OFF	ON value suppresses the display of the second extension line.
DIMSOXD	OFF	Suppresses display of dimension line outside extension lines.

Alternate Unit Dimensions
(These are active only when DIMALT = ON)

Variable	Value	Description
DIMALT	OFF	Controls the display of alternate units
DIMALTD	2	Specifies the number of decimal places for alternate units display.
DIMALTF	25.4000	Gives the scale multiplier for alternate units. Default translates inches to centimeters.
DIMALTRND	0.0000	Gives decimal places for rounding values, for alternate units.

Alternate Unit Dimensions
(These are active only when DIMALT = ON)

Variable	Value	Description
DIMALTTD	2	Gives decimal places for Tolerance dimension for alternate units.
DIMALTTZ	0	Gives zero suppression, Tolerances.
DIMALTU	2	Gives display units.
DIMALTZ	0	Dives zero suppression.
DIMAPOST	""	Adds text before or after dimension text. Use <> to represent default dimension.

Angular Dimensions

Variable	Value	Description
DIMAUNIT	0	Gives units for angular dimension.
DIMAZIN	0	Suppresses zeros for angular dimensions.
DIMADEC	0	Gives number of decimal places for angular dimensions.
DIMCEN	0.0900	Specifies size of center line or mark. Negative value is center line; positive is center mark arrows.
DIMASZ	0.1800	Gives arrow size (multiplied by value of DIMSCALE).
DIMBLK	""	Specifies the dimension block for arrowheads. Use a period to define the default. (DIMSAH must be off).
DIMBLK1	""	Gives dimension block for first arrowhead. (DIMSAH must be on).
DIMBLK2	""	Gives dimension block for second arrowhead (DIMSAH must be on).
DIMLDRBLK	""	Gives arrow type for Leaders.
DIMSAH DIMBLK2.	OFF	Off = Default DIMBLK arrows; ON = use DIMBLK1 and
DIMSD1	OFF	ON value suppresses the display of first arrowhead.
DIMSD2	OFF	ON value suppresses the display of second arrowhead.
DIMTSZ	0.0000	Angled tick size; zero value enables regular arrow display.

Color and Lineweight Settings

Variable	Value	Description
DIMCLRD	0	Color for dimension line and arrowheads
DIMCLRE	0	Color for extension lines
DIMCLRT	0	Color for text
DIMLWD	–2	Lineweight setting for dimension lines
DIMLWE	–2	Lineweight setting for extension lines

continues

TABLE 14.2 CONTINUED

Color must be an integer 0–256, where 0 represents the logical color Byblock and 256 represents the logical color Bylayer. Byblock or 0 is the default.

Text Display in Dimensions

Variable	Value	Description
DIMDEC	4	Number of decimal places to display in dimension text.
DIMDSEP	"."	Character used for decimal separation; default is a period.
DIMFIT	3	Obsolete, replaced with DIMATFIT and DIMTMOVE.
DIMFRAC	0	Setting for the fraction display format (when DIMLUNIT = 4 or 5).
DIMJUST	0	Alignment of text in relation to extension lines.
DIMLFAC	1.0000	Multiplier for calculated value in dimension text.
DIMGAP	0.0900	Definition for the space between a leader line and text; also minimum dimension line length.
DIMLUNIT	2	Linear units for dimension text display.
DIMPOST	""	Addition of text before or after Dimension text. Use <> to represent default dimension.
DIMRND	0.0000	Decimal places for rounding values.
DIMTAD	0	0 value puts text above the dimension line; 1 value breaks the dimension line.
DIMTIH dimension line	ON	ON value always draws text horizontally; OFF aligns text with
DIMTVP DIMTAD = OFF).	0.0000	Vertical position adjustment for dimension text (only when
DIMTXSTY	Standard	Text style for dimension text.
DIMTXT	0.1800	Text height, multiplied by the value of DIMSCALE when text style height = 0.
DIMUNIT	2	Obsolete. Replaced by DIMLUNIT and DIMFRAC.
DIMUPT	OFF	User-positioned text. OFF = dimension line only; ON = dimension and text.
DIMZIN	0	Zero suppression. 0 = suppress 0 feet and 0 inches; 1 = allow both; 2 = suppress 0 inches; 3 = suppress 0 feet.

When text is forced outside the extension lines because it doesn't fit, use the following variables.

DIMTIX	OFF	ON value forces text between extension lines; OFF allows AutoCAD to decide.
DIMTMOVE	0	0 = move dimension line; 1 = Add leader; 2 = No leader.

Text Display in Dimensions

Variable	Value	Description
DIMTOFL line.DIMTOH	OFF ON	ON value draws a dimension line; OFF = no dimension ON value displays text horizontally; OFF aligns text with dimension line.
DIMATFIT	3	0 = text and arrows move outside extensions; 1 = move arrows first; 2 = move text first; 3 = try both for best fit.

Tolerance Dimensions

Variable	Value	Description
DIMLIM	OFF	Generates dimension limits (turns DIMTOL off).
DIMTOL	OFF	Adds tolerance to dimension text (turns DIMLIM off).
DIMTDEC	4	Specifies number of decimal places to display in dimension text.
DIMTFAC	1.0000	Sets scale factor for text height.
DIMTM	0.0000	Sets minimum tolerance value for dimension text.
DIMTOLJ	1	Specifies justification for tolerance text. 0 = bottom; 1 = middle; 2 = top.
DIMTP	0.0000	Gives upper tolerance limit.
DIMTZIN	0	Zero suppression. 0 = suppress 0 feet and 0 inches; 1 = allow both; 2 = suppress 0 inches; 3 = suppress 0 feet.

This section of the chapter is primarily for reference. There is no way you can expect to digest all of this information simply by reading it. Use the preceding table whenever you need to find out which variable controls a particular setting, and then read about it in more detail in the AutoCAD Command Reference.

SPEEDING UP DIMENSIONING

By now, you should be very familiar with the basic dimensioning techniques available in AutoCAD 2000. It's time now to look at three dimensioning commands that will allow you to work even faster. These are grouped together at the center of the Dimension toolbar (see Figure 14.22).

Figure 14.22
These buttons on the Dimension toolbar access the speed-dimensioning commands: QDIM, Baseline Dimension, and Continue Dimension.

PART

IV

CH

14

These commands do not involve new types of dimensioning. Rather, they work along with the commands you are familiar with—linear, angular, ordinate, and so on. The Continue and Baseline Dimension commands allow you to repeat functions without having to repeat the dimensioning command each time; the Quick Dimension command allows you to dimension multiple objects at the same time. Open up a new practice drawing to practice the speed-dimensioning commands. On the CD that accompanies this book, locate the drawing file CH14EXO2.DWG and copy it to your system. This drawing is a simple architectural-type drawing, and the dimension style, layout, and floating viewport have already been set up. Now that you are familiar with how dimension styles are set up, you may want to browse through the Dimension Style Manager and check out how this style differs from the previous one that you created. A major difference is that this drawing is scaled. The Overall Dimension Scale is 48, which means it is set up to plot at 1/4 inch = 1 foot.

CONTINUE DIMENSION

The Continue Dimension command (Dimcontinue) is the rightmost of the three speed-dimension buttons. This command enables you to continue adding dimensions off the second extension point of the previous dimension. To create a continued dimension, you must first create (or select) a linear, ordinate, or angular dimension to serve as the base dimension. Then, the Continue command enables you to keep adding more dimensions simply by picking consecutive points.

EXAMPLE: USING CONTINUE DIMENSION

1. Open the CH14EX02.DWG and zoom to the top end of the plan.

2. Add a linear dimension from the top left corner of the plan to the midpoint or endpoint of the partition wall.

3. Click the Continue Dimension button, or select Dimension, Continue from the menu.

   A dimension is generated automatically, starting from the endpoint of the dimension you just added, and you are prompted with this:

   ```
   Specify a second extension line origin or [Undo/Select] <Select>:
   ```

4. Select a point at the next partition wall and then a farther point at the edge of the curved wall.

5. Press Enter to complete the command.

   The results are shown at the top of Figure 14.23.

Note

Although the Continue dimension command starts from the most recent dimension by default, you can also "continue" from dimensions you entered in an earlier dimensioning session. If you do not want to start from the most recent dimension, just press Enter at the Specify a Second Extension prompt, and select another dimension object. This option applies to the Baseline Dimension command also.

Figure 14.23
The Continue Dimension and Baseline Dimension commands enable you to repeat dimensioning commands.

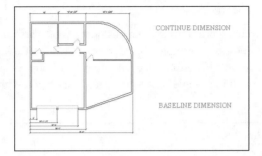

BASELINE DIMENSION

The Baseline Dimension command (Dimbaseline) works in a similar fashion to the Continue Dimension. This command either starts from the basepoint of last dimension created or prompts the user to select a dimension object to act as the base dimension. It enables you to create a series of dimensions from a single basepoint. For example, you might want to measure from the same exterior wall to each of the doors, windows, and interior walls along the same axis.

EXAMPLE: USING BASELINE DIMENSION

1. Zoom to the lower edge of CH14EX02.DWG, and add a linear dimension from the lower-left corner to the edge of the door.

2. Click the Baseline Dimension button, or select Dimension, Baseline from the menu.

   A dimension is generated automatically, starting from the same baseline as the dimension you just added, and you are prompted with this:

   ```
   Specify a second extension line origin or [Undo/Select] <Select>:
   ```

3. Select a point at the edge of the wall between the doors, then at the end of the second door, then at the intersection of the angled wall, and finally at the edge of the right exterior wall.

4. Press Enter to complete the command.

   The results are shown at the bottom of Figure 14.23.

The dimensions all share the same first extension line and have a different second extension line. Each dimension is automatically positioned below the previous dimension, offset by the same amount. The Baseline offset (or spacing) is controlled by the dimension variable Dimdli. This variable can be manipulated in the Dimension Style Manager. If you check the Lines and Arrows tab, you will see that Baseline spacing is set to 3/8 inch. You can override or modify the value here, or you can simply type **dimdli** at the command prompt and change the value there.

The Baseline Dimension command can create linear, angular, or ordinate dimension objects, depending on the original dimension in the series.

QUICK DIMENSION

The Quick Dimension command is a powerful dimensioning tool that is new with AutoCAD 2000. QDIM dimensions multiple objects with the same baseline and can be a real timesaver. With this command you can select any number of objects in the drawing and QDIM will dimension them all in a single pass. It is easier to use QDIM than to try to explain what it can do.

EXAMPLE: USING QUICK DIMENSION

1. Open a clean copy of CH14EX02.DWG.

2. Zoom to the top of the drawing again, and click the Quick Dimension button on the Dimension toolbar, or select Dimension, QDIM from the menu.

   You are prompted to select an object to dimension.

3. Use a selection window to select the entire top wall in the architectural plan. (Drag the selection window from left to right to make an inclusive window.)

   Before you press Enter, notice the options displayed at the command line:

   ```
   Specify dimension line position, or
   [Continuous/Staggered/Baseline/Ordinate/Radius/Diameter/datumPoint/Edit]
   <Continuous >:
   ```

4. Press Enter to accept the default <Continuous >. (Or type **c** and then press Enter if your default is different.)

Instantaneously, QDIM dimensions all the points it can find in the selection window. Your drawing should resemble Figure 14.24. The Quick Dimension command creates multiple dimension objects at once, possibly more than you need at times. However, you can edit or remove individual dimension objects after the command is complete.

Figure 14.24
Using the Quick Dimension command (QDIM), you can dimension multiple objects with a single click.

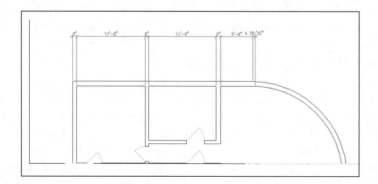

When you have finished admiring this instant dimensioning, erase (or undo) this dimension and repeat the procedure, testing each of the options shown in step 3. As usual with command-line options, you need to type only the capitalized part of the option. You should be familiar by now with most of these types of dimensions, except perhaps the Staggered dimension, which is a variation on a continuous dimension, in which the dimensions are nested inside each other.

Now that you are familiar with all of the basic dimensioning functions and with the speed dimensioning options, you have just about covered all of the bases. The remaining two commands on the toolbar are Quick Leader and Tolerance. These are not real dimensioning functions; they are annotation functions that share some common features with dimensioning.

LEADERS AND TOLERANCES

The Leader and Tolerance commands are located in the center of the Dimension toolbar, to the right of the Continue Dimension command.

- A leader is simply an arrow that points to a location in a drawing and then leads to one or several lines of text.
- Geometric tolerances specify deviations of form, profile, orientation, location, and runout of a feature.

Let's take a brief look at these annotation objects, starting with leaders.

SETTING UP A DIMENSION STYLE FOR LEADERS

For a professional-looking drawing, the leaders should have a consistent look, using the same arrows at the same size, perhaps using the same angle for the arrow. If you have a column of leaders, they should be aligned vertically so that the text portion of the leaders always starts in the same horizontal position. A dimension style is the obvious way to set standards for leader arrows and text.

Leaders are often drawn a little differently than regular linear and aligned-dimension objects. Architectural dimensions typically use diagonal ticks instead of arrows but require a solid arrowhead for the leader. The position of the text is typically different also: Text is usually above the line for a standard dimension and is aligned with the line for a leader.

To handle these differences in style, you can set up a subsidiary (or child) style for leaders only, within the current (parent) dimension style. For further information about this, see "Dimension Style Families," on page **329**.

EXAMPLE: SETTING UP A DIMENSION STYLE

1. Click the Dimension Style button on the Dimension toolbar, and then click the <u>New</u> button.

   The Create New Dimension Style dialog box is displayed.

2. In the Use For list box, click the down arrow and select Leaders and Tolerances; then click Continue.

The name in the New Style Name box changes to the parent dimension style name followed by Leader: ARCHITECTURAL: leader. The naming is automatic; even if you type in a name it will be overwritten. AutoCAD 2000 links the child style with its parent style via the name. If you rename the parent or child, you will lose the connection.

3. When the New Dimension Style dialog opens, click the Lines and Arrows tab and check that the leader arrowhead is a solid arrow. Change it to a solid arrow if necessary.

4. On the Text tab, select the Centered option on the vertical text placement.

5. Click OK and then close the Dimension Style Manager.

    The changes you made will be applied to the leader objects only.

QUICK LEADER

Now that you have a dimension style set up to handle leaders, go ahead and create some.

EXAMPLE: USING QUICK LEADER

1. Click the Quick Leader button (qleader) on the Dimension toolbar, or select Dimension, Leader from the menu.

2. Click anywhere onscreen to place the arrowhead.

3. Click a second point to define the end of the arrow and the start of the *hook line*. Rather than turn Ortho mode on (F8), draw a short line, and then turn Ortho mode off again—simply press Enter at this point.

    AutoCAD 2000 draws a standard-length hook line for you.

4. You will be prompted to enter text:

```
Specify text width <6'-2">:
Enter first line of annotation text <Mtext>:
```

    You can specify a value for the width of the text or indicate the desired width onscreen. (You can always resize the Mtext object later.) Add as many lines of text that you need to complete the leader label, and then press Enter to exit the command.

    If you prefer to use the Multiline Text Editor, press Enter at the first text prompt, without typing any text, to display the editor.

QUICK LEADER SETTINGS

You may have noticed that when you start the qleader command, you see a Settings option at the Command prompt:

```
Command: _qleader
Specify first leader point, or [Settings]<Settings>:
```

If you type **s** and press Enter, you open the Leader Settings dialog box. This enables you to set some additional Dimension Style settings for the Leader object only. The Leader

Settings dialog box contains the following two tabs, which enable you to preset the angle of leader lines and the position of leader text:

- Click the Leader Line & Arrow tab, and notice that you can constrain your leader to preset angles or allow any angle. The second segment or hook line can be similarly constrained, but a more standard setting would be horizontal.

- Click the Attachment tab, and you will see two columns of radio buttons controlling options when Mtext is on the left or right side of the leader arrow.

At this point, you can click Cancel because you are not going to make any more changes to the leader settings.

SPLINE LEADER

More leader options exist, although they are not available on the Dimension toolbar. The regular Leader command allows multiple types of leaders, including spline curve leaders and tolerance annotation.

EXAMPLE: USING SPLINE LEADER

1. To review the Spline Leader, type **leader** at the command prompt, and locate the arrowhead with your cursor.

2. Click the second leader point, and you will notice some options on the command line:
   ```
   Specify next point or [Annotation/Format/Undo] <Annotation>:
   ```

3. Type **F** and press Enter to bring up the Format options:
   ```
   Enter leader format option [Spline/STraight/Arrow/None] <Exit>:
   ```

4. Type **S** to select the Spline option.

   You will now see the spline curve onscreen, and you can make it as long as you like by entering more points.

5. Click Enter to complete the command.

The Spline option will remain in effect for leader objects until you change the format option to Straight. You also have the format option of a leader with No Arrow, and an Arrow option to put it back again.

LEADER ANNOTATION OPTIONS

The Leader command has some interesting annotation options. When you create a leader, type **a** at the command prompt and then press Enter. You will be offered a choice of annotation options:

```
Specify next point or [Annotation/Format/Undo] <Annotation>: a
Enter first line of annotation text or <options>:
Enter an annotation option [Tolerance/Copy/Block/None/Mtext] <Mtext>:
```

- The Tolerance option opens the Geometric Tolerance dialog box, as described in the next section.

- The Copy option enables you to copy the annotation from any other leader object, including a Tolerance control frame and its geometric tolerances.

- The Block option enables you to insert a block at an offset from the end of the leader (no hook line). The prompts are the same as the Insert command when you insert a block into a drawing.

TOLERANCE

In mechanical engineering and drafting, tolerances are a key part of a drawing's annotation. The Tolerance command (tolerance) offers a quick way to build standard feature control symbols, as shown in Figure 14.25.

Figure 14.25
Standard feature control notation.

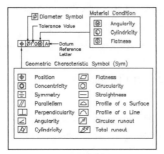

When you click the Tolerance button on the Dimension toolbar, or select Dimension, Tolerance from the menu, the Geometric Tolerance dialog box (see Figure 14.26) opens and enables you to build the feature control symbol by entering datum values and picking symbols from subsidiary icon menus.

Figure 14.26
The Geometric Tolerance dialog box makes it easier to develop standard tolerance annotation.

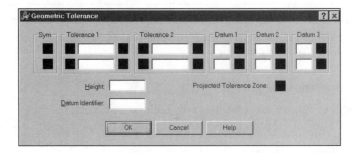

By this point in the chapter, you have learned all there is to know about creating all the different forms of dimensioning: linear, ordinate, angular, radial and diameter (as well as the quick dimension, continue, and baseline dimension options). In this section, you have additionally reviewed some dimensioning lookalikes, leaders, and tolerance notation, which share some of the features of dimensions. The only topic left to review is how to edit dimensions you have created.

EDITING DIMENSIONS

AutoCAD 2000 provides two sets of commands for editing dimensions: Dimension Edit and Dimension Text Edit on the Dimension toolbar; and Oblique and Align Text on the Dimension menu. After reviewing each of these commands, you will also try some alternative ways of editing dimensions.

EDITING THE TEXT IN A DIMENSION

The Dimension Text Edit command (Dimtedit) enables you to move the text component of the dimension relative to the baseline. On the Dimension menu, the same function is described as Align Text—a more accurate description of this command. You can use any of your practice dimensions to experiment with these commands.

EXAMPLE: USING DIMENSION TEXT EDIT

1. Click the Dimension Text Edit button on the Dimension toolbar, or select Dimension, Align Text from the menu.

   The sequencing of steps varies between the menu command and the toolbar command, but the final result is comparable. The menu command offers the text alignment options on a cascading menu, and the toolbar command offers the same options at the command prompt. Try each of these in turn. You should restart the text Edit command each time.
   ```
   Specify new location for dimension text or [Left/Right/Center/Home/Angle]:
   ```

2. When the Select Dimension prompt displays, select any dimension object on the screen.

   The dimension text will follow your cursor, allowing you to position the text with your mouse.

3. Type l for left; the text will position itself on the far left of the baseline.

   Try again with the Right and Center options.

4. Finally, use the Home option to position the text back where it was before you rearranged it.

The Angle option enables you to rotate text about its insertion point without rotating the dimension.

EDITING DIMENSIONS

The main editing function offered by the Dimension Edit command (Dimedit) is the capability of adding an obliquing angle to a dimension. If you check on the Dimension menu

PART

IV

CH

14

you will see that the command is called Oblique. The toolbar version of the Dimension Edit command also includes some text editing functions; it enables you to rotate text, change dimension text, and reposition it back to the home position—just like with Dimtedit.

The obliquing function is used to align the extension lines primarily; the rest of the dimension (text, arrowheads) remains in the same orientation, although their positions may change. The most useful application of this command is in isometric drawings. An isometric drawing (CH14EX03.DWG) is supplied on the CD that accompanies this book. Use this drawing to practice using the obliquing function as outlined in the following exercise.

EXAMPLE: USING OBLIQUING

1. Open CH14EX03 in AutoCAD 2000. It is a cube drawn using isometric snap mode. (See the Snap command in AutoCAD 2000's online help for more on isometric style.)

   Look at Figure 14.27. The dimensions on the right of the drawing look a little different from the ones on the left; the right dimensions give the visual impression of being in the same plane as the drawing object. This obliquing effect is accomplished by using the Oblique option of Dimension Edit, which applies an angle setting to the extension lines. You will now edit the dimensions on the left side to match.

Figure 14.27
This isometric drawing demonstrates both correct positioning of dimensions (on right side of cube) and incorrect positioning of dimensions (on left side of cube).

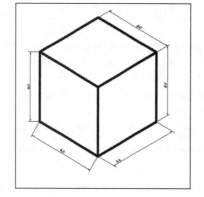

2. Click the Dimension Edit button on the Dimension toolbar, and type **o** at the command prompt; then press Enter. (Or select Dimension, Oblique from the menu.)

3. Select the dimension on the left of the cube. The command prompts for an oblique angle:

   ```
   Enter obliquing angle (press ENTER for none): 30
   ```

4. Type **30** and press Enter.

   The left dimension shifts to a more realistic position. Repeat the operation for the dimension object at the bottom left, giving it an oblique angle of 30° also.

OBLIQUING THE TEXT

You can complete the illusion by applying an oblique text style to the dimension text so it leans the same way as the dimension.

- Use the Style command to set up a new text style, and enter **30** in the Oblique box.
- The dimension object at the bottom right is set at an oblique angle of 330°. (You can also enter this number as –30°.) Make another text style with an oblique angle of –30°.

Apply the new text style(s) to your dimension objects using the Properties command. For further information about using the Properties command, see the section "Changing Dimension Properties," later in this chapter.

→ For more information on text styles, refer to Chapter 12, "Annotating the Drawing."

Tip 109 from
Paul Richardson

If your dimension objects don't stay together as one piece when you create them, they can be very hard to edit. The dimension variable that keeps dimensions as a single object (via associative dimensioning) is Dimaso. If your dimensions break apart, you need to change DIMASO to ON at the command prompt. Type **dimaso,** and then type **ON** or **1** (either will work). Now any new dimensions you create will be grouped as a single object. (Do not look for this adjustment in the Dimension Style Manager dialog box because the setting is not stored in a dimension style.)

The Edit Dimension commands have fairly specific applications: You can reposition and reorient text, and you can change the orientation of the actual dimensions. You can also edit dimensions using standard AutoCAD 2000 editing tools; you can accomplish many of the edits you require by using the *grips* or the Properties command via the right mouse button.

GRIP EDITING

This is the easiest way to edit almost anything, including dimensions. There's nothing to remember. Just click on the dimension object you are interested in, highlight what you want to move, and reposition it. If you click any linear or aligned dimension object, five grips are displayed: one to control text location, two for the control points at the end of the extension lines, and one at either end of the baseline. You can click any grip to make it active (hot) and then click somewhere else to reposition it.

Some applications for grips are not immediately obvious: For example, leaders are made up of two objects that retain a connection. (Create a leader object with the Quick Leader button to check out this option.)

- If you click the text part and then reposition the text object using the grip, the leader will reposition itself relative to the text.
- If you click the leader part, you can reposition it and leave the text object where it was.

PART

IV

CH

14

Stretching an object using grips is the default option, but you do have others. Click a dimension object and highlight a grip, and then look at the command line. You have the following options:

```
Specify move point or [Base point/Copy/Undo/eXit]:
```

You can type the first letter (B, C, U, or X) to start the command option in the usual way, or click the Spacebar and cycle through the options. The Copy option is particularly useful when you want to create multiple leader lines from a single leader object.

CHANGING DIMENSION PROPERTIES

Click any dimension object in your drawing, and then click your right mouse button anywhere in the drawing area. You should see the shortcut menu. Click on the Properties command at the bottom of the menu. The Properties window is displayed.

The Properties window shows you a list of properties you can change for the object you selected. The Properties window will give you menu options for typical object properties, such as layer color and linetype, and also dimension-specific properties, such as lines, arrows, and fit. All of the information embedded in the dimension style is accessible via the Properties window. You can even collect multiple dimension objects and apply a right-click edit to them. This provides an easy and intuitive way to modify your dimensions.

In this chapter, you have explored the full range of dimensioning commands. You have learned how to create dimension styles and how to modify and override them, and you have reviewed the editing options available via the Dimension menu and toolbar, and also the standard AutoCAD editing options you can use. This essentially completes the overview of dimensioning in AutoCAD 2000. A brief discussion of the relative merits of adding dimensions in model space and paper space concludes the chapter.

DIMENSIONING IN PAPER SPACE OR MODEL SPACE?

All of the dimensioning you have added in this chapter has been created in model space, but it is also possible to add dimensions in paper space. In this final section, you will have a chance to practice adding dimensions in paper space, and to evaluate the pros and cons of each approach.

Earlier sections of this chapter looked at some of the scaling problems that arise when you are dimensioning in model space—and how to solve these problems. Some users feel dimension-scaling issues are easier to resolve in paper space (layouts), but in fact each approach requires you to understand the scaling issues and manipulate dimension variables appropriately. You cannot sidestep scaling issues simply by adding your dimensions in paper space. The question of which method is easier for any user largely comes down to which way was learned and mastered first.

→ For more information on dimension scaling in model space, see "Scaling for Different Paper Space Layouts," on page **323**, and "Working with Multiple Scales," on page **336**, earlier in this chapter.

In this next exercise, you will add a dimension in paper space and learn how to make the appropriate scaling adjustments.

EXAMPLE: ADDING A DIMENSION IN PAPER SPACE

1. Clean all the model space dimensions from CH14EX02.DWG and then click the Layout1 tab.

   The viewport scaling has already been set for plotting at 1/4 inch = 1 foot.

2. Zoom to the top of the drawing and add a linear dimension from the top-left corner to the far edge of the first interior wall.

   If you are having trouble snapping to points in the drawing, click the SNAP button on the status bar. Because you have not made any adjustments to the scaling, a huge—and inaccurate—dimension appears on the layout (see Figure 14.28).

Figure 14.28
When you add dimensions in paper space you must adjust the dimension scaling or the measurements will not be accurate.

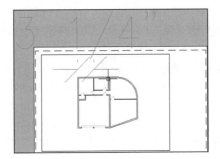

First, consider the text size. You may remember from an earlier section in this chapter, "Calculating a Scale Factor," on page **321**, that to compensate for viewport magnification, model space dimensions must be multiplied up by a corresponding factor. In this scaled drawing, the Overall Dimension Scale Factor is set at 48—so the paper space dimension has been magnified 48 times. You need to go into the Dimension Scale Manager and change this.

3. Open the Dimension Style Manager and select Modify or Override, depending on whether you want to temporarily or permanently change the style.

4. Open the Fit tab and click the Scale Dimensions to Layout (Paper Space) button.

   The Overall Scale value is zeroed out and also grayed out

5. When you return to the layout, click the Dimension Update button and select the oversized dimension.

   The dimension will shrink back to the appropriate size.

However, the calculated measurement is still inaccurate. It reads 3 1/4 inches, which is 48 times smaller than it should be. If you worked through the multiple scale drawings earlier in the chapter you probably have an idea as to how to rectify this. The problem clearly lies in the linear scale value. The model space drawing has been scaled to 1/4 inch = 1 foot, (that is, reduced 48 times) via the viewport, but the layout is effectively at 1:1 scale, which distorts the dimensioning.

6. Go back into the Dimension Style Manager, and this time click the Primary Units tab.

7. Change the Scale Factor to 48, and check the Apply to Layout Dimensions Only box.

8. Click OK and then Close to exit the Dimension Style Manager.

9. Click the Dimension Update button, and select the 3 1/4-inch dimension.

   It will now display the measurement correctly as 13 feet.

Whether you do your dimensioning in model space or in paper space (layout), it seems that there are scaling issues to be resolved that involve either the Overall Dimension Scale (Dimscale) or the linear measurement scale (Dimlfac). Each method is the reverse of the other, so you should probably choose one, set up the dimension style appropriately, and stick with it.

With all scaling issues being effectively equal, other factors might predispose you to choose model space for your dimensions:

- In paper space, you do not have access to the range of object selection methods available when you are dimensioning in model space. This effectively rules out using the Quick Dimension command and generally limits your productivity.

- When you revise or move dimensions in model space, you can edit and reposition the dimensions at the same time. Paper space dimensions must be reworked in a separate cycle.

Probably as a result of these factors, most users today dimension their AutoCAD drawings in model space. However, both options are available and the choice may come down to your personal preference or the dictates of your company standards.

SUMMARY

AutoCAD 2000 has provided some great tools for dimensioning. After you understand the basics of calculating a scale factor for your dimensions—either in model space or paper space—adding dimensions should be as easy as adding text to a drawing. Mastering dimension styles gives you the ability to manage and reuse a set of dimension variables. The AutoCAD DesignCenter enables you to quickly and easily transfer dimension styles from one drawing to another. This means you can reuse and standardize your dimension styles for yourself and perhaps your entire network. You might never have to wrestle with dimension variables again!

CHAPTER 15

MAKING DRAWING EASIER

In this chapter

USING THE INQUIRY TOOLS

With all the interface improvements and productivity enhancements that come with AutoCAD 2000, the user might well believe life could not get any easier for the AutoCAD user. But indeed there is more. Over the years, the development staff at Autodesk has listened to the requests (and complaints) from the trenches and has supplied extra utilities with the core program. The Express Tools package currently supplied with AutoCAD 2000 (some 60 tools in all) is the result of this effort and has built upon the very successful Bonus tools of Release 14.

Within the core package, users can additionally make use of the valuable Inquiry Tools to access the drawing database whenever they need to query an object or perform measurements and calculations concerning drawing objects. Let's take a look at this handful of practical and functional routines before tackling the wide-ranging Express Tools programs.

AutoCAD 2000 stores a list of data for each object in a drawing. In addition to layer, color, and linetype information for each object, AutoCAD 2000 stores geometric data, such as the x, y, and z coordinates of critical points, and the scale and rotation angle of blocks inserted in a drawing. You can query any object and extract this information via the AutoCAD 2000 Inquiry tools. The Inquiry tools are conveniently grouped together on the Tools menu (see Figure 15.1).

Figure 15.1
All the Inquiry tools can be started from the Tools menu.

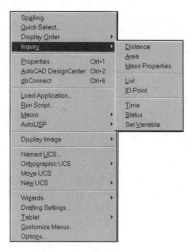

If you prefer to access commands via toolbar, you can load the Inquiry toolbar by choosing View, Toolbars and then selecting Inquiry. The Inquiry toolbar accesses the five main inquiry commands (see Figure 15.2). The remaining commands (Time, Status, and Set Variable) can be started from the menu or command line only.

The Inquiry tools are for information only—they provide measurements and other data about objects in the drawing, but they are not used to modify the objects. In the next several sections, you will have an opportunity to thoroughly test all the Inquiry tools. A practice drawing CH15 INQUIRY.DWG is supplied on the CD that accompanies this book. You should copy this drawing onto your hard drive so you can complete the Inquiry tools exercises.

Figure 15.2
The Inquiry toolbar accesses the five main inquiry commands.

Note

A set of drawing files is supplied for use in the practice exercises for this chapter. If you want to experiment with the Inquiry tools and also the Express Tools described later in the chapter, you should copy all of the CH15 drawings from the CD that accompanies this book into a practice folder on your hard drive.

MEASURING A DISTANCE

The Distance command enables you to measure the distance and the angle between two selected points. You can use the Distance command with OSNAP to facilitate point selection; you can turn on ORTHO to assure orthogonal measurement.

EXAMPLE: MEASURING A DISTANCE

1. Start AutoCAD 2000, open the practice drawing CH15 INQUIRY.DWG, and zoom in to the lower rectangle (see Figure 15.3).

2. Choose Tools, Inquiry, Distance, or type **dist** at the command line and press Enter. You are prompted to specify two points.

   ```
   '_dist Specify first point:  Specify second point:
   ```

Figure 15.3
The Distance command measures the distance and angle between two points.

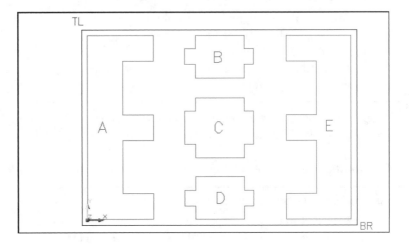

3. Pick the top-left corner and the bottom-right corner of the perimeter rectangle to measure the diagonal distance (TL to BR).

The Distance command measures the diagonal and provides the following read-out:

```
Distance = 475'-6 7/16", Angle in XY Plane = 325,   Angle from XY Plane = 0
Delta X = 391'-6 5/16",  Delta Y = -269'-10 3/4",   Delta Z = 0'-0"
```

If your command line window is set (in the Tools, Options, Display tab) to show fewer than three lines of text, you will not be able to read the full output at the command line. Press the F2 key to view the full listing in the AutoCAD text window. The diagonal distance measures approximately 475 feet; the Angle *in* XY Plane is 325° relative to the x-axis, and the Angle *from* XY Plane is 0°, which indicates that both points are located on the same plane. The Distance command also measures distances in three dimensions using a 3D vector.

Note

The measurement returned by the Distance command is stored as a system variable, DISTANCE. Type **distance** to view the last distance value. If you wish, you can include this distance data in a custom program or macro by retrieving it from the system variable.

CALCULATING A SPECIFIED AREA

The Area command gives you the area of a selected object or the area defined by a series of coordinates. This command can be used to find the area of any closed object, including polygons, closed polylines, regions, circles, or ellipses. The default version of this command prompts you to select the points that define the area you want to measure.

EXAMPLE: CALCULATING A SPECIFIED AREA

1. Still working with the drawing CH15 INQUIRY.DWG, choose Tools, Inquiry, Area, or type **area** at the command line and press Enter. You are prompted with this:
   ```
   Specify first corner point or [Object/Add/Subtract]:
   ```

2. Click in turn the top-right, bottom-right, bottom-left, and top-left corners of the outside rectangle; when you are finished, press Enter. The Area command calculates and displays the area and perimeter:
   ```
   Area = 15216730.67 square in. (105671.7407 square ft.),
   Perimeter = 1322'-10 1/8"
   ```

Where appropriate, you can simply pick an object in the drawing and the Area command will print its area and perimeter at the command line.

CALCULATING THE AREA OF AN OBJECT

EXAMPLE: CALCULATING THE AREA OF AN OBJECT

1. Repeat step 1 in the previous example. You are prompted with this:
   ```
   Specify first corner point or [Object/Add/Subtract]:
   ```

2. Type **o** (for object) and press Enter.

3. At the Select Objects prompt, select the outside rectangle. The area and perimeter measurements are instantly printed to the command line.

```
Area = 15216730.67 square in. (105671.7407 square ft.),
Perimeter = 1322'-10 1/8"
```

You can combine area calculations into a total by using the Add option. Likewise, the Subtract option calculates an area and subtracts from the total.

ADDING AND SUBTRACTING AREAS

EXAMPLE: ADDING AND SUBTRACTING AREAS

1. Repeat step 1 from the previous exercise. You are prompted with this:

```
Specify first corner point or [Object/Add/Subtract]:
```

2. Type **a** (to start Add mode) and press Enter.

3. Type **o** (for object) and press Enter.

4. At the (ADD mode) Select Objects prompt, select the outside rectangle again. The area and perimeter measurements are instantly printed at the command line.

```
Area = 15216730.67 square in. (105671.7407 square ft.),
Perimeter = 1322'-10 1/8"
```

5. When the (Add mode) Select objects prompt appears again, press Enter. You are again prompted with this:

```
Specify first corner point or [Object/Add/Subtract]:
```

6. This time, type **s** (to start Subtract mode) and press Enter. Then type **o** (for object) and press Enter.

7. At the (SUBTRACT mode) Select Objects prompt, select the building footprint labeled A. The area and perimeter measurements are displayed and then subtracted from the overall total.

```
Area = 2465950.87 square in. (17124.6589 square ft.), Perimeter = 866'-5"
Total area = 12750779.79 square in. (88547.0819 square ft.)
```

You can continue subtracting each of the building footprints—B through E—from the overall site area. The final result should be as follows:

```
Area = 2465950.87 square in. (17124.6589 square ft.), Perimeter = 866'-5"
Total area = 7908346.06 square in. (54919.0699 square ft.)
```

The area of the site that is not yet built is approximately 55,000 square feet, in contrast to the overall site measurement of 105,000 square feet. If you use Add mode to add the building footprint areas, they will total approximately 50,000 square feet.

The area calculation is also stored in the system variable AREA. Because the Area command and the system variable share the same name, you can't just type the name of the system variable to view its value. Instead, type **setvar** and press Enter. Then type **area** and press Enter to view the variable.

USING THE MASS PROPERTIES COMMAND

The Mass Properties command works with 3D solid objects. You can use the same drawing file CH15 INQUIRY.DWG to practice this command. First, however, zoom out and change the view from plan view to SW Isometric. This provides a 3D model for you to work with.

EXAMPLE: USING THE MASS PROPERTIES COMMAND

1. Zoom to Extents and then choose <u>V</u>iew, <u>3</u>D Views, <u>S</u>W Isometric. CH15 INQUIRY.DWG is displayed, as shown in Figure 15.4. The buildings in this drawing are shown as 3D solids for the purpose of this exercise.

Figure 15.3
The Mass Properties command is used to calculate the mass properties of solids and regions.

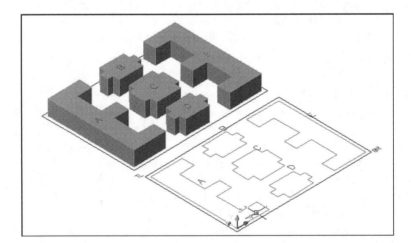

2. Choose <u>T</u>ools, Inquir<u>y</u>, <u>M</u>ass Properties, or type **massprop** at the command line and press Enter. You are prompted to select objects.

3. Select the building labeled A in the 3D model, and press Enter. The AutoCAD Text window pops up to display the following listing of the object's properties:

```
--------------      SOLIDS    ----------------

Mass:                    1232975437.2990 lb
Volume:                  1232975437.2990 cu in
Bounding box:       X:   3.5890    --    1117.8467 in
                    Y:   3640.4517  --   6679.2257 in
                    Z:   0.0000    --   500.0000 in
Centroid:           X:   450.3723 in
                    Y:   5159.8387 in
                    Z:   250.0000 in
Moments of inertia: X:   3.4006E+16 lb sq in
                    Y:   4.6228E+14 lb sq in
                    Z:   3.4263E+16 lb sq in
Products of inertia: XY: 2865247817076046 lb sq in
                     YZ: 1590488593509675 lb sq in
                     ZX: 1.3882E+14 lb sq in
Radii of gyration:  X:   5251.7282 in
                    Y:   612.3125 in
                    Z:   5271.5187 in
Principal moments (lb sq in) and X-Y-Z directions about centroid:
                    I:   1102543903351153 along [1.0000 0.0000 0.0000]
                    J:   1.3512E+14 along [0.0000 1.0000 0.0000]
                    K:   1186293512238423 along [0.0000 0.0000 1.0000]
```

4. If you wish to output this listing to a file, type **y** at the prompt.

   ```
   Write analysis to a file? [Yes/No] <N>:
   ```

   You can select a filename or accept the default, as shown in Figure 15.5.

Figure 15.5
You can output the
Mass Properties list-
ing to a text file.

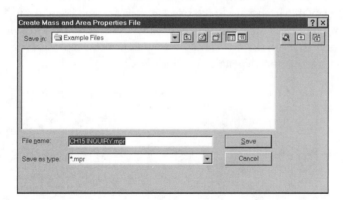

This 3D model is provided simply to demonstrate the use of the Mass Properties command; it does not represent a typical application for this command. You may wish to try this command on other three-dimensional models from the \ACAD2000\SAMPLE folder.

THE LIST COMMAND

The List command has survived from early versions of AutoCAD, when it was an essential tool for finding out the properties of any object in your drawing (layer; color; x, y, or z coordinates; and so on). In AutoCAD 2000, the Properties command performs the same function. However, the List command is still often used and will give you a quick listing of the properties of any selected objects.

EXAMPLE: USING THE LIST COMMAND

1. Choose Tools, Inquiry, List, or type **list** at the command line and press Enter. You are prompted to Select objects.

2. Select the building labeled A in the 3D model, and press Enter. The following listing of the object's properties is generated immediately:

```
3DSOLID   Layer: "BUILDING"
                          Space: Model space
                 Color: 132    Linetype: "BYLAYER"
                 Handle = CA
    Bounding Box: Lower Bound X = 0'-3 9/16", Y = 303'-4 7/16", Z = 0'-0"
    Upper Bound X = 93'-1 7/8", Y = 556'-7 1/4", Z = 41'-8"
```

The List command lists the object type; the object layer; the x, y, and z position of the object; and other properties.

You may wish to compare the output that is produced when you list an object using the Properties command. Select building A in the 3D model again, right-click to open the shortcut menu, and then choose Properties. The Properties window opens and displays a list of information (see Figure 15.5) that is slightly different from the data provided by the List command. Unlike List command, the Properties command enables you to access—and also change—the editable properties of the selected object. Some users like to keep the Properties window open at all times (docked as it is in Figure 15.6) so they can check and edit object properties on the fly. You can use either of these tools (List or Properties) to access object information, depending on your requirements at the time.

Figure 15.6
The Properties command overlaps and complements the functions of List command.

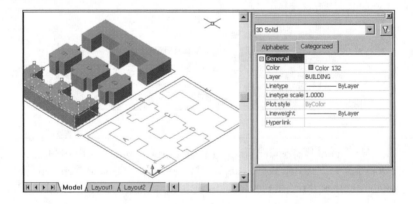

LOCATE POINT

This is a deceptively simple command, but one that is very useful. The Locate Point command prints the coordinate of any selected point at the command line.

Choose Tools, Inquiry, ID Point, or type **id** at the command line and press Enter. You are prompted with this:

`"Specify point:"`

When you click a point, the program instantly provides a read-out of the x, y, and z coordinates of the point. This read-out resembles the continuous read-out of points in the status bar. When used in conjunction with the snap overrides, the Id command will give the coordinates of the geometry that is snapped to, rather than the coordinates of the actual click point.

The coordinate information is also stored in the system variable LASTPOINT. If you use any drawing command that requests a point, such as Line or Circle, you can reference the coordinate stored in LASTPOINT by using the @ symbol. For example, if you wish to start a new line at 0.5 units to the right of a specific point, you should first ID the point. Then start the Line command and enter **@0.5,0** as the start coordinate. This starts the line 0.5 units to the right of the last point. You can specify other points on the line relative to the ID point in the same way, if appropriate.

Other Inquiry Tools

The remaining Inquiry tools—Time, Status, and Set Variable—represent a mixed bag of utilities. The Time and Status commands query the entire drawing rather than selected objects. The Set Variable command is simply a menu version of the setvar command.

- Time—This command displays the date and time statistics for the current drawing in the text editor, including the start date, elapsed time, editing time, time until next backup, and time until the next automatic save.

- Status—This command displays general information about the current drawing, modes, limits, and drawing settings, plus some additional information about your system. The Status listing for the CH15 INQUIRY.DWG is as follows.

```
172 objects in D:\EASY EXAMPLES\CH15 INQUIRY.dwg
Model space limits are X:      0'-0"    Y:      0'-0"   (Off)
                       X:      1'-0"    Y:      0'-9"
Model space uses       X: -264'-8 1/4"   Y: -14'-0 13/16" **Over
                       X:  405'-1 3/16"  Y: 564'-11 1/4" **Over
Display shows          X:  83'-0 5/8"   Y:   114'-1"
                       X: 110'-9 3/16"  Y: 127'-2 5/16"
Insertion base is      X:      0'-0"    Y:      0'-0"   Z:      0'-0"
Snap resolution is     X: 0'-0 1/2"   Y: 0'-0 1/2"
Grid spacing is        X: 0'-0 1/2"   Y: 0'-0 1/2"

Current space:        Model space
Current layout:       Model
Current layer:        "Text"
Current color:        BYLAYER -- 5 (blue)
Current linetype:     BYLAYER -- "Continuous"
Current lineweight:   BYLAYER
Current plot style:   ByLayer
Current elevation:       0'-0"  thickness:      0'-0"
Fill on  Grid off  Ortho on  Qtext off  Snap off  Tablet off
```

```
Object snap modes:    Center, Endpoint, Insert, Intersection, Midpoint,
                      Nearest, Node, Perpendicular, Quadrant, Tangent,
                      Appint, Extension, Parallel
Free dwg disk (D:) space: 2047.7 MBytes
Free temp disk (C:) space: 326.9 MBytes
Free physical memory: 5.7 Mbytes (out of 127.5M).
Free swap file space: 327.6 Mbytes (out of 422.9M).
```

- Set Variable—This menu option starts the Setvar command, which in turn enables you to view or modify system variables.

As was noted at the beginning of this tour of the AutoCAD 2000 Inquiry tools, these commands are for information only. You cannot use these commands to modify objects with the Inquiry tools. In the remainder of this chapter, you will have a chance to experiment with a completely different set of tools, the AutoCAD 2000 Express Tools.

EXPRESS TOOLS

The AutoCAD 2000 Express Tools are an enhanced and expanded version of the popular Bonus Tools introduced with AutoCAD R14. These programs are a mixture of AutoLISP, AutoCAD ARX, and Visual Basic routines that have been developed over the years by users and Autodesk employees. By all means, you should install the Express Tools; this package is an exceptional and comprehensive set of utilities, and you will find routines that you like and tools that you can't live without.

INSTALLING THE EXPRESS TOOLS

You may inadvertently have *not* installed the Express Tools because they do not install automatically as part of the typical install. You must either request the full installation, or specify them as part of a custom install.

If you did a typical install, you will now have to load the Express Tools from the installation CD. Run the Setup program again and add the Express Tools. Even after you have installed the Express Tools, you can run into a couple glitches, which are easily remedied.

- If you know that you have the Express Tools installed but can't see the menu, type **expressmenu** at the command prompt and press Enter. The Express menu is shown in Figure 15.7.

- If the Express menu is installed (see Figure 15.7) and you *still* cannot get the commands to work, type **expresstools** at the command prompt and press Enter.

LOADING THE EXPRESS TOOLS TOOLBARS

If you prefer to work from toolbars, some—but not all—of the Express Tools are available on toolbars. You can load all four of the toolbars or can choose to load each toolbar on an as-needed basis.

Figure 15.7
The Express menu gives you access to submenus of Express Tools, grouped by category.

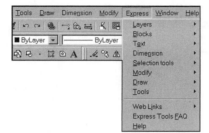

EXAMPLE: LOADING THE EXPRESS TOOLS TOOLBARS

1. Choose View, Toolbars, or type **toolbar** at the command prompt and then press Enter. The Toolbars dialog box is displayed (see Figure 15.8).

2. Select EXPRESS in the Menu Group list box, check the toolbar(s) that you wish to display in the drawing editor, and then press the Enter key or the Close button.

Figure 15.8
You can select Express toolbars from the Toolbars dialog box.

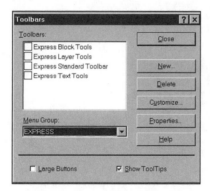

Tip 111 from
Paul Richardson

You can rapidly open the Express toolbars on the fly by right-clicking on the open area at the right end of the toolbar zone (see Figure 15.9). When the shortcut menu appears, highlight EXPRESS and then click on the name of the toolbar you wish to load.

EXPRESS TOOLS HELP AND WEB SUPPORT

The AutoCAD 2000 Express Tools come complete with their own Help system, Web page, and newsgroup support. Take a look at the Express Tools menu; the bottom three items are the relevant ones (see Figure 15.10).

Figure 15.9
You can also speed-load the Express toolbars via the shortcut menu.

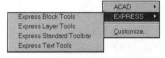

Figure 15.10
These three menu items directly open up the Express Tools support systems.

- Starting with the bottom item, click the Help item to open a full-blown Help system, which covers all the commands and programs included in the Express Tools.

- The next item, Express Tools FAQ, opens a Help page that specifically addresses frequently asked questions. Many of the responses to these questions lead back into the main Help system.

- The Web Links item offers two links that provide you with up-to-date information on Express Tools (see Figure 15.11).

Figure 15.11
The Web Links item offers two links that provide you with up-to-date information on Express Tools.

ACCESSING WEB SUPPORT FOR EXPRESS TOOLS   A single click will take you directly from the AutoCAD 2000 drawing editor to the Express Tools Web page or newsgroup.

Click the Express Tools Web Site link. Your Web browser starts up automatically and takes you to the Express Tools Web site (see Figure 15.12) at http://www.autodesk.com/expresstools.

The Express Tools Newsgroup item on the Express menu starts your newsreader, such as Outlook Express, and takes you to the Express Tools newsgroup. Here you can actually leave a question for other readers, and typically someone will have a solution for you. Very often someone has already asked the question you are about to ask, so it makes a lot of sense to browse previous questions before submitting yours.

Tip 112 from
Paul Richardson

For information on other Autodesk discussion groups, go to this Web address:
http://www.autodesk.com/support/discsgrp/index.htm

Figure 15.12
The Express Tools Web page provides up-to-date information and extra programs.

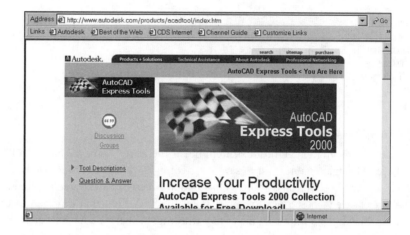

Now that you have had a chance to explore all the resources available to Express Tools users, it's time to start working with the tools themselves. The AutoCAD Express Tools menu organizes the tools into different categories. Each menu item has a group of related commands.

THE EXPRESS LAYERS MENU

All the layer-related commands are grouped together on the Layers menu item of the Express Tools menu. When you click Layers, a secondary flyout menu drops down, as shown in Figure 15.13.

Figure 15.13
The Layer Express Tools are grouped on the Layers submenu.

If you prefer to access commands from a toolbar, load the Express Layer Tools toolbar (see Figure 15.14), as described earlier in this chapter in the section "Loading the Express Tools Toolbars." Notice that there is not an exact correspondence between the menu and the toolbar: The menu has 12 commands and the toolbar has only 8.

Figure 15.14
The Layers submenu has 12 commands and the Express Layer Tools toolbar has only 8.

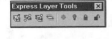

LAYER MANAGER

The first menu item and toolbar item opens the Layer Manager command (lman). The Layer Manager enables you to save layer configurations—in other words, the settings for your layers in terms of visibility (On/Off and Freeze/Thaw), linetype, lineweight, and color. You can save your settings to a layer state—or .LAY file—that can then be exported from your drawing and imported into other drawings. When you have layer states stored in your drawing, you can instantly switch between them and restore previous layer settings as required.

Take a look at the Layer Manager dialog box.

EXAMPLE: USING THE LAYER MANAGER

1. Start a new AutoCAD 2000 drawing.

2. Choose Express, Layers, Layer Manager, or type **lman** at the command prompt and press Enter. (Or, you can click on the toolbar button Layer Manager.) The Layer Manager dialog box opens, as shown in Figure 15.15.

Figure 15.15
The Layer Manager dialog box enables you to save and restore layer settings across different drawings.

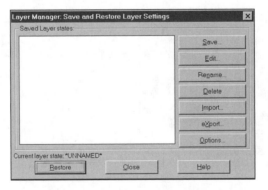

Note

The Layer Manager provides an easy way to define layers for plotting. If you have multiple drawings in a project that use the same layer settings, you can use the same layer state file (for example, PLOT1.LAY) just before you plot to make sure you have the correct layers on and off.

3. In the Layer Manager dialog box, select Import and browse to the \ACAD2000\EXPRESS folder. A set of saved layer files is stored in this folder. The layers are grouped by different disciplines: civil, plumbing, and so on. The layer names conform to the AIA standard layer naming conventions.

4. Click the file civil.lay, and press Open to load it into the Layer Manager Save and Restore Layer Settings dialog box.

5. Repeat steps 3 and 4 for any other disciplines that you would like to add to your drawing.

6. Press Close. The layers are loaded into your new drawing.

7. You new drawing started with only layer zero; open the AutoCAD 2000 Layer Manager to review the added layers that have been added (see Figure 15.16).

Figure 15.16
Civil and Landscape standard layers can be imported into a new drawing.

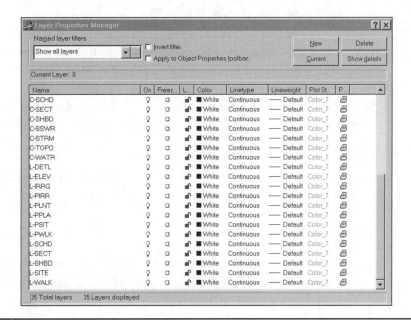

If these files meet the requirements of your discipline, you can use them to initialize your own layer standards. You will have to supply your own conventions for layer colors because there are no established standards for layer color at this time. After you have defined your layer names and colors in a drawing, create a new .LAY file and export it to a Standard folder to establish your own layer standards.

Subsequent practice exercises using the Express Layer Tools utilize CH15 LAYERS.DWG, which is located on the CD that accompanies this book. If you have not already done so, you should copy all the drawings that are prefixed CH15 into a practice folder (for example, \EASY EXAMPLES).

CH15 LAYERS.DWG drawing is a tile or grid section from a civil and landscape project. The layers utilized in this drawing are a slightly elaborated version of the AIA layers you imported in the previous exercise.

LAYER MATCH

The next menu and toolbar item, the Layer Match command (laymch), duplicates some of the functionality of the AutoCAD 2000 Property Painter. Essentially, you can select objects that are on the wrong layer, pick another object to define a target layer, and then change the selected group to the target layer. This command becomes more useful when combined with automated selection, thus enabling you to process a large group of objects. In this first exercise you will move one object to a selected layer.

EXAMPLE: MOVING AN ITEM TO A SELECTED LAYER

1. Open CH15 LAYERS.DWG and zoom in to the drawing, as shown in Figure 15.17.

2. Choose Express, Layers, Layer Match, or type **laymch** at the command prompt and press Enter. (Or, you can click on the toolbar button Match Object's Layer.) You are prompted to select objects.

3. Select the small magenta circular object adjacent to the index contour (20), and press Enter twice. (This object is presently on the general utilities layer U-GEN-BOX.) You are prompted with this:

   ```
   Select object on destination layer or [Type-it]:
   ```

4. Select the large blue circular object that is partially visible in the top-left corner of the drawing. The small circular object immediately changes to the target layer, turning blue in the process.

   ```
   One object changed to layer C-WATR-TANK.
   ```

Figure 15.17
The Layer Match command makes it easy to move objects from layer to layer and onto newly created layers.

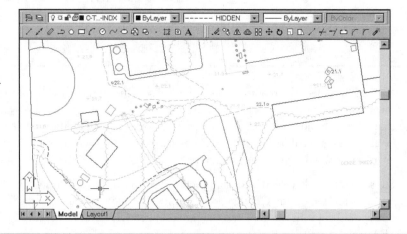

Not only can you move objects to an *existing* layer, but you also can *create* a layer on-the-fly and move the selected objects directly onto it. In this exercise, you move a building that is currently on C-BLDG-EXST to a demolition layer that has not yet been created.

EXAMPLE: MOVING A BUILDING TO A NEW LAYER

1. Start the Layer Match command and select the rectangular building at the top-right of the screen (see Figure 15.17). You are prompted with this:

   ```
   Select object on destination layer or [Type-it]:
   ```

2. This time, type **t** (for Type-it) and press Enter. You are prompted with this:

   ```
   Enter layer name:
   ```

3. At the prompt, type **C-BLDG-DEMO** and press Enter to complete the command. The Layer Match program adds a layer and moves the building to that layer.

The Layer Match program provides a speedy way to correct errors and regroup objects on drawing layers. The next command on the menu provides an even faster (one-step) procedure to move objects to a new layer.

CHANGE TO CURRENT LAYER

The next command on the menu and toolbar enables you to change a group of objects to the current layer. You can achieve the same result by selecting objects and then selecting a layer from the layer list box—but this method goes a little faster. In the practice drawing, the Index contour layer (C-TOPO-INDX) should be set as the current layer. In this exercise, you use the Current command (laycur) to change some objects on the C-TOPO-EXST (gray) layer onto the C-TOPO-INDX (black) layer.

EXAMPLE: USING THE CHANGE TO CURRENT LAYER COMMAND

1. Choose Express, Layers, Change to Current Layer, or type **laycur** at the command line and press Enter. You are prompted with this:

   Select objects to be changed to the current layer:

2. Zoom into the drawing, as shown in Figure 15.18.

3. Select the gray, dashed contour line (C-TOPO-EXST) at the right edge of the drawing, as shown in Figure 15.18. (You may have to select several times to collect all the objects—there are three objects in this contour.) Then press Enter.

The objects are immediately transferred to C-TOPO-INDX, and the layer color changes from gray to black.

Tip 113 from
Paul Richardson

When using the Express Layer Tools, you may select the objects first and then activate the command. In the preceding example, it is probably easier to use grips to select and highlight the whole contour line (see Figure 15.18) before activating the Current Layer command.

Figure 15.18
Using the Current
Layer command, you
can select any draw-
ing objects and move
them to the current
layer.

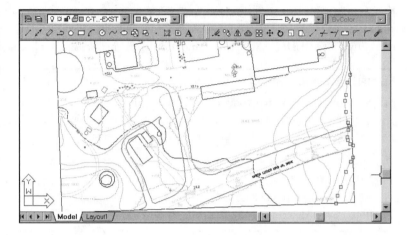

LAYER ISOLATE

The next command on the menu and toolbar, Layer Isolate, helps you to quickly isolate a layer so you can edit the items on a single layer. Or you can choose to isolate more than one layer. Essentially, this command (layiso) turns *off* all layers except the layer(s) of any object(s)that you pick. This remains in effect until you use the complementary Layer On command to turn on all layers again. (Layer On is described later in this section.)

Again, you can select objects and then start the command, or start the command first. Zoom to extents so you can see all the objects on the isolated layer.

Choose Express, Layers, Layer Isolate, or type **layiso** at the command line and press Enter. You are prompted with this:

```
Select object(s) on the layer(s) to be isolated
```

Select an object on the C-ROAD-SWLK layer (the cyan layer), and press Enter. All other layers turn off immediately when you press Enter.

With only one layer visible, you can perform edits more easily without accidentally selecting the wrong objects. You could now use the Match Layer command to change the quasi-rectangular objects to the layer L-SITE-CONC (the layer for concrete pads), and then select the semicircular objects and move them onto the L-SITE-PATH layer. After you have created new layers in this way, you should go to the AutoCAD 2000 Layer Properties Manager and set the color and linetype.

LAYER FREEZE

The next command on the Express Layer Tools menu and toolbar is Layer Freeze. Choose Express, Layers, Layer Freeze to start this command (or type **layfrz** at the command line), and then pick an object. The layer that object is on will be immediately frozen—except, of course, if you try to freeze the current layer. In that case, you would simply get an error message.

To un-freeze layers, use the Undo command, if appropriate. Otherwise, you will have to use the Thaw All Layers command, which is described at the end of this section. If the layer objects do not reappear, try View, Regen to redraw the objects.

LAYER OFF

As the name implies, the Layer Off command turns off a layer. It works in much the same way as the layfrz command, except that you can turn *off* the current layer if you cannot freeze the current layer. Choose Express, Layers, Layer Off to start the command (or type **layoff** at the command line), and then pick an object on the layer you want to turn off. The selected layer will be turned off. If it is the current layer, you will be asked whether you really want to turn off the current layer; answer Y if you actually want to do this. Otherwise, press Enter and select another object.

Tip 114 from
Paul Richardson

If you use Freeze and Thaw to control layer visibility for plotting, and On/Off to temporarily control layer visibility for editing, you will have a handle on layers settings. Freeze and Thaw cause a regen, which on large drawings can be time-consuming. On and Off work quickly because they don't cause a regen. If you are into customizing toolbars for yourself, you might consider adding the Layer On command (layon) to the Express Layer Tools toolbar. Create a button next to the Isolate (layiso) button, and you will be able to toggle layers on and off. This is very useful for isolating the objects on one layer for editing purposes.

LAYER LOCK

The next option on the Express Layer Tools menu and toolbar is Layer Lock. Choose Express, Layers, Layer Lock to start the command (or type **laylck** at the command line), and then pick an object. Nothing appears to happen, but look at the command line—it will tell you that the layer has been locked. If you click any objects on that layer, they will display grips but will not allow you to select again to make any grips hot. You won't be able to edit any objects on that layer (although you can still see them) until you unlock the layer.

LAYER UNLOCK

This is the reverse action to the previous command and unlocks a picked layer. Choose Express, Layers, Layer Unlock to start the command, or type **layulk** at the command line and press Enter.

LAYER MERGE

The Layer Merge command combines several operations into one clean command. You can put several layers of objects onto one layer and then remove the empty layers. In this exercise, you merge six different text layers into a single layer called TEXT. (This is not an approved AIA layer name, but you can forget layer standards for now.)

EXAMPLE: USING THE LAYER MERGE COMMAND

1. Use the AutoCAD 2000 Layer Properties manager (layer command) to add a new layer called TEXT in CH15 LAYERS.DWG. (Unlike the Match Layer command (laymch), this command does not allow you to create a new layer as you work.)

2. Zoom in close enough so that you can see all the different kinds of text in the drawing. There are seven different text layers in this drawing.

3. Choose Express, Layers, Layer Merge to start the command, or type **laymrg** at the command line and press Enter. You are prompted with this:
   ```
   Select object on layer to merge or [Type-it/Undo]:
   ```

4. Select an example of each text layer in the drawing, and press Enter. You are prompted with this:
   ```
   Select object on target layer or [Type-it/Undo]:
   ```

5. Type **t** and press Enter. Then type **TEXT** and press Enter.

At this point, you will receive some dire warnings advising you that objects will be merged and layers deleted:

```
******** WARNING ********

You are about to permanently merge the following layers into layer TEXT:
Do you wish to continue? [Yes/No] <No>:
```

The command also advises you of block definitions on the layers you are deleting, prior to redefining them on the target layer. Choose the Yes option to complete the command. All the text is merged onto a single layer, and the other text layers disappear. (If you change your mind immediately after you have merged the layers, you can always use the Undo command.)

You can doubtless appreciate how to quite easily merge layers that you did not intend to merge, and how much painstaking work could be involved in returning the objects to the correct layers. Used cautiously, however, this command is an excellent utility. Unfortunately, because it is a more recent addition to the Express Tools, it is not included on the Layer Tools toolbar.

LAYER DELETE

Like the previous command, the Layer Delete command is not on the toolbar—in this case, for a good reason. With one click, all the objects on the picked object's layer can be removed from the drawing. However, this command will ask you if you really want to kill a layer before it removes the layer. This is clearly not a command to be used casually, but it can be a real time saver when you do need it.

EXAMPLE: USING THE LAYER DELETE COMMAND

1. Choose Express, Layers, Layer Delete to start the command, or type **laydel** at the command line and press Enter.

2. At the prompt, select an object on the (green) tree layer. All objects on the layer immediately disappear, and you are prompted with this:

```
******** WARNING ********

You are about to permanently delete layer L-PLNT-TXST from this drawing.
Do you wish to continue? [Yes/No] <No>:y
```

3. Type **Y** and press Enter to remove this layer from the drawing.

At this point, you can still use the Undo command to retrieve the deleted layer and objects. You should probably do this before moving on to review the final layer commands.

TURN ALL LAYERS ON

This command should be used in conjunction with the Layer Off (layoff) and Isolate Layers (layiso) commands, as mentioned previously. The Turn All Layers On command simply turns on all layers that are turned off. It is currently available only on the Express Tools menu or via the command line. It is not accessible on any toolbar.

THAW ALL LAYERS

The Thaw All Layers command (laythw) thaws all layers that are frozen. This command also is not on the Express Layer Tools toolbar. You might wish to consider adding it to the toolbar, however, if you use this program a lot.

You have now worked through the entire suite of Express Tools layer utilities. The Express Tools contains 12-layer programs, which indicates how important efficient layer management is in production AutoCAD work. The next Express Tools menu item is Blocks. Take a look now at the Blocks programs.

THE EXPRESS BLOCKS MENU

All the block-related commands are grouped together on the Blocks menu item on the Express Tools menu. When you click Blocks, a secondary flyout menu drops down, displaying six Block Tools, as shown in Figure 15.19.

Figure 15.19
The Express Block Tools are grouped on the Blocks submenu.

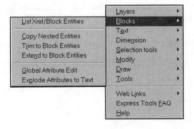

If you prefer to access commands from a toolbar, load the Express Block Tools toolbar (see Figure 15.20), as described in "Loading Express Tools Toolbars" earlier in this chapter.

Notice that there is not an exact correspondence between the menu and the toolbar: The menu has six block commands and the toolbar has seven. The toolbar contains a command from the Express Tools Modify commands called Extended Clip. This command will be reviewed along with the Modify Tools in a later section of this chapter.

Figure 15.20
The menu has six block commands and the toolbar has seven.

For the practice exercises using the Express Layer Tools, you should use the drawing CH15 BLOCKS.DWG, which is located on the CD that accompanies this book. Copy this file into a practice folder on your hard drive if you have not already done so. The CH15 BLOCKS.DWG drawing is derived from the AutoCAD 2000 sample drawing WIL-HOME.DWG.

LIST XREF/BLOCK ENTITIES

The first command on the Blocks menu—and the middle button on the toolbar—is the List Xref/Block Entities. When you run this command and select an object that is part of an inserted block, or xref, a dialog box displays the type of object you selected and some of its properties. A typical situation for using this program is when you want to find out the defined layer or color of an object nested within a block. You would normally have to explode the block, list the object, and then undo these steps to get back to where you were.

The process is even more complicated with an xref—so don't explode your xrefs! You *could* use the new Refedit command to pop objects out from an xref, but thanks to this List Xref/Block Entities command, you don't need to.

→ For more information on editing external references, see Chapter 17, "External Reference Files and Importing Images."

EXAMPLE: USING THE LIST XREF/BLOCK ENTITIES COMMAND

1. Open CH15 BLOCKS.DWG and zoom over to the A5 callout bubble at the top right of the drawing.
2. Choose Express, Blocks, List Xref/Block Entities to start the command, or type **xlist** at the command line and press Enter. You are prompted to select a nested block or xref.
3. Select the green arrowhead. A list window pops open and details the properties of the nested block, as shown in Figure 15.21.
4. Press OK to close the window.

Figure 15.21
The Express Tools List Xref/Block Entities command displays information about nested objects.

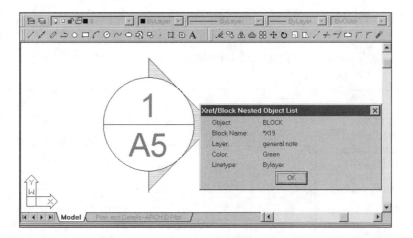

COPY NESTED ENTITIES

The next command on the Express Blocks submenu is the Copy Nested Entities command. (This is the leftmost button on the Express Blocks Tools toolbar, if you prefer to use the toolbar.) Use this command when you want to duplicate part of a block without having to explode the block.

In the CH15 BLOCKS.DWG is a composite washer-dryer block. In this exercise, you make a separate copy of only the washer for use in this or other drawings.

EXAMPLE: USING THE COPY NESTED ENTITIES COMMAND

1. Zoom to the laundry room at the left side of the drawing. Click on the washer. You will see that it is a part of the block WASHER-DRIER 01.

2. Choose Express, Blocks, Copy Nested Entities to start the command, or type **ncopy** at the command line and press Enter. You are prompted to select nested objects to copy.

Note
The washer portion of the WASHER DRIER 01 block is made up of a number of different objects. You may have to zoom in close to make sure that you have selected all the pieces, especially the front corners and the four lines that make up the handle.

3. Click on all the objects that make up the washer portion of this block (see Figure 15.22). Press Enter after you have selected all the objects that make up the washer. You are prompted with the following:

```
Select objects: Specify base point or displacement, or [Multiple]:
```

From here on, the Copy Nested Entities command works in exactly the same way as the AutoCAD 2000 Copy command.

4. Pick a baseline point and a displacement position for your new copy of the washer objects.

Figure 15.22
The Express Tools Copy Nested Entities command enables you to copy objects from within a defined block.

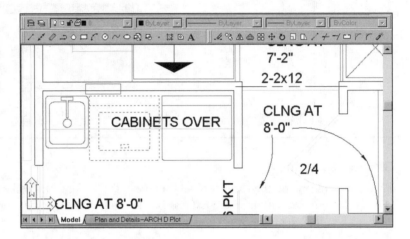

For another application, imagine that you are making multiple blocks using the same text attribute definition. You can pop out a copy of the text attribute and locate it away from the source block. This can then be used to define another block.

TRIM TO BLOCK ENTITIES

This command (btrim) is a variant on the standard Trim command. It enables you to pick objects nested in a block and use them to define a cutting edge for trim operations. Objects within an xref can also be used to form a cutting edge for trimming lines.

In this exercise, you select the front edge of the kitchen sink block and use it to trim a line that intersects this block.

EXAMPLE: USING THE TRIM TO BLOCK ENTITIES COMMAND

1. Zoom up to the kitchen area in CH15 BLOCKS.DWG.

2. Choose Express, Blocks, Trim to Block Entities to start the command, or type **btrim** at the command line and press Enter. You are prompted to select cutting edges.

3. Select the front edge of the kitchen sink block, as shown in Figure 15.23, and then press Enter. You are prompted to select the object that you wish to trim.

From here on, the Trim to Block Entities command works in exactly the same way as the AutoCAD 2000 Trim command.

4. Select the blue line that transects the sink block at any point to the left of the cutting edge. The line is immediately trimmed back to the front edge of the sink.

EXTEND TO BLOCK ENTITIES

Much like the preceding command, the Extend to Block Entities command (bextend) works with objects nested within a block definition. This is a variant on the standard Extend command. With the Extend to Block Entities command, you can extend objects such as arcs, lines, and polylines to intersect with nested objects within a block or xref.

Figure 15.23

You can now use a part of a block as a cutting edge when trimming other objects.

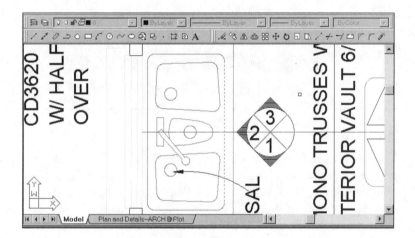

EXAMPLE: USING THE EXTEND TO BLOCK ENTITIES COMMAND

1. Zoom back to the A5 detail callout, as shown in Figure 15.24. As you may have noticed, the cross-section line does not extend fully to the edge of the callout bubble.

2. Choose Express, Blocks, Extend to Block Entities to start the command, or type **bextend** at the command line and press Enter. You are prompted to select edges to extend.

3. Select the circle object in the callout block and press Enter. You are now prompted to select an object to extend.

4. Select the cross-section line; the line immediately extends to meet the callout.

Figure 15.24
You can extend objects to intersect with objects within a block.

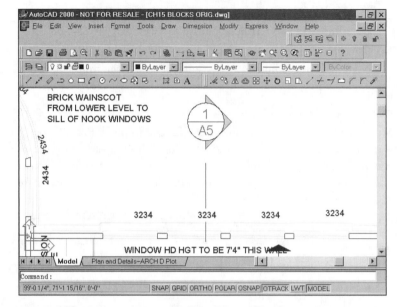

GLOBAL ATTRIBUTE EDIT

Editing attribute text in a block can be tricky. You can edit an individual attribute with the Attedit command, but if you need to do the same edit on multiple block references, this can get very tedious. The Global Attribute Edit command (gatte) performs the same edit, replacing a line of attribute text with your new definition on multiple block references. You can choose either to edit all the blocks of the same name or pick a selection set of the same block.

EXAMPLE: USING THE GLOBAL ATTRIBUTE EDIT COMMAND

1. Choose E**x**press, **B**locks, **G**lobal Attribute Edit to start the command, or type **gatte** at the command line and press Enter. You are prompted to select a block or attribute to edit.

2. Select the text attribute object A5. You are prompted with this:
   ```
   Enter new text:
   ```

3. Type **A19** and press Enter. You are asked whether you want this change implemented throughout the drawing. If you choose Yes, the attribute text in the six callouts in the drawing that use this attribute will be changed (see Figure 15.25).
   ```
   Number of inserts in drawing = 6   Process all of them? [Yes/No] <Yes>:
   Please wait...
   6 attributes changed.
   ```

AutoCAD 2000 does have alternative ways of accomplishing what the Global Attribute Edit command does:

- You can use the Quick Select (qselect) command to select multiple references of the same block, and then run the Find and Replace command from the Edit menu.
- You can also use the Attredef or AT command to redefine all the text attributes of all occurrences of a block.

However, this Express Tool accomplishes the same result with a minimum of effort.

Figure 15.25
The Global Attribute Edit command enables you to change the attribute text in one block, or in many simultaneously.

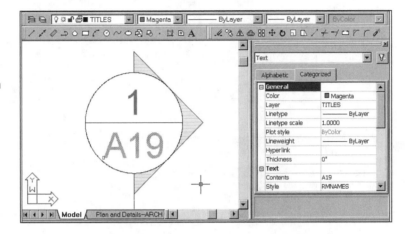

EXPLODE ATTRIBUTES TO TEXT

At times you will want to change the text of an attribute block but don't want to go to the trouble of redefining the block. For example, you might get a drawing from another company and need to make a couple of changes to the Title Sheet attribute block.

Normally, when you explode a block, the attribute text is lost. The Explode Attributes to Text program converts the attribute text to regular text that looks identical to the original. The command-line version of this program is *burst*, to distinguish it from the regular AutoCAD 2000 Explode command.

Choose Express, Blocks, Explode Attributes to Text to start the command, or type **burst** at the command line and press Enter. You are prompted to select objects. Select A19, the sheet number text, as shown in Figure 15.26, and press Enter.

The attribute text in this callout is immediately exploded. You can verify this by right-clicking on the object and selecting Properties for the shortcut menu. The Properties window shows that this object is now a text object and no longer a block object (as shown in Figure 15.25) prior to bursting.

THE EXPRESS TEXT MENU

All the text commands are grouped together on the Text menu item of the Express Tools menu. When you click Text a secondary flyout menu drops down, as shown in Figure 15.27.

Figure 15.26
The Burst command enables you to explode a text attribute without losing the current text value.

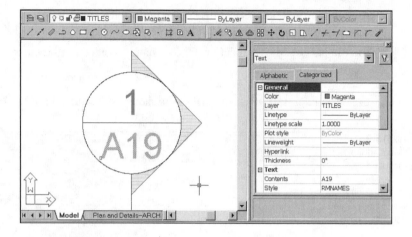

Figure 15.27
The Express Text Tools are grouped on the Text submenu.

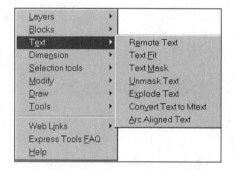

If you prefer to access commands from a toolbar, load the Express Text Tools toolbar (see Figure 15.28), as described in "Loading Express Tools Toolbars" earlier in this chapter. Notice that there is not an exact correspondence between the menu and the toolbar: The menu has seven text commands and the toolbar has only four.

Figure 15.28
Express Text Tools toolbar.

For the majority of the practice exercises using the Express Text Tools, you will use CH15 TEXT.DWG, which is located on the CD that accompanies this book. Copy this drawing to a practice folder on your hard drive if you have not already done so. CH15 TEXT.DWG drawing contains a random selection of engineering details with plenty of text to work with.

REMOTE TEXT

When you start using Remote Text, you won't be able to use AutoCAD 2000 without it. In its basic form, a remote text (or Rtext) object acts like an external reference, but it references a text file and not a drawing file. You can keep information such as a legend or any kind of list in a text file and then define an Rtext object that will import the latest version of the text file into the drawing.

EXAMPLE: USING THE REMOTE TEXT COMMAND

1. For this exercise, open a new drawing in AutoCAD 2000. Choose File, New, and Start From Scratch.

2. Choose Express, Text, Remote Text to start the command, or type **rtext** at the command line and press Enter. You are prompted with this:

   ```
   Current settings: Style=Standard  Height=0.2000  Rotation=0
   Enter an option [Style/Height/Rotation/File/Diesel] <File>:
   ```

   You can select from the following options:

   - Style—Type **s** and press Enter if you wish to change from the specified text style for the Rtext object.
   - Height—Type **h** and press Enter if you wish to change from the specified text height for the Rtext object.
   - Rotation—Type **r** and press Enter if you wish to change from the specified text rotation for the Rtext object.
   - File—Type **f** and press Enter if you wish to create an Rtext object using an ASCII text file as the source.
   - DIESEL—Type **d** and press Enter if you wish to create an Rtext object using DIESEL code.

   Rtext uses the current default for text style, height, and rotation angle. It optionally enables you to change them from the command line during the rtext command. After the rtext has been added to a drawing, you can change these text settings using the Properties command or the rtedit command.

3. Type **f** to choose the file option. The standard Windows Select File dialog box appears.

4. Browse to the \ACAD2000\EXPRESS folder and select AUGI.TXT; press Open.

   An outline box appears in the drawing editor to represent the remote text object, and you are prompted with this:

   ```
   Specify start point of RText:
   ```

5. Drag the top corner of the rtext object to the desired position, and click to select the insertion point. The text file is imported into your drawing.

6. You can press Enter at this point to complete the command, or you can again change the style, height, or rotation of the text. A further option, Edit, is offered as well. Type **e** and press Enter to review this option.

7. When you select the Edit option, the Windows Notepad opens so you can edit the text file from within AutoCAD 2000. You can make any changes that you choose from here. For example, you can add a few line breaks to the long text lines so the Rtext object resembles the one shown in Figure 15.29.

Figure 15.29
The Remote Text command enables you to reference external text objects in your drawing.

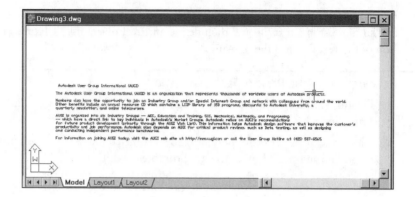

Changes and updates are transmitted in both directions between the AutoCAD 2000 drawing editor and the remote text file.

- Any changes you make from inside your AutoCAD 2000 drawing will be saved in the external text file.

- Likewise, any changes you make in the remote text file will be updated to your drawing the next time that you open or plot it.

Caution

> If you explode a Remote Text (Rtext) object, it will be converted to Mtext and you will lose the connection to the external text file. This may be an appropriate action to take when the remote text file has stabilize and is no longer changing—at the end of a project, for example.

DIESEL AND RTEXT   The DIESEL option offers an alternative for Rtext that enables you to do some very clever things. You can access the value of a DIESEL expression and insert it into your drawing as an Rtext object.

The DIESEL language is a string-based language built into AutoCAD 2000 chiefly for use in menus. It also gives you access to system variables; combined with Rtext, DIESEL commands can give you programmable text objects. You can set up your own title block external reference file, with diesel strings to automatically display date and time, filename, and a list of external references used in the current drawing. All this is documented in the Express Tools Help for Rtext in more detail than can be supplied here, and this is well worth reading.

Take a look at this short example of DIESEL coding that can be used in an Rtext object:

```
Drawing name: $(getvar, "dwgprefix")$(getvar, "dwgname")
External References:
$(xrefs,3)
```

The first line combines the drawing path (from the system variable DWGPREFIX) with the drawing name (from the system variable DWGNAME). The final line lists all the xrefs in the drawing, complete with their paths. This is a useful piece of code to put into a title block drawing.

You can even use such a drawing as an external reference, and the Rtext would pick up and display the drawing name and xrefs used in the current drawing.

Note
> If you wish to know more about the DIESEL programming language, refer to Chapter 5, "Using DIESEL—String Expression Language," in the *Customization Guide* in AutoCAD 2000 Help for a complete description.

TEXT FIT

The AutoCAD 2000 Text command provides two options for fitting text between two points: aligned and fit. Aligned text makes a line of text fit between two points by adjusting the height of the text; the Fit option maintains a fixed height and changes the width of the text.

→ The Align Text and Fit Text options of the Text command are reviewed in more detail in Chapter 12, "Annotating the Drawing."

The Text Fit command works very much like the Fit option of the Text command, but the text does not have to be defined with the Fit option. You might find the Text Fit command useful if you wish to compress or stretch the width of text to fit in a form or title block. Or you may simply need to fit text into a tight corner of a drawing. The command works by shrinking or stretching text width to match new start points or endpoints.

EXAMPLE: USING THE TEXT FIT COMMAND

1. Open CH15 TEXT.DWG and zoom to the detail depicting a street barricade, as shown in Figure 15.30.

2. Choose Express, Text, Text Fit to start the command, or type **textfit** at the command line and press Enter. You are prompted with this:
   ```
   Select Text to stretch or shrink:
   ```

3. Select the word END, and press Enter. You are prompted with this:
   ```
   Specify end point or [Start point]:
   ```

4. Type **s** (for start point) and press Enter. (If you do not specify a new start point, the command will use the current start point as a default.) You are now prompted to choose a start point and an endpoint.

5. Select two points, one on either side of the diamond-shaped board. The text stretches to match the length you have indicated (see Figure 15.30).

Caution

The stretched or shrunken text will not necessarily position itself at the correct start point. If the text was created with a Justify option of center or middle, the text center will jump to the new endpoint and you will have to move it back into position. If you are fitting a lot of text, you may wish to change its justification before you start to reposition it.

Figure 15.30
The Text Fit command enables you to stretch or shrink text to any width you specify.

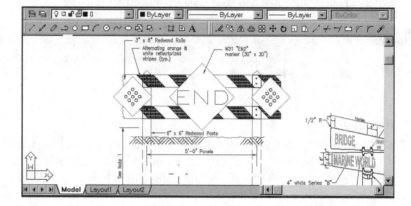

TEXT MASK

Text labels can often get lost in the complexity of a drawing. The Text Mask program gives the illusion of clearing the space behind and around a text object, while actually leaving the background objects intact. The surrounding objects do not actually move; they are covered by a mask, or wipeout object.

For example, you might want a text label to display in an area that has been hatched or that has a solid fill. When you run the Text Mask program on selected text, an area of hatch—or solid fill—surrounding the text will seem to disappear. It is still there, but a wipeout object has been created to mask it underneath the text. In the following exercise, you can see how this works.

Tip 115 from
Paul Richardson

The Text Mask command is very flexible. If you need to change text you have already masked, run the Text Mask command again after you have edited the text. The wipeout will be redefined.

EXAMPLE: USING THE TEXT MASK COMMAND

1. Zoom to the detail section at the lower-right side of the detail sheet (CH15 TEXT.DWG).

2. Choose Express, Text, Text Mask to start the command, or type **textmask** at the command line and press Enter. You are prompted with this:

```
Current settings: Offset factor = 0.3500, Mask type = Wipeout
Select text objects to mask or [Masktype/Offset]:
```

At this point, you can specify a new offset or choose a different type of text mask. Three different styles of text mask are available:

- Wipeout—This (default) option masks with a rectangular frame displaying in the background color of the drawing. A wipeout object is essentially an image tile that is the same color as your AutoCAD background.

- 3dface—This option places a 3D face behind the text.

- Solid—This masks with a 2D solid in a specified color.

3. Select the two CONCRETE text objects, and press Enter. The background disappears in the area of the wipeout. Zoom in close to the text if you want to see the effect more clearly.

A text mask is used most typically when text is placed on top of a hatch pattern or a solid fill. However, it can also be used to mask any drawing object. To demonstrate this, repeat steps 2 through 4, but this time select the text object Street Surface on the right of the detail and—after you have masked the text—move it on top of the line work. The line work appears to break around the text (see Figure 15.31). You can move the label about, and the lines and hatching will always break appropriately. The break is just an illusion created by the wipeout.

Tip 116 from
Paul Richardson

If your masked text seems to disappear when you move it around, try a regen and it will reappear.

Figure 15.31
The Text Mask command enables you to place text on top of objects in a drawing.

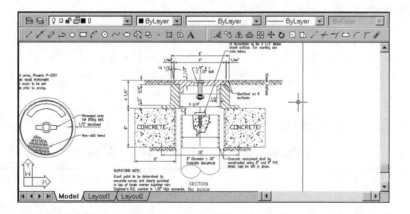

Caution

You can even use wipeouts in paper space to mask objects in model space. For the wipeout to plot correctly, the Plot Paper Space Last option must be clear in the Plot Settings tab of the Plot dialog box.

UNMASK TEXT

The Unmask Text command reverses the Text Mask command. Simply select the text or Mtext with the wipeout object, and then start the command from the Express, Text menu; or, type **textunmask** at the command line. In either case, the wipeout will be removed.

EXPLODE TEXT

The AutoCAD 2000 Explode command does not explode text objects; instead, this Express Tools command enables you to convert text objects to a polyline outline. Take a look at how the basic command works.

EXAMPLE: USING THE EXPLODE TEXT COMMAND

1. Still in CH15 TEXT.DWG, zoom to the view of the street signs shown in Figure 15.32.

2. Choose Express, Blocks, Explode Text to start the command, or type **textexp** at the command line and press Enter. You are prompted to select text to explode.

3. Select all six of the text objects on the actual street signs, and press Enter. The text objects are all converted to 2D polylines and are placed on layer zero. (You can check this using the Properties command.)

Figure 15.32
The Explode Text command enables you to convert text objects into lines and arcs.

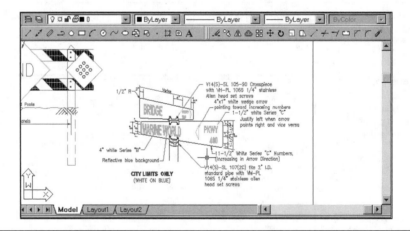

You will notice that the text has been converted to a polyline *outline*. When you have the polyline outline, you can edit it with regular AutoCAD 2000 editing tools. For a solid fill, you will need to use the Solid hatch pattern. (Choose Draw, Hatch, and select the Quick tab. Then click on the button with three dots on it. This in turn opens the Hatch Pattern Palettes tabs. The Solid hatch pattern is on the Other Predefined tab.)

This program is invaluable for working with company logos that are partly text or that are reversed out on a solid background.

CONVERT TEXT TO MTEXT

The Convert Text to Mtext command is available from the menu or the command line, but not from the Express Text toolbar. This utility is another time-saver, particularly if you have legacy drawings with multiple line text objects. If you need, for example, to adjust the column width of existing line text, you typically have to edit each line individually—a tedious task, at best. This command converts multiple lines of text objects to a single Mtext object. Then you can adjust a single object.

To practice this command, you can convert any of the text in CH15 TEXT.DWG. All the detail text is single-line text, created using the Text command.

EXAMPLE: USING THE CONVERT TEXT TO MTEXT COMMAND

1. Choose Express, Text, Convert Text to Mtext to start the command, or type **txt2mtxt** at the command line and press Enter. You are prompted to select text objects.

2. You can practice converting the text labels on the street signs. Select each line of text in one label, and then press Enter. You will be informed how many objects have been converted, for example:

   ```
   4 Text objects removed, 1 MText object added.
   ```

   You may have to do some minor alignment adjustments after the text has been converted because the line spacing or insertion point may vary slightly.

Caution

If by chance you select a line from an adjacent label as you convert the text, the line will be incorporated into the wrong Mtext object. If you notice this as you convert the text, use the Undo option and start again. Otherwise, you will have to do some cutting and pasting of Mtext at a later date.

3. To convert the two numbered Notes in CH15 TEXT.DWG, select the text for each numbered note and convert them one at a time.

Caution

Do not convert the item numbers along with the text; if you convert just the text, the Mtext object will line up appropriately. If you include the number also, you will lose the indent and will create a solid paragraph with the number embedded in it.

ARC-ALIGNED TEXT

Many AutoCAD users have a LISP program in their repertoire that positions text objects evenly along a curve. The Express Tools Arc-Aligned Text command does this and goes one step better. This command creates a single Arc Text object that can be selected and edited. Take a look at how you create and modify arc-aligned text.

EXAMPLE: USING THE ARC-ALIGNED TEXT COMMAND

1. Zoom to the detail of the monument marker at the bottom-left side of the detail sheet in CH15 TEXT.DWG (see Figure 15.33).

Figure 15.33
The Text Arc command enables you to position text along an arc object.

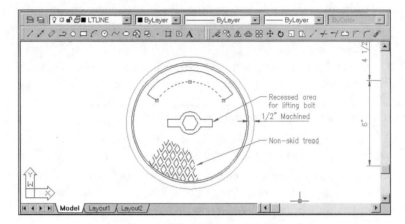

2. Choose Express, Text, Arc Aligned Text to start the command, or type **arctext** at the command line and press Enter. You are prompted with this:

```
Select an Arc or ArcAligned text
```

3. Select the lower arc within the marker, as shown in Figure 15.33. The ArcAligned Text Workshop dialog box is displayed (see Figure 15.34).

Figure 15.34
The Arc Text Workshop enables you to specify the text position, font, height, offset, and numerous text effects.

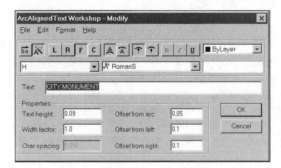

Most of the options offered in this workshop are self-explanatory:

- Pick boxes—These buttons control the text position relative to the arc; you can position the text above or below the arc and facing inward or outward. You can even reverse the order of the text as it is placed on the arc by using the first button (the ba icon). The Drag Wizard controls the text behavior when the arc is moved. You also can choose the text color, and if you are using a TrueType font, you can make the text bold, italic, or underlined.

- Text List Boxes—These list the Text Styles in the drawing, plus all the TrueType fonts and AutoCAD-compiled shape (SHX) fonts in the AutoCAD Fonts directory.

- Text Input Box—This is where you type the text string for arcing. You can modify or delete portions of the text at any time by reactivating the Arctext command.

- Properties Section—This panel enables you to override the height, width, and default character spacing to accomplish the arc text effect that you require. You also can manipulate the offset of your text and arc.

4. Enter the values and text shown in Figure 15.34, and press OK. (The Fit option is used to make the text fit to the arc.)

Because you do not get any graphical feedback in the workshop, it is difficult to position the Arc Text perfectly the first time. If the result is not to your satisfaction—the text sits too high or is too closely spaced, for example—start the Text Arc command again, but this time select the actual Arc Text, not the arc. When the Workshop dialog box reopens, you can make any necessary adjustments to the text properties.

Note

In some cases, you may not want the arc to be part of the completed geometry; you may need only the curving text. The arc does not have to remain in the drawing. When you have the text where you want it, you can erase the arc. The arc text will keep its position and can be modified using the Arc-Aligned Text command.

THE EXPRESS DIMENSION MENU

All the dimension commands are grouped together on the Dimension menu item of the Express Tools menu. When you click Dimension, a secondary flyout menu drops down containing three items, as shown in Figure 15.35. There is no toolbar for the Express dimension commands.

Figure 15.35
The Express
Dimension Tools are
grouped on the
Dimension submenu.

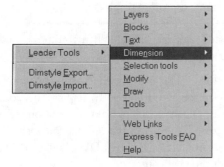

LEADER TOOLS

The first item on the Dimension submenu is Leader Tools. When you select this item, a fly-out menu opens and offers three leader options:

- Attach Leader to Annotation
- Detach Leaders from Annotation
- Global Attach Leader to Annotation

Each of these commands is discussed in the following sections.

ATTACH LEADER TO ANNOTATION   The first leader option enables you to create—or re-create—an association between a leader object and an Mtext object. When you create a dimension leader object from scratch, an Mtext object is associated with the leader object so that when the Mtext object is moved, the leader follows it. As a result of changes in the drawing, or human error, the Mtext and the leader can go their separate ways. This command resets the association between the separated leader and Mtext objects.

If you wish to practice this command, open practice drawing CH15 LEADER.DWG. Copy this file from the CD that accompanies this book into a practice folder on your hard drive.

EXAMPLE: USING THE ATTACH LEADER TO ANNOTATION COMMAND

1. Open CH15 LEADER.DWG. It contains a set of leaders and a set of Mtext objects. Most of the leaders and Mtext objects in this drawing are associated. Only the top-right leader object is not associated with the adjacent Mtext object (the label that starts with V14(S)–SL). If you move this label, the leader does not stretch with it.

2. Choose Express, Dimension, Leader Tools, Attach leader to Annotation to start the command, or type **qlattach** at the command line and press Enter. You are prompted with this:

   ```
   Select Leader:
   Select Annotation:
   ```

3. Select the leader at the top right of the diagram (as shown in Figure 15.36), and then select the text label beside it. The text does not highlight when you select but the command completes, and the command prompt displays.

This leader object is now associated with the Mtext. When you move the Mtext object, the leader should reposition itself to align with the text.

DETACH LEADERS FROM ANNOTATION   This is the reverse of the previous command and removes the leader association from the Mtext object. To activate this command, choose Express, Dimension, Leader Tools, Detach Leaders from Annotation, or type **qldetachset** at the command line and press Enter. Then select the objects you wish to separate. You may try this out with any of the leaders in CH15 LEADER.DWG. Detach a few of the leaders in this drawing so you can try out the next command.

Figure 15.36
The Express Leader Tools enable you to associate leader objects and Mtext objects.

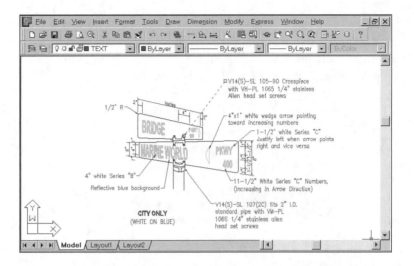

GLOBAL ATTACH LEADER TO ANNOTATION The third leader command enables you to associate a set of leader objects with their appropriate annotation objects. The command determines which leaders to link to which text based on distance. This command is intended primarily to update R13 leaders that did not create an association between leader and Mtext.

The Global Attach command operates in the same way as the Attach Leader to Annotation command, but you pick a group of objects rather than specifying one leader and one text object. To start the command, choose Express, Dimension, Leader Tools, Global Attach Leader to Annotation, or type **gqlattachset** at the command line and press Enter. Then select all the objects that are to be associated.

DIMSTYLE EXPORT

With this command, you can store all the settings and values from a dimension style in a .DIM file that can then be imported into other drawings. This enables you to transport dimension styles between your own drawings and also lets you share styles with other users. This command also provides an easy way to establish and manage project or company standards for dimension styles. For example, you could put your defined standard company dimension styles on a server so all users have access to them.

This functionality is also available in the new AutoCAD 2000 DesignCenter, which allows drag-and-drop importation of dimension styles.

DIMSTYLE IMPORT

This Express Dimension Tool enables you to import dimension styles created with the Dimstyle Export command.

→ Using the AutoCAD 2000 DesignCenter and the Dimstyle Export and Import commands is covered in more detail in Chapter 14, "Dimensioning."

THE EXPRESS SELECTION TOOLS MENU

All the Express Selection commands are grouped together on the menu item of the Express Selection Tools menu. When you click Selection Tools, a secondary flyout menu drops down as shown in Figure 15.37. There is no toolbar for the Express Selection commands.

Figure 15.37
The Express Selection Tools are grouped on the Selection Tools submenu.

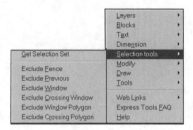

GET SELECTION SET

The Get Selection Set command (getsel) provides a quick filter to select specific objects and creates a temporary selection set. In this exercise, you use the Get Selection Set command to identify and then erase all the concrete hatching in a drawing. In the practice drawing, there are only four concrete areas—which could be erased easily without using a selection set. Other drawings, however, will present more complex scenarios, and you will find this filtering tool very useful.

EXAMPLE: USING THE GET SELECTION SET COMMAND

1. Open CH15 SELECT.DWG. (This drawing is on the CD that accompanies this book. Copy it into a practice folder on your hard drive if you have not already done so.)

2. Choose Express, Selection Tools, Get Selection Set to start the command, or type **get-sel** at the command line and press Enter. You are prompted first to identify a layer and then the exact type of object you wish to select:
   ```
   Select an object on the Source layer <*>:
   ```

3. Click on the herringbone hatch area at the street surface. This picks the layer LTLINE. All the objects drawn black are on this layer. You are prompted to be more specific:
   ```
   Select an object of the Type you want <*>::
   ```

4. Click one of the concrete hatched areas, as shown in Figure 15.38. This completes the selection routine. You have now selected all concrete objects on the LTLINE layer. You are advised of the following:
   ```
   Collecting all INSERT objects on layer LTLINE...
   11 objects have been placed in the active selection set.
   ```

5. Now start the Erase command. When you are prompted to select objects, type **p** (for previous) and then press Enter. The concrete is erased from the drawing.

Figure 15.38
Use the Get Selection Set command to create a temporary selection set while you are editing.

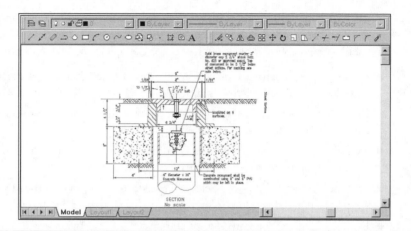

If you run any AutoCAD editing command and type **p** when prompted for a selection, the command will use the previously defined selection—which, in this case, would be the selection generated by getsel. In this exercise, the source layer and type of object were defined by picking the objects on screen; they can also be supplied by typing them at the command line.

Often, you want to repeat the same editing operation on multiple objects. For example, you might want to put all the text objects from one layer on a different layer. The Get Selection Set command enables you to group specific objects into a selection set, which can then be used by a command such as Chprop.

> **Note**
>
> AutoCAD 2000 has a number of other options for selecting and modifying objects:
>
> - The Quick Select command (Qselect) does the same job as getsel, but with a dialog box. It also offers the advantage of leaving the selected objects gripped for use by other commands.
> - You can use the Properties command in conjunction with Quick Select (via the filter on the Properties window) to select groups of objects and then edit them in the Properties window.

EXCLUDE SELECTION TOOLS

The Selection Tools menu includes an additional six commands, which at first glance look like the regular Select options. However, these commands all start with the word Exclude, which means that the selection set contains everything *except* the defined selection. In other words, you are picking the objects you *don't* want included in the selection set.

You can start the Exclude Selection commands from the menu, if you wish, by selecting Express, Selection Tools, and then clicking on one of the options listed here. However, it is probably faster to type the commands at the command prompt; just add **EX** at the front of the usual selection options that you use. You can use these commands transparently in the middle of another editing command. When you are prompted to Select objects, type the command with an apostrophe at the front. For example, type **'exf** and then press Enter.

- Exclude Fence—Select all objects in the drawing *except* those that cross a defined fence line. (Command-line version: **exf** or **'exf.**)

- Exclude Previous—Select all objects in the drawing *except* those selected in the previous command. (Command-line version: **exp** or **'exp.**)

- Exclude Window—Select all objects in the drawing *except* those fully within the defined window. (Command-line version: **exw** or **'exw.**)

- Exclude Crossing Window—Select all objects in the drawing *except* those fully or partly within the defined window. (Command-line version: **excw** or **'excw.**)

- Exclude Window Polygon—Select all objects in the drawing *except* those fully within the defined polygon. (Command-line version: **exwp** or **'exwp.**)

- Exclude Crossing Polygon—Select all objects in the drawing *except* those fully or partly within the defined polygon. (Command-line version: **excp** or **'excp.**)

Note

One selection command that is not on the Express menu or toolbars is SSX. This is a powerful and versatile command that allows you to create quite complex selection sets. At its simplest, you can start the command (type **ssx** and press Enter) and click on any object; SSX will add all similar objects to a selection set.

If when you start the SSX command you simply press Enter instead of picking an object, you are presented with the following options:
```
Select object <None>:
Enter filter option [Block
name/Color/Entity/Flag/LAyer/LType/Pick/Style/Thickness/Vector]:
```
You can then choose to make a selection set based on one filter, such as layer or color. Of course, this functionality is available in the AutoCAD 2000 Quick Select command, but at times you will find SSX the quickest way to make a selection set.

THE EXPRESS MODIFY MENU

All the Modify commands are grouped together on the Modify menu item of the Express Tools menu. When you click Modify, a secondary flyout menu drops down as shown in Figure 15.39.

If you prefer to access commands via a toolbar, load the Express Modify toolbar (see Figure 15.40) as described in "Loading Express Tools Toolbars" earlier in this chapter. The Standard toolbar contains some of the Express Modify commands along with some of the Express Draw commands and a couple Tools commands. Again, there is not an exact correspondence between the menu and the toolbar: The menu has six Modify commands and the toolbar has only four.

Figure 15.39
The Express Modify Tools are grouped on the Modify submenu.

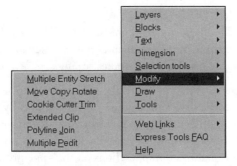

Figure 15.40
Express Modify tool-bar.

MULTIPLE ENTITY STRETCH

Using the regular AutoCAD Stretch command, you use a single window or polygon to define the area from which you want to stretch objects. The Multiple Entity Stretch command (mstretch) enables you to make as many windows or crossing polygons as you like. In this way, you can include all the objects that are to be stretched at one pass.

EXAMPLE: USING THE MULTIPLE ENTITY STRETCH COMMAND

1. Start the command from the menu (Express, Modify, Multiple Entity Stretch) or via the Express Standard toolbar, or by typing **mstretch** at the command line and then pressing Enter. You are prompted with this:

   ```
   Define crossing windows or crossing polygons...
   Options: Crossing Polygon or Crossing first point
   Specify an option [CP/C] <Crossing first point>:
   ```

2. When you have finished defining your objects and areas for stretching, press Enter. You are prompted with this:

   ```
   Done defining windows for stretch...
   Specify an option [Remove objects] <Base point>:
   ```

3. If you have included objects that you do not want to stretch, type **r** (for Remove) and press Enter; then click each of the objects to remove them from the selection set and press Enter again. You are prompted to select a basepoint and a second basepoint.

4. Specify or click on the screen to identify the distance and direction that the objects are to be stretched.

From step 4, this command works exactly like the regular Stretch command. You define your basepoint and then a relative point for the distance and direction of the stretch.

MOVE COPY ROTATE

The second command on the Modify menu combines several of the most popular edit commands into one operation. The name of the command (mocoro) is made up from MOve COpy and ROtate. The Mocoro command also handles scaling.

What makes this command special is that it retains the selected objects between editing commands. A green cross marks the basepoint you use for the initial copy or move operation. When you give the destination point for the move or copy operation, that point becomes the new base point for the transported objects, which remain selected. You can proceed to multiple move, scale, and rotation operations on the same group of objects. The practice exercises that follow utilize the CH15 MODIFY.DWG, which is on the CD that accompanies this book. Copy this file to a practice folder on your hard drive if you have not already done so.

EXAMPLE: USING THE MOVE COPY ROTATE COMMAND

1. Open CH15 MODIFY.DWG. Zoom in to the area of the concrete stairs in the bottom-right corner of the sheet. There is a concrete pad in front of the steps that you can practice moving, copying, scaling, and rotating.

2. Start the command from the menu (Express, Modify, Move Copy Rotate) or via the Express Standard toolbar, or by typing **mocoro** at the command line and then pressing Enter. You are prompted to select objects.

3. Pick the concrete pad (on layer L-SITE-CONC) and press Enter. You are prompted for a basepoint. When you select one, you are prompted with this:

   `[Move/Copy/Rotate/Scale/Base/Undo]<eXit>:`

4. Try out each of these options. First type **r** and rotate the pad 90°; then type **m** and move the pad to the position of the lower rectangle in Figure 15.41; then type **s** and scale it 1.1 times; finally, type **c** and copy the rectangle to the space above it, as shown in Figure 15.41. (Use the Base option if you want to shift the basepoint for the edit commands. Use Undo if you want to redo any of the options.)

5. Type **x** and press Enter twice to exit the command.

COOKIE CUTTER TRIM

With this command, you can trim objects using a specified boundary, just like the name suggests.

Start the command from the menu (Express, Modify, Cookie Cutter Trim) or the Express Standard toolbar, or by typing **extrim** at the command line and then pressing Enter. You are prompted to select an object to define a trimming boundary:

`Pick a POLYLINE, LINE, CIRCLE, ARC, ELLIPSE, IMAGE or TEXT for cutting edge...`

After you have selected your object, click *inside* or *outside* the shape to determine where the trimming will occur.

Figure 15.41
The Move Copy Rotate command enables you to perform multiple edits at the same time.

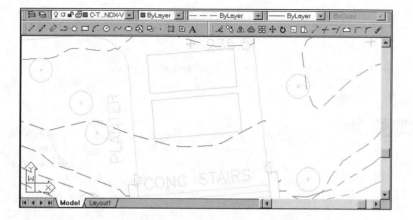

The command finishes off for you, trimming everything that can be trimmed.

EXTENDED CLIP

Both the AutoCAD 2000 boundary clip command (xclip) and the Express Tools Extended Clip command (clipit) enable you to view a portion of a block or xref and mask off the rest. The two commands differ significantly in their operation:

- Xclip uses rectangles, polygons, and non-closing polylines to create clipping boundaries; the Clipit command allows the use of circles, arcs, and ellipses when defining a clip window for an xref or block.

- When you use Xclip, the command prompts you to create the clipping boundary; Clipit prompts you to select an object that is already in the drawing. Thus, you should draw your clipping object, if necessary, before you start the command.

Using the current practice drawing, you can compare the way these two commands work. Because there are no xrefs in the current drawing, you can practice using a block—one of the tree symbols that are dotted about the drawing, for example.

→ For more information on boundary clipping and the xclip command, refer to Chapter 17, "External Reference Files and Importing Images."

EXAMPLE: USING THE EXTENDED CLIP COMMAND

1. In CH15 MODIFY.DWG, zoom to the trees to the left of the concrete steps area, where you practiced the MOCORO command (refer to Figure 15.41). Draw a circle or arc that intersects with one of the tree blocks.

2. Start the Clipit command from the menu (Express, Modify, Extended Clip), or by typing **clipit** at the command line and then pressing Enter. You are prompted to select an object to define a clipping boundary:

```
Pick a POLYLINE, CIRCLE, ARC, ELLIPSE, or TEXT object for clipping edge...
Select objects:
```

3. Select the circle (or arc) that you drew in step 1. You are prompted with this:

```
Pick an IMAGE, a WIPEOUT, or an XREF/BLOCK to clip...
Select objects:
```

4. Click the tree symbol. You are prompted with this:

```
Enter maximum allowable error distance for resolution of arc segments
<0.0500>:
```

> **Note**
>
> Clipit works by approximating the shape of a curve with a series of line segments. You can adjust the number of line segments to approximate a curve. There is a trade-off between accuracy and drawing and plotting time, however—the more segments you use, the more accurate, but the longer the regens and plotting time.
>
> The Express Tools Help entry for this command advises: "To increase performance, enter relatively large values at the Max error distance for resolution of arcs prompt while creating your drawing. When you are ready to plot your drawing, use CLIPIT again and specify a small error value for arc resolution at the CLIPIT prompt."

5. For now, simply press Enter to accept the default value.

   Only that portion of the tree block that is within the clipping boundary is displayed; the rest is masked.

POLYLINE JOIN

The standard Polyline Edit (pedit) command is most users' least favorite command, being both clunky to use and limited in its scope. Any command that improves or replaces pedit functions is worth investigating. The Express Tools Polyline Join (pljoin) improves on the corresponding pedit functions in the following ways:

- In the pljoin command, the grip editor has replaced the Pedit vertex editing functions.

- If you want to join sequential lines into a single polyline, you used to have to use Pedit, turn one of the lines into a polyline, and then add all the other lines to it. If one of the lines didn't quite match endpoints, then Pedit stopped work at that point. Pljoin enables you to select anything you like, including the All option, which selects the whole drawing and then connects everything it can into polylines.

- Pljoin even attempts to join lines that don't quite meet by letting you adjust the allowable gap (or *fuzz distance*) between line endpoints.

If you wish, you can try this user-friendly utility in the current drawing.

EXAMPLE: USING THE POLYLINE JOIN COMMAND

1. In CH15 MODIFY.DWG, zoom in to the building marked RESTROOM in the middle of the drawing. It is obvious that the line objects that make up the building do not intersect at the corners (see Figure 15.42).

Figure 15.42
The Polyline Join command lets you join objects that do not quite meet.

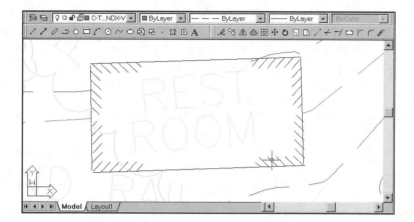

2. Start the Polyline Join command from the menu (Express, Modify, Polyline Join), or by typing **pljoin** at the command line and then pressing Enter. You are prompted to select objects.

3. Select the four sides of the rectangle. You are prompted with this:
```
Join Type = Both (Fillet and Add)
Enter fuzz distance or [Jointype] <0.000>:
```

4. If you press Enter to accept the default fuzz distance of 0.000, the lines will not be joined. You need to specify a new fuzz distance value. If you are not sure what fuzz value is enough to join the lines, you may pick two points onscreen to define the allowable gap. For this example, any value over 0.3 is sufficient to join the four sides of the rectangle.

The Polyline Join command joins the four original line objects and converts them into a single polyline object. You may check this via the List command or the Properties command. Type **list** and press Enter, or right-click the new polyline and select Properties on the shortcut menu to open the Properties window and display the new object properties.

MULTIPLE PEDIT

If you have to use the Pedit command, why not use Multiple Pedit command and edit all your polylines in one shot? The standard AutoCAD 2000 Pedit command works on only one selected polyline at a time; with mpedit, you may select as many lines and polylines as you want and edit them.

Experiment with this command in the current practice drawing. You will probably want to undo or abandon your changes at the end of this practice.

EXAMPLE: USING THE MULTIPLE PEDIT COMMAND

1. In CH15 MODIFY.DWG, zoom to Extents. Use the Express Layers Tool, Layer Isolate to turn off all layers except the L-PLNT-TXST, the trees layer.

2. Start the Multiple Pedit command from the menu (Express, Modify, Multiple Pedit) or via the Express Standard toolbar, or by typing **mpedit** at the command line and then pressing Enter. You are prompted to select objects.

3. Pick as many of the tree boundaries as you wish, and then press Enter. You are prompted with this:

```
Convert Lines and Arcs to polylines? [Yes/No] <Yes>:
Enter an option [Open/Close/Join/Width/Fit/Spline/Decurve/Ltype gen/eXit]
<eXit>:
```

4. Press Enter to accept the default Yes (although these objects are already polylines), and then experiment with the other Pedit functions. Type **x** to exit when you are finished.

THE EXPRESS DRAW MENU

All the draw commands are grouped together on the Draw menu item of the Express Tools menu. When you click Draw, a secondary flyout menu drops down, as shown in Figure 15.43.

Figure 15.43
The Express Draw Tools are grouped on the Draw submenu.

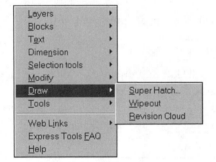

If you prefer to access commands from a toolbar, load the Express Standard toolbar as described in "Loading Express Tools Toolbars" earlier in this chapter. The Standard toolbar contains all three of the Express Draw commands, along with some Modify and some Tools commands (see Figure 15.43).

Figure 15.44
Express Draw toolbar.

SUPERHATCH

If you have ever tried to design a hatch pattern, you will love this program. SuperHatch enables you to create a hatch pattern from almost anything—including blocks, images, xrefs, and wipeouts. The possibilities are endless!

Working with regular AutoCAD 2000 hatch patterns, you are limited to straight lines with different linetypes at various angles. This makes anything approximating a curve very hard to do. If you have ever tried to make an irregular hatch pattern—to represent gravel, for example—you will know what a thankless task that can be. Under normal AutoCAD conditions, you end up with something that doesn't look very good and that takes forever to regen.

In the exercise that follows, you step through the SuperHatch process and create a pebbles hatch in just a few minutes. Use the CH15 DRAW.DWG that is supplied on the CD that accompanies this book.

EXAMPLE: USING THE SUPERHATCH COMMAND

1. Open the drawing CH15 DRAW.DWG. The large circle is the area you will hatch; the red box holds the objects you will use to create a block (see Figure 15.45).

Figure 15.45
With SuperHatch, creating a complex hatch pattern from a simple block requires very little effort.

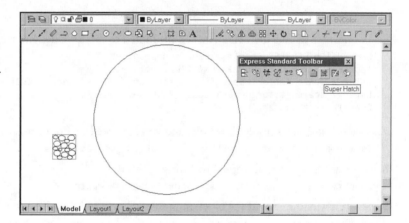

2. Create a block called Pebbles. Start the Block command; leave the insertion point at 0,0; and type the name **Pebbles** in the name edit box. Then click the Select Objects button and select all the objects within the red box. Press OK when you are done. Now you are ready to start the SuperHatch program.

3. Start the SuperHatch command from the menu (Express, Draw, Super Hatch) or from the Express Standard toolbar, or by typing **superhatch** at the command line and then pressing Enter. The SuperHatch dialog box opens, as shown in Figure 15.46.

4. Pick the Block button, and then pick the Block button on the SuperHatch–Insert dialog box and select Pebbles from the block list. In the options area, make sure Specify Parameters on Screen is checked.

5. Press OK and then click a point anywhere inside the circle.

Figure 15.46

The SuperHatch command enables you to use many different types of AutoCAD 2000 objects to define a hatch pattern.

6. Press Enter to take the defaults when prompted for scale values and rotation.

```
SUPERHATCH PEBBLES Specify insertion point or
[Scale/X/Y/Z/Rotate/PScale/PX/PY/PZ/PRotate]:
Enter X scale factor, specify opposite corner, or [Corner/XYZ] <1>:
Enter Y scale factor <use X scale factor>:
Specify rotation angle <0>:
```

7. The block appears inside the circle, and you are asked the following:

```
Is the placement of this BLOCK acceptable? {Yes/No] <Yes>:
```

8. Answer Yes. You are prompted with this:

```
Specify block [Extents] First corner <magenta rectang>:
```

9. Select a window around the block to define column and row tile distances. Keep close to the magenta outline. If you define a margin around the block, it will be replicated in the hatching. You are prompted with this:

```
Selecting visible objects for boundary detection...Done.
Specify an option [Advanced options] <Internal point>:
```

10. After you pick a point *inside* the circle, you will be offered the same prompt:

```
Specify an option [Advanced options] <Internal point>:
```

11. This time, press Enter to complete the command.

```
Preparing hatch objects for display...
Done.
```

You should now be able to view the completed hatch pattern. If not, you may have pressed Enter instead of picking a point inside the circle. Just work through the prompts again a little more slowly.

WIPEOUT

A wipeout object obscures geometry in a drawing without affecting the obscured objects. A wipeout object is what the Textmask command uses to mask any geometry behind and around the text object. The most common use of a wipeout is to clear the background when text is superimposed on a drawing. You can also use a wipeout to cover up any objects in a drawing on a temporary basis. The wipeout is essentially an image object with the same color as the current background color so it appears invisible. The hatched area you created in the previous exercise is a suitable candidate for a wipeout. Continue to use CH15 DRAW.DWG for this exercise also.

EXAMPLE: USING THE WIPEOUT COMMAND

1. Start the Wipeout command from the Express Draw menu (Express, Draw, Wipeout) or from the Express Standard Toolbar, or by typing **wipeout** at the command line.

   ```
   Select first point or [Frame/New from Polyline] <New>:
   ```

2. Pick a series of points to define your wipeout area. Make sure they fall at least in part over the hatched circle.

When you press Enter to complete the Wipeout command, the specified area is masked, as shown in Figure 15.47.

Figure 15.47
A wipeout object obscures all other objects in a defined area.

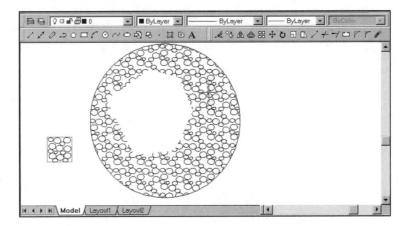

Your wipeout may look like the wipeout object in Figure 15.47 or it may have an outline (frame) around it. The presence (or absence) of a frame on the wipeout is determined by the Tframes setting in your system at the time you create the wipeout. The command Tframes, also on the Express Standard Toolbar, toggles the visibility of wipeout frames. Click the second button from the right on the toolbar a few times and you will see the wipeout frame turn on and off.

Typically, you want the wipeout frame to be invisible except when you need to edit the frame. Using grips is the simplest way to adjust the frame. Each time you move the frame, the wipeout will instantly be adjusted to match the frame. You may also use the wipeout frame to move or copy the wipeout just like any other AutoCAD 2000 object.

- Wipeouts don't have to be rectangular; you can make a wipeout from any shape of polyline as you just did. You can also use an existing closed polyline to define the wipeout location. Using the Wipeout command, at the first prompt, type **n** (for New) and press Enter. Then select the closed polyline. After the wipeout has been created, you can optionally remove the original polyline.

- You can also control the display of the frame defining the wipeout with the Frame option in the Wipeout command. Use the Frame option of the Wipeout command to display the frame: At the first prompt, type **f** (for Frame) and press Enter, and then type **off** or **on** to change the Frame setting. When the Frame is on, you can select the wipeout object and move it or copy it like any other AutoCAD object.

REVISION CLOUD

This is one the easiest and most fun programs in the Express Tools package. Architects and engineers use Revision Clouds to denote revisions in a drawing. You can start the program from the Express Draw menu or pick the button with the cloud icon on the Express Standard toolbar. After you click a start point, the program will draw an arc in the direction that you move your cursor. As you move your cursor counterclockwise, the program continues to draw a series of convex arcs; if you come back to your start point, the program will neatly complete the cloud.

CLOUD OPTIONS   This simple utility also offers a range of variations in cloud style. After you start the command but before you pick a start point, you can type **o** and press Enter to start the Revcloud Options dialog box (see Figure 15.48).

Figure 15.48
You can change the appearance of the Revision Clouds in the Revcloud Options dialog box.

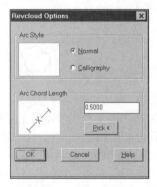

In this dialog box, you can redefine the arc length of the arcs used for the cloud. You can also change the look of the arcs by selecting the calligraphy style. This gives a varying width to the arc to resemble a calligraphic pen stroke. After you have made any desired changes to the cloud style, press OK. You are returned to the Revcloud prompt, and you can start drawing a cloud immediately.

Additionally, you can create concave clouds by moving the cursor in a clockwise rather than a counterclockwise direction. If you need to create a revision cloud in the shape of a donut (to demarcate an area where changes are to be made), you can use the typical convex clouds on the outer boundary and concave clouds to mark the inner boundary.

THE EXPRESS TOOLS MENU

All the Tools commands are grouped together on the Tools menu item of the Express Tools menu. When you click Tools, a secondary flyout menu drops down, as shown in Figure 15.49. Most of these utilities are available from the menu or command line only. Just two of these useful routines are included on the Express Standard toolbar: Pack 'n Go and Show URLs. In the sections that follow, each of these utilities is described in sequence as it appears on the Tools submenu.

Figure 15.49
The Express Tools tools are grouped on the Tools submenu.

PACK 'N GO

The first utility on the Tools submenu is Pack 'n Go. If you share drawings with other companies, you will know there is always a degree of uncertainty when you package drawing files for distribution. It's easy to overlook an xref, font file, or shape file that will be required by the recipient of your drawings.

Pack 'n Go groups all the support files needed for a particular drawing and puts them into a target folder for you. It can also create a report that you can print or save to a text file, and which describes all the support files and their expected locations.

To access the Pack 'n Go program, select Express, Tools, Pack 'n Go; or type **pack** at the command line and press Enter. You may also access this program from the Pack 'n Go button on the Express Standard toolbar. (The Pack 'n Go button is the one with the briefcase icon.)

You can then compact your files into a zip file for transmission as an email attachment or transfer to a floppy or zip disk.

FULL-SCREEN AUTOCAD

If you are working with a small monitor, this command enables you to work without the title bar and menu being displayed, increasing the relative size of your drawing area.

- Fullscreenon turns on the full-screen effect.
- Fullscreenoff turns off the effect.
- Fullscreenoptions opens a dialog box, which offers the single option of turning the status bar on and off.

To access the Full Screen AutoCAD program, select Express, Tools, Full Screen AutoCAD; or type **fullscreen** at the command line and press Enter.

This option turns on the full-screen effect; to access the other options, use the command line options; type **fullscreenoff** or **fullscreenoptions** to start these commands.

MAKE LINETYPE

The Make Linetype program provides a user-friendly approach to creating new linetype definitions. In AutoCAD, simple linetypes are defined as a series of line lengths, dots, and spaces. Complex linetype definitions may additionally include shapes and text objects. All linetype definitions are stored in linetype library files, with an extension of .LIN. The standard AutoCAD 2000 library of linetypes is stored in a file called ACAD.LIN.

Make Linetype takes all the tedium out of defining your linetypes. You don't even have to open a text editor. In AutoCAD 2000, simply draw a series of lines and dots to represent one complete segment of the linetype you want to create. This segment is repeated for the entire length of the linetype.

To access the Make Linetype program select Express, Tools, Make Linetype or type **mkltype** at the command line and press Enter. The program prompts you to specify the following information:

- The name and path of the library file in which to store the new linetype. Use the Select Linetype File dialog box that opens to browse to the \ACAD2000\SUPPORT folder, and add a new LIN file, for example, My Linetypes.LIN
- A name for the actual linetype, and a description, so that you will remember what the linetype represents or looks like, for example, Dash Dash Dot or Zigzag or Railroad.
- Start and End Point for the Linetype Definition
- The objects that you wish to include in the linetype definition: You can include lines, polylines, points, shapes and/or text objects in a linetype definition.

Once you have selected the required objects, press enter to complete the command. The linetype you have created is immediately available in the Linetype Control list box on the Object Properties toolbar.

The tricky part about defining linetypes is to make sure they scale consistently when you are working on scaled drawings. For more information, see the AutoCAD 2000 documentation for the system variable LTSCALE, which adjusts the scale on linetype definitions to match the drawing scale. Generally, you will want to draw your linetype at its plotted size, at 1-to-1 scale, and then use LTSCALE to adjust for drawing scale.

Complex linetypes are linetypes that include either a shape definition or a string of text. To make a complex linetype with embedded text, simply draw the lines and place a text object as you want to see it in the finished linetype. If you are using the Make Linetype program, select the text and lines in the correct sequence when prompted with <Select objects>:.

If you want to see a repeating graphic in your linetype, such as a fence post or an arrow, you must first create a shape file. The next command, Make Shape, assists you with creating the shapes. After you have the shape defined, draw your lines and then place the shape by using the Make Linetype program.

MAKE SHAPE

In AutoCAD 2000, shapes are used mainly in fonts and complex linetypes. In earlier versions of AutoCAD, when processing was more limited, shapes were sometimes used instead of blocks because they were more compact and could be drawn faster. Happily, that is no longer necessary. If you want to make a custom font for AutoCAD 2000, you can use this program as a starting point. If you want to create custom shapes to embed in complex linetypes, this program will do the job.

Creating shapes in AutoCAD 2000 is a task of some complexity. The Express Tools Make Shape program greatly simplifies matters by letting you create a shape definition based upon selected objects.

To access the Make Shape program, select Express, Tools, Make Shape, or type **mkshape** at the command line and press Enter. You will be prompted for the following:

- The name and path of the shape file (.SHP) in which to store the new shape definition. (Like linetype defintions, shape definitions must be stored in a type of library file.) Use the Select Shape File dialog box that opens to browse to the \ACAD2000\SUPPORT folder, and add a new LIN file—for example, My Linetypes.LIN.
- The desired resolution for the shape is a value between 0 and 32,767, which is rounded to the nearest factor of 8. The lower the resolution, the faster the shape will process; the higher the resolution, the better the appearance of the shape.
- The insertion base point, which is similar to block definition.
- The objects that you wish to include in the shape definition: You can include lines, polylines, arcs, circles, and ellipse objects in a shape definition.

Once the program has finished compiling the shape definition, you can delete the objects that were included in the file, if you wish. You can use the AutoCAD 2000 Shape command to place shapes in your drawing, or use the Express Tools Make Linetype program to include the new shape in a linetype definition.

PATH SUBSTITUTION

This is essentially a find-and-replace program for files that use paths, including xrefs, images, shapes, styles, and rtext. If you move drawing files from one location to another, it can take a little time to manually redefine these paths. With redir you can re-path all of them by using the wildcard option.

To access the Path Substitution program, select Express, Tools, Path Substitution, or type **redir** at the command line and press Enter.

```
Current REDIRMODE: Styles,Xrefs,Images,Rtext
Find and replace directory names
Enter old directory (use '*' for all), or ? <options>:
```

You are prompted to specify the name of the old directory (or type * to change all paths) and to specify a replacement directory name. If you want to strip all the paths, use the * option at the first prompt and press Enter at the second prompt.

Before you globally change any paths, you may wish to review the files that will be modified. At the first prompt, type **?** and press Enter. The program displays a listing of all the style, xref, image and Rtext files in the current drawing with complete path information.

SHOW URLS

Hyperlinks in an AutoCAD drawing contain URLs, or uniform resource locators, that describe a path to a file in World Wide Web format. This can include files within your company network (intranet) and even your personal computer. You can add a hyperlink to any object in your drawing by selecting Insert, Hyperlink. (The keyboard shortcut is Ctrl+K.)

The Show URLs command enables you to display all the URLs stored in a drawing; if necessary, you can edit individual links and find and replace a string.

To access the Show URLs program select Express, Tools, Show URLs, or type **showurls** at the command line and press Enter. You may also access this program from the Show URLs button on the Express Standard toolbar. (The Show URLs button is the one with the magnifying glass and world icon at the right end of the toolbar.)

This command opens the Show URLs dialog box, which enables you to both view and modify the URLs in the current drawing.

XDATA ATTACHMENT

As the name suggests, this command attaches extended entity data (xdata) to a selected object. The Xdata command is typically used by programmers rather than regular AutoCAD users.

Note

If you want to know more about xdata objects, call up the Visual LISP editor (type **vlide** at the command line and press Enter) and look up extended data in Visual LISP Help. Xdata is always associated with an application name. If you create your own xdata, you should follow consistent rules so you can recover the information when you want to.

To access the Xdata Attachment program, select Express, Tools, Xdata Attachment; or type **xdata** at the command line and press Enter. Then, select the object to which you want to attach data and enter an application name and then the data to be attached.

The Xdata command is used to store database links when drawing objects must be linked to an external database file, such as in GIS applications or tax assessor's maps and databases.

LIST ENTITY XDATA

This command lists the xdata (or extended data) associated with an AutoCAD object. See the previous section for more information.

To access the List Entity Data program, select Express, Tools, List Entity Xdata; or type **xdlist** at the command line and press Enter. Select an object and the program lists all of the associated extended data. If the object contains xdata associated with more than one application, you may specify only one application to view, or type * to view all xdata for that object.

SUMMARY

This chapter has covered a wide range of territory, including both the Inquiry commands and the Express Tools. The Inquiry tools, which are a part of the standard AutoCAD 2000 package, comprise a useful set of commands for querying objects in your drawing; they make it easy to obtain measurements of distance, angle, area and volume, as well as displaying the coordinates and other properties of objects in your drawing. The Express Tools add-on package addresses just about every area of AutoCAD 2000 functioning and provides close to sixty programs, each designed to make life just a little easier for AutoCAD 2000 users.

CHAPTER 16

CREATING AND USING BLOCKS

In this chapter

INTRODUCTION TO BLOCKS

A *block* is a set of AutoCAD objects grouped together as one object, known also as a *block reference*. When you define a set of objects as a block, it makes the drawing more manageable. Rather than numerous separate objects, many objects that form a particular part or fixture can be grouped together to create a block. For example, the lines that make up a door and the arc of the door swing can be combined to create a door block, just as the lines and arc drawn to make a pump or switch can be merged together to form a pump or switch block. Using this process, you can create a symbol library of discipline-specific blocks you can use within your drawing. Many other benefits are also gained by creating blocks, including higher productivity in the drawing, smaller drawing size, and simpler editing. Information in the form of block attributes can be assigned the block objects as well and then extracted from the drawing when finished to create a bill of materials or schedule.

In this chapter, you'll learn how to define, insert, and manage blocks and to master their use. You will also learn how to use the AutoCAD DesignCenter to create and extract block attributes.

BLOCKS VERSUS WBLOCKS

Blocks can be defined with two separate commands: Block or Wblock. The Block command creates a local block definition. This means the block can be inserted only into the current drawing file. The Wblock command creates a global block definition, which means the wblock can be inserted into any drawing file. The Wblock command actually creates a separate drawing file with a .dwg extension. Which block type you want to create depends on the intended purpose for the block object.

DEFINING BLOCKS

First, let's look at creating a Block, and then work through the Wblock command. You can access the Block command by choosing the Make Block button from the Draw toolbar, shown in Figure 16.1, or from the Draw pull-down menu, Block, Make... option.

Figure 16.1
The Block command is easily accessed from the Draw toolbar.

The Block Definition dialog box appears. From this dialog box, you will define everything that AutoCAD needs to create the block (see Figure 16.2).

Figure 16.2
Using the Block Definitions dialog box, you can specify the insertion point, objects, description, and insertion units needed to create the block.

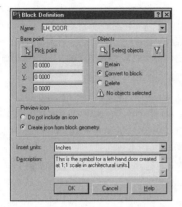

Tip 117 from
Ron House

You can also activate the Block command by typing **Block** at the command line and pressing Enter. If you precede the command with a hyphen (**-Block**), the Block Definition dialog box is suppressed, prompting you to provide the block specifics at the command line. This is a handy tip to remember when creating multiple blocks at one time. You might find it easier to type the command at the command line without the need for the dialog box.

The different sections of the dialog box are described as follows:

- Name—The name for the block, which subscribes to the standard Windows name conventions.

- Pick point—The base point, or insertion point, for the block is defined using this button. After the button is clicked, this dialog box temporarily closes, allowing you to pick a point on or near the objects that make up the block. When the block is inserted into the drawing, it uses this point as the placement point to position it. If you know the specific X, Y, and Z coordinates, they can be entered into the edit boxes provided.

Note

Think of the base point as the carrying point or handle of the object. It is more common to pick the base point graphically because the absolute coordinate is rarely known. However, when inserting other drawings or blocks into your current file, it's common to use as a base point X, Y, and Z coordinate values of 0,0,0 for the base point. This gives you an overall reference point throughout all drawings.

- Select objects—The objects that will be used to define the block can be selected by clicking the Select Objects button. Note that a button that activates the Quick Select command is immediately to the right of this edit box. This is available so you can filter through the drawing to specifically locate the objects used to create the block.

Note

The Quick Select, or Filter command is discussed in Chapter 10, "Selecting Objects." This command enables you to quickly select drawing objects based on their properties, such as color, lineweight, layer, and so on. Use this chapter as a reference for using the Quick Select command to select the objects that make up a block.

To remind you, a warning sign appears at the bottom of the Objects box if no block objects have been selected. After the objects have been selected, three options determine what happens to the original block object:

- Retain—This option will retain the objects you selected in the drawing, as well as use them to define the new block.

- Convert to block—This inserts a block to represent the objects, and uses them to create the block.

- Delete—The selected objects are deleted from the drawing after they are used to create the block.

■ Do not include an icon—By default, an icon is created at the same time the block is defined so it can be previewed within the AutoCAD DesignCenter. This option would disable that function so that no icon would be stored with the block, which would also make the preview feature for this block not available within DesignCenter.

■ Create icon from block geometry—The icon stored with the block is created from the select geometry to define the block.

Tip 118 from
Ron House

The Block icon command can be used to create icons for blocks that were created in earlier versions of AutoCAD prior to Release 14. Use the AutoCAD Help function to learn more about this feature.

■ Insert units—By selecting a unit from the select list, you can define the original unit for the block. This will be used later when the block is inserted into a drawing by using AutoCAD DesignCenter, and allows any block to be used within any drawing regardless of drawing units.

■ Description—This is the description you can assign to a block. The description can be used to assist others in determining how and what this block was created for. Information such as the creator and designed scale factor can be entered here to further describe the function of this block.

After entering the required information needed to create the block, click the OK button. The next example illustrates the process for creating a block.

EXAMPLE: CREATING A DOOR BLOCK

1. Open the drawing ch16_01.dwg that you copied from the accompanying CD. This is a simple door using an arc to define the door swing path. Although this may seem a

rather elementary example, a door was chosen because doors come in many different sizes that can typically vary from project to project. This example will assist you in creating a single door block that can be inserted at any scale factor at any size.

Tip 119 from
Ron House

The key to creating a block that can be inserted at any size is to draw the original object at equal proportions. By drawing the door 1" wide by 1" high, it can be inserted at any scale as long as the X and Y scale factors remain the same. Apply this tip to blocks that are part of your symbol library where they will be inserted in multiple drawings of varying scales.

2. Activate the Block command by typing **Block** at the command line. After the Block Definition dialog box appears, enter **LH_DOOR** for the name for your block in the Name edit box.

Tip 120 from
Ron House

When picking the insertion point of a symbol, choose a point on the object that can be used as a reference point. An example of this might be a connection point for a pump or switch, or the hinge for a door. Taking time to think through how your block will be used will save you having to edit the block after it is inserted. In this case, accept the default of (0,0,0) because that is the hinge of the door.

3. Next, select the arc and the lines that make up the door objects that will define the block. Choose the Select objects button to manually select the objects, or click the Quick Select button to use this feature to filter out of the drawing those objects you want to use to define the block. In this case, select all the objects in the drawing.

4. Select the Retain, Convert to block, or Delete button to indicate what to do with the objects after the block has been defined. In this case, choose Retain.

5. Make certain the Create icon from block geometry button is selected. This will help others in determining what this block looks like when using AutoCAD DesignCenter.

Note

AutoCAD DesignCenter is a tool that enables you to view and import blocks embedded within an external drawing. Each time you create a block, the icon that is saved with the drawing is displayed within AutoCAD DesignCenter. This enables you to preview the block before it is inserted into your drawing. Also when defining a block, AutoCAD allows for descriptions to be added to the block reference. These descriptions can aid in searching for blocks and when inserting them from the DesignCenter. You'll learn more about using DesignCenter in "Using AutoCAD DesignCenter" later in this chapter

6. Choose the Insertion units from the Insert Units list. Your block will automatically be rescaled for the units of the drawing you are inserting into. In this case, set the Insert Units to "Inches."

7. Type a description that will enable others to get a clear idea of the purpose for this block—for example "A door that opens to the left, three feet wide" (or whatever you feel is appropriate).

8. Click the OK button to finish creating the block. At this point, there is no need to save the drawing unless you wish to use this scalable block in a drawing of your own.

Note

It is also possible to create a block that is made up of other blocks. This type of block is commonly referred to as a *nested block*. For example, suppose you also created a block that represents the door frame. The door and frame block could easily be combined into one block, but here you probably need to re-create the block at a one-to-one scale factor to account for the different wall thicknesses you will encounter using the door frame.

After the block has been defined in a drawing, it can then be inserted wherever needed in that drawing. As a general rule, if you want to use this block in other drawings, the block must be converted using the Wblock command. This also allows a portion of your current drawing to be saved out as a drawing itself, which is important when creating details and symbols that will be used in other drawings.

USING THE WBLOCK COMMAND TO CREATE NEW DRAWINGS

The advantage of using Wblock, or write block, is that the block definition is no longer confined to the original drawing it was created in. The block is actually written to your local or network disk as a new drawing, thus the write block name. This enables drawing "parts" to be reused in any drawing, for they become drawing files themselves.

To use Wblock, type **Wblock** at the command line. The Write Block dialog box appears (see Figure 16.3).

Figure 16.3
Use the Write Block dialog box to convert blocks and individual objects into separate drawings. The Source object that is selected changes the options that are available from within the dialog box.

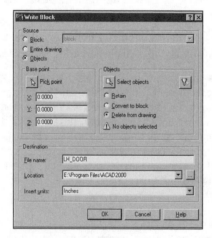

Although similar, notice that this dialog box looks different from the Block Definition dialog box used to create a block. The options that are available will change depending on what Source option is selected. These options are described in detail here:

- Block—This option is enabled only if there are blocks in the current drawing. This allows you to convert an existing block into a separate drawing, which can be selected from the compiled list of all blocks in the drawing. When this option is chosen, specific information is obtained from the block, which disables the Base point and Objects options.

- Entire drawing—This option allows the entire drawing to be saved as a new drawing with a different name, which also disables the Base point and Objects options of the dialog box.

| Tip 121 from
Ron House	You're probably wondering, "Why would I want to use the Entire drawing option when my current drawing is already saved as a .dwg file?" There are advantages to using this option, one of which allows you to eliminate any unused drawing components in your drawing, such as empty layers or unused blocks. Because this command writes a new drawing from scratch, using this option will eliminate those unused items, making your drawing smaller in file size. This can also be accomplished using the Purge command, which is discussed later in this chapter.

- Objects—You can select individual objects using this option to define the wblock, in which you will be specifying the insertion, or base point. You also are given the same options to select objects from the drawing that you were given when creating a block. Objects from the drawing can be selected by clicking the Select objects button or by choosing the Quick Select button. You can filter the objects you want to define the wblock. The options that will affect the original objects used to create the wblock are available as well, allowing you to Retain, Convert to block, or Delete from drawing.

- File name—The name of the drawing file that will be created.

- Location—This specifies the location or the path of the drawing to be created. Selecting the ellipsis button opens a Browse for Folder dialog box, which enables you to click on the directory or subdirectory folder from the tree to place the wblock.

- Insert units—This option sets the original unit for the wblock.

| Tip 122 from
Ron House	It is important to create block standards to standardize your block symbols within your company. Doing so creates consistency throughout your projects company wide, which avoids confusion and, even worse, misinterpretation. When defining blocks with the Wblock command, you can store your block symbols into common and logically named directories. For instance, on a network drive you could create a folder called Blocks. Within this folder you can create discipline-specific subfolders such as Plumbing, Electrical, Furnishings, and so on. Enforcing a directory structure similar to this helps alleviate multiple copies of a block being used on your projects. Changes are made to the source blocks and stored in their defined directory, ensuring that everyone in the company is using the most up-to-date block definition. This allows blocks to be retrieved quickly and easily, giving you and your co-workers one common location for all blocks used by your company.

Tip 123 from
Ron House

To make block insertion more efficient, you can add the network paths in which you store block symbols to your AutoCAD Options path settings. This will help eliminate browsing to search for block symbols, making this process more efficient. Right-click in the command line and select Options from the shortcut menu. Select the Files tab, and then open the Support Files Search Path folder. You can either modify the current search paths or add a new path to the list. To add a new path, simply select the Add button and type in the path. You can also click the Browse button to graphically specify the location of your blocks. You can repeat this step to add the multiple locations where your blocks reside. The more centralized your blocks are, the quicker the process is for locating your blocks, so try keep this list to a minimum. The AutoCAD DesignCenter, which will be discussed later in this chapter, will assist you in eliminating needless browsing as well.

INSERTING YOUR NEWLY CREATED BLOCKS

Now that you've learned how to create a block, let's discuss the steps to insert the block object into a drawing. This is done using the Insert command. Later, you'll learn how to use the AutoCAD DesignCenter, discussed later in this chapter, to insert blocks as well.

To start the Insert command, choose the Insert Block button from the flyout on the Draw toolbar, shown in Figure 16.4.

Figure 16.4
You can select the Insert Block command from the Insert flyout on the Modify toolbar.

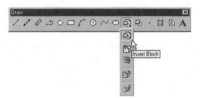

Tip 124 from
Ron House

The button is located next to the Make Block button, and could be enclosed within the flyout. The command can also be quickly accessed by typing **Insert** at the command line.

The Insert dialog box appears, from which you can specify the insertion properties of the block. The following is the list of available options:

- Name—Allows you to select from the list of blocks in the current drawing.

Tip 125 from
Ron House

When selecting from the list box, type in the first few letters of the block to quickly locate it in the list. This will help you find the block faster if there are several to choose from rather than scrolling down the list.

- Browse—Use this option to select any drawing you want to insert from the Select Drawing File dialog box.

- Insertion point—Specifies the insertion point for the block. Consider this the "handle" you'll use to locate where the block is placed into the drawing.

- Specify on-screen—When this option is selected, the parameters for Insertion point, Scale, or Rotation can be specified as the block is being inserted in the drawing.

- Scale—This is the scale factor for the block, in which separate scale factors can be entered for the individual X, Y, and Z directions.

- Uniform scale—If this option is selected, the value entered in the X scale factor edit box will be applied uniformly to the block in the Y and Z directions as well.

- Rotation—The rotation angle of the block as it is inserted into the drawing. This angle is based on the current setting of the ANGBASE system variable, which defines the base angle of the drawing.

- Explode—This option "explodes" the blocks back into the individual objects used to create the block.

The next example demonstrates the process of inserting a block into a drawing.

EXAMPLE: INSERTING A BLOCK

1. Using the drawing ch16_02.dwg that you copied from the accompanying CD, you will insert a block that already exists in the drawing.

2. Start the Insert command by choosing the Insert Block button from the Draw toolbar.

3. Select the block PHONE from the select list in the Insert dialog box.

4. Click the Specify on-screen buttons for the Insertion point and Rotation angle so these values can be provided graphically as the block is inserted into the drawing. Leave the X, Y, and Z scale values at their default settings.

Tip 126 from *Ron House*	The block can be inserted into the drawing as individual components by checking the Explode button in the lower corner of the Insert dialog box. This can also be achieved if the Insert command is activated at the command line by typing an asterisk (*) before the block name. The Explode command is discussed in detail in "Exploding a Block" later in this chapter.
Tip 127 from *Ron House*	When defining blocks, it is important to monitor the layers on which they are created. If you decide to create the entire block on layer 0, when the block is inserted it will always adopt the color of the layer it was inserted upon. This is true if the color of the layer 0 objects is set to Bylayer, which means the properties of the objects are set by the layer they reside on. If your entire block or components of the block are on another layer besides layer 0, those components will retain the color of the layer they were created upon, even if they are inserted onto a different layer.

PART
IV

CH
16

5. Click the OK button and the Insert dialog box disappears. An image of the block appears at the crosshairs, allowing you to place the block into the drawing visually. The following options appear at the command line:

```
Specify insertion point or [Scale/X/Y/Z/Rotate/PScale/PX/PY/PZ/PRotate]:
```

6. The P options allow you to preset the values before inserting the block into the drawing. Type **PR** at the command line and press Enter, which displays this prompt:

```
Specify preview rotation angle: 45 <ENTER>
```

7. Set the preview rotation angle to 45° by typing 45 and pressing Enter. You can now drag the block at the preview angle. Use any of the P options to preview a change to the X, Y, or Z scale values and rotation angle of the block.

Tip 128 from
Ron House

The Pscale option allows one scale factor value to be set for the X, Y, and Z axis, rather than independently using the PX, PY, and PZ options.

---

8. Insert the block by clicking the desired location.

Use the Insert command to insert individual block in the drawing. To learn how to place multiple blocks in the drawing at one time, use the Minsert command discussed in the next section.

INSERTING MULTIPLE BLOCKS WITH MINSERT

Multiple blocks can be inserted into the drawing in instances where the spacing between the blocks does not vary. This command can save time when using blocks to place columns or light fixtures on a floor plan, or a bolt hole pattern for a part. The Minsert command allows you to place the blocks given the number of columns, rows and the spacing between them. Essentially, the Minsert command is a combination of the Insert and Array commands.

To activate this command, type **Minsert** at the command line. After supplying the name of the block you want to insert, you are prompted to specify the insertion point as the insert options are displayed. After the X and Y scale factors and the rotation angle values of the first block are given, you'll need to provide the number of rows and columns of the block array, as well as the spacing between.

Any time multiple blocks need to be inserted into a drawing, the Minsert command can be used to save time and increase your productivity.

After you have placed blocks into a drawing, they can easily be edited by using the Refedit command, which is discussed in the next section.

EDITING AND REDEFINING BLOCKS USING REFEDIT

One of the great advantages of using blocks is that if a change is made to the block definition, every instance of that block in the drawing is updated. An example of when this could save a considerable amount of time is when a particular block reference changes during the life of a project. If a block has changed, a block definition can be modified and all block references in the drawing can be globally updated. The Refedit command allows you make minor changes to block definitions from within the current drawing.

Type **Refedit** at the command line or choose In-place Xref and Block Edit, Edit Reference from the Modify pull-down menu. Then select the block you want to edit. The Reference Edit dialog box opens, displaying the selected block and any nested references it might contain (see Figure 16.5).

Figure 16.5
The Refedit command allows changes to be made to a block or any of its nested references through the Reference Edit dialog box.

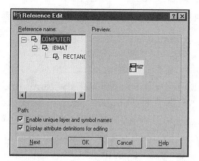

This dialog box enables you to select the block or nested reference to be modified from the Reference name tree listing displayed in the Preview window.

Note

The Refedit command can also be used to modify External Reference (Xref) files. This feature is new to AutoCAD 2000, enabling users to modify the Xref from within the current drawing. The option Enable unique layer and symbol names is unique to External Reference files, and is discussed in Chapter 17, "External Reference Files and Importing Images."

The Display attribute definitions for editing option is covered in "Attaching Attributes to Blocks" later in this chapter.

After a reference has been selected from the list, select the OK button. At the Select nested objects prompt, choose the block components you want to alter. The selected objects are added to a working set of objects to be modified, and depicted by a different color. After you press the Enter key to indicate completion of the working set, the Refedit toolbar appears, giving convenient access to the Refedit commands. You now have the ability to use the AutoCAD drawing and editing commands to modify the block.

Use the other options from the Refedit toolbar, shown in Figure 16.6, to add or remove objects from the working set, or to discard the changes made to the block. The block reference shown in the block name pull-down menu allows changes to be made to a block or any of its nested references through the Reference Edit dialog box. Any new objects that you add to the drawing are automatically added to the working set.

Figure 16.6
The Refedit toolbar contains options to modify additional blocks or to add and remove objects from the working set.

After you are finished altering the block type, use the `Refclose` command to complete the changes. You can also select the Save Back Changes to Reference button from the Refedit toolbar to redefine the block. Again, this will redefine the other blocks of the same name in your drawing.

EXPLODING A BLOCK

There are times when you want to modify a particular block without updating all other block references in the drawing, especially if the block is unique, separating it from all other blocks in the drawing. For example, suppose you have a door block that needs to be modified, and the changes you want to make to this block will make it different than any other door in the drawing. The Explode command will convert this block back into the original objects that were used to create it, allowing you to make the required changes.

You can access this command by choosing the Explode button from the Modify toolbar, shown in Figure 16.7.

Figure 16.7
The Explode command returns a block back into the original objects used to create the block definition and can be accessed from the Modify toolbar.

Select the blocks you want to explode, then press Enter when you are finished. Because a block is placed on the current layer when it is inserted into a drawing, when the block is exploded, the individual block objects will go back to the layer(s) they were created on. If those layers do not exist in the drawing, AutoCAD will automatically create them.

Note

When a block is exploded, and the objects used to compose the block return to the layers they were created on, and if those layers are frozen or turned off, it will appear as if the objects have disappeared from the drawing. Thawing or turning on those layers will reveal the whereabouts of the original block objects.

| **Tip 129 from**
Ron House | The Explode command will explode only the top nested block definition. A nested block will need to be exploded for each nested level to return the block to individual drawing objects. |

| **Tip 130 from**
Ron House | You cannot use the Explode command on blocks that have been inserted using the Minsert command. Because the blocks inserted with this command are grouped together as a whole, individual blocks within the group cannot be edited. You can only modify the blocks as a group using the Refedit command. |

If a block has been exploded and is not redefined, the block definition still remains in the drawing. The next section discusses the use of the Purge command to remove unused object definitions from the drawing.

PURGING UNUSED BLOCKS FROM THE DRAWING

When a block is exploded and no longer needed, and no other insertions of this block exist in the drawing, you will want to purge the drawing of this block definition. This not only removes object definitions no longer needed in the drawing, but also helps to reduce the file size of your drawing. The Purge command eliminates unused blocks, as well as unused layers, text styles, dimension styles, and more from the current drawing file. You can access this command by typing **Purge** at the command line, which displays the following prompt:

```
Enter type of unused objects to purge
[Blocks/Dimstyles/LAyers/LTypes/Plotstyles/SHapes/textSTyles/Mlinestyles/All]:
```

You can also select this command by choosing File, Drawing Utilities, Purge. Then a particular purge option can be selected from the menu. If the All option is chosen, all the drawing objects will be purged from the drawing. You will be prompted to enter the name of the individual objects you want to purge, separated by a comma. Accepting the default value at Enter name(s) to purge <*>: will purge all objects of that type. Each object can be verified before being purged from the drawing by replying Yes to the following prompt:

```
Verify each name to be purged? [Yes/No] <Y>:
```

The advantage of using this option is that each object will be displayed at the command line. If you have forgotten the name of the unused object, you can accept the default No value, which enables you to scroll through the list of available objects to be purged.

In order for an object to be purged from a drawing, no other instance of that object type can exist in the drawing. For example, to purge a layer, no object must reside on that layer. It is the same for a text style; no text objects can use this style in order for it to be purged. The purged object must not be referenced in any way by any other object in the drawing.

Tip 131 from
Ron House

It is good practice to purge after exploding a block if it will no longer be needed in the drawing. All other blocks of this type must either not exist or be exploded in order for this block definition to be purged from the drawing. This is considered a good maintenance practice that keeps your drawing purged of unneeded objects.

If you have exploded a nested block, the Purge command will need to be run for each unused block definition.

The Purge command can be used at any time during the drawing session and you can always undo it if necessary. So it's a good idea to use it liberally to keep your drawing free of any used objects.

Now let's look at a new feature in AutoCAD 2000 that enables you to manage wblocks and blocks, as well as other objects internal and external to the current drawing. The next section covers the AutoCAD DesignCenter and its options.

USING AUTOCAD DESIGNCENTER

The AutoCAD DesignCenter is an easy way to share information between drawings. It does not matter whether the drawing is currently open; AutoCAD DesignCenter allows you to share information from multiple external drawings. The available types of information that can be shared include Blocks, DimStyles, Layers, Layouts, Linetypes, Text Styles, and Xrefs. Developers of third-party tools can also add custom content to the AutoCAD DesignCenter.

STARTING DESIGNCENTER

To initiate DesignCenter, type **Adcenter** at the command line. It can also be accessed by selecting the AutoCAD DesignCenter button from the Standard toolbar (see Figure 16.8).

Figure 16.8
Select the DesignCenter button from the Standard Toolbar to open the DesignCenter dialog box. This opens the DesignCenter window shown in Figure 16.9.

You can use DesignCenter to view the content of open drawings and other sources and to display preview images and descriptions to help you identify the content before inserting it in the drawing. You can also use DesignCenter to browse content to locate specific drawing files. The AutoCAD DesignCenter window consists of four separate sections, or panes: Tree View, Element, Preview, and Description.

The functionality of these panes combine to allow sharing objects from external files from within the current drawing file.

Figure 16.9
The DesignCenter window is made up of four sections: Tree View, Element, Preview, and Description.

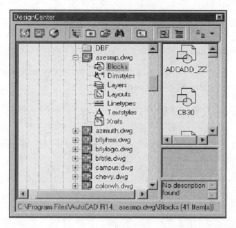

The DesignCenter window enables you to easily load other drawing files into DesignCenter and share the resources of that file. Each section of the window has a specific function that displays information about the selected shared object.

The DesignCenter window palette consists of four main panes: Tree View, Element, Preview, and Description. Each of these is described in detail in the following list:

■ Tree View window—Similar to Windows Explorer, this window enables you to browse local, network, Internet-based directories, drawing files, and object types. This window is also used to load content into the palette, allowing you to click the plus(+) and minus(-) signs to display portions of the hierarchy. As you select different items in this window, the other windows dynamically change to present the drawing information.

Tip 132 from
Ron House

Use the Adcnavigate command to specify the path you want to navigate to after the AutoCAD DesignCenter is opened.

■ Element window—In this window you can view the various elements that exist within the drawing loaded in DesignCenter.

■ Preview window—This window displays an icon of the selected object, giving you a graphic representation of the shared object.

■ Description window—Displays the description of a drawing or defined block.

The DesignCenter toolbar contains these various options to display information and navigate through the drawings:

- Desktop icon—This allows you to browse the elements of any drawing located on your local drive, network drive, or the Internet.

→ See Chapter 19, "Internet Publishing" for more information on how to access drawing files from the Internet.

- Open Drawings—Browses the elements of currently open drawings.

- History—Reveals a list of the last 20 locations that have been recently explored.

- Tree View—This option toggles the display of the Tree View window off and on. This option is not available during the History mode.

- Favorites—You can use the Favorites option button to create locations where you commonly go to retrieve information. For instance, if you have a few block directories where you store standard block symbols, these locations can be added as favorites so you do not have to browse from them.

- Load—This option opens the Load DesignCenter Palette dialog box, enabling you to load a drawing into DesignCenter.

Tip 133 from *Ron House*	Use the Locate button in the Load DesignCenter Palette dialog box to find drawings located within the current directories specified in the Support File Search path. Enter the name of the drawing you want to locate in the File Name box and click the Locate button. The dialog box display will update, showing you the directory structure of where the file is located.

- Find—This option opens the Browse\Search dialog box, allowing you to search for a specific file either by name or date created.

→ See Chapter 1, "Working with the Interface."

- Up—Use this option like you would in Windows Explorer to move you up one directory.

- Preview—This toggles the display of the Preview window in AutoCAD DesignCenter.

- Description—Toggles the display of the Description window in AutoCAD DesignCenter.

- Views—This option changes the way the elements are displayed within the Element window. Choose the display option from the select list to modify how the files are viewed.

You can right-click on any folder, drawing file, or drawing element in order to explore the different files and elements. On this menu you can also add any folder, drawing file, and drawing element to your Favorites list discussed earlier, or use the Find option to search for a particular file. The Organize Favorites option will open your Favorites folder to organize your folders.

INSERTING BLOCKS WITH DESIGNCENTER

After you have located a drawing file that contains objects you want to share, open the file by right-clicking and choosing the Open option. The Element pane is populated with the objects available within that drawing. Open the Blocks level to display the blocks in the file. Click on the block you want to share, and drag and drop it into the current drawing.

> **Note**
> You can only insert a drawing if no other command is active in the receiving drawing, and only one block at a time can be inserted.

PART

IV

CH

16

Using the drag-and-drop process to insert a block into the drawing does not allow you to scale the block. A feature called AutoScaling automatically compares the Insert units of the block, which were defined when the block was created, and adjusts the block to the new unit value if needed. For example, you can define a block created within an architectural drawing to be inserted into a metric drawing. The design units of the block are easily adjusted to accommodate for the difference.

To define a scale and rotation angle for a block being inserted from DesignCenter, right-click on the block in the Element pane and drag the file into the current drawing. When you release the pointer button to insert the block, a shortcut menu appears. Two options are available, Cancel and Insert Block. Choosing the Insert Block option opens the Insert dialog box, allowing you to define the insertion point, scale factors, and rotation angle of the block.

> **Tip 134 from**
> *Ron House*
>
> Drawing files can also be opened in the drawing editor from DesignCenter. After you have located the drawing in the Element pane, right-click on the Drawing icon and select the Open in Window option, which opens the file in the drawing editor. Note that you can also choose options to insert the file as a block, attach it as an external reference file, or copy it to the Clipboard.
>
> Images can also be previewed and inserted into the drawing from DesignCenter as well. Right-clicking on an image file from the Element pane gives the option to Attach Image. Selecting this option from the shortcut menu opens the Image dialog box, allowing you to specify the parameters of the image. Or you can drag and drop the image file onto the current drawing and provide the insertion options from the command line.

EXPLORING OTHER OBJECT DEFINITIONS USING DESIGNCENTER

As discussed previously, layers, linetypes, paper space layouts, dimstyles, text styles, and external references are also accessible from DesignCenter. Multiple object definitions can be added at one time using the Shift and Control keys to select them from the Element pane. The following list details specifics about sharing each of the available object definitions:

- Layers and Linetypes—If the layer already exists in the current drawing, that particular layer will still be the color it is in the current drawing file. If linetypes are inserted, the LTSCALE system variable will remains unaffected.

- Paper Space Layouts—When adding paper space layouts from one drawing to another, the title block will be added (if one exists) to the current drawing file in paper space. It will include the viewport configurations as well.

- Dimstyles and Text Styles—If a dimstyle or text style being added already exists in the current drawing file, it will retain its attributes from the current drawing file. Of course, AutoCAD DesignCenter is better suited to add these elements if they do not exist as a way of reducing setup time.

- External References—Right-clicking on a drawing file from the Element pane gives the option to attach the file as an external reference file. When this option is selected, the External Reference file dialog box opens, enabling you to specify the options for inserting the xref.

Whether you are creating a drawing from scratch or working with an existing drawing, you can gain time and increase your productivity using the DesignCenter, without the need to open external files to access their drawing content.

The next section discusses how to attach attribute information to blocks, enabling you to expand your use of blocks within a drawing.

ATTACHING ATTRIBUTES TO BLOCKS

Attributes can be defined as informational data that is attached to blocks and then extracted to create reports, Bill of Materials, and schedules. Not only does this allow you to assign specific information about the individual blocks in a drawing, but you or others can also gather details about all the blocks in the entire drawing. Attribute values can be assigned as blocks are inserted into the drawing, or they can be predefined as constant values. When attributes are created, they are actually saved as part of the block. When blocks with attributes are inserted into a drawing, data is assigned to each block attribute (see Figure 16.10). This is done by first creating each individual attribute, then using the Block or Wblock command to combine these with the objects that make up the block.

Figure 16.10
A block with attributes displayed, representing the telephone number and cube it is located in.

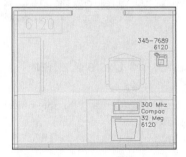

Tip 135 from
Ron House

When using the Refedit command to edit a block that contains attributes, check the option to Display attribute definitions for editing.

The Attdef command, short for attribute definition, is used to define the attributes. From the pull-down menus, choose Draw, Block, Define Attributes. The Attribute Definition dialog box appears, where the properties of the attribute can be determined (see Figure 16.11).

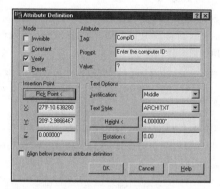

Figure 16.11
Attributes are defined and created using the Define Attributes dialog box, accessed by the Attdef command

The following is a list of states that can be assigned to a block attribute:

- Invisible—This mode turns off the display of the block attributes as they are inserted. This is typically used when you might want attribute information assigned to a block, yet not displayed in the drawing.

- Constant—This option assigns a fixed value to the block attribute.

- Verify—This option will prompt the user to verify the value of the attribute as it is inserted.

- Preset—The attribute value is preset when the attribute is inserted and is not prompted for.

- Tag—The Tag is a classification given to the attribute, which identifies each occurrence of the attribute in the drawing.

- Prompt—The prompt informs the user to enter the attribute data or value.

- Value—This allows a preset or default value for the attribute to be assigned.

In addition, if attributes are to be displayed, properties that determine how the textual information will be formatted can be defined. The insertion point and Text options such as justification and style can be set in the Attribute Definition dialog box. As many as 16 attributes can be assigned to a block. To assist you with placing multiple attributes to a single block, use the next option available from the Define Attributes dialog box, Align below previous attribute definition.

- Align below previous attribute definition—After the formatting of the displayed attribute is defined, use this option to enable the next attribute to take on the same formatting of the previous, locating it directly below the attribute before it.

To further illustrate this process, let's walk through an example assigning attributes to a block.

EXAMPLE: DEFINING ATTRIBUTES TO A BLOCK

1. Use the drawing ch16_02.dwg that you used in the previous example. First, you'll define attributes for a computer and save it as a block, and then enter specific attribute values as you insert it back into the drawing.

2. You will assign attributes to the computer block and then insert a computer block at each cubicle location. Access the Attdef command by typing the command name at the command line.

3. In the Define Attributes dialog box, click the Verify mode, and then enter **CompID** in the Tag edit box. As the block is inserted into the drawing, you will be prompted to verify the attribute value.

Tip 136 from
Ron House

Because attribute tag names cannot contain spaces, use underscores or dashes instead.

4. Next, type the prompt for the attribute by placing the statement **Enter the computer ID:** in the Prompt edit box.

5. Enter a default question mark in the Value edit box.

Tip 137 from
Ron House

By using a default value, like a question mark, for the attribute value, you can determine whether an attribute value has been entered. If not, you will see a question mark displayed next to the block, which will also appear in any reports you generate from the block attributes. This will assist you in making certain you have entered values for all the blocks.

6. Define a justification of Middle and a style of Architxt. Then, enter a height of 4°, and a rotation value of 0 for the text options.

7. Click the Pick Point button and locate the attribute text to the right of the block. You will also be assigning another attribute, so make sure to leave room for the next value.

8. Click the OK button and you will see the tag placed next to the computer. The Define Attributes dialog box disappears, and the tag is displayed next to the block because there currently is not a value for this attribute. After the block is saved and inserted into the drawing, a value will appear in its place.

9. Repeat steps 1–8 again, this time creating an attribute with a tag called **Price** and a prompt of **Enter the Computer Cost:**. Make this attribute invisible by selecting the Invisible mode button, so the price does not display on the drawing.

10. Select the Align below previous attribute definition button to place this attribute directly below the attribute you created previously.

11. Click the OK button to place the next attribute tag into the drawing. Then open the Attribute dialog box by entering Attdia at the command line, which enables you to enter the individual attribute values. If this setting is not set to a value of 1, you will be prompted for the attribute values at the command line. The advantage of doing this is that you can view the attribute values all at once within the dialog box, modifying them as many times as necessary before committing them.

Tip 138 from
Ron House

Use the Ddedit command to modify attribute tags, prompts, and default values before saving them with a block. The same and more can be accomplished if you select the attribute, activating Grips on the object. Right-click and select Properties, which opens the Properties dialog box for the attribute. From here you can also change the mode of the attribute.

12. Type the Block command at the command line, and name the block **Computer**. Click the Select Objects button and select the attributes and the drawing objects that make up the computer.

13. Click the Pick Point button to define a base point for the block of your choosing. Select the Convert to Block button to convert the objects into a block. This is done so attribute values can be given to the new block inserted at this location.

Tip 139 from
Ron House

The order that you select the attributes as you create the block also defines the order the user will be prompted for the attribute values. If you want the attribute values to be answered in a specific order, you'll need to consider this as you select them during the block definition process.

14. When you click the OK button, AutoCAD will display Edit Attributes dialog box, allowing you to enter the values for the computer attributes (see Figure 16.12). Click the OK button after the values have been entered.

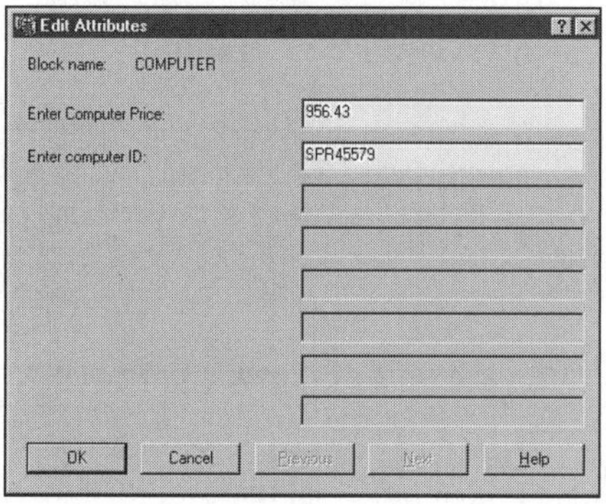

Figure 16.12
The Edit Attributes dialog box displaying the parameters discussed in this example.

<table>
<tr><td>Tip 140 from
Ron House</td><td>Regardless of the initial visibility setting of the attribute, you can toggle on the display of attributes throughout the drawing using the ATTMODE setting variable. If this variable has a value of 2, all variables are displayed; a value of 0 turns off the display of all variables. A value of 1 is Normal, which means that each attribute is displayed based on its visibility setting.</td></tr>
</table>

Now that the attributes have been saved with the block, the next example will insert the computers into the drawing with attribute values.

EXAMPLE: INSERTING BLOCKS WITH ATTRIBUTES AND ATTEDIT

1. Insert the block Computer into the drawing ch16_02.dwg using the Insert command. Access the Insert command by selecting the Insert Block button from the Draw toolbar.

2. Locate a computer on each of the cubicle desktops, each time entering different values for the computer identification number and price. As you insert the computer block, rotate the block as needed.

<table>
<tr><td>Tip 141 from
Ron House</td><td>When you associate an attribute to a block, the initial rotation angle for the attribute remains constant regardless of how the block is rotated when it is inserted into the drawing. The Attedit command can be used to rotate the attribute to the desired angle, as illustrated in the remainder of this example.</td></tr>
</table>

3. After you have located the eight computer blocks in the drawing, correct the rotation angle of the upside down attributes. From the Modify pull-down menu, choose Attribute, Global. This command will allow you to globally edit all attributes within a drawing, yet you are only interested in correcting the four upside down attributes. Press Enter to accept the default to edit the attributes individually. You will see the following prompt is displayed at the command line. Notice that the name of this command is -Attedit.

```
-ATTEDIT
Edit attributes one at a time? [Yes/No] <Y>: <ENTER>
```

<table>
<tr><td>Tip 142 from
Ron House</td><td>Only when you type a hyphen (-) before the command can you globally replace attributes and modify their properties. If you type Attedit at the command prompt, you can only edit the value of the attributes.</td></tr>
</table>

4. For this example, press Enter for each of the following prompts:

```
Enter block name specification <*>: <ENTER>
Enter attribute tag specification <*>: <ENTER>
Enter attribute value specification <*>: <ENTER>
```

Tip 143 from
Ron House

As you can see in step 4, the Attedit command is capable of selecting which blocks and attributes you want to edit by providing the block name, attribute tag, and value. After this information has been provided, AutoCAD will search the drawing for blocks and attributes containing these values, enabling you to edit only these objects.

5. Next you will be prompted to select the attributes you want to modify. Pick on each one of the upside down attributes. Press Enter when you are done.

6. AutoCAD will display the number of attributes selected, and then list the options available. You will first use the Angle option to set the angle of the attribute to zero, rotating it right side up. Type **A** and press Enter:

```
4 attributes selected.
Enter an option [Value/Position/Height/Angle/Style/Layer/Color/Next] <N>: A
<ENTER>
Specify new rotation angle <180.00>: 0 <ENTER>
```

7. You may also want to adjust the position of the attribute by typing a **P** to access the Position option. This will allow you to select a new location for the text:

```
Enter an option [Value/Position/Height/Angle/Style/Layer/Color/Next] <N>: P
<ENTER>
Specify new text insertion point <no change>:
```

8. Type **N** and press Enter to continue to the next attribute. Repeat the steps to correct the remaining attributes.

Tip 144 from
Ron House

Single attributes can also be edited using the Attedit command—from the <u>M</u>odify pull-down menu, choose Attribute, <u>S</u>ingle. You will be prompted to select the block reference to edit, which opens the Edit Attributes dialog box to modify the attribute values for that block. Notice that this command allows you to edit only the Values of the attributes, not the complete properties, as the -Attedit command did.

Tip 145 from
Ron House

You can only define the attribute values for the first block inserted by using the Minsert command. As the blocks are placed into the drawing, each block in the array will contain the same attribute values as the first block.

Note

When a block with attributes is exploded, the values for the individual attributes are lost, converting to the attribute tag name. The Express tools contain a command called Burst, which can explode a block without losing the attribute information. See Chapter 15, "Making Drawing Easier," to learn more about this command and the Express tools.

Now that you have placed the attributes into the drawing, the next section will show you how to extract the attribute information to create a bill of materials.

EXTRACTING ATTRIBUTE INFORMATION

After you have completed inserting blocks with attributes into a drawing, the information can be extracted from the attributes to create reports, such as schedules and a bill of materials. Before this can be done, a template must be created that defines what will be extracted and how it will be formatted. The template can be created using a text editor like Notepad. Using a text editor, enter the following information, placing each block field code or field classification to be extracted on a single line:

- Block Field Code—This is the information that can be extracted from blocks in the drawing. Each code begins with BL:, and these are shown in Table 16.1.

- Field Classification—This defines the classification for each field extracted from the drawing. There are two types available: Numeric and Character.

- Numeric—This is indicated by the letter N, which defines this attribute value as a numeric value. Only number values are allowed, and alphanumeric or special characters such as dollar signs must be omitted.

- Character—This field classification is indicated by the letter C, which accepts all character types except spaces within the value.

You can extract specific information about the block using the codes listed in Table 16.1.

TABLE 16.1   BLOCK FIELD EXTRACTION CODES

Function	Description and Field Classification
BL:NAME	Block Name (Character)
BL:X	X Coordinate of the block (Numeric)
BL:Y	Y Coordinate of the block (Numeric)
BL:Z	Z Coordinate of the block (Numeric)
BL:HANDLE	Block Handle (Numeric)
BL:LAYER	Block Layer (Character)
BL:LEVEL	Block Nesting Level (Numeric)
BL:NUMBER	Block Counter (Numeric)
BL:ORIENT	Block Rotation Angle (Numeric)
BL:XSCALE	X Scale Factor (Numeric)
BL:YSCALE	Y Scale Factor (Numeric)
BL:ZSCALE	Z Scale Factor (Numeric)
BL:XEXTRUDE	Extrusion Distance of block along X-axis(Numeric)
BL:YEXTRUDE	Extrusion Distance of block along Y-axis(Numeric)
BL:ZEXTRUDE	Extrusion Distance of block along Z-axis(Numeric)

Attribute information can also be extracted by listing the name of the attribute tag in the template. Each of the field classifications is followed by the field width, which also specifies the numeric accuracy of the numeric field. The following lines are three examples from a template:

```
BL:COMPUTER      C025000
BL:X             N010000
COMPID           C025000
```

The first line will extract the name of a block, and the width of the field is 25 characters wide. Second, the block's X-coordinate of its insertion point is extracted in a numeric field of 10 characters, and the last line gives the value of the attribute COMPID with a column field width of 25 characters. Tabs are used to separate the columns, and it is important that the field classification must match the attribute value being extracted. If not, the extraction will fail.

> **Caution**
>
> You can use tabs to separate the columns in a template only if you are using a text editor. If you create the template using a word processor, tabs will not be read correctly and the extraction will be terminated. The work around is to use spaces to separate the columns when using a word processor.

After the extraction template has been made, use the Attext command to extract the block and attribute information you want. At the command line, type **Attext** and press Enter. The Attribute Extraction dialog box appears, which is shown in Figure 16.13.

Figure 16.13
You can define which attributes will be extracted, the file format, and the extraction template file using the Attribute Extraction dialog box.

This dialog box allows you to specify the blocks, the template, and the output file for the extraction in one of three following formats:

- Comma Delimited File (CDF)—This option creates a text-based file where the field values are separated by a comma delimiter (,).

- Space Delimited File (SDF)—Creates a text-based file where each field value is separated by a single space.

- DXF Format Extract File (DXF)—A Drawing Interchange File is created of the blocks selected. This particular format does not require the use of a template.

The next example creates an SDF output file of the drawing ch16_01.dwg using the template you just created.

EXAMPLE: EXTRACTING BLOCK AND ATTRIBUTE INFORMATION

1. With the drawing ch16_01.dwg still open in AutoCAD, and using the template file ch16_att.txt copied from the companion CD, you will extract the computer ID number and price of each of the computers in the drawing.

2. Activate the Attext command by typing the command at the command line. Click the Space Delimited File (SDF) button.

3. Click the Select Objects button, which temporarily clears the dialog box. Select the eight computers you inserted into the drawing previously.

4. Click the Template File button and locate the template ch16_att.txt that you copied from the accompanying CD.

5. Specify the location where you want the output file placed after it is created by selecting the Output File button.

6. Select the OK button to start the extraction. Once finished, AutoCAD should display the following prompt:

   ```
   ATTEXT 8 records in extract file.
   ```

After the extraction output file has been created, you can import the file into a spreadsheet like Microsoft Excel, modify it however you want, and using Object Linking and Embedding (OLE), place it into your drawing file.

→ See "Embedding Data from Other Sources Using OLE" in Chapter 20, "Customizing Made Easy."

This gives you an easy way to generate information from attributes placed in the drawing, from bills of material to parts lists and room schedules. You can also use this process to check the placement of blocks by extracting the block X, Y, and Z coordinate values, and also to determine the number of blocks in a drawing.

SUMMARY

Using blocks can dramatically increase your productivity when working with repetitive instances of symbols in a drawing. Couple this with the use of attributes, and you also have a way to easily document the specifics of the drawing. After the information is extracted, it can be exported into a number of external software packages, modified, and imported back into the drawing using OLE.

EXTERNAL REFERENCE FILES AND IMPORTING IMAGES

In this chapter

UNDERSTANDING EXTERNAL REFERENCES

In today's design environment, AutoCAD 2000 users must be proficient with the workings of external reference files. Most AutoCAD projects involve the sharing of drawings between work groups within companies and with design team members in other companies. Using the external reference feature is the only way to allow multiple users to access the same drawing at the same time. Understanding how to use external references effectively is essential for productivity.

Although in principle, external references have long been the most efficient way to share drawings, in practice they were hampered by some performance issues. Many reference files were overly large; file paths and circular references caused problems; and users often resorted to inserting and exploding reference files, thereby defeating the very purpose of external references. AutoCAD 14 introduced clip boundaries, demand loading, and file unloading and reloading, and also resolved some of the circularity problems—all of this greatly improved the functionality of external references. AutoCAD 2000 continues to build upon these performance enhancements by adding reference editing to the capabilities of this suite of commands.

In itself, an external reference object (or *xref*) is identical to a block: Each is a collection of geometry that behaves as if it were a single entity; both are defined in the symbol table; and both can be nested (blocks within blocks and xrefs within xrefs). Both also are regular AutoCAD drawing files that are included in another drawing. Some critical differences exist, however:

- Typically blocks are smaller drawing files, and external references are larger and more complex objects.

- A more significant distinction is that blocks are typically fixed, whereas external references are often dynamic and subject to change during the life cycle of the current drawing.

- Blocks are *inserted into* a drawing. After being inserted, the block loses any connection to its original source drawing; if the source drawing changes, the block must be re-inserted into the drawing.

- External references are *attached to* or *overlaid on* the current drawing. Any changes that are made to a referenced file are updated to a host drawing that references it.

So an external reference is simply a reference to a regular AutoCAD drawing file. Any AutoCAD drawing file can be referenced into another, with a few minor qualifications. The reference to a drawing creates essentially a *read-only* copy of the original, which makes it available in multiple drawings and to multiple users at the same time. Use of external references conveys significant advantages in a production environment:

- Consistency—If you have multiple drawings that use the same geometry, external references allow all the drawings to reference a single drawing, such as a column grid or a title block. Sharing a single drawing means that you have built-in consistency. All your columns will refer to the same grid, and all your title blocks will have a uniform look.

- Simultaneous access—If you are collaborating with other users over a network and want to share a common background drawing such as a building outline, an external reference is the only way to allow multiple users to reference the same drawing at the same time.

- Design coordination—When architectural and engineering designers are concurrently working in the same space, as is typical, it is essential to overlay the different discipline plans to avoid design collisions.

- Current status ensured—Ongoing changes to a reference drawing are updated to all users who reference it. The changes are not made in real time; instead, each time that a host drawing is opened or plotted, or whenever an external reference file is reloaded into a drawing, AutoCAD 2000 loads the most recent version of the referenced drawing.

- Drawing size—Because the geometry for an external reference is stored outside the drawing that references it—and is *shared* rather than duplicated by many users—there is a considerable savings in drawing file sizes.

In this chapter, you will work with some real-world examples to demonstrate the features of external references. You will find the practice files for this chapter on the CD that accompanies this book. If you have not already done so, you should copy these examples to a practice folder, such as \XREF EXAMPLES, on your hard disk.

PART
IV

CH
17

Note

The example drawings for this chapter are adapted from the construction documents from the San Francisco New Main library (architects: Simon Martin-Vegue Winkelstein and Moris, San Francisco), which was completed in 1996. The structure of the external references for this project was vital. Every sheet in the project referenced the column grid drawing. This guaranteed that the grid lines would be in the same place on every drawing for every floor; each floor comprised a range of disciplines (reflected ceiling plan, equipment plan, and carpet plan), all of which referenced a common floor plan. To achieve a consistent look to the plotted set of drawings, each plotted sheet had an external reference to the same title block drawing.

ATTACHING AN EXTERNAL REFERENCE IN MODEL SPACE

As a practice exercise, you will simulate the xref structure of a typical architectural design project. Start up AutoCAD 2000, and begin by referencing a background floor plan into model space.

EXAMPLE: ATTACHING AN EXTERNAL REFERENCE

1. Choose File, New, or click the New Drawing icon to open a new drawing and then select Start from Scratch from the Startup screen. Save the new drawing as PLAN1.DWG in your practice folder.

2. Choose View, Toolbars (or right-click on any toolbar) to open the AutoCAD Toolbars list box, and then select Reference.

   The External Reference toolbar is displayed, as shown in Figure 17.1.

Figure 17.1
The Reference toolbar enables you to manage, attach, clip, and bind external references to an AutoCAD 2000 drawing.

The first five buttons on the toolbar access external reference commands. (The remaining buttons access options pertaining to imported images, which are reviewed later in this chapter.) If you glide your cursor over these buttons, the ToolTips read as follows:

- External Reference
- External Reference Attach
- External Reference Clip
- External Reference Bind
- External Reference Clip Frame

The first button opens the Xref Manager. If you try this now, you will see that the Xref Manager has no information to display because you have not attached any xrefs at this point. The second toolbar button starts the Attach command (see Figure 17.1).

Before you attach a reference drawing, you should add a layer to your current drawing to put the external reference drawing into. This will make it simpler to turn on or off the xref as you edit your current drawing. (Some users prefer to have a separate layer for each drawing they reference, but you should have at least one xref layer.)

Figure 17.2
It is a good idea to
add one XREF layer
(or more) to your
drawing when you
attach external
references.

PART

IV

CH

17

EXAMPLE: ADDING AN XREF LAYER

1. Using the Layer Properties Manager (choose Format, Layer, or type **layer** and press Enter), add a layer called XREF LAYER (see Figure 17.2) and set it as current.

2. Click the Attach button on the Reference toolbar. (You can also choose Insert, External Reference on the menu or type **xattach** at the command line and press Enter.) This opens the Select Reference File dialog box.

   Now reference the background floor plan for your practice project into model space.

3. Browse to your practice folder (\XREF EXAMPLES) and select CH17 FLOOR 4.DWG.

4. Click the Open button, and the External Reference dialog box is displayed (see Figure 17.3).

When you reference a drawing, you have two key decisions to make: whether to create a hard path, and whether to attach or overlay the referenced drawing. Some implications of these issues will be reviewed later in this chapter in the "Missing Reference Files" section on p. **450**, and the "Attachment Versus Overlay" section on p. **453**. For now, just familiarize yourself with the general concepts. Take a look at these options in the External Reference dialog box in Figure 17.3.

■ Retain Path—Unlike a block, an external reference can retain a hard path to the drawing file being referenced. This is appropriate if your drawings will always use the same path structure, such as a shared folder on a file server. Generally, if you are transferring drawings from one user's system to another, unselecting the check box is a better option. The directory structure often varies from user to user. If the Retain Path box is unchecked, AutoCAD 2000 will search for the named drawing throughout the AutoCAD Support File Search Path.

■ Reference type—You can choose between attaching an external drawing and overlaying it. Both provide a read-only copy of the drawing you require.

An attachment links the drawing you have selected, in addition to all its nested references to your drawing. These references are associated to your current drawing in a fairly permanent way; if your current drawing is referenced by yet another drawing, all the nested reference files are visible in the new host drawing.

An overlay enables you to view information from another file in your current drawing, but an overlaid xref will not show up in other drawings that reference your drawing. Otherwise, an overlay performs in exactly the same way as an attachment.

5. Clear the check box for Retain Path if it is checked.

6. In Reference Type, activate the Attachment button.

Figure 17.3
The External Reference dialog box shares some features with the Insert Block dialog box.

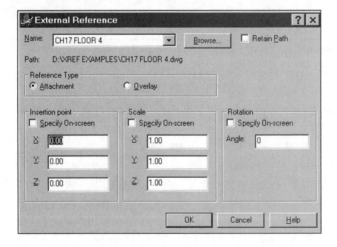

The lower half of the External Reference dialog box looks a lot like the Insert Block dialog box. As you attach an *xref*—just like a block—you can specify (or pick) an insertion point, scale, and rotation angle, or you can accept the default settings.

→ To compare the External Reference dialog box with the Insert Block dialog box and procedure, see Chapter 16, "Creating and Using Blocks."

7. Make sure the Specify Onscreen fields for Insertion Point, Scale, and Rotation are unchecked, as shown in Figure 17.3. Accept the default values of 0,0,0 for insertion coordinates, 1 for scale, and 0 for rotation.

8. Press OK. The floor plan now is attached to your new drawing in the XREF LAYER, but you probably won't see anything onscreen until you resize your view area.

9. Click the Zoom Extents button on the Zoom flyout. This should display the entire floor plan, as shown in Figure 17.4.

10. Save your drawing (PLAN1.DWG) in your practice folder.

Figure 17.4
The background floor plan is attached to the current drawing.

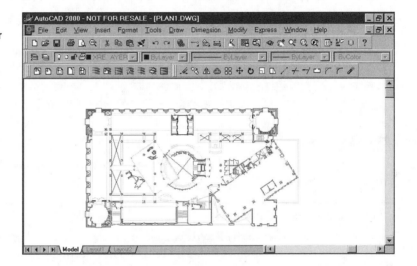

Tip 146 from
Paul Richardson

When you attach an xref in real life and your drawing does not align the way you expect it to, check the system variable INSBASE in the referenced drawing. The Base command sets the INSBASE system variable. Type **base** and press Enter to view or change this variable. INSBASE is typically set to 0,0,0. If it is set to different coordinates, you may have to make some adjustments either to the insertion point in the host drawing or to the base point in the reference drawing.

XREF INSERTION STANDARDS

Xrefs are a great way for workgroups to share common information. For Xrefs to work seamlessly, users must use a common insertion point, UCS, scale, and rotation angle. Typically, you want an xref to go into your drawing in exactly the same place it was originally drawn. The defaults for reference insertion (as described here and shown in Figure 17.3) are the most commonly used values:

- UCS—You will nearly always want to have your coordinate system set to World. This is the AutoCAD 2000 default, and the UCS icon displays a W when your coordinate system is set to this. Use the ucsman command or the UCS button on the UCS toolbar to check your setting.

PART
IV
CH
17

- Insertion point—The insertion point of an xref will nearly always be 0,0,0 unless you specifically know otherwise. You will have to make the appropriate adjustments if the reference drawing was created with a basepoint other than 0,0,0—for example, a background survey drawing that is based upon actual geographical coordinates.

- Scale and rotation—A scale of 1.0 and rotation of 0 should duplicate the orientation of the drawing being referenced. If the reference drawing was created using different drawing units, you will need to adjust the scale to match your drawing units.

- Insertion layer(s)—It is good practice to insert your xrefs on a layer separate from the geometry of the current drawing. That gives you more flexibility for turning off (or freezing) the xref, as needed. You gain even more flexibility if you put each external reference on a different xref layer. (You could name each layer according to the xref filename.) This latter approach gives great clarity and enables you to turn different xrefs on and off to meet varying needs, but it requires additional setup.

THE XREF MANAGER

Now that you have added an external reference to your drawing, you should open the External Reference Manager.

EXAMPLE: USING THE XREF MANAGER

1. Click the first button on the Reference toolbar (or choose Insert, Xref Manager; or type **xref** at the command prompt and press Enter). The Xref Manager dialog box opens, as shown in Figure 17.5.

Figure 17.5
The Xref Manager displays the status of all external references in the drawing.

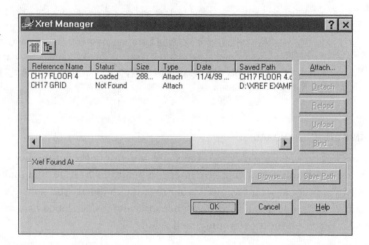

2. Glide your mouse across the two buttons at the top left corner of the list box. The ToolTip on the left button reads List View (F3), and the ToolTip on the right button reads Tree View (F4).

The Xref Manager displays whether xrefs in the current drawing are attached or overlaid, and whether they are loaded, unloaded, or even not found. The reference information is shown in two different formats; you can toggle between the two views.

3. Click the List View button (or press the F3 function key).

In List View, the Xref Manager shows a directory-style listing of all xrefs associated with this drawing (see Figure 17.5). By clicking any of the list box headings (name, status, type, file date, file size, or saved path), you can sort the list of external references in any way you want.

4. Click the Tree View button (or press the F4 function key).

Tree view (see Figure 17.6) displays the xrefs in a hierarchical fashion, which shows the relationships among xref definitions more clearly. Tree view shows how xrefs are nested and displays the type of reference graphically: The Attached icon is a single sheet with a paper clip; Not Found shows a gray icon with a question mark (?).

Figure 17.6
Tree View shows the type and relationships of the xrefs graphically.

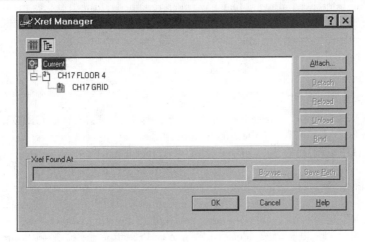

From the List View, it should be evident that AutoCAD 2000 successfully attached the floor plan drawing; however, AutoCAD also has searched for—and not found—a grid drawing that you did not ask it to load.

From the Tree View, you can clearly see the grid drawing was nested in the floor plan drawing. When you reference a drawing, AutoCAD also loads all *its* attachments into your drawing. In this case, AutoCAD looked for the grid drawing but was unable to find it for some reason.

Note

When you first attached the floor plan, you may have noticed a brief text message in the corner of your screen: "Xref D:\XREF EXAMPLES\CH17 GRID.dwg." For each external reference it cannot find, AutoCAD 2000 displays the path name of the missing reference at the insertion point, scale, and rotation angle of the original reference.

MISSING REFERENCE FILES

One problem with storing information externally to the current drawing is that this information does not always stay in the same place. If a drawing has defined xrefs and AutoCAD cannot locate them, these xrefs will not be loaded into the host drawing. This can happen for a number of reasons:

- The referenced drawing may not exist on your system. A work group or team member may forward a drawing file to a colleague and neglect to send the required xrefs. The only solution in this case is to request the reference file from the first group and load it onto your system.

- The referenced drawing may be in a different location or path than the paths searched by AutoCAD. If the file is stored outside your system's search paths, it will not be found. (This is probably the major problem users have with external references, and it is discussed in more detail in the following section.)

- The referenced drawing may have been renamed. If the xref files themselves are renamed, AutoCAD will not be capable of locating them. This is not an uncommon occurrence when multiple users access the same set of drawings without strong project controls.

REDEFINING AN XREF PATH

Take a look in your practice folder. You will see a file called CH17 GRID2.DWG, suspiciously similar to the filename you need. For the present practice exercise, assume that CH17 GRID2 is the xref you need—just that it has been erroneously renamed by some other user. You do not need to detach the original xref in the floor plan drawing and go through the process of attaching GRID2; in fact, you may not have permission to make such changes. Simply use the Xref Manager to identify GRID2 as the required xref. When AutoCAD 2000 is incapable of finding a reference drawing, you can use the Xref Manager to browse to an alternate folder or filename and redefine the path—as long as the required file exists somewhere on your system.

EXAMPLE: REDEFINING AN XREF PATH

1. In the Xref Manager, highlight the xref CH17 GRID and then click the Browse button. The Select New Path dialog box is displayed.

2. Browse to your practice folder and select CH17 GRID2; press Open (see Figure 17.7).

3. Select CH17GRID2.DWG and click Open. The new path and filename appear in the Xref Found At list box. This field shows where the xref is actually found; it is not necessarily the same as the saved path. Check the Save Path check box if you wish to save this new path.

4. Press OK to exit the Xref Manager, and the CH17 GRID2 drawing is loaded into your current drawing.

Figure 17.7
Use the Xref Manager to specify a new path or filename for a misplaced external reference.

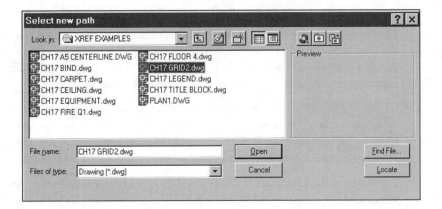

EXTERNAL REFERENCES AND SEARCH PATHS

A large percentage of user frustration with xrefs occurs when users share drawing files created at different computer sites. The xrefs may be working perfectly at one site, but when the files are forwarded to another site, the xrefs don't load. Often this is because the path for the xref needs to change—one site may load xrefs from a server with a different drive designation—or the general folder structure is completely different. If files are moving backward and forward between companies, this can become tedious very quickly if you have to redefine the xref paths each time the files are transferred.

AutoCAD goes through a specific series of steps when attempting to find and load an xref:

- If a user has checked (or neglected to uncheck) the Retain Path check box when a file is attached, AutoCAD will search for the drawing in that location *only*.

- If Retain Path is cleared, AutoCAD searches the following folders and paths, in the following sequence:

1. First, it attempts to load from the last folder from which it successfully loaded that reference.
   If the drawing file has moved, AutoCAD proceeds to the next step.

2. If the xref is not found in its previous location, AutoCAD searches the paths defined for this project. (This is an optional path specification and is described in more detail later.)

3. Finally, if the xref has still not been located, the AutoCAD Support Files Search path—as defined in the Options, Files tab—is searched.

If the xref is still not found, it is listed as Not Found at the command prompt and in the Status column of the Xref Manager. The xref path can be redefined in the Xref Manager, as shown in the previous section, but there is a more efficient way to preempt this situation: by adding a project name and path.

ADDING A PROJECT NAME AND PATH

One way to facilitate the transfer of xrefs between systems is to add a project name to each drawing. The PROJECTNAME system variable was added in AutoCAD 14 specifically to handle problems with xrefs and imported images. This system variable stores a search path for all external references or images associated with a specified project.

The power of the project name variable lies in the fact that it can be set differently on different computer systems. AutoCAD 2000 interprets the path associated with a project name by looking at values in the registry of the local computer. Each user of the same set of drawings can have different path and folder values associated with the same project name.

For example, the originator (user A) of a drawing may store the background drawing in the folder S:\DATA\PROJECTS\0092345\MAPS and will set this path in the project name. The second user (B) may store all the project files in D:\PIER39 and will set that value in the project name. Users A and B can then pass the drawings and xrefs back and forth between their systems, and AutoCAD will automatically search the paths in the PROJECTNAME variable and load the references.

Using the project name and path approach allows faster retrieval of xrefs. The alternative is to add each of your data folders to the AutoCAD 2000 Search path, a less desirable option. AutoCAD 2000 can find the reference files more efficiently based upon the PROJECTNAME search path.

EXAMPLE: ADDING A PROJECT NAME AND PATH

1. Select Tools, Options, or type **options** at the command prompt. (Or right-click and select Options from the shortcut menu.)
2. Select the Files tab and click Project Files Search Path.
3. Press the Add button, and type **LIBRARY** in the empty box. Then press Enter. This creates the project name variable (PROJECTNAME). Now you can define the desired paths.
4. With the project name highlighted, press Add again, and a second box displays.
5. Browse to the folder where you put the practice files for this chapter, and press OK. (This practice exercise uses \XREF EXAMPLES, but you may have copied the files into another folder.) The folder that you select is displayed in the Options tab (see Figure 17.8).
6. Press OK to complete the Options command.

You have now created an entry in the Windows Registry defining your Library project folder. You can add multiple folders for each project name, and AutoCAD will search all of them to find an xref for that project.

Figure 17.8
The Project Files
Search path is set in
the Options dialog
box.

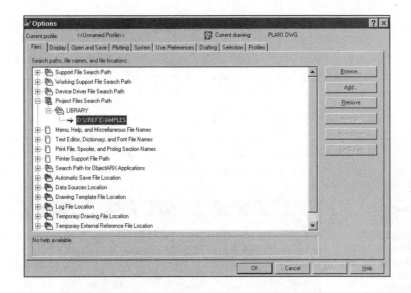

You can create any number of project names with associated folders in AutoCAD 2000, but each drawing can have only one project name—stored in the PROJECTNAME system variable.

ATTACHMENT VERSUS OVERLAY

Overlays behave in a very similar fashion to attached external references. Conceptually, an overlay is more typically used when you want to access information but not make it a permanent part of your drawing. In the previous example, the floor plan and grid become an integral part of your drawing and are plotted with your data; if another user references your drawing, these nested attachments will be included.

When you want to refer to another team member's plans for design consistency, an overlay works equally well. Any nested overlays will not be read into your current drawing or into any future drawing that references your current drawing. For example, if you were working on the reflected ceiling plan, you might want to check your design against the grid. But you may not want to make the grid a permanent part of the drawings that you send to other team members. In that case, an overlay would suffice.

The procedure for overlaying a drawing is almost identical to the steps for attaching an external reference you followed in the first practice exercise—only step 4 is different.

EXAMPLE: OVERLAYING A DRAWING

1. Keep your first practice file (PLAN1.DWG) open, and now open CH17 CEILING.DWG.

2. Make XREF LAYER the current layer. (The CH17 practice drawings already have this layer added.)

3. Click the Attach button on the Reference toolbar, or choose Insert, External Reference.

4. Select the GRID drawing CH17 GRID2.DWG; the External Reference dialog box is displayed.

5. Under Reference Type, select Overlay, as shown in Figure 17.9.

6. Uncheck the Specify On-Screen check boxes to accept the default insertion point, scale, and rotation—and remember to uncheck the Retain Path box also. Click the OK button, and then save the file CH17 CEILING.DWG.

Figure 17.9
Use the Overlay option in the External Reference dialog box to reference the grid into the reflected ceiling plan.

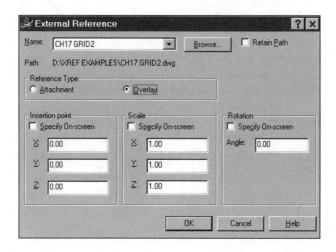

> **Note**
>
> The grid reference you have now added to the reflected ceiling plan drawing is not visible to other users who may reference this drawing. Because the grid reference is an overlay, not an attachment, it will not be loaded automatically with the host drawing when other users access the host drawing.

7. Without closing the reflected ceiling drawing, now open the CH17 EQUIPMENT.DWG and overlay the CH17 CEILING.DWG onto this drawing (following steps 2 through 6).

8. Because the reflected ceiling drawing is in use, you will receive the message shown in Figure 17.10. Press OK, and load the reflected ceiling into the equipment plan. Save CH17 EQUIPMENT.DWG.

Notice that when you load the reflected ceiling, the nested grid overlay is not referenced into the equipment drawing. If you now open the carpeting plan CH17 CARPET.DWG and overlay the equipment plan into the carpet plan, the reflected ceiling plan is not nested in the equipment plan.

Figure 17.10
Even when a drawing is in use, you can reference a read-only copy of the drawing in your current drawing.

> **AutoCAD Message** ☒
>
> File D:\XREF EXAMPLES\CH17 CEILING.dwg is open for editing. Unable to demand load it. Performing a full read instead.
>
> OK

If you had attached all the previous drawings, each time you referenced a drawing, all the previous nested references would also have loaded.

You can repeat this exercise using attachments if you wish to review the nesting process. First detach all the overlays (using the Detach button in the Xref Manager) to return the drawings to their original state, and then reference them again as attachments.

A further advantage of using an overlay is that this eliminates the possibility of a self-referencing drawing (circular reference).

PART
IV
CH
17

CIRCULAR REFERENCES

A circular reference is one that references itself. This can occur when attached references are nested repeatedly. In the previous exercise, you overlaid the grid into the reflected ceiling, the reflected ceiling into the equipment plan, and the equipment plan into the carpet plan. If you were now to overlay the carpet plan into the grid, you would have completed the circle. Because these drawings are overlaid, this causes no problem at all. If the references were attached one to the other, the circle could not be completed. However, in AutoCAD 2000, circular references are less an issue than they used to be.

In earlier versions of AutoCAD, a circular reference stalled the xref process until it could be resolved. Since AutoCAD 14, if a circular reference is detected, AutoCAD displays a warning. You can choose to stop and resolve the circularity problem, or you can continue. If you continue, AutoCAD 2000 loads all the nested references until it reaches the circular reference. Thus, the circular reference is effectively detached from the current drawing.

XREF DRAWING CONTENT

As you can see, when you attach an external reference to your drawing, all the geometry is displayed in your drawing editor. Additionally, all the nongraphical objects, such as text styles, layers, linetypes, and blocks, are included in your drawing.

Go back and open your practice drawing (PLAN1.DWG), and take a look at what has been added.

■ If you open the Linetype Control dialog box by selecting Other from the linetype drop-down menu on the Object Properties toolbar, you can see the dependent linetypes, prefixed with the xref name (see Figure 17.11). In their present state, there is little you can do with these linetypes because you cannot make them current or apply them to new drawing objects. (Of course, you could use the DesignCenter to drag and drop linetypes from the xref drawing into your current drawing, and they would then be usable with new drawing objects. But that is a different story.)

Figure 17.11
Linetypes from external references are added to the current drawing information.

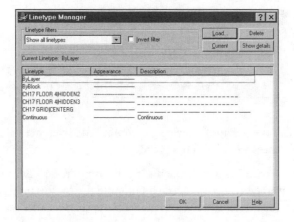

- If you open the Layer Properties Manager on the Object Properties toolbar, you will observe a similar situation. The xref-dependent layers are shown prefixed with the xref name (see Figure 17.12); again, you cannot make them current or add objects to these layers. However, you can manipulate these reference layers extensively.

LAYERS AND EXTERNAL REFERENCES

You have a variety of options with the layers in your xrefs. You can change the visibility, color, and linetype either globally, by manipulating the xref insertion layer, or by selecting the individual layers or subsets of layers.

MANIPULATING THE INSERTION LAYER   When you attached the practice reference drawings, you referenced them into a specific layer (XREF LAYER). This enables you to freeze and thaw all the xref layers (both the floor plan and the grid) at once. If you reserve a layer for each xref used in a drawing, you will have even better control of the visibility of those xrefs: You will be able to freeze and thaw (or turn on and off) all the layers of each xref by freezing and thawing its insertion layer.

Tip 147 from
Paul Richardson

If you want your xrefs to be visible but don't want any xref objects moved or deleted, you can set the xref insertion layer to Locked using the Layer Properties Manager on the Object Properties toolbar.

CHANGING XREF LAYER SETTINGS

When you attach an external reference, it is included in your drawing with all the layer settings of its original drawing. You will probably find that you prefer to view and plot these layers differently. In some drawings, you will wish to view only certain xref layers, and you may want to plot xref layers in different colors than those specified. A fairly common practice is to screen background xrefs when they are plotted. This requires changing the layer settings.

External reference layers are changed in exactly the same way as layers in the current drawing. You can experiment with PLAN1.DWG in the Layer Properties Manager. Turn different layers on and off, and change the colors. If you zoom in to look at the grid bubbles and dimensions, you will see that there are in fact two sets—for two different drawing scales. The appropriate bubbles for this scale of drawing are the larger bubbles and dimension text. You should freeze the layers that contain the smaller versions.

→ If you want to learn more about the Express Layer Tools you can use to manipulate layers, see Chapter 15, "Making Drawing Easier."

You also can use the layer filters at the top-right corner of the dialog box to change whole sets of layers (see Figure 17.12). In the next practice exercise, you will change the grid layers to gray and the floor plan layers to yellow using the preset layer filters.

Figure 17.12
You can use the layer filters to select different sets of xref layers.

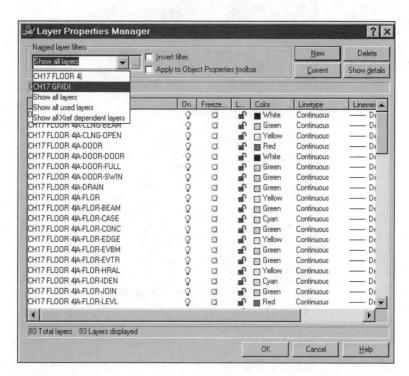

PART

IV

CH

17

EXAMPLE: CHANGING XREF LAYER SETTINGS

1. In PLAN1.DWG, click the Layers icon on the Object Properties toolbar, or type **layer** at the command prompt. The Layer Properties Manager dialog box opens.

2. Open the Named Layer Filters list box and select CH17 GRID1.

3. When the grid layers are displayed, press Ctrl+A to select all the layers; click the color button of any of the layers and select standard gray (#9) in the Select Color dialog box. All the grid layers are displayed as gray.

4. Repeat steps 1 to 3, but this time select the CH17 FLOOR 4I filter and change the layers to standard yellow.

Now the grid layers display as gray and the floor plan layers display as yellow.

CREATING CUSTOM LAYER FILTERS   You can filter the layers even more selectively by developing your own selection sets. Click the button with three dots (...) next to the preset layer filters. This opens the Named Layer Filters dialog box. The example shown in Figure 17.13 adds a filter specifically for the xref door layers. When you have selected a subset such as this, you can lock or unlock, freeze or thaw, or change the linetype or color to the entire group rather than one at a time.

Figure 17.13
You can create custom filters to control the display and plotting of different sets of xref layers.

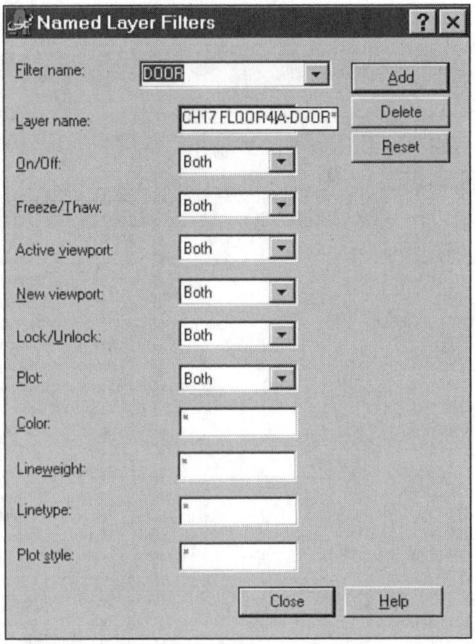

VISRETAIN AND XREF LAYERS

The changes you are making affect the current drawing only; you are not editing the original drawing. So what happens when you reload the same xref at a later date?

Fortunately, thanks to the powerful VISRETAIN system variable, you can store your custom xref layer settings and they will be restored each time you load the reference. This variable is set in the Options command, Open and Save tab. Choose Tools, Options, and click the Open and Save tab. A check box labeled Retain Changes to Xref Layers provides a deceptively simple On/Off switch, which works as follows:

- Visretain=On (1)—When Visretain is on, the current drawing retains all the layers settings for xrefs. You can edit the settings for visibility, color, and linetype. In AutoCAD 2000, the new layer settings for lineweight and plot style can also be retained. (Plot styles are remembered only if the system variable equals 0.)

- Visretain=Off (0)—When Visretain is set to 0, the layer settings for an xref are determined by the settings in the xref itself. Even if you make changes to the layer settings for the xref, such as changing colors, these changes will be lost when you exit the drawing. The next time you call up the same drawing, the xref layer colors will be however they are defined in the xref.

You can have completely different layer settings for the same xref in different drawings, and each will remember its own xref layer settings. Open CH17 CEILING.DWG and change its grid layers to magenta. You now can open the original CH17 GRID2.DWG, PLAN1.DWG, and CH17 CEILING.DWG simultaneously, and each will display the grid layers differently. All these drawings have Visretain set to On.

None of the changes made in this section need to be saved, so you can close these drawings without saving the layer changes.

REFERENCING A TITLE BLOCK IN A LAYOUT

A standard title block can be added to a drawing either as a block (as the name suggests) or as an xref. For smaller projects in which you control the title block and the model drawings, you may find it easier to insert a block rather than attach an xref. However, there are definite advantages to using an xref on larger-scale projects:

- If you insert the title block as a block, any changes made to the title block require you to call up each drawing and edit each title block drawing individually. The larger your project, the more efficiency you gain from using an xref.

- Conversely, any changes you make to a drawing are automatically updated in any drawings that reference it. For example, you might change a date field in an attribute block prior to plotting. Then every drawing you plot that references that title block will have the same plot date.

CREATING THE LAYOUT

Layouts are generally used for setting up the plotted drawing. Thus, you will reference the project title block (CH17 TITLE BLOCK.DWG) into a layout. First, however, you need to create a layout. The following exercise takes you through defining a layout and referencing a title block to your practice drawing. You might also use the Create Layout Wizard to accomplish this.

→ For further information on using the Layout Wizard, refer to Chapter 18, "Plotting and Layouts."

Note   If you decide to use the Layout Wizard to reference in the title block, place a copy of the project title block (CH17 TITLE BLOCK.DWG) in the \ACAD 2000\TEMPLATE folder. This is where the wizard looks for a title block. Also, don't forget to select the Xref option at the fifth wizard screen.

PART
IV

CH
17

EXAMPLE: CREATING THE LAYOUT

1. Open the reflected ceiling plan (CH17 CEILING.DWG) in model space.

2. To create a new layout, choose Insert, Layout, New; or type layout at the command prompt and press Enter, and then type **n** and press Enter.

3. At the Enter New Layout Name prompt, type Library and press Enter. A new layout tab appears with the name "Library."

4. Click on the new layout tab to display the layout. The Page Setup dialog box opens automatically at this point (see Figure 17.14).

Figure 17.14
You must set up your page specifications each time you create a new layout.

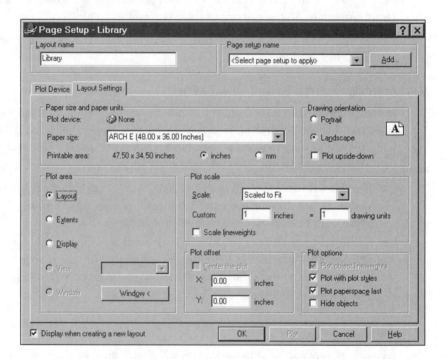

5. The library drawings are E-size drawings. On the Plot Device tab, select an E-size plotter if you have one installed for your system; otherwise, select None from the top of the list of plotters. You will not be able to plot the drawings, but it doesn't matter for the purposes of this exercise.

Note

The Plot Device list box displays only the system printers installed on your system. The size of the plot device selected determines the size of layout you may specify; if you select a letter-size printer, AutoCAD 2000 will allow you to create layouts for that size only. The None option allows you to define a layout, even when you do not have a printer available on your system.

6. Click the Layout Settings tab, and enter the following information:

   - In the Page Size field, choose ARCH E (48X36 Inches).

   - In Drawing Orientation, select Landscape.

   - In Plot Area, select Layout.

7. Press OK to return to the layout. (The remaining fields should be left with their default settings, as shown in Figure 17.14.)

Note

You can create a new layout by simply clicking on one of the default layout tabs (Layout1 or Layout2) and then re-configuring the layout. The Page Setup dialog box will not automatically open when you do this. To open it, choose File, Page Setup, or type **pagesetup** and press Enter.

PART

IV

CH

17

ATTACHING THE TITLE BLOCK

Now that you have set up a layout for a page size of 48 by 36 inches, you can reference the project title block into the layout.

EXAMPLE: ATTACHING THE TITLE BLOCK

1. On the Reference toolbar, click the Attach button.

2. Browse to your practice folder and select CH17 TITLE BLOCK.DWG.

3. When the External Reference dialog box opens, deselect the Retain Path check box and all the Specify Onscreen check boxes. In Reference Type, choose Attachment.

4. Press OK to complete the command.

The project title block will be inserted in the layout at 0,0,0—at scale 1.0 and rotation angle 0.0.

ADJUSTING THE VIEWPORT

The location of the initial viewport is generated automatically and often needs a little adjustment. Click the viewport to activate its grips. Click again to highlight the top-left corner of the viewport. Click again at the top-left corner of the title block. Notice that the viewport retains its rectangular shape when you move a single point. Make the bottom-right corner of the viewport hot and stretch it into the title block so your layout looks like Figure 17.15.

This example is complete, and you can save CH17 CEILING.DWG. The layout is set up for plotting, and you can return to model space to modify any of the model space xrefs, if required.

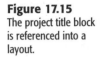

Figure 17.15
The project title block is referenced into a layout.

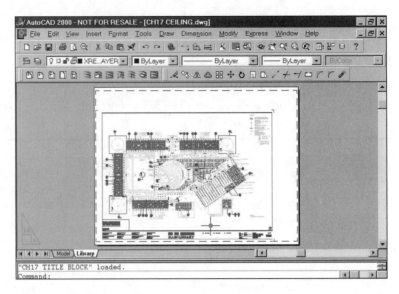

UNLOADING AND RELOADING EXTERNAL REFERENCES

At times, it may help you to have an external reference visible, and at other times you may prefer to turn it off for a shorter or longer period. If you wish to remove an external reference entirely, the best way is to use the Xref Manager and detach the attachment or overlay. If you simply want to turn off the reference for a period, you can use the Unload and Reload options on the Xref manager. When you reload an external reference, any changes that have been made to the source drawing are updated to the current drawing. For this practice exercise, you should use a new example drawing: CH17 FIRE Q1.DWG.

EXAMPLE: UNLOADING AND RELOADING EXTERNAL REFERENCES

1. Open CH17 FIRE Q1.DWG, and then click the first button on the Reference toolbar to open the Xref Manager. This screen shows that the floor plan and nested grid are referenced into the FIRE drawing.

2. Highlight the floor plan drawing and click the Unload button to unload the reference, as shown in Figure 17.16.

Figure 17.16
The Unload and
Reload options in the
Xref Manager enable
you to temporarily
detach external
references.

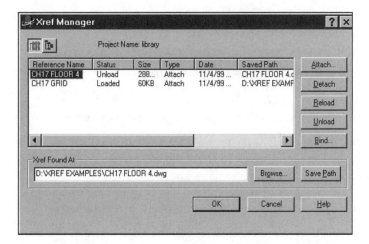

3. Press OK to return to your drawing. The floor plan has been unloaded.

Look at the FIRE drawing; you will notice a couple of items:

- The nested grid drawing is also unloaded, although you did not specifically unload this file. If you check back in the Xref Manager, you will see that it is listed as orphaned.

- The underlying FIRE drawing occupies only a part of the area covered by the floor plan.

Because the FIRE drawing covers only the top-left quadrant, having the full floor plan displayed onscreen is not particularly helpful. You can enhance your performance a little by displaying only the portion that you require. This is accomplished by using the external reference clipping boundary command.

SETTING XREF CLIPPING BOUNDARIES

When you create a clipping boundary, you can view just part of a block or xref. You can use a rectangle or a closed polygon shape, or even a polyline, to define the clipping boundary. You should continue to use CH17 FIRE Q1.DWG for this example:

EXAMPLE: ADDING A RECTANGULAR CLIPPING BOUNDARY

1. If it is not already open in the drawing editor, open CH17 FIRE Q1.DWG. (If you unloaded the xrefs in the previous example, you should reload them at this point. In the XREF Manager, highlight the floor plan drawing again and click the Reload button.)

PART

IV

CH

17

2. Click External Reference Clip on the Reference toolbar, or type **xclip** at the command line and press Enter. You are prompted with this:

```
Select objects:
```

3. At the prompt, click the floor plan to select it and then press Enter to complete the selection. The following prompt appears:

```
Enter clipping option
[ON/OFF/Clipdepth/Delete/generate Polyline/New boundary] <New>:
```

None of these options except New will work at this point; when you have added a clip boundary, you can experiment with the other options.

4. Press Enter to select the default New.

```
Specify clipping boundary:
[Select polyline/Polygonal/Rectangular] <Rectangular>:
```

5. You want to create a rectangle around the FIRE drawing. Press Enter to select the default Rectangular.

6. Give two points to specify a rectangle that includes the entire FIRE drawing in the top-left quadrant.

```
Specify first corner: Specify opposite corner:
```

After you click the second corner of the boundary, the area of the xref that lies outside the boundary disappears, as shown in Figure 17.17. The clipping applies only to the xref selected; any other geometry in the drawing is unaffected by the clipping boundary. In this particular case, there should be no drawing objects outside of the clip boundary.

DISPLAYING THE CLIP FRAME   If you want to see and plot the clip boundary, you can turn on the Clip Frame from the toolbar or at the command line.

■ Click the Clip Frame button on the Reference toolbar; this is the fifth button from the left. This buttons toggles the clip frame off and on.

■ At the command prompt, type **xclipframe** and press Enter. This enables you to enter a value for the system variable XCLIPFRAME:

```
Command: _xclipframe
Enter new value for XCLIPFRAME <1>:
```

The current setting for XCLIPFRAME is 1, which turns on the display of the clip frame, as shown in Figure 17.17; conversely, 0 turns off the display of the clip frame.

REMOVING THE CLIPPING BOUNDARY

You can remove clip boundaries and frames either temporarily or permanently, depending on your requirements. In the previous section you saw how easily clip frames can be turned on and off; typically, you will wish to have the frames on when you need to select them, but do not need them otherwise. You can turn clip boundaries on and off also; while you are working in a detail area, you may turn off the clip boundary temporarily in order to refer to information contained elsewhere in the xref.

Figure 17.17
The rectangular clipping boundary around this image is displayed with the clip frame set to On.

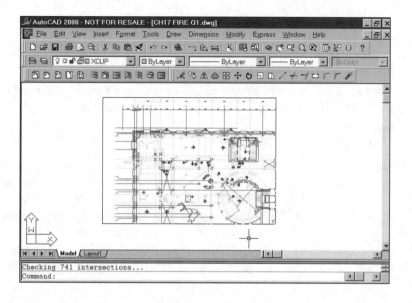

EXAMPLE: REMOVING THE CLIPPING BOUNDARY

1. Activate the Clip command by clicking the Clip button on the Reference toolbar, or by typing **xclip** and pressing Enter.

2. Select the floor plan again and press Enter. The clipping options are displayed at the command prompt.

   ```
   Enter clipping option
   [ON/OFF/Clipdepth/Delete/generate Polyline/New boundary] <New>:
   ```

3. First type **Off** and press Enter. The xref reappears in its entirety.

4. Repeat steps 1 and 2; this time, type **On** and press Enter. This returns you to the clipped drawing.

   The On and Off options toggle the display by the clip frame. On enables the clip frame to mask parts of the xref or block; Off removes the effect of the clip frame.

5. Repeat steps 1 and 2; this time, type **d** and press Enter. The clip boundary and clip frame are removed permanently.

Two additional options are available with the xclip command:

- The Generate Polyline option enables you to create a polyline that matches the outline of the clipping boundary. This object is separate from the clipping boundary and remains even if you delete the clipping boundary.

- The Clipdepth option enables you to specify two clip planes in 3D perpendicular to the current clip boundary. You must have defined a clip boundary for an xref or block before using Clipdepth. You then are prompted for the perpendicular distance to the front clipping plane and then the distance to the back clipping plane.

Before leaving the topic of clipping boundaries, you should try the other options for creating boundaries.

ADDING A NONRECTANGULAR BOUNDARY

The Clip command provides two additional options for creating clipping boundaries. When you create a New clipping boundary, you are prompted with this:

```
Specify clipping boundary:
[Select polyline/Polygonal/Rectangular] <Rectangular>:
```

- Select polyline—The current example drawing does not contain any polylines for you to use. If you wish to test this option, you must first draw a polyline to approximate your clipping area. Start the Clip command; at the Specify Clipping Boundary prompt, type **s** and press Enter; then select the polyline. The Clip command closes the polyline, if required, and clips the xref along the path of the polyline.

- Polygonal—At the Specify Clipping Boundary prompt, type **p** and press Enter. Using your cursor, pick a series of points to define a closed polygon resembling the one shown in Figure 17.18.

Figure 17.18
The Polygonal option of the Xclip command enables you to define an irregular clip boundary.

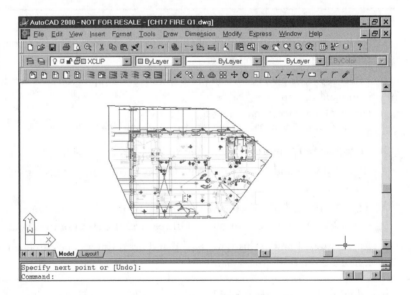

SOME LIMITS OF CLIPPING BOUNDARIES   As you have probably discovered in the previous exercises, there are a couple limitations to the Clip commands.

- It would be nice if you could adjust the clip boundary using grips, but unfortunately this is not the case. If you want to adjust a clip frame, you must delete it and make another one.

- You may wish to have more than one clipping boundary active in your drawing at a time, but you cannot have more than one boundary per xref. To create a second clipping boundary, you must load a second copy of the xref into your drawing. Depending on the size of the xref, this could impact your performance.

Enabling Demand Loading

When you use the Clip command, the actual data that is loaded into your drawing is not changed, but the display of the objects outside the boundary is suppressed. In the architectural drawing samples you have been using, the external references are very small and have little impact on the overall performance. In civil engineering and mapping projects, however, the external reference drawings can be of considerable size. Clipping the xrefs may give some small gains in screen regeneration, but you still have the entire xref loaded into your drawing.

To significantly improve performance in these situations, you should use the demand loading feature in conjunction with the Clip command. When the demand loading system variable is enabled, AutoCAD 2000 loads only the part of a drawing that is specified; the area masked by a clip frame is not loaded into the drawing. Demand loading can also be used in conjunction with the Freeze/Thaw layer settings to reduce the amount of data that is loaded into a drawing.

Part

IV

Ch

17

Example: Enabling Demand Loading

1. To enable demand loading, choose Tools, Options, or type **options** at the command prompt.

2. Click the Open and Save tab, and locate the External References (Xrefs) section in the top-right panel.

3. In the Demand Load Xrefs list box, choose Enabled and press OK.

Figure 17.19
Demand loading of external references is set via the Options command.

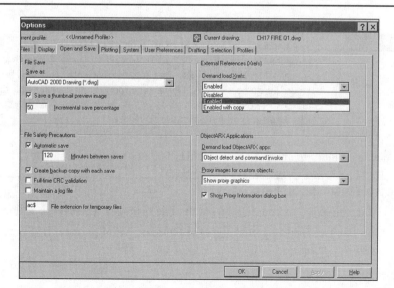

The drop-down list for Demand Load Xrefs allows three choices: Disabled, Enabled, and Enabled with Copy. This corresponds to the values 0, 1, and 2 for the system variable XLOADCTL.

- The default value is Enabled (XLOADCTL=1). When demand loading is enabled, the file that is being referenced is locked to other users. This means other users can open a copy of the xref but cannot save any edits back to it.

- If other users need to be allowed to modify the xref, you should set demand loading to Enabled with Copy (XLOADCTL=2). This enables you to work from a copy of the XREF while allowing other users to modify the original xref.

- The Disabled option (XLOADCTL=0) turns off demand loading.

For either the Enabled or Enabled with Copy option to work, the drawings that are being referenced must be saved with layer or spatial indexes.

CREATING SPATIAL AND LAYER INDEXES

Layer and spatial indexes are an integral part of demand loading. They contain lists of objects by layer or by location, which are accessed only when an xref is demand loaded. There is no advantage to creating an index in a drawing that will not be used as an xref. The following is a description of both:

- Spatial index—This records location information about all the objects in a drawing and organizes objects based upon this information. When a clipping boundary has been set and demand loading is enabled, the spatial index determines which objects in an xref lie within the clipping boundary. Only those objects are loaded into the host drawing.

- Layer index—This stores freeze and thaw layer information about each drawing object. When demand loading is enabled, xref objects on a frozen layer are not read into the host drawing.

Note   Spatial indexes can be used three-dimensionally. When you are working with a 3D model, it is common to define front and back clipping planes via the Clipdepth feature of the Xclip command. Spatial indexes also work in conjunction with a front and back clipping plane to reduce the number of objects loaded into your current drawing. Only the objects between the specified clipping planes are loaded, which can afford a considerable performance improvement in resource-intensive 3D models.

Adding an index to an existing AutoCAD 2000 drawing is very simple.

EXAMPLE: ADDING AN INDEX

1. Start the Save As command from the File menu, or type **saveas** at the command line.

2. In the Save As dialog box, press the Options button to open the Save As Options (shown in Figure 17.20).

3. Click the DWG Options tab, and then click the Index Type list box to display the index choices.

4. You can select either a layer index or a spatial index—or both, if you prefer.

Figure 17.20
Layer and spatial indexes are set in the Saveas Options dialog box.

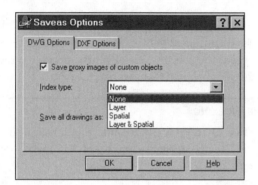

To add indexes to drawings from earlier releases of AutoCAD, you should first call them up and save them as AutoCAD 2000 drawings. Then you can go ahead and add layer and s patial indexes.

EDITING EXTERNAL REFERENCES

Prior to AutoCAD 2000, if a change was required in an external reference, the modification had to be made to the xref in a separate editing session. AutoCAD 2000 introduced in-place reference editing to enable users to modify any external reference files as they work. Using in-place editing, minor changes can be accomplished without having to open and close different drawings.

In the next practice example, you move an object in an xref. When reference editing is not activated, all the geometry of the xref drawing behaves as a single object—in fact, all the geometry of all the nested xrefs behaves as a single object. If you try to select and move a single grid line, for example, the entire set of nested xrefs will highlight and move with it.

The reference editing command (Refedit) enables you to separate and select parts of the xref to work with. This is such a powerful feature it merits its own toolbar, distinct from the regular Reference toolbar. To load the Refedit toolbar, right-click on any toolbar and select Refedit from the drop-down toolbar menu.

When the Refedit toolbar appears (as shown in Figure 17.21), run your mouse along the buttons to review the toolbar options. The first button starts the editing command and enables you to select objects to edit; the second and third buttons enable you to modify the selection set; and the final two buttons pertain to saving back the changes to the xref drawing.

Figure 17.21
Reference editing has its own toolbar separate from the Reference toolbar.

ESTABLISHING THE WORKING SET

The actual editing commands used to modify objects in an xref are standard AutoCAD 2000 commands. Before you can get to the editing, you must first specify the xref to be edited and also identify to AutoCAD the set of objects that you plan to edit.

EXAMPLE: ESTABLISHING THE WORKING SET

1. Open drawing CH17 FIRE Q1.DWG, and zoom to the top left of the drawing. You will edit the leftmost grid line and move it a foot to the left; make sure you have a good view of the grid bubble #0.7.

> **Note**
> You also can activate the Reference Edit command from the Modify menu or from the command line: Choose Modify, In-Place Xref and Block edit, Edit Reference, or type **refedit** at the command line and press Enter.

2. Click the first button on the Refedit toolbar (Edit block or Xref). This starts the Refedit command and prompts you to select a reference.

   ```
   Command: _refedit
   Select reference:
   ```

3. Click any part of the grid xref in the drawing. This opens the Reference Edit dialog box (see Figure 17.22).

   Because you have selected a nested reference, the dialog box displays a view of both references. The floor plan drawing in turn references the grid drawing.

Figure 17.22
The Reference Edit dialog box displays all the nested xrefs.

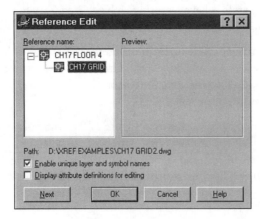

4. Select the CH17 GRID drawing and press OK. The drawing editor is redisplayed. Notice that the grid drawing name is displayed in the Refedit toolbar. Now you can select individual objects for editing. You are prompted with this:

```
Select nested objects:
```

5. Click the leftmost grid bubble (#0.7), the vertical grid line, the diagonal slash, and the dimension baseline, as shown in Figure 17.23. The prompt should return this:

```
4 items selected
```

Figure 17.23
Before you begin to edit, you must select the working set of objects.

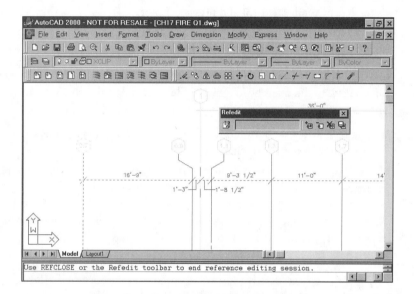

PART

IV

CH

17

Caution

At this point, you have simply identified the objects you plan to edit. The Refedit command extracts these objects and makes them available for editing. Your selected items are now part of a working set of objects you can change and that can then be saved back to the source drawing. You are warned at the command prompt you must close the editing session after you have completed your changes.

```
Use REFCLOSE or the Refedit toolbar to end reference editing
session.
```

Note

You may notice that all unselected objects in the xref are faded to 50% intensity to indicate that they cannot be edited. The percent intensity is under the control of the system variable XFADECTL, which you can define at any value from 0% to 90%.

EDITING THE XREF OBJECTS

This part of the Refedit process involves straightforward AutoCAD editing.

EXAMPLE: EDITING THE XREF OBJECTS

1. Select the four objects again, as shown in Figure 17.23. This time, you are actually going to edit them.

2. Start the Move command from the Modify toolbar. At the prompt, click your mouse anywhere to establish a base coordinate; then enter a relative coordinate 12 inches to the left by typing **@-12,0** and pressing Enter.

ENDING THE EDITING SESSION

Now that a change has been made to the grid drawing, you can choose whether to save the changes back to the referenced drawing file or abandon the changes. Select from the two right buttons on the Refedit toolbar:

■ The second-to-last button discards any changes you have made. Press OK to confirm that you wish to discard changes.

■ The last button on the Refedit toolbar saves any changes back to the referenced drawing. Press OK to confirm that you wish to save the changes.

If you save the changes you have made, they will affect all the other drawings that reference the grid, so it is probably better to discard the changes at this point.

Tip 148 from
Paul Richardson

Rather than using the toolbar options, you also can right-click to open a shortcut menu and close the Refedit session, as shown in Figure 17.24.

Figure 17.24
You can save or discard your changes at the end of the reference editing session.

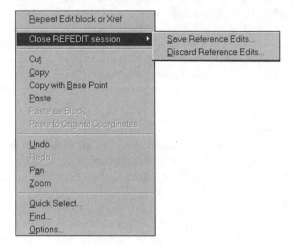

ENABLING AND DISABLING REFEDIT   If you attempt to edit an xref and AutoCAD gives you a message denying access, this is probably because reference editing is disabled in the source drawing. You have reviewed the settings in the Tools, Options dialog box a couple times already. Take a look at one more setting. Click the Open and Save tab again. In the External References panel is a check box Allow Other Users to Refedit Current Drawing, as shown in Figure 17.25. This check box toggles the XEDIT system variable: 0 = disable Refedit and 1 = enable Refedit.

Figure 17.25
Reference editing is enabled in the Options dialog box.

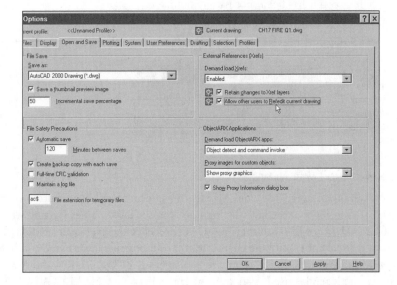

If editing is denied in the xref you are using, open the source drawing and check the Xedit variable; you $ may have to change it to 1.

BINDING AN EXTERNAL REFERENCE

Binding an xref makes the referenced drawing a permanent, unchanging part of the drawing that previously referenced it. The xref is converted to a block within the host drawing and loses its connection to the externally defined drawing. Usually this is done at the end of a project, when the dynamic relationship with the external drawing is no longer relevant or desirable.

In the next example, you will bind a reference drawing into the current drawing.

Open the drawing CH17 BIND.DWG. This is a version of the familiar equipment plan. At the bottom-right corner is the equipment legend xref. While the drawing was under development, the legend was subject to changes. This—and the fact that the same legend was used in several floors—made it productive to keep the legend in the form of an xref. Now that the drawing is complete, the legend will not need to be changed, so it is appropriate to bind it to the drawing.

EXAMPLE: BINDING A REFERENCE DRAWING INTO THE CURRENT DRAWING

1. Click the first button on the Reference toolbar, or type **xref** at the command prompt to start the Xref Manager.

2. Select CH17 LEGEND, and then press the Bind button. You will be offered a choice of Bind or Insert, as shown in Figure 17.26.

3. Select Bind, and press OK. The CH17 LEGEND xref disappears from the list of xrefs, telling you it has been successfully bound.

4. Press OK to exit the Xref Manager.

Figure 17.26
When a project is complete, you may wish to permanently bind an xref into the host drawing.

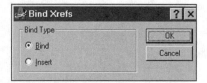

BINDING AND LAYER NAMES

Now start the Layer Properties Manager by clicking the Layers button on the Standard toolbar. Scroll down the layer listing until you see layer names starting with CH17 LEGEND. You will recall that AutoCAD precedes the xref layer name with the xref name and a vertical bar (|) or pipe character, to avoid possible layer name conflicts within a drawing. In the xref LEGEND, there are two layers A-FLOR-FURN and A-SHBD-TEXT. When the legend is used as an xref, the layers become CH17 LEGEND|A-FLOR-FURN and CH17 LEGEND|A-SHBD-TEXT.

These layer names are handled differently, depending upon whether you bind or insert the xref.

■ When the xref is bound in the conventional way, those layers become CH17 LEGEND0A-FLOR-FURN and CH17 LEGEND0A-SHBD-TEXT. Note that the vertical bar is replaced with 0. A similar naming convention is applied to text and dimension styles, linetypes, and blocks—they are renamed with the xref name, 0, and the old name combined.

■ If you choose the Insert option instead of the Bind option, the xref-name prefix is removed. If the layer names already exist in the drawing, the original name takes precedence. For example, the layer name A-SHBD-TEXT exists in both the current drawing and the xref, so the contents of the A-SHBD-TEXT layer in the xref would be moved to that layer in the host drawing. Similarly, the definitions for text and dimension styles, blocks, and linetypes are defined by the open drawing. Any definitions in the xref that use the same name will be overruled by the open drawings settings.

In this chapter so far, you have worked extensively with external reference files. You have learned how to attach and detach them; when to attach and when to overlay external references; how to reference a title block into a drawing; how to clip external reference files; how to edit them; and finally how to bind them into your drawing. The balance of this chapter will review the comparable commands used to manipulate raster images in AutoCAD 2000 drawings. The image commands are located on the same toolbar as the xref commands and share many features with external reference commands.

IMPORTING IMAGES IN AutoCAD DRAWINGS

Graphical data can be stored in either raster or vector format. AutoCAD 2000 drawing data is typically stored in vector format because vector format files are much smaller and more accurate than raster files. Raster files (such as .TIF, .BMP, and .GIF files) store every point in an image as a series of dots or pixels, whereas vector files store only critical information such as start point, endpoint, or radius values.

AutoCAD 2000 enables users to import raster images in many formats and overlay these images on the native vector format drawings. Raster applications come in many forms:

- Scanned architectural and engineering drawings—Raster files may be scanned versions of existing building drawings or detail sets you wish to include in your current drawing.

- Municipal block and lot maps—Most cities have huge archives of tax maps that can be matched to vector drawings to optimize the information available.

- Aerial photos—These images provide real-world backgrounds for civil and mapping projects.

ATTACHING AN IMAGE

AutoCAD 2000 enables you to attach, clip, and manipulate these images within your vector drawing using the image commands included on the Reference toolbar. In this practice exercise, you will open a supplied vector drawing; then you can experiment with importing an image.

Note

The example drawings for this chapter are adapted from the drawings and images from the San Francisco Basemap Digitizing Project, which was completed in 1997. A critical part of the project involved matching the digitized centerline map to the aerial photographs of the project area. This was accomplished by overlaying the unified centerline drawing on the corresponding aerial images (.TIF files). In this example, you will work with one image (A5) only and the matching segment of the centerline map. The two files that you will need (CH17 A5 CENTERLINE.DWG and CH17 A5.TIF) are supplied on the CD that accompanies this book. Copy these files into a practice folder on your hard drive.

PART
IV

CH
17

EXAMPLE: ATTACHING A NOTE

1. Locate the drawing file CH17 A5 CENTERLINE.DWG in your practice folder, and open it in the drawing editor. This extracted piece of the centerline drawing (see Figure 17.27) corresponds to a specific aerial image. You will use the yellow outline (on the IMAGE POSITION layer) to help you position the imported .TIF file.

If you do not have the Reference toolbar loaded, right-click on any toolbar and select Reference from the toolbar list box. The Reference toolbar is displayed. The image commands and variables are displayed at the right side of the Reference toolbar. (By dragging the edge of the toolbar, you can group the xref and image commands into two mini-toolbars, as shown in Figure 17.27.)

Figure 17.27
The Image Editing commands are available on the Reference toolbar.

2. Run your mouse over the toolbar buttons to review the available image commands. Notice the resemblance between these commands and the xref commands.

   The commands (Attach, Clip, and Clip Frame) perform in a very similar fashion to the xref commands. There is even an Image Manager that looks just like the Xref Manager. Click the first button, Image, or choose Insert, Image Manager to preview this dialog box. At this point, you have no images loaded, so there is nothing to manage.

3. Now click the second button, Image Attach, and browse to your practice folder and select CH17 A5.TIF. A thumbnail image is displayed in the Preview screen. Press Open, and the Image dialog box appears, as shown in Figure 17.28.

Figure 17.28
The Image dialog box enables you to specify the insertion parameters for the image, including insertion point, scale, and rotation.

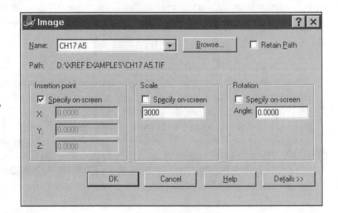

4. If you have worked through any of the external reference examples, you will be quite familiar with the layout of this dialog box. You need to specify the Insertion Point, Scale and Rotation values. This time, however, you must manually select an insertion point and also supply a scale value. Use the values shown in Figure 17.28.

   • Insertion point—The centerline map and aerial images are part of a drawing set that is based on real-world coordinates—actual labeled points on the world's surface—so you cannot use 0,0,0, as the insertion point. Rather than using the actual geographical coordinates, you will check the Specify On Screen box and position the image relative to the AutoCAD drawing. You will match the corner of the photo to the corner of the rectangle that outlines the centerline segment. Positioning will be easier if you have the Object Snaps on.

   • Scale—Enter **3000** in the Scale input box to scale the photo image to the real-world dimensions of the centerline map.

   • Rotation—There is no need to adjust the rotation angle for this image.

5. When you have entered these values, press OK to return to the drawing editor. Move your cursor to select the bottom-left corner of the yellow outline rectangle. This is your insertion point. The aerial image is now displayed in the AutoCAD drawing editor. The only problem is that the image is displayed on top of the vector drawing.

6. To reverse this, choose Tools, Display Order, Send to Back. When you are prompted to select an object, type l (for "last"). The drawing regenerates to position the line work on top of the image, as shown in Figure 17.29.

PART

IV

CH

17

Figure 17.29
The AutoCAD 2000 drawing is displayed on top of the imported aerial image.

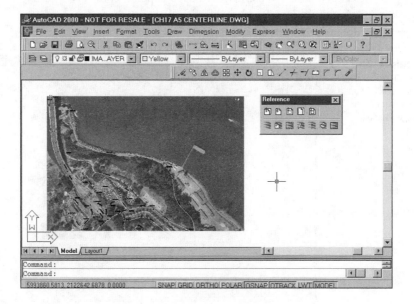

Tip 149 from
Paul Richardson

If you are having trouble selecting the image—especially if all 250 vector objects keep getting selected instead—you can change the process. Select the vector objects and then choose the Send to Front option in the Display Order command.

You also may find that the outline box you used to position the image gets in the way when you are selecting the image. If so, you can turn this IMAGE POSITION layer to Off.

CLIPPING AN IMAGE

Raster images are generally very heavy on computer resources because of their size. Hence, the Image Clip command can be a very useful option. If you want to work on the pier area in this drawing, for example, you could mask off the remainder of the aerial image.

EXAMPLE: CLIPPING AN IMAGE

1. Start the Image Clip command by clicking the third button on the Reference/Image toolbar. (You also can choose Modify, Clip, Image, or type **imageclip** at the command prompt to start this command.) You are prompted with this:

   `Select image to clip:`

2. Select the aerial image—a crossing window seems to be the easiest way to select this image. When the image has been selected, the Imageclip command works in practically the same way as the Xclip command you experimented with earlier in this chapter. Press Enter twice to create a New Rectangular clipping boundary.

3. Select two points to define your image-clipping boundary, as in Figure 17.30. Only the portion of the image within the clipping boundary is displayed.

Figure 17.30
The Image Clip command enables you to mask areas of the image you do not require.

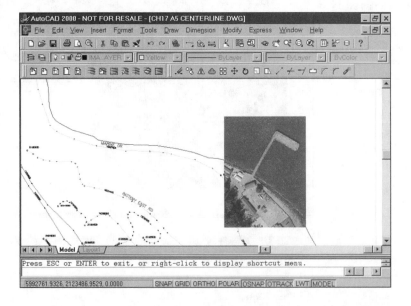

MANIPULATING IMAGE DISPLAY

The Reference toolbar contains a number of additional options that give the user control over the display of images in an AutoCAD 2000 drawing.

- Image Adjust—This toolbar option enables you to manipulate the brightness, contrast, and fade values of each image in your drawing. The default settings are 50% for brightness and contrast, and minimum for fade. You can change these via slider bars in the Image Adjust dialog box, and you can observe the impact in a preview window (see Figure 17.31).

- Image Quality—This option enables you to choose either High or Draft quality for the display of imported images—this can have a considerable impact on display performance but has no impact on the plotted output. Images are always plotted using the high-quality setting.

- Transparency—This variable controls whether the background of an image is transparent. This option is not available for all file formats.

- Image Frame—You can toggle the display of the Clip Frame on or off via the Image Frame button at the right end of the toolbar. This works in the same way as the external reference clip frame toggle.

PART

IV

CH

17

Figure 17.31
The Image Adjust dialog box enables you to manipulate display characteristics of imported images.

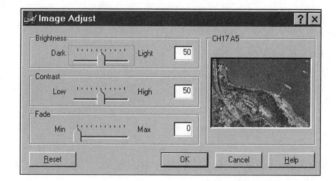

SUMMARY

In the past, both external references and imported raster images have had the status of second-class citizens in the AutoCAD production environment. This is clearly no longer the case. Numerous enhancements have made these once somewhat limited objects flexible and easy to incorporate into AutoCAD 2000 drawings.

The combination of clip boundaries and demand loading has improved the performance of oversize external references, and the addition of in-place reference editing has added greater flexibility to the use of xrefs. Images can be positioned, cropped, and scaled with accuracy like any other drawing object—and most importantly, the user can now draw on top of imported images and use them as a practical basis for their vector drawings.

PLOTTING AND LAYOUTS

In this chapter

PLOTTING IN AUTOCAD 2000

Chances are good that almost every drawing you spend any time on at all is destined to end up on paper. AutoCAD 2000's powerful plotting features will let you plot your drawing any way you want to plot it, from a simple print of the current page to setting up your own pages and layouts with multiple views.

With AutoCAD 2000, Autodesk has greatly enhanced plotting in AutoCAD. For the first time, plotting is completely built upon the Microsoft Windows standards for printing. Familiarity with other Windows products and how to print in them will help you use AutoCAD's plotting commands as well.

Tip 150 from	If you have used previous versions of AutoCAD, you will have a lot to learn about the new interface. You can learn from scratch by going through the entire chapter, but you will also be interested in the section "Changes to Plotting in Release 2000," later in this chapter, for a comparison.
Dylan Vance	

The new interface includes the introduction of wizards for performing common but difficult tasks. Wizards exist for configuring plot devices, creating page layouts, working with plot styles, and importing settings from previous releases of AutoCAD. This chapter shows you how to use the wizards and, when applicable, how to go beyond the wizards.

Note	Many of AutoCAD's new plotting-related Wizards are the only way to do certain things, so this chapter does go into detail about them. In the case of the Page Layout Wizard, both the wizard and the more detailed standard way of layout are described.

THE BASICS OF PLOTTING IN AUTOCAD

Plotting includes more than simply outputting the drawing to your printer. It also includes configuring the paper settings, laying out the page, creating titles and other common graphics in title blocks, and configuring AutoCAD to work with your printer or plotter. This chapter starts by teaching you how to set up a plotter in AutoCAD. Next, you learn how to set up the page and lay out the graphic elements. Many of these topics are new to users of previous releases of AutoCAD, although they will seem very familiar to many users of the Windows operating system.

Topics that will not be familiar to most users are discussed in the "Using Advanced Plotting Features" section. These include the new Plot Styles feature, which lets you plot the same drawing in different ways, as well as other uses for plotting and other ways to output your drawings.

USING THE ADD-A-PLOTTER WIZARD

AutoCAD now automatically supports whatever printers you have set up to work in Windows. This means you do not have to add them as plotters—you can just use them. However, AutoCAD also includes support for many common plotters, usually better support than the Windows drivers for the same plotters. In this section, you learn how to set up and configure an AutoCAD driver for a plotter. You will use the plotter configuration that you set up here throughout the rest of the chapter, so the plotter that you use will match the one in the examples.

AutoCAD 2000 plotter drivers are called Heidi drivers and have the extension hdi. The configurations for plotters are stored in pc3 files, for "plotter configuration file version 3" (previous versions were used by earlier versions of AutoCAD). Each pc3 file is associated with one plotter driver, but each driver can have anywhere from zero to many pc3 files associated with them. This means you can have as many configurations for the same device as you would like. Or, you can have more than one device that uses the same Heidi driver.

Tip 151 from
Dylan Vance

You can also use pc3 files to store additional configurations for Windows system printers. This enables you to have configurations that are specific to AutoCAD as well as multiple saved configurations for a single printer. For example, many people tend to print in portrait mode from most Windows programs (MS Word, for example), but landscape mode from within AutoCAD. If you are like this, you could make a configuration that used landscape as the default.

PART

IV

CH

18

Creating a configuration for a plotter is very easy in AutoCAD 2000. The Add-A-Plotter wizard takes you through all the steps, asking you for the information necessary to configure the plotter. The following example walks you through setting up a Hewlett-Packard LaserJet 5si printer. Although you may have a completely different type of printer, this ez shows you the steps to configure a printer to work with AutoCAD:

EXAMPLE: USING THE ADD-A-PLOTTER WIZARD

1. To start, choose the Plotter Manager option from the File pull-down menu, which brings up the Plotter Manager dialog box, shown in Figure 18.1.

Note

The Plotter Manager is actually a Windows Explorer window. It shows you the contents of the Plotters folder: your pc3 files and a shortcut to the Add-A-Plotter wizard. Double-clicking a pc3 file edits that plotter configuration file, and double-clicking the wizard shortcut creates a new plotter configuration file.

2. Double-click the Add-A-Plotter wizard icon. This brings up the Add-A-Plotter wizard.

3. The first screen of the Add-A-Plotter wizard is purely informational. Click Next to continue to the second screen, as in Figure 18.2.

Figure 18.1
The Plotter Manager lets you edit and create plotter configurations.

Figure 18.2
The second screen of the Add-A-Plotter wizard asks you to select how you will connect to the plotter.

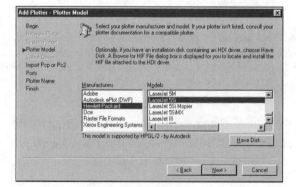

4. Choose the My Computer option on this screen, and then click Next to continue. The plotter uses the third and fourth screens to ask you questions about Network or Windows System plotters. Figure 18.3 shows the fifth screen of the wizard:

Figure 18.3
The fifth screen of the Add-A-Plotter wizard asks you to select a plotter model.

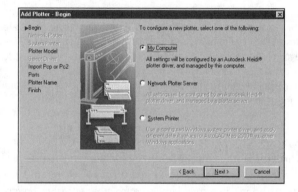

5. On the fifth screen of the wizard, you are asked to choose the plotter model for the plotter you are configuring. Choose Hewlett-Packard from the list of manufacturers, and choose LaserJet 5Si from the list of models. Finally, click <u>N</u>ext to continue to the seventh screen of the wizard, shown in Figure 18.4.

Note The plotters listed include both real plotters (such as the HP LaserJet that you chose here) and file formats (such as JPEG and DWF). These "file" drivers are very useful for using the plotting engine to output drawings as raster images for publication or to put on the Internet. Both the raster file formats and Autodesk ePlot drivers are discussed in detail in the "Using Advanced Plotting Features" section at the end of this chapter.

Figure 18.4
The seventh page of the wizard enables you to import settings from previous versions of AutoCAD.

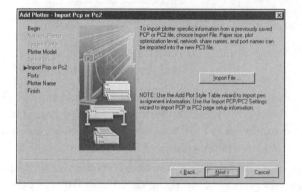

6. The seventh screen of the Add-A-Plotter wizard enables you to import older pcp or pc2 settings from earlier versions of AutoCAD. This is useful if you have been using AutoCAD before AutoCAD 2000 and already have your plotter configured the way you want. In this case, you will not use older settings, so click <u>N</u>ext to continue to the next screen, as shown in Figure 18.5.

Figure 18.5
The Add-A-Plotter wizard asks you for the port settings for your plotter.

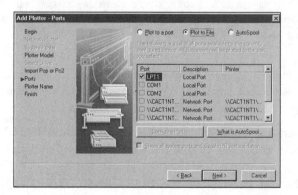

PART

IV

Cʜ

18

7. For this configuration, you will use the plotter only to plot to file. Choose the Plot to File option, and click Next. Figure 18.6 shows you screen nine of the Add-A-Plotter wizard.

Figure 18.6
The Add-A-Plotter wizard allows you to give your plotter configuration a name that is easy to remember.

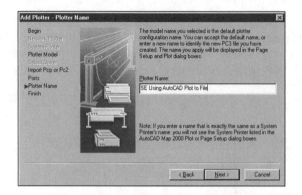

8. In the ninth screen, you give a name to your plotter configuration. This is the name that you see in AutoCAD when choosing a plotter. In this case, type **SE Using AutoCAD Plot to File** for the plotter name, and then click Next to continue to the final page of the Add-A-Plotter wizard.

9. The final page of the Add-A-Plotter wizard enables you to edit the plotter configuration or calibrate the plotter. At this point, click Finish. You can delete the plotter setup from the plotter manager later if you do not want to use it after the exercises in this chapter.

Tip 152 from
Dylan Vance

You will probably never need to calibrate a plotter unless you are making plots where the scale is very important. For example, if you are plotting a very precise drawing that needs to overlay on top of another drawing *exactly*, you may want to calibrate the plotter's scale. Calibrating the plotter corrects errors in the hardware scaling of the output. Errors in hardware (plotter) scaling can cause slight variations in scale from one plotter to another, and can cause two drawings plotted by different hardware to not match up exactly.

You have now configured a plotter driver to work with AutoCAD. Configuring any plotter is identically simple because AutoCAD automatically asks you all the questions it needs within the wizard. You will configure another plot driver later in this chapter.

The Add-A-Plotter wizard is the first of several wizards that AutoCAD 2000 introduces to make plotting easier. In the next section, you learn about the Create Layout wizard.

CREATING A SIMPLE PLOT WITH YOUR PLOTTER CONFIGURATION FILE

Plotting what you see in the Model tab of a drawing is easy. The following exercise takes you through opening a drawing and plotting its extents. In this case, you are plotting to a file, but the same instructions will let you plot to paper if you have set up a plotter to do that or are using a Windows system plotter.

1. Open the ch18_01.dwg that you installed from the companion CD, or use a drawing of your own.

2. From the View pull-down menu, choose Zoom, Extents. This zooms to the extents of the drawing. If you wish to plot only part of the drawing, zoom to that part of the drawing.

3. Choose File, Plot, or use the shortcut key Ctrl+P. This brings up the Plot dialog box, as in Figure 18.7.

Figure 18.7
The Plot dialog box allows you to configure your plot.

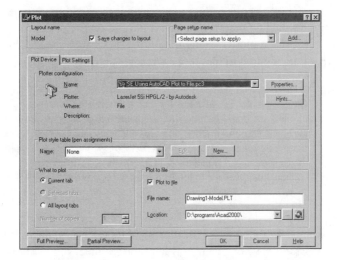

4. In the Plot dialog box are two tabs. Choose the Plot Device tab.

5. You choose the plotter configuration you wish to use for your plot from the Plotter configuration frame. Select the SE Using AutoCAD Plot to Filepc3 plot configuration file.

6. Give the plot file a name and path in the Plot to file frame. This step is unnecessary if you are plotting using a pc3 file that does not specify Plot to file.

7. Select the Plot Settings tab.

8. Because you started by zooming to display exactly what you wanted to plot, you should now choose Display in the Plot Area frame. This tells AutoCAD to plot exactly what you see in the window.

9. In the Plot Scale frame, choose Scaled to Fit. This forces whatever plot area you have chosen fit to a single page.

PART
IV
CH
18

Caution

Ninety percent of the time, when you are plotting from AutoCAD and are not worried about the exact scale a drawing prints on the screen, you will use Scaled to Fit. This option always takes the plot area you have chosen and makes it fit to the page or, as you shall see, to a view of your drawing on the page.

10. Finally, click OK to plot the drawing.

You have just plotted to a file. The plt file that was created could be copied to a printer (from a DOS prompt, use the command "Copy MyPlotFile.plt LPT1:" where LPT1: is the port for your printer), and the printer would plot the drawing without having to open AutoCAD again. Of course, the printer you copied it to would have to be an HP LaserJet 5Si, or the plt file would be the wrong format. Plotting to the printer directly is just as simple: Instead of choosing a plotter configuration that is set to automatically plot to a file, choose one that is configured to plot to an actual plotter.

Tip 153 from
Dylan Vance

Creating plt files can be useful if you do not have a plotter set up on your AutoCAD machine and don't have AutoCAD set up on your plotting machine. You can create the plt file on the AutoCAD machine and copy it to your plotting computer (using a floppy, for example, if you do not have a network setup). On the plotting computer, you can then use the copy command to plot the drawing. This is useful when the plotter is in one office (without AutoCAD) and AutoCAD is at a remote office or at home.

Most of the plotting you do in AutoCAD will probably be very similar to this, printing exactly what you see on the screen. However, at times you will want your plot to include more than just a single view of a your drawing. For example, you might want multiple views, titles, and other information. In these cases, you will need to use AutoCAD's layout functionality.

USING THE CREATE LAYOUT WIZARD

Taking what you have onscreen and outputting it to your printer is a fundamental function of a CAD package, but there are many ways in which you can customize the look of your plots—for example, adding legends or titles to your plot. AutoCAD gives you complete flexibility over what you can plot. Figure 18.8 gives an example of how you might want your plot to look (this particular plot is from one of the sample files that ships with AutoCAD 2000):

Whenever you want to create a plot that is not simply a view of the drawing—for example, if you want a title, legend, or multiple views of your drawing—you use *page layouts*. By default, AutoCAD 2000 has two layouts associated with each drawing that you can customize, but you can also add as many as you need.

A page layout enables you to place text or graphics wherever you want on the page. A page layout includes *viewports*, which are different views of your drawing. You can think of a viewport as a window in the paper into your drawing. Figure 18.9 shows a viewport containing a drawing on a piece of paper. In this case, the paper also has some text and graphics on it.

Figure 18.8
A plot can be more than just a simple presentation of your drawing using layouts.

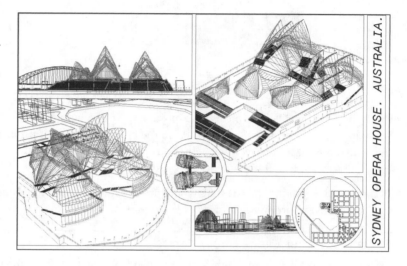

Figure 18.9
Viewports are windows into your drawing.

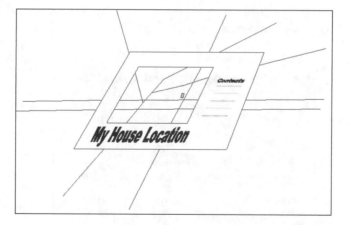

You can also have multiple viewports. For example, suppose you had a drawing that was an architectural view of an addition to a house. One viewport could show an overview of the entire house, while another might show a close-up view of just the addition with more detail. Within each viewport, you can zoom in and out, pan, or rotate the perspective individually, as if each were a separate drawing window. You can change the layer settings so a viewport shows only the layers you want.

Layouts show up in the drawing window as tabs across the bottom. Choosing a different tab shows you that layout. The Model tab is always there and represents the actual data, or contents, of your drawing. Figure 18.10 shows the default tabs on a new drawing. In the following sections, you will learn how to work with one of these existing layouts, but first you will create a new one.

Figure 18.10
The Layout tabs let you easily switch between layouts.

Creating a new layout is easy with the Create Layout wizard. Of all the plotting wizards, this is the one you will probably use the most. This wizard automates the process of laying out graphic elements on the screen. Later in the chapter, you will learn how to do all the things that the wizard does for you without using the wizard, but you will probably end up using the wizard most of the time.

In this exercise, you use the Create Layout wizard to create a layout for one of the drawings that you have seen previously in this book:

EXAMPLE: USING THE CREATE LAYOUT WIZARD

1. Open the ch18_02.dwg file that you installed from the CD that came with this book.

2. Choose Tools, Wizards, Create Layout. This displays the Create Layout wizard. You can also type **LayoutWizard** at the command line. Figure 18.11 shows you the first screen of the Create Layout wizard.

Figure 18.11
You can use the Create Layout wizard to create a new layout quickly and easily.

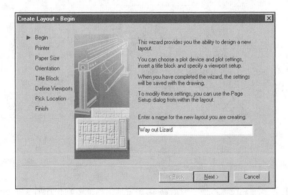

3. Enter a name for your new layout—in this case, type **Way out Lizard** for the name, and then click <u>N</u>ext to continue to the second screen of the wizard. Figure 18.12 shows you the second screen of the wizard.

4. The second screen of the wizard asks you for a printer. Choose the SE Using AutoCAD Plot to Filepc3 plotter configuration that you created earlier in this chapter (your list will probably not match the one in the illustration). Then click <u>N</u>ext to continue to the third screen of the wizard, as in Figure 18.13.

Figure 18.12
Choose a plotter
configuration to use
for your new layout.

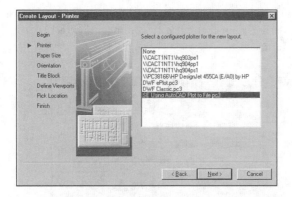

Figure 18.13
Choose a paper size
for your layout.

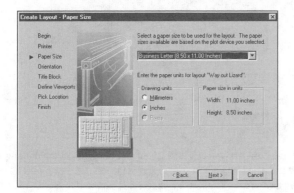

PART

IV

CH

18

5. Because a layout is the AutoCAD representation of a page, the wizard needs to know the size of the paper to which you will be plotting. Choose Business Letter (8.50 × 11.00 inches). Also, choose Inches for the drawing units. Finally, click Next to continue to the fourth screen of the wizard, as in Figure 18.14.

Figure 18.14
Choose a paper orien-
tation for your new
layout.

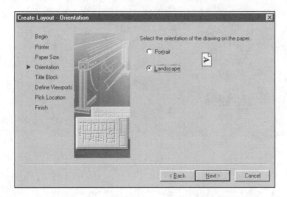

6. The fourth screen of the wizard asks you to choose the orientation of your page. Choose Landscape and then click <u>N</u>ext to continue. Figure 18.15 shows you the fifth screen of the wizard.

Figure 18.15
Choose a drawing to use as a block for the graphics of your layout.

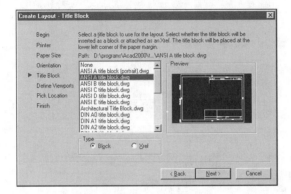

7. In the fifth screen, the wizard asks you to choose a title block. Choose the ANSI A title block drawing, and choose Block for the type of insertion. Click <u>N</u>ext to continue to the sixth screen of the wizard, as shown in Figure 18.16.

Tip 154 from
Dylan Vance

You can draw any graphics on a layout, but using an existing drawing as a block enables you to create standards or use existing standards. The title blocks listed in the Create Layout wizard are standard title blocks that ship with AutoCAD. You can also create your own and add them to the list in the wizard. For more information, see the section "Working with Title Blocks," later in this chapter.

Figure 18.16
Choose the setup of the viewports in your layout.

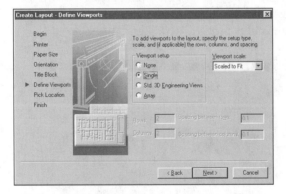

8. This layout will have a single viewport that shows the entire drawing. Under Viewport setup, choose Single. In the Viewport scale, select Scaled to Fit from the drop-down list. Click <u>N</u>ext to continue in the wizard. Figure 18.17 shows the seventh screen of the wizard.

Figure 18.17
The seventh screen of the Create Layout wizard enables you to specify the location of the viewport or viewports.

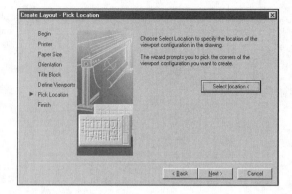

9. AutoCAD needs to know where to place the viewport or viewports on the layout. Press the Select location button and draw a viewport in the middle of the title block. Choosing this button creates the layout and enables you to draw the viewport(s) on it. When you have finished drawing the viewport, you will automatically be taken to the last screen of the wizard, as shown in Figure 18.18.

Figure 18.18
The last screen of the Create Layout wizard lets you know when you are done.

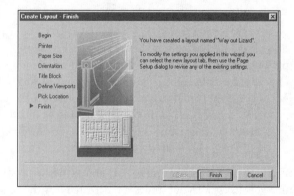

PART
IV

CH
18

10. The eighth and final screen is simply informational, letting you know you are done. Press the Finish button to exit the wizard.

When you are done, you should have a new layout that looks something like Figure 18.19.

Note

Your viewport may look different from the one in Figure 18.19 if you did not draw it the same way. If you want, you can edit the viewport by selecting its outline.

If you wanted to plot this layout just the way it is now, you could choose the Plot command and accept the defaults in the Plot dialog box because they would match the layout settings that you just created.

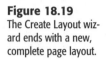

Figure 18.19
The Create Layout wizard ends with a new, complete page layout.

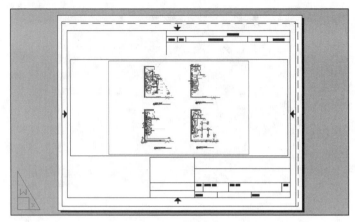

Later in this chapter, in the section titled "Working with Layouts," you will learn how to modify the view of your drawing that shows up in the viewport, as well as how to create new viewports and edit the rest of the layout. But first, you will learn about setting the preferences for the way you want a page to plot.

SETTING UP THE PAGE

Page layouts are used to plot your drawings in different ways. For example, you might have one page layout for plotting the electrical wiring plans for a house (using a subset of layers and one legend), and another for plotting the plumbing diagrams (using a different subset of layers and legend). When you create a new page layout from scratch, the first thing you must do is set up the page. It is important to do this first because so many of the things you do when creating a page layout (adding a title block, graphics, or viewport, for example) rely on the size of the page and the page units to work properly.

Setting up the page first is so important that AutoCAD automatically displays the Page Setup dialog box the first time you access a layout (unless you created it with the wizard). You can also edit the page setup of an existing layout. You can access the Page Setup command from the File menu, Page Setup option; from the command line (type **PAGESETUP**); or from the shortcut menu on the layout tabs at the bottom of the drawing.

Figure 18.20 shows the Page Setup dialog box.

Each page layout has a page setup associated with it. You can tell by looking at the top of the Page Setup dialog box, where it shows you the name of the page layout you are viewing. The dialog box shows the setup for the layout that was active when you called the command, and any changes you make apply only to that layout.

Tip 155 from
Dylan Vance

If you use the same page setup for multiple layouts, even across drawings, you can use them without having to recreate all the settings. Use the Page setup name frame to choose a page setup from within the drawing. Be careful when choosing the page setup from the drop-down list—choosing it automatically applies the changes to the current page setup, losing whatever changes you might have already made.

Use the Add button to save the current page setup with a new name, or to import a page setup from another drawing.

Figure 18.20
The Page Setup dialog box enables you to modify the page and plot settings for a layout.

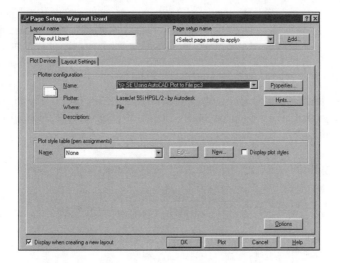

The important part of the dialog box is in the large tabbed part at the bottom. This is where you set the plotter that you wish to use, the paper size, and the other settings that control what and how you wish to plot. Figure 18.21 shows you the Plot Device tab.

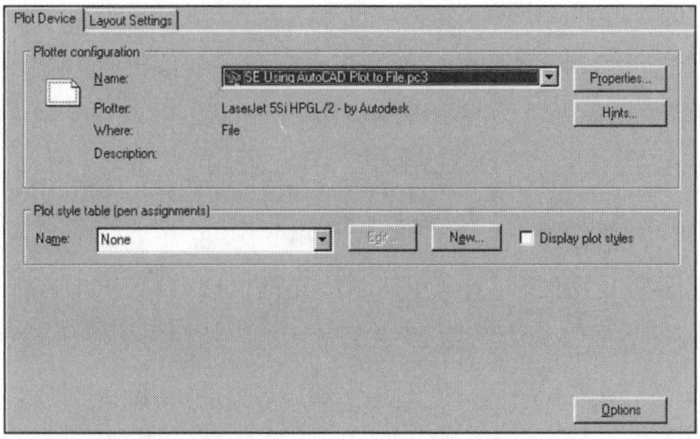

Figure 18.21
The Plot Device tab enables you to choose the plot device and change its settings.

This tab enables you to choose which device (plotter) AutoCAD will use to plot. Besides changing the plotter itself, you can also change the properties of the plotter. In most cases, using the plotter properties is unnecessary; the properties that are most likely to require changing are also on the Layout Settings tab.

Changing the settings in the plotter properties is the same as editing the plotter configuration. Changing the same settings in the Layout Settings tab changes only the page setup you are currently editing. The Plot Device tab also enables you to specify the plot style table to use. You will learn more about plot styles in the section "Using Advanced Plotting Features," later in this chapter.

Tip 156 from
Dylan Vance

You may want to make a few typical changes that require using the properties of the plot device: If you want to change the print area (the unprintable borders of the page), create a custom paper size, modify the options for optimizing pen plotters, or change the paper source (upper tray to lower tray, for example), you will need to use the plotter properties.

Now look at the Layout Settings tab in Figure 18.22. This part of the dialog box includes all the settings that affect the page, and hence the layout view. It also controls which part of the layout will plot.

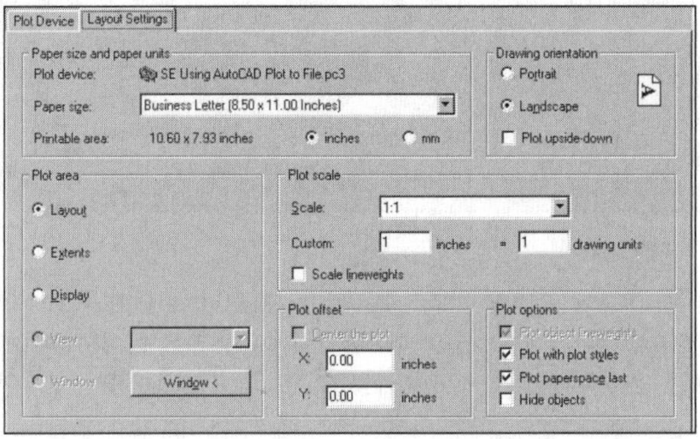

Figure 18.22
The Layout Settings tab is where you will make most changes when working with a page setup.

The top part of the tab is similar to most Windows programs that print. The Paper size and paper units frame enables you to choose the size of the paper AutoCAD will plot (such as letter, legal, and so on) and the units for the paper width and height. The Drawing orientation frame enables you to choose either portrait or landscape. The Plot upside-down option simply rotates the entire drawing by 180° when plotting.

The rest of the dialog box is more specific to AutoCAD. The Plot area frame enables you to choose which part of the current layout you wish to print, and it has the following options:

- Layout—This plots the entire layout as you have set it up in the layout view.
- Extents—This plots the entire extents of the all objects in paper space (or model space, if the Model tab is the currently active view).

- Display—This plots whatever you are currently zoomed to.

- View—This plots all the objects in a specific named view. If you select this option, you will need to choose the named view from the drop-down list.

- Window—This enables you to specify a rectangular area of the layout to plot. To choose this option, you must press the Window button and then draw a rectangle on the screen to define the area to plot.

These options may not all be available all the time. The Plot scale frame is very important when plotting. This sets the scale of drawing units to the paper. For example, if you are printing model space and the extents go from 0, 0 to 1000, 1000, you will not want to print at a 1:1 scale because the paper would have to be 1,000 inches tall and wide to accommodate the whole drawing.

Usually, you will use a scale of 1:1, and in the Plot area frame choose Layout, when you want to plot a layout view in its entirety. With the other options, you will probably want to plot using the Scaled to Fit option in the Plot scale frame. This option takes whatever you have selected to plot and adjusts the scale to fit the entire printed page.

The Plot offset frame enables you to move the origin of the plot on the page. This rarely used option allows you to move the origin of the plot on the paper. When not printing using the layout option (in the Plot area frame), you have the useful option to center the plot. You would use this most often with plots that are to a specific scale and do not plot the entire layout.

Finally, the Plot options frame provides the following options:

- Plot object lineweights—This includes the lineweights of the objects when plotting. With some older plotters, this would slow the printing. With printers and most newer plotters, turning this on does not affect printing time.

- Plot with plot styles—This is the option to use plot styles, which are discussed later in this chapter. When this option is checked (the default), the Plot object lineweights option is not available because the lineweights will be plotted based on the plot styles.

- Plot paperspace last—This option plots paper space objects on top of model space objects in viewports. If this is not checked, the model space objects will be plotted on top of the paper space objects. For more information on paper space and model space, see the section "Model Space and Paper Space," later in this chapter.

- Hide objects—This option sets the hidden line removal option for the paper space three-dimensional objects. This applies to paper space only; each viewport also has this as a property to affect the model space in that viewport.

At the bottom of the Page Setup dialog box is a check box that enables you to show the Page Setup dialog box automatically when creating a new layout. In most cases when you create a new layout, the first thing you should do is set up the page, so it is probably a good idea to leave this checked.

PART

IV

CH

18

Caution

It is always a good idea to set up the page the way you want to use it before making other changes to a layout. Changing the page setup after putting graphics or viewports on the layout may change the layout, forcing you to redo the graphics.

Finally, at the bottom right of the dialog box, you have the option to cancel your changes, accept them by clicking OK, or plot directly from this dialog box.

WORKING WITH PAGE LAYOUTS

You have already seen how to create a page layout using the wizard. In this section, you learn how to work with existing page layouts and how to create new ones from scratch.

EDITING EXISTING PAGE LAYOUTS

Across the bottom of a drawing are the layout tabs. Each one represents a view of your data. The first tab is always labeled Model. This tab is the data tab and is where most of your work will take place. All the other tabs (and there can be as many as you need) are plotting layouts.

By clicking a Layout tab, you switch to that view. What you see is the representation of a piece of paper. A new layout looks like that shown in Figure 18.23.

Figure 18.23
A new layout is simply a blank piece of paper with a viewport.

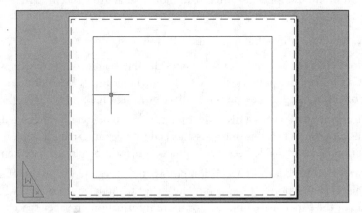

The white area with the shadow border is the paper, which, of course, means the gray area is off the paper. The dotted lines just inside the edge of the paper are the margins, which define the printable area on the paper. The size of the paper and the printable area are set up by your printer driver and the page setup you have defined for the layout. The black square in the paper is the first viewport. By default, AutoCAD creates a single blank viewport in any new layout.

Tip 157 from
Dylan Vance

If you are using another color paper in your plotter (or even if you are not), it is possible to change the background color of the paper in layout views. To do this, go to the Tools pull-down menu, select Options, and in the Display tab, click the Colors button. You may remember that this is the same place you changed the background color in the Model tab earlier. Changing the background color does not change the way AutoCAD plots your drawing.

Having a blank layout is not much better than simply plotting the Model tab, so you should now learn to add something to it. The following exercise will show you how to use one of the two default page layouts in a drawing and how to add a title across the bottom of the page. Adding text or any graphics to a page layout is the same as doing it in the Model tab, so this exercise gives you an example by adding an Mtext object for the title:

EXAMPLE: ADDING AN MTEXT OBJECT FOR THE TITLE

1. Open the ch18_03.dwg file that was installed from the CD that came with this book.

2. Click Layout1. The Page Setup dialog box automatically opens when you switch to a page layout for the first time.

Note

If the Page Setup dialog box does not automatically open, this page layout has been used before. Simply right-click the Layout tab and choose Page Setup from the shortcut menu that appears.

PART

IV

CH

18

3. Make the following selections in the Page Setup dialog box:
   - Choose any printer you want.
   - Choose the letter page size and set inches as the units.
   - Make the drawing orientation landscape.
   - Choose Layout for the plot area.

4. Click OK to close the Page Setup dialog box and save the changes you made. You should now have a blank layout.

5. Choose Draw, Text, Multiline Text to create an Mtext object.

6. Click and drag a wide, short box under the viewport in the Layout tab. This defines the extents of your title.

7. The Multiline Text Editor will appear. Type **My Drawing Title** into the text box. Change the font to any font you like, and click OK.

You have just added a title to the bottom of your page layout.

Tip 158 from
Dylan Vance

If you would like to change the style of the text, you can do that, or you can move it around to make it more centered on the page. If you would like to try these things on your own, use the Properties window (from the Tools pull-down menu, Properties option; or by pressing Ctrl+1) to change the text properties. You also can try selecting and moving the text. To learn more about editing text and other types of entities, refer to Chapter 2, "Drawing Setup."

Figure 18.24 shows the page layout with the new title across the bottom. Your page should look similar to this.

Figure 18.24
The blank layout now contains your title.

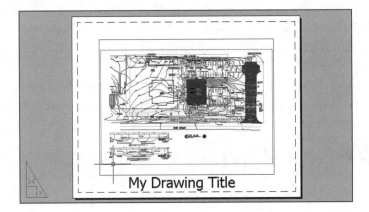

USING CUT, COPY, AND PASTE BETWEEN LAYOUTS

You may create something in your model that you want to use in your layout. Or, you may have something in one layout that you would like to appear in another. For example, you may have a logo you have drawn on one tab that you want to appear on another tab. Similar issues arise many times when you want something that is in the model to appear on the page instead.

In this case, the simplest way to put the objects on another tab is to copy and paste them. While in one tab, select the objects you want to appear in another and press Ctrl+C to copy them to the clipboard. Then, in the new tab, press Ctrl+V to paste the objects onto the screen. The new objects will be on the same layer as the old ones but will now be in the new tab only.

If you do not want the original objects to remain in the original tab at all, you can delete them after copying them. Or, you can use Ctrl+X to cut instead of Ctrl+C to copy, which copies the objects to the Clipboard and deletes them at the same time.

As you learned in Chapter 1, "Working with the Interface," you can even use copy (or cut) and paste to move objects between drawings.

WORKING WITH VIEWPORTS

The layout you were just looking at has one large viewport. In many cases, you want to have more than one viewport. For example, if your drawing were a map of a city you might want one that is small and that shows the city location on a country map, and you also might want one or more others that show detailed views within the city.

> **Note**
>
> Viewports in the Model tab (discussed in Chapter 13, "Hatching,") are called tiled viewports. Tiled viewports divide the screen into multiple views of your drawing. In page layouts, the viewports are called *floating viewports*. Floating viewports can be independently moved and resized. You can even overlap floating viewports. Both types of viewports are created, managed, and worked with using the VPORTS command, although you can also edit floating viewports as if they were geometry.

In the following exercise, you start with a blank layout that has one viewport (you can use the layout from the previous section, if you want), and you will add another. Before you can add the new one, however, you must edit the existing one to make room for it. Editing a viewport is very simple—it acts just like a piece of geometry on the page. When you are done, you should have two viewports:

EXAMPLE: ADDING A VIEWPORT

1. Click the outline of the viewport in the page layout.
2. Using grips, resize and move the viewport so that it matches the larger viewport.
3. Choose View, Viewports, 1 Viewport. This enables you to draw a new viewport on the screen. Click the two corners that define the smaller viewport.

Viewports are actually an entity type, and you can edit them just like any other entity. You have already seen that you can edit the size and shape with grips. In the following exercise, you will change the color of the smaller viewport border.

EXAMPLE: CHANGING THE COLOR OF THE SMALLER VIEWPORT BORDER

1. Deselect any objects you currently have selected.
2. Select the smaller viewport by clicking any part of its border (the rectangle around the outside edge).
3. If you do not already have the Properties window showing, press Ctrl+1 to show it.
4. Change the Color property to Red.
5. Right-click the page layout and press the Deselect All menu item on the shortcut menu.

The viewport outline is now red. You can also change the linetype and weight, layer, and other object properties of the viewport. You can make the viewport look however you want—to match the way you want your final plot to look.

You have changed the way your viewports look, but the larger viewport is showing only part of your drawing. You want to see the whole drawing in this viewport, so the following exercise takes you through changing the view of the drawing in the viewport:

EXAMPLE: CHANGING THE VIEW OF THE DRAWING IN THE VIEWPORT

1. Double-click anywhere in the larger viewport. This makes the viewport active and lets you edit what you see in it. The viewport outline becomes thick to let you know it is in this new mode. This new mode is called Model. If you want to modify anything *inside* the viewport, including the view, you will have to go into this mode.

2. Choose View, Zoom, Extents to zoom to the extents of your drawing within this viewport.

3. Double-click anywhere on the page (but not on a viewport) to return to the normal page layout mode, which is called Paper.

In Model mode, all the zoom commands work as they do on the Model tab, but they apply only to the viewport, not to the entire window. In this example you used Zoom, Extents, but you could just as easily have used zoom in or out, or even the realtime pan and zoom.

When you are in the Model mode, you can edit all the entities in your drawing, just as if you were on the Model tab (hence, the name Model). When you are in the Paper mode, you can edit all the entities on the page. For a more complete description of the Model and Paper modes, see the section "Model Space and Paper Space," later in this chapter.

Now you will change the layers shown in each viewport. As you shall see, this is trickier than it sounds:

EXAMPLE: CHANGING THE LAYERS SHOWN IN EACH VIEWPORT

1. Try to freeze layer Shade in the larger viewport. Select the viewport by clicking the outside border, and then use the layer control in the toolbar to freeze layer Shade.

Note For this example to work, the layer Shade must not be the current layer.

2. Notice that layer Shade was frozen in both viewports, instead of just the one you were interested in. This was not what you wanted to do, so choose Edit, Undo to undo the freeze.

3. Obviously, the normal method for freezing a layer will not work in this case. AutoCAD also provides a tool for changing the state of layers in individual viewports. That method is the VPLAYER command, short for "viewport layer." Type **VPLAYER** at the command line.

Tip 159 from
Dylan Vance

If you work with multiple viewports often, you can add the VPLAYER command to your menu or toolbars. For more information on how to add commands to the menu or toolbar, see Chapter 22, "External Database Connection."

4. At the first prompt, type **F** for "freeze." The other options are thawing a layer; resetting the entire viewport; creating a new, frozen layer; and resetting the visibility of a layer to its default.

5. The next prompt asks you to enter a layer (or more than one). You may enter layers separated by commas (but not spaces because a space would be interpreted as an Enter). In this case, type **Shade**.

6. The next prompt asks you to select the viewport to change. Type **S** to select a viewport, and then select the larger viewport by clicking its border.

7. The next prompt is simply the command starting again (this command enables you to change the settings of many layers without having to call the command again). Simply press the Enter key to complete the command. You should now have a layout that looks like that shown in Figure 18.25. Notice that the shading in the middle of the drawing is gone in one of the viewports, but not the other.

PART

IV

CH

18

Figure 18.25
You can control the settings of layers in each viewport independently.

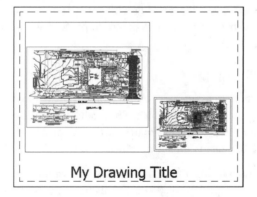

Now you have the skills necessary to edit a layout to look the way you want it, including editing the graphics on the page and modifying the views of your drawing data that you see on the page.

Tip 160 from
Dylan Vance

Viewports do not have to be square. You can create a viewport by drawing a polygon, using View, Viewports, Polygonal Viewport. Or, you can convert an existing polyline, ellipse, circle, region, or spline object into a viewport with the View, Viewports, Objects command. Both these commands can be accessed on the command line with options on the **–VPORTS** command (Note: the standard VPORTS command (without the dash) does not have the Polygonal Viewport options.)

Now that you have learned about modifying existing layouts, including viewports in the layouts, you can learn how to create a new layout.

MAKING NEW LAYOUTS

Each AutoCAD drawing starts with two blank layouts. However, you might want to have many layouts. For example, you might want one layout that is used for plotting your entire project and twenty layouts for plotting separate detail views of different parts of your project.

So far, you have been working with layouts that already exist. Now you will learn how to create them yourself. The following exercise steps you through creating a new layout:

EXAMPLE: CREATING A NEW LAYOUT

1. Right-click any of the tabs at the bottom of the drawing window. From the shortcut menu, choose New Layout. A new tab should appear, titled Layout2.

2. Click the Layout2 tab to activate it. Unless you have changed the default settings, the Page Setup dialog box will now appear. For this exercise, simply choose the defaults and press the OK button.

Now that you have seen how to create viewports, modify them individually, and put graphics around them, you have all the basics for working with paper layouts. In the next section, you learn about model space and paper space, and a common practice for standardizing the layout of your drawings.

MODEL SPACE AND PAPER SPACE

In AutoCAD, all the objects that are part of your drawing are part of what is called model space. When you are using the Model tab, you are in model space. The coordinates you see onscreen and that you enter are model coordinates (with the constraints given by the User Coordinate System, or UCS, when you have modified it).

When you print, you are introducing a new kind of coordinates for AutoCAD to work with—the coordinates on the paper. AutoCAD calls this paper space. Paper space is usually in inches or millimeters, and represents the location on the printed page for a specific layout.

Paper space is not just the coordinates used. When you are looking at a layout view (which represents a piece of paper) and are in the Paper Space mode, anything you draw will appear in that spot on the paper, not in your model.

Each layout has its own paper space, and each contains its own set of objects. In other words, if you put a title block in one layout, it will not appear in another.

Viewports are the interface between paper space and model space. A viewport sits on the page and has paper space coordinates that describe its location on the page. It also contains a view of the model, so it has model space coordinates that describe what you see inside its boundaries. When AutoCAD is in layout mode, you can switch the viewports between paper mode and model mode. In paper mode, you can edit the position of the viewport on the paper, as well as add, delete, and modify graphics on the page. In model mode, you can modify the view of the objects in the viewport as well as add, delete, and modify objects in your model.

When AutoCAD is in model mode, you have the same functionality that you normally have in the model window. Of course, if you are going to be doing a lot of work in model space (for example, when you are initially creating your drawing), you will probably want to switch back to the Model tab.

You have several ways to switch between model space and paper space when you are in a layout view. By far the easiest way to switch to model space is to double-click inside the viewport you want to work in. Similarly, when you wish to switch to paper space, simply double-click outside any viewport.

The mode you are in is shown at the bottom of the AutoCAD window, in the status bar. The last button in the status bar is the paper-space/model-space toggle button. This button provides an easy visual cue for whether you are in paper or model space (it always says the one you are in), and it also provides an alternative way to switch between paper and model space. Pressing this button when you are in model space switches AutoCAD into paper space. Pressing this button when AutoCAD is in paper space toggles to model space for the current viewport.

When you are in model space, the outline of the active viewport becomes thicker. Figure 18.26 shows a viewport in model space and shows you the location of the model/paper space toggle button in the status bar. When you are in model space and there are multiple viewports on the page, you can switch to the model space of a particular viewport by simply clicking anywhere in the viewport you want to activate.

As discussed previously, blocks are a collection of objects, much like a drawing is a collection of objects. What you think of as a drawing is represented inside AutoCAD as a special block called model space. Paper space is represented internally as a block as well. This is fairly technical, and it may not seem like something you need to know, but it helps in two ways. First, it makes it much more obvious that anything you can do in model space you also can do in paper space (or blocks). This is important when you are trying to learn how to create page layouts. Secondly, if you are ever programming AutoCAD using any of its programming interfaces, it is much easier to program if you realize that each of these seemingly different parts of the program is really the same thing as the others.

WORKING WITH TITLE BLOCKS

AutoCAD gives you all the tools to make a different page layout for every drawing that you create, but you will probably want to create one or several standard template layouts to use

PART

IV

CH

18

for most of your drawings. In fact, you might even work in an office that already has standard layouts for the drawings you create. Luckily, AutoCAD also provides functionality to make this easy.

Active
viewport

Figure 18.26
The active viewport has a thicker boundary to show you it is active.

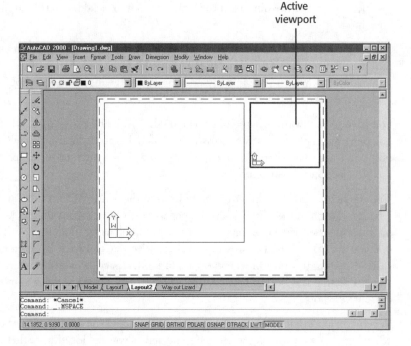

Blocks and xrefs can be used to put objects from other drawings into your current drawing. By using blocks or xrefs, you can use a drawing as a standard template for layouts. AutoCAD comes with many template drawings you can use. You saw these drawings in the Create Layout wizard when you inserted a title block. The following exercise takes you through inserting a title block into your drawing (without using the wizard):

EXAMPLE: INSERTING A TITLE BLOCK INTO THE DRAWING

1. Create a new layout. In the page setup, make it letter size, in inches, and set its orientation as Portrait.

Note

Remember that you can create a new layout with the Insert, Layout, New Layout command. The Page Setup dialog box (which appears automatically when you switch to the new layout tab) will enable you to make the paper setting changes.

2. Just as you did in model space, add a block to paper space using the Insert command. Type **INSERT** at the command line, or choose Insert, Block from the menu. This brings up the Insert dialog box, as shown in Figure 18.27.

Figure 18.27
The Insert dialog box is used to insert blocks into paper space as well as model space.

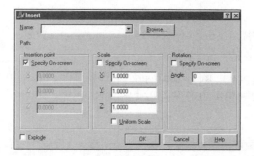

3. Press the Browse button to select a file to insert as a block. In the Select Drawing File dialog box, choose the file ANSI A title block (portrait).dwg, which is in the Templates folder under the AutoCAD folder. Click Open to return to the Insert dialog box.

4. In the Insert dialog box, click OK.

5. Position the cursor so the title block is centered on the page layout. (Note: The cursor position will be near the bottom left of the layout.) Click the mouse to set the block instance in place.

Now you have used another drawing as a template for a page layout. To finish this layout, you would probably want to move the viewport to make it fit into the title block and fill in the information such as drawing name and revision number in the template. Filling in the information is done by using the Mtext or Dtext commands, which are discussed in Chapter 14, "Dimensioning."

Creating your own drawings to use as title blocks is easy. You should create a drawing that contains all the objects you want in your layout. The objects should be in model space because the Insert command uses the objects that are in model space to create the block.

When creating the objects, remember that you should make the total size of the objects fit within the space of a single page. For example, if you are making a template title block for legal-size paper, the object should be 8 1/2 units wide by 14 units tall (assuming that your page will be in inches). Also, just to make your work easier, the lower-left corner of the drawing should be at the origin. This is because when you insert the new block as a title block, if the origin of the drawing is 0,0, you can position it perfectly by typing **0,0** at the command line for the insertion point.

After you have finished creating the objects, you should save your drawing file (with a descriptive name) into the Drawing Template File location (usually the Template folder under your AutoCAD folder, although to be sure, you should check the AutoCAD Options). This makes the drawing show up in lists for title blocks automatically (for example, in the Create Layout wizard).

If you follow these rules, you should not have any trouble creating your own title block templates.

PLOTTING

After you have set up your layout the way you want it, plotting can be as easy as clicking the Plot icon and then choosing OK.

When you plot, all of the options are set through the Plot dialog box, shown in Figure 18.28. Plotting is started by either choosing the File, Plot menu item, or by typing **PLOT** at the command line.

Figure 18.28
The Plot dialog box looks very similar to the Page Setup dialog box.

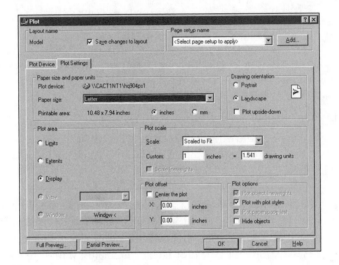

You should notice a couple things about the Plot dialog box. The most obvious thing is that it is almost identical to the Page Setup dialog box that you saw previously in the chapter. Look at the differences: First, you cannot change the name of the page setup. However, you can choose whether to save the changes back to the actual page setup for the layout. When you plot, AutoCAD creates a temporary page setup that matches the page setup for the layout. You can make any changes you wish to the setup of the page, and then when you plot (or choose Cancel), the changes will be applied or not, based on the choice you make in the Layout name frame.

Next, in the Plot Device tab are two new frames asking for information that was not in the Page Setup dialog box. In the What to Plot frame, you can choose which layouts (tabs) to plot and how many copies there should be. In the Plot to File frame, you can send the plot to a file, if you wish. Some plotter configurations and some plotter drivers in AutoCAD force you to plot to a file.

There are no changes at all to the Plot Settings tab of the dialog box. However, there are new options at the bottom of the dialog box that apply to Plot Preview. The next section discusses these options.

Plotting from this dialog box is as simple as verifying your options and then pressing the OK button.

USING PLOT PREVIEW

The plot preview commands found on the Plot dialog box are extremely useful for making sure that you have set up all your page and layout settings the way that you want them. If you are plotting to a quick printer, having a few mistakes may not be a big deal. However, when you are plotting a drawing that takes an hour to plot, you'll want to make sure it is correct before you send it to the plotter. Plot preview does everything plotting will do. It should show you exactly what your plot will look like, as well as give you any error message that might come up. This gives you an opportunity to change the plot settings before you actually plot.

Tip 161 from
Dylan Vance

You can also use plot preview without going into the Plot command. Choose File, Plot Preview, or use the **PREVIEW** command to see a preview of your plot.

The following exercise shows you how you can use plot preview effectively. Assume that instead of showing the whole page, you want to show only a small part of the page, but show it larger to see more detail:

EXAMPLE: USING PLOT PREVIEW

1. Open the ch18_03.dwg file, if it is not already.
2. Click the tab for the Preview Layout page layout.
3. Choose File, Plot to bring up the Plot dialog box.
4. On the Plot Settings tab of the Plot dialog box, in the Plot Area frame, press the Window button. From here you can select a window of the page to plot.
5. Draw a rectangle around the words My Drawing Title and the bottom parts of the two viewports, as in Figure 18.29.

PART
IV
CH
18

Figure 18.29
Draw a window around this part of the layout.

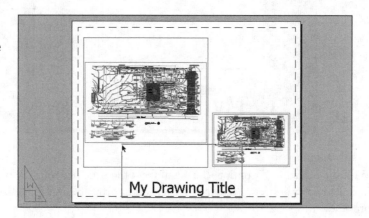

My Drawing Title

6. Back in the Plot dialog box, press the Full Preview button. You should get a preview that looks like Figure 18.30.

Figure 18.30
Previewing your page
before plotting can let
you know that you
have not set up your
page properly.

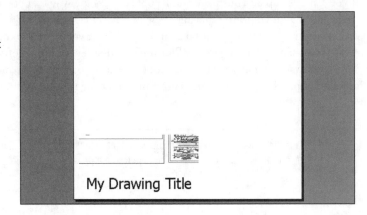

My Drawing Title

7. Because the intent was to show the area larger, this is obviously not what you wanted; this shows only the area that you are interested in, but it shows it at the normal size. Press Enter to return to the Plot dialog box.

8. In the Plot Scale frame, choose Scaled to Fit in the Scale drop-down list box, and then press the Full Preview button again. You should now see a plot preview more like Figure 18.31.

Figure 18.31
The preview shows
you that the page
setup is correct.

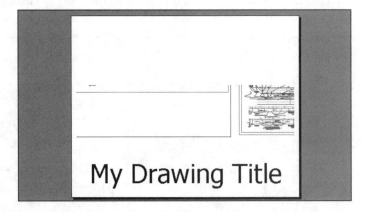

My Drawing Title

9. With the Scaled to Fit option, the detail from the page now fills the plot. Press Enter to exit the plot preview. Press the OK button to print it exactly as you saw it in the preview.

From the beginning of the chapter, you learned about the Create Layout wizard. Now you have learned how to do all the things that the Create Layout wizard does for you, without using the wizard. The wizard is a great way to get up and working quickly, but at times you will need to know how to do these things yourself because the wizard does not give you exactly the plot you want.

Now you know the basics of the way AutoCAD plots. If you have used AutoCAD's plotting before and wonder where all the configuration you are used to has gone, the next section is for you. It details the changes that have happened to plotting in AutoCAD 2000 from previous releases.

CHANGES TO PLOTTING IN RELEASE 2000

Plotting changed considerably in this release of AutoCAD. If you have ever used plotting in previous versions of AutoCAD, you have probably already noticed that there are many differences. Although this is not meant to be a comprehensive comparison of the differences between previous versions and AutoCAD 2000, this section gives you a few details that might help you make the jump from one version to the other. For more information, AutoCAD has a built-in set of help instructions just for you. The first time you try to plot, AutoCAD asks if you would like to see the Fast Track to Plotting Help. This is help designed specifically for users who are familiar with previous releases.

NEW PLOTTER DRIVERS

The biggest change from previous releases is the removal of the old ADI drivers. These have been replaced by HDI (Heidi) drivers, as well as by better support of the Windows system drivers. AutoCAD ships with a few HDI drivers, including one for HPGL/2, but some older plotters (ones that do not emulate HPGL/2 and that do not have Windows system drivers) are no longer supported by AutoCAD. They will work if someone writes an HDI or Windows system driver for them in the future.

This lack of backward-compatibility may seem bad at first, but HDI offers many advantages over ADI. First, it allows AutoCAD to have "what-you-see-is-what-you-get" (WYSIWYG for short) display for the first time. This means that, by default, the way that drawing looks while you are editing it is also the way it will look when you print it. Secondly, all the drivers now support features that were previously supported only by high-end third-party ADI drivers. This includes features such as line-end style, line-join style, line fills, and color screening. Of course, some plotters—especially pen plotters—have hardware reasons why they cannot support all the new features, but devices that cannot handle a feature simply ignore it. Thirdly, this version is faster—both printing and plotting speeds are faster with AutoCAD 2000. Finally, the interface for configuring and managing plotters is much simpler.

PLOTTING CONFIGURATION

AutoCAD Release 14 had three basic components to plotting configuration: the Device Configuration, the What to Plot Settings, and the Pen Assignments. These were stored in .pcp files, .pc2 files, and the acadr14.cfg file. When you install AutoCAD, the program optionally reads the existing configurations and converts as much as possible to the newer formats. AutoCAD also provides tools for individually importing different aspects of configuration from previous releases. The following information will help you if you ever need to import information on your own.

DEVICE CONFIGURATION

Device Configuration has changed names to Plotter Configuration, and it is now stored in pc3 files. Two new UI components can be used to manage and configure plotters. The Add-A-Plotter wizard enables you to add a plotter simply and easily. The Plotter Configuration Editor enables you to modify the settings of a specific configuration after you have created it. You learned about setting up plotters at the beginning of this chapter. The Add-A-Plotter wizard has the option of importing information from the older pcp and pc2 files, if you need to restore information from previous releases of AutoCAD.

Device configuration for Windows system printers also is much easier. Windows system printers now work automatically in AutoCAD, without having to individually configure each one. You need to configure only a system printer if you want to change its default settings when used by AutoCAD.

WHAT TO PLOT SETTINGS

The What to Plot settings are now stored as part of the page setup information for each layout view. This information is stored in the drawing itself, although you can import the settings from one drawing into another. You have learned about this functionality already in the Page Setup section. If you need to import the plot settings in a pcp or pc2 file from a previous release of AutoCAD, there is a wizard for doing so available from Tools, Wizards, Import R14 Plot Settings.

PEN ASSIGNMENTS

Pen assignments are handled completely differently in this release of AutoCAD. Pen assignments are now part of what is called Plot Styles. Pen assignments correlate closely with color-based plot styles, which are stored in ctb files (Plot styles are discussed more fully in the "Plot Styles" section, later in this chapter). You can convert older pen assignments from pcp, pc2, or cfg files into plot styles using one of the two wizards discussed in that section.

PAPER SIZES

Paper sizes have also been changed in this release of AutoCAD. In previous releases, page sizes were defined as the printable area on a page. Now, paper size is defined by the total size of the paper, its nonprintable area (the margins), and its orientation. If you change the default settings for a plotter, the changes are stored in a .pmp file. All the changes for a single plotter are stored in the same pmp file (separate from the pc3 file or files for the plotter). This means that all plotter configurations (pc3 files) for the same physical plotter can share the same paper sizes without you having to recreate them each time.

Although it may take you a little time to get used to the new plotting tools, you will soon find them much easier to use, better organized, and better integrated with the Windows environment than ever before.

USING ADVANCED PLOTTING FEATURES

Now that you have learned all about plotting from AutoCAD, you are ready to learn about the advanced features in the plotting engine. This section includes discussion of several advanced topics involved with plotting. New in AutoCAD 2000, plot styles let you change the look of a drawing without modifying your data—with just a change of configurations, you can create different plots in the blink of an eye. This section also includes using the plotting engine to get other output from AutoCAD. Finally, this section describes alternatives to plotting.

PLOT STYLES

AutoCAD uses a new feature, called *plot styles*, to control the way an object will look when it plots. The default for plot styles in AutoCAD makes objects plot the same way they look on the screen. Up to now, this chapter has ignored plot styles and has used them in exactly this default way. However, plot styles grant you lots of flexibility when you are plotting to change the way your drawings look.

Plotting styles for objects in AutoCAD have traditionally been assigned by color. The color of an object decided the pen used to plot. This was true of pen plotters, where the pen would be an actual physical pen, as well as other plotters, where "pen" is simply a designation for a line style that includes line color, line weight, and line type. This was called *Pen Assignment*. The problem with this is that it limited the use of colors, and made "what you see is what you get" plotting more difficult because the color of an object would not necessarily match how it would plot.

In AutoCAD 2000, pen assignments have been replaced with plot styles. Plot styles work in one of two modes: *Named* or *Color-Dependent*. Color-Dependent mode is very similar to the old Pen Assignment method of controlling plots, and this is the initial default in AutoCAD. Named plot styles add a new property to objects, which allows color to be separate from the plot style. With this property, each object can have a plot style that is associated with it by name.

In either Named or Color-Dependent mode, the plot style on the object is simply a reference used for association; it does not actually contain the style information. The style information is contained in a style table, which is simply a list of all the available styles, and a definition for each one. Separating this into a different place enables you to replace the entire table if you want. In fact, in AutoCAD, the style tables are contained in separate files from the drawing or configuration files. This enables you to easily share plot style tables between drawings as well as with other AutoCAD users.

You can use plot style tables to create standards for your department. And changing from one department to another one that has different standards can be as simple as changing the plot style table. However, this does require that all of the people sharing these drawings use the same naming conventions for Named plot styles.

The default style tables (in either mode) simply tell AutoCAD to plot the features as they appear on screen. Because of this, the default in AutoCAD is to have WYSIWYG plotting.

CHANGING THE PLOT STYLE TABLE

Take a look at the effects of replacing one style table with another. In the following exercise, you use the ch18_03.dwg file that you have seen earlier in this chapter, and you preview it with no style table. Then you will see it with two other styles tables just to see how they can affect the way your drawing is plotted:

Tip 162 from *Dylan Vance*	If you have two plotters that require different pen assignments, you can use plot styles to set them up. Then, changing between those plotters can be as simple as using a different plot style table.

EXAMPLE: CHANGING THE PLOT STYLE TABLE

1. Open the ch18_03.dwg file, if it is not already open. This drawing uses Color-Dependent plot styles, so assigning or changing the plot style table will affect the way that it looks.

2. Click the layout tab marked PreviewLayout at the bottom of the drawing window.

3. Choose the File, Plot menu item. This brings up the Plot dialog box.

4. Click the Plot Device tab. Notice the Plot Style Table (Pen Assignments) frame in the middle of the tabbed area of the dialog box. It should say None, meaning no plot style table is associated with the drawing, and AutoCAD will simply use the styles associated with the individual objects.

5. Press the Full Preview button at the bottom of the dialog box. You should see a preview of the page that looks almost identical to the page layout that was previously onscreen, as in Figure 18.32. Press the Enter key to return to the Plot dialog box.

6. In the Plot Style Table (Pen Assignments) frame, choose Monochrome.ctb from the list of plot style tables. Now press the Full Preview button again. The preview should be all black. Press the Enter key to return to the Plot dialog box.

Figure 18.32
The plot preview with
no plot style table is
WYSIWYG.

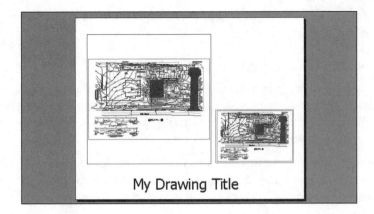

7. Now choose the Screening 50%.ctb plot style table. Press the Full Preview button again to see a lightly screened preview, as in Figure 18.33.

Figure 18.33
The plot preview with
the Screening 50%
plot style table is
lighter.

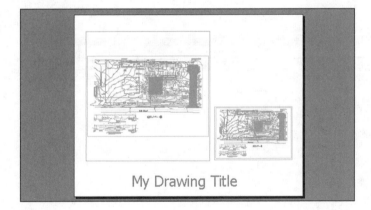

PART

IV

CH

18

8. Press the Enter key to return to the Plot dialog box, and then press the Cancel button to exit the Plot command.

From this, you can tell that changing a plot style table can greatly affect the way your objects are plotted. As you might guess from the fact that the plot style table choice is on the Page Setup and Plot dialog boxes, a plot style table is associated with each layout. This means that you can set up each layout to plot the way that you would like and, without affecting the other layouts, set each one to plot with their own colors and linestyles.

Tip 163 from
Dylan Vance

You can also display plot styles in any layout view by selecting Display Plot Styles in the page setup for that layout.

Now that you have an idea of what plot style tables do, you can learn more about what they are and how to create and edit them.

CREATING AND MODIFYING PLOT STYLE TABLES

To really learn what a plot style table is, you will now define a new one. Two types of plot style tables exist, to go along with the two modes in which plot styles can work: Color-Dependent and Named. Each type is basically a table of style definitions—one for each color or name—based on the type of plot style table.

A plot style table is stored in a file with either a ctb (Color-Dependent) or stb (Named style) extension. Both are created in the same way. The following exercise creates a Color-Dependent plot style table where each of the colors is 50% screened and converted to grayscale:

EXAMPLE: CREATING A PLOT STYLE TABLE

1. Choose File, Plot Style Manager to bring up the Plot Style Manager, shown in Figure 18.34.

Figure 18.34
The Plot Style Manager is a Windows Explorer window.

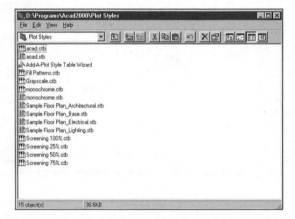

2. The Plot Style Manager, like the Plotter Manager, is actually just a Windows Explorer window that shows you the files in the Plot Styles folder. This is where all the .ctb and .stb files are located. There is also a shortcut to the Add-A-Plot Style Table wizard. Double-clicking a style table enables you to edit that table, and double-clicking the wizard shortcut enables you to create a new table. Double-click the Add-A-Plot Style Table wizard icon to bring up the first page of the Add-A-Plot Style Table wizard, as shown in Figure 18.35.

3. The first page of the wizard is simply informational text. Click Next to continue to the second page of the wizard, as shown in Figure 18.36.

Figure 18.35
The Add-A-Plot Style
Table wizard enables
you to create a new
plot style table.

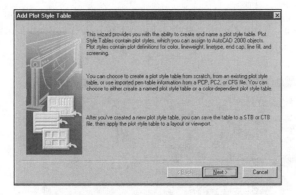

Figure 18.36
The second page of
the wizard asks you
how to start the plot
style table.

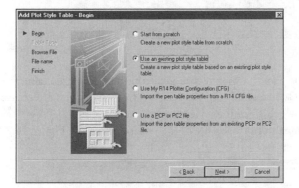

4. In this case, you will start with the 50% screened plot style table because that is similar
to the one you want to create. Choose the Use an Existing Plot Style Table option, and
then click Next. This takes you to the fourth page of the wizard (the third page, which
asks you the type of table to create, is skipped because the existing one you chose makes
that choice for you). Figure 18.37 shows the fourth page of the wizard.

Figure 18.37
The next page asks
you to choose the file
to copy.

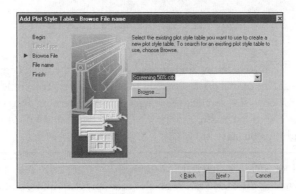

5. On the fourth page, choose the Screening 50%.ctb file from the drop-down list. Because this is a ctb file, the plot style table is Color-Dependent. Click <u>N</u>ext to continue to the fifth page of the wizard, shown in Figure 18.38.

Figure 18.38
This page asks you to enter a name for the new plot style table.

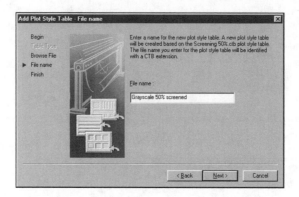

6. On the fifth page of the wizard, you give your new plot style table a name. Type **Grayscale 50% screened** into the text box (remember you are creating a new plot style table in which all of the styles are grayscale and dimmed by 50%), and then click <u>N</u>ext to continue to the last page of the wizard, shown in Figure 18.39.

Figure 18.39
Here, you can finish the plot style table.

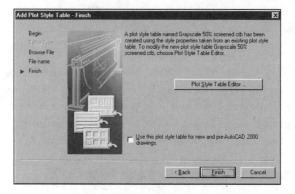

7. At this point, all you have left to do is the actual edits to the table (right now you have an exact copy of the original 50% screened plot style table). You could do that from this page, but for now, simply click the Finish button. The next exercise will take you through editing the (now) existing table. The Plot Style Table Editor works the same way, whichever way you start it.

When the Add-A-Plot Style Table wizard is complete, you are returned to the Plot Style Manager (remember that the Plot Style Manager is simply an Explorer window for the Plot

Styles directory. From here, you can edit any of the style table files. This next exercise shows you how to edit the Grayscale 50% screened Color-Dependent style table that you just created:

EXAMPLE: EDITING A PLOT STYLE TABLE

1. Double-click the Grayscale 50% screened.ctb file in the Plot Style Manager. This brings up the Plot Style Table Editor, shown in Figure 18.40.

Figure 18.40
The Plot Style Table Editor enables you to make the real edits to your plot style table.

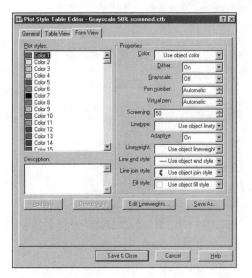

2. The Plot Style Table Editor has three tabs. The General tab gives you information about the plot style table and enables you to enter a description for the table, if you would like. The other two tabs show two different views of the same information. For this exercise, you will use the Table view. Click the Table View tab at the top of the dialog box. This brings up a tabular view of the plot styles in the file, shown in Figure 18.41.

Tip 164 from
Dylan Vance

> The Form view is good if you are creating a number of individual styles, such as for standards in your company or in order to create pen assignments for your plotter. It makes modifying or adding a single plot style easy. In this case, the Table view is used because it makes it easier to modify the entire set of styles at once.

3. Because this is a Color-Dependent plot style table, there are style settings for each color. You can set all the style properties that will be used to plot objects of that color. Many of the settings in this plot style table are set to the Use object setting. This means the plot style does not change the way the object will be plotted for those

PART

IV

CH

18

settings. Right now the only setting that is changed is the screening, which has been set to 50% for every color style. To complete this plot style table, you want to change every style to include the Convert to grayscale setting. After this exercise is a list of each of the settings and what they mean. In the first column of the Convert to grayscale row, click the check box so it is checked.

Figure 18.41
The Table view enables you to view and modify all the styles simultaneously.

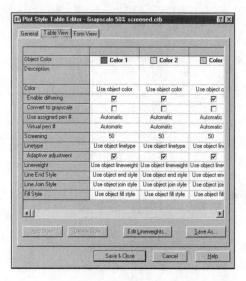

4. Press the right arrow key to move over one column, and then press the spacebar to check the next check box.

5. You could continue to press the right arrow and spacebar until every column has been checked (there are 255), but there is an easier way. Right-click one of the two cells that you just checked. On the shortcut menu, choose Copy. Then right-click again and choose Paste to All Styles. This means every column will have Convert to grayscale checked.

Tip 165 from
Dylan Vance

Using the right click menu item "Paste to All Styles" is a quick way to modify all of the styles in a plot style table at once.

---

6. At the bottom of the Plot Style Table Editor, press the Save & Close button. This saves your changes and closes the editor.

7. Press the X button at the top right of the Plotter Manager window to close it and return to AutoCAD.

You have now created a useful new plot style table. You may use this to plot any drawings that use Color-Dependent mode. Many settings exist for a plot style, and some may be confusing. The following list describes each one and what they do:

- Name—This is the name of the style. For Color-Dependent plot styles, this is the name of the color and is not modifiable. For Named plot styles, you can have any name you want (except Normal, because that is reserved, as you shall see). There is a limit of 255 characters, and you cannot have duplicate names.

- Description—This is the description of the style. Again, you can put any text you want into this setting.

- Color—This is the color in which objects that use this style will be plotted. The default is Use object color, which simply means to use the color assigned to the object.

- Enable Dithering—Dithering means approximating colors by using patterns of other colors overlaid. This gives the impression of plotting with more colors than are available. Dithering is usually turned off for several reasons. The first is that thin lines that are dithered often appear as a series of dots and dashes rather than as continuous lines. Secondly, dim colors may appear even dimmer when dithered. When dithering is turned off, AutoCAD automatically chooses the closest color available. The default is on.

- Convert to Grayscale—This setting converts the color in which the object would plot to a gray color that has the same value (darkness). The default is off.

- Use Assigned Pen Number—This setting applies only to pen plotters. It specifies a pen to use when plotting objects that use this plot style. Pens range from 1 to 32, although if the pen plotter has fewer pens, the pens should range only through the actual physical pen numbers. Setting the value to 0 sets this to Automatic. In Automatic mode, AutoCAD chooses the best pen by looking at the pen characteristics in the plotter configuration. For more information on plotter configuration, see the section "Using the Add-A-Plotter wizard," at the beginning of this chapter, and the section "Changes to Plotting in Release 2000."

- Virtual Pen Number—Some non-pen plotters can simulate pen plotters using virtual pens. If you want to use this feature of your plotter, you can set the virtual pen number between 1 and 255. Choosing 0 sets this to Automatic. In Automatic mode, AutoCAD will make the virtual pen assignment based on the color mode. Because a virtual pen includes all the style information for drawing, using virtual pens ignores all other settings in the plot style.

- Screening—This setting determines the amount of ink used on the paper. This is a percentage from 0 to 100. Zero means that no ink will be placed on the paper, and 100 means that the color will be printed normally (at full intensity). Basically, this means if you set the color to less than 100, it will be lighter than normal. The default is 100.

- Linetype—This is a linetype used to print a line. The default is Use object linetype, which uses the linetype defined with the object.

- Adaptive Adjustment—This setting adjusts the scale of a linetype to complete the linetype pattern at the end of the line. For example, if a linetype is made up of two dashes with a long space between them, a line drawn with this pattern may end in the middle of a space (and, therefore, you would not be able to see the end of the line). Using this

PART

IV

CH

18

setting would automatically make the pattern end on a dash. Use this setting if it is important to see the entire line. Do not use this setting if it is more important that the scale of the linetype pattern be the same throughout. The default is on.

- Lineweight—This is the thickness of a plotted line in millimeters. The default is Use object lineweight. This setting can be any value, although AutoCAD gives you only a small number of choices. To add your own setting to the choices, use the Edit Lineweights button in the Plot Style Table Editor.

- Line End Style—This option enables you to choose a line end style for objects plotted with this plot style. The default setting is Use object end style.

- Line Join Style—This option enables you to choose a line join style for objects plotted with this plot style. The default setting is Use object join style.

- Fill Style—This option enables you to choose a fill style for objects plotted with this plot style. The default setting is Use object fill style.

USING NAMED PLOT STYLES

Up to this point, all the exercises have taught you about Color-Dependent plot styles. Named plot styles are very similar to Color-Dependent plot styles, but there are a couple of differences you should learn to help you work with them.

Named plot styles are more flexible than Color-Dependent plot styles. You can have as many or as few styles in a Named plot style table as you want. Named plot styles are not based on color, so objects that are the same color can have different plot styles. For example, you might have a plot style called Support Walls and another called Non-support Walls. You might want objects on your drawing that are support walls to be red, and you might also want features on your drawing that are non-support walls to be red. However, when they plot, you might want to differentiate them in a way not shown onscreen. By assigning each one a different Named plot style, you can do this.

Named plot styles also involve a little bit more work than Color-Dependent plot styles. Named plot styles add another property to each object that you can set with the Properties window, the Properties toolbar, or using the PLOTSTYLE command.

The default Named plot style for objects is ByLayer. This implies, correctly, that each layer has a plot style associated with it. The default Named plot style for layers is the Normal plot style, which you will learn more about later in this section. You can change the plot style for a layer with the Layer command.

Every drawing is either in Color-Dependent mode or Named mode when it is first created, and you cannot change it. The only exception to this is drawings from previous versions of AutoCAD, which have a mode assigned to them the first time you save them in AutoCAD 2000.

There are two ways to create drawings in the mode that you want. A setting in AutoCAD's options (Tools, Options, Plotting tab, Default Plot Style Behavior for New Drawings frame) enables you to change the default behavior when you create a new drawing. Also, if you use File, New, you can choose from different templates that are either Color-Dependent or Named.

The following exercise takes you through creating a new drawing that uses Named plot styles, chooses a plot style table for the new drawing, and adds a new plot style to the plot style table:

EXAMPLE: USING NAMED PLOT STYLES

1. Create a new drawing by choosing the New option from the File pull-down menu.

2. In the Create New Drawing dialog box, press the third button across the top (the Use a Template button). This should give you a list of templates similar to those shown in Figure 18.42.

Use a Template button

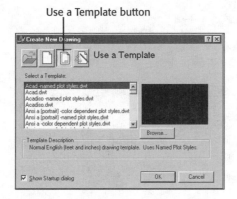

Figure 18.42
You can choose templates in Named plot style mode or Color-Dependent plot style mode.

3. Choose the Acad –named plot styles.dwt file from the list. This is the standard AutoCAD drawing template, but it uses Named styles rather than Color-Dependent styles. Press OK to close the dialog box and create the new drawing using that template.

4. Choose Format, Plot Style from the menu. This brings up the Current Plot Style dialog box, shown in Figure 18.43.

5. In the Active Plot Style Table frame, choose the ACAD.STB from the drop-down list of plot style tables. This automatically sets the Model tab of the drawing to use that style table. Press the Editor button to modify the plot style table. This brings up the Plot Style Table Editor for acad.stb, as in Figure 18.44.

Look at the differences between this plot style table and the Color-Dependent plot style tables you saw earlier. First, notice that there are only two plot styles in this table. A Named plot style table can have as few as one plot style, or as many as you would like. Also, notice that the first plot style is called Normal and is grayed out. Every Named plot style table has a Normal plot style, which is simply set to use the object's style settings.

This plot style is read-only and cannot be modified. Modifying Named plot styles works exactly the same as modifying Color-Dependent ones, except that you can also modify the name of the plot style. However, you can add new plot styles to a Named plot style table. For the completion of this exercise, you will create a new plot style called Dimmed, which will have 50% screening.

Figure 18.43
The Current Plot Style dialog box enables you to choose the style to use for new entities and the plot style table that is active.

Figure 18.44
When editing Named plot styles, the Plot Style Table Editor is almost identical to when it is used to edit Color-Dependent plot styles.

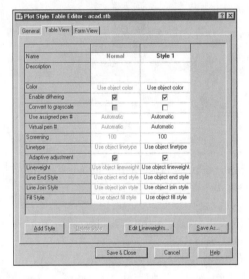

6. Click the Add Style button at the bottom of the Plot Style Table Editor. You will automatically be placed into the Name field of the new style. Type the name **Dimmed** into the Name field.

7. Click in the Screening row for the new style, and type **50**.

8. Press the Save & Close button at the bottom of the Plot Style Table Editor.

9. Finally, press OK to exit the Current Plot Style dialog box.

Now you have a drawing setup that uses Named plot styles, and you have modified the plot style table that is associated with the Model tab. As a final exercise, you will create some objects, set their plot styles, and then see how that affects the plot:

EXAMPLE: SETTING OBJECT PLOT STYLES

1. Use the Line command to quickly draw some lines in the drawing. Press Enter when you are done. You should have something that looks similar to Figure 18.45.

Figure 18.45
Draw some lines for this exercise.

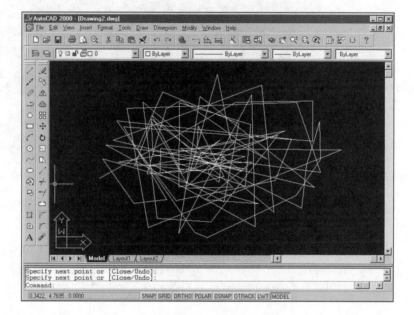

2. Select all the objects you just created by drawing a rectangle around them.

3. Press Ctrl+1 to bring up the Properties window (if it is already visible, it will go away when you hit Ctrl+1; you may have to use Ctrl+1 to make it visible again).

4. In the Properties window, in the Plot Style field, choose Normal from the drop-down list. This sets all the lines to Normal. This is not strictly necessary, but it is useful for this exercise.

5. Press Esc twice to deselect all the lines, and then draw a new rectangle to select only the middle two lines.

6. Type **PLOTSTYLE** at the command line to bring up the Select Plot Style dialog box. Select Dimmed from the list, and then press OK. This changes the plot style only for those objects that you have currently selected.

7. Select a different set of objects (for example, the bottom half of the screen), and change their color to red (you could use the Object Properties toolbar, the Properties window,

or any other method you want). You should have a drawing that looks something like that in Figure 18.46.

Figure 18.46
You should now have some red and some white lines, but they should all be full color.

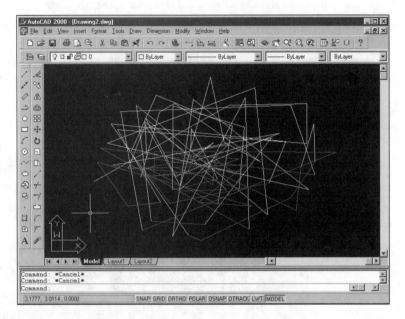

8. Finally, choose File, Plot Preview to see a preview of the Model tab using the plot styles you just chose. Your screen should look like the one shown in Figure 18.47. Notice that the color (red or black) is separate from the plot style (normal or dimmed).

Figure 18.47
Half the objects are lighter than the others, as defined by the Dimmed plot style.

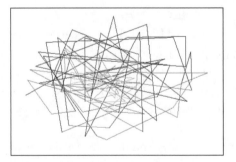

If you had another plot style table that defined Dimmed as full screening but grayscale, you could assign that to the model, and those objects that were dimmed would be gray. In fact, you could have as many different plot style tables as you want, each defining Dimmed in a different way, and you could assign them to different layouts—or, each time you plot you could assign a new plot style table to the plot. Because plot style tables are defined outside the drawing, you can now use the acad.stb and its new Dimmed plot style in any other drawing that is in Named plot style mode.

Now, you have a good working knowledge of plot styles. Next, you will look into another advanced topic dealing with plotting: using the plotting engine for creating files rather than paper output.

PLOTTING RASTER FILES

AutoCAD enables you to use the plotting engine to create raster images from your data. Although we traditionally think of plotting as creating paper output, it turns out that the majority of the process is the graphics processing that tells the plotter how to print. The same graphics processing applies to creating raster images or drawing Web format (dwf) files.

You can create files in many raster formats, although you must set up a plotter configuration for each one. The following exercise takes you through setting up a pc3 file for JPEG output:

PART IV

CH

18

EXAMPLE: SETTING UP A FILE FOR JPEG OUPUT

1. Choose Tools, Wizards, Add Plotter to start the Add-A-Plotter wizard. Previously in this chapter, you did this by starting the Plotter Manager first, although this is not necessary if you know you want to add a new plotter without going to the Plotter Manager. In the first screen, click Next.

2. In the second screen, select the My Computer option, and press the Next button to display the fifth screen (remember that the third and fourth screens are skipped when you choose the My Computer option).

3. In the fifth screen, choose Raster File Formats from the Manufacturers list, and choose Independent JPEG Group JFIF (JPEG Compression) from the Models list. Notice that there are many other raster file formats to choose from as well. Click Next to continue to the seventh screen of the wizard.

4. In the seventh screen, simply click Next because you do not want to import settings from previous versions of AutoCAD. This brings up the eighth screen.

5. For the raster file format drivers, there is no port option; you must choose the Plot to File option. Click Next to continue to the ninth screen.

6. In the ninth screen, give the new driver configuration the name AutoCAD JPEG File, and then click Next to continue to the final screen in the wizard.

7. In the final screen, press Finish to complete the plotter setup.

You have now set up this driver to allow you to plot to JPEG files directly from the Plot dialog box. The following exercise shows you how to create a JPEG file from your drawing, for example, to use on a Web page:

EXAMPLE: CREATING A JPEG FILE TO USE ON A WEB PAGE

1. Open a drawing and choose the layout that you want to convert to JPEG.

2. Choose File, Plot command. Press the No button if AutoCAD asks you to see the Fast Track to Plotting Help.

3. On the Plot Device tab, choose the AutoCAD JPEG File plotter.

4. On the same tab, choose the filename and path that you want to create (the default is the name of the drawing and the name of the layout, in the folder where the drawing is located).

5. On the Plot Settings tab, choose the resolution for the file you want to create.

6. In the Plot Scale frame, choose Scaled to Fit. You will probably always want to use this option for raster image plotting, or else you will need to create new title blocks that match the resolution at which you want to create JPEG's files.

7. In the Plot Area frame, choose Extents.

8. Press the Full Preview button to see how the raster image will look when plotted.

9. Press Enter to exit the preview.

10. Click OK to plot.

With this, you have created a JPEG file that can be used in Web pages or imported into graphics programs to be viewed and modified.

Creating JPEG files for use on the Internet simply creates a static file that shows your drawing. For a more dynamic file that allows users to zoom and pan in your drawing, you can use the Drawing Web Format, as described in the next section.

MAKING YOUR DRAWING FILES VIEWABLE FROM THE INTERNET

Just as you use the plotting engine to create JPEG files, you can also use it to create a special kind of drawing file called a dwf file (dwf stands for "drawing Web format.") This is similar to the dwg drawing format, but it is designed to be used on the Internet. If you did a full install of AutoCAD, two plot configurations were created automatically for working with dwf files: the DWF Classic and DWF ePlot configurations. DWF Classic creates DWF files that resemble model space (they have black backgrounds). The DWF ePlot configuration creates dwf files that resemble paper space; they have white backgrounds and a paper boundary.

If you publish a dwf file to the Internet, the people accessing your Web site will require a special viewer called the Whip! viewer.

You have now learned much that there is to know about plotting in AutoCAD. You can do a lot of exploring with the features that you have learned about so far in this chapter. The last section of this chapter tells you about alternatives to plotting.

Outputting Your Drawing in Other Ways

This chapter has been all about plotting, but there are times when you must find an alternative way to output your drawings, whether it is to another application (for example, a word processing or page layout program) or to another person (for example, a service bureau).

When you are trying to get your drawing into another program, there are several ways to go about this. You have already learned about exporting to raster graphics programs by plotting raster images such as JPEG that can be imported into other programs.

Another way to get your drawings into other programs is to use the built-in graphics export commands in AutoCAD. You can learn and type each graphics export command independently, but it is much easier to remember the single command EXPORT, which combines them all into one.

> **Note**
>
> Using the Export command, you can create bitmap files (BMP) and Windows metafiles (WMFs), which is the Windows standard for simple graphics that is supported by most Microsoft programs, such as Word or PowerPoint, as well as many other Windows software programs. You can also create EPS files, which are used or imported by many high-end vector graphics programs, such as Adobe Illustrator. The Export command also exports other file formats that enable you to work in other CAD-like programs, such as 3DS (3D studio file), SAT (ACIS solid object file), STL (stereo lithography file), and DXX (attribute extract DXF file).

Finally, you can use Copy and Paste to copy drawings into such programs as Word, which supports embedding OLE objects. In this case, what you actually get is a DWG file embedded into the (in this case) Word document. It will display like a graphic object, but it can be edited if you double-click it. If you do this, you bring up AutoCAD to do the editing, but you update the Word document when it is done.

If you plan to create high-end graphics for publications, you may want to send your output to a service bureau for the actual plotting. If you do this, you should ask the service bureau what format they want the drawings in. They may want you to plot to a specific plot device but plot to file. They may be able to plot directly from the DWG file. The most likely case is that they will ask for an EPS file. You can use the Export command to create an EPS file, although a shortcut is to use the PSOUT command, which has the same functionality but takes you directly to the EPS export part of the command. The other advantage of using EPS (besides its widespread use) is that you can use Adobe Illustrator or another vector drawing program to get the exact look you want. The most common thing people want to do in their drawings but often have trouble doing is creating the proper fills for polygons.

Vector graphics programs, such as Adobe Illustrator, are filled with tools for fine tuning the look of graphics, including the fills.

AutoCAD provides many ways to get your drawings onto paper or into presentations. Chances are that you will learn and use one or two of these methods on a regular basis, but continue to experiment with everything you learned in this chapter. You will become better at getting what you want out of AutoCAD.

SUMMARY

Plotting in AutoCAD 2000 has changed drastically from previous releases. It is now very well integrated with the Windows printing system, and configuration has gotten much simpler than it was in previous releases. Similarly, the interface and drivers have become simpler, faster, and easier to use.

With all this ease of use, Autodesk has also made obsolete all of the knowledge that long-time users of AutoCAD have gained over years of using the product.

Whether you are a new user or have been using AutoCAD for years, hopefully this chapter answers your questions, and shows you how easy and powerful plotting can be in AutoCAD.

CHAPTER 19

INTERNET PUBLISHING

In this chapter

USING THE INTERNET TO ACCESS AND VIEW DRAWINGS

With the popularity of the Internet and corporate intranets growing at a phenomenal rate, it only makes sense to expand AutoCAD's Internet-based functionality. You'll find this has been accomplished by adding several Internet-aware tools that make working with the Internet easier. Whether you want to collaborate on a project over the Internet or just open files from a corporate intranet site, this chapter will show you how to use the features in AutoCAD 2000 to accomplish these tasks.

WEB-ENABLED FILE DIALOG BOXES

Most of the file dialog boxes within AutoCAD 2000 recognize Internet file addresses, or uniform resource locators (URLs), which means you can easily access files from Internet sites. Just as with opening a file from your hard drive or from a network, you need to know the file's path or location. In the case of using URLs, these indicate the location of the Internet Web server and indicate where a file resides on the server.

The commands Open, Save As, and Xref provide the capability to open or save drawing files via the Internet. In addition, you can also open and save to several other Internet-based file types, such as DWF, LSP, SCR, MNU, and MNX. The following examples show you how to access different files from the Internet using these commands, in addition to incorporating Web-based files into your drawing using AutoCAD DesignCenter.

EXAMPLE: OPENING AN AUTOCAD FILE VIA THE INTERNET

1. From the File pull-down menu or the Standard toolbar, select the Open command. Rather than entering a filename, click the Search the Web button (see Figure 19.1).

Figure 19.1

Click the Search the Web button instead of entering a filename.

2. This opens the Browse the Web–Open dialog box, shown in Figure 19.2.
3. The Look in: edit box is useful when you are not certain of the complete URL and you want to browse the directory for the file you want, or if you want to avoid typing in a long URL. Use the File name: edit box to type in the full URL of the file you want to open. Make certain to include the full address of the file. The following are examples of what an Internet address should look like:

    `http://www.autodesk.com/exercise/expo98e.dwg`

    or

    `ftp://www.autodesk.com/exercise/expo98e.dwg`

Figure 19.2
The Browse the Web–Open dialog box can be used to download files from an Internet site or to upload files to a remote site.

Note

When using the Open command, there is no difference between using http or ftp to access a drawing file. Ftp stands for File Transfer Protocol, which can be used to download a file from an Internet site. The protocol that is used is determined by the administrator of the site from which you are accessing the file, depending on the rights you have been assigned. Check with the site administrator for the correct protocol to use.

PART
IV
CH
19

4. This places the filename in the File Name box of the Select File dialog box. Clicking the Open button opens the file from the Web-based site into the Drawing Editor.

Tip 166 from
Ron House

To save a file to a Web-based site, simply use a URL with the Save or Save As commands with the ftp protocol format. The http protocol cannot be used to save a drawing file, so you must use the ftp protocol.

To save a location to your Favorites folder from within the Browse the Web–Save dialog box, click the Favorites button. This opens a list of your saved favorites, and at the top of the list is the Add to Favorites… option. Selecting this option enables you to type in the name of the shortcut for your favorite, which is then added to the list of Favorites.

ATTACHING AN EXTERNAL REFERENCE FILE FROM THE INTERNET

The process for attaching an external reference file is similar to opening a file from the Internet.

→ You can learn more about external reference files in Chapter 17, "External Reference Files and Importing Images."

There are a number of advantages to referencing files from a Web-based server, especially if you are collaborating with multiple consultants on a single project located in various cities throughout the world. Because all drawing files for the project are saved on a single server, changes being made to the consultant's files enables you to see the most up-to-date modifications by reloading the external reference files attached to your drawing. The project is more dynamic, and it enables you to quickly view updates to the overall project as the work continues. No more waiting to receive files from the consultant to view their changes—you can view them as soon as they are saved to the server.

The next example walks you through the process of attaching an external reference file from a site on the Internet. Imagine you want to attach the latest version of the changes to a building elevation available from a consultant's Web site. (To further illustrate attaching a file via the Internet, you will attach an example exercise file from Autodesk's Web site).

EXAMPLE: ATTACHING AN XREF FROM A WEB SITE

1. Create a new drawing using an ANSI D size template.

2. Toggle to model space by clicking the Model tab.

3. From the pull-down menus, select Insert, External Reference.

4. Type **http://www.autodesk.com/exercise/expo98e.dwg** in the File Name edit box in the Select Reference File dialog box. Another option is to select the Search the Web button and type in the URL in the Browse the Web dialog box.

5. Click the Open button to start downloading the file.

6. Use the External Reference dialog box to set the insertion point, scale factor, and rotation angle of the file. For this example, do not select any of the Specify On Screen check boxes, but use the default values for each parameter. Then click the OK button.

7. When the file has finished loading, use the Zoom Extents command to view the extents of the external reference file.

8. Double-click the Paper/Model tile from the status bar, toggling to model space. Repeat the Zoom Extents command in model space to fit the external reference file inside the architectural border.

9. Select from the status bar the Paper/Model tile to return to paper space.

→ Refer to Chapter 18, "Plotting and Layouts," for information on using paper space and model space.

→ The section "Project Collaboration and Buzzsaw.com" later in this chapter, shows how you can easily collaborate with your colleagues across the globe using the Internet and Autodesk's new e-commerce venture, Buzzsaw.com. You can sign up to host your project on this site by pointing your browser to http://www.buzzsaw.com.

On Buzzsaw.com and other Internet-based project-collaboration Web sites similar to it, you can actually download and insert blocks from various vendor symbol libraries off the Internet right into your drawing. The next section discusses how to do so by using AutoCAD Design Center.

OPENING INTERNET-BASED FILES USING AUTOCAD DESIGNCENTER

Loading a drawing into the AutoCAD DesignCenter from the Internet gives you the capability to attach layers, blocks, other external reference files, linetypes, and much more. This allows you to obtain current information from the source drawing file and enables you to obtain the most up-to-date blocks in your symbol libraries.

The next example shows you how to insert a block from a file located on a Web server.

EXAMPLE: INSERTING A BLOCK USING AUTOCAD DESIGNCENTER FROM THE INTERNET

1. Open the AutoCAD DesignCenter in your current drawing. Right-click in the DesignCenter window, and choose Load from the shortcut menu.

2. Select the Search the Web button from the Load DesignCenter Palette dialog box.

3. Open the file located at this address: `http://www.autodesk.com/exercise/arch01.dwg`

4. After the file is loaded, expand the tree listing for this drawing to access the various components of the file.

5. Click on the Blocks component, and then drag and drop the P90-17 door and door swing from this file into your drawing.

Use this process to access into the AutoCAD DesignCenter objects from other drawings without the need to open the file to access blocks and other objects.

In addition to inserting blocks located on the Internet, you can also attach hyperlinks to drawing objects that link to other project files. The next section will show you how to place and edit hyperlinks in your drawings.

INSERTING HYPERLINKS INTO DRAWING FILES

Hyperlinks can be inserted into drawing files to link to other associated files, such as other drawing files, Windows documents (Excel, Word, PowerPoint, and so on), and URLs. This provides an efficient way of integrating all the documents related to a project into your AutoCAD drawings. These documents can come from a local or network drive as well as an Internet site.

Begin by opening the Insert Hyperlink dialog box. Using the pull-down menus, choose Insert, Hyperlink, which opens the Insert Hyperlink dialog box.

PART

IV

CH

19

Tip 167 from
Ron House

The Insert Hyperlink command can also be accessed by selecting the Insert Hyperlink button from the Standard toolbar (see Figure 19.3).

This command can also be quickly activated by pressing Ctrl+K.

Figure 19.3
Access the Insert
Hyperlink button from
the Standard toolbar.

It is a good idea to save your drawing before inserting a hyperlink, which AutoCAD will prompt you to do before continuing, as Figure 19.4 illustrates. If the drawing is not saved, AutoCAD cannot determine the default relative directory for the new hyperlink.

Figure 19.4
AutoCAD will alert
you if the drawing
has not been saved
before attaching a
hyperlink to a
drawing.

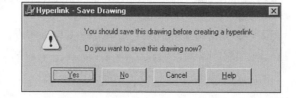

After the drawing has been saved, select the objects you want to attach the hyperlink to and press Enter. The Internet Hyperlink dialog box opens, as shown in Figure 19.5.

Figure 19.5
The Insert Hyperlink
dialog box contains
all the options
available for creating
hyperlinks in a
drawing.

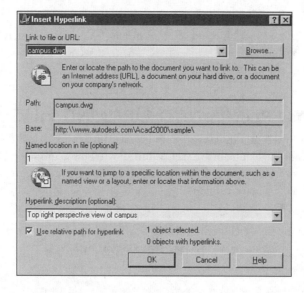

These are the options available:

■ Link to File or URL—This is the filename or URL to which you want to link.

Tip 168 from
Ron House

You can set the default path for all links by setting the HYPERLINKBASE setting variable to the desired default Internet address. When the HYPERLINKBASE setting variable has been set, only the filename needs to be entered at the Link to File or URL box. Then the base path address will appear in the Base edit box for every new link you create and will be appended automatically.

- Browse—This option enables you to define the location of the file. Browse to the location of the file located on you local disk, or use the Search the Web button to specify a URL.

- Path—The path and filename are displayed here, unless the Use Relative Path for Hyperlink option is checked—then only the filename is shown.

- Base—This sets the default path for all hyperlinks in the drawing. If the HYPERLINKBASE setting variable has been previously set,that path is shown. This can be defined in the project template file to read from a default project directory.

Tip 169 from *Ron House*	You can preset system variables such as HYPERLINKBASE in a template file designated for a specific project. When drawings for the project are created using this template, these settings would already be defined and would not need to be set by the individual project members. This will help to ensure consistency throughout the project drawings. Refer to Chapter 2, "Drawing Setup," for more information on creating drawing templates.

- Named Location in File—You can specify a saved view in the linked drawing that you want to view after the drawing opens. This enables you to further define an area of interest using the link. This might be a specific detail or note in the linked drawing.

- Hyperlink Description—This option enables you to add a description to your URL to further explain to the user what the link refers to. When the cursor passes over the linked object, a ToolTip appears displaying the link description.

- Use Relative Path for Hyperlink—When this option is set, AutoCAD refers to the value set in the HYPERLINKBASE variable to determine the path. The path is saved with the drawing. If this option is toggled off, the full pathname is saved.

PART

IV

CH

19

DEFINING THE HYPERLINK

You may enter the link to a file or URL that contains both the base path and the filename of the link. If the URL is used, you must precede the site name with `http://` or `ftp://`. The filename will be listed in the Path edit box, and the base path name will be listed in the Base edit box. The file can be selected from a file dialog box by picking the Browse button. This opens the Browse the Web–Select Hyperlink dialog box.

The Named Location in File edit box enables you to enter a specific location within the document you want jump to. For example, this could be set to a view saved in a drawing with the View command. This would then open the drawing at that view when the link is activated.

You can also type in a hyperlink description to assist in identifying the link you have assigned to an object. When the cursor passes over an object that has a hyperlink attached to it, a ToolTip appears displaying the linked URL if no description has been defined (see Figure 19.6). If a description has been provided, the description is displayed by the ToolTip.

Figure 19.6
Pointing to an object with a hyperlink displays the hyperlink filename or description.

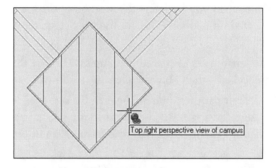

Top right perspective view of campus

Tip 170 from
Ron House

The display of hyperlink ToolTips, as well as the display of the hyperlink menu and cursor, can be toggled off using the options available from the User Preferences tab in the Options dialog box. Consider this option when a file has a number of hyperlinks and you find it difficult to edit the file with the hyperlinks displayed. Right-click in the drawing editor while no object is selected, and choose Options from the shortcut menu. Select the User Preferences tab. The hyperlink display options are located in the lower-left corner of the Options dialog box, shown in Figure 19.7.

Figure 19.7
The hyperlink display options are available from the Options dialog box, User Preferences tab.

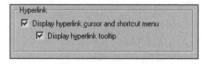

Note The Use Relative Path for Hyperlink button toggles the use of the base path set by the HYPERLINKBASE setting variable. If you wish to override that variable so the path is not automatically attached to the link filename, make certain this option has not been checked.

Note also that when you select a number of objects that are to be assigned a hyperlink, the dialog box lists how many have been selected and how many already have been hyperlinked to. This is important information to have so you do not accidentally overwrite any previously defined hyperlinks.

After the link is saved with the drawing file, the AutoCAD file can essentially be used to manage the other documents related to the file. Better yet, if the file is saved in Drawing Web Format, or DWF, those who view your file over the Internet can also jump to your supporting documentation via hyperlinks if those files are accessible. Since DWF files are considerably more compact than drawing files, they are ideal for transferring information to others involved with the project.

HYPERLINKING TO A FILE BY AREA

The options described in the previous section detailed how to link to a particular object or a group of objects. This section looks at what you do when you want to link to an entire area of a drawing rather than just objects. Use this feature to hyperlink entire areas of a drawing, such as using a site plan to link to individual lots or sections of the overall site, or using detail sheets linked to specific corresponding areas of a house plan. This can be accomplished by running the Hyperlink command at the command line. Type **–Hyperlink** at the command line, and the following prompt appears:

```
Enter an option [Remove/Insert] <Insert>:
```

Tip 171 from *Ron House*	Typing a dash before the command name activates the command at the command line without the use of a dialog box. This is important to remember if you are accessing commands via a macro assigned to a custom toolbar or pull-down menu. You can read more about creating custom macros and interfaces in Chapter 20, "Customizing Made Easy."

At this point, you are prompted to remove or insert a hyperlink. For now, accept the default option to insert a link; more will be discussed on removing hyperlinks in the next section. The following steps outline the process of inserting a link to an area:

1. Using the Area option available at the next prompt, you can specify an area to be linked. Type **A** at the command line, and press Enter:
   ```
   Enter hyperlink insert option [Area/Object] <Object>: A <ENTER>
   ```

2. You will then be prompted to pick the opposite corners of the area you want to link to. After selecting the corners, you can enter the hyperlink drawing name:
   ```
   Enter hyperlink <current drawing>:
   ```

3. Supply the name of the drawing you want to hyperlink to, and press Enter. The prompt for the path appears next:
   ```
   Enter named location <none>: http:\\www.autodesk.com\exercise
   ```

4. And then the hyperlink description:

   ```
   Enter description <none>: This will link you to a file on the Internet.
   ```

The process is now complete. After hyperlinks have been placed in a drawing, they can easily be modified, as the next section demonstrates.

ACCESSING MULTIPLE HYPERLINKS WITHIN A NESTED BLOCK

Hyperlinks can also be attached to blocks, and because blocks can be made up of multiple objects, each object used to define the block can also have a hyperlink attached to it. To

PART

IV

CH

19

access hyperlinks attached to objects nested within a block, you'll need to use the Hyperlink shortcut menu. The shortcut menu is specific to the individual hyperlinks and the objects they are attached to. The menu shows only the hyperlink attached to the block and the hyperlink attached to the nested object within the block, depending on which object the cursor is over when the menu is accessed. The following example will help illustrate this process.

EXAMPLE: ACCESSING A HYPERLINK NESTED INSIDE A BLOCK

1. Let's create a sample block with nested hyperlinks. Launch AutoCAD, if not already started, and create a new drawing.

2. Next, draw a small rectangle, although the size of the rectangle is irrelevant for this example. Then attach a hyperlink to the rectangle. Use one of the sample AutoCAD drawings from the Sample subdirectory under the ACAD2000 directory. If you like, also type in a hyperlink description.

3. Now, define the rectangle and associated hyperlink as a block named Rectangle.

→ Refer to Chapter 16, "Creating and Using Blocks," for information on how to create a block, if needed.

4. Repeat the process for a new circle. Draw a circle near the rectangle you just created, attach a hyperlink to both the rectangle and circle, and make those items into a block as well. Give the block a simple name, such as Circle for this example, and select both objects when defining the block.

5. At this point you should have two blocks, each with separate hyperlinks attached to them. Create a new block that consists of these two blocks, and call it **Linked_Objects**.

6. After you have created the nested block, select the block, activating grips on the block object. Right-click in a clear area away from the block, and then select the Hyperlink shortcut menu option. Note that not only is the overall block hyperlink shown, but the nested object hyperlinks also appear (see Figure 19.8).

By creating a nested block, you can maintain the hyperlinks associated with the nested objects that define the block. When a block is inserted into a drawing, the hyperlinks are converted to relative links whose path information is controlled by the current setting of the HYPERLINKBASE setting variable in that drawing.

Note
You can edit only the hyperlink attached to the overall block definition. To remove or edit those hyperlinks associated with nested objects, you must first explode the block. Refer to Chapter 16 for more information on the Explode command.

HYPERLINK EDITING

Editing a hyperlink is as easy as creating one, and the Edit Hyperlink command uses a dialog box similar to the one used to create the hyperlink. To edit, select the linked object and right-click. Choose Hyperlink, Edit Hyperlink. The major difference between the two dialog boxes is that the Edit Hyperlink dialog box contains a <u>R</u>emove Link button in its lower–left corner (see Figure 19.9). This Remove Link option is covered in the next section.

Figure 19.8
The Hyperlink short-cut menu gives you access to hyperlinks within nested blocks.

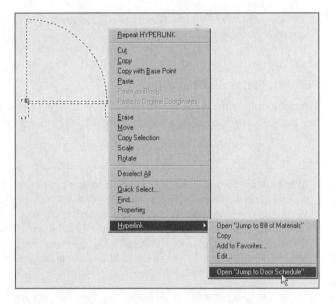

Figure 19.9
The Edit Hyperlink dialog box contains a Remove Link button to remove unwanted hyperlinks from the drawing.

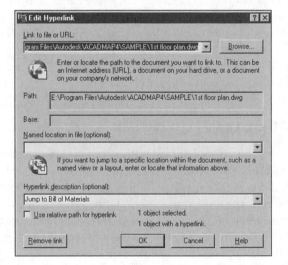

If the drawing hasn't been saved since creating the hyperlink, the Hyperlink–Save Drawing dialog box appears. If the drawing has been saved, the Edit Hyperlink dialog box opens. All other options are the same, allowing you to modify the current values for the hyperlink.

Tip 172 from	A hyperlink can also be edited using the Properties command. Right-click on an object after it has been selected, and choose Properties from the shortcut menu. The Properties dialog box appears, in which you will see only the description shown in the Hyperlink edit box. If a description is not given, click in the edit box and an ellipsis button appears. Select the ellipsis button and the Edit Hyperlink dialog box opens, enabling you to edit the parameters of the hyperlink.
Ron House	

REMOVING A HYPERLINK FROM A DRAWING

To remove a hyperlink, follow the steps to edit a hyperlink to open the Edit Hyperlink dialog box. Click the Remove Link button to remove the hyperlink attached to the selected object.

Tip 173 from	If you begin the practice of assigning hyperlinks to your project drawings to access other project-related documents, make it a habit to check all links in your drawing before allowing other project members to view them. Edit or remove broken links to avoid confusion, and test them in an environment similar to the one used by outside consultants (for example, a dial-up connection). This will assist in making your project run smoothly, and ensuring that your links are correct will help eliminate unwanted frustration.
Ron House	

Two different formats allow viewing AutoCAD drawing files over the Internet. The first file format, the Drawing Web Format (DWF), can be described as an uneditable view of a drawing file. A new product Autodesk is introducing will eventually replace the DWF format, however. This new product is called Volo View Express, and you can use it to view DWF files as well as other files. This product can be run as a standalone product or via the Internet. (It is discussed in "Introduction to Volo View Express," later in this chapter.) First, look at creating DWF files using your completed drawings.

DRAWING WEB FORMAT

Using the *WHIP!*™ 4.0 plug-in from Autodesk with a browser, you can save AutoCAD drawing files in a format that allows users to view a drawing file without the need for AutoCAD or the actual drawing file itself. To do this, you must first save the original drawing file in DWF format. To save a drawing as a DWF file, you must use the AutoCAD Plot command, using the new ePlot (or electronic plot) feature. The Plot command can be accessed from the File pull-down menu or the Standard toolbar. The Plot dialog box is shown in Figure 19.10.

In the case of creating a DWF file, rather than generating a hard copy of your drawing, you will be plotting to a file that can be viewed from the Internet. You can choose two types of DWF plot configurations from the Plot Configuration tab:

- DWF Classic—This is the original Release 14 DWF file type, which is being replaced by the newer ePlot version discussed in the next point. The option to create a DWF file from the Plot command is new with AutoCAD 2000, and DWF Classic files can be generated using the DWF Classic.pc3 plotter configuration. You can also type **DWFOUT** at the command line to create a DWF file—but only in the Classic version.

Figure 19.10
The Plot dialog box contains plot configurations for DWF files, which allow you to create "electronic plots" that can be viewed over the Internet.

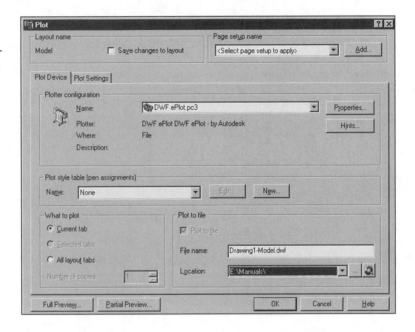

PART
IV
CH
19

> **Note**
>
> The original DWF type creates a file that is only two-dimensional and has few options for customizing the plot. Because this is the Release 14 DWF format, lineweights are not supported with this file type; it is available for backward-compatibility only and will not be supported by future releases of AutoCAD. This format still exists because there still are a lot of users who have custom applications built around the WHIP! 3.0 DWF format, and Autodesk still wants to supply this version without forcing them to update. You can read more about it and download the WHIP! software utility at http://www.autodesk.com/whip.

- ePlot—The new DWF format, or electronic plot, has numerous features that add to the existing functionality of the original DWF file format. Most notable of these features is the capability to view three-dimensional files and control the display of the DWF file, which includes being able to view lineweights assigned within the file. This format also views the file with a paper boundary on a white background. Unlike its predecessor, using ePlot is the only way to create the new DWF format.

The following steps outline the process to create a DWF file in ePlot format:

1. Open a sample drawing from the Sample subdirectory under the ACAD2000 directory. After the file opens, select Plot from the File pull-down menu.

2. From the Plot dialog box in the Plotter configuration section, choose the DWF ePlot.pc3 from the Name selection list.

3. The Plot to File button is automatically selected. A default filename is provided based on the name of the current drawing in the File Name edit box. The path can be set in the Location edit box. The location can be set either to a network drive or to an Internet/intranet URL by selecting the Browse the Web button.

Note

If you are plotting from a Layout set in your drawing, AutoCAD may issue a warning stating that the paper size in the layout is not supported by the plot device, and it will use the paper size defined by the plot device. Choose the desired paper size by clicking the Plot Settings tab to set the plotted paper size. This typically is not a concern unless you are plotting the DWF to a specific scale factor. Paper size must be considered when assigning a specific scale to fit the entire drawing onto the plot area.

4. Click the Plot Settings tab and define the plot parameters, such as scale, plot area, and drawing orientation, just as you would a standard AutoCAD plot.

Tip 174 from
Ron House

Only the Current Tab button in the What to Plot box grants access to the Plot Settings tab. From this tab, you can change specific plot options, such as paper size, drawing orientation, and plot area, and options such as lineweight display. Selecting the All Layout Tabs radio button will plot all layouts you have in the drawing.

5. Adjust the options for offsetting the plot as desired, and then click the Full or Partial Preview buttons to view how the drawing will look when displayed as a DWF file. A Partial Preview illustrates how the overall drawing will fit onto the printable area, and the Full Preview actually displays the drawing in the given area.

6. Click the OK button. When the DWF file has been created, test the file by first launching a browser, and then drag and drop the file into the browser viewing area. The file should load, and you can navigate the file using the right-click shortcut menu.

Tip 175 from
Ron House

To be able to view DWF files from a browser, you must first install the *WHIP!*™ 4.0 plug-in from Autodesk, which you will find on the companion CD.

Tip 176 from
Ron House

By default, AutoCAD 2000 includes lineweights during plotting. If you haven't specified lineweight values in the Layer Properties Manager, a default lineweight of .06 inches is applied to all graphical objects when you plot a drawing. Areas of your ePlot DWF files may look significantly different from the way they display when you view them in an Internet browser, particularly during zoom operations. Clear the Plot with Lineweights options on the Plot Settings tab in the Plot dialog box to avoid this problem.

Another setting that can affect the display of a DWF file is the resolution of the file itself. The next section discusses how to determine what the resolution should be and how to set that value.

SETTING THE FILE RESOLUTION AND COMPRESSION OF A DWF FILE

The amount of detail of the file you want to output will determine the resolution of a DWF file. Although a medium resolution setting will work for most files, the higher the amount of detail needed, the higher the resolution you will want. A higher resolution results in a larger compressed DWF file. The lower the resolution, the smaller the file size. By default, DWF files are automatically compressed, which does not result in a loss of data.

To set the resolution of a DWF file, select Plot from the File pull-down menu. Choose the ePlot plotter configuration from the Plotter Configuration Name list, and then select the Properties button. Click Custom Properties from the Device and Document Settings tree list, which displays a Custom Properties button. Selecting this button opens the DWF Properties dialog box, shown in Figure 19.11.

Figure 19.11
The resolution and compression of a DWF can be set from the DWF Properties dialog box.

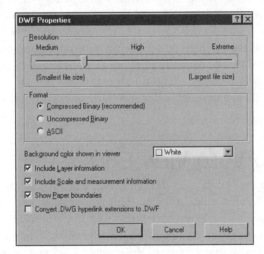

These options are available from within this dialog box:

- Resolution—This option controls the resolution for the DWF file.
- Format—Three formats are available for DWF files using ePlot:
  - Compressed Binary—This is the default setting and is recommended for most DWF files.
  - Uncompressed Binary—This allows the DWF to be output in an uncompressed format.

- ASCII—This creates the DWF file as text, which can be read and modified using a standard text editor such as Notepad.

■ Background color shown in viewer—This sets the background color for the file. Any color can be selected from the color palette available from the list.

■ Include Layer information—This allows layers that are on and thawed to be manipulated within the DWF file. If this option is toggled off, then the layer information is not available when the file is viewed within an Internet browser.

■ Include Scale and measurement information—This information is available in the output DWF file.

■ Show Paper boundaries—This enables you to show the paper boundaries displayed within the drawing's layout.

■ Convert .DWG hyperlink extensions to .DWF—This converts the .DWG hyperlinks that exist in the drawing to .DWF hyperlinks. This allows an entire project to be output to DWF format, keeping the hyperlinks intact by referencing them to the associated project DWFs.

Using the *Whip!*™ plug-in to view DWF files is ideal when you want others to be able to view your drawing files without having to actually give them a copy of your files. Yet you may want to give your colleagues the ability to view your drawing files without the need to convert to a DWF file, and without needing AutoCAD to open the drawing file. Maybe you want to show management the progress on a particular project you are working on, and the time or need to learn AutoCAD or to create paper plots is not available. A new product from Autodesk, Volo View Express, gives you the ability to view not only DWG files, but also DWF and DXF files. The next section discusses how to use this product to view DWG files via the Internet.

INTRODUCTION TO VOLO VIEW EXPRESS

Autodesk's Volo View Express product is a DWG, DWF, and DXF viewing package that makes it easy for anyone to view AutoCAD data. This is advantageous for those who need to view AutoCAD drawings but who do not have access to AutoCAD to view the files. Using this product, files do not need to be converted into DWF format to be viewed, saving time and the need to verify that you have converted the most up-to-date drawing file into DWF format. Volo View Express is a great way for those without access to the AutoCAD software to view drawing files both locally and via the Internet. The similarity between the navigation commands in Volo View Express and AutoCAD makes the product easy to use and makes it a natural drawing viewing tool for AutoCAD users.

Volo View Express is one of three products in the Volo View family, which also includes Volo View and Volo View Explorer. The functionality of each software product is listed here:

■ Volo View Express—This software allows 2D and 3D drawing files to be viewed either running as a standalone application or via the Internet using a browser.

- Volo View—This application combines the viewing capability of Volo View Express with a set of markup tools utilizing AutoCAD components and ActiveShapes technology from Autodesk's Actrix Technical software product.

- Volo View Explorer—This software product is a drawing manager for small design teams, enabling them to collaborate on the project's drawing and related files. This allows tracking, version control, and the administration of the project files for a Windows NT LAN.

For the context of this book, this chapter covers only the features available in the Volo View Express product, which can be downloaded from this site: `http://www.autodesk.com/products/volo/index.htm`. After installing the software and launching the program, you will find the interface very straightforward, as shown in Figure 19.12, and will discover that many of the functions are similar to those in AutoCAD 2000.

Figure 19.12
The navigation tools of the Volo View Express interface mirror those found in AutoCAD, making the software easy to use.

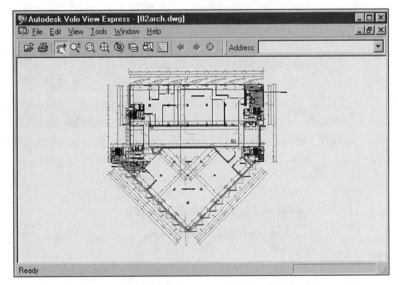

Using Volo View Explorer, you can open DWG, DWF, or DXF files in any of the following ways:

- Open them via the File dialog box.

- Open them by dragging and dropping from Windows Explorer

- Open them by entering the URL for the file in the Address field. Drawings viewed previously can be quickly revisited by selecting the file location from the Address pull-down menu. When the site is visited using a URL, Back and Forward buttons also become available, making navigation through the site history easy.

PART

IV

CH

19

After you open a file, many of the navigation tools mirror those found in AutoCAD 2000. Pan, Zoom (Window and Extents), and 3D Orbit are available, making the software easy to use if you are familiar with navigating AutoCAD drawings.

MANIPULATING THE FILE WITHIN VOLO VIEW EXPLORER

Three additional options available enable you to change the display of the drawing based on how the drawing was created. You can control which layers, views, and layouts are displayed. Let's look at the commands that are available from the View pull-down menu:

- Layers—A dialog box appears that lists all the layers in the drawing (see Figure 19.13).

Figure 19.13
You can toggle the visibility of the layers in the drawing to view the drawing in multiple ways.

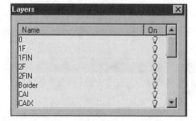

Corresponding with each of the layers is the light bulb symbol. Clicking on the light bulb toggles the layer off or on, depending on its current state. When the layer visibility has been modified, close the dialog box to view the drawing in that state.

- Named Views—If the drawing contains saved views, you can toggle those views on via the Named Views dialog box (see Figure 19.14).

Figure 19.14
Views saved with the drawing can be quickly viewed within Volo View Explorer using the Named Views option.

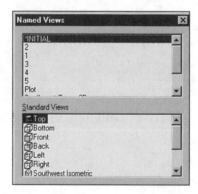

Selecting the view name from the list changes to that view in the viewer.

- Layouts—The different layouts created with the drawing can also be viewed using Volo View Express (see Figure 19.15).

Figure 19.15
The layouts used to plot the drawing can also be viewed.

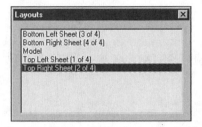

USING VOLO VIEW EXPRESS TO VIEW A DRAWING FILE IN MICROSOFT WORD

Because Volo View Express is actually an ActiveX control, the viewing functionality can be embedded into other Windows applications, such as Word and PowerPoint. ActiveX controls are small components that expand the functionality of Microsoft Office software products and are similar to plug-ins. Using these components enables you to include drawing files in presentations or handouts that emphasize a specific point or idea.

Tip 177 from
Ron House

Currently, the Autodesk Volo View Explorer is available only as an ActiveX control, which is not supported within the Netscape Navigator browser. Netscape Navigator users can still use the application as a standalone viewer, and it is Autodesk's intent to support that browser in the next release of the software.

Here are the steps you can follow to embed a drawing into a Word 97 document using Volo View Express:

1. After opening Word 97, choose the Object option from the Insert menu, which opens the Object dialog box.

2. From the Create New tab, select Autodesk Volo View Control from the list and pick the OK button. This places a Volo View drawing area into your document.

3. Right-click inside the drawing area and select Options. From the General tab File Name box within the Options dialog box, type in the path and the filename or browse to locate the drawing you wish to embed. Click the OK button.

PART
IV

CH
19

The embedded Volo View drawing area can be resized and repositioned in the document. When the document is saved and distributed, users of the document who have the Volo View software installed can navigate within the Volo View drawing area to view the drawing. You can also copy a drawing shown in Volo View Express to the Clipboard and paste it into another Windows document.

Tip 178 from *Ron House*	The accuracy of the drawing is lost when the drawing image is copied to the Clipboard, which is mostly due to the image conversion to the Windows Meta File format. Also, a file cannot be copied while you are viewing a file in 3D Orbit mode.

The ability to view drawing files over the Internet using software products such as Volo View Explorer and the use of new advances in Web-based technology open up a new realm in the computer-aided design market: Project Collaboration Web sites. In the next section, the offerings of one such site, Buzzsaw.com, are presented as an alternative to the current practices used to convey project information.

PROJECT COLLABORATION AND BUZZSAW.COM

Project Collaboration Web sites enable team members to jointly discuss ideas and concerns using chat rooms, white boards, drawing viewers, and other Web-based technologies to relay information about a project. These sites are especially advantageous when the members of the project team are working in various locations throughout the world.

One of these sites, called Buzzsaw.com, was formed as a venture collaboration with Autodesk and other vendors to provide businesses with a Web site designed to be a focus point for the building design industry. Here, companies can collaborate with others involved on their projects and can quickly access various building design e-commerce services. Here are just a few of the services buzzsaw.com has to offer:

- Project Hosting—Sign up for a free, secure, Web-based project workspace to collaborate on your projects.
- Online Meetings—With this feature, made possible by WebEx, who provides Web-based collaboration services for the site, you can host interactive online meetings, complete with the capability to red-line documents.
- Cad Tools—Gain access to tools you can use to complete a project.
- Web Camera—Using tools offered by Inet Architects, Inc., you can display actual photos of your project as it is being built to monitor job progress and resolve site issues.

To access this site, point your browser to `http://www.buzzsaw.com` (see Figure 19.16).

Sign up and use this site to manage projects when you need to collaborate with multiple colleagues in various cities throughout the world—or just across town.

Figure 19.16
Use the Web site at Buzzsaw.com to collaborate on a project and gain easy access to building design services via the Internet.

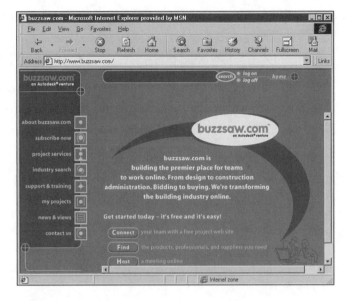

SUMMARY

This chapter discussed the numerous ways to access drawings and DWF files using the Internet functionality built into AutoCAD and other Autodesk products. With the use of the Web-enabled file dialog boxes, you are no longer limited to opening files from your local or network hard disk—any drawing file you have access to, as well as sample files on the Internet, are available to you. Furthermore, with sites such as buzzsaw.com, you can share your files and collaborate with colleagues across the world using the Internet.

Here are some additional sites and discussion groups you can visit to learn more about AutoCAD, *WHIP!*™, Volo View, Architectural Desktop, and Mechanical Desktop:

- AutoCAD Web site—*http://www.autocad.com*
- AutoCAD discussion groups—*http://www.autodesk.com/support/discsgrp/acad.htm*
- WHIP!™ home page—*http://www.autodesk.com/whip*
- Volo View home page—*http://www.autodesk.com/products/volo/index.htm*
- Discussion groups for WHIP!™ and Volo View—*http://www.autodesk.com/support/ discsgrp/internet.htm*
- Architectural Desktop home page—*http://www.autodesk.com/products/archdesk/index.htm*
- Architectural Desktop discussion groups—*http://www.autodesk.com/support/discsgrp/ aec.htm*
- Mechanical Desktop home page—*http://www.autodesk.com/products/desktop/index.htm*
- Mechanical Desktop discussion groups—*http://www.autodesk.com/support/discsgrp/ mech.htm*

PART

IV

CH

19

- Autodesk Learning Assistance Discussion Groups—*http://www.autodesk.com/support/discsgrp/learnassist.htm*
- The Customer File Exchange—*news://adesknews.autodesk.com/autodesk.autocad.customer-files*

BECOMING A MASTER OF AUTOCAD

CHAPTER **20**

CUSTOMIZING MADE EASY

In this chapter

CUSTOMIZING AUTOCAD TO FIT THE WAY YOU WORK

The capability of customizing AutoCAD to optimize the way you work is a powerful feature, and AutoCAD 2000 is very flexible in how it enables you to accomplish this. This chapter shows you how to customize AutoCAD, whether by creating your own toolbars, automating processes using scripts, integrating AutoCAD with any of the Microsoft Office products, or using a combination of any of these features.

After you have spent some time working with AutoCAD, you'll start to think of ways that you might want to tweak the software to further enhance your productivity. Luckily, AutoCAD is easy to customize and, with some work, can quickly be tailored to fit your needs. To start, let's look at creating scripts, which can enable you to automate simple processes done within AutoCAD. In the next section, you'll look at how scripts can be used to create simple objects and automate a slide show.

USING SCRIPTS TO AUTOMATE AUTOCAD

Scripts can be quickly created to automate a process, and then run to set AutoCAD into a standalone mode, where it can run unattended. For example, you have a set of drawings that need to have the project titleblock attached. A script can be produced to open a drawing, externally reference the titleblock given a specific insertion point, scale, and rotation angle, and then saved and used to open the next drawing and repeat the operation.

A script file is simply a text file created using Microsoft Windows Notepad or a similar text editor. It is made up of a series of commands needed to complete a task or operation. Each command can be placed on a separate line for clarity's sake, making it easy to debug your script, and the individual lines would contain all of the parameters required to complete the command. Comments can be added to a script file by preceding the line with a semicolon, which indicates that the line is to be ignored when the script file is processed.

The following is an example of a script file that creates a circle enclosed within a simple box:

```
Line 0,0 0,1 1,1 1,0 close
Circle .5,.5 Diameter 1.0
```

Note that a space in the line acts the same as pressing the Enter key during the command, as does transitioning from one line to the next in the script. Script files have an .SCR extension and are launched using the Script command, or by selecting the Run Script option from the Tools pull-down menu. AutoCAD opens the Select Script File dialog box, where you can select the script to be run. Each line in the script is then read and each command is completed until it reaches the end of the script file.

Script files offer little user interaction and only the following commands can be used within a script:

- Delay—This command can be used to delay the script, and the command is followed by the number of milliseconds you want the script to be delayed. For example, Delay 1000 will delay the script for one second, the maximum delay being 33 seconds, or 32767 milliseconds. Use this to pause a script for visual verification, such as to view a magnified portion of the drawing before continuing on with the rest of the script.

■ Rscript—The Rscript command repeats the script continuously until the user presses Esc key. This is commonly used if a process needs to be repeated in a continuous loop, such as a benchmarking test.

You can also use AutoCAD as presentation software to display slide shows by creating a script to exhibit a series of slides. The following section discusses the creation of slides and how to view them using a script.

CREATING A SCRIPT FOR A SLIDE SHOW

A slide is a snapshot of the current screen that can be saved to a file with an .SLD extension. The Mslide command, short for Make Slide, is used to create the snapshot and is activated by simply typing Mslide at the command line. You can use this command to "capture" the shaded rendering of a drawing, or a particular area of interest or concern, which can then quickly be displayed.

Slides can be viewed using the Vslide command, short for View Slide, which is also activated at the command line. This command can be used within a script to create a slide show, as shown in the following sample slide file:

```
; This is a sample slide show that repeats.
; Note that slides 2 and 3 are preloaded.
VSLIDE SLIDE_A
DELAY 2000
VSLIDE *SLIDE_B
DELAY 2000
VSLIDE
VSLIDE *SLIDE_C
DELAY 2000
VSLIDE
DELAY 2000
RSCRIPT
```

Tip 178 from *Ron House*	Preceding the slide with an asterisk (*) preloads that slide, and the Vslide command following a delay simply displays the preloaded slide. Because the slide is preloaded, it is quickly displayed, making the transition to the next slide smoother.

Tip 179 from *Ron House*	When working with a drawing that contains multiple paperspace viewports, a script can be run independently within the active viewport. This enables you to display the slide show along with several "static" viewports showing other areas of interest in the drawing.

PART

V

CH

20

In addition to this customizing feature, AutoCAD contains a number of ways to customize the AutoCAD interface, which can be modified to match how you work. The following sections each illustrate how to customize a specific portion of the interface. Let's start by discussing how to create your own keyboard shortcuts.

MODIFYING THE KEYBOARD SHORTCUTS

When you begin to learn the commands and how to access them, you may want to expedite some of the processes to activate some of these functions. If you know your way around a keyboard, and especially if you can type without looking at the keyboard, you should consider creating your own keyboard shortcuts, which is one of the easiest methods to customize AutoCAD.

Note

Even if you aren't proficient at typing, contemplate creating shortcuts using keys you can quickly type without having to "hunt and peck." Also, consider the amount of time it takes to access a command from the toolbars or pull-down menus. If you can immediately launch that command using either of these interfaces, there really isn't much to gain by creating a keyboard shortcut.

As you gain more experience working with AutoCAD, you'll find it useful to review the shortcuts you've created and replace them with other commands that take more time to access.

If you favor accessing commands from the toolbars and pull-down menus, check out the "Customizing the AutoCAD Interface" section later in this chapter. Here you'll learn to customize the interfaces you prefer to use.

Making your own shortcuts, rather than selecting them from a toolbar or pull-down menu, can greatly enhance your productivity. Let's begin by first examining the format you'll use to create the shortcut, then you'll add some of your own keyboard shortcuts (or, command aliases, as they are often called) to the standard list of shortcuts that comes with AutoCAD.

The Acad.pgp file, found in the AutoCAD 2000 Support subdirectory, contains all the definitions that make up the command aliases.

→ Examine Appendix A, "Taking Advantage of AutoCAD's Keyboard Shortcuts," for a complete list of the default shortcuts shipped with AutoCAD. Use this list to model your own command aliases from.

To view the Acad.pgp file, you'll need to use a text editor like Windows Notepad, which is convenient because it is easily accessible on any Windows-based computer.

Caution

Remember, it is very important to make a backup of your Acad.pgp file. Any error in the file could lead to error messages similar to this one:

```
Syntax error in acad.pgp file on line 93 in field 3
(memory size specification missing)
```

Having a backup of this file will enable you to recover the backup Acad.pgp file and continue working until you locate the error in your modified file.

Caution

Avoid using a word processing software program, such as Microsoft Word, to edit text-based files such as the Acad.pgp or Acad.mnu. These programs typically embed formatting codes into the text, making the file unreadable by AutoCAD. Use only a text editor to edit these files.

While viewing the Acad.pgp file, scroll through to the section on command aliases. Command aliases have the following format:

```
<Alias>,*<Full command name>
```

First comes the alias, followed by a comma and an asterisk, and then the full command name. Also notice that Autodesk has supplied guidelines for creating new command aliases that are embedded in the Acad.pgp file:

```
The following are guidelines for creating new command aliases.
1. An alias should reduce a command by at least two characters.
Commands with a control key equivalent, status bar button, or function key do not
require a command alias.
Examples: Control N, O, P, and S for New, Open, Print, Save.
2. Try the first character of the command, and then try the first two, then the
first three.
3. When an alias is defined, add suffixes for related aliases:
Examples: R for Redraw, RA for Redrawall, L for Line, LT for Linetype.
4. Use a hyphen to differentiate between command-line and dialog box commands.
Example: B for Block, -B for -Block.
Exceptions to the rules include AA for Area, T for Mtext, X for Explode.
```

These guidelines well document the process for creating aliases. It's a good idea to first examine the Acad.pgp file to see whether the command to which you want to assign an alias has already been created.

Using keyboard shortcuts to access commands can save you time and greatly increase your productivity. When you have modified and saved your ACAD.PGP file, you will need to reload the file to see if the aliases work as expected. To do this, use the Reinit command to reinitialize the ACAD.PGP file. Use the process outlined here to reinitialize the modified ACAD.PGP file:

Open the Re-initialization dialog box by typing **Reinit** at the command line and pressing Enter (see Figure 20.1).

In the Device and File Initialization section, you will see a check box marked PGP File. Select the check box, and click the OK button. AutoCAD reloads the file, making the changes you made available.

The keyboard shortcuts are fine if you are used to typing, yet some memorization is needed to gain substantial productivity from their use. In addition, there are no hints or ToolTips, such as you will find on the toolbars, to guide you to the correct shortcut. You can expand the productivity you gained with the keyboard shortcuts by customizing the toolbars. The next section discusses how to create and modify your own toolbars.

PART

V

CH

20

Figure 20.1
A modified
ACAD.PGP file can be
reinitialized without
exiting AutoCAD
using the Reinit
command.

CUSTOMIZING THE AUTOCAD INTERFACE

By modifying the ACAD.MNU file, you can make changes to the different tools that make up the AutoCAD interface. Although the other menu tools must be altered manually, the Toolbars section can be dynamically generated through a drag-and-drop process and can be automatically saved in a separate ACAD.MNS menu file. When you are certain that you like the changes that have been made, you can incorporate them into the ACAD.MNU file.

DYNAMICALLY CUSTOMIZING THE TOOLBARS

The capability to customize and create your own toolbars is one of AutoCAD's best customizing features. It's easy to create your own toolbar: No programming experience is required, and it's a simple drag-and-drop process. By quickly creating a toolbar and assigning to it those commands you use most often, you can become even more productive. For example, you can combine the commands you use the most into one toolbar rather than having to select the same commands from multiple toolbars. This gives you one location to choose the commands you use the most.

The fastest way to customize the toolbars is to right-click a toolbar button and select the Customize option from the menu, as shown in Figure 20.2.

Figure 20.2
Selecting Customize
from the right-click
menu makes cus-
tomizing toolbars
easy.

This launches the Toolbars dialog box. From here, you can create, customize, or delete toolbars (see Figure 20.3).

Figure 20.3

You can create, cus-
tomize, or delete
toolbars from the
Toolbar dialog box.

These options are available from within this dialog box:

- Close—Closes the dialog box and saves the updates to the menu files.
- New—Creates new toolbars.
- Delete—Enables you to delete toolbars from the list.
- Customize—Opens the Customize Toolbars dialog box, enabling you to populate new toolbars with buttons from existing toolbars.
- Properties—Enables you to modify the toolbar properties, such as name and helpstring.
- Large Buttons—Enables you to see large buttons on the toolbars.
- Show ToolTips—Displays ToolTips when the cursor pauses on the button.

Selecting the New button brings up the New Toolbar dialog box, enabling you to create a new toolbar by typing its name in the Toolbar Name edit box. After you click the OK button, a new toolbar is created and you are returned to the Toolbar dialog box.

Tip 180 from *Ron House*	You can also choose the menu to which you wish to append your toolbar from the Menu Group list. This defines which menu file will be altered. See the section "Modifying the ACAD.MNU File" later in this chapter, to learn how the menu file is modified by the custom menu process.
Tip 181 from *Ron House*	You might need to look closely for the empty toolbar after it is created. Sometimes the toolbars can be hard to find, especially if you are not quite sure what to look for.
Tip 182 from *Ron House*	Your new toolbar should look like the empty toolbar shown in Figure 20.4. It may be necessary to relocate dialog boxes and toolbars to see the newly created toolbar, which you will need for the drag-and-drop process to populate your toolbar.

PART

V

CH

20

Figure 20.4
Your new toolbar
should look like this.

ADDING COMMANDS TO YOUR NEW TOOLBAR

Say for example you have a defined process to check project drawings to see if they are complete. This process consists of zooming to the extents of each drawing, checking the attached reference files, and creating layouts for and saving the individual drawings. Independently, you would need to access four separate toolbars for all of these commands. You can easily increase your productivity and save time by creating a toolbar that contains all of the command buttons to activate each of these functions.

Now you can choose which buttons you want to add to the empty toolbar that you just created. Click the Customize button, and choose the command buttons you wish to use from the current list of toolbars (see Figure 20.5).

Figure 20.5
Add commands to
your newly created
toolbar with a simple
drag-and-drop
function.

First, select from the Categories list which group of buttons you wish to choose from existing toolbars. Drag and drop the buttons from the Customize Toolbars dialog box onto your new toolbar. When all the dialog boxes are closed, the menu file is updated to contain your changes.

Tip 183 from *Ron House*	You can automate the process of creating a new toolbar by dragging and dropping a button icon from a toolbar category in the Customize Toolbars dialog box onto the drawing area. After you've completed adding buttons to the toolbar, you can then modify the toolbar properties by clicking the Properties button in the Toolbar Properties dialog box.

Tip 184 from *Ron House*	More than one toolbar can be opened during this process. This enables you to move buttons from one toolbar to another. To copy rather than move buttons across toolbars, hold down the Ctrl key while you drag.

Follow the process outlined in the following steps to create your own toolbars:

EXAMPLE: CREATING TOOLBARS

1. Right-click on any toolbar and select the Customize option.

2. From the Toolbar dialog box, click the New button.

3. Type **Custom** for the name of this toolbar in the Toolbar Name edit box. From this dialog box, you can also assign your new toolbar to a menu group, which means that the toolbar definition will be added to the ACAD menu file ACAD.MNS. This file contains the user-defined modifications to the menu and is constantly updated during an AutoCAD session. Leave this set to the ACAD menu group. Now choose the OK button. An empty toolbar appears near the top of the graphics screen, and the name of your toolbar is added to the list.

4. Select the Properties button on the Toolbar dialog box to modify the current properties of the new toolbar, or select Customize to add icons to the newly created toolbar.

5. When you select Customize, the Customize Toolbars dialog box appears. From the Categories pop-up list, you can select commands or button icons from the list of current toolbars. Note that the description of a button appears when it is selected, making it easy for you to associate a command with a button. To add an icon, select the icon of your choice, and drag and drop it onto your toolbar. This makes a copy of the button and places it into the custom toolbar you created.

6. Click the Close button on the Customize Toolbars dialog box when you are finished adding command buttons to your toolbar. The Properties button on the Toolbar dialog box enables you to change the name of the toolbar and also to define the helpstring that will be used in conjunction with the toolbar.

> **Note**
>
> Helpstrings are the text that is displayed at the status bar when the cursor pauses on a toolbar button or on a pull-down menu option. Helpstrings help relay to the user what action will take place when the button or menu option is selected. Refer to the section "Modifying the ACAD.MNU File," later in this chapter, which discusses how to define the helpstrings associated with the pull-down menu options.

7. Select the Close button on the Toolbars dialog box to update the menu files.

LOADING A MODIFIED .MNU FILE

Changes to the toolbars are automatically saved to the ACAD.MNS file, which is a temporary menu that contains user changes to the Toolbar menu file during a drawing session. To make the changes to the toolbars permanent, append the changes from the Toolbars section in the menu ACAD.MNS file to the same section in the ACAD.MNU file found in the Support subdirectory. Then type **menu** at the command line, and select the ACAD.MNU file from the list. You may need to switch the Files of Type pull-down list to list all .MNU files to locate the file. When this file is selected, an alert box appears, as shown in Figure 20.6.

Figure 20.6
AutoCAD alerts you that reloading the ACAD.MNU file will result in the loss of any changes you may have made to the toolbars.

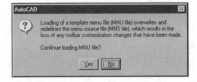

If you have not copied your changes from the ACAD.MNS toolbar section into the ACAD.MNU, they will be lost during reloading of the .MNU file. It is wise to make a copy of the ACAD.MNU file and rename it ACAD.BAK, indicating that this is the backup of the original menu file.

Note

It is extremely important to make a backup of your ACAD.MNU file! If any changes that you make to the menu do not work, reloading the ACAD.MNU file will restore this file to its original condition.

CUSTOMIZING A BUTTON'S APPEARANCE

You can also assign your own custom graphics to a button, especially if you have assigned a specific macro or AutoLISP function to the button and you want to create a new button icon that represents what the function does. AutoCAD's built-in Button Editor makes modifying the appearance of the buttons easy. To do so, right-click on your toolbar and select Customize. This brings up the Toolbar dialog box to modify the toolbar properties; in this case, you want to make changes to the individual button properties. Right-click on the toolbar button you wish to modify, which opens the Button Properties dialog box for that button. This dialog box is shown in Figure 20.7

Figure 20.7
You can modify the individual toolbar button properties via the Button Properties dialog box.

The Button Properties dialog box enables you to modify the button name that pops up in the button ToolTip, the Help statement, or the helpstring that appears in the status bar when the icon is highlighted and also enables you to modify whatever command or macro you want assigned to the icon. You can also modify the bitmap associated with the icon by selecting a new button from the Button Icon list, or you can create your own by choosing the Edit button.

Tip 185 from
Ron House

You can also edit the button graphics as you create a custom toolbar. As you drag buttons onto your new toolbar, right-click on the button you wish to modify. This opens the Button Properties dialog box, giving you access to the Button Editor so you can modify your buttons to stand out from the default buttons that ship with AutoCAD.

Figure 20.8
You can change the appearance of a button using AutoCAD's built-in Button Editor.

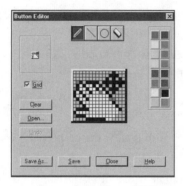

This dialog box contains the tools needed to modify the bitmap. These tools are available:

- Pencil—Use this tool to apply a color to the individual graphic pixels.
- Line—The Line tool colors in the pixels between the selected beginning point and endpoint.
- Circle—This places a circle with an invisible fill onto the graphic.
- Eraser—Erase any mistakes with the Eraser tool by selecting the individual button pixels.
- Grid—Use the Grid option to toggle a grid onto the button. This assists in modifying specific pixels that need to be changed.
- Color Palette—Select the colors you want to apply to the graphic by choosing the color before selecting the tool.

Tip 186 from
Ron House

Because of the limited size of the graphic, you may find it hard to draw a completely diagonal line or a perfect circle. Remember that you are looking at a magnified view of the button and that what you see at this enlarged view may not be completely apparent when the button is viewed at normal size. Use the button previewer to get a glimpse of what the button may look like as you edit the graphic. Also consider that if the Large Buttons option within the Toolbars dialog box has been selected, more button detail will be shown.

In addition, these options are also available within the Button Editor dialog box:

- Open—This option enables you to open an existing .BMP button icon for editing. This helps you customize your own icons assigned to the buttons.

- Undo—This undoes the last operation.
- Save As—With this option, you can save the icon as a .BMP file. This also prevents you from overwriting the default icon for a specific button.
- Save—This saves the changes you've made to the icon.
- Close—This closes the dialog box and returns you to the Button Properties dialog box.

Your modifications are applied to the menu when you close the various customizing dialog boxes. The following paragraphs review the steps required to modify a button's appearance.

First, right-click any toolbar and select the Customize option. Right-click again on the button you want to modify from its toolbar.

From the Button Properties dialog box, you can change the graphic associated with the button to another, or you can modify the button graphics using the Button Editor.

Use the tools available in the Button Editor to modify the graphics, or use the Open button to select a bitmap you want to map to the button.

Select the Save As button to save this graphic with a different name, or use the Save button to overwrite the existing button graphic.

Close all dialog boxes to update the toolbar.

CHANGING A BUTTON'S MACRO

Now that you know how to create a toolbar and modify the graphics associated with the buttons, let's look at how to modify the macro, or specific commands associated with the button. From the Button Properties dialog box, access the Macro edit box, which contains the command or commands that will be activated when a button is selected. Use the toolbar buttons to automate those processes or commands that you use on a consistent basis by combining them into a macro.

A macro can contain multiple commands, although you must provide the parameters for each command option or prompt to complete the action. Each value or command must be followed by a semicolon to simulate pressing the Enter key. For example, let's create a macro to automate the process of placing a border edge around an 8.5-by-11 portrait drawing. First, create a layer called MyBorder, make it current, and give it a color property of red and a line weight of 0.3. Then draw a rectangle with specific start and end corner points of 0,0 and 8.5,11 on the layer.

This is how that macro would look:

```
^C^C_-layer;m;MyBorder;c;red;;lw;0.3;;;Rectangle;0,0;8.5,11
```

First you have the ^C^C notation. This is the same as canceling twice to exit a command, and it is a good idea to assign it to this macro to cancel any command you might be in before executing your macro commands.

Tip 187 from
Ron House

The symbol pair ^C refers to Ctrl+C, which is what you had to type to cancel a command in versions of AutoCAD prior to Release 14. Typing a C while holding down the Ctrl key was the typical way to cancel the active command rather than pressing the Esc key. Canceling using the Esc key was the preferred way to cancel a command in Windows, and AutoCAD adopted this method when the software was ported to that operating system. The operation in Windows activates the Copy command, which forced the change.

The option of using Ctrl+C to cancel a command is still available in AutoCAD 2000. By opening the Options dialog box and accessing the User Preferences tab, you can toggle between using the Windows standard accelerator keys and the older key combination shortcuts available in AutoCAD. Refer to Appendix A, "Taking Advantage of AutoCAD's Keyboard Shortcuts," for more information on the settings available through this interface.

Also note that there is a hyphen before the Layer command. This differentiates commands that are run at the command line from those that are run via dialog boxes. Because the use of dialog boxes is not allowed in the macros, it forces the use of command-line input only. Thus, all the options for the commands are displayed via the command line rather than through dialog boxes. The Layer command is one of these commands. Then the Layer Make option is used to create the layer and set it current at the same time.

Tip 188 from
Ron House

When creating layers within a macro, it is desirable to use the Make option rather than the New option of the Layer command. The Layer Make option has a built-in "layer-checking" mechanism, which checks to see whether the layer already exists. If the macro specifies that a layer should be created and that the layer already exists in the drawing, this option will set that layer to be the current layer. If the layer does not exist, the Make option will create the layer. The Layer New option however, will crash the macro if instructed to create a layer that already exists.

Then the properties for the layer are set, and finally, the Rectangle command is used to draw the border in the desired location.

Now that the macro is finished, you may have realized that it is too specific: It creates a border only for an 8.5-by-11 portrait drawing. How could this macro be modified to create a border for any size drawing? One way is to allow for user interaction within the macro. This is done by using a backslash (\) whenever you want the user to provide input. Using this approach, the code for the macro would be modified to look like this:

```
^C^C_-layer;m;MyBorder;c;red;;lw;0.3;;;Rectangle;\\
```

This macro can now be used in multiple situations, pausing for drawing specific coordinates or user-supplied pick points to define the size of the drawing. Taking this one step further, the macro could be easily modified to create a rectangle of any size on any layer using the following code:

```
^C^C_-layer;m;\c;red;;lw;0.3;;;Rectangle;\\
```

PART
V

CH
20

Note that the macro now has a backslash that has been added in place of the layer name and its following semicolon, enabling you to type in the name of any layer on which you want the rectangle to be placed.

Tip 189 from *Ron House*	Although using ^C^C is sufficient to cancel most commands, in some cases this will not work. Specifically, you must consider the use of grips and noun/verb selection when designing your macro. To illustrate this, examine the following macro:
	
	`^C^C_Erase;\;`
	
	This simple macro enables the user to select one object to erase, requiring no keyboard input or shortcut menu interaction. If grips are applied to an object before activating this macro, using ^C^C would not cancel the grips, so the Erase command would be applied to the selected object. This may be acceptable, but you must pay attention to which objects have grips applied to them before activating the macro. If not, the objects highlighted with grips will be erased rather than enabling you to select an object. To force the macro to ignore objects selected with grips, use the Pickfirst setting variable to turn off the noun/verb selection, run the macro, and then turn the setting variable back on after you finish with the Erase command. Therefore, the macro would now look like this:
	
	`^C^C_Pickfirst;0;Erase;\;_Pickfirst;1;`
	
	Although this may not be the solution for all scenarios, the point is to consider how you work when designing a macro. A macro that works well in one instance may not work well in other operations.

Macros are a great way to add functionality to AutoCAD without needing to have programming experience. Rather than having to activate each command separately, you can write a macro to string together the commands needed to complete a repetitive task. Since these commands are group together as a macro, they are activated during one click of the button, saving you valuable time and increasing productivity. However, if you want to add logic or user interaction and be able to use and access system variables from within your macros, you'll need to resort to writing AutoLISP functions. Then the AutoLISP functions themselves can be assigned to a button. In the next section, you'll learn at a basic level how to do this.

ASSIGNING AN AUTOLISP ROUTINE TO A BUTTON

Let's take toolbar customizing one step further by running an AutoLISP routine from a toolbar button. The process is relatively simple: You can either recreate the code shown later using a text editor, or you can copy the sample routine from the companion CD. You'll find the code located in the directory of the same name as this chapter. Begin by creating an AutoLISP routine to add to a new toolbar.

EXAMPLE: ASSIGNING AN AUTOLISP ROUTINE TO A TOOLBAR BUTTON

1. Make certain that AutoCAD is not running. You will be modifying files that AutoCAD loads upon opening, so you will change these files first and then launch AutoCAD.

2. Using a text editor such as Notepad, open the file called SEUACAD2000.lsp from the Chapter 20 directory that you copied from the companion CD. You may also opt to type in the code using a text editor exactly as you see it listed here:

```
(defun zoomW ()
(Command "_zoom" "w" pause pause)
)
(defun zoomx10th ()
(Command "_zoom" ".1x")
)
(defun zoomx2 ()
(Command "_zoom" "2x")
)
```

3. These are the three functions you will access from the toolbar. Each function is defined by the defun, or define function statement. After you have opened the file or duplicated the code, save this file using the same name (SEUACAD2000.lsp) to a directory on the AutoCAD search path. To determine which directories are on this search path, right-click at the command line and select Options from the menu. Click the Files tab from the Options dialog box, and then expand the Support File Search Path (see Figure 20.9).

Figure 20.9
You can view the directories in the AutoCAD support file search path from the Options dialog box.

4. From the AutoCAD Support directory, open the file acad2000doc.lsp using your text editor. Append the following code to the end of this file:

```
(load "SEUACAD2000.lsp" (princ))
```

5. Save the file, start AutoCAD, and open a drawing from the Sample directory.

6. Right-click on a toolbar and select Customize from the menu.

7. Select the New Button from the Toolbar dialog box, and enter **SEACAD2000** for the name of the toolbar. Click the OK button to create the toolbar (see Figure 20.10)

Figure 20.10
Commands, custom macros, and AutoLISP routines can be assigned to a new toolbar created with the New Toolbar dialog box.

8. A new toolbar will appear in the drawing editor. Select the Customize button and drag and drop from the list of existing toolbars at least three buttons to your new toolbar.

9. Right-click on a button from the new toolbar to access the Button Properties dialog box. Add the following code to the Macro edit box:

   `(zoomW)`

10. Repeat the last step for each function contained in the SEUACAD2000.lsp file for each button. When you finish, you will have assigned the (zoomx10th) function and the (zoomx2) function to separate buttons on the new toolbar. Change the individual button names and, if you wish, the helpstring for each button.

11. Close all the dialog boxes to update the toolbar.

12. As you click each button, the associated AutoLISP routine should now run, enabling you to quickly navigate the drawing with a single button click.

Note

If you want to add more advanced functionality to toolbars beyond what is covered in this section, check out Chapter 21, " A Primer for AutoLISP and VBA." Look to this chapter for insight on how to create your own AutoLISP functions and routines.

Tip 190 from
Ron House

Use the AutoCAD Customization Reference that ships with AutoCAD 2000 as an additional resource for learning how to write AutoLISP functions.

As you finished modifying the toolbars, you may have noticed that certain messages were displayed at the command line. These messages indiscreetly notified you that several menu files were updated and automatically modified as you made changes to the toolbars. These menu files are text-based files, which can easily be customized to activate a command when a specific interface tool has been selected. The next section deals with modifying these interfaces.

MODIFYING THE ACAD.MNU FILE

The ACAD.MNU file consists of nine different sections, each defining how a specific part of the AutoCAD interface will function.

These sections, which are separated in menu groups, are described here:

- Menu group—A string of 32 characters (no spaces or punctuation marks allowed) that define the contents of a section of the menu file. This is the unique label that distinguishes this portion of the menu from other partial menus, which are all combined to make the entire menu.

- Auxiliary—This is the system pointing device menu, which contains the commands that are assigned to the buttons on the device.

- Buttons—This is the section for pointing devices with multiple buttons, other than the system pointing device, such as a digitizer puck or stylus. This is defined by the section label BUTTONSn, where n indicates the number of button menu groups. Only the numbers 1 through 4 are allowed.

- Pop—This section defines the pull-down and shortcut menus shown in the menu bar. These are labeled as POPn, where n can be a number from 1 through 16.

- Toolbars—This section determines the makeup of the toolbars; the correlation between button icon and command; whether the toolbar is a flyout, docked or undocked, and hidden or visible; and the position of the toolbar. These have a label of TOOLBARS.

- Image—This defines the text and corresponding image used in an image tile, such as with the Hatch and Point Style commands. This menu section's label is IMAGE.

- Screen—This section describes the various menus accessed from the Screen menu, labeled as the menu group SCREEN.

- Tablet—This menu group defines the tablet section of the menu and associates the command with the section of the tablet that activates it.

- Helpstrings—This section defines the helpstring shown in the status bar associated with a pull-down or toolbar menu function. This is labeled HELPSTRINGS.

- Accelerators—This menu section lists the keyboard accelerators that are defined in the menu and accessed via the keyboard.

Note

The *AutoCAD Customization Reference* should be used as a reference for a broader understanding of each of the menu files and their sections.

MODIFYING THE BUTTON MENU GROUP

This menu section enables you to customize the key and button combinations that are possible using a pointing device with multiple buttons, such as digitizer tablets. The functionality of digitizer tablets that typically utilize a puck or stylus can take advantage of this menu section. To illustrate this, let's examine the following code from the ACAD.MNU file:

Note

The format for the Button and Aux menu sections are the same, although they have differing functions. The Aux menu section defines the functionality of the main pointing device, while the Buttons section determines the commands accessed from an alternate pointing device, such as a digitizer puck.

Tip 191 from
Ron House

Comments can be placed within the menu by placing two forward slashes (//) before the text in that row. These rows are then ignored when the menu is compiled. It is a good idea to thoroughly document your menu to remind yourself of the changes you have made.

Examine the following sample snippet of button menu code:

```
***BUTTONS1
// Simple + button
// If a grip is hot bring up the Grips Cursor Menu (POP 500), else send a carriage
return
// If the SHORTCUTMENU sysvar is not 0 the first item (for button 1) is NOT USED.
$M=$(if,$(eq,$(substr,$(getvar,cmdnames),1,5),GRIP_),$P0=ACAD.GRIPS $P0=*);
$P0=SNAP $p0=*
^C^C
```

For example purposes, only the first three buttons are shown in the sample code. The first line contains the header label defining the button section. This is indicated by three asterisks before the section name. After this, each row represents a specific button and what action will occur when a button is selected. The button actions are listed in order, beginning with Button 1, Button 2, and so on.

The first button checks to see whether grips are active—if not, then it displays nothing. If the grips are active and you choose a hot grip, the Grip command mode is displayed in the status bar. Not every button menu row will look similar to this. This particular row uses the Diesel macro language to add a bit of logic to this button action. This can greatly enhance the functionality of menus, and with some work you can master working with the language.

Note

> More information can be obtained by referring to the section later in this chapter called "Implementing the Diesel Macro Language in Your Menu Files."

The second button utilizes the code $P0=SNAP to display the Snap pop-up menu when pressed. This same menu can be accessed by holding down the Shift key and the right mouse button. The third button issues a cancel by using the control key combination ^C^C string when pressed. Other control key combinations can be used to toggle different settings; some of these are shown in Table 20.1.

TABLE 20.1 EXAMPLES OF CONTROL KEY COMBINATIONS

Control Key	Function
^B	Toggles the use of Snap in the drawing
^O	Toggles the use of Ortho in the drawing
^G	Toggles the display of the Grid in the drawing
^D	Toggles the display of the Coordinates at the status bar
^E	Sets the active Isometric Isoplane (either Right, Top, or Left) in the drawing
^T	Toggles the Tablet mode off or on in the drawing

The buttons can also be combined with certain keys to increase the tablet button functionality. The button-key combinations are shown in Table 20.2.

TABLE 20.2   THE AVAILABLE BUTTON-KEY MENU COMBINATIONS AND CORRESPONDING BUTTON SECTION

Button Section	Button-Key Combination
***BUTTONS2	Shift + button
***BUTTONS3	Ctrl + button
***BUTTONS4	Ctrl + shift + button

One of the best reasons for modifying the Button or Aux menus is that you can have a number of commands available at your fingertips. With either a mouse or a digitizer puck, neither pointing device has to be moved to access a command if a function is assigned to a button.

CREATING YOUR OWN PULL-DOWN MENU

Of all the menu types, pull-down menus are among the easiest to create. You may wish to create a pull-down menu of your own that contains specific commands you use on a daily basis. For example, you could compile into a single pull-down menu all the commands you used most often from all the pull-down menus. This would keep you from having to memorize the location of these commands in the pull-down menus, and would provide you with one pull-down menu to access the commands you use most. The following code illustrates an example of a custom pull-down menu. Use this code to model your own pull-down menu:

```
***POP12
**CUSTOM
ID_MnSE2000   [&SE2000]
[->Drawing]
ID_Line       [&Line]^C^C_Line
ID_Circle     [<-&CircleTtr]^C^C_Circle ttr \\\
[--]
[->Editing]
ID_Erase      [&Erase]^C^C_Erase
ID_Move       [&Move]^C^C_Move
ID_Copy       [<-Co&py]^C^C_Copy
```

Let's examine the code here briefly to give you a better idea of what happens when you select a menu option. First, the ***POP12 indicates the order of the menus placed across the menu bar. In this case, this will be the 12th pull-down menu from the left side of the screen. The submenu name is preceded by two asterisks, allowing the menu to be referenced by name. The ID_Mn is the nametag, which identifies the header of the menu file. Immediately after the nametag is the text that will be displayed in the menu bar, enclosed within square brackets. Similarly, text placed within brackets defines the text for each item that will be displayed on the menu. The item name should indicate the command that will be activated when that option is chosen. The ampersand placed before a character in the name specifies the hot key for that menu.

PART

V

CH

20

Placed after the control characters to cancel the current command (^C^C) is the command that will be activated. Each space in the command string indicates a carriage return, so each parameter or value is separated by a space. Text used within the command string must be enclosed inside double quotes.

Cascading menus can be placed in the menu by using the <- and -> symbols inside the option name brackets. The first -> symbols indicate where the menu starts to cascade, and you must have a corresponding <- symbol to allow the menu to close. Also, the [—] symbol defines a menu separator.

FORCING A MENU TO PAUSE FOR USER INPUT

You can expand the use of a menu option by allowing the menus to pause for user input. For example, look at the Circle TTR command in the POP12 sample menu code. Backslashes are inserted to pause for user input, in this example to enable the user to select the tangent objects and to specify the circle radius.

Tip 192 from *Ron House*	Because a backslash is used to pause for user input, it cannot be used anywhere else in the macro. If you want to specify a path, you must use the forward slash instead.

Experiment with modifying this sample code to create more complex pull-down menus. Place this segment of code before the Toolbars section in the ACAD.MNU file. Save the file, and use the Menu command to reload the ACAD.MNU file.

MODIFYING THE TABLET MENU SECTION

The tablet menu section works hand in hand with a tablet overlay. The tablet overlay divides a digitizer tablet into multiple spaces, defined by column and row designations. Each space is related to a row in the tablet menu. To see a sample tablet overlay, open the drawing Tablet 2000.dwg (see Figure 20.11). This template is shipped with AutoCAD, so you can modify the tablet menu section and update the table overlay to match your changes.

Figure 20.11
The AutoCAD tablet overlay located in the Sample directory displays the four menu areas and the screen pointing area.

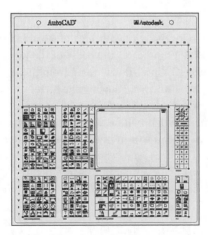

The tablet overlay is split up into four main menu areas and a screen pointing area. When a tablet overlay has been created, you'll need to map the location of the area corners to define the columns and rows.

CONFIGURING A TABLET OVERLAY

The following steps outline the setup procedure for those users who work with digitizer tablets.

EXAMPLE: CONFIGURING A TABLET OVERLAY

1. Secure the tablet overlay to the digitizer tablet. If the overlay shifts at any time during the setup process, you'll need to reconfigure it again.

2. From the pull-down menus, select Tools, Tablet, Configure. During the tablet configuration process, you will specify the number of rows and columns of each of the four menu areas. Then you will be prompted to pick points on the digitizer that define three corners of each of the four menu areas. After you have entered the number of rows and columns for the menu areas, this prompt appears:

   ```
   Digitize upper left corner of menu area 1:
   ```

3. Pick the three corners of each menu section. When you have completed this, you will be prompted to specify the fixed screen pointing area:

   ```
   Do you want to respecify the Fixed Screen Pointing Area? <N>:
   ```

4. Answer Yes, and pick the upper-left and lower-right corners of the fixed screen pointing area.

5. Next, the prompt to specify the floating screen menu area appears:

   ```
   Do you want to specify the Floating Screen Pointing Area? <N>:
   ```

6. This allows you to disable the tablet menu areas to trace a drawing with your tablet. You must define a floating screen pointing area to access the status bar and pull-down menus.

7. Type **Y** and press Enter; this prompt appears:

   ```
   Do you want the Floating Screen Pointing Area to be the same size as the Fixed
   Screen Pointing Area? <Y>:
   ```

8. This enables you to specify that the floating screen area should be the same as the fixed screen area you defined earlier. Entering **N** at the prompt enables you to define a different location for the floating screen area.

9. Then the final prompt is displayed:

   ```
   The F12 key will toggle the Floating Screen Pointing Area ON and OFF. Would
   you like to specify a button to toggle the Floating Screen Area? <N>:
   ```

10. Replying No uses the default F12 function key to toggle the use of the floating screen area. Answering Yes enables you to set a different function key for this action.

AutoCAD stores this configuration until you reconfigure the tablet. Test your tablet menu by selecting a command from each of the menu areas to see whether the correct command is activated.

PART

V

CH

20

HELPSTRINGS

The helpstrings menu section uses the name tag to determine the helpstring associated with the menu item. Helpstrings assist the users to determine what command or feature will be activated if a menu item is selected. For example, say that you have a pull-down menu that looks like this:

```
***POP12
**SAMPLE
ID_MnSE2000  [&SE2000]
ID_Line      [&Line]^C^C_Line
ID_Circle    [&Circle]^C^C_Circle
ID_Rectangle [&Rectangle]^C^C_Rectang
```

A corresponding helpstring section would look like this:

```
***HELPSTRINGS
ID_Line [This activates the Line command]
ID_Circle [This activates the Circle command]
ID_Rectangle [This activates the Rectangle command]
```

Note that the ID_Name name tag is the unique identifier to link the helpstring to the menu item. You can use this feature to provide users of custom applications with hints or tips as to what the custom menu items do or provide.

ACCELERATOR KEYS

Accelerator keys can be defined in the ACAD.MNU file to give more flexibility than the keyboard shortcuts defined in the ACAD.PGP file.

→ The keyboard shortcuts are covered in the "Modifying the Keyboard Shortcuts" section, earlier in this chapter.

Those shortcuts referenced by the keyboard are limited to the use of alphabetic keys, while the accelerator keys can use the alphabetic keys in conjunction with the Shift, Ctrl, and Function keys, which are called modifiers. This gives you a broader base of key combinations to work from, thus enabling you to activate more commands quickly using the accelerators via the keyboard. These combinations are typically a single character or a virtual key, such as a function key, that is enclosed within double quotes.

Actually two distinct types of accelerators exist: the Name-tab Value and the Explicit command sequence. Although these formats are similar, the latter format gives you some greater flexibility because you can string together multiple commands, much like the macros defined in using the toolbars.

Tip 193 from
Ron House

You may find that those commands requiring more user interaction might be best activated by the Explicit command sequence accelerators, which enable you to quickly initiate the command. You could then utilize the Name-tab Value accelerators for those commands that require little or no interaction, such as Zoom All or Erase Previous. Then these commands can be combined and run in sequence using the accelerator.

CREATING NAME-TAB VALUE ACCELERATORS

Name-tab accelerators are defined in the menu structure first by a name-tab, which is used to dictate which command will be activated by the character combinations. This is followed by a label containing modifiers with a single character. Multiple modifiers can be used by specifying a "+" sign to concatenate the string together. The following are examples of Name-Tab Value accelerators:

```
ID_Line    [Shift+Control+"L"]

ID_ZoomW   [Control+"F12"]
```

In both of these examples, each accelerator is initiated with an ID, the name of the command to be activated, and finally the modifier and virtual key. Note that because the command is defined in the name tab, this format doesn't really allow for multiple commands to be activated at once. The next format allows a bit more flexibility.

DEFINING AN EXPLICIT COMMAND SEQUENCE ACCELERATOR

Explicit command sequence accelerators are formatted to look like this:

```
[SHIFT+CONTROL+"M"]midpoint

[CONTROL+"E"]zoom all erase all
```

The Explicit command sequence accelerators are in reverse order from the name-tab value format. The modifiers and virtual key combinations are defined first, and then the associated command string. This format makes it easier to concatenate multiple commands together, as shown in the last example. Table 20.3 displays the available virtual keys.

TABLE 20.3	VIRTUAL KEYS
Key	**Function**
F1	Toggles the display of the Help function
F2	Toggles the display of the text screen
F3	Toggles the use of Osnap in the drawing
F4	Toggles the Tablet mode off or on in the drawing
F5	Sets the active Isometric Isoplane (either Right, Top, or Left) in the drawing
F6	Toggles the display of the Coordinates at the status bar
F7	Toggles the display of the Grid in the drawing
F8	Toggles the use of Ortho in the drawing
F9	Toggles the use of Snap in the drawing
F10	Toggles the use of Polar Tracking in the drawing
F11	Toggles the use of Object Snap Tracking in the drawing

PART

V

CH

20

continues

TABLE 20.3   CONTINUED

Key	Function
F12	Can be used to toggle the use of the floating screen menu area if one is defined during the tablet configuration
Insert	Unassigned
Delete	Unassigned
Escape	By default, this button is assigned the Cancel function, and it is not recommended that this be altered. You can use this button in combination with the Shift modifier, but not with Shift+Ctrl+Escape or Ctrl+Escape, which define Window functions.
Up Arrow	Can be used only with the Control modifier
Down Arrow	Can be used only with the Control modifier
Left Arrow	Can be used only with the Control modifier
Right Arrow	Can be used only with the Control modifier
NUMPAD0-9	Unassigned

Utilize these virtual keys with the Shift or Control modifiers to define any command you want to an accelerator key. For example, you could assign the various Zoom commands you use on a frequent basis, such as Zoom Extents, Zoom Previous, and Zoom Window, as Explicit Command Sequence Accelerators. You could combine the function keys F1, F2, and F3 with the Shift key to activate these commands with ease.

Tip 194 from
Ron House

When creating Name-tab Value or Explicit Command Sequence Accelerators, carefully choose the keys you use to activate the commands. They should be quickly typed with one hand if possible and located to make memorizing these keyboard combinations an easy task.

To expand the functionality of the menu files, the Diesel macro language can be used to add some evaluation capabilities to enhance the somewhat static menu files, as illustrated in the next section.

IMPLEMENTING THE DIESEL MACRO LANGUAGE IN YOUR MENU FILES

DIESEL is an acronym for Direct Interpretively Evaluated String Expression Language, a macro language for changing what can be displayed at the status line. Although this language is used mainly to alter the status line, Diesel string expressions can also be used in all menu sections, as you saw in the sample Button code. Diesel can be used to make evaluations based on the value of certain settings, which can then be used to toggle the display of menus off and on.

The easiest way to learn Diesel is to first experiment with sample code within the ACAD.MNU file at the command line, using the MODEMACRO command. This command can be run by itself or transparently within the operation of another command. Examine the following examples to get a better feel for using this macro language.

→ Use the AutoCAD Help function to gain more information on the use of Diesel in the menu files and elsewhere in AutoCAD.

THE BASIC USE OF DIESEL   Examine the following sample Diesel expressions:

```
$(/,25,5)
```

```
$(getvar,clayer)
```

```
$(if,$(getvar,orthomode),"Off","On")
```

Diesel expressions are enclosed within parenthesis preceded by the dollar sign ($); this indicates to AutoCAD that the following information is in Diesel. Inside the parentheses, an operator must be used to determine the value of the expression. In the first sample, the division sign is the operator used to divide 25 by 5. Try this sample code by first typing Modemacro at the command line and then entering the expression. When you press Enter, the resulting value will appear in the lower-left corner of the status bar.

In the second expression, getvar is the operator, which retrieves the variable of the argument, the setting variable within the parenthesis. In this example, the getvar is the Clayer variable, which stores the name of the current layer. Testing this expression using the Modemacro command displays the current layer in the status bar. This can be expanded by placing **Current layer:** before the expression to further define what is being displayed at the status bar, as the following code illustrates:

```
[$(eval,"Current layer: " $(getvar,clayer))]
```

In this case, the EVAL operator is used to display the text, which is enclosed within double quotes and is the result of the nested Diesel expression.

The third expression is a little more complicated because it is used to determine the value of a current setting. Note that Diesel expressions can be nested, with the inside expression being evaluated first. In the case of this expression, the current setting of the Orthomode is found and then compared with the values Off or On. If the current Orthomode setting is off, a value of 1 is returned and the word Off is displayed in the lower left corner of the status bar. Toggling the Orthomode back on displays On.

These three examples are very basic and can easily be incorporated into your menu code to display messages informing you of the state of certain settings, like the last Orthomode expression. The next section shows you how to accomplish this.

PART

V

CH

20

USING DIESEL IN A MENU

Preceding a Diesel expression with the $M= command allows the expression to be evaluated with a menu macro. Let's look at the next sample expression, which not only toggles the Orthomode setting off and on, but also dynamically changes the text displayed in the menu itself:

```
[$(eval,"Snapmode " $(if,$(getvar,snapmode),"Off","On"))]'SNAPMODE $M=$(-
,1,$(getvar,snapmode))
```

Diesel expressions are used in both the name and in the display of the snapmode variable. In using the expression in the menu name, you do not need to use the $M= command. The menu item name will display whether the snapmode is on or off, depending on the current setting of the variable. The later part of the expression displays the current Snap mode in the menu.

Diesel expressions can be used to make your menus more dynamic, allowing them to display settings or values. Although this chapter only starts to represent what can be done with Diesel, you'll find more examples and information in the AutoCAD Help files by searching for the keyword Diesel.

You can quickly check whether your menu works by creating a smaller custom menu to load. These menus are called partial menus and can be easily loaded and unloaded, enabling you to further enhance the AutoCAD interface. The next section discusses partial menus in further detail.

LOADING PARTIAL MENUS

You can define any portion of a menu file as a separate .MNU file and load that portion of the menu file by itself, allowing it to be dynamically combined with the current loaded menu. This allows a greater degree of flexibility and enables you to create menus that are discipline-specific and that can easily be changed when needed. To illustrate this, let's look at the following menu example:

```
***POP12
**CUSTOM
ID_MnARCH   [&Architectural]
ID_Walls        [&Walls]^C^C_Mline


***TOOLBARS


**TB_DIMENSION
ID_TbDimensi [_Toolbar("Dimension", _Floating, _Show, 100, 130, 1)]
ID_Dimlinear [_Button("Linear Dimension", ICON_16_DIMLIN,
ICON_16_DIMLIN)]^C^C_dimlinear
ID_Dimaligne [_Button("Aligned Dimension", ICON_16_DIMALI,
ICON_16_DIMALI)]^C^C_dimaligned
ID_Dimordina [_Button("Ordinate Dimension", ICON_16_DIMORD,
ICON_16_DIMORD)]^C^C_dimordinate
             [--]
ID_Dimradius [_Button("Radius Dimension", ICON_16_DIMRAD,
ICON_16_DIMRAD)]^C^C_dimradius
ID_Dimdiamet [_Button("Diameter Dimension", ICON_16_DIMDIA,
ICON_16_DIMDIA)]^C^C_dimdiameter
ID_Dimangula [_Button("Angular Dimension", ICON_16_DIMANG,
ICON_16_DIMANG)]^C^C_dimangular
             [--]
ID_QDim        [_Button("Quick Dimension", ICON_16_QDIM, ICON_16_QDIM)]^C^C_qdim
ID_Dimbaseli [_Button("Baseline Dimension", ICON_16_DIMBAS,
```

```
        ICON_16_DIMBAS)]^C^C_dimbaseline
ID_Dimcontin [_Button("Continue Dimension", ICON_16_DIMCON,
ICON_16_DIMCON)]^C^C_dimcontinue
            [--]
ID_Leader    [_Button("Quick Leader", ICON_16_QLEADER,
ICON_16_QLEADER)]^C^C_qleader
ID_Tolerance [_Button("Tolerance", ICON_16_TOLERA, ICON_16_TOLERA)]^C^C_tolerance
ID_Dimcenter [_Button("Center Mark", ICON_16_DIMCEN,
ICON_16_DIMCEN)]^C^C_dimcenter
            [--]
ID_Dimedit   [_Button("Dimension Edit", ICON_16_DIMNEW,
ICON_16_DIMNEW)]^C^C_dimedit
ID_Dimtedit  [_Button("Dimension Text Edit", ICON_16_DIMHOM,
ICON_16_DIMHOM)]^C^C_dimtedit
ID_DimUpdate [_Button("Dimension Update", ICON_16_DIMUPD, ICON_16_DIMUPD)]^C^C_-
dimstyle _apply
```

This menu named ch20_ex2.mnu, which is included on the companion CD, will load a partial menu that deals specifically with creating and dimensioning walls. The Architectural pull-down menu can be used to activate the Multiline command, and the menu displays a custom toolbar that contains those dimensioning commands that could be used to dimension walls.

Tip 195 from
Ron House

You could take this example one step further by loading an architectural multiline style before launching the command. For example, say that you have a multiline style name loaded in the drawing called WallInt2x4, used to create interior 2-by-4 walls. The pull-down menu code would then look like this:

```
***POP12
**CUSTOM
ID_MnARCH  [&Architectural]
ID_Walls    [&Walls]^C^C_Mline St WallInt2x4
```

This could also be used to set the justification and scale of the multiline.

As you saw earlier in the chapter, after a change was made to the ACAD.MNU file, the Menu command was used to recompile and reload the menu. This command is used to load only what could be called the base menu, which in this case actually is the ACAD.MNU file. When you want to load a smaller, partial menu, incorporating it with the already loaded base menu, use the Menuload command.

Tip 196 from
Ron House

The Button and Aux menu sections are ignored when a partial menu is loaded.

This command is accessed from the pull-down menus by choosing Tools, Customize Menus, or by typing **Menuload** at the command line. This opens the Menu Customization dialog box, shown in Figure 20.12.

PART
V

CH
20

Figure 20.12
The Menu
Customization dialog
box is used to load
partial custom menu
files.

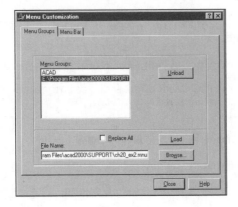

Select the Menu Groups tab, using the Browse button to locate the menu file you want to
load; then click the Load button. After the menu is loaded, and if a pull-down menu is
defined in the custom menu, you can define where the menu is located on the menu bar.
Select the Menu Bar tab, which displays the options shown in Figure 20.13.

Figure 20.13
The Menu Bar tab
contained within the
Menu Customization
dialog box can be
used to position a
custom pull-down
menu anywhere in
the menu bar.

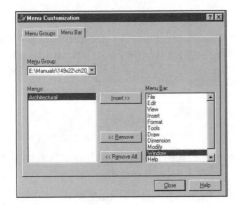

Choosing the custom menu from the Menu Group select list displays and highlights the
name of the custom menu in the Menu Bar list box. The list on the left contains the names
of the pull-down menus available from the recently loaded menu file. The list box on the
opposite side displays the names of the currently loaded pull-down menus. Select the name
of the pull-down file you want to insert into the currently loaded menu, then select where
you want the menu to be inserted. Only the selected menu is inserted preceding the pull-
down object you choose when you click the Insert button. You should automatically see the
name of the custom pull-down menu appear in the menu bar. You can also use the Remove
Button to remove a single pull-down menu, or the Remove All button to remove all pull-
down menus from being displayed in the menu bar. The following example reiterates the
process of loading a partial menu using the code listing earlier in this section.

1. From the pull-down menus, choose Tools, Customize Menus.

2. Select the Menu Groups tab after the Menu Customization dialog box appears. Use the Browse button to locate the custom menu ch20_ex2.mnu that you copied from the companion CD.

3. Click the Load button to load the menu. You should see the Wall Dim toolbar appear.

4. Next, select the Menu Bar tab. Select the custom menu from the Menu Group; the Architectural menu name appears in the Menus list.

5. From the Menu Bar list, select the pull-down menu you want to insert into the current menu. Click the Insert button. The Architectural menu should appear as one of the available pull-down menus.

Loading partial menus gives you the flexibility to access custom specific menus that enhance the standard AutoCAD menu. Consider creating custom menus that allow quick and easy access to blocks, macros, scripts, and AutoLISP routines designed around a specific function or discipline.

In the next section, you'll learn how to broaden the use of AutoCAD by integrating it with data from other sources, such as data created using the Microsoft Office products.

EMBEDDING DATA FROM OTHER SOURCES USING OLE

The functionality of AutoCAD is definitely enhanced when you utilize the power of Windows object linking and embedding, or OLE, to link and import data from outside sources. Because the data is linked, if the outside source is updated, the data displayed in AutoCAD also is updated. Accessing and modifying the data is a simple process: Just double-click on the data object in AutoCAD to launch the software in which the data is stored. Importing this data is also an easy task; follow through the next example to see how it is done.

EXAMPLE: EMBEDDING AN EXCEL SPREADSHEET INTO AUTOCAD

1. This example uses Microsoft Excel for Windows NT or 95/98. The important thing to remember is that if you wish to use another spreadsheet application, that application must support OLE for it to work. Open the drawing ch20_1.dwg you copied from the companion CD.

2. Open Excel and the spreadsheet ch20_ex3.xls. Click cell A:1, and drag to H:35 to highlight the spreadsheet data.

3. In Excel, choose Copy from the Edit pull-down menu.

4. Switch to AutoCAD by selecting the AutoCAD tab from the Windows desktop taskbar. Then, from the Edit pull-down menu, select Paste Special, which opens the Paste Special dialog box (see Figure 20.14).

Figure 20.14
The Paste Special dialog box imports data from other applications into AutoCAD via the Windows Clipboard.

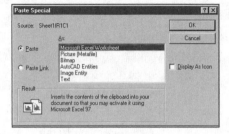

5. Click the Paste Link radio button. Microsoft Excel Worksheet should be highlighted in the <u>A</u>s list.

6. Select the OK button, and the spreadsheet is imported into the current drawing (see Figure 20.14).

7. Note that the size of the spreadsheet is too large due to the scale of the current drawing. Right-click and select the Properties option from the shortcut menu to adjust the size.

Figure 20.15
The properties of a data object imported into AutoCAD may need to be adjusted, depending on the scale of your drawing.

8. The OLE Properties dialog box opens. Set the size height and width to 25%, making certain that the <u>L</u>ock Aspect Ratio check box is selected.

Tip 197 from
Ron House

To restore an OLE object to its original size, right-click the object and select <u>P</u>roperties. Then click the Reset button.

9. You can also adjust the text font and size from this dialog. Click the OK button to apply the changes to the imported data object.

10. With grips still applied to the spreadsheet, move the object to the desired location in the drawing.

Note

Other paste options are available from the Edit pull-down menu as well:

- Paste—Imports data on the Clipboard into the AutoCAD drawing. Using this option creates no link with the source document, so the source document can be updated without modifying the OLE object in AutoCAD.
- Paste as Block—Inserts objects from the Clipboard inserted into AutoCAD as a block.
- Paste as Hyperlink—Pastes a hyperlink to the object you select.
- Paste to Original Coordinates—Pastes the objects from the Clipboard to the same coordinates as in the original drawing.

Other applications can be used to embed OLE data objects into AutoCAD. Word documents, PowerPoint slide shows, or even Microsoft Project timelines can be imported and displayed.

Tip 198 from
Ron House

Text from a document can be copied to the Clipboard and pasted into AutoCAD by using the Ctrl+C/Ctrl+V key combination. The text automatically will be inserted into AutoCAD, and the OLE Properties dialog box will appear, allowing you to modify the properties of the inserted text. This process can save time when you wish to import text into AutoCAD.

Beyond the use of Microsoft Office products, you can also embed animations, sound, and video clips into AutoCAD, turning your drawing into a presentation showpiece to present your ideas.

EXPORTING AN AUTOCAD DRAWING USING THE CLIPBOARD

You may also want to export your drawing into other types of software applications to illustrate a point or concept. This can be done using the Clipboard and the Cut and Paste commands. To export an AutoCAD drawing, three copy functions are available from the Edit pull-down menu:

- Copy—The Copy, or Copyclip command, can be used to copy drawing objects or text from the drawing, depending on the location of the cursor at the time the Copyclip command is activated. Placing the cursor at the command line or text screen while pressing Crtl+C copies text to the Clipboard. Pressing the same set of keys while the cursor is in the graphics screen enables you to select drawing objects to copy.

- Copy with Base point—This copies the object from the current drawing with a user-specified base point. This means that the copied object can be accurately placed in the original drawing or another drawing.

- Copy Link—This copies the current view to the Clipboard.

After the AutoCAD objects have been copied to the Clipboard, use the Paste Special command to insert them into another application.

EDITING AN EMBEDDED AutoCAD DRAWING OBJECT

After an OLE object has been embedded into your drawing, you may need to edit the linked object. You can access the many OLE editing options by right-clicking on the object. Here you can choose options that enable you to toggle the selectability and display order of the data object.

Tip 199 from *Ron House*	When an OLE object is imported into AutoCAD, you can also use the Olehide command to toggle the display of the object off and on in model space and paper space. Refer to Chapter 18, "Plotting and Layouts," for more information on model space and paper space.

Also from the shortcut menu is a cascading menu name Linked Document Object that contains specific options for editing these objects:

- Edit—This switches you to the application in which the OLE data object was created for editing. The application should be open when this occurs—if not, you might see an alert message stating "Failed to launch server application."
- Open—This opens the OLE object in its original application.
- Convert—This converts the OLE object so that it can be opened by another application. This option can be used to convert an object to be edited by an application that is different from its source application.

Other options are available for maintaining the OLE object through the use of the Olelinks command. Selecting this option from the Edit pull-down menu displays the dialog box shown in Figure 20.16.

Figure 20.16
Use the Links dialog box to manage the links within your drawing.

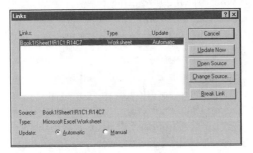

From here you can manage all the links placed into your drawing, allowing you to update and change applications, and break the link if you do not want the OLE object in AutoCAD to be updated. An example of when you might break a link is when a project is complete, yet you have an active embedded OLE object that is continually updated when the updates no longer apply to the finished project drawings.

Use this command and its options to easily maintain a drawing with embedded links. However, you also must take certain limitations into consideration before embedding a data object using OLE:

- Objects embedded into AutoCAD can be printed only using Window system printers.

- OLE typically embeds the data object as a raster image, which does not print using a pen plotter. A workaround to this is to embed the object instead as a Windows metafile.

- Excel spreadsheets embedded into AutoCAD are limited in size. Only a portion of the spreadsheet will be imported if it is too large. A workaround to this is to break the spreadsheet into multiple smaller parts.

- The Landscape mode of the system printer must be used to rotate the embedded object instead of using plot rotation. An OLE object will not display, will not plot correctly, and will lose its aspect ratio if rotated to an angle other than 0° or 90°.

SUMMARY

As you can see, there are many ways to customize the AutoCAD interface, using not just one tool, but multiple tools. This gives you the ability to customize AutoCAD depending on how you work, using the interface tool you prefer or using multiple tools to increase your productivity. Whether you are an experienced programmer or a beginner, it is well worth your time to investigate customizing the AutoCAD menu. You'll find the time well spent and the productivity you'll gain invaluable.

PART

V

CH

20

A PRIMER FOR AUTOLISP AND VBA

In this chapter

USING VBA AND AutoLISP

With AutoCAD 2000, the range of programming options available to the CAD user has been significantly extended. Historically, AutoLISP was the engine that drove AutoCAD. Until Release 13, AutoLISP was integrated into the core code of AutoCAD. The world of software has since gone through a revolution known as *object-oriented programming*, and AutoCAD has kept pace with this revolution. With AutoCAD 2000, the conversion of AutoCAD to a fully object-oriented program is complete. The AutoCAD 2000 model enables multiple interfaces with a range of programming languages, including Visual Basic for Applications (VBA). Although AutoLISP still retains its popularity, VBA is being increasingly used as a programming environment for AutoCAD customization.

This chapter takes a look at the basic features of these two application programming interfaces (API's): AutoLISP and VBA. Whether you are experienced in AutoLISP or are a new developer, you will want to take a look at both of these environments in AutoCAD 2000. In this chapter, you will develop a set of programs in the AutoLISP environment; then you will review the same programs in the VBA environment. This approach is designed to give you a direct feel for the possible strengths and limitations of each programming environment. At the end of this chapter, you should be able to decide which environment is best suited to your purposes.

All the programs you work with in this chapter are available on the CD that comes with this book. You should make yourself a folder for your programming exercises (for example, create one called "My Programs") and copy all the programs that begin with CH21 into that folder. You should then add this folder to the AutoCAD search path, using the Options command.

→ If you want to learn more about the AutoCAD search path, see the section "Adding a Folder to the AutoCAD Search Path," later in this chapter.

ONCE AND FUTURE LISP

Even within LISP, you can choose from a range of programming options. The LISP language was originally designed as a language for efficiently processing *lists*, such as series of numbers or text. AutoLISP is an adaptation of LISP for AutoCAD. The language easily handles (x, y, z) coordinate geometry and is well suited to programming in a CAD environment. This is still the quickest and easiest way to customize AutoCAD.

Visual LISP was developed as an enhancement to standard AutoLISP. It was introduced as an add-on product for AutoCAD Release 14 and is now included as part of the package with AutoCAD 2000. Visual LISP is a fully integrated development environment (IDE) for AutoLISP. This new environment includes all the capabilities of the original AutoLISP, in addition to a compiler, a debugger, and various productivity tools.

Most LISP developers who are starting out now prefer to work in the Visual LISP environment. However, it is worth your while to familiarize yourself with the workings of the original AutoLISP. You will undoubtedly encounter situations in which it is more efficient to type in a quick LISP routine or macro.

GETTING STARTED WITH AUTOLISP

AutoLISP is the most versatile API for AutoCAD. Almost every AutoCAD user has a library of LISP routines that are used to speed up every aspect of production work—drawing walls, inserting blocks, calculating areas, and plotting drawings. You can jump right in and start some basic programming by simply typing in LISP statements at the command prompt. The built-in AutoLISP interpreter immediately understands LISP statements, so no compiling is required. You can interact with your drawing, assign values, or run programs, all from the command prompt, and get results immediately.

Let's give it a try. Here, you will type in a simple statement to add two numbers.

EXAMPLE: ADDING TWO NUMBERS

1. Open the AutoCAD 2000 Drawing Editor. At the command prompt, type:

   (+ 3 4)

2. Press Enter.

If all went well, the interpreter read your statement and returned the value 7 to the command line. But even this elementary statement contains pitfalls. You need to carefully observe the conventions pertaining to spacing and parentheses, or else this simple addition will fail or return erroneous results. The conventions are as follows:

- Spaces—Make sure you put a space after the plus sign and a space between the two numbers. If you omit the space after the plus, AutoCAD will return an error message; if you omit the space between 3 and 4, AutoCAD will—correctly—return a value of 34.

- Parentheses—Every AutoLISP statement must be enclosed in parentheses. These parentheses may be nested to any level—that is, a LISP statement may contain other LISP statements, which in turn are enclosed in parentheses. Left and right parentheses *must* balance. If they don't, your statement or program will not run.

If you enter a statement at the command prompt that doesn't balance, you will see the following prompt:

(_>

Here, the interpreter is giving you a chance to complete the statement. You can type in the missing parenthesis at this prompt, or you can press the Esc key to cancel and start over.

SIMPLE EXPRESSIONS, FUNCTIONS, AND ARGUMENTS

An AutoLISP program consists of a series of *expressions*. The simple calculation you have completed demonstrates the basic elements of an AutoCAD expression, a *function*, and an *argument*—and don't forget the parentheses. Table 21.1 shows some examples of elementary arithmetic functions (also known as *operators*).

PART

V

CH

21

TABLE 21.1   EXAMPLES OF AUTOLISP ARITHMETIC FUNCTIONS

Function	Description
+	Returns the sum of all numbers
-	Subtracts the second and following numbers from the first
*	Returns the product of all numbers
/	Divides the first number by the product of the following numbers
1-	Returns the number reduced by 1
max	Returns the largest number
rem	Divides the first number by the second and returns the remainder

The values supplied to a function are called *arguments*. These follow the function separated by spaces. You should observe the following conventions:

- The function (or operator) always goes first, followed by the arguments.

- With arithmetic functions, the arguments are typically numbers. If you type **(+ a b)**, the expression will generate an error because the function is expecting to add numbers.

- Most of these functions accept multiple arguments: Try the following expressions and check the results. The first four functions process the multiple arguments; the rem function ignores all arguments beyond the first two; and the final function (1-) cannot process more than one argument.

```
(+ 1 2 3 4)
(- 1 2 3 4)
(- 3 2 4 1)
(max 1 2 3 4
(rem 1 2 3 4
(1- 1 2 3 4)
```

Each function has its own rules, or *syntax*, for the arguments it is expecting. If you supply the wrong type or the wrong number, the interpreter will do one of two things: It may ignore extraneous information—as with (rem 1 2 3 4), where rem requires only two numbers. Or, it may give an error message and the function will not run, as in the final example (1- 1 2 3 4).

Tip 200 from
Paul Richardson

When you are working at the command prompt, you have a very limited window in which to review your work. To review earlier transactions, use the F2 key to open the AutoCAD text window. You can maximize the text window to give yourself even more room to review.

When you are adding (+ operator) and multiplying (* operator), the order of the numbers is not crucial. When you are subtracting (- operator) or dividing (/ operator), however, the syntax makes it crucial to enter them in the right order. In more complex expressions, you can define the precedence of operations by nesting parentheses.

```
(/ (+ 5.9 7.32) 3.247)
```

This statement will process the inner pair of parentheses—the add expression—and then divide the sum by the number 3.247. The innermost parentheses are processed first, and then the interpreter moves out from there. This rule applies to all AutoLISP expressions, not just the arithmetic ones.

> **Note**
>
> Notice in the preceding expression that one of the arguments is itself an expression (+ 5.9 7.32). Just remember as you develop complex nested expressions such as this that the parentheses must balance. This error happens to everyone more often than they would care to admit.

Of course, AutoLISP does a great deal more than perform numerical calculations. A full library of functions are fully described in the AutoCAD Help system—as long as you know how to find your way around it! The following section reviews the Help sections that you will find most helpful.

AutoLISP Help

You will need to refer to the AutoCAD online Help frequently while you are learning the idiosyncrasies of LISP syntax. It's a good idea to keep Help open continuously while you work so you can switch among AutoCAD, Help, and your programming environment.

Example: Using AutoLISP Help

1. From AutoCAD, select the Help button (or press the F1 key).

2. In the Contents tab, click Visual LISP and AutoLISP, and then select the shortcut link to the AutoCAD Visual LISP Help. This takes you to LISP and ActiveX Help.

   You will find it helpful to familiarize yourself with both the AutoLISP Reference and the Visual LISP Developer's Guide. Appendix A in the Developer's Guide provides a useful overview of the different types of LISP functions and what they do. Let's look at this first.

3. Click Visual LISP Developer's Guide to open the online manual, and select Appendix A, "AutoLISP Function Synopsis."

4. Take a moment to browse a few of the different categories: Basic Functions and Utility Functions, for example (see Figure 21.1). Each of these categories has additional subcategories. If you get lost in the nested levels, click the Help Files tab to return to the table of contents.

PART
V

CH

21

Figure 21.1
The Visual LISP Developer's Guide contains a summary of all the AutoLISP functions.

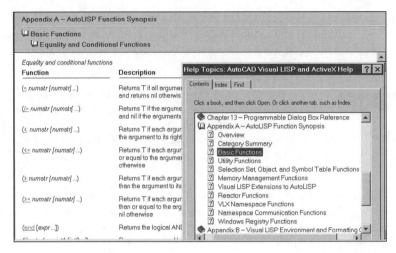

5. If you have closed Help, repeat steps 1 and 2 of the current procedure. Otherwise, browse back to the top of the Help Files tab, click AutoLISP Reference, and select AutoLISP Reference Overview. All the functions are organized alphabetically in this document, not by type of function.

6. Click the A–Z buttons at the top of the screen to navigate through this reference (see Figure 21.2).

Note

The purpose of this exercise is not to confuse you, but to give you a sense of the range of options available in AutoLISP and to show you how to locate information about these functions when you need it. For more detailed information about each function, you must access the AutoLISP Reference.

Figure 21.2
The AutoLISP Reference Overview provides detailed information about the use of each function.

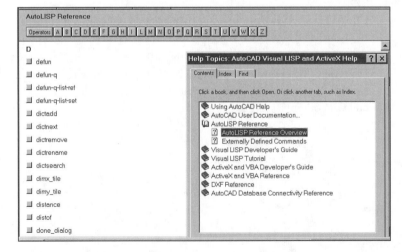

Note

You can download a full-color poster of AutoLISP and Visual LISP Functions from the AutoCAD Web site at `http://www.autodesk.com/products/acad2000/devres/ vlisp.htm`. The file is in Portable Document format (PDF), so you can view it onscreen with Adobe Acrobat software. You will need a "D-"size color plotter to print the file.

You will spend a lot of time in the AutoLISP Reference while you are learning AutoLISP. Some of the function names—such as *getangle* or *length*—give you a clue as to what that function does, but often the names are obscure, such as *terpri* and *mapcar*. In the course of this chapter, you will learn to use a few of the more common functions.

VARIABLES AND DATA TYPES

So far, you have been executing AutoLISP expressions and getting results, but you haven't done anything with the results. The values returned by the calculations were essentially throwaway information. However, in real life and in real programming, the same operations tend to come up repeatedly. You need to be able to store and reuse the same information again and again. This is where variables come in. In AutoLISP, as in most programming languages, you can assign a value to a variable. A *variable* is a temporary storage location for data in your program. For example, you might extract the dimension scale value from the current drawing and store it in a program variable, and then use this variable to manipulate another object's properties, like text size.

To assign a value to a variable, use the setq function, followed by the name of the variable and the value you want to give it. For example, type the following expressions:

```
(setq a 30)
(setq b 26)
```

LISP will store these values in a and b for the duration of your drawing session or until you tell it otherwise. If you type the expression (+ a b), LISP will return a value of (56), not an error code, because a and b are effectively numbers now.

You also can assign the output from any AutoLISP function to a variable. It makes sense to assign the output of any repetitive, complex expressions to a variable—you don't want to have to type complex expressions more than once. Remember the nested expression you used earlier: (/ (+ 5.9 7.32) 3.247). Let's assign that whole expression to the variable a.

```
(setq a (/ (+ 5.9 7.32) 3.247))
```

The new value (4.01745) replaces the old value (30). If you type **(+ a b)** now, the expression will return a new result of (30.0715).

Tip 201 from
Paul Richardson

If you need to check the value of a variable at any time, type an exclamation point followed by the variable name (for example: **!a**) at the command prompt and then press Enter. The

PART

V

CH

21

continued

value of the variable will be displayed on the next line. The exclamation point is needed only when you are working at the AutoCAD command prompt; when you are working in the Visual LISP editor, there is no need to use the exclamation point. Just type the variable name at the prompt to display its value.

Thus far, you have been using variables in a fairly elementary way. Variables can be assigned values in many ways. They can be set up to capture the results of another operation, to combine the output of several expressions or other variables, or to hold information that a user enters as the program runs. You should read further about both variables and the setq function in the AutoLISP Reference in the AutoCAD Help System (see Figures 21.1 and 21.2). You will return to setq in the context of some real programming later in this chapter. For now, let's take a closer look at another aspect of LISP variables: data types.

If you are accustomed to programming in other environments, you will have noticed how easy it is to create a variable in AutoLISP. You may be surprised that you do not have to specify the type of data it contains. Data types are significant in AutoLISP. The LISP interpreter recognizes many different types of data and processes expressions sequentially according to data type. However, you do not have to declare the type. Each variable automatically assumes the data type of the value it receives. You can check this using the two variables you recently created. Use the type function to determine what kind of data each variable holds. Type the following statements and observe the results:

```
(type a)
(type b)
```

The command prompt should have returned the value REAL for *a*, showing that *a* holds a real number containing a decimal point. Likewise, it should have returned INT for *b*, to indicate that it contains an integer or whole number.

Let's try one more example before concluding this overview of variables and data types. This time, you will assign a piece of text (or a "string") to a variable. Notice that the text string must be enclosed in quotes. If you omit the quotes, you will get a syntax error. Also be careful with the parentheses and quotes: They both must match perfectly for the expression to evaluate. Type the following two statements at the command prompt.

```
(setq fn "First Name")
(type fn)
```

The command prompt should have returned the value STR, to show it identified the data type as a STRING. AutoLISP recognizes several more data types, which you should review in the Help Files described in the previous section.

USING THE COMMAND FUNCTION

A lot of limitations and inconveniences are involved in programming AutoCAD at the command prompt: You are pretty much restricted to single-line programs, although they may achieve a fairly high level of complexity and sophistication. If you make any errors (whether in syntax or typing), you must re-enter the whole expression again. Most significantly, all the work you have done, including all the values you assigned to variables, is lost when you quit the current drawing. However, it is useful at times to be able to quickly check out a command sequence without opening a program editor. You also need to be familiar with how AutoCAD commands function. Before starting to write LISP programs in an editor, let's work a little longer at the command line.

Most AutoLISP programming involves running sequences of standard AutoCAD commands. In earlier versions of AutoCAD, many commands were run from the command line, and the user was prompted through the process step by step. Now most commands automatically open dialog boxes, and all the underlying processes are invisible to the user. In this chapter, you will develop some layer utilities using the AutoCAD Layer command, so you will need to understand the actual steps the Layer command goes through. If you type **layer** at the command prompt, this opens the Layer Properties Manager dialog box, which doesn't help at all. To see what is really going on, you need to type **–layer** ("minus" layer) and step through the prompts.

→ To learn more about using the Layer command, see Chapter 3, "Working with Layers and Linetypes."

When you are editing a drawing, it is often helpful to isolate the layer you are working with. The example that follows shows the inputs involved in turning off all layers except the current layer:

EXAMPLE: USING THE COMMAND FUNCTION

1. Open City base map.dwg from the AutoCAD 2000 \SAMPLE folder (or one of your own drawings) so you can follow the process.

2. For the purposes of this exercise, change the current layer to one that has something visible on it. In the Layer drop-down list, click the "Freeways" layer to make it the current layer.

3. Type **–layer** at the command prompt and enter the responses shown (in bold) here. Press the Enter key to complete the command. All layers except the current layer should turn off.

   ```
   -layer
   Current layer:  "Freeways"
   Enter an option
   [?/Make/Set/New/ON/OFF/Color/Ltype/LWeight/Plot/Freeze/Thaw/LOck/Unlock]: off
   Enter name list of layer(s) to turn off: *
   Really want layer "Freeways" (the CURRENT layer) off? <N> n
   Enter an option
   [?/Make/Set/New/ON/OFF/Color/Ltype/LWeight/Plot/Freeze/Thaw/LOck/Unlock]:
   Command:
   ```

4. When you are finished, you can click the Undo button on the Standard toolbar to return the drawing to its original state.

In this exercise, you selected the layer off option and then typed an asterisk (*) to turn off *all* layers. You typed an **n** to leave the current layer (Freeways) on, and you pressed Enter to finish the command.

When you have grasped the steps involved in the command, it is a relatively easy step to include them in an AutoLISP expression using the command function. The command function runs standard AutoCAD commands and their options. (Review the AutoLISP Reference in the AutoCAD Help system for more information about the command function.)

This one-line expression replicates your input in the preceding exercise.

```
(command "layer" "off" "*" "N" "")
```

In this example, the command function is followed by a series of text strings as its arguments. Each text string is enclosed in quotes that define the beginning and end of the string. The command function treats each text string as if it were a line of text typed at the command prompt and followed by an Enter key. The last string is an empty, or null, string (") and is equivalent to pressing the Enter key.

When you are developing and testing expressions such as this, it is often more efficient to work at the command prompt rather than migrating in and out of your editor. Although the command prompt is still a great place for running single statements, you can't edit code there, of course.

USING THE VISUAL LISP EDITOR

It's time to start creating some programs you can use repeatedly. To write AutoLISP programs, all you need is an ASCII editor or any word processor. You can write your code, save it as an ASCII file, and then load that file directly into AutoCAD. Despite this appealing simplicity, most developers prefer to use the Visual LISP Editor.

Visual LISP was created to provide an AutoLISP development environment that was closer in style and functionality to other contemporary programming environments—for example, the Visual Basic Editor. Visual LISP provides an easy-to-use environment for writing and maintaining AutoLISP code. The "integrated development environment" (IDE) has many productivity enhancements: color-coded display, automatic formatting and indenting, and syntax checking and source code debugging. Visual LISP has all the existing AutoLISP functions plus an extended function set of its own.

Note

The Visual LISP extended function set is beyond the scope of this chapter. The Visual LISP functions and extensions enable you to access the AutoCAD object model, add reactors to AutoCAD objects, interact with Windows, and have many other advanced features. The functions that are not a part of standard AutoLISP begin with vl–, vlr– or vlax–.

USING THE DEFUN FUNCTION

Using the Visual LISP Editor, you now will develop the simple command function you wrote in the previous exercise into a loadable program:

```
(command "layer" "off" "*" "n" "")
```

This turns off all layers except the current layer, which is accomplished by putting the LISP statement into a named subroutine, using the defun function. Before you open the Visual LISP Editor, you need to do a couple of things.

- Set up a new folder for your LISP programs.
- Open the City base map.dwg from the AutoCAD 2000 \SAMPLE folder again. Set the "Rail Roads" layer as the current layer.

Note

As you develop useful programs, you will want to have them easily accessible. You should store your programs in one place, but don't clutter your AutoCAD folders with custom files. You can easily lose things in there, especially when you upgrade AutoCAD from one version to the next. If you have not yet done so, take some time to create a personal programming folder (called "My Programs," for example) under the Program Files folder. If you plan to work through the examples in this chapter, you should copy all the files that begin with CH21 from the accompanying CD into this folder also.

Now that you have a folder set up and a drawing to work with, you are ready to start using Visual LISP.

EXAMPLE: USING VISUAL LISP

1. To open the Visual LISP interface, select Tools, AutoLISP, Visual LISP Editor, or type **vlide** at the command prompt. If this is the first time you have opened the editor, the display should look like Figure 21.3. If someone has previously worked with your copy of the Editor, the last program worked with will be displayed in an Edit window below the toolbars.

Figure 21.3
The Visual LISP User Interface contains a menu, five toolbars, the Console window, and a status bar.

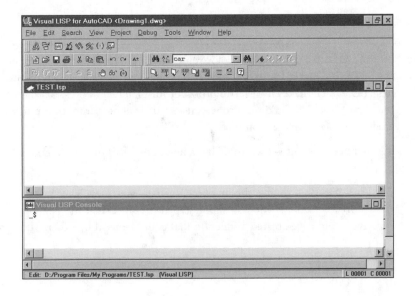

PART
V
CH
21

2. If any previous programs are displayed in the Editor, close them by clicking the Close button in the top right of the Edit window.

Note

The Visual LISP Console window acts in exactly the same way as the command prompt. You can check this by typing in your command function: **(command "layer" "off" "*" "n" ")**. If you flip back to the AutoCAD window, you will see that all the layers (except the current layer) have been turned off. Click the Undo button to cancel the changes and go back to the Visual LISP interface. You could also perform this function in the Console window by typing **(command "undo" ")**.

3. To open the Editor, select File, New File, or click the New File button (the first button at the left of the Standard toolbar). This opens the Edit window. Notice that the grayed-out toolbar, above the right side of the window, is now active. This is the Tools toolbar.

4. Click the Save file button, browse to your LISP folder, and then save your file. Visual LISP gives your file a temporary name, something like Untitled-0, but you will want to assign your own program name.

Tip 202 from
Paul Richardson

A good habit to adopt is to distinguish your programs with a unique identifier: Use your initials as the first three letters of your program name, or use a project code to group all the programs written for a particular project. Anything will work as long as you are consistent. LISP source files should always be stored with the .LSP extension.

5. Enter the following four lines of code into the Visual LISP editor:

```
(defun C:OF ()
(command "layer" "off" "*" "n" ")
(princ)
)
```

Notice the varied colors. Each color represents a different coding element. Words that Visual LISP reserves for itself—mostly function names—are shown in blue. Text strings are magenta, which makes it easier to proof for mismatched quotes. Parentheses are shown in red. The Visual LISP Editor also uses its Smart Indent feature to arrange the text into an easily readable format as you type.

The defun statement is used to define a new AutoLISP function. Take a look at its component parts:

■ First, you need to give the function a name—your new layer program is called OF (short for "off"). If you had simply typed (**defun OF** at the beginning of the program, you would have created a function that could be used by other LISP programs. By adding **C:** in front of the name—which has nothing to do with your C: drive, by the way—the new function becomes an AutoCAD command. After the LISP program is loaded, simply type **OF** at the command prompt to start the command.

- Any arguments expected by the function would be appended here, enclosed within parentheses. You do not need any arguments in this exercise. Nonetheless, you must include the empty parentheses **( )**, or your program will not run.

- The second line contains the actual operations to be performed by the function. You should be very familiar with these by now.

- The **(princ)** statement is just good housekeeping. It standard procedure to terminate AutoLISP routines with princ to eliminate the nil statement, which otherwise is output at the end.

CHECKING YOUR SYNTAX

Check your program before you load and run it. Nothing beats consistently checking your typing and matching of parentheses and quotes as you go. Visual LISP additionally includes a number of syntax- and format-checking routines on the Tools toolbar, which are worth trying.

EXAMPLE: CHECKING THE SYNTAX

1. Make sure the Edit window is active. If your cursor is in another window, the Tools toolbar will be grayed out. (It's the one with the arrow and check mark icons—the lower-right toolbar in Figure 21.4). Click the Check Edit Window button as shown in Figure 21.4.

Figure 21.4
The Visual LISP Editor provides a variety of tools for locating syntax and formatting errors in programs.

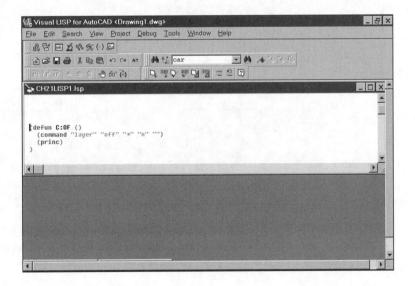

Note

The output from the Check Edit function is often not very helpful. A message such as "error: malformed string on input" appears in the Console window. Position your cursor in the error message and right-click. If you select Show Error Source from the shortcut menu, the cursor will jump to the line where the error was detected. This narrows the field a little.

2. This time, click the Format Edit Window button on the Tools toolbar (see Figure 21.4). If the Formatter finds unbalanced quotes, it issues the message "Unbalanced token" and stops work; if it finds unbalanced parentheses, it will offer to add one. Click No, and check your program line by line.

Caution

The Visual LISP Formatter will offer to *correct* mismatched parentheses that it finds. Do not accept this offer. It is unlikely to put the required parenthesis in the correct place; you are better off locating and replacing it yourself. If you are having trouble matching your parentheses, you also can use the Edit Menu's Parentheses Matching option (Ctrl+M). Using the Match forward (Ctrl+]) and Match backward (Ctrl+[) functions, you can successfully pair up your parentheses.

3. Now click the Load Active Edit Window button (see Figure 21.5) to load the program into AutoCAD. You are about to perform the final error check—does the program run in AutoCAD?

Figure 21.5
You can load your LISP program into AutoCAD directly from the Visual LISP Editor.

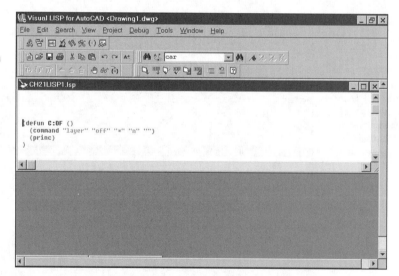

4. Click the Activate AutoCAD button (see Figure 21.5) to return to AutoCAD.

5. Type **of** at the command prompt. All layers except the current layer in the city base map drawing will be turned off. (Remember to use the Undo key to return this drawing to its original state if you want to test this program again.)

You have effectively created your own unique AutoCAD command.

ADDING COMMENTS TO YOUR PROGRAM

Now that your layer program is functional, you should take care of some details before you finalize it. Go back to the Visual LISP editor and add some comment lines similar to the ones shown here:

```
;;;;Author: Your Name and date
;;;;Program: OF to turn off all layers except the current layer
;;;;
(defun C:OF ()
(command "layer" "off" "*" "n" ")
(princ)
)
```

Your comments should include authorship and creation date; program title and description; instructions on using a routine, if required; and explanatory notes throughout.

To distinguish comments from actual code, you must precede each comment with at least one semicolon. AutoLISP uses different combinations of semicolons and dashes to identify different types of comments. If you wish to know more about commenting conventions, refer to the Visual LISP Developer's Guide, Chapter 2, in the AutoCAD 2000 Help system. For now, just make sure you have at least one semicolon in front of the comment so the line will not be evaluated as code. Notice that visual LISP highlights all comments.

Tip 203 from
Paul Richardson

Two buttons are located at the far right of the Tools toolbar: "Comment Block" and "Uncomment Block." If you prefer, you can type in your comments *without* all the semi-colons, and then use the Comment Block button to add the semicolons and highlighting. If you change your mind or accidentally comment out a piece of code, use the Uncomment Block button to remove the semicolons. At times you may want to "comment out" lines of code while you are testing and debugging programs.

Comments have no function other than to describe the program, but it's a very good habit to date and describe each step in your programs. After you have written a few hundred routines, the details of each individual program can become dim and distant.

When you are satisfied with your comments, click the Save File button.

EXPANDING YOUR PROGRAM REPERTOIRE

Now that you have a working program to turn off layers (OF.LSP), you can consider some other options. How about adding a command to turn the layers *on* again? This can be accomplished with some judicious cutting and pasting.

PART

V

CH

21

EXAMPLE: TURNING LAYERS ON AGAIN

1. In the Visual LISP Editor, open the OF program again.

2. Select the whole program (Ctrl+A). Click the Copy button, and then click the Paste button *twice* to make a duplicate copy of the OF program.

3. In the second program, change OF to ON everywhere you see it. Then delete the "n" in the fifth line of the program and fix the comments so that what you have looks like this:

```
;;;; Author: Your Name and date
;;;;Program: OF to turn off all layers except the current layer
;;;;
(defun c:OF ()
  (command "layer" "off" "*" "n" " ")
  (princ)
)
;;;; Author: Your Name and date
;;;;Program: ON to turn on all layers
;;;;
(defun c:ON ()
  (command "layer" "on" "*" " ")
  (princ)

)
```

With very little additional effort, you now have two programs, ON and OF, in the LISP file. These two programs are included in CH21LISP1.LSP on the CD that accompanies this book. You could now add two more routines to this file, to freeze (FR) and thaw (TH) layers—if you have a lot of layers to freeze or to thaw, it's more efficient to type a couple of characters than to open the Layer Properties Manager and perform multiple clicks.

You can experiment on your own as well: Copy the existing routines and make the necessary edits, check the syntax, load the programs, and try them out. When you are finished, review the file CH21LISP2.LSP on the accompanying CD. This file contains the ON, OF, FR, and TH programs.

LOADING AUTOLISP PROGRAMS

In the preceding exercises, you used the Load Active Edit Window button (see Figure 21.5) to load your programs from the Visual LISP editor into AutoCAD. Of course, you will not always be in the Editor when you want to load a program. There are several different ways to load a LISP program from within AutoCAD 2000.

LOADING LISP FROM THE COMMAND PROMPT   You can enter a load statement at the command prompt. The load statement is quite simple:

```
(load "myfile.lsp")
```

This will work as long as your LISP file is in the AutoCAD search path. If you attempt to load a file called myfile.lsp and AutoCAD can't find it, you will get an error message similar to this one:

```
; error: LOAD failed: "mylisp"
```

If you want to load a LISP file from a folder not in the AutoCAD search path, you can add the path to the load statement. You may not use the backslash in the usual fashion. This is because the LISP interpreter reserves the backslash for its own use. To specify a path, use either a forward slash or a double backslash:

```
(load "c:\\Projects\\Lisp Folder\\mylisp")
```

It is often easier to add the folder to the AutoCAD search path and be done with it. (Later in this chapter, you will experiment with AutoLISP dialog files (*.DCL). DCL files *must* be in the AutoCAD 2000 search path to work.

EXAMPLE: ADDING A FOLDER TO THE AUTOCAD 2000 SEARCH PATH

1. Select Tools, Options, or type **options** at the AutoCAD command prompt. (You also can right-click anywhere and get the Options menu item.)

2. Click the plus sign beside Support File Search Path (on the Files tab) to expand the display. Check whether the folder containing the LISP file is shown.

3. Click the Add button, if you need to add the folder, and then click the Browse button to browse to your folder. The folder will be added to the bottom of the list of files in the search path.

4. Click the OK button when you are done.

If you prefer a menu and dialog box approach, you can also load LISP programs via the Load Applications dialog box in AutoCAD 2000.

EXAMPLE: LOADING LISP VIA THE LOAD APPLICATIONS DIALOG BOX

1. Choose Tools, AutoLISP, Load, or type **appload** at the command prompt and press Enter.

2. Browse to the folder that contains your LISP programs.

3. Select the .LSP file to load, and then press the Load button. You can load more than one program at this point.

4. Click the Close button to return to AutoCAD 2000. All programs you have loaded will be functional in the current drawing until you close the drawing.

You will have to load the LISP programs again each time you open a new drawing.

PART

V

CH

21

AUTOMATIC LOADING OF LISP FILES You would probably prefer to have your LISP files available every time you open a drawing and not have to load them each time. To accomplish this, you will have to create a file called ACADDOC.LSP. AutoCAD 2000 searches for an ACADDOC.LSP file each time it opens a drawing; ACADDOC.LSP contains a list of LISP routines that will be automatically loaded into each drawing.

You can use the Visual Lisp Editor to create your own ACADDOC.LSP file.

EXAMPLE: CREATING AN ACADDOC.LSP FILE

1. Start a New file and save it as ACADDOC.LSP to the AutoCAD 2000 Support folder. (This will typically be c:\Program Files\ACAD2000\SUPPORT.) If you already have an ACADDOC.LSP file, do not overwrite it. Instead, you should add the new load statements to the existing statements in this file.

2. Add as many load statements as are required to load all your programs:
```
(load "myfile")
(load "ch21LISP1")
(load "ch21LISP2")
```

3. Save the file and exit the editor.

Notice that you do not need to include the .LSP file extension in the load statement. If your LISP folder is not in the AutoCAD search path, remember to include the path in your load statement (see "Adding a Folder to the AutoCAD 2000 Search Path," earlier in this section).

Caution

You may be familiar with the ACAD.LSP file from earlier versions of AutoCAD. Prior to AutoCAD 2000, the ACAD.LSP file performed the automatic load function that is now performed by ACADDOC.LSP file(s). Do not expect ACAD.LSP to perform the same way in AutoCAD 2000 as it did in prior versions. It is now intended for application-specific startup routines; LISP functions loaded by ACAD.LSP will be available only to the first drawing opened.

INTERACTING WITH THE AUTOCAD DRAWING DATABASE

The programming you have done so far has involved sequencing pre-existing AutoCAD commands and options. All the steps involved would be intuitively obvious to most AutoCAD users. To take LISP any further, you will have to interact directly with AutoCAD drawing objects. You will need to learn more about how AutoCAD stores information and how you can retrieve the data you need and pass it to your programs.

RETRIEVING INFORMATION ABOUT DRAWING OBJECTS

Suppose that rather than turning off all layers, you want to be able to turn off a single layer at a time by clicking on it. Accomplishing this will involve a few more LISP functions. You will have to learn how to select an object (using entsel), how to "get" the list of information that defines the object (using entget), and how to extract the exact items you need (using car, cdr, and assoc). The logic here is fairly tortuous to explain. It is actually easier to perform each step and then figure out what each step has accomplished.

> **Note**
>
> The AutoLISP programming in this section is more complex than in the exercises completed above. You can check your results against the programs supplied on the accompanying CD at three points in the program. First, you will learn how to extract the relevant layer information from the drawing database. You can check your work to this point with CH21LISP3A.LSP. Then, you will use the AutoLISP *while* function to test for user input (check this with CH21LISP3B.LSP). Finally, you will use the AutoLISP *if* function to test whether the user has selected the current layer and also learn how to exit cleanly from a program (check this using CH21LISP3C.LSP).

Before you start, open the \AutoCAD 2000\SAMPLE drawing City base map.dwg again. (You may use any drawing you choose, but this exercise refers to the \SAMPLE drawing.) You can complete the following steps either at the AutoCAD command prompt or in the Visual LISP Console window.

EXAMPLE: RETRIEVING INFORMATION ABOUT DRAWING OBJECTS

1. Type the following expression, and press Enter:

   ```
   (setq DwgObject(entsel))
   ```

   This expression contains two LISP functions.

   - You are familiar with setq from earlier exercises, where you assigned specific numerical values and calculations to variables. In this example, you are assigning the output from another function to the variable DwgObject.

   - The entsel function prompts the user to pick a drawing object (line, block, circle, or text) by entering a point or clicking on it. If you type **(entsel)** and press Enter, you will be prompted "Select Object:." On its own, this would serve no useful function, but it is fundamental to many AutoLISP programs.

   The previous expression prompts you to pick an object in your drawing.

2. Click anywhere on the "Street Curbs" layer. The data returned consists of a *list* of two items:

   ```
   (<Entity name: 147b918> (1439.69 1781.21 0.0))
   ```

   This output from the entsel function is assigned to your new variable, DwgObject. The first item of the list gives the "entity name," and the second part is the coordinate of the cursor click. You don't need the second part. So the next step is to extract only the first item from the list and pass it to another variable, ObjName.

> **Note**
>
> You may have noticed the terms "object" and "entity" are used somewhat interchangeably to refer to AutoCAD elements. Since AutoCAD 13, the correct usage is to refer to everything as "objects." In Release 12 and earlier, these "objects" were called "entities." Because of this legacy, many of the embedded functions, prompts, and system variables refer to *ent*-this or *ent*-that, which creates a slight awkwardness at times.

3. Type the following expression and press Enter:

```
(setq ObjName(car DwgObject))
```

You may recall that LISP language was originally designed to process lists. As a result, it has a number of built-in functions for retrieving data from lists. The car function returns the *first* element in any list that is supplied to it. In this case, it extracts the "entity name" and passes it to ObjName:

```
<Entity name: 147b918>
```

You now have the information required to proceed to the next step, where you will use the function entget to "get" the data that you want—entget requires the "entity name" of the object.

> **Note**
>
> The CD that accompanies this book contains a bonus LISP file (CH21GROUPCODES.LSP), which displays any object's "group codes" in an easy-to-read dialog box. Use Tools, AutoLISP, Load to load this file. Type **GC** at the command prompt to start the program. This program simply displays the group code data in a more accessible way. To understand it, you should refer to the AutoCAD 2000 Help files, under DXF Reference.

4. Type the following expression and press Enter.

```
(setq AssocList (entget ObjName))
```

This expression assigns the output from entget to yet another variable, called AssocList. Let's take a closer look at what entget has produced. (If you are working at the command prompt, press F2 to see the whole list; if you are working in the VL Console, the data is output to a single long line.)

```
((-1 . <Entity name: 147b918>) (0 . "LWPOLYLINE") (330 . <Entity name:
147b0f8>) (5 . "3D03") (100 . "AcDbEntity") (67 . 0) (410 . "Model") (8 .
"Street Curbs") (100 . "AcDbPolyline") (90 . 35) (70 . 1) (43 . 0.0) (38 . 0.0)
(39 . 0.0) (10 2433.65 3995.88) (40 . 0.0) (41 . 0.0) (42 . 0.0) (10 2472.64
3964.43) (40 . 0.0) (41 . 0.0) (42 . 0.0) (10 2584.74 3971.61) (40 . 0.0) (41 .
0.0) (42 . 0.0)
```

The output looks like gibberish until you decipher that it is a list made up of a series of pairs of elements, each enclosed in parentheses and separated by a period or dot. The first four items in the list are shown below:

```
 ((-1 . <Entity name: 147b918>)
(0 . "LWPOLYLINE")
(330 . <Entity name: 147b0f8>)
(5 . "3D03")
```

Entget has output the "association list" of the object you selected. This is how AutoCAD objects look to AutoLISP: Each object is a series of "dotted pairs."

- The first part of the dotted pair is a number called a *group code*. Each group code has a consistent meaning. The group code 0, for example, is always "Object Type." Different types of objects use codes that are unique to that object. If you want to look up the group codes for any object, look in the AutoCAD 2000 Help system under DXF Reference.
- The second part of the dotted pair contains the actual data that defines the object. Group code 0, in this example, is "LWPOLYLINE." In step 2, you picked an object on the "Street Curbs" layer, a lightweight polyline.

Table 21.2 provides a partial list of the "dotted pairs" that define this lightweight polyline:

TABLE 21.2   AUTOLISP GROUP CODES FOR A SELECTED OBJECT

Group Code	Value	Description
−1	\<Entity name: 147b918	Object name
0	"LWPOLYLINE"	Object type
330	\<Entity name: 147b0f8>	Soft pointer handle
5	"3C9B"	Handle
100	"AcDbEntity"	Subclass marker
67	0	Model space/paper space marker
410	"Model"	Layout tab name
8	"Street Curbs"	Layer name
100	"AcDbPolyline"	Subclass marker
90	3	Number of vertices
70	0	Polyline flag (optional)
43	0.0	Constant width (optional)
38	0.0	Elevation (optional)
39	0.0	Thickness (optional)
10	126.681	Vertex coordinates
	6040.25	
40	0.0	Starting width (optional)
41	0.0	Ending width (optional)

PART
V

CH
21

continues

TABLE 21.2   CONTINUED

Group Code	Value	Description
42	0.0	Bulge (optional)
210	0.0 0.0	Extrusion direction (optional)
	1.0	

The dotted pair that contains group code 8 is the only one you need for your current program. (Layer name is always group code 8.) Now that you have the association list, you need to extract the layer name information and pass it to your program. This is accomplished in two steps.

5. Type the following expression and press Enter.

```
(setq DottedPair (assoc 8 Associlist))
```

The assoc function searches the association list (contained in AssocList). It looks for the element containing 8 and passes the result (8. "Street Curbs") to the new variable, Dotted Pair. Now you have narrowed the search down to the dotted pair level. One more step will retrieve the actual layer name.

6. Type the following expression, and press Enter.

```
(setq LayerName (cdr DottedPair))
```

The dotted pair is a list of two elements. In step 3, you used the car function to extract the first element from a list. The cdr function will return everything *except* the first element of a list. In a dotted pair list, cdr returns the second element of the dotted pair, the layer name.

That involved a whole lot of steps to get to the layer name. In reality, you wouldn't create so many unnecessary variables if you were writing a production program. In fact, you could compress all the previous statements into a single complex statement. This one eliminates all the temporary variables you created between selecting the object and extracting the layer name, but the logic is very dense:

```
(setq LayerName (cdr (assoc 8(entget (car (entsel)))))))
```

In practice, you might condense the six steps of the previous exercise to a reasonable number of variables and statements, but not to the point where the logic becomes murky.

Tip 204 from
Paul Richardson

If you have complex expressions with many nested levels, you can use indentation to track each nested expression. Don't worry about positioning your parentheses exactly while in the Visual LISP Editor. As long as you have separated out the code onto separate lines, clicking the Format Edit Window button will align all the left and right parentheses exactly above each other.

```
(setq LayerName
   (cdr
      (assoc 8
         (entget
            (car (entsel)
               )
            )
         )
      )
   )
)
```

This ten-line version of the program works exactly the same as the single-line version.

So now you have identified the layer name of the layer you picked. Your original goal was to turn off a selected layer. You are now in familiar territory. A few more statements will accomplish that objective. Start a new file in the Visual LISP Editor and type the following lines (or edit one of your previous files).

```
(defun c:OFP ()
  (setq LayerName (cdr (assoc 8 (entget (car (entsel))))))
  (command "layer" "off" LayerName "")
  (princ)
)
```

You will notice that there are no quotes around LayerName in the command statement because this is a variable and not a text string. The Visual LISP Editor helpfully colors it black to distinguish it from the (magenta) text strings.

Check the syntax, check the formatting, load the program into AutoCAD, and type **OFP** at the command line. (A copy of the program so far is contained in the file CH21LISP3A.LSP on the CD that accompanies this book.) You now have a functioning program to turn off layers on the fly. Or do you?

CHECKING USER INPUT

In the earlier programs you wrote, you had total control over all the inputs to your programs. In this routine, you are asking for input from a user, so you will additionally have to build in some checks and tests to protect your program from user error or inaction, as in the following situations:

- What if the user accidentally doesn't click on an AutoCAD object? Your program will respond to the click, find nothing, give an error message, and fail.
- What if the user inadvertently selects the current layer? Do you allow the user to turn it off? This might depend on whether your routine is part of a larger program that requires the current layer to be on.

To complete the program, you need to add some error checking (using the while, if, and progn functions).

USING THE WHILE LOOP

The first task is how to keep the program looping until the user successfully clicks on an object and entsel returns a value. With a bit of adjustment you can use the AutoLISP *while* function to perform this task.

The standard *while* function in AutoLISP repeats as long as the expression that it is testing evaluates to anything other than nil. This is the reverse of what you want to do; you need to keep repeating the selection as long as entsel returns nil (or the user fails to select an object).

The logic of the while function can be reversed by using the = (equals) function to test the result of the entsel selection and compare that to nil. With this additional step, the while loop now evaluates each expression and, if the expression is *nil*, the while loop repeats; if the expression is *not nil*, the while loop completes and the program continues. In this way you can use a while loop to test whether a drawing object has been selected.

```
(while (= (setq DwgObject (entsel))nil ))
```

As long as a nil value is returned to the DwgObject variable—no object has been selected by the click—the entsel function will keep prompting "Select object:". Of course, this could go on for quite a while and, if the user does not figure what to do, there is no way out except by hitting the Esc key.

This while loop needs a little improvement. You could give the user a better prompt than the standard "Select object:"—you can add any desired prompt (in quotes) after entsel.

```
(while (= (setq DwgObject (entsel "\nSelect layer to turn OFF: ")) nil ))
```

This expression adds a more direct message to the user: "Select layer to turn OFF." (The \n simply tells the program to put the message on the next line.) You could emphasize this even more by adding an alert box. An alert box is easily programmed: Just add the alert function, followed by a string containing a warning message. Take care to insert it before the final parenthesis of the while loop.

```
(while (= (setq DwgObject (entsel "\nSelect layer to turn OFF: ")) nil )
(alert "Nothing Selected")
)
```

SOME EXTRA PROGRAM ADJUSTMENTS

You are almost in shape with the while loop addition to your program. Just a couple modifications should be made to allow your program to process smoothly.

REMOVE DUPLICATE FUNCTIONS   You have just moved the entsel function into the while loop, so it is redundant in the (entget (car (entsel))) function further down the program and you should remove it. You can now pass the DwgObject variable to this function. Car will extract the first element "entity name" from DwgObject and pass it to entget. Edit the setq statement as follows:

```
(setq LayerName (cdr (assoc 8 (entget (car DwgObject)))))
```

TURNING OFF THE COMMAND ECHO You may have noticed a quick flurry of activity at the command prompt as your program terminates. As your program becomes more professional, you should eliminate these signs of the internal workings of your routines. What you are seeing is "command echo." As you are developing programs, it can be useful to see AutoCAD commands going through their motions, but these should not be displayed in your finished product. The display is controlled by the cmdecho system variable. Use the setvar function to write a new value to cmdecho. Setvar sets any system variable to a specified value.

```
(setvar "cmdecho" 0)
```

This statement turns off command echo at the command prompt by setting the "cmdecho" system variable to 0. Zero is equivalent to "off" for all system variables that hold on/off values. The number one (1) is equivalent to "on."

All the code to date is included in the file CH21LISP3B.LSP on the CD that accompanies this book. The program will function quite respectably as long as the user does not select the current layer.

Note

AutoCAD stores values for various drawing settings in *system variables*. You can view the complete list in the AutoCAD 2000 Help system under the "Command Reference" entry. You can also view all the system variable settings by typing **setvar ?** at the command prompt and pressing the Enter key twice. The variables and their values will scroll onto the AutoCAD text window, but you won't get much explanation as to what they do. It is well worth your time to familiarize yourself with the system variable documentation.

The current settings for drafting defaults generally start with the letter "C." At the command prompt, type **setvar ?** and press Enter, and then type **c*** and press Enter. This will list all the system variables that start with a "C":

CECOLOR	"BYLAYER"	Default color
CELTSCALE	1.0000	Default linetype scale
CELTYPE	"BYLAYER"	Default linetype
CELWEIGHT	–1	Default lineweight
CLAYER	"0"	Default layer

USING THE IF FUNCTION

The final problem to solve is how to alert the user who (perhaps inadvertently) selects the current layer. AutoCAD would usually prompt the user "Really want layer "Xxxxx" (the CURRENT layer) off?" Of course, because you have turned cmdecho off, you don't get that prompt, and the program goes awry at this point. You need to include a test for the current layer in your program, using the if function. The if statement syntax is superficially similar to the while loop syntax:

```
(if (= LayerName CurrentLayer)
    (alert "Cannot turn off Current Layer")
    (command "layer" "OFF" LayerName ")
)
```

The if function here tests whether LayerName is *equal to* the "CurrentLayer."

- If they are equal, the if function evaluates the first expression and an alert is issued: "Cannot turn off Current Layer."
- If LayerName is different from "CurrentLayer," the if function passes to the second expression, and the command function turns off the selected layer.

Note

In a full-fledged program, you would probably allow the user a choice as to whether to turn off the current layer or not. However, because users typically do not wish to turn off the current layer, this step has been omitted in the interest of brevity.

As you have no doubt noticed, the variable "CurrentLayer" is included in these expressions, and you have not assigned it a value. Fortunately, this can be easily accomplished. The current layer information is held in a system variable called clayer. You saw how to change system variables using setvar. In the same way, you can view the contents of any system variable by using the getvar function. Try typing **(getvar "clayer")**. You also can assign the output from getvar to a variable:

```
(setq CurrentLayer (getvar "clayer"))
```

Insert this statement into your program—before the if function—and your program is complete.

Caution

Not all system variables can be changed; some are read-only. You must take care to supply the expected data type to the system variable, or your assignment will be rejected. Sometimes the value required is not obvious. The variable CLAYER, which holds the current layer, expects a string. If you assign a new value to CLAYER, it must be enclosed between quotation marks. Even layer zero is a string—"0"—not a number.

ENDING YOUR PROGRAM

The only remaining criticism of this program might be that it terminates rather abruptly. If a user was not paying close attention, that user might not be sure what had been turned off. You could rectify this situation by adding another alert function—after the command function—to give feedback as to what has happened. The alert would look something like this:

```
(alert (strcat "Layer: " LayerName " turned off")
```

The only new element here is the strcat function, which concatenates multiple strings and returns a single string. The output would be something like this: "Layer: "Rail Roads" turned off."

THE PROGN FUNCTION   Unfortunately for this plan, an if statement in AutoLISP evaluates only one expression for any condition. What happens when you want it to run more than one statement? Progn function comes to the rescue: You can use progn to evaluate several expressions where only one expression is expected. Insert the progn function before the first expression, and don't forget the closing parenthesis:

```
(if (= LayerName CurrentLayer)
    (alert "Cannot turn of Current Layer")
    (progn
      (command "layer" "OFF" LayerName " ")
      (alert (strcat "Layer: " LayerName " turned off"))
    )
)
```

PRINC FUNCTIONS   Two final statements will close out your program neatly at the command line:

```
(princ "\nOFP Done")
  (princ)
```

The first princ statement prints a "Done" message to the command prompt, and the second princ returns a null symbol to the command prompt, avoiding the usual nil value. If you have been working along in this chapter, you can test and then run your own version of this program. If not, all this code for the completed OFP program is included in the file CH21LISP3C.LSP on the CD that accompanies this book. This file additionally contains the code for FRP, a comparable program that freezes any selected layer. You should review both finished programs.

The group of programs you have developed in this chapter are all command-line based; they are started from the command prompt, and all the error messages and prompts are issued at the command line. In the next section, you will review the processes involved in creating a graphical user interface for an AutoLISP program.

ADDING A DIALOG BOX IN AUTOLISP

To complete the suite of layer utilities you have been developing, you need a final program that will turn on layers, or thaw frozen layers selectively. You can't just modify your pick programs (OFP and THP) because the layers are not visible to the user. Your program will need to generate a list of the layer names that are frozen or off so the user can select the layers to turn on (or thaw). This means a dialog box.

In this section, you will focus primarily upon the programming involved in creating a dialog box in AutoLISP. This time you don't need to do all the coding for this program. Instead, starting with the finished product, you will step through the processes involved in getting this dialog box to work. All the code for the dialog box and the new program ONS is available in the file CH21LISP4.LSP on the CD that accompanies this book. If you have not already done so, you should copy this file into your personal LISP/programming folder.

EXAMPLE: ADDING A DIALOG BOX IN AUTOLISP

1. Start AutoCAD 2000 and open the City base map.dwg from the \SAMPLE folder (or any drawing of your choice).

2. Load both CH21LISP4.LSP and the practice programs you have worked with into the drawing.

3. Turn off a few random layers and freeze a couple layers using the OFP and FRP programs. The ON OF FR TH and OFP programs are supplied in CH21LISP3C.LSP if you have not been working along in this chapter.

4. Type **ONS** at the command prompt and press Enter. The dialog box shown in Figure 21.6 appears onscreen.

5. Click the radio button "Show Turned Off Layers." The layers you turned off in step 3 will be displayed.

6. Select a layer (or layers) to turn back on, and press OK.

The layers will turn back on. You can repeat the process for the frozen layers.

Figure 21.6
A dialog box enables the user to select off or frozen layers.

→ If you get an error when you try to load your programs, review the section "Loading AutoLISP Programs," found earlier in this chapter.

USING DIALOG CONTROL LANGUAGE (DCL)

With AutoCAD 2000, you can design and implement dialog boxes to use with your applications. The dialog boxes are loaded and unloaded by AutoLISP commands, and the inputs and outputs from the dialog boxes are managed by AutoLISP functions. However, the actual dialog boxes are not developed in AutoLISP per se.

The appearance of a dialog box is defined by ASCII files written in AutoCAD's Dialog Control Language (DCL), which has a slightly different syntax and conventions from AutoLISP. DCL programming is a lengthy topic in itself and will not be covered in detail here. For a complete description of dialog boxes, go to the AutoCAD 2000 Help system, Visual Lisp Developers Guide, Chapters 10 through 13. DCL programs are not written in a special programming environment; they are typically written in an ASCII editor, such as Windows Notepad.

For the purposes of this exercise, you are not expected to learn Dialog Control Language. It is sufficient for you to read through this section, review the definitions for the ONS dialog box and become familiar with the basic process. Dialog box definitions are stored in a separate text file with a .DCL extension. Although they are not LISP files, you can view and edit DCL files in the Visual LISP Editor. The DCL file that defines the dialog box in Figure 21.6 is CH21LAYERS.DCL. To view the dialog box definitions follow these steps:

EXAMPLE: VIEWING THE DIALOG BOX DEFINITIONS

1. To open the Editor, select Tools, AutoLISP, Visual LISP Editor, or type **vlide** and press Enter at the command prompt.

2. Click File, Open File, and select CH21LAYERS.DCL from your LISP/programming folder.

3. If you want to preview the dialog box, choose Tools, Interface Tools, Preview DCL in Editor. (Make sure that the Edit window is *active* (your cursor is in the window), or you will not be able to select Interface Tools.)

If you choose Preview, the dialog box appears in the AutoCAD drawing editor. The radio buttons click on and the OK and Cancel buttons work, but the AutoLISP file does not function.

Take a look at the dialog box code for ONS. The DCL file is shown in Figure 21.7. It contains two dialog boxes: one for the ONS program, and one for the GC (CH21GROUPCODES.LSP) program you used earlier.

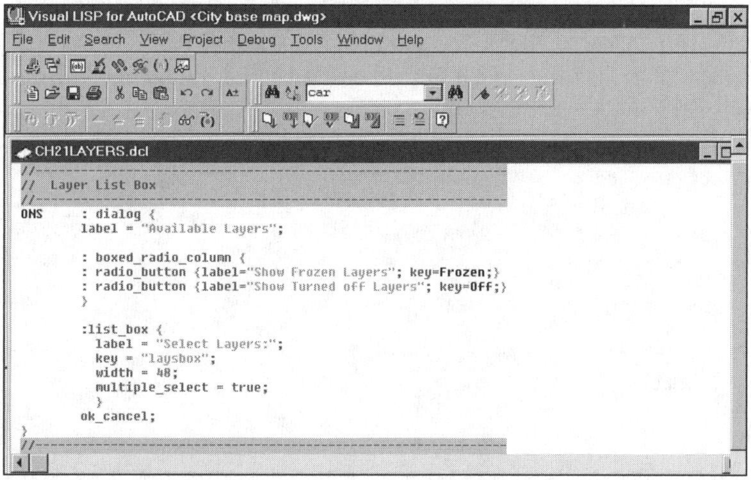

Figure 21.7
You can view and edit a DCL file in the Visual LISP Editor.

In DCL, AutoCAD provides you with a set of prepackaged dialog parts (text boxes, radio buttons, and so on), called DCL "tiles." The ONS program uses the following parts: one

PART

V

CH

21

dialog box, two radio buttons, and a list box, plus OK and Cancel buttons. You don't have a lot of control over the size or look of these tiles; the spacing is more or less automatic. You can specify a width for one tile, and the rest of the tiles will adjust to fit the shape of your dialog box. In the code listing in Figure 21.7, you will notice that a width of 48 was selected for the list box to accommodate layer names.

Each tile is described by a colon and its type, such as :radio_button, and it is followed by a list of its properties. Labels for each of the tiles are shown as text strings (magenta) within quotes. The coding, so far, is pretty transparent. The "key" following each tile is the link into the AutoLISP program. The keys for the radio buttons are "Frozen" and "Off." The key for the list box is "laysbox." You will see how these "keys" become arguments in specialized AutoLISP commands later in this chapter in the section called "Using the Action_Tiles Function." You will probably want to open the DCL file again or refer to Figure 21.7 at that point.

Close the DCL file and open the CH21LISP4. LSP file in the Editor. You will analyze the different parts of this program, but not necessarily in the order in which they appear in the program. The following overview of the program points out the LISP functions that you are familiar with and introduces you to some new ones. By now you are fairly conversant with AutoLISP functions and should have little difficulty in understanding this program. The program is fully commented in the file, although the comments have not been included in the text version shown in this section.

LOADING A DCL FILE

The DCL file is a separate file from the LISP file, created independently, but you do not need to load it separately. Any LISP file that uses a DCL file will also contain a simple load statement to load the DCL file and then test whether the required dialog box is in the named DCL file (using the if function). Take a look at how this works in the following lines of code:

```
(Defun c:ONS (/ DCL_ID)
  (setvar "cmdecho" 0)

  (setq DCL_ID (load_dialog "CH21LAYERS"))
(if DCL_ID

  (new_dialog "ONS" DCL_ID)
  (progn
    (alert "Dialog box not found!")
    (exit)
  )
)
```

AutoCAD first looks for the DCL file "CH21LAYERS." (As long as the file is in a folder in the AutoCAD search path, it will be found.) After the DCL file is found, the program checks for the specified dialog box. If the dialog box ("ONS") can't be found a message (alert) is displayed to the user and the program exits. There is no problem here because the ONS dialog box is defined in the referenced DCL file.

Note

Loading the dialog box is clearly a function that is performed at the start of the program. But from now on you will not necessarily be reviewing the ONS program in exactly the same order as in the accompanying CD file, CH21LISP4.LSP. The sections that follow review in turn the major components of the ONS program. Once you have read through the sections and have an understanding of the different activities that are going on, you should review CH21LISP4.LSP, which is fully commented.

CREATING THE LISTS FOR THE LIST BOX

The AutoLISP program now has to build two lists: a list of the frozen layers in the drawing, and another of the layers that are off. It accomplishes this using a method like the one you used to retrieve layer information in the OFP and THP programs from the "dotted pairs."

This time however, AutoLISP must extract the ON/OFF and FROZEN/THAWED status of each layer, as well as the layer name. The entget function cannot provide all this data. You will need to use a new function, tblnext. AutoLISP keeps layer information in the form of a layer table, with a dotted pair list for each layer. The specific layer group codes you need to extract are shown in Table 21.3:

TABLE 21.3   AUTOCAD LAYER GROUP CODES

Group Code	Description
2	Layer name
6	Linetype name
62	Color number (if negative, layer is off)
70	Standard flags (bit-coded values):
	1 = Layer is frozen.
	2 = Layer is frozen in new viewports.
	4 = Layer is locked.
	8 = Not used.
	16 = Xref flag.
	32 = Xref resolved.
	64 = At least one object is on the layer.

This represents an abbreviated list of the layer group codes. You should refer to the AutoCAD 2000 Help System, DXF Reference, Chapter 4 for full information about these tables of codes. For current purposes, code 62 and code 70 in the layer table provide the necessary information to test whether a given layer is off or frozen. Code 62 holds the layer color, and a negative value shows that the layer is off. Code 70 is in binary code, but the first code (0000001) indicates that a layer is frozen.

The ONS program cycles through all the layers in the drawing and compiles two lists, "OffLayers" and "FrozenLayers."

```
(setq record (tblnext "layer" T))
  (while record
    (setq b70 (cdr (assoc 70 record)))
    (setq next (cdr (assoc 2 record)))
    (setq col (cdr (assoc 62 record)))
    (if (< col 0))
      (setq OffLayers (cons next OffLayers))
    )
    (if    (= (logand b70 1) 1)
      (setq FrozenLayers (cons next FrozenLayers))
    )
    (setq record (tblnext "layer"))
  ) ;end while
  (if (> (length FrozenLayers) 0)
    (setq NoFrozenLayers nil)
    (setq NoFrozenLayers T)
  )
  (if (> (length OffLayers) 0)
    (setq NoOffLayers nil)
    (setq NoOffLayers T)
```

This code looks daunting at first glance, but in fact you have worked with most of the functions already (setq, while, if, cdr, and assoc).

In the first line, the tblnext function simply fetches the next sequential entry from a specified table—in this case, the "layer" table. The secondary argument T instructs tblnext to start at the first entry in the "layer" table. When a table record is returned, the while loop fetches each record and extracts the layer information. The tblnext function is called again at the bottom of each loop. When tblnext returns nil, the while loop finishes.

In the next three lines, the assoc function pulls out the group code information from each layer. Then a series of if statements tests for frozen, xref, and off layers. Within the if statements you see the following expression:

```
(= (logand b70 1) 1)
```

This statement performs a logical AND of group code 70 and the number 1 or 0000001. If the result is equal to 1, the layer is frozen. If the test of the frozen flag shows the layer is frozen, the layer name is added to the FrozenLayers list. The cons function simply adds the layer name (variable "next") to the list.

```
(if    (= (logand b70 1) 1)
      (setq FrozenLayers (cons next FrozenLayers))
```

Testing which layers are off is a lot easier than testing which layers are frozen. From group code 62, you get the color; then you can test whether the color is negative or less than zero. If the layer is off, you can add it to the OffLayers list.

```
(if (< col 0)
  (setq OffLayers (cons next OffLayers))
```

Then the cycle starts all over again as the program gets the next record.

```
    (setq record (tblnext "layer"))
  ) ;end while
```

The lists for the dialog box have now been created. A final test checks that there are entries in each list. If the FrozenLayers list has no values, the variable NoFrozenLayers is set to True.

```
(if (> (length FrozenLayers) 0)
    (setq NoFrozenLayers nil)
    (setq NoFrozenLayers T)
  )
```

A similar variable NoOffLayers records whether there are no Off Layers.

```
  (if (> (length OffLayers) 0)
    (setq NoOffLayers nil)
    (setq NoOffLayers T)
  )
```

When the lists are assembled and checked, the next step is to develop the interaction with the dialog box.

USING THE ACTION_TILE FUNCTION

Now you can start dealing with the dialog box. In this section you will review how the user inputs (such as clicking the radio buttons) are processed by AutoLISP, and how the LISP program passes information to the layer list box in the dialog box.

AutoLISP uses the action_tile function to define how the program responds to a user clicking buttons in the dialog box. Each element, or potential click point, in a dialog box is assigned a "key" in the DCL file. For example, you may remember when you viewed the DCL file (CH17LAYERS.DCL) the radio buttons had the following keys: "Frozen" and "Off."

In AutoLISP, the first argument to an action_tile function is the "key." The string that follows the key argument assigns the action that will occur when the named "tile" is clicked. For example, in the next two lines, LISP defines actions that will occur when either of the two radio buttons is clicked:

```
(action_tile "Frozen" "(setq Thaw 1)(LayersFrozen)")
(action_tile "Off" "(setq Thaw 0)(LayersOff)")
```

When the Frozen button is clicked, it stores 1 in the variable Thaw and calls the LayersFrozen function. LayersFrozen fills the list box with the names of the frozen layers from the FrozenLayers list, which was described in the previous section.

The Off button does a similar job, setting Thaw to 0 and running the LayersOff function. LayersOff fills the list box with the names of the layers from the OffLayers list, which also was described in the previous section.

PART

V

CH

21

The list box action_tile is a little more complicated. In the DCL file, the list box key was defined as "laysbox." The following line defines what happens when a layer in the list box is clicked:

```
(action_tile "laysbox" "(setq pickf $value)")
```

This line instructs the program to store the $value of the selection in the variable pickf. ($value is always the name of the value returned by a dialog box, and it is always in the form of a string.)

The list box has a property defined in the DCL file: the multiple_select property is set to *true*. This means the user can use the Shift or Ctrl keys with the mouse to select multiple layers from the list in the list box. When multiple items are selected, the value of pickf becomes a string with multiple numbers separated by spaces. These numbers represent the position of the item(s) picked or highlighted in the list box.

EXITING THE DIALOG BOX   Before you continue with the main program, take a look at the remaining action_tile functions in this program. The last two action_tile functions respond to the user clicking the OK or Cancel buttons. These are standard AutoCAD DCL components, and the bottom row of every DCL file will have some version of OK_Cancel to securely exit the program.

The predefined LISP function done_dialog closes the dialog box and passes an integer to the start_dialog function to say whether OK or Cancel was pressed.

```
(action_tile "accept" "(done_dialog 1)")
(action_tile "cancel" "(done_dialog 0)")
(if (= (start_dialog) 1)
```

The start_dialog function returns the value passed by the done_dialog function. If start_dialog equals 1, the program then knows the OK button was pressed and it proceeds to modify the selected layers; If start_dialog equals 0, the program then knows the Cancel button was pressed and it exits the program without further processing.

TURNING ON (OR THAWING) THE LAYERS

By the end of the section before last, the program had generated lists of Off and Frozen layers, and could display the correct list in the dialog box when the appropriate radio button was activated. All of this, of course, is preliminary to the actual work of the program, which is to turn on selected Off layers, and/or to thaw selected Frozen layers. The remaining lines of code accomplish this task:

```
(if        (= Thaw 1)
     (progn
   (setq retlist (LayerList FrozenLayers pickf))
   (command "Layer")
   (foreach layern retlist (command "Thaw" layern))
   (command "")
     ) ; progn
     (progn
   (setq retlist (LayerList OffLayers pickf))
```

```
(command "Layer")
(foreach layern retlist (command "On" layern))
(command " ")
```

First of all, the program tests whether the Thaw variable is set to 1 to see if it is thawing frozen layers or turning on layers that previously were turned off. Once again the progn function allows the AutoLISP if statement to evaluate more than one expression. (You used the progn function in the OFP program earlier in this chapter.)

Next, the program has to get the layers that the user picks in the dialog box. The variable pickf contains the indexes for the picked items on the list box. The LayerList function retrieves the equivalent Layer Names from the FrozenLayers list or, if you are processing Off Layers, it retrieves them from the OffLayers list.

```
(setq retlist (LayerList FrozenLayers pickf))
```

After the picked layers have been retrieved by the program, it simply runs the AutoCAD Layer command and either thaws or turns on the required layers. The foreach function repeats the same action on all the items in a list, so you run this in the middle of the Layer command.

COMPLETING THE PROGRAM

After the Layers have been processed, the only tasks remaining are to unload the dialog box and exit the program cleanly by using the princ statements that should be very familiar to you by now.

```
(unload_dialog DCL_ID)
  (princ "\nOns done")
  (princ)
```

Then you're done. If you have all your programs loaded, you should be able to run through all of them now: OF, ON, FR, TH, OFP, FRP, and ONS. All these programs are combined into a single, commented file CH21LAYERS.LSP on the CD. In the future, you need to load only this one program into your drawings or include it in your ACADDOC.LSP file. In the remainder of this chapter you will see how to tackle the same programs using Visual Basic for Applications (VBA).

VISUAL BASIC FOR APPLICATIONS

Visual Basic for Applications (VBA) is an object-oriented programming environment. It was initially available in the Microsoft Excel and Microsoft Project environments and has more recently been added to AutoCAD. As with Visual LISP, VBA offers an "integrated development environment" to help you design and test your programs.

To give you the opportunity to compare the different approaches of VBA and AutoLISP, the second half of this chapter replicates the AutoLISP programs from the first half of the chapter, but this time in VBA. All the programs created and reviewed in the VBA part of this chapter are available on the CD that accompanies this book. The VBA versions of the layer

PART

V

CH

21

programs are located in the file CH21LAYERS.DVB. If you have not done so already, you should copy this file into your programming folder (\My Programs).

> **Note**
>
> Although the focus in this chapter is on developing relatively elementary layer utilities, the potential range of VBA programming spans the whole spectrum from simple utilities, linking databases and drawings, and connecting files across intranets and the Web. To get a sense of what developers are doing with VBA and AutoCAD 2000, you should take a look at the Application Gallery in the ActiveX and VBA Developer's Guide in the AutoCAD 2000 Help system. The projects demonstrated there range from a Parking Utilities program that draws parking lots and an I-beam construction program that creates I-beam drawings to a Facility management program that links blocks in an AutoCAD drawing to records in a Microsoft Access database.

AN OVERVIEW OF THE VBA MODEL

One of AutoLISP's advantages is that you can just jump right in and start programming. Before starting with Visual Basic for Applications, you need to become familiar with *objects* and *object-oriented programming* (OOP). Starting with AutoCAD Release 13, the core of AutoCAD has been rebuilt. AutoCAD's new ActiveX interface enables any compatible programming language to interact with an AutoCAD drawing. This includes not only languages such as C++, Java, and Delphi, but also any application that includes VBA—all these languages and applications now have full access to AutoCAD drawings. Conversely, from AutoCAD VBA you have full access to any other applications that support VBA, such as the Microsoft Office programs. Figure 21.8 shows a schematic representation of the ActiveX technology (abstracted from AutoCAD 2000 online help).

Figure 21.8
AutoCAD ActiveX technology allows many different programming languages and environments to access AutoCAD drawings.

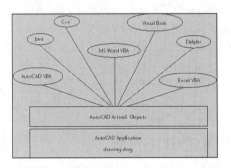

If you are new to VBA, you will find a lot of useful material in the AutoCAD and VBA help files to familiarize you with the object hierarchy known as the AutoCAD Object Model.

EXAMPLE: USING HELP FOR THE OBJECT MODEL

1. Open AutoCAD 2000 Help, and select VBA and ActiveX Automation. You will then need to double-click the shortcut offered.

2. Then select ActiveX and VBA Reference. The first item in the drop-down list is "Object Model" (see Figure 21.9)

3. Select Object Model to see a graphical representation of the AutoCAD Drawing Database ActiveX Object Model.

Figure 21.9
This graphic represents the AutoCAD Drawing Database ActiveX Object Model.

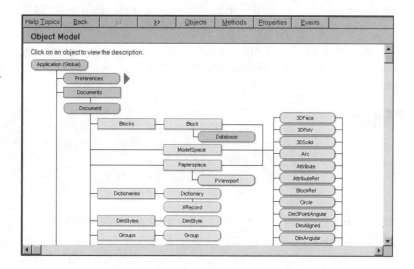

You can click any of the graphic elements to find out more about each element in the object hierarchy. If you scroll down to the bottom, you will see the legend: The rounded shapes represent "objects" and the rectangular shapes represent "collections" of objects.

All objects exist in a hierarchy with the application object (AutoCAD) at the top. When you have established a reference to the application object, you have access to all the other objects. (You can also establish references to other application objects such as Microsoft Word or Excel, and this will give you access to all their ActiveX objects. For the purposes of this chapter, you will stay within the AutoCAD application.)

AutoCAD drawings are "objects" within this framework; a drawing is a document object, which contains other graphical elements (lines, text, and dimensions); style elements (Dim styles and linetypes); and so on. All these elements are also objects, which are organized into "collections." Everything in an AutoCAD drawing is an object, and most objects are contained within other objects.

A "collection" is a special type of object. Its function is to simplify working with a set of similar objects as a group. You can use collections when you want to look up a particular item in a group or process an entire collection. Later in this chapter you will use the Layers collection to look up the properties of individual layer objects (see the section called "Declaring the Variables," later in this chapter). Objects can even be members of multiple

PART

V

CH

21

collections. For example, a block would be a member of the Blocks collection and—once inserted into model space (as a BlockRef)—a member of the ModelSpace collection.

When you click any object in this diagram, the relevant Help screen opens. You see immediately that every object and every collection object has its own "methods," "properties," and "events." Methods, properties and events are reviewed in the next section. In VBA, you use the object model to access the properties and methods of any AutoCAD object. All you have to do is set a reference to the appropriate object.

After this brief tour of the object model, take a look at the development environment. You will have a chance to further examine the object model within the VBA "integrated development environment."

Note
You can download a full-color poster of the ActiveX Object Model chart from the AutoCAD Web site, at http://www.autodesk.com/products/acad2000/devres/vba.htm. The file is in PDF format, so you can view it onscreen with Adobe Acrobat software. You will need a "D"-size color plotter to print the file.

EXPLORING THE VBA INTEGRATED DEVELOPMENT ENVIRONMENT

The VBA IDE is comparable to the Visual LISP editor, which is also and integrated development environment (IDE). The VBA IDE enables you to edit, run, and debug programs interactively. In addition to providing an intelligent editing environment, the IDE is plugged directly into AutoCAD 2000 so you can run programs, watch values, and debug. To open the VBA IDE from AutoCAD, follow these steps:

Choose Tools, Macro, Visual Basic Editor, or type **vbaide** at the command prompt. The shortcut key Alt+F11 also gets you there and is a little faster. The Visual Basic Editor opens (see Figure 21.10).

Let's explore the environment. You are not in AutoLISP anymore: There is no command-line access to AutoCAD, and your only access to AutoCAD is through the ActiveX interface—in other words, the AutoCAD Object Model. You have already navigated through the object model via the AutoCAD/VBA Help System. Now you can use the Object Browser in the VBA Editor (see Figure 21.10) to familiarize yourself further with this model. Before you start into actual VBA coding, take a look at how layer objects are organized via the Object Browser.

THE OBJECT BROWSER

The Object Browser acts like the Windows Explorer, in that it allows you to view successive hierarchies of objects. It gives a useful overall view of the objects that can be accessed in a given application, as well as their properties, methods, and events.

Start the Object Browser in the VBA Editor by pressing the F2 key. You also can start the Object Browser from the toolbar, or by selecting View, Object Browser.

Figure 21.10
The Object Browser in the VBA IDE provides easy-to-access information about AutoCAD collections and objects.

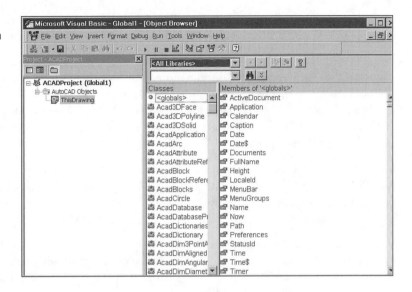

PROJECT/LIBRARY LIST BOX The list box at the top left corner of the Object Browser contains the Project/Library list box. This list box shows whatever current projects you have in the IDE and all the type libraries (.TLB files) referenced by these projects.

Because you have not yet created any projects, the list box shows only the default "AcadProject." The remaining entries in the list box are "type libraries." Each VBA application uses a different set of templates to define its ActiveX objects, and these templates are called "classes." The class definitions for an application are usually grouped into a single file called a type library (.TLB). A number of type libraries come preloaded in the VBA IDE. In this chapter, you will primarily use the AutoCAD library plus a few elements from the MSForms library.

Select AutoCAD in the list box. This limits your view to AutoCAD classes only. "Acad" should now prefix all the classes listed in the browser windows. (If you browse down to the bottom of the list, you will also see some other objects with yellow icons, which are prefixed by AC—not Acad. These are not classes, but enumerated constants. Constants are beyond the scope of this chapter.)

Tip 205 from
Paul Richardson

If you don't see AutoCAD in the Project/Library list box, you can reference the AutoCAD library by clicking Tools, References, and then browsing to locate the ACAD.TLB file. A typical location would be C:\Program Files \ACAD2000 \ACAD.TLB. If you want to be able to reference AutoCAD objects, you must make sure the appropriate type library is referenced in VBA.

"CLASSES" LIST Immediately below the Project/Library list box is the "Classes" list. As you browsed through the options in the Project list box, you probably noticed that the contents of this list change. Currently the left panel displays the "classes," or templates, for all objects available in AutoCAD. What you are actually looking at are the class definitions stored in a type library.

Users are frequently confused about the distinction between a "class" and an "object." The common analogy is that of a cookie cutter (class) and a cookie (object). The class specifies the type of data that can be contained in an object and also defines the properties, methods, and events available to that object class. You will always use the class to create an *instance* of the class, which is the object.

You may notice that there are classes for AcadBlock and Acad Linetype, and also for AcadBlocks and AcadLinetypes. The first class defines the individual block or linetype object; the second is the class for the "collection" of blocks or linetypes. (You will recall that objects are usually grouped into "collections" in the AutoCAD Object Model.)

Because you are planning to write some layer programs, take a look at the AcadLayer class and the AcadLayers collection class. Click AcadLayer in the Classes list and notice the information in the bottom window (the Details pane) of the Object Browser: The class is described as "a logical grouping of data, similar to transparent acetate overlays on a drawing." If you now click Acadlayers, the Details pane shows "a collection of all layers in the drawing."

THE "MEMBERS OF" LIST As you click each class, the right pane displays all the "members" available to that class of object. Members include properties, methods, and events. Most programming of AutoCAD with VBA has to do with defining the objects you are interested in, then manipulating their methods and properties, and specifying what the object does when a given event occurs.

PROPERTIES For any object you work with, the members you will most often access and manipulate are its Properties. Properties are values of an object that can be read and sometimes changed. For example, every AutoCAD graphical object in a drawing has a property for layer, color, and linetype. You will remember that in AutoLISP, this type of information is buried in tables and group codes. In VBA, the information is held more accessibly in the object's properties. For the purposes of the layer utilities that you are about to develop, you should take a look now at the properties that affect visibility: Freeze and LayerOn.

EXAMPLE: LOOKING AT THE FREEZE PROPERTY

1. Select Acadlayer in the Class pane.

2. Browse the properties, methods, and events available to this class of object. In the "Members Of" pane, the pointing finger icon indicates object properties.

3. Highlight the Freeze property in the Members Of pane, and then click the yellow Help button at the top of the Object Browser. This opens a typical Help screen containing a description of the Freeze property and allowed values. The page also contains links to a code example and to similar objects.

4. Click the Example link. The example provided is a full procedure you can cut and paste into a code window, and run.

METHODS Methods are the actions that an object knows how to perform. The code for the method is a part of the object. When you have a defined an object in your program, you can call the object's methods.

In the Object Browser, a flying green brick icon indicates the methods available to a given object. Again, select AcadLayer and view the methods available to it. Layers do not have an extensive range of methods available, although objects such as a line or a circle have a lot more actions available. Click AcadCircle, for instance, and you will see a whole range of methods: copy, mirror, offset, and rotate, to name but a few.

EVENTS An event is something that happens to an object. The VBA application (AutoCAD 2000, in this case) specifies the events to which an object will respond. Your program tells the object what action to take when an event occurs.

In the Object Browser, the lightning bolt icon shows events. Most AutoCAD objects have only a Modified event so your program can check whether objects have been changed. If you check the AcadLayer class and a few others, you will see that this is the case. Check AcadApplication or AcadDocument to see a wider range of "events."

You will not be using AutoCAD events in this chapter. However, you will have a chance to review some MSForms events later. Most controls on a form, such as buttons and list boxes, have events so that a signal can be sent to your program. This is how your program knows a user has clicked a button.

Spend a little time browsing the items in the Classes window and looking at the corresponding properties and methods available to each class. The AcadDocument object contains a wide range of properties, including viewports, layers, model space, selection sets, and so on. All of the values from these properties can be accessed through the AcadDocument. The AcadPreferences object contains all the information you set in AutoCAD 2000 when you run the Options command, including grips and pick settings.

SEARCH BOX The Object Browser can also locate objects for you. If you know what object you are interested in, you can type it into the Search combo box (next to the binoculars) to see all the relevant objects.

Type **circle** in the text box, and press Enter. The Search function opens the Search Results pane and returns the results shown in Figure 21.11.

The search has located the AcadCircle object, three versions of AddCircle method (for blocks, paper space, and model space) and a constant value acCircle.

To obtain more information on any of these items, select the item and then click the yellow Help button.

PART

V

CH

21

Figure 21.11
The Object Browser Search function can locate the library, class, and member for any search item..

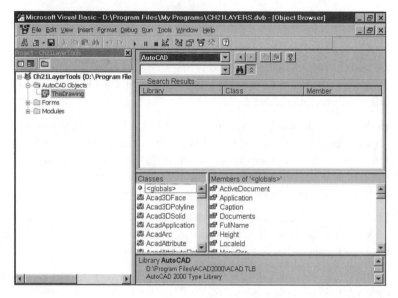

STARTING A NEW VBA PROJECT

A project in VBA is a collection of code modules and form modules that work together to perform a specified function. You will develop some layer utilities, so you should establish a project called "LayerTools." If you do not give your project a name, it will be automatically assigned the default name ACADProject.

1. If you don't have your VBA IDE open, press Alt+F11 in AutoCAD or select Tools, Macro, Visual Basic Editor.

   This time, look at the window on the right side of the Editor; this is the Project Explorer. The Project Explorer displays a hierarchical view of the components of your VBA project. These include forms, modules, and classes. These are displayed in collapsible folders similar to the Windows Explorer. You can browse through the folders and double-click any item to bring it up in the Editor.

   When you first open the VBA Editor, it displays a default project, named ACADProject. You should give this project a new name and save it as your project before you start writing code. Project names are set in the Properties window.

2. To change the project name, highlight "AcadProject" in the Project Explorer and then press the F4 key. This opens the Properties window, which displays all the properties of any selected object. The default "project" has only one property—the default name given to it by VBA.

3. Click "Name" in the Properties window. The default name (ACADProject) is selected. Type the new project name **LayerTools**, and press Enter.

Note

Notice that you have changed the Name property of the default project, but the project has not yet been saved under that name or any other name. It is very important to save your project under an appropriate filename.

4. Select File, Save, and then browse to your programming folder (\My Programs). Before you save a project, VBA assigns it the default name of Project.DVB. You must give it a new name; otherwise, your project will become the default project.

5. Type in an appropriate name for your project file, such as **LayerTools** or **Layers**. This does not need to be the same as the "Name" property.

Tip 206 from
Paul Richardson

If one of the windows in the VBA IDE does not display, use the function keys to activate the windows as follows: Ctrl+R for the Project Explorer; F4 for the Properties window; F2 for the Object Browser; and F7 for the Code window.

BEGINNING YOUR FIRST MODULE

Now that you have named your project and saved it to a .DVB file, you should add a new module to the project to contain your VBA code. Your first VBA module will replicate the AutoLISP program "OF" from the earlier part of this chapter.

EXAMPLE: BEGINNING YOUR FIRST MODULE

1. Highlight your project in the Project Explorer, and then select Insert, Module. "Module1" is added to your project in the Project Explorer.

2. Select "Module1," and press F4 again to open the Properties window. Click the "Name" property, and give your module a more meaningful name, such as **Lay1**; then press Enter. The module name automatically changes in the Project Explorer. (You should be aware that module names, and also form names, are limited to 40 characters with no spaces.)

Note

In this practice VBA project, you will create one module to contain all of the VBA layer routines you develop. When you review the finished VBA file (CH21LAYERS.DVB) from the accompanying CD, you will see a separate module for each part of the program (CH21VBA1, CH21VBA2 and so on). These modules were created for tutorial purposes only, and to provide a correspondence with the LISP programs (CH21LISP1, CH21LISP2, and so on). For a suite of simple utilities such as this, you need only one module.

3. Save your project.

4. Double-click the Lay1 module in the Project Explorer (or press the F7 key). An empty Code window is displayed.

PART
V

CH
21

5. Before you start your program, you should set your options so that variable declaration is required. (The reason for this will be clear when you actually declare some variables later in this exercise.) Select Tools, Options, and check the box labeled Require Variable Declaration on the Editor tab. Then click the OK button. This automatically puts the statement "Option Explicit" at the beginning of every new module.

6. On this occasion, you will need to type it in yourself. In the Code window, type **Option Explicit** and press Enter. Notice that the words turn blue and become capitalized, showing that VBA recognizes them as keywords, and formats them accordingly.

> **Note**
>
> If you wish to learn more about the color-coding and formatting conventions used by VBA, select Tools, Options, and then click the Editor Format tab. The Code Colors window lists all the different kinds of text that VBA recognizes: keyword text, execution point text, comment text and so on. If you highlight any item in the Code Colors window, a sample of the formatted code is displayed in the Sample window.

7. Type the statement **Sub AllOff ( )**, and press Enter. VBA responds by leaving a blank line and then typing End Sub. (If you forgot the parentheses, VBA will add those for you also.)

```
Sub AllOff ()

End Sub
```

You have now added a Sub procedure, named AllOff, to your module. This sub procedure has no arguments, but you still need to include the empty parentheses. The sub declaration tells where the procedure starts.

All VBA program code is contained in sub or function procedures. Contrary to logic, VBA sub procedures carry out the main business of the program; they are not necessarily subsidiary to other procedures. Sub procedures carry out instructions but do not return a value. VBA functions, or function procedures, always return a value.

Declaring the Variables

Before you can use an AutoCAD object, you need to establish a reference to it. In formal Visual Basic terminology, this is called "instantiating an object." For the AllOff program, you need to reference the Layer collection (Layers) and reserve layer objects to store a test layer and the current layer. This could be simply done with the following three statements:

```
Layercollection = ThisDrawing.Layers
testLayer = ThisDrawing.ActiveLayer
currentLayer = ThisDrawing.ActiveLayer
```

This is not advisable, however. Although VBA will let you use variables without declaring them, you can get into some very tricky debugging situations. Before you use a variable in VBA, it is good practice to declare it with the Dim statement. This "explicit" declaration lets VBA know what data type to expect and reserves room in memory for the variable when the program runs. (This is why you set the Option Explicit flag at the beginning of your code. "Option Explicit" won't let your program run unless you declare each variable with a Dim statement.)

The preferred practice is to use a Dim statement and a Set statement, per the following model:

```
Dim VariableName As ClassName
Set VariableName = ObjectName
```

The Dim statement references the appropriate "class" of object, and the Set statement creates an instance of the class, or "instantiates" the object. Enter the following three lines in the Code window:

```
Dim layerCollection As AcadLayers
Dim testLayer As AcadLayer
Dim currentLayer As AcadLayer
```

> **Note**
>
> When you add these statements to your program in the VBA Editor, remember to type them after the Sub Alloff () statement and before the End Sub statement. These two lines (Sub and End Sub) mark the beginning and end of a sub procedure.

Notice that after you type the word **As**, VBA tries to help by opening a list box from which you can select objects. This is VBA's IntelliSense at work. You can browse the list box and select the class of object you require.

> **Caution**
>
> Make sure you select the correct item from the list. For example, do not confuse AcadLayer the class with ACAD_LAYER data type. Look for the class icon, with the red/blue/yellow blocks on it, to be sure you are selecting the class and not the data type.

> **Note**
>
> Dim not only declares the type of the variable, but also describes its scope. *Scope* refers to the visibility of the variable. Depending upon the location of the Dim statement, the variable can be limited to a single procedure (Sub or Function) or can be available to an entire module. The Dim statements in your AllOff program are confined to this specific Sub.

Next, you must assign an object reference to each variable using the Set statement:

```
Set layerCollection = ThisDrawing.Layers
Set testLayer = ThisDrawing.ActiveLayer
Set currentlayer = ThisDrawing.ActiveLayer
```

ThisDrawing is the object that refers to the current AutoCAD 2000 drawing, and it is automatically available to VBA. Notice when you type the period after ThisDrawing that VBA IntelliSense kicks in and displays a list of the properties and methods available to the ThisDrawing object. You can scroll down the list to "Layers" or to "ActiveLayer" and either click or press Enter to complete the line. (You also can use the Tab key, which enters the value without putting the cursor on the next line.)

> **Note**
>
> If you are a working in Visual Basic (not VBA) and are starting from outside AutoCAD, you will need to connect to the AutoCAD application before you can access AutoCAD objects. Before you can have access to an AutoCAD drawing, you first must declare the AutoCAD application as an object. This is a nonspecific type of object and is generally not good practice. However, for this technique to work you must use nonspecific "late-binding," as shown here:
>
> ```
> Public AcadApplication As Object
>
> On Error Resume Next
>     Set AcadApplication = GetObject(, "AutoCAD.Application")
>     If Err Then
>         Set AcadApplication = CreateObject("AutoCAD.Application")
>         AcadApplication.Visible = True
>         Err.Clear
>     End If
> ```
>
> If AutoCAD is already running, the GetObject statement works, and the AutoCAD application object is assigned to the Object Variable AcadApplication. If AutoCAD is not running, GetObject doesn't work and an error is generated. You then can run the CreateObject statement to start a new AutoCAD application, assign the application object to the AcadApplication variable, make AutoCAD visible, and clear the error.

TURNING OFF THE LAYERS

Now that you have all your objects in place, you can cycle through the Layers collection and turn off all layers except the current layer. The actual program is very short.

Type the following five lines into the Code window:

```
For Each testLayer In layerCollection
        If testLayer.Name <> currentLayer.Name Then
            testLayer.LayerOn = False
        End If
    Next
```

In Visual Basic, the For Each...Next statement repeats a group of statements for each element (or object) in a collection. In this case, the program checks two properties of each layer object in the Layer collection: the "Name" property and the "LayerOn" property. It checks the Name property for the layer name, to see whether this layer is the current layer. If the layer being tested is *not* the current layer, the LayerOn property is set to "False."

Notice that when you refer to a property of an object (for example, the Name property of the testLayer or currentLayer object), it is appended to the object with a period between the object and the property, as in testLayer.Name. Methods are appended to their objects in the same way.

CONCLUDING THE PROCEDURE

All that remains is to set your variables to Nothing. This frees up the system and memory resources that were allocated to these object variables. Type the following three lines of code into the Code window:

```
Set layerCollection = Nothing
    Set testLayer = Nothing
    Set currentLayer = Nothing
```

SAVING YOUR PROJECT FILE

You have completed your first module. Click the Save icon on the toolbar in the VBA IDE, or select File, Save to save your project. The module is saved as a part of this project.

You could go straight ahead and load this project into AutoCAD 2000 to see if it performs, but you should take advantage of VBA's debugging tools before you do that.

RUNNING AND DEBUGGING YOUR VBA PROGRAM

You should test your program prior to loading it into AutoCAD 2000. Make sure there is a drawing open in AutoCAD before you try to run the program. Even if there is no drawing in the editor, the program will run, but it will not be tested. As with most VBA actions, there are several ways to accomplish what you want. Select one of the following methods to test-drive your program.

- The F5 key runs the procedure or form you have currently highlighted.
- On the main toolbar are the VCR-type buttons, Run(play), Break (pause), and Reset (stop).
- These three options are also available from the Run menu: Choose Run, Break, or Reset.

When you run your program, it is compiled before it is loaded and run. At this point, if there are errors in your code, the program will not load and you will get an error message. VBA highlights the line where the error occurred, and you can choose to click OK to correct the error, or click the Help button to get a message from VBA with its idea of the problem.

Even if your program loads, it may still have execution errors; VBA has a number of tools to help you locate the error.

You can select a break point by simply clicking to the left of your code at the point where you want to pause your program. Try inserting a break point on the For Each line in your code:

1. Move your mouse to the left of the line and into the gray margin. When the mouse cursor changes from a right arrow to a left arrow, click in the gray margin. You will see a brown dot; this is your break point. You can simply click it again when you want to clear it.

2. Press F5 to run the program. The program will run up to the break, and the line in your code with the break point will be highlighted.

3. From here you can press F5 again to run at full speed, or press F8 to single-step through your program one line at a time.

If you are still having problems with this program, you should compare it to the first module, CH21VBA1, in the CH21LAYERS.DVB project file on the CD that accompanies this book. Notice that the module is not saved separately from the project. You can review this program in the VBA Editor, but first you will have to load the program.

LOADING A VBA PROJECT

As with LISP programs, VBA programs (or projects) must be loaded before you can run them. When a program is loaded, it is automatically available in the VBA Editor. All the programs you will work with in this chapter are available in a single project file CH21LAYERS.DVB on the accompanying CD-ROM.

On the Tools Menu, select Macro, VBA Manager. From here you can see which projects are loaded, and you can either load or unload VBA files. To be even faster, you can select Tools, Macro, Load Project, or type **vbaload** at the command line. You should become familiar with both methods.

EXAMPLE: LOADING A VBA PROJECT

1. If you have not already done this, copy the CH21LAYERS.DVB file from the CD into your programming folder (\My Programs).

2. In AutoCAD 2000, select Tools, Macros, VBA Manager.

3. Click the Load button in the VBA Manager dialog box (see Figure 21.12).

4. When the Open VBA Project dialog box appears, browse to your programming folder.

4. Select CH21LAYERS.DVB and press Open. The program returns to the VBA Manager.

5. Press Close to return to AutoCAD 2000, or press the Visual Basic Editor button to open the project in the Editor. The sample project contains all the modules that you will be working with.

6. Highlight the module CH21VBA1, and double-click to open the Code window. (You may also press the F7 key to open the code window.)

You can now compare this file to the program you have just written. In addition to the program code, this file also contains a full set of comments (in green).

Figure 21.12
The VBA Manager dialog box enables you to load and unload project files.

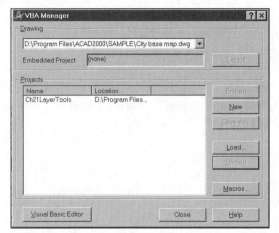

EXPANDING YOUR PROGRAM REPERTOIRE

You can expand your suite of VBA layer utilities with some judicious copying and editing, in the same way you did with the AutoLISP programs.

- You can add an AllOn program to turn on all the layers in a drawing. This program is almost the same as AllOff, except that this time the LayerOn property is set to True for all layers.

- You can very easily create AllFreeze and AllThaw programs to freeze and thaw all the layers in a drawing. Use the Freeze property instead of the LayerOn property, but the code is very similar: In the first procedure, the Freeze property is set to True; in the second procedure, the Freeze property is set to False.

You can develop these procedures, if you wish, and then check them against the supplied files. The programs are all extensively commented. If you want review AllOn, it is located after AllOff in the CH21VBA1 module. If you wish to review AllFreeze and AllThaw, highlight the second module in the project (CH21VBA2) and double-click or press the F7 key.

USING MORE OBJECTS, METHODS, AND PROPERTIES

Following the same sequence as the AutoLISP programs you created, you will now add a layer utility to turn off specific layers, picked by the user. Again, the programming here is a little more complex. The program must wait for the user to do something before it can start its cycle: it has to prompt the user, if necessary, and then it must respond to a screen pick by a user and turn off the correct layer.

PART
V

CH
21

Rather than entering this program as you go, you should open it in the VBA Editor and follow along as the text moves through the program. Open the CH21VBA3 module in the VBA Editor. Open a drawing in AutoCAD so you will be able to test the program, and then return to the VBA Editor (press Alt+ F11) to review the program.

BEGINNING THE PICK PROGRAM The overall framework of this program is identical to the AllOff program. It begins with an "Option Explicit" statement to force the declaration of all variables and then starts the procedure Sub PickOff:

```
Option Explicit
Sub PickOff()


End Sub
```

The procedure concludes with an End Sub statement. The sequence of events in between is a little more involved than in your previous program, AllOff. Let's follow it through section by section.

DECLARING THE VARIABLES

Take a look at the Dim statements first. There are few new elements here:

```
Dim AcadObject As Object
Dim testLayer As AcadLayer
Dim currentLayer As AcadLayer
Dim layerCollection As AcadLayers
Dim strlayerName As String
Dim SelectPoint As AcadPoint
```

- AcadObject is declared as an object to enable you to select any kind of AutoCAD object. Because you don't know what the user will pick, you can't be specific about the object type.

- testLayer and currentLayer are both AcadLayer objects, and layerCollection is the collection of layer objects. You should be familiar with all these objects from the AllOff program you wrote.

- strlayerName is defined as a simple string data type, not an object.

- SelectPoint is declared as an AcadPoint. This is required by the GetEntity method.

You will notice in the program that there are only two Set statements for the six Dim statements:

```
Set currentLayer = ThisDrawing.ActiveLayer
Set layerCollection = ThisDrawing.Layers
```

This is because AcadObject and SelectPoint are required by the GetPoint routine only—they are not used by the main procedure (Sub PickOff); layerName is a String and not an object; and the testLayer variable is set later in the program. Only two objects need to be "instantiated" for the main procedure.

Selecting an Object

Take a look at the first seven lines:

```
SELECTION:
    On Error Resume Next
    ThisDrawing.Utility.GetEntity AcadObject, SelectPoint, "Pick object to turn
off its layer: "
    If Err <> 0 Then
        Err.Clear
        MsgBox "Nothing Selected, Please try again"
        GoTo SELECTION
```

The first thing you want to do is prompt the user to select an object. If the user doesn't successfully pick an object, you must keep cycling back to give the user another chance. This is accomplished using a label to mark the start point of the cycle, the GetEntity method to select an object, and an Err object to verify that an object has been picked. These three processes are described as follows:

- In VBA, a label is a word with no spaces, followed by a colon—in this case, the word SELECTION:. This label is inserted at the start to enable the program to go back and repeat the object selection code sequence.

- The GetEntity method performs the same task as the entsel function you used in the AutoLISP version of this program. GetEntity is a method of the Utility Object for the AutoCAD drawing (ThisDrawing). It requires the user to select an object by picking a point on the graphics screen. If the user picks a point that is not an AutoCAD object, GetEntity will generate an error.

- To find out whether the GetEntity method successfully picked an object, you can make use of the Err object. You do not need to declare this object because it is always available to VBA programs. If an error occurs in a VBA program, a number is stored in the Number property of the Err object. If no error occurs, the Number property remains zero. (The Number property is the default property of the Err object, so you don't have to code "If Err.*Number* <> 0 Then"—"If Err <> 0 Then" is sufficient.)

If the user does generate an error and the Number property of the Err object is not zero, the program clears the error and prompts the user to try again. Then the GoTo statement returns the procedure to the start point.

If GetEntity successfully picks an AutoCAD object, you have access to its properties.

```
Else
        strLayerName = AcadObject.layer
```

First, you assign the layer property from the selected AcadObject to the string variable strLayerName.

Getting Objects from Collections

Now that you have the name of the layer, you want to get the actual layer object from the Layer collection so you can look at its properties.

```
Set testLayer = layerCollection(strLayerName)
```

If you look at any of the collections in the AutoCAD Application object, you will see that each has a very similar set of methods and properties. Press F2 to open the Object Browser and try clicking AcadLayers, AcadLayouts, AcadLinetypes, or anything that ends in an "s." The properties and methods are pretty much the same. The default method in all cases (shown by a blue dot) is the Item method. The preceding statement in the program uses the Item method. Fully expanded, this statement would read:

```
Set testLayer = layerCollection.Item(strLayerName)
```

Because Item is the default method, it does not need to be spelled out. The Item method returns the single member of the collection corresponding either to a numerical index or to a string key name. This procedure uses the string layer name, which it got in the previous step in the program, to get the actual layer object of the picked object.

You can now compare the Name property of the layer objects for the current layer and the picked layer. If the layer names don't match, you can safely turn off the selected layer by setting its LayerOn property to False.

```
If testLayer.Name <> currentLayer.Name Then
        testLayer.LayerOn = False
```

If the picked object is on the current layer, a message box displays "Cannot turn off the Current Layer" and the program goes back to the SELECTION label.

```
Else
    MsgBox "Cannot turn off the Current Layer"
    GoTo SELECTION
End If
```

Note

As in the AutoLISP version of this routine (OFP) described earlier in this chapter, the Pickoff program does not allow the user to turn off the current layer. This part of the program could be further developed to warn the user (Are you sure you want to turn off the current layer?), and then allow the user the option (Yes/No) of turning off the current layer.

Concluding the Program

The program then sets any objects used to Nothing.

```
Set AcadObject = Nothing
Set testLayer = Nothing
Set currentLayer = Nothing
Set layerCollection = Nothing
```

The PickOff program is now complete. The PickFreeze procedure is almost identical, except that it freezes the layer of a picked AutoCAD object. After a reference to the layer object has been obtained, its Freeze property is set to True. Both programs are included in the CH21VBA3 module.

CREATING A FORM IN VBA

You are now at the same point as you were with the AutoLISP programs, and you are facing the same problem. To complete the suite of layer utilities, you need to create a procedure that will enable you to selectively turn on or thaw layers that are presently off or frozen. Because you cannot select an object on a layer that is off or frozen, however, you cannot use the GetEntity method. You need to access a list of layers that are off or frozen. This means you must develop some type of dialog box, known as a "form" in VBA.

The final module in this set of layer utilities will combine the On and Thaw utilities because the coding for each is so similar. Two radio buttons will be used to select either the On or the Thaw procedure, the same as in the AutoLISP dialog box you created.

You can type in the code for this program or open the supplied file in the VBA Editor and follow along. To open the file in the Code window, select the CH21VBA4 module in the Project Explorer and press F7.

LOADING THE FORM

This program uses a form, so most of the code will go into the form's event procedures. A sub procedure is required to load the form:

```
Sub OnThaw()
  frmLayers.Show
End Sub
```

In this statement, the OnThaw procedure calls the Show method of the frmLayers form. This is the entire program. The rest of the coding is in the form, and you will review the form code later in this chapter. Before you can write the code, however, you must build the form.

BUILDING A FORM

This is actually the easy part. Building a graphical user interface is much simpler and more flexible in VBA than in AutoLISP. VBA enables you to visually build a dialog box, or "form," simply by dragging and dropping the elements that you want onto a blank form.

EXAMPLE: BUILDING A FORM

1. To create a new form, highlight your project (LayerTools) in the Project Explorer and then select Insert, UserForm.

2. "UserForm1" is added to your project in the Project Explorer, under "Forms," and an empty form appears in the Code window (see Figure 21.13). Select "UserForm1" and press F4 to open the Properties window.

3. Highlight the (Name) field in the Properties window; tab to the current value (UserForm1); overtype with a more meaningful name, such as **frmLayers**; and press Enter. The form name automatically changes in the Project Explorer. (If you call your form something different, you will have to change the name in the Sub procedure also.)

4. Highlight the Caption field in the Properties window; tab to the current value (UserForm1); overtype with a more meaningful name, such as **AutoCAD Layers**; and press Enter. The new form caption appears at the top of the form as you type.

You have now created a basic form named frmLayers and titled "AutoCAD Layers." You can see in the Properties window that your new form has many preset properties, but you do not need to alter any more of the default values for this program. If you cannot see your form at any time, double-click the frmLayers form in the Project Explorer.

Figure 21.13
VBA form controls can be dragged from the Forms Toolbox onto the form.

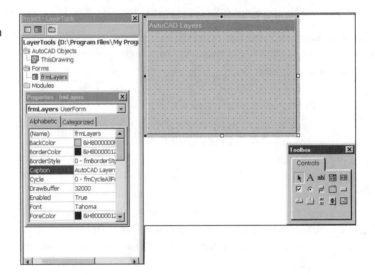

SIZING A FORM   Click the form itself and notice the tiny squares on the corners and mid-points around the edge of the form. These are called sizing handles, and you use these to change the size of the form. You don't need to change the width of this form, but you should stretch it until it is about twice as deep. Precision is not important because you can adjust the size at any time. Click the bottom midpoint handle, and drag down until the window is twice as deep as it was originally.

ADDING A FRAME   It's time to add some controls to the form. If your form is visible, you should also be able to see the Toolbox (see Figure 21.13). If your Toolbox is turned off and does not appear when you click the form graphic, select View, Toolbox to make it visible. First add a frame for the option (or radio) buttons.

EXAMPLE: ADDING A FRAME

1. Move your mouse over the Toolbox controls and observe the names on the ToolTips. This gives you the name of each control. Locate the "Frame" control.

2. Click the Frame control and then click the form and hold down the mouse. Drag until you see a window approximately 2 inches across and one-half-inch deep.

Again, don't worry about getting it just right—you can adjust at any time, or you can simply click an object and press the Delete key to start over.

ADDING A FRAME CAPTION   When you have the frame in place, click the frame again so the Properties window shows the properties for Frame1. Double-click the Caption property, and Frame1 becomes highlighted. Type **"Select Frozen or Off Layers."** As you type, you will see that the caption for the Frame changes—no waiting here. You can change the Name property if you wish, but because the object is not referred to directly in code, you don't need to.

ADDING RADIO BUTTONS   The purpose of the frame is to act as a container for your radio buttons so they act as a group. With radio buttons, you want only one to be active. If the user clicks one, you need the others to become deselected.

EXAMPLE: ADDING RADIO BUTTONS

1. Click the form again so its handles become highlighted.

2. Now, click an option (radio) button on the Toolbox and drag a rectangle in the top half of the frame. The rectangle you drag includes your button and its associated text. (Leave room for a second option button below the first.)

3. When you are satisfied with the position of your button, click it to highlight it, and then change its name in the Properties window to **optFrozen**.

4. Change its Caption property to **Show Frozen Layers**.

Repeat steps 2 through 4 to add a second option button. This time, change its name to **optOff** and its caption to **Show Turned Off Layers**.

ADDING A LIST BOX   Next, add a list box to the form to contain a list of either frozen or off layers.

EXAMPLE: ADDING A LIST BOX

1. Select Listbox on the Toolbox, and then drag a rectangle underneath the option buttons approximately two inches square.

2. Adjust the list box up, if you don't have a half-inch free at the bottom of the form. Alternatively, you can drag the form down, if you like.

PART

V

CH

21

3. Change the Name property for the list box to **lstLayers**.

When selecting layers from the list box, you want to be able to select multiple times using the Shift or Ctrl keys to select and deselect layers. This is handled by simply changing the MultiSelect property of the list box.

4. Find MultiSelect in the Properties window, click the down arrow opposite MultiSelect, and pick the last option 2-frmMutiSelectExtended.

ADDING COMMAND BUTTONS   Now, you just need to add a couple of command buttons, and you are done with the form.

EXAMPLE: ADDING COMMAND BUTTONS

1. Click the form and then click CommandButton on the Toolbox. Drag a rectangle an inch long by a "quarter inch high underneath the list box.

2. In the Properties window, change the Name property to **cmdOn** and the Caption property to **Thaw or On**.

3. Add a second command button to the right of the first one; try and make it the same size, and center the two buttons horizontally in the form.

4. Click the second button and change its Name property to **cmdCancel** and its Caption property to **Cancel**.

Finished!

NAMING FORMS CONTROLS   Before moving on to the code part of this program, a word about object naming conventions is appropriate. When you are writing code, it is easy to forget what you called a particular control on a form. Thus, it is important to give your controls meaningful names. Microsoft has recommendations for consistent prefixes for control object names in its Visual Basic Programming Guide. Table 21.4 is derived from the Microsoft guide.

TABLE 21.4   RECOMMENDED PREFIXES FOR NAMING FORMS CONTROLS

Prefix	Form Control
chk	Check box
cbo	Combo box
cmd	Command button
dat	Data control
dir	Directory list box
fil	File list box
frm	Form

Prefix	Form Control
fra	Frame
grd	Grid
hsb	Horizontal scrollbar
img	Image
lbl	Label
lst	List box
mnu	Menu
pic	Picture
spn	Spin
txt	Text box
tmr	Timer
upd	UpDown
vsb	Vertical scrollbar
sld	Slider
ils	ImageList
tre	TreeView
tlb	Toolbar
tab	Tabstrip
sta	StatusBar
lvw	ListView
prg	ProgressBar
rtf	RichTextBox

EVENT-DRIVEN PROGRAMMING

In the AutoLISP environment, code tends to run in a linear fashion, starting at the beginning, following a predictable path, and finishing at the end. When you use a Visual Basic form, you enter the world of event-driven programming. When a form is loaded and displayed on the computer screen, nothing happens until the user does something, clicking a button with a mouse or entering a value from the keyboard. When this happens, the control on the form raises an event to inform the program that something happened. Your program responds to the event (called *sinking the event*) with an event procedure. At this point, all the event procedures for your form are empty. You need to add code to them to direct the program.

ADDING CODE TO THE FORM

Click your form and then press the F7 key. This should bring up the Code window. You can also get to the Code window via the View menu or by double-clicking the form itself.

Start coding here by declaring your module-level variables—that is, variables that are available to all other procedures within this module.

EXAMPLE: ADDING CODE TO THE FORM

1. At the top-left side of the Code window is a drop-down list box (the Object list box). If the Object box doesn't say (General), click the box and scroll down to select (General). When you select (General), the cursor jumps to the General section of at the top of the program. Variables that are defined in the General section are available to all sub procedures in the program.

2. In the General section, type in the following statements after the Option Explicit (if you don't have Option Explicit displayed, type that in, too):

```
Option Explicit
    Dim currentLayer As AcadLayer
    Dim layerCollection As AcadLayers
    Dim testLayer As AcadLayer
```

   That has reserved memory for your two layer objects and the Layer collections object. You will want to instantiate these objects when the form is loaded and set them to Nothing when the program finishes.

3. A list of the objects in your form displays. Select UserForm from the Object box.

4. At the top-right side of the Code window is a drop-down list box (the Procedure list box). The Procedure box shows a list of events to which the form can respond. Select the Initialize event. The code for the event is dumped into the Code window. Every time this form is loaded, the code in this event procedure will be run.

```
Private Sub UserForm_Initialize()

End Sub
```

5. Your cursor should be positioned on the blank line within the Initialize event. Now instantiate the Layer collection and the layer object for the current layer. The testLayer is used within a For Each loop only and does not need to be set for the main procedure.

```
Private Sub UserForm_Initialize()
    Set layerCollection = ThisDrawing.Layers
    Set currentLayer = ThisDrawing.ActiveLayer
End Sub
```

Whenever a control is displayed in the left list box (the Object box), the events for that control are listed in the right list box (the Procedure box). You can step through the controls in the Object list box and fill out the appropriate event procedures.

Alternatively, you can double-click each control on the form in turn. (To open the form, press Ctrl+R to open the Project Explorer, and then double-click the form name.) Double-clicking a control on the form has the same effect as starting the Code window and selecting the control from the list box.

ACTIVATING THE OPTION BUTTONS

Let's do the option buttons on the form. (These are also known as radio buttons, outside the VBA environment). Sometimes it's hard to tell exactly where the limits of a control are. Because the limits of the control are not displayed on the form, it helps to single-click the control to mark it and highlight the grips and then double-click to display the Code window.

EXAMPLE: ACTIVATING THE OPTION BUTTONS

1. Double-click the first option button. If the Object list box displays optFrozen, you selected the right button. If you don't see optFrozen, either go back and try again, or simply select optFrozen in the Object list box.

2. Then select the Click event procedure.

```
Private Sub optFrozen_Click()

End Sub
```

3. Your cursor should be placed in the optFrozen Click event. Type in the code for the Frozen button:

```
lstLayers.Clear
    For Each testLayer In layerCollection
        If testLayer.Name <> currentLayer.Name Then
            If testLayer.Freeze = True Then
                lstLayers.AddItem testLayer.Name
            End If
        End If
    Next
```

When the Click event occurs, the program cycles through the following steps. First, the layer list box must be cleared to display either frozen or off layers. Calling the Clear method of lstLayers does the job. Then a For Each Next loop runs through the Layers collection and checks for Frozen Layers (Freeze property = True). The Additem method adds the name of any frozen layers to the list box.

Repeat these steps for the second option button. This option loads the layer list box with layers that are off.

EXAMPLE: LOADING LAYERS THAT ARE OFF

1. Go back to the form, and double-click the lower option button.

2. When optOff is displayed in the Object box, select the Click event from the Procedure box.

3. Type in the code for the Off button:

```
Private Sub optOff_Click()
    lstLayers.Clear
    For Each testLayer In layerCollection
        If testLayer.Name <> currentLayer.Name Then
            If testLayer.LayerOn = False Then
                lstLayers.AddItem testLayer.Name
            End If
        End If
    Next
End Sub
```

THE LIST BOX

The list box itself doesn't require any code; it keeps track of the items that have been selected. When you added the list box to the form, you set the MultiSelect property to value 2. If Multiple Selections is enabled, this allows the user to select more than one item (or layer) from the list box.

THE COMMAND BUTTONS

The main work of the program occurs after the user has pressed the "Thaw or On" command button (cmdOn). Up to that point, the user has a chance to change his mind and exit the program without making any changes in AutoCAD. After the Thaw or On button has been pressed, the program must change the properties of the selected layers.

Let's add the code for the cmdOn click event. Go back to the form and double-click the Thaw or On button. Then enter the following:

```
Private Sub cmdOn_Click()
    Dim i As Integer
    Dim testname
```

First, you must declare a couple variables for use locally in this procedure.

- The integer i will be used as an index to the list box Selected property. (The list box Selected property shows (True/False) whether any object in the list box has been selected or not.)

- Variable testName is declared without specifying a type, so it will default to a variant type. (A variant is a variable type that will accept any other type. In other words, you can use a variant to store objects, arrays, integers, or strings.)

You now test every layer in the list box to see whether any are selected. The index for the first item is zero, so the index for the last item is the total count minus 1. The listCount property of the lstLayers list box gives the total count.

```
For i = 0 To lstLayers.ListCount - 1
```

Each element in the list box is tested to see if its Selected property is True. If the Selected property is set to True, the program goes to the next test.

```
If lstLayers.Selected(i) = True Then
```

Assign the text from the current index of the list box to testname.

```
        testname = lstLayers.List(i)
```

Find the layer object that matches the layer name in the Layers collection.

```
            For Each testLayer In layerCollection
                If testLayer.Name = testname Then
```

If the option button for Frozen layers is highlighted, unfreeze the layer.

```
                    If optFrozen.Value = True Then
                        testLayer.Freeze = False
                    Else
```

If the option button for Off layers is highlighted, turn on the layer.

```
                        testLayer.LayerOn = True
                    End If
                End If
            Next testLayer
        End If
    End If
Next i
```

REGEN THE VIEWPORTS

When frozen layers are thawed, you should activate a regen of all the viewports. (This is equivalent to the AutoCAD Regenall command.)

```
ThisDrawing.Regen acAllViewports
    End
End Sub
```

ACTIVATING THE CANCEL BUTTON

Only one more control is left: the Cancel button.

EXAMPLE: ACTIVATING THE CANCEL BUTTON

1. Go to the form and double-click the Cancel button.
2. Type **End** in the Click event.

```
Private Sub cmdCancel_Click()
    End
End Sub
```

That's all there is to it. Now, you should load and run this program.

RUNNING VBA PROGRAMS

Before you can run a VBA program, you must load its project into your drawing.

EXAMPLE: RUNNING VBA PROGRAMS

1. If you have not yet loaded your project, select Tools, Macro, and then choose either Load Project or VBA Manager; or, use the vbaload command.

2. Browse to your programming directory (\My Programs), and load the required project, either your own or the demo project supplied on the CD (CH21LAYERS.DVB).

3. To run a program, select Tools, Macro, and then choose Macros; or, type **vbarun** at the command prompt. Either of these options will open the Macros dialog box.

4. Select any of the programs shown in the list box, and press the Run button.

Each time you want to run the program, you will have to repeat the vbarun process. It is probably worth your while to create a simple LISP file to run VBA macros you use regularly with a simple command-line statement. For example, the following lines of code will create keyboard commands to run the VBA macros contained in CH21LAYERS.DVB:

> **Caution**
>
> If you have worked through the practice VBA project in this chapter and created your own VBA module, the following LISP program will not work with your project. Even though the sub procedure names are the same in your project, the vbarun command will not find them without the correct module name. In the practice project, there is only one module (named Layers or Lay1, for example). Replace the CH21VBA1–4 references with the name of the module you created.

```
(defun c:vbOf()(command "vbarun" "CH21VBA1.AllOff"))
(defun c:vbOn()(command "vbarun" "CH21VBA1.AllOn"))
(defun c:vbFr()(command "vbarun" "CH21VBA2.AllFreeze"))
(defun c:vbTh()(command "vbarun" "CH21VBA2.AllThaw"))
(defun c:vbPf()(command "vbarun" "CH21VBA3.Pickfreeze"))
(defun c:vbPo()(command "vbarun" "CH21VBA3.PickOff"))
(defun c:vbOt()(command "vbarun" "CH21VBA4.OnThaw"))
```

These LISP statements are saved in a LISP file (CH21VBARUN.LSP) you can find on the CD that accompanies this book. You may load this file into the current drawing each time you need it; or, you may want to add this LISP file to your ACADDOC.LSP file so it is available each time you open a drawing. Then you can type **vbfr** to freeze all the layers in your drawing, or **vbpf** to pick a layer and freeze it. When you have commands to run VBA programs, you can also assign those commands to AutoCAD 2000 toolbars. That way, you don't even have to remember the names of the commands you created.

→ For instructions on creating or editing an ACADDOC.LSP refer to the section "Automatic Loading of LISP Files," earlier in this chapter.

→ For information on customizing toolbars in AutoCAD 2000, refer to Chapter 20, "Customizing Made Easy."

SUMMARY

This chapter was designed to help you compare the two different programming environments of AutoLISP and VBA, and to help you draw your own conclusions as to how you can most effectively customize AutoCAD. The chapter does not represent an exhaustive analysis of either environment. Instead, it has attempted to give you a feel for the overall approach of each language via typical functions and procedures. The chapter also explored the differing methodologies used by LISP and VBA to design graphical user interfaces.

The choice is a tough one. AutoLISP is easy to learn and still does pretty much everything you can do with AutoCAD. With the Visual LISP extensions, you can even access the AutoCAD Object Model and interact with Windows. VBA offers the stability of an object-oriented approach (but you must master the object concepts), gives you easy access to other applications that support the ActiveX interface, and is more flexible than AutoLISP/DCL when you are designing dialog boxes, or "forms." Both environments have a lot to offer, and you won't go wrong whichever one you choose.

CHAPTER 22

EXTERNAL DATABASE CONNECTION

In this chapter

ACCESSING EXTERNAL DATA WITH dbCONNECT

Since Release 12 and the introduction of AutoCAD SQL Extension (ASE), AutoCAD users have had the capability to connect to external databases. This capability has been greatly expanded throughout the years and has been enhanced considerably within AutoCAD 2000. What was previously accomplished using numerous commands is now accomplished using a single command called dbConnect. With this feature, you can easily connect to external databases, view and edit row information within tables, and create queries to search for information linked to drawing objects to create selection sets.

Tip 207 from *Ron House*	dbConnect now replaces the ASE commands available in older versions of AutoCAD. The AutoCAD Migration Assistant can convert data within older drawing files to the new format for use in AutoCAD 2000.

→ See Appendix C, "AutoCAD Migration Assistance," for more information on how to convert files linked to a database using ASE to the new database connection format.

After drawing objects have been linked to an individual table in a database, specific information about those objects can be exported and brought back into the drawing as a report or a Bill of Materials. This chapter covers how to do this and more.

CONNECTING TO A DATABASE

First, let's discuss how to connect a drawing to a database. You can use two methods to access an external database: either ODBC or OLE DB. Both of these methods allow a connection to be made to the database, acting as a sort of translator to get to the data regardless of specific platform or database structure.

USING ODBC TO MAKE THE CONNECTION

The first method is to use the Microsoft Windows Open Database Connection (ODBC) by creating a Data Source Name (DSN). The DSN is essentially the name given to the ODBC connection for a particular database. You can think of the DSN and ODBC combination as an administrator who controls the specifics of how to connect to the database. A DSN can be created through the Windows Control Panel using the ODBC Data Source Administrator. Clicking the ODBC Data Sources icon launches a setup routine that prompts you for the DSN and for the details of connecting to your database. Using ODBC, you can connect to the following types of databases or spreadsheets:

- Microsoft Access 97
- dBASE V and III
- Microsoft Excel 97

- Oracle 8.0 and 7.3
- Paradox 7.0
- SQL Server 7.0 and 6.5
- Microsoft Visual FoxPro 6.0

Note

Refer to the Microsoft Help files for more information on connecting to databases using ODBC.

The second method is discussed in the next section. OLE DB, which is new to users working with releases prior to AutoCAD 2000, can be used to quickly connect to a particular database, although it cannot be used with as many databases as ODBC.

CONNECTING TO A DATABASE USING OLE DB

The OLE DB software enables you to bypass the ODBC software by using direct drivers to connect to a specific database. The OLE DB direct drivers that are shipped with AutoCAD 2000 allow you to connect to these databases:

- Microsoft Access
- Oracle
- Microsoft SQL Server

The next section describes how to connect to one of these databases using the dBConnect Manager.

CONNECTING TO A DATABASE VIA THE dbCONNECT MANAGER

The dbConnect Manager manages the existing DSNs, links, queries, and labels, in addition to listing the drawings open during the current session. The tree structure conveniently displays these items, making it easy to view the linked databases and related information. Start the dbConnect Manager by selecting dbConnect from the Tools pull-down menu. You can also activate dbConnect by clicking the dbConnect button from the Standard toolbar (see Figure 22.1) or by typing **DBC** at the command line.

When the dbConnect Manager window is open, you'll notice a dbConnect pull-down menu is now available from the menu bar. This menu is added to allow quick access to all the operations associated with the command. When you connect to a data source, a Data View pull-down menu also is available, providing many of the Data View commands and options.

Figure 22.1
You can activate dbConnect by using the dbConnect button from the Standard toolbar.

Tip 208 from
Ron House

If you are working with an Access or Excel database file, or other types of databases that have an actual filename, you can easily link that database with the drawing using a drag-and-drop process. Drag the database file from Windows Explorer onto the dbConnect Manager window of your drawing and drop it there. The database is connected and automatically creates the Data Link File for you. For those databases without a specific filename, you must either use OLE DB or create a DSN to use ODBC to connect.

The following example walks you through connecting to an Access database using the Microsoft Access direct driver.

EXAMPLE: CONNECTING TO AN ACCESS DATABASE USING OLE DB

In this example, you will connect to an Access database that is included on the companion CD.

1. Copy the database SE_Acad_2000.mdb from the CD to the C:\Program Files\AutoCAD2000\Sample directory.

Note

You must make certain this file has Archive rights assigned to it. You can check this by right-clicking on the file in Windows Explorer and selecting Properties. Look in the Attributes section of the Properties dialog box: Only the Archive check box should be selected. If not, check the appropriate boxes to make it so.

2. Open the drawing ch22_01.dwg. This is an office floor plan you will use with the database file mentioned in step 1.

3. From the Tools pull-down menu, select the dbConnect option. This opens the dbConnect Manager, displayed in Figure 22.2

Figure 22.2
The dbConnect Manager window displays the tree structure of drawings, links, Data Source Names, and linked tables within in the database.

4. When the dbConnect Manager is open, right-click on the Data Sources node and select Configure Data Source, as shown in Figure 22.3.

Figure 22.3
You can easily configure a data source within the dbConnect Manager window.

5. The Configure a Data Source dialog box opens, as shown in Figure 22.4. Type in **SE_ACAD_2000** for the name of the data source and click the OK button.

Figure 22.4
The Configure Data Source dialog box enables you to create a new data source, and it also displays a list of all the data sources currently available within the drawing.

6. Select the desired OLE DB provider from the list to connect to your database within the Data Link Properties dialog box, shown in Figure 22.5. For this example, choose the Microsoft Jet 3.51 OLE DB Provider, and then click the Next button.

Figure 22.5
The Provider tab within the Data Link dialog box gives a list of OLE DB providers that can connect to your database.

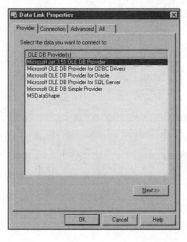

Tip 209 from
Ron House

> For connection to databases other than Access, Oracle, or SQL Server, use the Microsoft OLE DB Provider for ODBC Drivers. This enables access to your database via a DSN link.

7. The provider you choose determines the information you will need to provide to link to your database on the Connection tab, shown in Figure 22.6. Browse and select the SE_Acad_2000.mdb database from the C:\Program Files\AutoCAD2000\Sample directory by clicking the button to the right of the edit box.

Note

> If your database requires a user name and password, type that information in the appropriate boxes. If the password is blank, click the Blank password check box. If you provide a password, you may click the Allow saving of password check box to avoid typing the password in the future.

Figure 22.6
Type in the specific information needed to connect to your database under the Connection tab in the Data Link Properties dialog box.

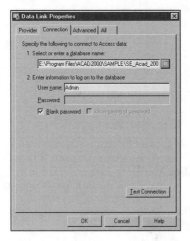

8. Click the Test Connection button to attempt a trial connection to your database. You will get an alert box displaying either that the test was successful or that the attempt failed.

The Advanced tab contains information specific to network connections and database access rights, as shown in Figure 22.7. You need not modify anything under this tab.

9. The All tab, shown in Figure 22.8, displays the settings for connection to your database that can be modified from here. First select the property, and then click the Edit Value button.

10. After you click the OK button in the Data Link Properties dialog box, the data source is added to the Data Source Manager tree.

Figure 22.7
Network settings, access remissions, and connection timeout values can be set from the Advanced tab of the Data Link Properties dialog box.

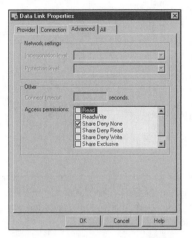

Figure 22.8
The All tab in the Data Link Properties dialog box enables you to view and edit the information needed to connect to your database.

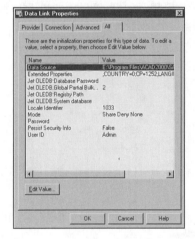

Tip 210 from
Ron House

The information contained within a DSN is saved in a file with the same name and with a .UDL extension. These files are kept in the directory specified in the Files tab of the Option dialog box. This can be accessed by right-clicking in the command line and selecting Options from the menu. The path can be set in the Data Sources Location folder. If you modify the location of the DSNs, you must close and restart AutoCAD.

11. Select the data source you just created, and right-click. Choose Connect from the menu. If AutoCAD is capable of connecting to your database, a list of tables will appear under your DSN, as shown in Figure 22.9.

Figure 22.9
A connected data source will display the tables available within the dBConnect Manager.

Tip 211 from
Ron House

A small red X will appear next to the DSN in the dbConnect tree list to indicate that the corresponding database is not connected. After you are connected, you may need to select the plus sign next to the DSN to view the linked tables.

Various dbConnect options are available from the dbConnect Manager (see Figure 22.10) can be applied to the items within the tree structure.

Figure 22.10
The options available from the dbConnect Manager enable you to view and edit tables, create and execute queries, and create link and label templates.

These options are listed as follows:

- View Table—Click this icon to view the records and columns in the table via the data view window, shown in Figure 22.11.

- Edit Table—If you have the rights to edit the database, this option opens the table data in the data view window and enables you to make changes to the database.

- Define Link Template—This enables you to create a link template to link objects in the drawing to a row in the connected table. Link templates specify the location of a table and the key column to be used for that database. A key column contains a specific identifier that is unique for each field in the table.

→ The section "Using a Link Template to Link Objects to a Database," later in this chapter, explains the process of creating a link template and linking in more detail.

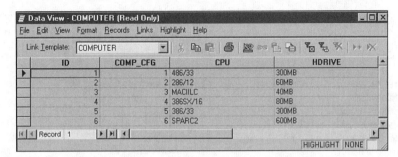

Figure 22.11
The data view window displays the rows and columns of the linked table.

- Define Label Template—This option creates a label template that can be used to label objects linked to data within the database. See the example, "Creating Labels as You Link Drawing Objects," later in this chapter.

- New Query—The New Query option enables you to create a query to be run against the current linked table. The information returned by the query can be displayed within a data view, thus defining what data is shown for this table.

After you have connected to a database, you can view and edit information from a specific table after a query has been defined.

CREATING A NEW QUERY

A query can be created to view specific information within a table and can be displayed within a data view window. You can easily create new queries using the Query Editor. To access the Query Editor, first select a table from the dbConnect Manager window. Then right-click and select the New Query option. This opens the New Query dialog box, which displays the current table the query will be run against (see Figure 22.12).

Figure 22.12
Using the New Query dialog box, you can define a new query name as well as view existing query names.

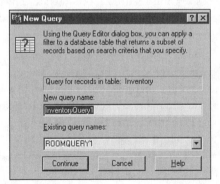

Using the list of all the existing query names to determine the new name, enter the name of the new query. After you specify a name and click the Continue button, the Query Editor appears (see Figure 22.13).

Figure 22.13
Four different tabs, each defining a specific query device such as Quick Query, enable you to narrow your query to find exactly what you want.

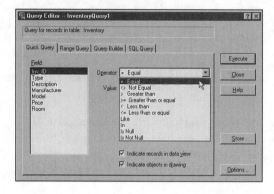

From within this dialog box, you can choose from four different types of queries, each available by clicking the associated tab. Each tab contains two check boxes named Indicate records in data view and Indicate records in drawing; these enable you to define how the queried information is displayed, either in the data view or in the drawing, by highlighting the linked objects to the data queried.

- Quick Query—Quick Query lets you define a field from the table and create a Boolean search for information based on that field. After a Boolean operator has been selected, you may click the Look up values button to search for a specific value available in the selected field. Figure 22.13 displays the Quick Query Tab and the various Boolean operators that can be selected.

- Range Query—A Range Query allows you to query for a range of data rather than for a specific value. The dialog box shown in Figure 22.14 illustrates how a range query would be implemented in searching for all employee names whose identification numbers fall between 1019 and 1044.

- Query Builder—The Query Builder also queries for a range of data, yet with this option you can construct a query statement over a series of rows, using the AND and the OR Boolean operators to combine the individual rows. Up to four sets of parentheses can be included within a query statement. Each row of a multiple-row query must be grouped inside parentheses. Parentheses can be used to group query statements by selecting the Field column to the left of the starting field and also the column to the right of the ending Value field for that row. Double-clicking inside a cell drops down a list of fields available from the table. Selecting within the Logical column toggles you between the AND and OR operators. This is represented in Figure 22.15.

Figure 22.14
Using the Query Editor to define a range query for data that falls within a specified range of values.

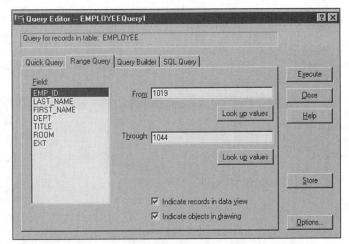

Figure 22.15
Using the Query Builder, you can create a query quickly and easily.

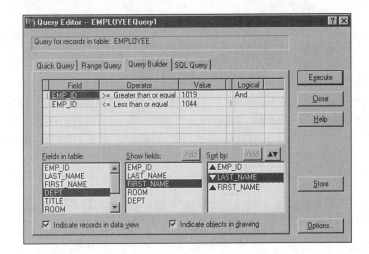

Tip 212 from
Ron House

One feature that sets the Query Builder option apart from the Range Query option is that you can define how the returned information will be displayed. Using the Show fields and Sort by columns, you can toggle which fields will display and then sort them as a result of your query. If no Show fields are specified, all fields in the table are displayed.

Tip 213 from
Ron House

You can also drag and drop field names into the Show fields and Sort by columns. Once in the Sort by column, a field can also be dragged into its desired sort order. The first field in this list is the main sort field. By default, a field is displayed in ascending order. Use the ascending/descending sort button to reverse this order, or double-click on the field to toggle to the opposite sort order.

- SQL Query—Selecting this tab enables you to enter and view the SQL statement defined for the query. In addition, there are tools to construct the statement. When you have completed entering the SQL statement, you can check the syntax by clicking the Check button. This portion of the New Query dialog box is shown in Figure 22.16.

Figure 22.16
You can enter SQL statements to define a query by clicking the SQL Query tab in the New Query dialog box.

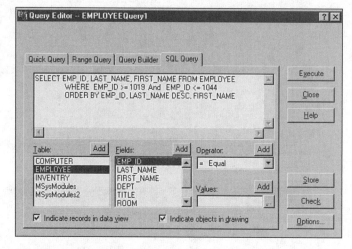

Click the Store button to save your query and add it to the dbConnect Manager window. When the query is displayed from here, it can easily be run again by right-clicking the query name and selecting Execute from the shortcut menu. Selecting the Execute button runs the query against the table and returns the data in a data view, as shown in Figure 22.17.

Figure 22.17
A data view displays the data returned from a query. From here, objects can be linked to a row in the table.

The next example walks you through the process of defining a new query to define what table data you want to view.

EXAMPLE: DEFINING A NEW QUERY

1. Reopen the drawing ch22_01.dwg, if it is not already open. Connect the Data Link SE_ACAD_2000 you created in the previous example. Right-click SE_ACAD_2000 from the dbConnect Manager tree listing and select Connect. You will use this drawing

and example database throughout the rest of the chapter, so what is done in the example will assist you in completing the following dbConnect examples.

2. Right-click the Employees Table listed in the dbConnect Manager window and select New Query.

3. From the New Query dialog box, name the new query **EMP_QUERY** and click Continue.

4. Select the Range Query tab in the Query Editor to define the following query. Say, for example, that you want to view all the employees who occupy rooms 6020 through 6060. Pick the Room field from the list, and then either choose the Look up values button or type in the value **6020** in the From edit box. Do the same for the Through edit box, but enter a value of **6060**. The finished dialog box is shown in Figure 22.18.

Figure 22.18
Defining the query within the Query Editor using a range query for employees who occupy rooms 6020 through 6060.

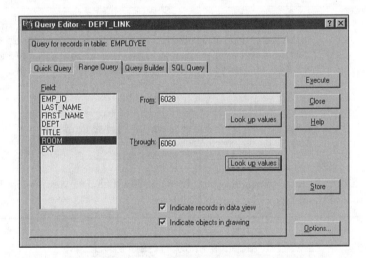

5. Next, click the Query Builder tab to limit the amount of data shown in the data view. Drag the fields EMP_ID, LAST_NAME, FIRST_NAME, DEPT, and ROOM from the Fields in table column to the Show fields column (see Figure 22.19).

Tip 214 from
Ron House

To remove a field name from the Show fields column, select the field and press the Delete key.

6. From the Show fields column, drag the Room field into the Sort by column. You will want to view room numbers in descending order, so double-click on the Room field in this column to toggle the ascending arrow so it is pointing downward, or in Descending mode.

PART
V

CH

22

Figure 22.19
You can determine which columns will be displayed in the data view window using the Show fields column within the Query Builder tab.

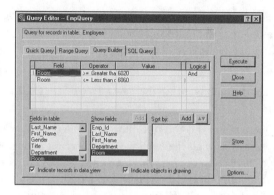

> **Note**
>
> After you have defined the query using the Query Builder or SQL Query options from within the Query Editor, do not return to the Quick Query or Range Query tabs. If you do, the query you just created will be reset to its default setting and then cleared. Fortunately, AutoCAD will warn you before continuing with this action.

Tip 215 from
Ron House

If this is a query you will want to run again and again, click the Store button to add the query to the dbConnect Manager window.

7. Click the Execute button to open the data view. The data view should be as you specified and should look like Figure 22.20.

Figure 22.20
The queried data in the data view window displays information about the employees who are assigned to rooms defined within the query.

Tip 216 from
Ron House

The table information displayed within the data view window can be set to read-only mode by right-clicking in the command line and selecting Options... from the list. Selecting the System tab displays the dbConnect Options section, which contains the Open tables in read-only mode option. This would enable a CAD Manager to ensure that the database information is not being modified accidentally, and can be set within the individual CAD user profiles. If a user attempts to modify the data, an alert box will appear, stating that the column is not editable and cannot be edited. See Appendix B, "AutoCAD Environment Options," for information on how to create user profiles.

In the following section, you learn more about the functionality of the data view window and how to apply it to the data you've queried.

WORKING WITH THE DATA VIEW WINDOW

The data view window displays the queried table data similar to a spreadsheet. Figure 22.21 displays the column shortcut options of the data view grid window.

Figure 22.21
You can right-click in the column header of the data view grid window to access table column shortcut menu.

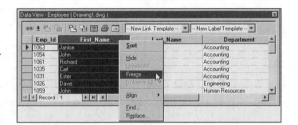

Tip 217 from
Ron House

Use the Record number indicator located in the lower-left corner of the data view window to scroll to a specific numbered row in the query. Just type the number of the row you wish to scroll to in the edit box, and press Enter.

You can control the display of the data within the columns by right-clicking on a column header and accessing the desired function from the menu. The following options allow you to modify how the column data is viewed:

■ Sort—The values within the columns can be sorted in ascending or descending order with the Sort dialog box.

Tip 218 from
Ron House

When you do not want to sort all the columns in the entire table, you can sort specific groups of columns by using the Ctrl and Shift keys. Then right-click to access the shortcut menu and choose Sort.

■ Hide—Hiding a column temporarily turns off the display of the column in the data view window. The display of the column can be restored by right-clicking on any column header and selecting Unhide All.

■ Freeze—Selecting a column and choosing Freeze from the right-click shortcut menu keeps this column from scrolling when using the horizontal scrollbar. To unfreeze the column, right-click on a column header and select Unfreeze All from the shortcut menu.

Tip 219 from
Ron House

You can freeze only multiple columns that are consecutive. If you cannot freeze the desired columns, move the columns by clicking the column header and dragging the column to the correct location; then freeze those columns.

- Align—The alignment of the column (Left, Center, or Right) can be modified with this option.

- Find—This option enables you to search for a specific text value in the column.

- Replace—You can search for and replace a text value in the column.

These options are great for modifying column-specific settings. Now take a look at the options to change an individual cell. These options give you the ability to change data stored in the database from within AutoCAD, without the need to access a database application. This saves you considerable time and effort.

MODIFYING A CELL'S VALUE

When you want to make changes to a table row, double-click in the cell and type the new value, or right-click in the cell and select Edit from the shortcut menu shown in Figure 22.22.

Figure 22.22
The cell shortcut menu enables you to modify a value or find and replace a specific cell value.

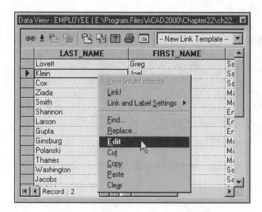

The following list gives detailed descriptions for each of the available options:

- View linked objects—This option enables you to view the objects linked to this row.

- Link!—The data view window temporarily closes, enabling you to select the objects you want to link to this row.

- Link and Label Settings—This menu contains those options specific to linking and labeling, covered later in the chapter.

→ The View linked objects and Link! options are covered in more detail in the section "Linking Drawing Objects to the Table" later in this chapter. The option for Link and Label Settings is discussed in the section called "Creating Labels as You Link Drawing Objects."

- Find—This enables you to search for a particular text value in the column.

- Replace—This replaces the searched-for text items in the column with another value.

- Edit—The value in the cell is highlighted and can be edited with this option.

PART

V

CH

22

- Cut—The value can be cut to the Clipboard.

- Copy—This enables you to copy the value to the Clipboard.

- Paste—This enables you to paste the value on the Clipboard into the cell.

- Clear—The value currently in the cell is cleared.

After a change has been made to a row, note that a symbol appears in the record header on the left side of the row, as well as in the grid header. This indicates the table has been modified, but changes have yet to be committed to the database.

SAVING CHANGES MADE TO A DATABASE TABLE

When changes are made to a cell and the focus is changed to a different cell, a triangular-shaped symbol appears in the row header for that row as well as the grid header.

Figure 22.23
The data view window displays a triangular-shaped symbol to indicate that changes made to the table need to be saved and to indicate which row was edited.

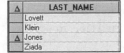

The triangle indicates the row has been modified since the changes were last committed to the database. To commit the changes to the entire database, right-click on the grid header and select Commit from the shortcut menu. The changes will be saved and the data view window will close. To reopen the data view window with your query, double-click on the query name from the dbConnect Manager window.

You may have noticed other options available from the grid cell menu as well:

- Restore—Restores the table rows to their original values.

- Unhide All Columns—Unhides all hidden columns in the data view window.

- Unfreeze All Columns—Restores all frozen columns to their original unfrozen setting.

- Clear All Marks—Clears any highlights from the rows in the data view window.

- Print Preview—Previews the data displayed in the data view window for printing, as shown in Figure 22.24.

- Print—Prints the data view window.

- Format—Opens the Format dialog box to modify the format of text within the data view window.

Figure 22.24
The Print Preview dialog box previews the data view window for printing the queried data.

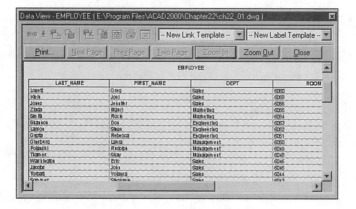

In addition to the grid cell menu options, there are also many options that deal mainly with editing and viewing data in the Data View window. In addition, the Data View toolbar contains the various commands needed to link the queried table to drawing objects and to view linked records, which are discussed in the next section.

THE DATA VIEW TOOLBAR

While the grid header options dealt mainly with displaying and editing the queried data in the table, the Data View toolbar commands enable you to link to drawing objects and to view the rows that are linked. The toolbar buttons are shown in Figure 22.25.

Figure 22.25
The various toolbar buttons access the commands to link and view linked records from within the data view window.

You'll find out about linking rows to drawing objects in the next chapter, but one feature will be covered here: the Data View and Query Options dialog box (see Figure 22.26).

These options are accessed by selecting the Data View and Query Options button from the Data View toolbar (see Figure 22.26). The Data View and Query Options dialog box is split into four separate categories, two of which you'll learn about in this section. The first section is called Record Indication Settings. The options in this section indicate how the linked rows in the data view window will be displayed:

- Show only indicated records—This displays only those records linked to objects in the current selection set in the data view window.

- Show all records, select indicated records—All records are shown in the data view window, and those records linked to drawing objects are selected.

Figure 22.26
The Data View and Query Options dialog box contains the settings that control the display of linked records within the data view window.

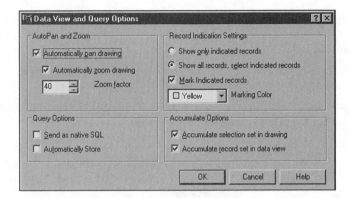

- Mark indicated records—The records that are linked to an object are highlighted with a marking color in the data view window.

- Marking Color—This option enables you to set the color used to mark the linked records.

The next section covered in the Data View and Query Option dialog box is the Query Options section. This section contains two options:

- Send as native SQL—Queries are sent in the native format of the current table to the database rather than in an SQL 92 format.

- Automatically Store—If this was not done previously, queries are automatically stored after execution when this option is checked.

The remaining two sections of this dialog box will be discussed more appropriately after you learn how to link rows in the table to objects in the drawing. Part of the process leading up to this is learning how to create a link template, which is covered in this next section.

USING A LINK TEMPLATE TO LINK OBJECTS TO A DATABASE

Before any linking can take place, a link template must be created. A link template determines the location of the table and the field you want as the key column. The key column, or index column, defines each row in the table with an individual number or indicator specifically used to relate to data in that row.

Unlike attributes assigned to blocks, the advantage of linking drawing objects to an external database is that the data can be edited outside of AutoCAD. For example, suppose you have linked all door blocks in a drawing to an external database. Information linked to these blocks, such as manufacturer or fire rating, can be edited as often as needed without opening AutoCAD. If this information were stored as attributes, the block attribute defining the information would need to be edited each time the data was changed. If you have a drawing with numerous doors and various fire ratings, you can start to envision the amount of time you can save by linking to an external database.

→ Chapter 16, "Creating and Using Blocks," contains information about assigning attribute information to blocks. Refer to that chapter for more information on this feature.

The next example walks you through the process of creating a link template and then shows you how to apply it when linking drawing objects.

Tip 220 from
Ron House

Although it is not necessary to query the items in the table prior to linking to objects in the drawing, it does help to limit the number of rows displayed in the data view window. This makes it easier to find what you want to link.

EXAMPLE: CREATING A NEW LINK TEMPLATE

Now that you have created a query that narrows the list of objects you want to view in the data view window, let's link specific rows in the table to objects in the drawing:

1. Using the drawing and connected table from the preceding example, right-click on the Employees table in the dbConnect Manager window and select New Link Template.

2. This opens the New Link Template dialog box (see Figure 22.27). Here, you can create a new template called **EmpLink**, and then click the Continue button.

Figure 22.27
The New Link Template dialog box enables you to use an existing template to create new link templates to the same table, yet use the same or a different key field.

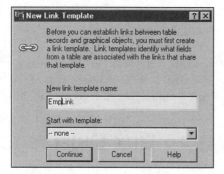

Tip 221 from
Ron House

Similar to using a template drawing to create a new drawing, you can select an existing template from the start. Using a template list, you can duplicate an existing template and use it to create a new link template.

3. The Link Template dialog box opens, listing all the fields within the selected table. Click in the check box to the left of the field in the Key Fields listing, shown in Figure 22.28, to indicate that this field is unique in defining the individual rows of the table.

Figure 22.28
The Link Template dialog box displays all the columns in the table you want to link so a key field can be set.

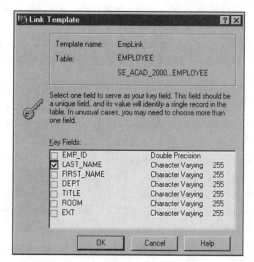

Tip 222 from
Ron House

Be careful if multiple fields in your table can be defined as key fields and you want to link to more than one key field. Choosing more than one key field will affect the performance of many database functions, including queries. You must determine whether having multiple key fields is worth the wait you might encounter while accessing the table.

4. When you click the OK button to finish creating the link template, the new template name is added to the list of link templates shown in the dbConnect Manager window.

After the link template is created with a column defined as the key field, drawing objects can be linked to individual rows in the table.

LINKING DRAWING OBJECTS TO THE TABLE

Now that you have created the link template, you are ready to link to drawing objects to the table using the key field you specified.

Note

Before linking objects in the drawing to records in the table, you should consider placing labels with the objects as you link; this is covered in the section "Creating Labels as You Link Drawing Objects" later in this chapter. If you don't do so, you may need to relink these items for the label to be applied.

EXAMPLE: LINKING TO OBJECTS IN THE DRAWING

You have already created a query that narrows the list of objects you want to view in the data view window, so now you will link specific rows in the table to objects in the drawing:

1. First, restore a view in the drawing used in the previous examples called Emp_Offices.

2. If it's not already open, start by opening the data view window containing the DEPT_LINK query information by double-clicking on this query name from the dbConnect Manager window.

3. When the Data View window opens, make certain the Select a Link Template list from the toolbar is set to Emp_Link. Then find and select the row for cubicle 6060 in the Room column. Use the Find option, if needed, to locate the row. Right-click within a cell in that row and choose the Link! option. This is an empty cubicle, so the record will list the employee name as Vacant.

4. The data view window temporarily closes so you can select the drawing object to link. Select the polyline surrounding the empty cubicle marked 6060. Press Enter to complete the linking process.

That's all there is to linking a drawing object to a record in the table—and you'll link more objects in the examples to follow. A few tools need to be mentioned beforehand so you can use them in linking more records. Earlier in the chapter, the Data View and Query options were discussed. Only two of the sections in that dialog box were covered; now that you have linked a record to a drawing object, let's examine the remaining options. Return to the data view window, and click the Data View and Query Option button to open its associated dialog box.

First, examine the AutoPan and Zoom section. These functions zoom or pan to the location of the drawing objects linked to the selected record in the data view window. These options make it easy to locate the linked object:

- Automatically pan drawing—This option automatically pans to the location of the linked objects in the drawing.

- Automatically zoom drawing—This automatically zooms to the location of the linked objects that can be viewed within the drawing.

- Zoom factor—You can set the zoom scale factor to determine how closely you zoom in to the linked object. The default value is 50% and can vary from 20% to 90% of the current window.

The Accumulate Options section also accumulates the linked drawing objects into a selection set or accumulates the linked records in the data view window. These are the options for this feature:

- Accumulate selection set in drawing—Every time you select a record in the data view window, the corresponding linked object in the drawing is selected and added to the current selection set.

- Accumulate record set in data view—Each record that is selected in the data view window remains selected until cleared. If this options is not chosen, AutoCAD clears the previously selected record when another record is selected.

These options make linking objects easier, enabling you to view the linked objects in the drawing and by creating selection sets of those objects.

VIEWING LINKED OBJECTS IN THE DRAWING

Now that you know the options in the last section are available, you will link two more drawing objects to records in the database and automatically zoom to their location in the drawing. Follow the steps in the next example.

EXAMPLE: AUTOMATICALLY VIEWING LINKED OBJECTS

1. Picking up where you left off, you'll need to finish linking the remaining cubicle polylines in the drawing. But first, let's turn on the AutoPan and Zoom options available in the data view window.

2. Select the Data View and Query button from the data view window. Click both the Automatically pan drawing and Automatically zoom drawing check boxes in this dialog box. Set the zoom factor to 40, and then click the OK button.

3. Link the polylines belonging to cubicles 6020 and 6021 to their respective rows in the table.

4. Now when you select one of the linked records for cubicles 6020, 6021, or 6024, you are zoomed to the location of the linked polyline in the drawing (as shown in Figure 22.29).

Figure 22.29
You can use the AutoZoom function to zoom to the location of a linked object in the drawing by selecting the associated record in the data view window.

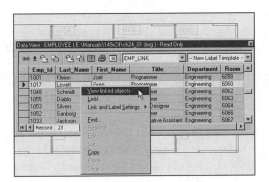

In the next section, as you link the remaining cubicle polylines to the table, you'll also create a selection set of the linked drawing objects.

CREATING A SELECTION SET USING THE DATA VIEW WINDOW

Extending the use of the Data View and Query options, now create a selection set of the linked objects through the data view window. The following example shows you how.

EXAMPLE: CREATING SELECTION SETS VIA THE DATA VIEW WINDOW

1. Open the Data View and Query dialog box again, and toggle on both options for Accumulating selection set in drawing and Accumulate record set in data view.

Caution

The options for setting the Accumulate record set in data view and the Mark indicated records options are grayed-out when the Show all records, select indicated records option is toggled off.

2. Turn on the Mark indicated records option and set a highlight color. After you link the remaining polylines, this creates a selection set of the linked drawing objects and highlights the records in the data view window.

Tip 223 from
Ron House

When you turn on the Mark indicated records option, AutoCAD places the current highlight color in the lower-right corner of the data view window. If you are using multiple link templates, you can switch to a different color for each template, making it easy to distinguish among the different colored records.

3. Link the polylines for cubicles 6023 and 6022 by selecting the corresponding record from the table, right-clicking, and choosing Link! from the shortcut menu. Then press Enter after selecting the drawing objects you want to link to the record.

4. After the polylines have been linked, select the records for cubicles 6020 through 6024.

Note

After completing the previous step, note that in addition to zooming to the location of the linked drawing object, the next selected record adds the linked drawing object to the selection set. The zoom window now encompasses all the selected objects and continually adjusts, as more records are selected, to include the newly added objects to the selection set.

5. To illustrate the use of the next option, clear the current drawing selection set by pressing the Esc key until no objects are selected. Also clear the selected records from the data view window by right-clicking on the grid header and selecting the Clear All Marks option.

6. Now, reverse the process this time by first selecting the linked polylines in the drawing to show which records are linked. Select the polylines for cubicles 6020 through 6024. As you click on each drawing object, note that the corresponding record is highlighted in the data view window.

As you can see, these options make it easy to assess the correlation between objects in the drawing and records in the connected database. This also can be used as a visual check to verify you have the desired objects linked in the drawing.

So, after you have linked the drawing objects to records in the database, now what? Continue on to the next section, where you'll learn how to create a table that can be inserted into the drawing using information from the objects you just linked.

EXPORTING LINKS

After the process of linking objects in a drawing has been completed, it is easy to create a table, such as a room schedule or bill of materials, from the linked objects. Using object linking and embedding (OLE), you can insert the table into the drawing, enabling you to enhance your drawings with information gained by linking the objects.

→ Refer to Chapter 20, "Customizing Made Easy," for information on using OLE with AutoCAD.

EXAMPLE: USING LINKED OBJECTS TO CREATE A TABLE

1. Continuing with the previous example, select all the records queried in the data view window; this should be cubicles 6020 through 6060.

2. At this point, the associated cubicles should also be selected in the drawing. Now select the dbConnect, Links, Export Links. The Select a Database Object dialog box appears, shown in Figure 22.30.

Figure 22.30
The Select a Database Object dialog box enables you to select a link template to export, which determines the linked information that is exported to a file.

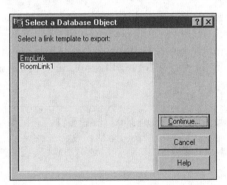

3. Click Emp Link from the list and then click the Continue... button to export. This determines what linked row information is exported.

4. The Export Links file dialog box appears, in which you can set the export filename and directory. Note the Include Fields list at the right of the dialog box, enabling you to select each of the fields you want to export (see Figure 22.31). Select all the available fields and enter the name **emp_export** for the export file. Place the file in a directory that you can easily recall.

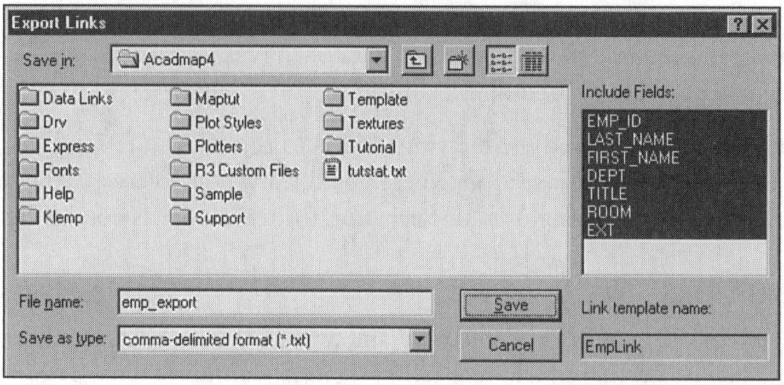

Figure 22.31
You can select the fields to be exported to create a report from the Export Links dialog box.

5. Launch Excel and import the file emp_export.txt you just created.

6. You may wish to add table and column headers or other annotations to the table. When you are finished modifying the file in Excel, save the file as an Excel worksheet (or spreadsheet, depending on the version of Excel you are using) and toggle back to AutoCAD.

7. From the pull-down menus, choose Insert, OLE Object, which opens the Insert Object dialog box.

8. Click the Create from File radio button and browse to the table you saved in Excel. Then click the OK button to import the file.

9. The OLE Properties dialog box appears, which enables you to set the object properties, such as size and scale, as well as the overall text height for the OLE object. You will want to adjust the scale factor of the OLE object to 25% of its original size. To make the object more readable, set the OLE plot quality to Line Art (that is, spreadsheet). Then click the OK button.

Note

Depending on the scale of your drawing, the size of the imported spreadsheet may need to be adjusted to fit onto your drawing. Use the OLE Properties dialog box to make these corrections as needed.

→ For more specific information about use OLE in AutoCAD, refer to Chapter 20, "Customizing Made Easy."

10. The table is inserted into the drawing where it can be moved to its desired location.

Note

If the information in either the drawing or the database changes, the table will need to be updated. The OLE object cannot be linked because the table was originally exported as a text file and must be converted into a spreadsheet format before it can be inserted back into the drawing.

Combining the Link Export command with OLE gives you a great deal of flexibility in creating tables using the external database information via the linked drawing objects. Although this is valuable when you might want an overall table to reference the linked objects, you may want to place labels to more distinctly identify objects in the drawing. For this, you will want to create labels for the individual linked drawing objects. The following section shows you how to create these labels.

PART

V

CH

22

CREATING LABELS AS YOU LINK DRAWING OBJECTS

With drawing objects linked to records in a table, you can also generate labels for those linked objects. Labels display database information associated with the linked objects. Before you can create the labels, you must produce a label template. A label template defines which fields will be used to make the label. The next example demonstrates the process of creating a link template.

Tip 224 from
Ron House

To place labels into the drawing, you must create both a link and a label template. Remember, you can use only fields that are part of the link template for them to be used to define the label.

EXAMPLE: GENERATING A LABEL TEMPLATE

1. Right-click on the Employee table in the dbConnect Manager window, and select New Label Template. This opens the New Label Template dialog box, shown in Figure 22.32.

Figure 22.32
Use the New Label Template dialog box to name a new label template.

2. Enter **EMP_LABEL** for the name of the template, and click the Continue button.

   This opens the Label Template dialog box, shown in Figure 25.33, which looks very similar to the one used by the Mtext command.

3. Select a field from the Fields list, and then click the Add button to define the table columns to be used for the label. Each field added is placed on a separate row for the label.

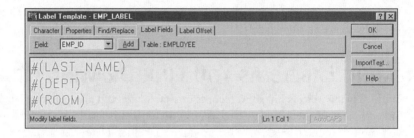

As you add fields to the label, you can also add any additional text to supplement the label text. Highlighting and right-clicking on the text opens a formatting shortcut menu. The label text can be modified using any of these options, such as changing the case, stacking, and combining paragraphs. When this option is used, the label becomes a long string of text rather than being placed on separate rows. Before you activate this option, AutoCAD will prompt you to determine that you really want to continue.

4. After the label and the properties for the label have been defined, click the OK button to finish creating the label template.

After you define the label template, you can place the labels into the drawing. Two types of labels are available to you: attached and freestanding labels.

ATTACHED LABELS

Attached labels are labels actually attached and linked to the drawing object. If the object moves, so does the label. The same is true if the object is copied to the Clipboard—the label is copied as well. Likewise, if the object is erased from the drawing, the label also is erased. Attached labels use leader lines to indicate the object to which they are linked. For the examples in this chapter, the leader line beginning is placed at the center of the area defined by the polyline because you are linking to a polyline object.

CREATING FREESTANDING LABELS

Freestanding labels are the opposite of attached labels. These labels can be placed anywhere the user desires, regardless of the location of the linked object. Freestanding labels have no leader lines and, when placed into a drawing, become the linked object rather than the selected drawing object with the attached labels.

Because a label can be attached only when the object is being linked, you'll need to first delete the existing link and then create the label when the object is relinked. The next section shows you how.

ATTACHING A LABEL TO A DRAWING OBJECT

Before placing a label in the drawing, you must delete the existing link attached to the object. To do so, you will need to use the Link Manager. The Link Manager manages the links between the drawing objects and the records in the table. It also enables you to edit links in the drawing. (This is discussed in detail in the next section.) For now, you'll use the Link Manager to erase links within the drawing so the object can be relinked with a label. This example walks you through the process.

PART

V

CH

22

EXAMPLE: RELINKING A DRAWING OBJECT WITH AN ATTACHED LABEL

1. In the drawing you have used in the previous examples, select dbConnect, Links, Link Manager. You are prompted to select an object, so select the polyline for cubicle 6023.

2. The Link Manager dialog box opens, as shown in Figure 22.34. Select Emp Link from the Link Templates list, and then click the Delete button to remove the Emp Link link from the polyline. Click the OK button to complete deleting the link.

Figure 22.34
You must delete a link from a drawing object using the Link Manager before placing a label.

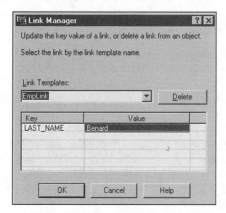

3. You are now ready to relink the polyline. From the data view window, first toggle the Link and Label Setting button to Create Attached Labels (see Figure 22.35).

Figure 22.35
The Link and Label Setting button is used to toggle between creating Attached or Freestanding Labels, or to place a link in the drawing.

4. Then locate the record for cubicle 6023 in the data view window. Right-click in any cell in that row, and select Link! from the shortcut menu.

5. Select the polyline surrounding the cubicle 6023. After it is selected, the label you defined in the label template appears at the center of the enclosed polyline along with its leader line. You can use grips to locate the label as desired.

6. Experiment with moving the polyline to see how the label follows the object. Make certain to undo the move to return the polyline to its original position.

Next, follow through the process of creating a freestanding label.

CREATING FREESTANDING LABELS

The process for creating freestanding labels is similar to the you just worked through for attached labels. The difference occurs when you place the freestanding label into the drawing. Rather than automatically locating the label on or near the linked object, you can place the label where you want it to be.

Repeat steps 1 and 2 from the previous example to place a freestanding label by first deleting the existing link. This also erases the label from cubicle 6023 as the link is deleted. In step 3, this time choose Create Freestanding Labels from the Link and Label Settings list. Then right-click the record in the data view window and select Link!

The following prompt appears at the command line:

```
Specify point for label:
```

As you pick where you want the label to be placed, the label, not the polyline, now becomes the linked object.

Using either of these types of labels gives you the flexibility to define how linked objects in the drawing will be annotated with data from a linked external database. After the labels are placed into the drawing and information in the database is changed, you will want to update the existing labels with the new information.

RELOADING LABELS TO UPDATE YOUR DRAWING

As information in the database is updated, the labels placed in the drawing will need to reflect the new information. This is easily accomplished using the Reload Labels command. From the pull-down menus, choose dbConnect, Labels, Reload Labels. The Select a Database Object dialog box appears (see Figure 22.36).

Select a label template from the list to update, and then click the OK button. The labels placed with the selected label template are updated throughout the drawing. To ensure data integrity, you will want to reload the labels every time changes to the database are made.

As your drawing changes, the links placed in the drawing will need to be modified as well.

EDITING INDIVIDUAL LINKS IN THE DRAWING

Earlier in the chapter, you saw how to use the Link Manager to delete an existing link. The Link Manager also can be used to edit the links to a record in the table. To access this command, select dbConnect, Links, Link Manager. After selecting a linked object to edit, the Link Manager dialog box enables you to edit the value for a link.

Figure 22.36
The Select a Database Object dialog box enables you to select the label template to reload.

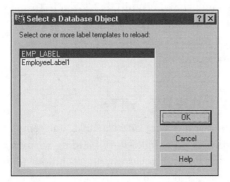

When a drawing contains a large number of links, it is wise to verify the links throughout the drawing by synchronizing the link.

SYNCHRONIZING DATABASE LINKS IN THE DRAWING

To check the overall integrity of your links, you can run the Synchronize command. The Synchronize command ensures that the links you have in your drawing are connected to a valid table. Suppose, for example, that the database file you were linked to has been accidentally moved. You can use the Synchronize command to determine whether the link you created is still valid.

This is activated from the dbConnect Manager window. Right-click on a link template from the list and select Synchronize. AutoCAD runs a check to verify the link. If no link errors are detected, AutoCAD displays a message box indicating that the drawing and external databases are in a consistent state.

If errors are detected, they are listed in the Synchronize dialog box. From here you can choose to do one of the following options at a time:

- Indicate Drawing Objects—This highlights the drawing object, enabling you to quickly identify objects with broken links.
- Fix—This option attempts to fix the broken link.
- Delete—The broken link is deleted.

Although this command makes it easy to verify the links within a drawing, at times a link is no longer needed. The next section discusses the need for the Delete Links command.

DELETING LINKS FROM THE DRAWING

Links can be deleted from the drawing using the Delete Links command. For example, you might use this command when a link contains multiple broken links and you want to delete it completely from the drawing. To accomplish this, select the link from the dbConnect Manager window, right-click and select Delete from the shortcut menu. This also deletes the link from the dbConnect Manager window.

EXPORTING LINK AND QUERY SETS

You can save valuable time when working with queries, links, and templates that apply to multiple drawings. If you are working on a multi-story building where a common query or template set can be applied to each floor (in this scenario, each floor represents a different drawing), you can reuse your queries and templates instead of recreating them for each drawing. This is done by exporting the query and template sets. If the database structure is such that the same table applies to each floor of the building, you can create the query and templates in one drawing, export them, and then import them into the next floor drawing.

In another scenario, you might want to share your query and link templates with a colleague. You can easily export the queries and templates from your drawing, allowing a colleague to import them into any other drawing, as long as the database is also being shared.

Note

If you export your query and template sets to be used on another computer, the receiving computer must be configured to use the shared database using one of the external database connection methods discussed in the "Connecting to a Database" section earlier in this chapter.

To export, right-click on the drawing that contains the queries or templates you want to export in the dbConnect Manager window, and then choose the Export Template Set or Export Query Set from the shortcut menu. Enter the name of the set into the Export File dialog box; query sets are saved with a .dbq extension, and templates are saved with a .dbt extension. By default, the files are saved in the Data Links subdirectory under the AutoCAD 2000 directory on your hard drive.

To import, right-click on the drawing from the dbConnect Manager and select Import Template Set or Import Query Set. After you select the file from the Import File dialog box, the queries and templates are imported into the receiving drawing file.

SUMMARY

As you have seen in this chapter, there are a number of uses for linking a drawing to an external database. Although you worked through various types of examples, this chapter only scratches the surface of what can be accomplished by linking. Apply these examples to your projects when an external database contains specific information about the project. Using this feature will help you become more productive, not only in creating tables and annotating the drawing, but also in updating the labels to maintain data integrity for your project.

CHAPTER 23

VISUALIZATION

In this chapter

AUTOCAD'S 3D CAPABILITIES

One of the many advantages of working with the Autodesk Architectural and Mechanical Desktop software products is the ability to work in two dimensions, yet generate a three-dimensional drawing. This is possible through unique features such as multi-view blocks and view-dependent display, both of which make it easier and reduce the learning curve required to work in base AutoCAD 3D, especially if you are accustomed to working in a 2D-only environments. Aside from this fact, you can also create three-dimensional models within AutoCAD 2000. Although you do not have the built-in 3D functionality of Architectural or Mechanical Desktop, once you start working and thinking in three-dimensions, you'll find it is an easy transition from the 2D world.

A good portion of this chapter is dedicated to walking you through the process of creating a three-dimensional model, describing the use of many 3D AutoCAD modeling commands. After the part is finished, you'll examine the 3D Orbit command and its options, which are designed specifically for viewing three-dimensional objects. Then, on to rendering and visualization, applying materials and lighting to the part to make it photo-realistic, or as if a photograph were taken of the finished part.

Let's begin by thinking of how you can create the 3D model, which is referred to simply as "model" in the rest of this chapter. The easiest way to create a model in AutoCAD is to look at the part you want to create and find a primary feature that all other sections of the part stem from. For an architectural model, maybe it's a focal point like an atrium, facade, or elevation that the rest of the building is modeled around. A primary feature for a mechanical drawing might be a cylinder or base that makes up the major portion of the model.

After you've selected or created the main feature, you can combine other features with the primary section of the part. To combine the pieces or primitives together as one, you may use four different Boolean operations: Intersection, Subtraction, Union, and Interference. Intersection yields the intersection of two pieces, Subtraction subtracts one object from another, and Union joins the objects as one. Interference is a combination of Intersection and Union, if you can imagine such a process. When the Union command is used to join two primitives, the original shapes are lost when the two are made into one. Interference not only allows you to keep the original shapes but also creates a solid from the area the two primitives intersected.

Now that the basic of Boolean operations have been discussed, the following exercise demonstrates the use of these operations to create a grinder vise base, shown in Figure 23.1.

Most of the commands that you will use to create the part are available from the Solids toolbar, which contains 3D commands that can be used to create objects such as cylinders, boxes, cones, and spheres, all of which can be used as base primitives to build upon. More often than not, the model you want to build doesn't contain these primitive objects, and you must generate your own base primitive. This can typically be accomplished by using a polyline or region that represents the profile of the base primitive, which can then be extruded to give the profile thickness and corresponding volume.

Figure 23.1
A base for a grinder vise created in one of the examples in this chapter.

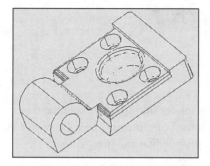

When you want to create an irregularly shaped object that is bounded on all sides by other objects, use the Boundary command, available from the Draw pull-down menu. Similar to creating a hatch pattern in the drawing, this command can generate a polyline or a region out of the determined or found boundary. A region differs from a polyline object, although both represent two-dimensional closed areas. The main difference is that you can analyze the properties of this shape. Using the Massprop command, the area, centroid, and moments of inertia of the shape can then be determined and analyzed before being extruded.

Note

You'll find the Massprop command available from the Tools pull-down menu in the Inquiry submenu.

CREATING SOLIDS FROM 2D POLYLINES

Let's start by drawing the cylinders and arched slot. You will want to create the primitives, or the basic features that make up the part. In this case, the primitives are the two cylinders, the arm and the reinforcing web part of the arm. Then you'll use the Boolean operations to join them together.

EXAMPLE: CREATING THE PRIMITIVES

1. Open the drawing ch23_01.dwg that was copied from the accompanying CD. In this example you'll create the base for the grinder vise shown in Figure 23.1.

2. Using the polyline profile for the base, you'll extrude the polyline to form the base primitive. From the Solids toolbar, select the Extrude button shown in Figure 23.2.

Figure 23.2
Choose the Extrude button from the Solids toolbar to give the profile thickness.

AutoCAD displays the current Isolines setting at the command line, which indicates the number of lines that will be used to represent the solid object. A value of 4 should be sufficient for now, so select the polyline and press Enter.

Tip 226 from
Ron House

Although increasing the number of isolines for a part increases the amount of detail, it also increases the amount of time needed to regenerate the object, such as when toggling from model space to paper space layout. See "Model Space and Paper Space" in Chapter 18, "Plotting and Layouts," for more information on using this feature.

This should be taken into consideration when adjusting this value and balanced between the level of detail you need shown in the drawing and the time it will take to regenerate, which mainly depends on the size of the model and the design and speed of your computer. Generally, you'll want to adjust this value when needed, setting it to a low value when you are not working on this particular part, and then increasing the number of isolines when working on or near this part.

4. At the Specify Height of Extrusion or [Path] prompt, type **3.25** and press Enter.

5. Type **0** at the Specify Angle of Taper for Extrusion <0> prompt and press Enter to complete the extrusion. The angle of taper allows the part to become narrower, based on the angle and thickness of the part.

6. At this point, the polyline has been extruded into the screen, which you cannot see at this moment. Use the Viewports command to split the screen into two viewports, and then change the view in the right viewport to view the primitive from the Southeast direction. Type **Viewports** at the command line to open the Viewports dialog box.

→ See Chapter 11, "Viewing the Drawing," for more information on working with viewports.

7. Select Two: Vertical from the Standard Viewports list to create two vertical viewports. Choose 3D from the Setup list, and then from the Change to View list click SE Isometric. Click the OK button to create the viewports. You screen should look similar to the one shown in Figure 23.3.

Figure 23.3
To assist you in drawing in three dimensions you can create two viewports from which to work from and view your model.

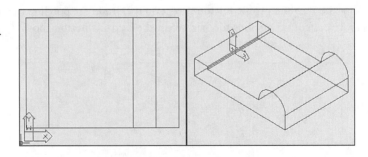

After your drawing viewports have been set up, let's talk briefly about the UCS, or User Coordinate System, discussed in the next section.

DEFINING THE USER COORDINATE SYSTEM

The user coordinate system, or UCS, is a movable coordinate system that can be determined by the user, depending on the face or axis you wish to work on. AutoCAD requires that you work within this user-defined "working plane" because many of the editing commands are dependent on the UCS location and orientation. The UCS defines the direction of the x, y, and z axis, or current working plane, which can easily be moved to any orientation and saved with a specific name. Once saved, the UCS working planes orientations can then be individually restored when you return to work on that portion of the part or face. Use the UCS icon as a visual reference to remember where the UCS working plane is located.

The "W" shown on the icon refers to the World UCS, which is the original coordinate system for the drawing, and appears on the icon when you return to this orientation. This gives you a frame of reference among the many UCS working planes that can be defined in a drawing, and allows you to quickly return to this orientation should you become disoriented working in three dimensions.

There are many options for the UCS command, and the easiest option to use is the UCS Face option. Available from the Tools pull-down menu, New UCS submenu, the Face option enables you to define the face you wish to work on by first selecting it and then flipping the UCS along the x and y axis to locate it into its desire position. It's a good idea to save your UCS working planes as you go along by using the UCS Save option. This makes it easy to return to a previous UCS orientation and location without the need to align the UCS with the plane you want to work on.

Now that you are familiar with the basics of the user coordinate system, you are ready to start adding and subtracting from the base primitive to create the part using the Boolean operations.

CREATING A COMPLEX PRIMITIVE

A *complex primitive* is one that has been generated by combining multiple, individual primitives using Boolean operations. In the next example you'll add cylinders to the part and subtract them using the Subtract Boolean operation to create the holes in the primitive.

EXAMPLE: SUBTRACTING CYLINDERS FROM THE BASE PART

1. You'll create the large hole near the center of the part by first creating a cylinder, and then using the Subtract Boolean operation to remove the cylinder from the part. Select the Cylinder button from the Solids toolbar (see Figure 23.4).

Figure 23.4
Create a hole in the part by first creating a cylinder by selecting the Cylinder button from the Solids tool-bar.

2. You are prompted to specify the center point for the base of the new cylinder, and because the hole is 1.75 inches off of the left end of the part, use the From and Midpoint Object Snaps to locate it. Press Shift and right-click to open the Object Snap pop-up menu and choose the From option. This will allow you to place a temporary point to locate the center of the cylinder from the base primitive edge. Open the Object Snap shortcut menu again to select the Midpoint object snap when you see the Base point: prompt.

3. Select the left-hand edge in the Top viewport to place the From base point, which selects the midpoint of that edge. At the Offset prompt, type **@1.75,0** and press Enter.

4. Specify a diameter for the cylinder of **1.5** and a height of **1.0**.
```
Specify diameter for base of cylinder: 1.5 <ENTER>
Specify height of cylinder or [Center of other end]: 1 <ENTER>
```

> **Caution**
>
> Look at the position of the UCS, or User Coordinate System, icon in the viewport you are using to create the part. This indicates the plane you are working in, which also sets the direction of the x, y, and z axes. Also note that the UCS icon is located differently in the viewports. Each viewport can have a separate UCS assigned to it, allowing you to view and work on the drawing from any angle. You must be careful which viewport you are working in, or you may end up with an object created in the wrong location or direction.

5. Next, select the cylinder in the right SE Isometric viewport and move it down .25 units along the y-axis to make certain the cylinder protrudes out the bottom plane of the base primitive. This will ensure the cylinder goes all the way through the base. Select the cylinder to apply Grips to the object, and right-click to choose Move from the shortcut menu.

6. At the Specify Base zpoint or Displacement prompt, type **0,-.25** and press Enter to set the displacement. At the Specify second point of displacement prompt, press Enter to use the first point as the displacement. The cylinder is moved down .25 units along the y-axis.

7. Open the Solids Editing toolbar by choosing the View pull-downpull-down menu and selecting Toolbars. Click the toolbar name from the list and select the Close button. Select the Subtract button from the Solids toolbar to remove the volume of the cylinder from the base.

8. First you will need to select the object to subtract from, and then the object to subtract. At the prompt select Solids and Regions to Subtract From, select the base primitive, and press Enter. The select the cylinder at the next prompt:

```
Select solids and regions to subtract ..
```

9. Your part should now look like the one in Figure 23.5.

Figure 23.5
The base primitive after the cylinder has been subtracted.

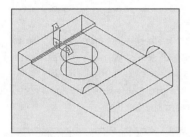

PLACING OBJECTS ALONG THE Z-AXIS

Now as you place the cylinders to create a mold for the countersunk holes, you'll place them by specifying an elevation with a z coordinate point. Because you need to create the four countersunk holes, you can adjust the elevation of the cylinders to create the area to subtract from the part.

Tip 227 from
Ron House

You can also use the Elev command, rather than the z coordinate, which can be set independently for each viewport you have in the drawing. This is convenient when you have multiple objects that are going to be placed at the same level in a viewport. The elevation can then be set to that level, enabling you to avoid having to key in a z-coordinate value. If you have an object that needs to be set at a different level, the z-coordinate can be entered in relation to the current elevation. This gives you added flexibility to change the elevation of objects as needed.

After you change to a different viewport, the elevation is set back to the current elevation for that viewport. You must be aware of the current elevation setting to avoid locating objects at the wrong position in the vertical plane.

EXAMPLE: MODIFYING THE ELEVATION TO PLACE THE CYLINDERS AT DIFFERENT LEVELS

Earlier, you had placed a cylinder in the drawing and moved the cylinder down a quarter unit to make certain it passed through the bottom plane of the part. By setting the z coordinate to a negative .25 units below the base primitive, you can avoid the need to repeat that step for the other cylinders. This will place their starting plane at that level.

1. Create the first cylinder for the countersunk hole by selecting the Cylinder button from the Solids toolbar again. Taking advantage of the multiple viewport display, view the part from the right side viewport to locate the cylinder, but work from the left viewport.

Tip 228 from	Another unique advantage of working with viewports is being able to set a different view in one viewport while you have another viewpoint set in the other. The advantage of working in an isometric view while creating a three-dimensional part is that very seldom are you looking straight down an edge at this viewpoint. This is extremely important when using object snaps to select a point in the drawing. When you are viewing a part where multiple edges are on top of each other, it is hard to determine on which edge the object snap has been selected.
Ron House	

2. Locate the first cylinder 1.125 units from the left edge and .5 units up from the bottom edge of the part, with a z coordinate of -0.25. At the prompt to specify the center point for the base of the cylinder, press the Shift key and right-click to access the From Object Snap again. At the Base Point prompt, press Shift and right-click again and select the Endpoint Object Snap from the list.

Tip 229 from	Because you are working from the left viewport, you can't really see the bottom edge of the left side of the base part. You could change the viewpoint in that view, but there really isn't any need because you already have the right hand viewport set at a viewing angle where you can see the edge you want to select. Click inside the right-hand viewport to make it active, select the point you want, and then return the focus back to the top view by clicking in the left viewport.
Ron House	

3. Pick the lower-left corner of the base primitive in the right hand viewport, and then click back into the left viewport to complete the command. If you don't do this, the wrong UCS will be used to create the cylinder and it will be positioned incorrectly.

4. At the Offset prompt, enter **1.125,.5,-.25** and press Enter.

   `<Offset>: @1.125,.5,-.25 <ENTER>`

5. Enter a radius of **0.2344** for the cylinder, and a height of **1** unit.

   `Specify radius for base of cylinder or [Diameter]:0.2344 <ENTER>`
   `Specify height of cylinder or [Center of other end]:1 <ENTER>`

6. Check to see if the cylinder did actually pass through the bottom of the part by switching your current view in the left viewport to the Front view. From the View pull-down menu, choose 3D Views, Front to see if the columns are in the correct location. The view should look like the one in Figure 25.6.

Figure 23.6
The base viewed from the front shows the column protruding through the bottom.

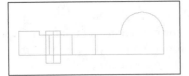

7. Switch back to the previous viewing angle by choosing the Top view again from the 3D View options. You may find it advantageous to open the View toolbar from the Toolbars dialog box used earlier and shown in Figure 23.7.

Figure 23.7
You can use the View toolbar to quickly toggle the viewpoint you are using to view the model.

PART

V

CH

23

8. Place the other cylinder used to create the countersunk hole similar to the last one. Start the Cylinder command again, using the center of the previous cylinder to locate this one. At the Center Point prompt, press Shift and right-click to open the Object Snap menu and choose the Center Object snap. Click in the right viewport to locate the cylinder, selecting the top end of the last cylinder.

9. Supply a radius of **0.315** and height of **-0.5** for the cylinder.

10. Next you'll use the Union Boolean operation to join the two cylinders together to complete making the mold for the countersunk hole. Select the Union button from the Solids Editing toolbar, shown in Figure 23.8. Select both of the cylinders and press Enter.

Figure 23.8
Select the Union button from the Solids Editing toolbar to combine two solid objects into one.

11. Now you can array the combined cylinders to position the other holes. Type **AR** at the command line and press Enter. Choose the combined cylinder, and then create a Rectangular array with two rows and columns, with a row spacing of **2.25** and a column spacing of **1.25**:

```
Enter the type of array [Rectangular/Polar] <R>: R <ENTER>
Enter the number of rows (— -) <1>: 2 <ENTER>

Enter the number of columns (¦¦¦) <1>: 2 <ENTER>

Enter the distance between rows or specify unit cell (— -): 2.25 <ENTER>
Specify the distance between columns (¦¦¦): 1.25 <ENTER>
```

12. Use the Subtract command to remove the combined shape for the countersunk hole and remove them from the base primitive. After activating the command, first select the base primitive, and then at the Select solids and regions to subtract prompt, select the four cylinders you just arrayed and press Enter. You should see something similar to the model shown in Figure 23.9.

Figure 23.9
The model after subtracting the four countersunk holes from the base.

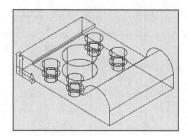

For the next part of this example, click in the right viewport. You will create two cylinders that will be subtracted from opposite sides of the base primitive.

EXAMPLE: WORKING IN A DIFFERENT VIEWPORT

1. Start the cylinder command from the Solids toolbar, and at the center point prompt press Shift and right-click to choose the Center Object snap from the shortcut menu. Snap to the center of the half cylinder at the right-hand side of the base.

2. Create a cylinder that has a radius of **1.0** and a height of.**75** units:

   ```
   Specify radius for base of cylinder or [Diameter]: 1.0 <ENTER>
   Specify height of cylinder or [Center of other end]:.75 <ENTER>
   ```

3. Next you'll want to mirror this cylinder to the opposite side of the base. Activate the Mirror command by typing **MI** at the command line and pressing Enter.

4. At the Select Objects prompt, type **L** at the command line to select the last object you created: the cylinder. Press Enter to finish adding objects to the selection set.

5. Specify the first point of the mirror line by accessing the object snap menu and selecting the Midpoint shortcut menu option. Select the lower edge of the right-hand side of the base; you should see the Midpoint icon appear as you near the edge.

6. Repeat this process to select the opposite midpoint of the left-hand bottom edge. You will not want to remove the original cylinder from the drawing, so answer No to the prompt to delete source objects and press Enter.

   ```
   Delete source objects? [Yes/No] <N>: <ENTER>
   ```

7. Subtract the cylinders from the base using the Subtract command.

8. Create one final cylinder again using the center of the half cylinder at the right-hand side of the base. Make this cylinder with a radius of **0.345** and a height of **1.8** units.

9. Again, subtract this cylinder from the base using the Subtract command. Your part should now look like the one in Figure 23.10.

Figure 23.10
The part after the completion of adding and subtracting the other primitives from the base primitive.

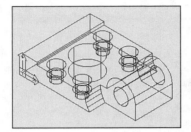

USING THE FILLET COMMAND TO SMOOTHE EDGES

The edges of your 3D model now need to be rounded. For this you can use the Fillet command.

→ See "Using The Fillet Command to Round 3D Edges," p. **188**, in Chapter 9, "Not All Objects Can Be Edited This Way," for more information on creating fillets on three-dimensional objects.

EXAMPLE: FILLETING THREE-DIMENSIONAL OBJECTS

1. Activate the Fillet command from the Modify pull-down menu. AutoCAD will display the Select first object prompt at the command line. Select one of the edges shown in Figure 23.11.

Figure 23.11
Fillet these edges on the model with a fillet radius of 0.125.

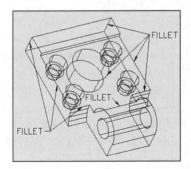

2. When an edge is selected, you'll be prompted for the fillet radius. Set a radius of **0.125** for all edges on the model.

3. Select the additional edges at the Select an Edge or [Chain/Radius] prompt.

4. After all the edges have been selected, press Enter. The finished part should look like the model in Figure 23.12.

Figure 23.12
The completed base for a grinder vise after applying a Gouraud shade from the View pull-down, Shade option.

When you create a three-dimensional (3D) model you need to be able to view this model in a number of different ways to visualize draw and edit geometry easily. AutoCAD provides you with tools that you can use to set up different views of the model. One of these tools is the 3D Orbit command.

3D ORBIT

The 3D orbit command activates an interactive 3D orbit view in the current viewport, which is accessed from the Standard toolbar (see Figure 23.13).

Figure 23.13
Access the 3D Orbit from the Standard toolbar.

You may also open the 3D Orbit toolbar by right-clicking any toolbar and selecting 3D Orbit from the list (see Figure 23.14). This 3D viewing feature enables you to view the object in either wire-frame mode or shaded mode from any angle.

Figure 23.14
The 3D Orbit command, in addition to many other viewing commands, can be accessed from the 3D Orbit toolbar.

This is accomplished by manipulating the rotation of an "arcball" circle using the pointing device (see Figure 23.15).

Figure 23.15
The 3D Orbit command displays an arcball, allowing you to rotate the model about a stationary target point.

The 3D orbit view displays a large circle, or *arcball*, divided into four quadrants by smaller circles. By holding down the left mouse button and moving the cursor, you can dynamically rotate the model around a stationary point, which is the target view at the center of the large orbit circle. Placing your cursor over the smaller circles of the "arcball" changes the shape of the cursor, indicating the direction of rotation. You can view the entire model or magnify an area from different viewpoints. You cannot, however, enter commands on the command line while the 3D orbit command is activated.

The options for the 3D Orbit command are available by right-clicking when the 3D Orbit command is active. These options are discussed in the next section.

THE 3D ORBIT VIEWING OPTIONS

From the 3D Orbit shortcut menu, you can select options that enable you to locate the camera position to determine the target point you want to rotate around. You are able to reposition the camera before starting the 3D Orbit command to change your target location view.

There are also a set of options available that allow you to zoom in and out on the object and also to move the camera in or out to allow for close-ups of different areas of the object. You can also access the Pan command in 3D Orbit to shift the position of the object view on the screen while viewing it at the desired angle.

3D Orbit will also allow you to view your object in two distinct projection views: Parallel and Perspective. Parallel changes the view so that two parallel lines never converge at a single point. The Parallel default option enables you to zoom in close while making the object not appear distorted. The Perspective option changes the view so that all parallel lines will eventually converge to a point. This type of view gives an impression of what the eye sees in the real world. This is illustrated in Figure 23.16.

Figure 23.16
Viewing the model with the Perspective viewing mode turned on, one of the options during the 3D Orbit command.

Tip 230 from
Ron House

If you want to use AutoCAD to present your finished model to others, use the Continuous 3D Orbit mode. Choose the 3D Orbit command from the Standard or 3D Orbit toolbar, and then right-click and select More, Continuous Orbit. Use the pointer to drag the model into motion, rotating it in the direction you want to view. The model will continue rotating in the direction you originated until stopped or sent in another direction.

Another great feature available in the 3D Orbit command is Adjust Clipping Planes. This option opens a floating window that enables you to dynamically drag a clipping plane to view a clipped section of your model, shown in Figure 23.17.

Figure 23.17
The Adjust Clipping Planes option, available within the 3D Orbit command, clips the front or back viewing plane of the model dynamically from a separate clipping window.

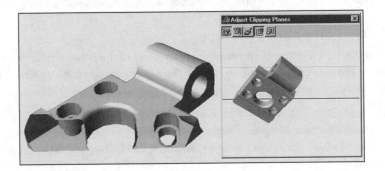

After the model is complete, you can easily generate two-dimensional working drawings from the model. The next section explains how.

GENERATING 2D WORKING DRAWINGS FROM A 3D MODEL

The Solids toolbar also contains commands to create 2D working drawings after the 3D model is complete. Select the Setup View button from the toolbar, shown in Figure 23.18.

Figure 23.18
Commands such as Setup View, available on the Solids toolbar, allow you to create two-dimensional drawings from the finished 3D model.

This activates the Solview command. This command assists you in creating Ortho, Auxiliary, Sectional, or a view from the location of a defined User Coordinate System from the three dimensional model. After specifying the desired view, you are prompted to choose a side or edge to define the type of view you want to create. You can also draw the viewport window edge around the view to create a floating viewport in the layout. Figure 23.19 illustrates a layout created using the Solview command.

Figure 23.19
A layout generated using the Solview command provides an easy way to create multiple views of a 3D model.

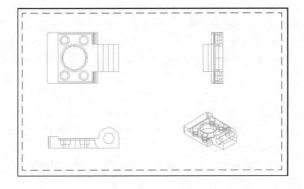

ENHANCING YOUR 3D IMAGE

There are a number of tools AutoCAD provides you with to greatly enhance your 3D model to help you visualize your final design much more clearly than viewing a basic wireframe representation. With a complex wireframe shape, it becomes very confusing trying to distinguish whether you are looking at the model from the back, front, top, or bottom given all the tessellation lines (lines that help visualize ruled surfaces) are visible. There are three different types of visual images available: Hidden, Shaded, and Rendered.

Of the many visual image types available in AutoCAD 2000, the simplest form is the hidden-line image. A hidden line image makes a three dimensional shape much easier to visualize because all the back faces of the image are not displayed.

Shading automatically removes hidden lines and assigns flat colors to only the visible surfaces. If you can shade or render your image, you can greatly enhance the realism of the image.

Rendering attaches materials and adds adjustable lighting to the surfaces to give a more photo-realistic image. Rendering also can add effects like background images and colors, shadows, fog, and blurring effects.

Which kind of image you choose is dependent upon its purpose and the amount of time you have. If you are preparing your design for a presentation to customers/marketing, you may decide to go for a full rendering. If, however, you merely want to view the image to check the integrity of your design, you may decide only to work with a hidden line or flat shaded image.

Let us look at the different visualization tools in a little more depth to give you a good overall understanding of what can be done and how you can apply it to the 3D model you have created on the screen.

HIDDEN LINE IMAGES

After you create your 3D object you will notice that in the Wireframe mode the object appears very cluttered with so many lines that it is almost impossible to fully understand what the object should look like and from which plane you are viewing it. The Hide command, chosen from the <u>V</u>iew menu, displays 3D objects with all the background lines removed. This simplifies the display, making it easier to define and clarify the design.

SHADED IMAGES

Hidden line images enhance your image sufficiently to clarify the design, but to achieve a more realistic image of your model you can use the Shade mode. The Shade mode gives you an image with a fixed ambient light and a light source located from behind you and over your left shoulder. You are able to edit your design while in the Shade mode and can also save the object and open it with the object still shaded.

There are essentially seven shade settings you can use when shading your object. Shading is accomplished with the Shade command, accessed from the View pull-down menu. Each of these options is described in the following list:

- 2D Wireframe—Objects are displayed using lines and curves that represent boundaries, where raster images and OLE objects are visible (see Figure 23.20).

Figure 23.20
Wireframe models are quick and easy to work with but can get complex and hard to visualize.

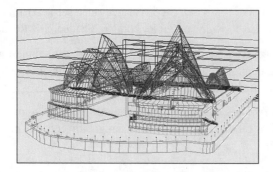

- 3D Wireframe—Objects are also displayed using lines and curves, yet this option does not allow raster images and OLE objects to be displayed.

- Hidden—The backfaces of the object are hidden in this 3D representation of a wireframe model, shown in Figure 23.21.

Figure 23.21
Using the Hidden Shade command, backfaces from a 3D wireframe object are hidden. This image is an example of the results.

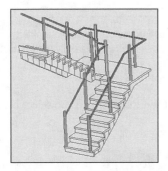

- Flat Shaded—Shades the objects inside the polygon faces. This makes the objects appear flatter and less smooth than Gouraud Shaded objects. Materials that have been attached to the objects will also be shown.

- Gouraud Shaded—Shades the objects and smoothes the edges between polygon faces, giving the objects a smooth, realistic appearance. Materials that have been applied to objects are shown.

- Flat Shaded, Edges On—Combines the Flat Shaded and Wireframe options. The objects are flat shaded with wireframe showing through.

- Gouraud Shaded, Edges On—Combines the Gouraud Shaded and Wireframe options. The objects are Gouraud shaded with the wireframe showing through.

Of all the visual images that can be produced using AutoCAD 2000, the most impressive are the rendered images. The next section briefly discusses the process of creating these realistic images.

CREATING RENDERED IMAGES

When a designer wants to present his design in a realistic image form, traditionally he would have had to possess the artistic skills to finish his conceptual design using a number of techniques like watercolors, colored pencils, air-brushing, and so on. With the Rendering tools available in AutoCAD 2000 you can achieve the same effects without acquiring the skills of an artist.

Here are the three different rendering types:

- Render—This is the basic render. It allows you to adjust and add lights, add background images or colors with output file options such as *.GIF, *.TIF files, and so on.

- Photo Real—This is a photo-realistic renderer that will display transparent materials and mapped shadows.

- Photo Raytrace—This is a photo-realistic raytraced renderer that generates reflections, refraction and more precise shadow effects.

Note

When you use the basic render option you can render your object without attaching materials or adding any lights. The renderer will automatically use a virtual over-the-shoulder light source that you cannot adjust.

Each of these options can be selected from the Rendering Type select list in the Render dialog box, shown in Figure 23.22.

Figure 23.22
The Render dialog box pulls all aspects of rendering together. The scene to render, the background, the fog depth, and rendering type are set from this dialog box.

In the next example, you'll open a drawing and render the file to see what you get using a basic render.

EXAMPLE: QUICK-RENDERING THE DRAWING

1. Open the file ch23_02.dwg, one of which was copied from the accompanying CD. This is a drawing of the Sydney Opera House, which you will use for the examples in this chapter.

2. From the View pull-down menu, choose Render, Render. The Render dialog box appears, shown in Figure 23.22. Select Render from the Rendering Type select list, and then click the Render button.

Figure 23.23
The Render dialog box contains the options to create one of the three different types of rendered images.

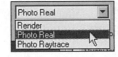

To illuminate the model better, let's apply some light to the model.

LIGHTING UP YOUR MODEL

There are three types of lights that can be defined in a three dimensional model to illuminate the rendered image. These can be selected from the Light dialog box by choosing the Light button from the Render toolbar. This opens the Lights dialog box, which allows you to define a new light or modify an existing light (see Figure 23.24).

Figure 23.24
The Ambient light or defined light sources are set and created within the Lights dialog box.

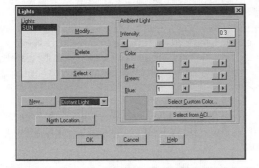

The types of lights available are

- Point light—This option can be used to define a general light source within the model.

- Distance light—Used to create illumination from a far off light source, this option is typically used to define sunlight in the scene. This allows the position of the light to be determined by the Sun Angle Calculator.

- Spotlight—Using this option, you can define a target position and light location to define the direction of the spotlight.

The amount of ambient light in the scene can be set from this dialog box using the Ambient Light Intensity slider bar, in addition to the color of the light. The color can be chosen from a Custom color palette or the standard AutoCAD Color Index (ACI) by selecting the appropriate button. To create a new light, select the type of light from the list and click the New button. The type of light chosen defines the appearance of and options available within the dialog box. The dialog box for a spotlight source is shown in Figure 23.25.

Figure 23.25
The New Spotlight dialog box. Values for specific attributes of a spotlight, such as the size of the hotspot and falloff and the values for shadows produced by this light source can be set.

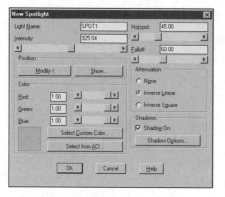

Tip 231 from
Ron House

You can specify coordinates to locate the lights inserted into your model. You can also use the Move command to position them after they are placed in the scene. The Light Icon may be hard to locate on your drawing depending on drawing scale. To increase or decrease the size of these icons, enter the desired scale from the Render dialog box and render the scene. To transfer from the rendered image to a wireframe image, use the 3D Views command from the View pull-down menu to refresh the model and to see the updated Light icons. This will make it easier to find the positioned lights in the model.

Use lighting to illuminate highlights of your design or to illustrate how the finished product would look at a certain time of day. The Sun Angle calculator, discussed in the following example, makes this task easy.

EXAMPLE: CREATING A DISTANT LIGHT SOURCE USING THE SUN ANGLE CALCULATOR

1. Open the file ch23_02.dwg, one of which was copied from the accompanying CD. This is a drawing of the Sydney Opera House, which you will use for the examples in this chapter.

2. From the View pull-down menu, choose Render, Render. The Render dialog box appears; select Render from the Rendering Type select list, and then click the Render button.

3. After a few minutes, the shaded image appears. The image is extremely dark and very hard to see. At this point you will need to create some lighting for the drawing to improve the image. From pull-down menus, select View, Render, Light to open the Lights dialog box (see Figure 23.26).

4. Select Distant Light from the Light Source select list, and then click the New button to open the New Distant Light dialog box (see Figure 23.27).

5. Type **SUN** for the name of the light, and then click the Sun Angle Calculator button. The Sun Angle Calculator dialog box opens, shown in Figure 23.28.

Figure 23.26
Using the Light option, you can specify a Distance, Point, or Spotlight source from the Light dialog box.

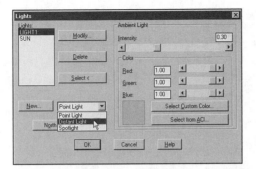

Figure 23.27
Create Distant Light sources using the New Distant Light dialog box, which allows you to specify the Light Source Vector and Intensity of the light.

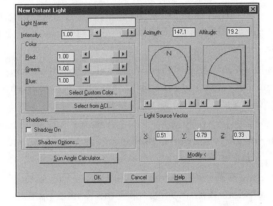

Figure 23.28
The Sun Angle Calculator creates a distant light source in the drawing, calculated by setting a Date, Clock, Time, Latitude, and Longitude.

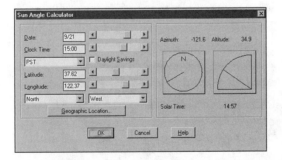

6. Click the Geographic Location button, which opens the Geographic Location dialog box (see Figure 23.29). This option allows you to set the location anywhere in the world, and the sun position is calculated to provide the correct lighting for the image. First, select Australia from the Continent select list, and then click the Nearest Big City button. This allows you to choose a city that best represents the location you desire.

Figure 23.29
The Geographic Location dialog box calculates the Latitude and Longitude for any location in the world.

7. Choose Sydney, Australia from the City select list. Note that a blue crosshair appears over the location of the city in the continent preview box, and the Latitude and Longitude values are provided.

8. Click the OK button to return to the Sun Angle Calculator dialog box. In this dialog box, set a date of your choosing and time of 12:00 noon. Choose Queensland from the Time Zone select list.

9. Set the Hemisphere select lists to Southern and Western. Note the azimuth and altitude displays update to reflect the current settings. Click the OK button. Click again to close out of the Light dialog box.

10. Select the Render button from the Render toolbar. Click the Smooth Shade option from the Rendering Options box, and then click the Render button.

What you should see is something similar to the rendering in Figure 23.30.

Figure 23.30
The appearance of the Opera House after a base render. The next step is to add materials to the model to make it more visually interesting.

Up to this point, you have rendered a model based on the colors defined by the layers of the drawing. The next section discusses how to assign materials to three-dimensional objects in the drawing to achieve more realistic effects.

USING MATERIALS TO PROVIDE RENDERED DETAIL

AutoCAD allows you to attach materials to your object in three different ways. You can attach a material directly to the object so that every time you render the view the material attached will be displayed. You can also attach your material to a color. AutoCAD refers to this as ACI (AutoCAD Color Index). In other words, you attach a material to a color that you want to use for constructing the object.

For example, suppose you construct several objects on different layers and you have chosen magenta as your line color for all the objects; when you render those objects they will have the material assigned to the color attached to them. Other objects constructed using different line colors will be displayed rendered with its original line color.

The third method you can use to attach a material to objects is by attaching it to layers. Any objects that reside on those layers with a particular material attached to it will, when rendered, display the material attached to that layer.

If you have objects that are blocks, they will always display the material that is saved with that block. You will have to explode that block and re-attach a material if you want a different material displayed.

Let's look at the process of assigning a material to an object. Select View pull-down, Render, Materials, which opens the Materials dialog box (see Figure 23.31).

Figure 23.31
The Materials dialog box enables you to assign a material from a bitmap image or a procedural material to a three-dimensional object.

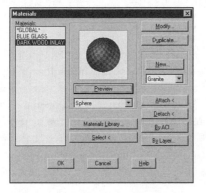

Two methods exist for assigning a material to a three-dimensional object: using a bitmap image or a procedural material. Using a bitmap image, a raster image such as .TGA, .PCX, .JPG, .GIF, or other graphic file is chosen to be applied to the surface. With a procedural material, the computer generates the appearance of the material onto the surface rather than using a pre-generated image. In the Materials dialog box, this is done by clicking the Materials Library button and opening the Materials Library dialog box, shown in Figure 23.32.

Figure 23.32
Graphic images can be imported into a drawing from an image library to be assigned to a surface for rendering from the Material Library dialog box.

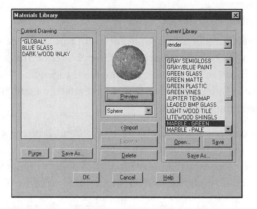

Images can be selected and previewed from an image library on a basic sphere or cube object by first selecting the image, choosing the object to apply the image to, and clicking the Preview button. This will quickly render the image, allowing you to see roughly how the image will appear in the rendering. After you have found the images you want to use, select the Import button, which adds the image to the list of images to be used in the drawing. Then click the OK button to return to the Material dialog box.

As you return to the Material dialog box, you see that the materials you selected are now listed in the Materials list box. Now you are ready to apply them to surfaces or three-dimensional objects using one of the three methods previously mentioned.

ASSIGNING A PROCEDURAL MATERIAL TO A SURFACE

To assign a procedural material to a surface, choose one of the four material types from the select list on the right-hand side of the Materials dialog box. The available material types are Standard, Granite, Marble, and Wood. Each material will open a different dialog box that will allow you to set the specific attributes defining how the material will appear on the surface. These attributes determine the properties of the material based on color or another image. At rendering time, a 3D pattern is generated in two or more colors and applied to the object. The pattern is controlled by attributes that vary with the kind of material.

> **Note**
>
> Procedural materials cannot be imported with the AutoCAD model into 3D Viz or 3D Max, two rendering software packages offered by Autodesk. These software packages contain their own computer generated material processes similar to the process in AutoCAD. Remember that if the model is imported into one of these packages, you'll need to redefine the material on the 3D object.

The dialog box shown in Figure 23.33 displays the different settings for the Marble material.

Figure 23.33
Specific attributes can be assigned to a procedural material through the New Marble, Granite, or Wood Material dialog boxes. The dialog box for a New Marble Material is displayed here.

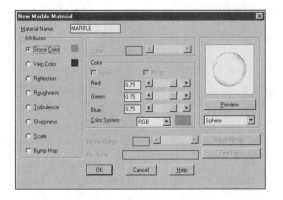

Note

Your rendering must be Photo Real or Photo Raytrace to utilize bitmap effects.

After a material has been assigned to an object, the image or material is mapped to the surface. This process is described in the next section.

MAPPING

This is the term used for projecting a 2D image onto a 3D surface and configuring the image for that surface. You already learned how to assign an image to a 3D object, yet the default size of the image may be too large or small for the object you are applying it to. Mapping allows you to define the size and location of the image onto the surface. Clicking the Mapping button from the Render toolbar and selecting objects from the drawing displays the Mapping dialog box shown in Figure 23.34.

Figure 23.34
There are four mapping projection types that can be applied to three-dimensional objects using the Mapping dialog box.

Here you can set one of four different types of mapping projections, depending on the size and shape of the object you are mapping to. The name of the projection type gives you a pretty good idea what type of objects you should apply them to:

- Planar—Applied to flat or large surfaces

- <u>C</u>ylindrical—Applied to cylindrical objects
- <u>S</u>pherical—Used to map spheres or round surfaces
- So<u>l</u>id—Applied to cubes or thick, solid objects

Although the names of the mapping projection may be somewhat obvious, you'll still need to think about the object and how you want the mapped image to appear on the object. For example, applying a spherical mapping projection to the stairs in Figure 23.34 would distort the image of the applied wood material, where a planar mapping projection would be best for the flat treads of the stairs.

A planar projection might work for the entire stair assembly if looking at it from a distance, but might need some adjusting if used in a close-up view. To adjust the position of the mapped image, click the <u>A</u>djust Coordinates button. This will open the Adjust Planar Coordinates dialog box. The appearance of this dialog box depends on the projection option you chose (see Figure 23.35).

Figure 23.35
Adjust the coordinates and size of the mapped image from the Adjust Coordinates dialog box, which changes depending on the mapping projection chosen.

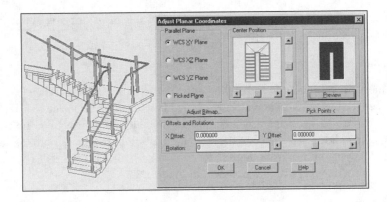

The plane the bitmap is mapped to and the offset and rotation of the bitmap on the object can be adapted for the surface. Slider bars can also be used to adjust the positioning of the image in relation to the 3D object. To adjust the size of the bitmap image, click the Adjust <u>B</u>itmap button, which opens the Adjust Object Bitmap Placement dialog box (see Figure 23.36).

This dialog box offers three image-tiling options that determine how the image will be mapped to the object:

- <u>D</u>efault—The image is mapped to the entire object.
- <u>T</u>ile—The original size of the image is maintained and matched edge to edge and mapped to the 3D object.
- <u>C</u>rop—This tiling option does not tile the image, yet uses the edges of the image to render the sides of the 3D object.

Figure 23.36
The Offset scale and Tiling options for a mapped bitmap image is set through the Adjust Object Bitmap Placement dialog box.

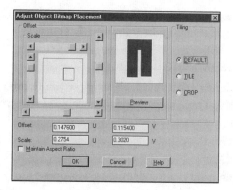

By defining a tiling method and adjusting the offset size and scale of the mapped image, you can tweak the appearance of a three-dimensional object and the bitmap image applied to it. Beyond mapping, there are special material effects that can be used to achieve photo-realistic rendering.

MORE ADVANCED RENDERING EFFECTS

Photo-Realistic rendering combines a number of effects to achieve near picture-perfect renderings. Unfortunately, AutoCAD 2000 is not capable of producing some of these effects, yet they are available in higher-end rendering packages like 3D Viz and 3D Studio, both available from Autodesk.

Note

You can find more information about these products by viewing the 3D Viz demo on the accompanying CD, or by visiting the Kinetix Web site at `http:\\www.ktx.com`.

Photo-realistic rendering supports the following kinds of maps:

- Texture maps—In AutoCAD, you can define surfaces as if a bitmap image were painted onto the object. For example, to simulate a brick pattern on an object, you may apply an image consisting of long rectangles, and then edit the colors to look like bricks.

- Reflection maps—Simulate a scene to be reflected on a shiny object. If the object has materials assigned to it that have shiny surfaces then the amount of reflection can be adjusted. If the object you have is a glass or transparent object the amount of refraction can be adjusted using a set of refraction values.

- Opacity maps—Specify areas that you want to be transparent or opaque, such as windows that are not reflecting light or a clear glass vase.

- Bump maps—Create an embossed or bas-relief effect. These maps add to the realism of the object by supplying the look of a natural or applied texture like the roughness of stone or gravel.

There are however, some interesting features available in AutoCAD 2000 that allow you to create very realistic renderings you'll find in the following section.

ADDITIONAL RENDERING EFFECTS IN AUTOCAD 2000

There are several different rendering effects available to allow you to produce a near photo-realistic image in AutoCAD 2000. Three effects available enable you to create Backgrounds, Fog, and even Landscaping for your rendered scene.

CREATING A BACKGROUND SCENE

Selecting the Background button from the Render dialog box opens the Background dialog box, from which you can choose one of four background options:

- Solid—Specifies a one-color background to be used in the rendered scene. This is a consistent color of your choosing to illustrate a specific object.

- Gradient—Up to three colors can be applied to the background for the scene. Gradient provides a varying color background for adding visual interest to your overall rendered image.

- Image—A bitmap image can be selected to create a backdrop. This is used when you have an actual image, such as a sunset or clouds, that you want to have in the background.

- Merge—Allows the use of the current AutoCAD image as the background image, available only when the current viewport is selected as the rendered image destination. This option enables you to select an object from the drawing and render it with the image set with the Image option. The Merge option is convenient when you want to render and view a specific object against a background without rendering the entire scene.

As mentioned earlier, you may want to have a background color to your rendering or a background image like a sky or landscape. These background images can be imported from your own personal files in various formats, *.JPG, *.TIF, and so on. As mentioned earlier, you can add shadows to an image.

And finally, you can use this feature to place your object or objects in a scene and create a complete photo-realistic picture, for presentation, as a computer-generated photographic image of a complete product.

USING SCENES IN RENDERING

A scene is a "snapshot" of a rendered view with all the lighting and effects set up to your requirements. You are able to save a number of scenes with your drawing allowing you to show the object viewed from different angles and with different effects. Scenes save you time because you do not have to set up viewpoint and lights from scratch every time you render.

SAVING, PRINTING, AND EXPORTING RENDERED MODELS

To view your rendered image AutoCAD gives you three options:

- Viewport
- Render Window
- File

When you render to a viewport, the image will appear with all the default render command settings. This is generally the option you would use to check out all the parameters you have set up for your image. In my opinion, it tends to render quicker to viewport so that's why I use it as my first pass.

I use the Render window to manipulate my rendered image to appear how I would like the printed copy to appear. When you go to the print option from the Render window, a small picture of your rendered image is displayed in the Print dialog box. The image is shown represented on the paper size you have selected. By various tweaking of the image edges, you can size the picture to suit the kind of print you want.

After creating your rendered image you can redisplay your rendering at a later time providing you save the rendering to a file. Rendering can be a very time-consuming process but AutoCAD will allow you to save directly to a file. When you want to redisplay the saved rendered image, the rendering is instantaneous.

You may want to save your rendered image to a particular file format that will allow you to insert it into a document of some kind. It does not matter how your display is configured. You are able to save your rendered image to a file that will allow you to render your image to a much higher resolution for use with other displays. Some of the file formats you can render to are .BMP, .TGA, .TIFF, .PCX, and postscript.

RELATED APPLICATIONS

Several Autodesk products have export options with the AutoCAD renderer, including 3D Studio Max, 3D Viz, AutoCAD Architectural Desktop, Advanced Modeling Extension (AME), Autosurf, AutoCAD Designer, and of course Mechanical Desktop. Only the first two software products, 3D Studio Max and 3D Viz, require that you save you model into another format. AutoCAD has a built in feature for specifically importing and exporting AutoCAD drawing file to and from these products. These commands, called 3dsin and 3dsout, are available from two separate pull-down menus. To import a 3D Viz or Studio file, which have a .3DS extension, click on the Insert pull-down menu and select 3D Studio. To export a drawing to 3D Studio Max or Viz, select Export… from the File pull-down menu. Make certain that you change the file type in the Save as Type select list to 3D Studio(*.3DS) before saving your file. Both commands can also be activated from the command line by typing in the desired command name and pressing Enter.

SUMMARY

Although this chapter is only a quick overview of the commands that assist you in working in the three dimensions, you can start to envision to what is possible in the 3D world using AutoCAD 2000. The next two chapters deal with discipline specific software products built upon the AutoCAD 2000 base functionality that make working in three-dimensions easier. You'll find out how in the following introductory chapters on Architectural and Mechanical Desktop.

PART VI

BEYOND AutoCAD

CHAPTER 24

INTRODUCTION TO ARCHITECTURAL DESKTOP

In this chapter

INTRODUCTION TO PART VI

The two chapters in this section are dedicated to two AutoCAD-based, discipline-specific software products called Architectural Desktop and Mechanical Desktop. The intent of these chapters is to give you a basic idea of what these products have to offer. I will then point you to additional information and examples that can be applied to your own specific projects by using the trial versions of these products (included on the companion CD). Although covering both of these products in more detail is beyond the scope of this book, it is provided in this format to be a resource for those who are considering using either Architectural Desktop or Mechanical Desktop.

Although both software products contain the same basic functionality and AutoCAD commands found in the first twenty-three chapters of this book, they are geared toward designing and creating drawings in their respective fields. Each chapter illustrates how this is accomplished by describing the terminology and processes that are specific to each product. For example, Architectural Desktop contains features designed to enhance architectural productivity, such as model-based design and space planning (enabling the architect to visualize and lay out the building space in three dimensions). The same can be said for Mechanical Desktop, whose parametric design and capability to generate working drawings from the three-dimensional model give the designer the ability to quickly create parts.

Both of these products allow the capability to draw in 2D, yet the result is a model created in three dimensions. This unique functionality enables you to focus on your design without the need to learn how to work in 3D. It also gives you the added advantage of being able to view your drawing in three-dimensions where flaws or overlooked areas of the design can easily be seen, and where two-dimensional flat drawings often make it harder to visualize the end result. This type of functionality extends beyond what is available within the basic AutoCAD product and is typical of what will be emphasized in the next two chapters, starting with the Architectural Desktop package.

In this chapter I will introduce the AutoCAD Architectural Desktop 2.0, or ADT for short. ADT is a version of AutoCAD 2000 that has been enhanced for the AEC industry. In addition to containing a complete version of AutoCAD 2000, many new features & objects have been added, such as model-based design and multiview blocks, that are specifically built around the building design industry. Because all of the new objects work like standard AutoCAD objects, anyone familiar with AutoCAD can quickly master ADT.

TRANSITIONING TO ARCHITECTURAL DESKTOP

One of the most difficult tasks people face in the building design industry is progressing from traditional design techniques, where CAD is treated much like an electronic pencil, to using a software product like AutoCAD Architectural Desktop. Using built-in design features such as model-based design, the thought process of working with standard 2D drawings shifts to working with three-dimensional models. After you are accustomed to this transition, great leaps in productivity are made possible using ADT because it cuts the degree of effort on many levels.

One such level is the ability to create complex wall styles that can be represented in both two and three dimensions, depending on the angle from which they are being viewed. If the components that make up a wall style changes for a project, all walls created with this style are automatically updated throughout the drawing. Without the wall style functionality, you would need to manually update each wall segment, which is a tedious task regardless of building size.

Because the walls can also be viewed in three dimensions, you might not want to show every object that makes up the wall to decrease the overall complexity of what is being displayed. Using the view-dependent display feature, you can toggle off the display of these items in 3D views, yet make them visible in two—dimensional views. The point being illustrated here is that by using the various built-in features of Architectural Desktop, you can use one object that can be viewed in two or three dimensions and this object can look different, depending on how it is viewed.

As you go through this chapter, the many other features of Architectural Desktop will be discussed and the benefits to be gained using these features. To start, let's discuss the features available during the beginning of the design process.

CONCEPTUAL DESIGN

The process of designing a building normally starts in one of two ways: outside-in using massing studies or inside-out using space planning. ADT supports both of these design methods.

MASSING STUDIES

Massing studies takes an outside-in approach to building designs in which the designer manipulates simple 3D shapes to form the exterior of a building.

One specific feature that can greatly increase productivity that ADT supports is the capability to generate model-based designs. *Model-based designing* is the process of using three-dimensional models to define and modify a concept. There are predefined geometric shapes (*mass elements*) for which you can control the height, width, and length, can be placed into the drawing to represent specific features of the building, such as office areas, facades, towers, or anything else that can be conceptually portray a building space (see Figure 24.1).

Figure 24.1
The Add Mass Element dialog box enables you to add three-dimensional solid elements to the drawing to represent features of the building for model-based design studies.

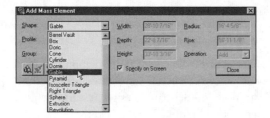

The mass elements can then be combined, using Boolean operations like add, subtract, or intersect, to create mass groups. Using these three-dimensional solids elements and groups, the overall volume of a building space can be generated and analyzed from all angles. Alternative design schemes to the original design can quickly be created and easily presented for consideration by both you and the client. The model can be viewed and manipulated in hidden-line, shaded, and rendered modes dynamically, as shown in Figure 24.2.

Figure 24.2
A simple three-dimensional solid model defining a building space can be analyzed using a 3D Orbit tool similar to the one found in AutoCAD 2000.

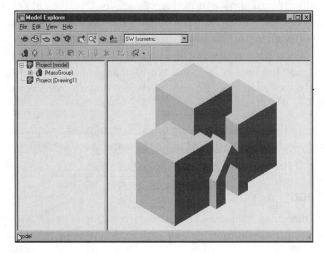

Model-based design also gives a designer and building owner a much better understanding of the building than a 2D plan allows (see Figure 24.3). Some reasons for this are as follows:

Figure 24.3
This figure represents the relationship between the model-based design and the completed drawing by overlaying the mass group design elements on top of the completed first floor.

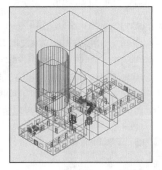

Two-dimensional plans lack the three-dimensional interaction that can be easily visualized using ADT. Because the human eye can better comprehend three-dimensional shapes than two-dimensional, flat illustrations; model-based design, in turn, helps reduce change orders and improve client satisfaction (see Figure 24.4).

Figure 24.4
Viewing a model in two and three dimensions can assist you in realizing design flaws in the conceptual stage of building design.

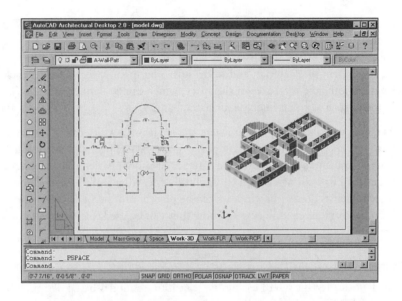

Note

Although there are numerous advantages to using model-based design, which will be pointed out as you continue to read this chapter, it is not mandatory to use ADT in this manner. If you find working in three-dimensions overwhelming, ADT is flexible enough to accommodate the traditional two-dimensional design process as well. It is the author's opinion that you will find ADT to be an exceptional design and drafting tool, whether you are working in three dimensions or two. The benefits that are gained by using model-based design will significantly outweigh the effort needed to change the way you currently design.

One of the best features of AutoCAD Architectural Desktop is that you can choose how you want to work with the software. You can work in 2D, 3D, or a combination of the two at the same time. View-dependent display, which is discussed in more detail in the section "View-Dependent Display" later in this chapter, gives you the ability to utilize the best of both worlds. This enables you to set what will be visible when you view the drawing in two or three dimensions. ADT also uses layouts and viewports to present one or both display modes, allowing you to choose the mode that gives you what you need to see.

ADT makes it easy to switch from one display mode to another, allowing you to easily visualize concepts to assist you during all phases of the project.

Mass studies are frequently followed by space planning to define the interior spaces of the building—this is discussed in the following section.

SPACE PLANNING

Space planning is the inside-out approach, in which a building designer compiles a list of space requirements and creates simple rectangular shapes to represent all the spaces that are needed. The designer then arranges the spaces into a usable floor plan. This can easily be done by creating a space style, which is defined as the properties of a new space placed into the drawing. Some of the space styles included in Architectural Desktop are libraries, office areas, kitchens or cafeterias, and restrooms. The space style properties include the desired length, width, and total area of the space, which can be defined as a specific line or polyline property such as color, linetype, or hatch pattern.

As spaces are placed into the drawing, the length and width of each space is confined by the total area specified within the associated space style. This helps keep initial room or area design parameters intact. After the room or area boundaries are set, you can convert the boundaries to walls based on a chosen wall style. After walls have been created, intelligent objects such as doors and windows can be placed into the walls. In the next section, you'll learn about intelligent objects and how they can be used to create and quickly modify a drawing.

WORKING WITH OBJECTS

ADT does a terrific job of easing the transition to model-based design. The key to the benefits of ADT is the new intelligent objects that are the core of ADT. These intelligent objects actually take on the properties of the objects they represent in the drawing. In other words, a wall acts like a wall, and a door acts like a door, so if a door is removed from a wall, the wall realizes the hole the door initially made no longer exists and fills the hole. The door, on the other hand, realizes it is constrained to the extents of the wall it has been placed into, so a door can be moved within the wall but not outside of it. Now, on hearing this you may think it sounds a bit like science fiction, but in actuality this is how objects "think" in ADT. The building design objects, which are referred to as AEC objects, can easily conform to each situation because very specific design rules have been built into the software, rules that you can control through parameters, similar to adjusting the values of setting variables in AutoCAD 2000.

In previous versions of AutoCAD-based architectural design software, simple objects such as lines were used to represent a wall. This was very inefficient because every line had to be created individually. Unlike objects, the individual lines that made up a wall didn't understand how to behave at wall intersections so every intersection had to be cleaned up manually. Adding to the problem, you could not easily change the style of the wall. If you wanted to change the width of the wall, you would have to adjust all the lines. Because every intersection and door insertion breaks the lines that make up the wall, there was no way to automatically determine the total length of walls in the building for estimation purposes.

The new objects in ADT, such as Wall Styles, were created to solve these problems (see Figure 24.5).

Figure 24.5
Wall Styles are only one of many different types of intelligent objects built into AutoCAD Architectural Desktop.

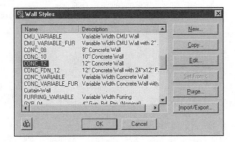

For example, a single wall object can represent multiple lines and hatch patterns; it can determine how it should intersect with other walls. A wall's width or style can be changed just by changing its properties, and you can also extract the length of walls by using the schedule command. Adjusting to working with intelligent objects instead of simple entities is the first and largest hurdle to mastering ADT.

VIEW-DEPENDENT DISPLAY

One of the most unique features of the new objects is that they do not force you to choose between 2D and 3D. As mentioned before, ADT could be used solely as a 2D design and drafting tool. In fact, the productivity enhancements that Architectural Desktop offers to standard 2D design and drafting alone is considerable. This includes the use of intelligent objects that automatically "clean up" the walls they are inserted into, avoiding the time-consuming editing of wall openings for each inserted door and window.

Regardless of this feature, the majority of novice users would prefer to work in 3D if it could be intuitive and not hamper their productivity. Working in three dimensions can be a tremendous aid in design, visually and conceptually. In addition, after a model is created, the building elevations and sections can easily be extracted from the model, decreasing the amount of time needed to produce working drawings.

In ADT, the objects you create are simultaneously 2D and 3D objects. To help illustrate this, think of the many different ways a single object is represented in traditional architectural design during the different stages of the design process. For example, a door is drawn differently for a floor plan, a ceiling plan, an elevation, and an isometric view of the drawing. In ADT, each object has these multiple modes of display built into it, so when a door is viewed from a plan view the objects display only as 2D entities. When viewed from the front or side, objects display in elevation mode. From any other angle the objects display as 3D. This is called View-Dependent Display and it is one of the most important features of ADT. Although the object shown is a three dimensional object, only the portion of the object that needs to be represented at that view is displayed. These properties can easily be configured in ADT, giving you control over how specific items are displayed in relation to how they are viewed.

A single object such as a door, when viewed from plan, could be represented as a simple double-line panel with an arc for the door swing, as shown in Figure 24.6.

Figure 24.6
View-Dependent Display enables you to modify how an object is viewed depending on the angle it is viewed from, for example the plan view.

This same door, when viewed from another angle, can be displayed as a three-dimensional door along with a header, as shown in Figure 24.7.

Figure 24.7
The display of a door and header in a three-dimensional view can be controlled through the use of View-Dependent Display.

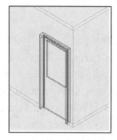

When viewed from the front, this door can be represented as a 2D elevation (see Figure 24.8).

Figure 24.8
The elevation view of the door displays only the portion of the door that needs to be displayed at this angle.

This is not achieved by manipulating hundreds of layers; rather, it is simply a native behavior of ADT's intelligent door object. This intelligence gives you the benefits of 2D and 3D without having the drawbacks of either.

MULTIVIEW BLOCKS

To expand on the use of view-dependent display, blocks in Architectural Desktop have been modified to display differently in different views. These blocks are called multiview blocks, and act just like the standard blocks you would create in AutoCAD 2000. The main difference between them is that there are actually multiple blocks, which can be referred to as child blocks, used to make one multiview block, or parent block.

The child block that is displayed depends on the view from which the multiview block is viewed. Each multiview block can consist of a top, front, side, and model view child block, which is referred to as the display representation of the parent block. As each child block is defined as part of the overall multiview parent block, you also specify the Display Representation (the child block to be viewed) and the View Direction—when a child block is displayed (see Figure 24.9).

Figure 24.9
Multiview blocks consist of individual blocks, for which you define the direction they are viewed from.

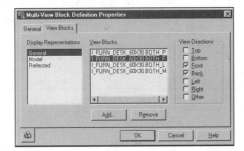

DISPLAY REPRESENTATIONS

Display Representations enable the user to control the display settings of various object components, such as layer, color, and linetype. Using Display Representations, you can define what is displayed in the drawing, depending on what stage of the project you are working on.

OBJECT TYPES AFFECTED BY DISPLAY REPRESENTATION

In addition to multiview blocks, there are also standard object types that are displayed based on the display representations shown in Table 24.1.

TABLE 24.1   OBJECT TYPES AVAILABLE IN ARCHITECTURAL DESKTOP AND THEIR ASSOCIATED DISPLAY REPRESENTATIONS

Block or Object	Display Representation
Anchor Bubble to Column Grid	Model, Plan, Reflected
Anchor Free	General

continues

TABLE 24.1 CONTINUED

Anchor Lead Entity To Node	General
Anchor Tag To Entity	General
Bldg Elevation Line	Model, Plan, Reflected
Bldg Section	Model, Subdivisions
Bldg Section Line	Model, Plan, Reflected
Camera	General
Ceiling Grid	Model, Plan, Reflected
Clip Volume	Model, Plan
Clip Volume Result	General, Subdivisions
Column Grid	Model, Plan, Reflected
Door	Model, Plan, Reflected, Elevation, Nominal, Door Threshold Plan
Entity Reference	General
Layout Curve	General
Layout Grid 2D	General
Layout Grid 3D	General
Mask Block Reference	General, Reflected
Mass Element	Model, Sketch, Reflected
Mass Group	Model, Plan, Reflected
Multiview Block Reference	Model, General, Reflected
Opening	Model, Plan
Railing	Model, Plan
Roof	Model, Plan, Reflected
Schedule Table	General
Slice	General
Space	Model, Plan, Reflected, Volume
Space Boundary	Model, Plan, Diagram, Sketch
Stair	Model, Plan, Reflected
Wall	Model, Plan, Reflected, Sketch, Graph
Window	Model, Plan, Reflected, Elevation, Nominal, Window Sill Plan

Displaying objects based on Display Representations gives you control over when an object will be viewed in a drawing or in an entire project. Display Representations can also be saved to a template, allowing you to define project standards for when specific objects are displayed.

In the rest of this chapter you will look at many of the new objects in ADT as well as how they fit into the building design process.

SPECIFIC FEATURES OF ARCHITECTURAL DESKTOP

Now that you know a little more about the basic built-in functionality of Architectural Desktop, here is a list of some of the individual features that make ADT unique:

- Layer Groups and Snapshots
- Grid Configuration and Layout
- Wall Styles and Cleanup
- Door & Window Objects
- Stairs Generator
- Roof Generator
- Expansive Library of Documentation Symbols
- Construction Documents
- Automatic Scheduling
- Annotation Routines
- Details and Elevation Generation
- Camera Angle Display

Each of these features is discussed in the following sections.

LAYER GROUPS

Layer Groups enable you to bundle sets of layers together to create working views that display only the information needed for that active layer group toggling specific layers off and on depending on what you are working on. For example, a layer group called Model displays only the layers needed for viewing the model elements and groups used for the building, whereas one called Work–Reflected will show only those layers related to working with the reflected ceiling plan. There are two methods to create layer groups such as those just mentioned: user-defined groups and filter-based groups.

User-defined groups (or *user layer* groups) are created when a "snapshot" is taken of the current layers displayed in a drawing. This process is covered in more detail in the next section. *Filter-based groups*, (*filter layer groups*), are groups of layers that have been filtered out of the drawing based on a particular set of properties. For example, suppose you want to create a layer group by filtering the drawing for all layers that are currently displayed that have "arch" as the first word in their name and have a default linetype of continuous. This would enable you to capture and easily restore those architectural layers that have these properties during a particular time when working on a drawing.

In addition, layers can be dragged and dropped in the layer group from the Layer Manager to add additional layers to the group. You can define which layers are displayed when a specific layer group is made active also using the Layer Manager, shown in Figure 24.10.

Figure 24.10
The layers contained within a Layer Snapshot and their properties can easily be edited in Architectural Desktop.

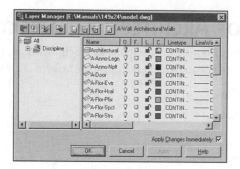

To take this feature one step further, you can also create Layer Snapshots, which are essentially project-specific layer groups.

LAYER SNAPSHOTS

Layer Snapshots allow the designer to take a "snapshot" of the current layer and view the configuration. After they have been saved, these snapshots can be edited and restored any time during a project. This can save a tremendous amount of time manipulating the layers to display specific information in the drawing. One instance were snapshots can be utilized is if a designer wanted to view the location of all of the furniture in relation to the location of the telephone and data jacks. The furniture, telephone, and data layers could be turned on, with only the needed background layers visible to provide enough information to the installers to locate the equipment, such as the exterior and interior walls. The drawing can then be quickly returned to this display state to convey this information in the drawing.

Layers can be added and deleted in addition to modifying the individual properties of the layers from within the snapshot (see Figure 24.11).

This allows snapshots to be extremely flexible and customized beyond their initial configuration.

Figure 24.11
The layers contained within a Layer Snapshot and their properties can easily be edited in Architectural Desktop.

GRIDS

Numerous grid configurations can be quickly generated and edited in ADT using grid objects designed to create rectangular and radial column grids and ceiling grids (see Figure 24.12).

Figure 24.12
Using grid objects, rectangular or radial grids can quickly be created, labeled, and edited in ADT.

This allows you to quickly lay out a column reference grid using rectangular or cylindrical column symbols which can be placed at the grid intersections as the grid is placed in the drawing. Then the grid can be automatically labeled based on the grid configuration, shown in Figure 24.13.

Figure 24.13
Grid objects can be automatically labeled using the Column Grid Labeling feature.

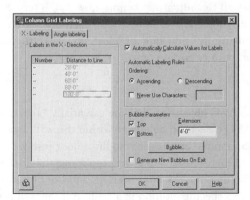

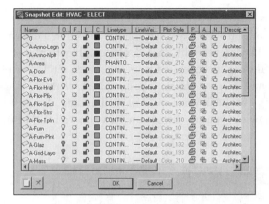

PART
VI

CH
24

WALLS

The AEC wall objects built into ADT are dynamically placed in a drawing based on standard or user-defined wall styles. Straight, curved, or a combination of straight and curved walls can be created. Walls can be generated from lines, arcs, circles, or polylines from line diagrams or sketches from the space planning design phase, enabling you to capitalize on work already done laying out the interior space of the building. As the wall objects are being placed into the drawing, you can also define how the wall will be dimensioned (see Figure 24.14)

Figure 24.14
Dimensions can easily be placed on wall objects as they are placed into a drawing.

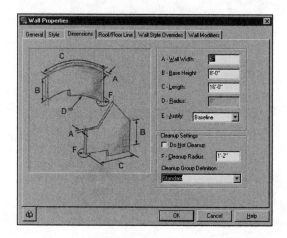

The wall style and end caps, as well as how the wall will meet with the roof or floor, can be defined in ADT.

WALL CLEANUP

Because the walls are intelligent objects, they can interact with other walls placed within their wall cleanup group. A wall cleanup group defines how wall intersections will be handled when walls of the same group come in contact with each other. So as you place walls into the drawing, they automatically know how to "clean up" when they touch or overlap, saving you a considerable amount of editing time.

DOORS AND WINDOWS

Doors and windows are also AEC objects, so they are essentially "aware" of how they are placed within a wall. The AEC object can be moved within the wall, but cannot be moved outside of the wall itself. An example of this is to modify a door inserted into a wall six feet long with windows placed on each side. If you attempt to move the door one foot in either direction, ADT alerts you, stating that the door overlaps another object. Doors and windows can also be anchored to a specific location in a wall, so if the wall is modified or moved, the location of the door or window remains the same.

One of the best features of ADT is the use of Door and Window Styles, where specific design rules can be built into the object that define how it will be used within the drawing (see Figure 24.15).

Figure 24.15
Design rules can be added to a Door or Window object, defining exactly how it will be used within a drawing.

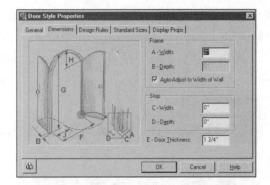

The Door and Window Styles enable you to create the AEC object from any user-defined shape, giving you the flexibility to design anything you can imagine.

STAIRS

Stairs are objects that can be placed in any number of configurations, at any angle into the drawing using the dialog box shown in Figure 24.16.

Figure 24.16
There are numerous parameters that can be applied to a stair object to define exactly how you want the stair to be placed into your drawing.

Stairs are defined by code-based styles that you can modify to adjust the tread and riser dimensions based on height and length (see Figure 24.17). This enables you to quickly place stairs based on code specifications, depending on type or function.

ROOFS

The roof generator can be used to create complex roof configurations from polyline objects in the drawing, like the one shown in Figure 24.18.

Figure 24.17
Stair Styles are used to determine the properties of a stair and how it is placed into the drawing.

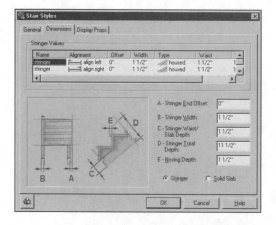

Figure 24.18
Complex roof structures can be created from existing polyline objects using the roof object generator in ADT.

The slope, rise, and overhang characteristics of the roof can be easily modified when placing a roof into a drawing. After the roof is drawn, you can edit the edge and faces that make up the roof.

DESIGN CONTENT LIBRARY AND ANNOTATION SYMBOLS

The Design Content Library contains many AEC drawings that can easily be inserted into your drawing. Using Design Center, you can also insert any graphics symbols needed to annotate your drawing, including blocks and leaders (see Figure 24.19).

Figure 24.19
The numerous ADT annotation and AEC symbols can quickly be placed into the drawing using AutoCAD Design Center.

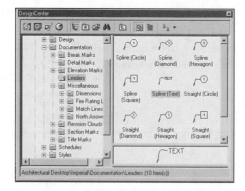

Here are the different groups of AEC symbols you can insert into your drawing:

- Appliances
- Casework
- Ceiling fixtures
- Electric fixtures
- Equipment
- Furniture
- Plumbing fixtures
- Site content

And these are the various annotation symbols available to you using ADT:

- Break marks
- Detail marks
- Elevation marks
- Leaders
- Revision clouds
- Section marks
- Title marks

SCHEDULING

Data can be attached to any AEC object and extracted to create schedules of any kind, which can then be edited and automatically updated (see Figure 24.20).

Figure 24.20
Schedule data attached to any AEC object can be easily edited so the associated schedule can be updated automatically.

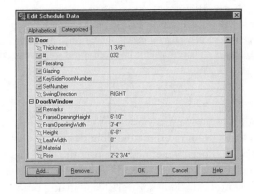

The schedules that can be generated easily in ADT include door, equipment, furniture, room, room finish, room finish matrix, space inventory, wall, and window. You can define these schedules to be manually or automatically updated (see Figure 20.21).

Figure 24.21
There are nine different schedules included in ADT, and you can create your own schedule type for specific schedules.

ELEVATIONS

Because the drawing content using ADT can be placed into the drawing as 3D objects, elevations for the drawing can easily be generated and updated when the drawing changes. The height from which the elevation is viewed and the objects shown in the elevation can also be selected. The advantage to this is that if changes are made to the model, the elevations can quickly be re-created to show those changes.

GENERATE PERSPECTIVES

Using the Camera feature, you can view your model from any angle by placing a camera into the drawing. The camera properties can be edited to adjust the viewing angle and height, as well as camera and target location. This gives you yet another feature that can be used to present your design to the client and others, allowing you to choose the angle that best represents your ideas and concepts.

These are just a few of the many features you will find in Architectural Desktop. These features speed up many of the mundane tasks that can bog down the architectural design process.

Tip 232 from
Ron House

To learn more about using Architectural Desktop, visit the Que Web site at `http://www.mcp.com`. Using the Search feature, type the keyword `autocad` and click the Search button. Select this book from the Search Results list to go to the *Special Edition Using AutoCAD 2000* Web page. Here, you will find information about a document created by Autodesk that details information and examples on specific Architectural Desktop features. This is an excellent source for details about many undocumented features and tips, with many examples on how to get the most out of this software package.

SUMMARY

Using Architectural Desktop can make architectural design easier, making you more productive while allowing you to focus more on the building design than on creating the working drawings. After the model has been generated, creating the working drawings is a snap, which also enables you to make changes quickly and easily through the project. ADT is definitely a step above the base AutoCAD 2000 software, capitalizing on its basic functionality while making the software more of a design than drafting tool. Whether you work in two or three dimensions, you'll find that the features and functionality built into ADT can save a considerable amount of time, regardless of the project. This software is definitely a must-have for you to be competitive in the architectural and building design fields using AutoCAD 2000.

CHAPTER 25

INTRODUCTION TO MECHANICAL DESKTOP

In this chapter

FROM CONCEPT TO REALITY

Mechanical Desktop is the three-dimensional solid modeling program that enables you to turn your concepts and ideas into reality.

This state-of-the-art three-dimensional solid modeling software enables the designer to fully develop products in a virtual computer environment. Mechanical Desktop will turn your ideas or existing 2D data into 3D solid models, modify existing files, and prepare data for prototyping or production. With Mechanical Desktop's powerful advanced assembly features, you can manage your complete product assembly structure and all drawings while maintaining full association among the three-dimensional master model, the assembly, and all drawings.

When an idea in AutoCAD has been developed as a 2D layout or shape, the next stage is to build a prototype (3D solid model) using the tools of Mechanical Desktop.

With Mechanical Desktop, a prototype can be generated to do the following:

- Help the designer evaluate the quality of the design in form, fit, and function.

- Define every geometric aspect of a component or assembly, minimizing the possibility of misinterpretation on the shop floor.

- Enable the customer/marketing department to see and feel a "real" working product. For many nontechnical people, a 2D drawing is confusing and difficult to understand.

- Provide data for downstream operations, such as rapid prototyping, stress analysis, mold flow-shrink, and warpage analysis.

Figure 25.1
A simple three-dimensional solid model prototype of a cellular phone casing created using Mechanical Desktop.

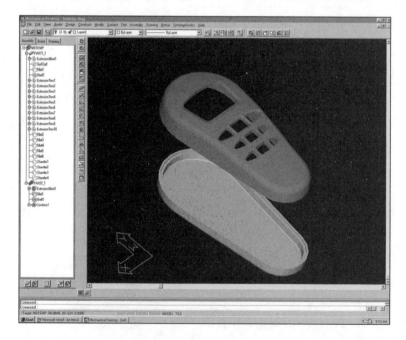

Mechanical Desktop enables you to build a prototype in two ways:

- As a 3D fully rendered image of the product—This is similar to a photographic image of the final product that can be rotated and viewed from any angle while still being just a computer-generated image.
- As a stereolithography model—This process allows parts to be constructed directly from the 3D files generated in Mechanical Desktop in just a matter of hours.

→ The stereolithography process is explained in the "Stereolithography and Rapid Prototyping" section later in this chapter.

Mechanical Desktop is the tool that enables you to create 3D models to evaluate the form, fit, and function of your designs. With the addition of analysis and simulation software that will work within Mechanical Desktop, you can understand and evaluate how your products will perform and function under varying circumstances before incurring the costs of manufacturing a quantity of prototypes. These software packages enable you to define exactly how the part will perform under stress and strain conditions in extreme temperatures based on different material types, all of which can be determined before the final prototype is created.

After evaluation is complete and modifications have been made, the 3D files can be used to generate:

- 2D detailed engineering drawings
- Assembly drawings
- Parts lists (in Microsoft Excel, if required)

PART

VI

CH

25

In addition, a complete documentation package can be generated to begin the manufacturing process, all within the familiar environment of AutoCAD.

One of the major advantages of using Mechanical Desktop is that all the drawings generated through the 3D software are first and foremost AutoCAD drawings that can be modified and stored just as if they had been produced in the 2D AutoCAD CAD software.

If the engineering detail drawings and assembly drawings are linked to the 3D file through parametric dimensional constraints, the same drawing can be used to produce multiple parts.

Note

The term *parametric* refers to a solution method that uses the values of part parameters to determine the geometric configuration of the part. A parametric dimension created during the sketch phase of a part creation controls the size of the part, and you can update the part by changing its value. If you wish to create a part with variables, you can add the parametric dimensions as a formula.

To elaborate on this even more, parametric constraints can confine a particular object that defines how you want it to relate—such as horizontal, vertical, or tangent—to adjacent objects or to the drawing as a whole. They can also be dimensions that contain equations that are related to other sections of the part, such as the length or width. If one or both of these parameters are altered, the part is updated based on these constraints.

For example, let's say that we have a lever arm that has a hole that is constrained by length and width (see Figure 25.2).

Figure 25.2
Hole in a lever arm, constrained by length and width.

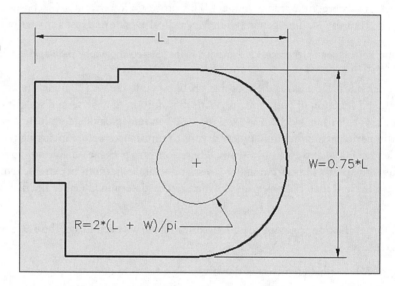

The radius of the hole is determined by this equation:

```
R=2*(L + W)/pi
```

This is the sum of the length and width times 2, divided by the value of pi, or 3.1416. Therefore, if the length and width of the part increase, so does the radius of the hole. The inverse is true if the length and width decrease, although we would need to further constrain the part to keep the size of the length and width in check. In other words, what would happen if the width of the part were substantially larger than the length? The radius might exceed the length; consequently you would need to constrain the part so the width could only be three-quarters the value of the length with a parametric equation such as this:

```
Width=0.75 * Length
```

By allowing the radius of the hole to be determined by the length and width of the part, this drawing can be used to create other parts that are similar. Expanding on the use of parametrics, entire assemblies or parts to make up complex pieces of machinery or equipment can be drawn with interrelated parts using parametric equations embedded inside dimensions. Any modifications to the 2D drawing, and subsequently to the 3D model, are automatically updated in the working or assembly drawings, and vice versa.

It is a fact that the use of this kind of software, hand-in-hand with computer automated design, are the keys to shortening time to market.

→ See "Case History" later in this chapter for a specific example of this.

As you can see, there are many reasons why companies are moving toward 3D modeling, so let us take a simplified look at the methods used in Mechanical Desktop.

CONSTRUCTING A 3D SOLID MODEL

The simplest way to describe how to produce a solid model is first to construct a sketch or profile of the base shape you want to model. Several different tools in Mechanical Desktop aid you in producing your 3D shape:

- Extrusion—The profile is extruded along a linear distance perpendicular to the profile plane.
- Lofted Feature—A parametric shape is created from a series of profile sketches defining the cross-sectional shape of the feature at each section.
- Revolve—A profile is revolved about an axis of revolution.
- Face Split—This tool supplies the capability to split an object's face using either a planar or a projected method to create two parts.
- Sweep—A profile is moved along a defined path.
- Boolean—In this solid modeling technique, two solids are combined to form one solid. Boolean operations include cut, join, and intersect. Cut subtracts the volume of one solid from the other; join unites two solids; and intersect leaves only the volume shared by the two solids.

After you have established your base solid, you start to chip away, similar to a sculptor creating a statue out of marble, to achieve the final shape using additional tools such as fillet, chamfer, shell, and surface cut.

With all these modeling tools available, a complete solid model can generally be used to generate a completely designed part.

PART
VI

CH
25

Caution

No 3D modeler currently on the market will give you perfect results every time; it depends on the complexity of the shape you are trying to construct. In my experience working with Mechanical Desktop, I can produce approximately 95% of the solids exactly as I designed them. In the case of a very complex nongeometric part where I cannot get the solid exactly as I designed it, I will either design around it or just include in the 2D engineering detail, drawing the correct dimensions to achieve the desired design. This typically allows the conceptual model to answer approximately 95% of my evaluation questions.

Some models are created by a process called *surface modeling*, in which the surface of the model changes constantly, such as a plastic bottle or a topographical terrain model. The next sections discuss this process in detail, starting with a more in-depth definition of surface modeling.

SURFACE MODELING

Surface modeling, as the term depicts, is the process of creating a surface (or, as some people refer to it, "a skin") to produce a completed model. This is more explicitly defined as a collection of individual surfaces that, when brought together, can represent a 3D model that looks similar to a solid, where it appears as if the entire model is one surface. This can better be defined by visualizing a plastic container, such as a milk bottle, which is actually made up of multiple surfaces welded together to complete the finished part. This method is widely used by industrial designers and stylists to establish a product shape or style.

Although surface models may be more complex to construct, parametric solid part models are easier to manage when changes are required. So why use surface modeling in engineering?

Well, some solid models require very complex surfaces—think of some of the new cellular phone shapes today. The only way to build these shapes is to construct the surface and then subtract it from the solid, leaving the shape you require behind.

As previously stated, imagine that you are a sculptor chipping away at the block. These tools are like your chisel. Think about what you need to take away to leave the shape you want. Then you will have a good understanding of what constructing a 3D-computer model is all about.

As with solid or part modeling, several tools are available in Mechanical Desktop to allow you to construct the surface. This list gives a brief explanation of each:

- Extrude—Creates a surface by moving a defined profile or shape in a specified direction for a specified distance.
- Sweep—Creates a surface by moving one or more cross-sections along one or two wires or rails.
- Revolve—Revolves a wire about an axis of revolution.
- Tubular—Constructs a surface around a wire that represents the axis of the tube.
- Lofted Surface—Creates a surface from a series of cross-sectional curves. The surface is created by exactly representing these curves at their specific locations.
- Planar and Trimmed Planar—Constructs a surface to adjoin existing surfaces.
- Ruled—Creates a surface between two polylines or splines using straight elements.

Additional tools help with blending surfaces and stitching them together. These are in the form of blends, fillets, and offsets. With these tools at your disposal, you will be able to generate complete, fully geometric 3D images.

Taking this one step further; rather than focusing on an individual part, let's combine a series of parts together to form an assembly, which is described in more detail in the next section.

ASSEMBLY

This set of tools in Mechanical Desktop enables you to assemble your 3D parts and create fully ballooned assembly drawings, illustrating how the individual parts interact with each other, which can also produce a parts lists and a bill of materials, and complete your final documentation ready for production.

The assembly process brings together a collection of parametric parts and surface models, tied together with assembly constraints, which creates a complete assembly.

Mechanical Desktop catalogs local and external parts and subassemblies for the top assemblies, which can be instanced, copied, renamed, replaced, externalized, removed, localized, and sorted.

To assemble the parts relative to each other, you apply assembly constraints to each part or subassembly. Although assembly constraints (which are similar to the parametric constraints mentioned previously) reduce the degrees of freedom of each part, they affect the entire assembly. By assigning assembly constraints, Mechanical Desktop can perform rigid body interference checking. In other words, if the parts don't fit, Mechanical Desktop will tell you.

DEGREES OF FREEDOM

PART

VI

CH

25

In part modeling, degrees of freedom determines how a geometric object such as a line, arc, or circle can change shape or size. For example, a circle has two degrees of freedom: center and radius. When these values are known, the degrees of freedom are said to be eliminated.

After the parts have been placed into the assembly drawing, the next step in bringing the parts together is applying the assembly constraints. Four types of constraints are available. The simple explanations that follow will help illustrate each type of constraint.

- Mate Constraint—This option causes a plane, face, or axis on one part to be coincident with a plane, face, or axis on another part in a specified direction. It removes a translational degree of freedom.

- Flush Constraint—This option makes two planes coplanar, with their faces aligned in the same direction.

- Angle Constraint—This option creates alignment between two planes at specified angles to each other.

- Insert Constraint—This option aligns center points and planes of two circles in a specified direction. It solves translation degrees of freedom. This constraint is used to constrain a bolt in a hole, for example.

From the data generated in the assembly, you have the necessary tools within Mechanical Desktop to automatically produce the parts list and the assembly hierarchy. As mentioned earlier in this chapter, because the assembly models are dynamic, any changes you apply to a part that is included in an assembly results in changes to the entire assembly.

When working with assemblies, it is advantageous to track how the assembly is constructed to get a clear picture of how the parts interact with each other. Mechanical Desktop includes a feature called the Desktop Browser, which is discussed in the next section.

THE DESKTOP BROWSER

When you start Mechanical Desktop, the Desktop Browser appears in a docked position at the left side of the your screen. This is where Mechanical Desktop keeps a hierarchy of the steps you have taken to produce either a part or an assembly (see Figure 25.3).

Figure 25.3
The Desktop Browser dialog box shows the hierarchy.

When you begin an assembly, Mechanical Desktop starts a new drawing in the Part/Assembly environment. The assembly is named after the current file. When you create the first sketch, a part is automatically named and represented in the browser. Because the first thing you create is a sketch, it is nested under the part. As you can see, these objects are automatically created in a hierarchy, essentially documenting how the assembly is created.

When you start a new drawing in the Single Part environment, or when you open an existing Single Part file, the Desktop Browser contains two tabs: Part and Drawing. In the Part/Assembly environment, the browser contains three tabs: Assembly, Scene, and Drawing. Picking the tabs at the top of the browser window allows you to easily navigate from one mode to another.

WHY YOU NEED A DESKTOP BROWSER

The browser not only gives you a hierarchy of how you have built your part or assembly, but it also gives you a shortcut to many commands. Most of the commands in Mechanical Desktop can be accessed using the browser menus. Two types of menus exist: those that you activate by right-clicking in the browser background, and those that you activate by right-clicking on an existing object in the browser.

This also means you can select a modeling or assembly operation in the hierarchy and modify it, or delete it and then allow the model to update itself. If the model/assembly consists of multiple parts, then as you move your cursor over the hierarchy, the part is highlighted.

You can activate the highlighted part as the one you wish to modify, select the operation you wish to modify or delete, and proceed.

This feature in Mechanical Desktop really allows you to directly design a 3D part, modifying certain aspects as you go through the design phase.

After the assembly is complete, you may have a need to include a rendering of the finished product into a brochure or for a client or company presentation. The next section discusses the various aspects of rendering or visualizing the assembly.

VISUALIZATION

Another set of tools within Mechanical Desktop falls under the heading of visualization. This gives you the ability to render your 3D parts or a collection of parts, called *assemblies*, using a large library of materials and colors. In addition, you can add backgrounds of images or colors and produce a photographic image of your design.

These rendered pictures can be printed or exported to graphic-type presentation software such as Corel or PhotoShop to present to customers or marketing groups as an illustration of your concepts (see Figure 25.4).

Figure 25.4
A rendered image greatly enhances the concept to the client.

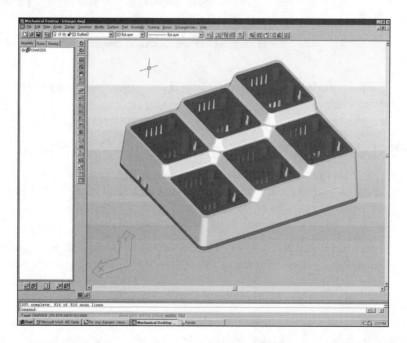

When you are constructing your models, Mechanical Desktop has a set of very effective shading and rotational commands that enable you to view the wire frame models as solid forms and rotate them to any position you require on the screen (see Figure 25.5). This is a very useful tool because it allows you to see exactly what you are modeling and shows any defects not seen in the wire frame mode.

Figure 25.5
A shaded and rotated view of a top cover created using the built-in visualization features of Mechanical Desktop.

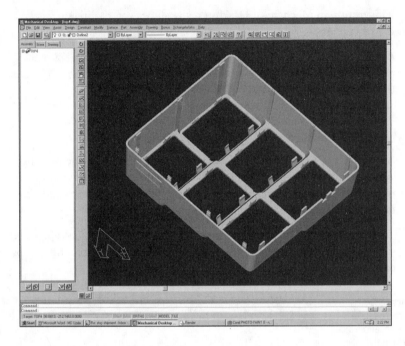

The next step in the design process is to create a prototype, and the methods available for accomplishing this are covered in the following section.

STEREOLITHOGRAPHY AND RAPID PROTOTYPING

So now that you have completed your models in Mechanical Desktop, what is the next step? The next step is having parts in your hand to build your first product prototype within a matter of hours, using one of the most cutting-edge forms of rapid prototyping available to industry and research today: stereolithography.

Stereolithography (SLA) is one of the most popular and widely used forms of rapid prototyping. *Rapid prototyping* is the process of quickly generating a prototype during the design phase, and SLA is a unique form of technology that allows for the translation of CAD 3D files to three-dimensional solid objects within hours.

An ultraviolet laser beam guided by the CAD data solidifies successive cross-sections of a transparent container filled with liquid resin forming the prototype. These prototypes are ideal for use as visualization conceptual tools, design evaluators, and functional test models.

EXPORTING DRAWINGS IN STL FORMAT

Mechanical Desktop has the capability to output the 3D files in an STL format, which defines the boundary surface of the object as a mesh of interconnected triangles. *.STL is the format used by the stereolithography computer system to download the information on the file geometry to its manufacturing system. Prior to producing your *.STL file, you need to define the accuracy you require for your part, or the facet resolution.

FACET RESOLUTION

Mechanical Desktop also enables you to set the facet resolution on your part, which defines the accuracy based on the number of facets required for your part. This value can be set between 1 and 10, with 10 being the highest resolution. The degree of accuracy you set depends on the complexity of the part and the amount of time required in production. The higher the resolution, the more time will be required by the SLA machine to make the part. So what you need to do with this part—presentation, testing, or making a pattern for a low-volume molding tool—determines the type of finish you require on the SLA part. Of course, the longer the SLA process, the more it costs.

Stereolithography replaces traditional prototyping methods and provides you with the following benefits (and more):

- Reduced cost and time for developing prototypes
- Capability to create a series of test models
- Reduced number of design steps and iterations
- Fit and function tests performed on prototypes
- Die casting, investment casting, and spray metal modeling patterns or molds developed

In addition to prototyping, a finished product can be created using Mechanical Desktop through another process (discussed in the next section).

MANUFACTURING CONCURRENT ENGINEERING

The 3D files created in Mechanical Desktop are not just used for prototyping. In fact, a growing number of manufacturers such as tool shops, sheet metal companies, and machine part manufacturers are capable, with the use of CAM (computer-aided manufacturing) software, to take your 3D files exported into their specific CAM format. A definite advantage of this is that these manufacturers can use the parameters already saved in your 3D model files to manufacture the parts using CNC (Computer Numerical Control)-related machinery. This process is described in the next section, and is basically the beginning of what is known as concurrent engineering.

COMPUTER NUMERICAL CONTROL (CNC)

A very simple explanation of CNC machinery is that a manufacturing machine, such as a lathe or a mill, can be programmed to complete the tasks normally carried out by a skilled machine operator automatically. These machines read data that is programmed directly into the machine by the operator. CNC machinery also interprets data directly from 3D files, allowing the CNC operator to input the machining data to manufacture the part. This process can be defined as *concurrent engineering*, where the part can be designed and quickly generated.

CONCURRENT ENGINEERING

Concurrent engineering is the capability through CAD/CAM systems to manufacture a part or component directly from the original data as supplied by the designer. It eliminates the need for documentation, such as 2D engineering drawings, and in theory should be error-proof.

In other words, the designer designs the part, produces the 3D data, and at the end of the line the machine pops out the part. Because no interpretation problems or explanations (hopefully) have occurred, the machine manufactures the part exactly as you designed it.

CASE HISTORY

To illustrate how Mechanical Desktop has worked for me, take a look at an actual case where I was able to save a lot of time and cost in getting a product to market (see Figure 25.6).

I was designing a product for a large telecommunications corporation whose manufacturing facilities are located in the Far East. The product I was designing was a complex plastic housing that was to be a new concept and that needed to be stylish as well as contain some very sophisticated electronics. The company wanted to be one of the first to market and had a large deal depending on the outcome of the design, so time and cost were of the essence.

The normal procedure in the past for this company was to have the 2D layouts approved and then produce a working model. The layouts would then be used to generate fully dimensioned 2D detail drawings, and these would be sent to a model maker in the Far East who would manufacture the parts by machining each one from plastic blocks and gluing other parts together. This was a very skilled and time-consuming procedure. After the models were complete, a design review would take place; if extensive design changes were required, the 2D drawings would be modified and a new model would be generated. There was no other alternative but to proceed in this manner because injection-molding tooling is a very expensive and time-consuming process. On a project this large, it is essential to ensure that by the time you are ready to start tooling, the design works.

Figure 25.6
The 3D part file of the base created in Mechanical Desktop.

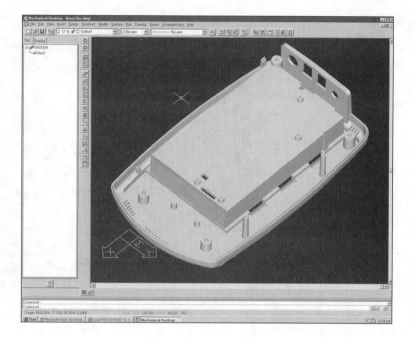

The time normally taken to complete this design procedure would have been as follows:

- Two weeks for the 2D layout and approval.
- Three weeks for the 2D detail drawings to be produced and checked.
- Eight weeks for the first model to be generated.
- One week for evaluation.
- One week for drawing modifications.
- Eight weeks for the final model.
- The total time to the final model would be 23 weeks.
- The costs for the models would have been $8,000 each.

USING MECHANICAL DESKTOP TO FACILITATE THE PROJECT

Now take a look at the process I followed using Mechanical Desktop, and notice how project time and cost was minimized.

As in the normal procedure, I produced a very complex 2D layout where the parts were designed around the electronics. After a design review and approval, I produced all the parts in 3D. After the 3D modeling was completed, I assembled the parts on the computer and checked for form, fit, and function; then I produced the STL files for stereolithography (see Figure 25.7). This was all completed within four weeks using Mechanical Desktop, which enabled the three-dimensional part to be rapidly produced.

Figure 25.7
The completed set of three-dimensional parts that make up the assembly—all created using Mechanical Desktop.

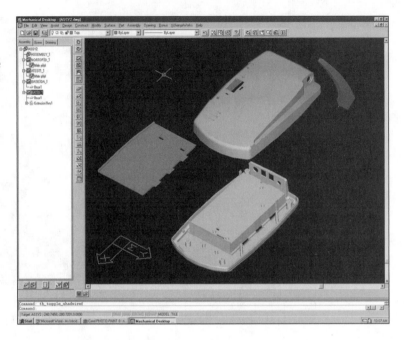

The files were downloaded via modem to the stereolithography company that afternoon. After checking with the vendor that the files were received, the vendor was prepared for the SLA process. I received the parts back on my desk within two business days.

REWORKING THE MODEL

At that time, a design review was held. Due to some major electronic changes, modifications were required to the model, and a new set of SLAs was required. I modified some of the files and rebuilt some small parts and sent the files to the SLA vendor. The final model was received in four days, when it was subsequently approved and ready for detailing and tooling.

The actual time and costs for this new procedure were as follows:

- Two weeks for 2D design layout and approval.
- Two weeks for the production of the 3D files.
- Four days (two working days) for SLA model.
- One week design evaluation and 3D modification.
- Four days for the final SLA model.
- Total time to the final model was 5.5 weeks.
- Approximate SLA costs was $3,000 total.

THE END RESULT

At the end of the project, calculations estimated that I had shaved four months from the normal project schedule and had saved approximately $13,000 on mechanical development costs.

Another advantage of using Mechanical Desktop for this project was that the company wanted to exhibit a working model at an industry trade show to launch the product prior to completion of the first production. I was able to have plastic parts produced using rapid prototyping techniques that entailed using SLA parts as patterns for soft tool molds (see Figure 25.8. The parts were produced, painted in a range of colors, and imprinted with the customer's silk-screen logo on the top cover. This enabled the company to host a successful launch of the product at the show several months before the final tools were completed.

Figure 25.8
The final assembly presented to the client at one-third of the cost and in one-quarter the amount of time normally required.

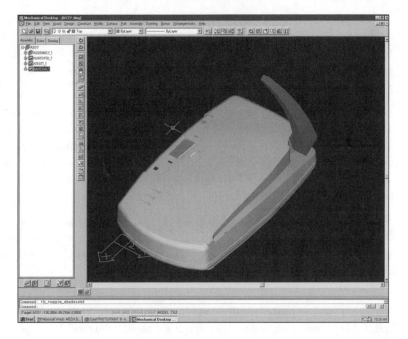

The normal time from concept to production was around 14 months. This product was in full production 10 months from its first concept.

This product also had to obtain FCC approval prior to being available to the market—FCC approvals can take up to four months. The company was able to submit units to the FCC using parts produced from the SLAs, and approval was obtained just prior to the first production run, allowing immediate delivery to the customer for sales distribution.

With the speed of technology advances today, the time to market for most companies is priceless.

THE HISTORY OF AUTODESK'S SOLID MODELING SOFTWARE

Many 3D solid modeling packages are on the market, some of which are extremely sophisticated, versatile, and very powerful, for the designer to use. With so many different mechanical design software packages available, why choose Mechanical Desktop?

Autodesk has a history of involving the customer to better define a software product such as Mechanical Desktop. Using user group wish-lists and extensive beta testing, and allowing users to provide feedback on the product before it is released, Autodesk has been able to develop products around users' needs. This has been very instrumental in the evolution of mechanical design software at Autodesk. To get a better understanding of how Mechanical Desktop grew into the product it is today, let's look at its brief history.

As a designer with some years of experience (yes, I even remember drafting boards and lightboxes), I was very critical of CAD in general when it first appeared. Many different software packages were available, but generally they were slow, difficult to understand, and generally designed by people who had no idea what drafting techniques were required to produce an engineering detail drawing.

AutoCAD was one of the first to recognize that designers wanted a say in how this software should be presented. They listened to designer feedback and went on to construct the most comprehensive, simple-to-learn 2D CAD software on the market today. The software designers were a little naïve, in my opinion, when it came to 3D—bringing out packages such as AME and AutoCAD Designer to compete against the more expensive mechanical design software products such as Pro-E and Unigraphics.

Advanced Modeling Extension (AME) was Autodesk's first step into the world of 3D. It used Boolean construction techniques and was incapable of constructing complex geometric shapes with draft angles and complex fillets, so it was followed by a more advanced 3D modeling package called AutoCAD Designer.

AutoCAD Designer was introduced to try to bring AutoCAD into the world of 3D modeling with a more industry-based 3D modeler, and this was a vast improvement over AME. AutoCAD Designer was a parametric, feature-based solid modeling tool. Although by using Designer we were able to produce some complex shapes using this software, it was still very limited and required additional proprietary software to produce *.STL files. Still, it was a step in the right direction leading to Mechanical Desktop.

AME and Designer fell well short of what the industry required and were literally ridiculed as being nothing more than an introductory level of 3D software with little practical use in the world of complex shapes and design.

As before, Autodesk listened and developed Mechanical Desktop, a powerful 3D tool that was easy to learn at a cost that was a fraction of the large 3D packages dominating the 3D CAD world. Mechanical Desktop also has a distinct advantage: Generally, the major 3D CAD companies put a lot of resources into their 3D software but tended to neglect the 2D side, resulting in companies usually having separate 2D stations in addition to their 3D station. Since Mechanical Desktop has the base AutoCAD 2000 functionality built-in, Autodesk has combined the best of both worlds.

As of the writing of this book, Autodesk introduced another mechanical design product called Autodesk Inventor. Inventor is a three-dimensional modeling system, enabling you to create and easily modify large assemblies containing hundreds of individual parts. Although Mechanical Desktop is great for individual parts, surface modeling, and small assemblies for specialized design and analysis, Inventor was designed specifically for large assemblies. Inventor takes you one step further by also allowing you to import assemblies from other mechanical design packages, such as Pro Engineer, SDRC, CATIA, and Solid Works.

As the history of Autodesk mechanical design solutions evolve into another era with the Inventor product, you have a clear path for expanding your mechanical design needs. Mechanical Desktop is great software to use if you need 2D and 3D design functionality and surface modeling, and then if you find yourself needing the ability to create large assemblies, you can easily work with your designs created in Mechanical Desktop using Autodesk Inventor.

When comparing Mechanical Desktop with other 3D solid modeling software, Mechanical Desktop satisfies all the requirements that the mechanical designer needs to generate:

PART
VI

CH
25

- Conceptual designs and ideas
- Complex parts with many different geometric shapes
- Stereolithography files
- Form, fit, and function analysis
- Complex, small assemblies and related documentation
- 2D drawings in a worldwide-recognized format, such as AutoCAD dwg and dxf
- Information for the production of rapid prototypes and full production parts

This enables you to go beyond the base functionality of AutoCAD 2000, but to capitalize on AutoCAD's familiar commands and features while using the mechanical design specific utilities like parametric driven dimensions and surface modeling design capabilities.

SUMMARY

Mechanical Desktop easily enables you to transition from designing mechanical parts in AutoCAD 2000 to an integrated mechanical design 2D and 3D environment. This provides a way to quickly generate three-dimensional models and working drawings from two-dimensional layouts created using base AutoCAD functionality. Rather than facing the steep learning curve of many 3D only mechanical design software products, Mechanical Desktop offers the user the ability to work in a familiar environment yet gain the mechanical design enhancements and productivity discussed in this chapter.

PART VII

APPENDIXES

Taking Advantage of AutoCAD's Keyboard Shortcuts

In this appendix

This is a quick reference for the default shortcuts available in AutoCAD 2000. These are contained in a file called ACAD.PGP and are loaded at the initial launch of an AutoCAD session. If you prefer to type commands rather than select them from toolbars or pull-down menus, these shortcuts give you an alternative.

QUICKER ACCESS TO YOUR FAVORITE COMMANDS

Because of the large number of shortcuts available, you will want to memorize the shortcuts for only the commands you use most often. Of course, the commands used by one user might differ considerably from those used by another.

> **Note**
>
> Some of the keyboard shortcuts listed here, such as PR and MO, exist to assist users who have worked with the previous versions of AutoCAD to transition to using AutoCAD 2000. These have been indicated in the list by an asterisk (*). You might wish to replace them with shortcuts of your own—you can learn how by referring to Chapter 20, "Customizing Made Easy."

TABLE A.1   KEYBOARD SHORTCUTS

Shortcut	Command
3A	3DARRAY
3DO	3DORBIT
3F	3DFACE
3P	3DPOLY
A	ARC
ADC	ADCENTER
AA	AREA
AL	ALIGN
AP	APPLOAD
AR	ARRAY
ATT	ATTDEF
–ATT	–ATTDEF
ATE	ATTEDIT
–ATE	–ATTEDIT
ATTE	–ATTEDIT

Shortcut	Command
B	BLOCK
–B	–BLOCK
BH	BHATCH
BO	BOUNDARY
–BO	–BOUNDARY
BR	BREAK
C	CIRCLE
CH	PROPERTIES
–CH	–CHANGE
CHA	CHAMFER
COL	COLOR
COLOUR	COLOR
CO	COPY
D	DIMSTYLE
DAL	DIMALIGNED
DAN	DIMANGULAR
DBA	DIMBASELINE
DBC	DBCONNECT
DCE	DIMCENTER
DCO	DIMCONTINUE
DDI	DIMDIAMETER
DED	DIMEDIT
DI	DIST
DIV	DIVIDE
DLI	DIMLINEAR
DO	DONUT
DOR	DIMORDINATE
DOV	DIMOVERRIDE
DR	DRAWORDER

continues

Table A.1 Continued

Shortcut	Command
DRA	DIMRADIUS
DS	DSETTINGS
DST	DIMSTYLE
DT	DTEXT
DV	DVIEW
E	ERASE
ED	DDEDIT
EL	ELLIPSE
EX	EXTEND
EXIT	QUIT
EXP	EXPORT

Note

If you have the Express Tools loaded, this keyboard shortcut actually launches Exclude Previous command from the Selection Tools, rather than the Export command using base AutoCAD. You may wish to modify this to avoid confusion or remove it altogether if you find that you rarely use the Export command.

Shortcut	Command
EXT	EXTRUDE
F	FILLET
FI	FILTER
G	GROUP
–G	–GROUP
*GR	DDGRIPS
H	BHATCH
–H	–HATCH
HE	HATCHEDIT
HI	HIDE
I	INSERT
–I	–INSERT
IAD	IMAGEADJUST

Shortcut	Command
IAT	IMAGEATTACH
ICL	IMAGECLIP
IM	IMAGE
–IM	–IMAGE
IMP	IMPORT
IN	INTERSECT
INF	INTERFERE
IO	INSERTOBJ
L	LINE
LA	LAYER
–LA	–LAYER
LE	QLEADER
LEN	LENGTHEN
LI	LIST
LINEWEIGHT	LWEIGHT
–LO	–LAYOUT
LS	LIST
LT	LINETYPE
–LT	–LINETYPE
LTYPE	LINETYPE
–LTYPE	–LINETYPE
LTS	LTSCALE
LW	LWEIGHT
M	MOVE
MA	MATCHPROP
ME	MEASURE
MI	MIRROR
ML	MLINE
*MO	PROPERTIES

continues

TABLE A.1 CONTINUED

Shortcut	Command
MS	MSPACE
MT	MTEXT
MV	MVIEW
O	OFFSET
OP	OPTIONS
ORBIT	3DORBIT
OS	OSNAP
–OS	–OSNAP
P	PAN
–P	–PAN
PA	PASTESPEC
–PARTIALOPEN	–PARTIALOPEN
PE	PEDIT
PL	PLINE
PO	POINT
POL	POLYGON
*PR	OPTIONS
PRCLOSE	PROPERTIESCLOSE
PROPS	PROPERTIES
PRE	PREVIEW
PRINT	PLOT
PS	PSPACE
PU	PURGE
R	REDRAW
RA	REDRAWALL
RE	REGEN
REA	REGENALL
REC	RECTANGLE

Shortcut	Command
REG	REGION
REN	RENAME
–REN	–RENAME
REV	REVOLVE
RM	DDRMODES
RO	ROTATE
RPR	RPREF
RR	RENDER
S	STRETCH
SC	SCALE
SCR	SCRIPT
SE	DSETTINGS
SEC	SECTION
SET	SETVAR
SHA	SHADE
SL	SLICE
SN	SNAP
SO	SOLID
SP	SPELL
SPL	SPLINE
SPE	SPLINEDIT
ST	STYLE
SU	SUBTRACT
T	MTEXT
–T	–MTEXT
TA	TABLET
TH	THICKNESS
TI	TILEMODE
TO	TOOLBAR

continues

TABLE A.1 CONTINUED

Shortcut	Command
TOL	TOLERANCE
TOR	TORUS
TR	TRIM
UC	DDUCS
UCP	DDUCSP
UN	UNITS
–UN	–UNITS
UNI	UNION
V	VIEW
–V	–VIEW
VP	DDVPOINT
–VP	–VPOINT
W	WBLOCK
–W	–WBLOCK
WE	WEDGE
X	EXPLODE
XA	XATTACH
XB	XBIND
–XB	–XBIND
XC	XCLIP
XL	XLINE
XR	XREF
–XR	–XREF
Z	ZOOM
AV	DSVIEWER
CP	COPY
DIMALI	DIMALIGNED
DIMANG	DIMANGULAR

Shortcut	Command
DIMBASE	DIMBASELINE
DIMCONT	DIMCONTINUE
DIMDIA	DIMDIAMETER
DIMED	DIMEDIT
DIMTED	DIMTEDIT
DIMLIN	DIMLINEAR
DIMORD	DIMORDINATE
DIMRAD	DIMRADIUS
DIMSTY	DIMSTYLE
DIMOVER	DIMOVERRIDE
LEAD	LEADER
TM	TILEMODE
*SAVEURL	SAVE
*OPENURL	OPEN
*INSERTURL	INSERT

You can also add to this list of shortcuts, if the command you want is not listed here, by modifying the ACAD.PGP file.

To learn more about modifying this file, see Chapter 20, "Customizing Made Easy."

Refer to this table often—you do not need to be an expert typist to take advantage of these shortcuts. When you have committed the shortcuts for your favorite commands to memory, you can easily increase your productivity by gaining quick access to the commands.

AutoCAD Environment Options

In this appendix

There are numerous options available that will enable you to become more efficient working in AutoCAD. These options vary from specifying search paths to customizing the AutoCAD display. You have seen many of these options in the form of setting variables, or *setvars*. AutoCAD also provides a series of dialog box tiles that make setting these preferences easier. This appendix will briefly describe the parameters available in each of the tabs within the Options dialog box.

OPTIONS AT A GLANCE

To access the AutoCAD Environment Options, right-click in the command line and select Options from the shortcut menu. This will open the Options dialog box, shown in Figure B.1.

There are nine tabs that contain hundreds of options. The name of each tab is listed in the following sections, with a brief description of what can be set within each tab.

THE FILES TAB

This tab controls which directories AutoCAD will search to find fonts, linetypes, hatch patterns, menus, and more. If AutoCAD cannot find the files specified in the current directory, it then searches the directories indicated here (see Figure B.1).

Figure B.1
You can set the directories AutoCAD will search when it does not find what it is looking for in the current directory.

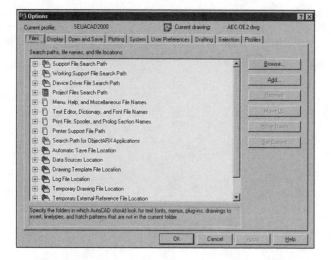

THE DISPLAY TAB

The various settings that affect the AutoCAD display can be set from this tab. Settings like crosshair size and text screen options, such as the use of scroll bars, fonts, display resolution, and performance are specified in the tab shown in Figure B.2.

Figure B.2
You can configure AutoCAD display settings by using the Display tab.

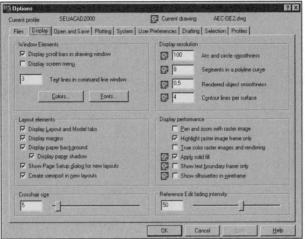

THE OPEN AND SAVE TAB

This tab contains the parameters that determine the default version type and file type for the Save and Save As commands. Also, File Safety Precautions, such as creating a backup file with every save and automatic save time and extension, and controlling how external reference files and ObjectARX applications will be loaded are accessed from here (see Figure B.3).

Figure B.3
The settings that determine how a file will be saved within AutoCAD, File Safety Precautions, and the loading of External Reference files and ObjectARX applications are available from the Open and Save tab.

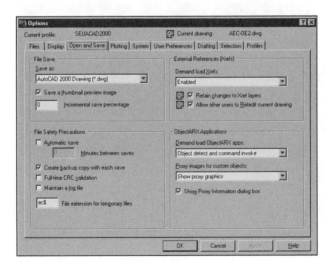

THE PLOTTING TAB

The options for plotting, such as the default plot device, adding and configuring new plotters, general plot options, and setting plot styles are available from this tab, shown in Figure B.4.

Figure B.4
Add or Configure
Plotters, Plot Styles,
plot style behavior,
and general plot
and OLE plot quality
options can be set
within the
Plotting tab.

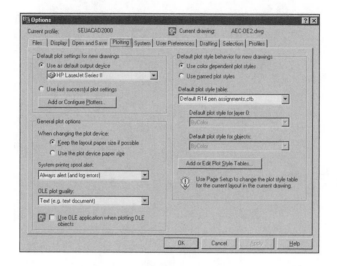

The System Tab

From within this tab you can set the current 3D graphics display and its properties, and specify the current pointing device. General options, such as loading the ACAD.LSP file with each drawing and beeping on error, as well as the dbConnect option open tables in read-only mode, are easily accessed from here (see Figure B.5).

Figure B.5
The various system
settings, like setting
the current pointing
device, and general
options, such as
allowing long symbol
names, are set from
the System tab.

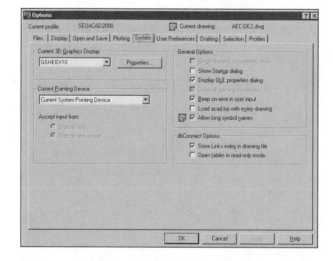

The User Preferences Tab

Options like enabling the use of the shortcut menus, defining the source and target drawing Insert units, and the display of the hyperlink ToolTip and cursor can be set from this tab (see Figure B.6).

Figure B.6
How AutoCAD responds to coordinate data and object sorting methods that determine how objects are selected are only two of the options available within the User Preferences tab.

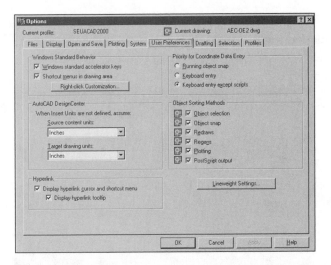

Clicking the Right-Click Customization button opens the Right-Click Customization dialog box. Here, options for defining the right-click in the default, editing, and command modes are available (see Figure B.7).

Figure B.7
Setting how AutoCAD will act when the right-click button on the pointer is clicked can be set from the Right Click Customization dialog box.

You can also set the specific Lineweight settings by clicking the Lineweight Settings button, which opens the dialog box shown in Figure B.8.

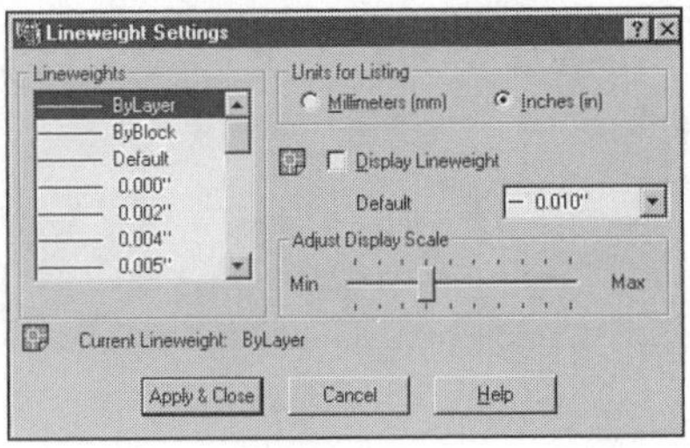

Figure B.8
The display settings and units for lineweights can be set from the Lineweight Settings dialog box.

THE DRAFTING TAB

Drafting settings such as the AutoSnap and AutoTrack settings, as well as the size of the Aperture, can be set from this dialog box (see Figure B.9).

Figure B.9
You can toggle the display of the AutoSnap and AutoTrack ToolTips, and set the color of the AutoSnap marker within the Drafting tab.

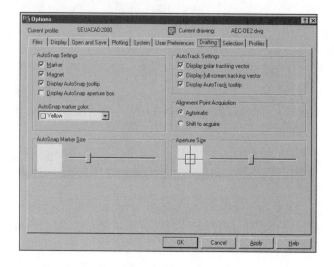

THE SELECTION TAB

The options for determining the Selection modes, such as Noun\verb selection and Implied windowing, and enabling grips are available in this dialog box, shown in Figure B.10.

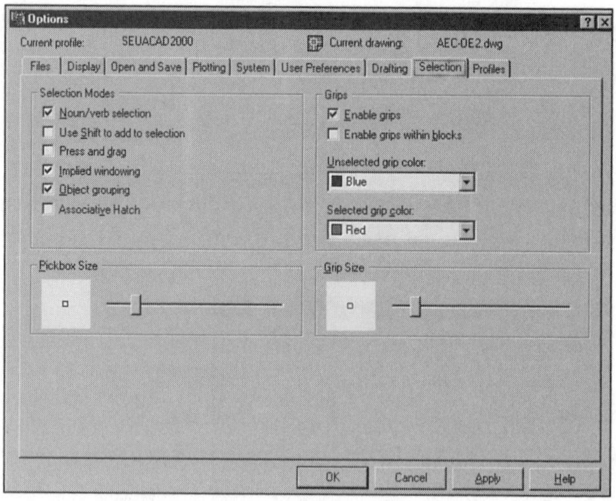

Figure B.10
The size of the standard Pickbox and Grip Pick boxes can be set from within the Drafting tab.

THE PROFILES TAB

This tab allows you to manage the different profiles that might be used on an AutoCAD system. Profiles are the AutoCAD Environment settings that are specific to a particular user. Multiple profiles can be set if different users share a single AutoCAD workstation, or they can be set for different project settings. To create or add a profile, adjust the options as desired and then click the Profiles tab (see Figure B.11).

Figure B.11

Profiles can be managed from the Profiles tab, which allows you to add, delete, modify, and set the different user profiles on your computer.

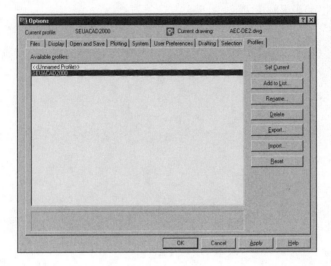

Select the Add to List button to open the dialog shown in Figure B.12, in which you can enter a particular username and description.

Figure B.12

User profiles can be defined with a name and description within the Add Profile dialog box.

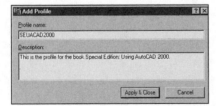

Clicking the Apply & Close button saves the options currently set in the Options dialog box to this user profile. The different user profiles can be activated by selecting the profile desired from the list and selecting the Set Current button.

The Options dialog box not only gives you quick and easy access to a large number of AutoCAD environment settings, but also allows you to define user profiles that can save user-specific settings for different projects and users. You'll find this is an efficient way to manage the AutoCAD settings that affect how you work.

AutoCAD Migration Assistance

In this appendix

To assist users of AutoCAD prior to AutoCAD 2000, and to ease their transition to the use of this software, several easy-to-use functions were bundled together into a package called the AutoCAD Migration Assistant. This product, which is included with AutoCAD 2000 but installed separately, contains nine tools that convert, analyze, and help the user upgrade their existing drawings, menus, toolbars, and AutoLISP routines to work with AutoCAD 2000. This appendix will aid you in determining what these tools are used for and to give you a brief explanation of how each one works, without having to load the software first.

CONVERTING FILES WITH THE MIGRATION ASSISTANT

The Migration Assistant analyzes and upgrades files to work within the AutoCAD 2000 environment. Which Migration Assistant function you use depends on which file you want to convert for use in AutoCAD 2000. To install the AutoCAD Migration Assistant, double-click the Setup.exe file from the Migration directory on the AutoCAD 2000 CD. Then the individual tools can be accessed from a single program interface and launched from the Start button Program Files list on the desktop. The interface is displayed in Figure C.1.

Figure C.1
The tools included in the AutoCAD Migration Assistant can easily be accessed from this interface.

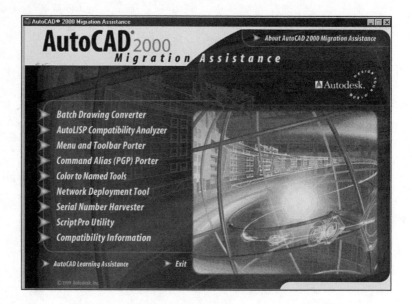

The various Migration Assistant tools are accessed by clicking on the individual tool names from the interface:

- Batch Drawing Converter—This tool will convert numerous drawing files at one time. This can be used to convert files between the AutoCAD 12, 13, 14, and 2000 file formats. A Drawing Previewer is included to view the drawings, and if you are converting to AutoCAD 2000 format, options allow you to convert pen width settings to lineweights via a user-supplied plotter configuration file (.PCP, .PC2, or .CFG). This is accomplished through the AutoCAD Batch Convert dialog box, shown in Figure C.2. AutoCAD 2000 must be installed on the computer before the Migration Assistant Tools can work.

Figure C.2
Multiple drawing files can be converted between AutoCAD Release 12, 13, 14, and 2000 formats using the AutoCAD Batch Convert dialog box.

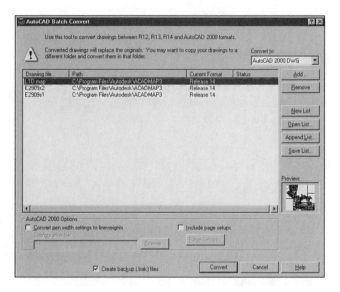

- AutoLISP Compatibility Analyzer—Easily analyze AutoLISP routines in AutoCAD 14 format and determine what needs to be done to make them work in AutoCAD 2000. Using the AutoLISP Compatibility Analyzer dialog box (see Figure C.3), you can open and analyze a single file or multiple files contained within a folder. The file can be modified using the built-in editor, or comments can be added for modification later in a text editor of the user's choice.

Figure C.3
The AutoLISP Compatibility Analyzer analyzes AutoLISP files in AutoCAD Release 14 format and recommends suggestions detailing how the file can be made AutoCAD 2000–compatible.

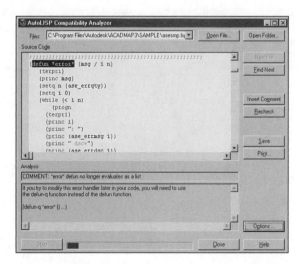

- Menu and Toolbar Porter—If you have menus from AutoCAD 12, 13, and 14, this tool will assist you in converting them so they will work in AutoCAD 2000. The Menu and Toolbar Porter dialog box displays the files in a tree-like structure, allowing you to view the make-up of the menu (see Figure C.4). Commands available within the menus can be viewed along with associated Diesel code.

Figure C.4
The Menu and Toolbar Porter easily displays the structure of your menu files, enabling you to transfer and upgrade menu and toolbar syntax between files.

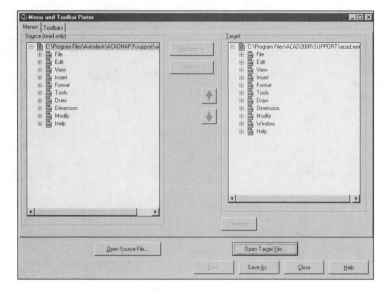

- Command Alias (PGP) Porter—This tool will assist you in upgrading any Command and External Aliases you have to format for AutoCAD 2000 use. Once loaded, the ACAD.PGP files are automatically compared, and the aliases that are missing in either file are denoted with a keyboard icon, enabling you to quickly find those aliases to import into the new format, shown in Figure C.5.

Figure C.5
The Command Alias (PGP) Porter displays those command aliases missing from either file, allowing you to transfer the alias syntax between files.

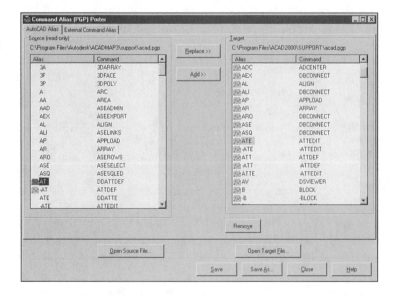

■ Color to Named Tools—You can convert color-dependent files, such as those created prior to AutoCAD 2000, to the new plot-style files with this tool. Two commands are included to upgrade files to the new plot-table standard. CONVERTCTB converts the older color-dependent plot style table (.CBT) into the new .SBT plot style table. CONVERTPSTYLES upgrades a color-dependent plot styles drawing into a drawing that names plot styles (see Figure C.6).

Figure C.6
Two commands,
CONVERTCTB and
CONVERTPSTYLES,
enable you to
upgrade color-
dependent drawings
and table to the new
plot style drawing
and tables.

■ Network Deployment Tool—A 30-day trial edition of the PictureTaker Enterprise software by Lanovation enables you to automatically install and configure AutoCAD 2000 on multiple workstations across a network. Selecting the link from the AutoCAD Migration Assistant interface connects you to the Lanovation Web site, where you can download the trial version of the PictureTaker software to assist you in installing AutoCAD 2000 (see Figure C.7).

Figure C.7
Connect to the
Lanovation Web site
to download a 30-day
trial version of the
PictureTaker software
to easily install
multiple seats of
AutoCAD 2000 across
a network.

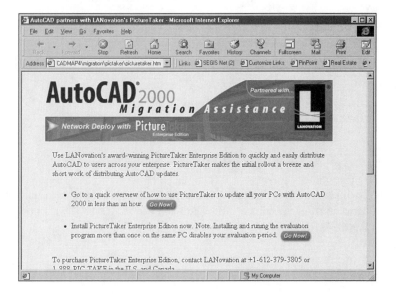

- Serial Number Harvester—The Serial Number Harvester tool, shown in Figure C.8, enables you to easily obtain the AutoCAD 2000 software serial numbers used within a network environment of multiple versions of AutoCAD.

Figure C.8
The Serial Number Harvester tool easily gathers shown in Figure C.8, enables you to the serial numbers of multiple versions of AutoCAD installed across a network.

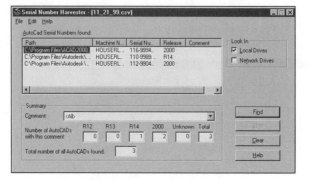

- ScriptPro Utility—Use this tool to effortlessly run scripts created in AutoCAD on multiple drawing files. Simply select the script, choose the drawing files you want to run the script on, and then click the Run this project button (see Figure C.9)

Figure C.9
The ScriptPro Utility runs a script on multiple drawing files using this easy-to-use dialog box.

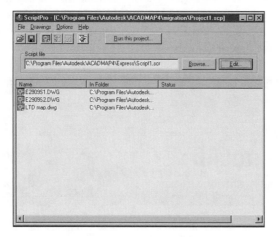

- Compatibility Information—This gives you more information on compatibility issues between older versions of AutoCAD and AutoCAD 2000 via a browser, shown in Figure C.10.

Figure C.10
More compatibility issues of using AutoCAD 2000 are addressed using this link.

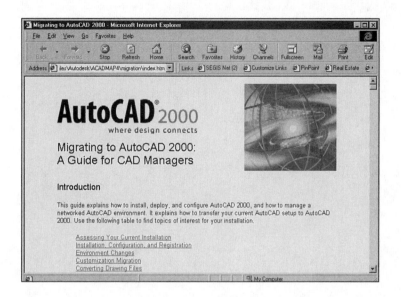

PART

VII

APP

C

The AutoCAD Migration Assistant can save you a considerable amount of time upgrading your existing AutoCAD files to AutoCAD 2000 format. As you upgrade to AutoCAD 2000, look where you might be able to use these tools to increase your everyday productivity.

INDEX

Symbols

P

Pack 'n Go command (Express, Tools menu), 409

page layouts, moving, 500

Page Setup command (File menu), 461

Page Setup dialog box, 494-506

pages
layouts, 494-507
modifying, 495

Pan command, 221-222

panning, 51-53

paper
adding dimensions, 354-356
blocks, 507
scaling, 323-325
selecting, 491
sizes, 512
space, 504-505

parallel lines. See multilines

parameters, Arc command, 81-82

parent blocks, 727

parent dimension styles, 329

Parentheses Matching option, 602

partial menus, loading, 580-583

Partial Open/Partial Load commands, 25-26

parts, rendering, 745

Paste Special command (Edit menu), 583

Paste Special dialog box, 583

pasting. See also copying
command-line text, 13
data, 585
moving objects between drawings, 24-25
page layouts, 500

Path Substitution command (Express, Tools menu), 412

paths
adding, 452
search, 605

Select New Path dialog box, 450
xref, 450-452

patterns, hatching. See hatching

PDMODE/PDSIZE variables, 94-95

PE command, 102. See also polylines; editing

Pedit command, 102. See also polylines, editing

Pen assignments, 512

Perspective viewing mode, 700

perspectives, Architectural Desktop, 736

photo-realistic rendering, 713-714

Pick program, 638

PickFirst, 138

PickOff program, closing, 640

pictures
3D, 701-703
hidden line, 702
rendered
attaching objects, 709-710
creating, 703-705
effects, 714
exporting, 715
lighting models, 705-706, 708
mapping, 711-714
saving, 715
scenes, 714
viewing, 715
rendering, 745
shading, 702-703

placing
line coordinates, 48
objects (z-axis), 693-696

planning space, 723-724

pljoin command, 402-403

Plot command (File menu), 487, 508

Plot Device, 495

Plot Device list box, 460

Plot dialog box, 487, 508-511

Plot Offset frame, 497

Plot Preview command (File menu), 526

plot preview commands, 509-511

Plot Style command (Format menu), 523

Plot Style Table Editor, 518-519, 524

plot styles, 513-521
linetypes, 62
named, 522-526
tables, 514-521

Plotter Manager dialog box, 483

plotters
Add-A-Plotter wizard, 483-488
configuring, 483-488
Create Layout wizard, 488-494
dwf files, 528
modifying, 495
new features, 511-513
plot styles, 513-523, 525-526
page layouts, 494-511
properties, 496
raster files, 527-528
selecting, 491

plotting, 482-483, 769-770
Add-A-Plotter wizard, 483
DWF files, 542-546

PO command, 94

Point Style dialog box, 94-95

points, 94-95
destination/source, 165-168

POL command, 84

Polar format, 160

polars
angles, 45-46
tracking, 44

polyarcs, 98-101
combining polylines and polyarcs, 100-102
options, 100-101

Polygonal Viewports command (View menu), 503

polygons, 84-86
defining bolt heads, 85-86
inscribed versus circumscribed, 84-85
selecting (selection set filters), 196